# INTRODUCTION

## TO THE

# Chemical Process

# Industries

RICHARD M. STEPHENSON
*Professor of Chemical Engineering*
*The University of Connecticut*
*Storrs, Connecticut*

*New York*
REINHOLD PUBLISHING CORPORATION

# Preface

This book discusses the most important of the chemical process industries. Emphasis is on the basic chemical and thermodynamical principles of the individual processes and the interrelationship of one process with another. It is not intended as an encyclopedia, but includes only those processes which any chemical engineer or chemist might reasonably be expected to be familiar with. The book can be used either as an undergraduate text or as a reference book for a practicing chemical engineer or chemist.

Information given here has been taken almost exclusively from the published literature. Because of the competitive nature of the process industries, I have been completely unsuccessful in obtaining any proprietary information from individual manufacturers. For this reason some of the information may be incorrect, and I would welcome any constructive criticism or suggestions for improvement.

I would like to thank the following people for the assistance they have given me: (1) Dr. Richard Goldstein of British Oxygen Co., Ltd., for his suggestions as to possible sources of technical information. (2) D. H. Porter of Hooker Chemical Corp. for supplying information on chlorine cells. (3) G. T. Waggy of Union Carbide Corp. for supplying information on "Tergitol" surfactants. (4) R. W. Lewis of the U.S. Bureau of Mines for supplying preprints of the 1964 "Minerals Yearbook." (5) D. P. Thornton, Jr., of Universal Oil Products Co. for furnishing information on their separation processes. (6) Robert Habermehl of Catalysts and Chemicals, Inc., for furnishing information on their catalysts. (7) Prof. Lewis Hatch of the University of Texas for furnishing information on biodegradable detergents. (8) The technical staff of Esso Research and Engineering Co. for their suggestions concerning sources of technical information on petrochemicals. Special thanks go to the staff of the Wilbur

Cross Library and to Dean Arthur Bronwell and Prof. Leroy Stutzman who made it possible for me to spend a year's sabbatic leave in the preparation of this material.

*Storrs, Connecticut*                                          RICHARD M. STEPHENSON
*May 1966*

# Contents

# CHAPTER 1

# Introduction

In studying the chemical process industries, certain elementary facts must always be remembered. First, the chemical process industries are both dynamic and highly competitive. Thus, no textbook can possibly describe all the important industrial processes, since these are continually changing as new processes are developed and older ones are abandoned. Also, because of the competitive nature of the process industries, it is very difficult in many cases to determine precisely what process is used to produce a given product. The information given in this book is taken from sources which are considered to be reliable, and it is hoped that all processes described here are essentially correct. However, it must be emphasized that often the exact processing conditions such as temperature, pressure, type of catalyst, yield, etc., are known only to those having access to the confidential files of the particular manufacturer.

It is also important to remember that the actual process which is used in a given situation will always be determined by economics. This requires a careful balance of such factors as plant location, cost and availability of raw materials, transportation costs, energy requirements, possible process obsolescence, etc. Since these factors are highly variable, they can only be discussed here in the most general way. Of necessity, this book will emphasize the technical features of the various processes; however, the reader should remember that only a small percentage of the chemists and chemical engineers employed in industry are engaged in fundamental process research.

## SEARCHING THE LITERATURE

In most cases, the latest information on a particular product or process can only be obtained through a search of the technical literature. It is extremely important that chemists and chemical engineers have some

1

familiarity with the literature, since a knowledge of previous work in a given field can save a lot of time and money in the planning of new experiments. Also, in the case of a patent, a literature search is absolutely essential since the existence of any published document describing a particular invention is prima facie evidence for denying a patent application.

The general method of searching the literature is somewhat as follows. First consult a technical encyclopedia such as the Kirk-Othmer "Encyclopedia of Chemical Technology" to gain a general knowledge of the subject and determine what should be stressed in the search. Second, go to the card catalog to see if there are any references to the particular subject; if the searcher is lucky, there may be a book or monograph which will cover the literature up to about a year prior to publication. Third, for the latest information it is necessary to go directly to abstract journals.

In the field of chemistry and chemical engineering, the most comprehensive abstract journal is *Chemical Abstracts* (1907-   ) which covers some 10,000 technical periodicals plus foreign and United States patents. The annual index (now semiannual) includes authors, subjects, patents and chemical formulas; in addition, dicennial indexes cover the period from 1907-56 and five-year indexes from 1957-date. The chief disadvantage of *Chemical Abstracts* is the fact that the abstracts are fairly brief and the reader must go to the original article for more detailed information.

The older chemical literature is covered by the *Chemisches Zentralblatt* (1830-   ). Also, the *Engineering Index* (1906-   ) covers most engineering journals published in English and a few foreign journals. It does not, however, cover patents. More specialized abstract journals include *Nuclear Science Abstracts* (1948-   ), *Science Abstracts* (1903-   ), and the *Industrial Arts Index* (1913-   ). Note that *British Chemical and Physiological Abstracts* (1926-53) has now ceased publication.

### Patents

The patent literature is an extremely important source of technical information. If a patent is to be valid, the disclosure must be complete enough for anyone skilled in the art to reproduce the particular results described in the patent. For this reason, much work appears in patents before it is described in technical journals or press releases, and often the details of a new and supposedly secret commercial process can be worked out fairly well merely by consulting the patents recently issued to the particular manufacturer.

United States patents are described briefly in the *Official Gazette* of the United States Patent Office (1872-   ). If this is inadequate, a copy of the patent can be obtained at a cost of 25 cents from the Commissioner of Patents. In the case of foreign patents, directions for obtaining copies are given in *Chemical Abstracts*. Often the most convenient procedure is to order a photostatic copy of the foreign patent from the United States Patent Office.

### Sources of Information

Often *Chemical Abstracts* will give a reference to a journal that is not available in the local library. By referring to the *List of Periodicals* abstracted by *Chemical Abstracts* and the *Union List of Serials*, it is possible to determine where the particular journal is available. If a large number of journals must be consulted, it may save time to visit one of the larger chemical libraries such as the Chemists' Club of New York or one of the larger university libraries. It is also possible to write for photostatic or "Xerox" copies of any desired journal articles, although this frequently necessitates a delay of several weeks before obtaining the information. For the chemical literature, and particularly the older European literature, unusually good service is given by The Chemical Society, Burlington House, London, which provides "Xerox" copies at a cost of half a shilling per page, usually within 24 hours of receipt of order.

Often the first announcement of a new product will be in the trade literature. Thus, all manufacturers will supply information bulletins giving the availability, properties, and uses of their products; unfortunately, these usually give no information on the methods of production. Trade associations such as the American Petroleum Institute are often a very good source of technical information. Several periodicals such as *Chemical and Engineering News* and *Chemical Week* are very good at picking up the latest gossip about new products, plant expansions, etc.; often they have valuable survey articles which review the status of one particular product or industry. Recent industrial developments are often published in *Industrial and Engineering Chemistry* and *Chemical Engineering Progress;* particularly valuable for their articles on petroleum refining and petrochemicals are the *Hydrocarbon Processing and Petroleum Refiner* and the *Oil and Gas Journal*. Government documents may be useful, especially those published by the Bureau of Standards, the Bureau of Mines, and the production figures available from the Tariff Commission. Chemical prices are given in the *Oil, Paint, and Drug Reporter*. Even financial reports such as the yearly reports to stockholders may be of interest, since these sometimes include information on new products or new production facilities.

*CHAPTER 2*

# Review of Thermodynamics and Kinetics

Two important questions which must be answered for any process under consideration are the energy requirements and the maximum possible yield of the desired product. Both of these can be determined from the thermodynamics of the particular reactions. It is assumed that the reader is familiar with the principles of thermodynamics,[1] and the purpose of this chapter is to summarize certain basic information which will be used later.

## Units and Nomenclature

Plant practice in the United States usually involves the use of English units, namely, mass in lbs-mass, force in lbs-force, distance in ft, and time in sec. However, most tables of thermodynamic data are given in scientific units, and these units are also used more commonly in the laboratory. The scientific units used most commonly in chemistry are mass in gm, distance in cm, and time in sec. Force is measured in dynes, and is a derived quantity in this system of units.

Because of the different units employed, a certain amount of confusion is perhaps inevitable. In general, we shall use scientific units for the calculation of such things as free energy and enthalpy, where temperatures in °K and heat in cal/gm mole must be used to be consistent with the usual equations of thermodynamics. However, much of the plant operating data will be given in English units such as temperature in °F and pressure in $lb/in.^2$

---

[1] For example, see G. N. Lewis and M. Randall, revised by K. S. Pitzer and L. Brewer, "Thermodynamics," New York, McGraw-Hill Book Co., Inc., 1961.

## Heat Capacity

Heat capacities are of great practical importance because they determine the amount of energy required to heat up a material and they also appear in the equations for free energy and heat of reaction. Heat capacities may be measured at constant volume $(C_v)$ or at constant pressure $(C_p)$. They are expressed either in cal/(gm mole) (°K) or in Btu/(lb mole)(°F); note that the numerical value of heat capacity is the same for both sets of units.

Since practically all industrial processes occur at essentially constant pressure, we shall be interested only in the value of $C_p$. Heat capacities vary both with temperature and pressure. However, the variation with pressure is small, and in the case of an ideal gas the heat capacity is independent of pressure. Tabulated values of heat capacity are based on a suitable standard state. For liquids and solids, the standard state is the pure material at 1 atm pressure; for gases, the standard state is the perfect-gas state (theoretically zero pressure for a real gas). When a property is referred to the standard state, a superscript is sometimes applied to the symbol, i.e., $C_p°$ represents the heat capacity in the standard state.

The numerical value of the heat capacity depends on the number of degrees of freedom possessed by the molecules of the material. In the case of gases at about room temperature, the energy of the molecules is largely translational and rotational. However, as the temperature is raised, the individual atoms in the molecule start to vibrate and thereby increase the number of degrees of freedom. Hence, heat capacities normally increase with temperature, depending on the relative fraction of the vibrational energy which is effective.

Empirical equations are commonly used to express heat capacity as a function of temperature. K. K. Kelley and his co-workers at the Bureau of Mines favor an equation of the type

$$C_p° = a + bT + cT^{-2} \tag{2-1}$$

where $T$ is the absolute temperature in °K and $a$, $b$, and $c$ are empirical constants. However, many others have used a simple power series, namely,

$$C_p° = p + qT + rT^2 \tag{2-2}$$

where $p$, $q$, and $r$ are, of course, different constants than above. The chief advantage of Eq. (2-1) is that integration gives a reciprocal temperature term whereas Eq. (2-2) gives a more complicated cubic term.

Regardless of which form of the equation is used, it must be remembered that these are empirical equations and hence have only a limited range of validity for any given material. Extrapolation outside of this range may lead to considerable error. Heat capacity data for many common materials are summarized in the Appendix.

### Enthalpy

One of the most useful thermodynamic functions is the heat content or enthalpy $H$ defined by the equation

$$H = E + PV \tag{2-3}$$

where $E$ is the internal energy, $P$ the absolute pressure, and $V$ the volume in consistent units. Enthalpy is a state function, dependent only on the state of the material and independent of the path taken to achieve that state. Usually enthalpies are measured in cal/gm mole; these can be converted to Btu/lb mole by multiplying by 1.8.

The great value of the enthalpy is the fact that in a flow process where there is no electrochemical or shaft work and where changes in potential and kinetic energy are negligible, the heat absorbed is equal to the change in enthalpy. This is almost always true in the process industries, since these are usually continuous operations involving substantial quantities of heat. Thus, it is standard practice to carry out a heat balance from the difference in enthalpies of the products and the reactants, and use this as a direct measure of the heat requirement of the particular system.

### Heat of Reaction

When a chemical reaction occurs, there is either an evolution or an absorption of heat as a result of the different chemical nature of the products and the reactants. For a reaction at constant pressure where no other forms of energy are included, the heat absorbed is equal to the change in enthalpy. Thus, if we consider a chemical reaction such as the hydration of ethylene,

$$H_2O \text{ (g)} + H_2C{=}CH_2 \text{ (g)} \rightleftharpoons C_2H_5OH \text{ (g)} \quad \Delta H^{\circ}_{298} = -10,938 \tag{2-4}$$

the heat absorbed is simply equal to the difference between the enthalpy of the products and that of the reactants.

As in the case of heat capacities, a superscript $^{\circ}$ refers to the reactants and products in the standard state. For solids and liquids, the standard state is the pure material at 1 atm pressure. For gases and vapors, the standard state is the perfect-gas state or the limit for a real gas as the pressure approaches zero. The heat of reaction under these conditions is known as the standard heat of reaction $\Delta H^{\circ}$. Since heats of reaction vary with temperature, a subscript is used to designate the absolute temperature in $^{\circ}K$ at which the reaction occurs. From the definition of enthalpy, $H$ is positive when heat is absorbed; hence, $\Delta H$ is negative for an exothermic reaction and positive for an endothermic reaction.

It is very convenient, especially in tabulating data, to know the heats of reaction when various materials are formed from the elements. If all materials are in the standard state, the change in enthalpy under these conditions is known as the standard heat of formation. Consider the reaction

$$2C \text{ (graphite)} + 2H_2 \text{ (perfect gas)} + \tfrac{1}{2}O_2 \text{ (perfect gas)} \rightarrow$$

$$\underset{\displaystyle H_2C\!\!-\!\!-\!\!-\!\!-CH_2}{\overset{\displaystyle O}{\triangle}} \text{ (perfect gas)} \quad \Delta H^{\circ}_{298} = -12{,}190 \quad (2\text{-}5)$$

The heat of formation of ethylene oxide at 298°K is thus $-12{,}190$ cal/gm mole, the negative sign designating an evolution of heat.

Tabulated values of heats of formation are given in the Appendix. Note that these are given as cal/gm mole at 298°K, and that the enthalpies of all elements in the standard state are assumed to be zero. The heat of formation of a given material depends on its physical state; for example, the heat of formation of liquid water is greater by the latent heat of vaporization than the heat of formation of steam. Thus, in writing chemical reactions, the physical state of each material is usually designated in parentheses after the chemical symbol, i.e., s = solid, c = crystal, g = gas, l = liquid, etc. Note that tabulated values of heats of formation or reaction may be converted to Btu/lb mole by multiplying by 1.8.

### Effect of Temperature on Heat of Reaction

The heat of reaction at 298°K can be calculated from tabulated values of heats of formation, but most industrial reactions occur at higher temperatures. The heat of reaction varies with temperature according to the Kirchhoff equation

$$\left(\frac{\partial \Delta H}{\partial T}\right)_P = \Delta C_p \quad (2\text{-}6)$$

where $\Delta C_p$ represents the heat capacities of the products less the heat capacities of the reactants. Note that $\Delta H$ represents a single quantity and that the partial derivative is taken at constant pressure.

If Eq. (2-6) is integrated

$$\Delta H_T - \Delta H_{298} = \int_{298}^{T} \Delta C_p \, dT \quad (2\text{-}7)$$

where $\Delta H_T$ is the heat of reaction at any absolute temperature $T$. For a small range of temperature or where $\Delta C_p$ is constant

$$\Delta H_T = \Delta H_{298} + \Delta C_p(T - 298) \tag{2-8}$$

For greater temperature intervals, $\Delta C_p$ can be expressed in a power series and then integrated term by term. Thus, if heat capacities are given by Eq. (2-1),

$$\Delta C_p = \Delta a + \Delta bT + \Delta cT^{-2}$$

and Eq. (2-7) becomes

$$\Delta H_T = \Delta H_{298} + \Delta a(T - 298) + \frac{\Delta b}{2}(T^2 - 298^2) - \Delta c\left(\frac{1}{T} - \frac{1}{298}\right) \tag{2-9}$$

If the constants are combined, Eq. (2-9) can be written

$$\Delta H_T = \Delta H_I + \Delta aT + \frac{\Delta b}{2}T^2 - \frac{\Delta c}{T} \tag{2-10}$$

where $\Delta H_I = \Delta H_{298} - 298\Delta a - 4.44 \times 10^4\Delta b + 3.36 \times 10^{-3}\Delta c$. If Eq. (2-2) is used to express heat capacities, the only difference will be in the final term of Eq. (2-9) which becomes a cubic.

In the use of the above equations, it is customary to assume that all reactants and products are in their standard state. This assumption is valid unless there are gases showing large deviations from the ideal-gas law, in which case the heat capacities would show a pressure dependence. However, the experimental data relating heat capacity and pressure are usually unavailable, so that in practice this correction is usually ignored.

### Free Energy

The free energy* $F$ is defined by the equation

$$F = H - TS \tag{2-11}$$

It is obvious that $F$ is a state function since $H$, $T$ and $S$ are themselves state functions. The importance of the free energy is that it can be used to determine equilibrium conditions for various systems. Suppose, for example, that we are considering the catalytic dehydrogenation of ethanol to produce acetaldehyde according to the equation

$$C_2H_5OH \text{ (g)} \rightleftharpoons CH_3CHO \text{ (g)} + H_2 \text{ (g)} \tag{2-12}$$

Assume that equilibrium is established at constant temperature and constant pressure. At constant temperature, the change in free energy is

---

* In the past, there has been considerable confusion over the definition of free energy. Actually the term "free energy" was first introduced by Helmholtz who used it to define the quantity $A = E - TS$. The free energy as defined above is the Gibbs free energy, which some writers define by the symbol $G$. However, most tables of thermodynamic data use the symbol $F$ for free energy, and this is also used more commonly in engineering.

$$\Delta F = \Delta H - T\Delta S = Q - T\Delta S \tag{2-13}$$

since the heat absorbed $Q = \Delta H$ for a constant pressure process.

Consider now the change in entropy for the reaction. By definition

$$\Delta S = \int \frac{(dQ)_{rev}}{T} = \frac{Q_{rev}}{T} \tag{2-14}$$

where $Q_{rev}$ is the heat absorbed in a reversible process. When the ethanol first starts to dissociate, the reaction is not reversible and Eq. (2-14) would not apply. However, when equilibrium is established, Eq. (2-14) will give the change in entropy for a differential quantity of material reacting in either direction. Thus, at equilibrium, combining Eqs. (2-13) and (2-14)

$$\Delta F = Q - T\frac{Q_{rev}}{T} = 0 \tag{2-15}$$

Thus, the general rule is that the change in free energy is zero for any physical or chemical process in equilibrium at constant temperature and pressure.

### The Fugacity

Suppose we have a perfect gas which expands isothermally and reversibly from a standard pressure $P_0$ to a lower pressure $P_1$. For a perfect gas, $\Delta E$ and $\Delta H$ are both zero for an isothermal expansion. The change in free energy is thus from Eq. (2-14) and the first law for $\Delta E = 0$,

$$\Delta F = \Delta H - T\Delta S = -Q = -\int_{V_0}^{V_1} P\,dV = -RT\int_{V_0}^{V_1} \frac{dV}{V}$$

$$= -RT\ln(V_1/V_0) = RT\ln(P_1/P_0) \tag{2-16}$$

As the pressure $P_1$ approaches zero, the free energy from Eq. (2-16) approaches minus infinity. This is a severe disadvantage in the use of free energy for gases, since the zero of pressure is the point at which all real gases become ideal.

This problem can be eliminated by defining a new function known as the fugacity, $f$, namely,

$$F = RT\ln f + \alpha \tag{2-17}$$

where $\alpha$ is a constant at any given temperature. Differentiating at constant temperature

$$\left(\frac{\partial F}{\partial P}\right)_T = RT\left[\frac{\partial(\ln f)}{\partial P}\right]_T \tag{2-18}$$

By comparing Eqs. (2-16) and (2-17), it can be seen that the fugacity is simply a corrected pressure. For ideal gases, the fugacity is at all times equal to the pressure in atmospheres. For real gases, the fugacity is arbitrarily set equal to the pressure as $P \rightarrow 0$, and the fugacity at higher pressures must be evaluated from experimental P-V-T data.

From the definition of free energy and enthalpy,

$$dF = dH - T \, dS - S \, dT \tag{2-19}$$

$$dH = dE + P \, dV + V \, dP \tag{2-20}$$

but from the first and second laws, for a reversible process

$$dE = dQ - dW = T \, dS - P \, dV \tag{2-21}$$

Combining Eqs. (2-19) through (2-21)

$$dF = V \, dP - S \, dT \tag{2-22}$$

or at constant temperature

$$\left(\frac{\partial F}{\partial P}\right)_T = V \tag{2-23}$$

Thus, from Eqs. (2-18) and (2-23)

$$\ln \, (f_1/f_0) = \ln \, (f_1/P_0) = \frac{1}{RT} \int_{P_0}^{P_1} V \, dP \tag{2-24}$$

where the fugacity at zero pressure $f_0$ is equal to the pressure. Equation (2-24) can be integrated graphically if experimental data are available, or integrated directly by substituting a suitable equation of state for $V$ as a function of $P$.

## CHEMICAL EQUILIBRIUM

As in the case of the other thermodynamic functions, tables of free energies and fugacities are also based on a standard reference state. Free energies for solids and liquids are normally based on the pure material at 1 atm pressure. In the case of gases, free energies are based on the hypothetical perfect-gas state at 1 atm. In most cases there is very little difference between the free energy of a gas in the standard state and the free energy of a real gas at 1 atm. Note that with this definition, all gases have unit fugacity in the standard state.

Let us now determine the change in free energy for a chemical reaction. Suppose we have equilibrium established at some temperature and pressure for a general reaction

$$m\text{M} + n\text{N} + \cdots \rightleftharpoons q\text{Q} + r\text{R} + \cdots \tag{2-25}$$

If $\Delta F$ is the change in free energy when the substances are in any given state, then

$$\Delta F = (qF_Q + rF_R + \cdots) - (mF_M + nF_N + \cdots) \qquad (2\text{-}26)$$

Similarly, if $\Delta F^\circ$ is the change in free energy when each substance is in the standard state, then

$$\Delta F^\circ = (qF_Q^\circ + rF_R^\circ + \cdots) - (mF_M^\circ + nF_N^\circ + \cdots) \qquad (2\text{-}27)$$

If $f^\circ$ and $f$ represent fugacities in the standard and nonstandard states, then from Eq. (2-17)

$$qF_Q - qF_Q^\circ = qRT \ln (f_Q/f_Q^\circ) = RT \ln (f_Q/f_Q^\circ)^q \quad \text{etc.} \qquad (2\text{-}28)$$

Subtracting Eq. (2-27) from Eq. (2-26) and substituting

$$\Delta F - \Delta F^\circ = RT \ln \frac{(f_Q/f_Q^\circ)^q (f_R/f_R^\circ)^r \cdots}{(f_M/f_M^\circ)^m (f_N/f_N^\circ)^n \cdots} \qquad (2\text{-}29)$$

For a gaseous reaction, all fugacities in the standard state are unity and

$$\Delta F - \Delta F^\circ = RT \ln \frac{f_Q^q f_R^r \cdots}{f_M^m f_N^n \cdots} \qquad (2\text{-}30)$$

The quotient in the last term of Eq. (2-30) is known as the fugacity quotient or equilibrium constant for the reaction. If the gases can be treated as ideal, the fugacities become equal to the pressure in atmospheres and

$$\Delta F - \Delta F^\circ = RT \ln \frac{P_Q^q P_R^r \cdots}{P_M^m P_N^n \cdots} \qquad (2\text{-}31)$$

### The Equilibrium Constant

We have seen that $\Delta F = 0$ for a system in equilibrium at a given temperature and pressure. Under these conditions Eq. (2-30) becomes

$$\Delta F^\circ = -RT \ln \frac{f_Q^q f_R^r \cdots}{f_M^m f_N^n \cdots} \qquad (2\text{-}32)$$

Since $\Delta F^\circ$ is a constant at a given temperature, the condition of equilibrium is that the fugacity quotient must also be constant for a system in equilibrium. This quotient is usually referred to as the equilibrium constant $K$, and hence

$$\Delta F^\circ = -RT \ln K \qquad (2\text{-}33)$$

For a system involving only ideal gases,

$$K = \frac{P_Q^q P_R^r \cdots}{P_M^m P_N^n \cdots} \qquad (2\text{-}34)$$

In practice, several types of equilibrium constant are commonly used.

The "true" equilibrium constant is the one defined on the basis of the fugacity ratios or activities as given by Eq. (2-29), namely,

$$K = \frac{(f_Q/f_Q^\circ)^q (f_R/f_R^\circ)^r \cdots}{(f_M/f_M^\circ)^m (f_N/f_N^\circ)^n \cdots} \tag{2-34}$$

This definition of $K$ will always be correct. However, for convenience the equation is often simplified. Thus, for a homogeneous gas reaction, the fugacities in the standard state are equal to unity and

$$K_f = \frac{f_Q^q f_R^r \cdots}{f_M^m f_N^n \cdots} \tag{2-35}$$

where $K_f$ is the equilibrium constant based on fugacities. If the gases are ideal, the fugacities become equal to the pressures in atmospheres and

$$K_p = \frac{P_Q^q P_R^r \cdots}{P_M^m P_N^n \cdots} \tag{2-36}$$

where $K_p$ is the equilibrium constant based on pressures. Equation (2-36) may also be written in terms of the composition of the mixture. Thus, if $P$ is the total pressure and if $x_Q$ = mole fraction of Q in the mixture of ideal gases, etc., then $P_Q = Px_Q$ and

$$K_p = \frac{x_Q^q x_R^r \cdots}{x_M^m x_N^n \cdots} P^{q+r+\cdots-m-n-\cdots} \tag{2-37}$$

The quotient on the right side of Eq. (2-37) is the equilibrium constant based on composition. Thus,

$$K_x = \frac{x_Q^q x_R^r \cdots}{x_M^m x_N^n \cdots} \tag{2-38}$$

Equation (2-38) is also commonly used for solutions, since the fugacity ratios or activities for an ideal solution are usually equal to the mole fractions of the various components present.

Note that the true equilibrium constant is a function of temperature only, but is independent of pressure and composition. However, this is not necessarily true for $K_f$, $K_p$, and $K_x$. In actual practice, $K_p$ is used almost exclusively since most industrial processes involve gaseous reactions where the gases are either close to ideal or else where the fugacities are not known and there is no alternative but to assume the gases are ideal. Note that if there is no change in the total number of moles on each side of the chemical equation, then $K_p = K_x$ and the equilibrium constants are independent of pressure as long as the gases are ideal.

The great value of the free energy is that it permits the determination of the maximum possible yield in a given chemical process. Thus, from tables of standard free energies, it is possible to calculate $K$ at a given temperature; the maximum theoretical yield of product can then be determined from Eq. (2-36) if the reaction involves ideal gases or from Eq. (2-34) or (2-35) if fugacities are known for the particular system under consideration.

## Change of Equilibrium Constant with Temperature

Tables of standard free energy are normally given at room temperature whereas most commercial processes occur at elevated temperatures. The change in free energy with temperature can be determined in the following way. Writing Eq. (2-22) for all reactants and products taking part in a chemical reaction, then at constant pressure

$$\left(\frac{\partial \Delta F}{\partial T}\right)_P = -\Delta S = \frac{\Delta F - \Delta H}{T} \tag{2-39}$$

since $\Delta F = \Delta H - T\Delta S$ for a given reaction. Equation (2-39) is a simple differential equation which may be solved for $\Delta F$ as a function of temperature. Thus changing to ordinary derivatives and remembering that subsequent equations are valid only at constant pressure

$$\frac{d\Delta F}{dT} - \frac{\Delta F}{T} = -\frac{\Delta H}{T}$$

Multiplying by the integrating factor $1/T$,

$$\frac{1}{T}\frac{d\Delta F}{dT} - \frac{\Delta F}{T^2} = \frac{d(\Delta F/T)}{dT} = -\frac{\Delta H}{T^2} \tag{2-40}$$

which can be integrated if $\Delta H$ is known as a function of temperature. Thus, if the heat capacities of reactants and products can be expressed in an equation similar to Eq. (2-10), then

$$\frac{\Delta F}{T} = \int \left(-\frac{\Delta H_I}{T^2} - \frac{\Delta a}{T} - \frac{\Delta b}{2} + \frac{\Delta c}{T^3}\right) dT$$

$$= \frac{\Delta H_I}{T} - \Delta a \ln T - \frac{\Delta b T}{2} - \frac{\Delta c}{2T^2} + I \tag{2-41}$$

The integration constant $I$ can be evaluated if $\Delta F$ is known at any temperature within the temperature range for which the heat capacities are valid. If standard heats of formation and free energies of formation are known at 298°K, then substituing the value of $\Delta H_I$ from Eq. (2-9) and simplifying gives

$$I = \frac{\Delta F^\circ_{298} - \Delta H^\circ_{298}}{298} + 6.697\,\Delta a + 298\,\Delta b - 5.63 \times 10^{-6}\,\Delta c \tag{2-42}$$

If heat capacities are expressed in the form given by Eq. (2-2), the only effect on Eq. (2-41) is to change the fourth term on the right to a $T^2$ term. There is also, of course, a similar change in the last term of Eq. (2-42).

The effect of temperature on the equilibrium constant can also be determined from the above equations. Thus, from Eqs. (2-33) and (2-40), we have the well-known equation of van't Hoff

$$\frac{d(\ln K)}{dT} = \frac{\Delta H^\circ}{RT^2} \qquad (2\text{-}43)$$

From Eq. (2-43) we can see that exothermic reactions ($\Delta H^\circ$ negative) become less favorable at higher temperatures whereas endothermic reactions ($\Delta H^\circ$ positive) become more favorable. A similar conclusion would also be obtained from Le Chatelier's principle. Over small ranges of temperature or where $\Delta H^\circ$ is constant, Eq. (2-43) can be integrated to give

$$-R \ln K = \frac{\Delta H^\circ}{T} + \text{Constant} \qquad (2\text{-}44)$$

where the constant can be evaluated if the equilibrium constant is known at any one temperature. If heat capacity data are available for reactants and products, Eq. (2-41) gives

$$-R \ln K = \frac{\Delta H_I}{T} - \Delta a \ln T - \frac{\Delta b T}{2} - \frac{\Delta c}{2T^2} + I \qquad (2\text{-}45)$$

**Plotting Equilibrium Data**

Experimental values of the equilibrium constant are available for many chemical reactions. If $-R \ln K$ is plotted as a function of the reciprocal of the absolute temperature, over small temperature intervals a straight line should be obtained having a slope equal to $\Delta H^\circ$ from Eq. (2-44). This value of $\Delta H^\circ$ can then be compared with the value from thermal data at the corresponding temperature.

If heat-capacity data are available for all reactants and products, a better correlation of equilibrium measurements can be obtained in the following way. Rewriting Eq. (2-45)

$$\frac{\Delta H_I}{T} + I = \Sigma = -R \ln K + \Delta a \ln T + \frac{\Delta b T}{2} + \frac{\Delta c}{2T^2} \qquad (2\text{-}46)$$

The quantity $\Sigma$ represents the entire right side of Eq. (2-46). If $\Sigma$ is determined at every temperature for which $K$ is known, a plot of $\Sigma$ as a function of $1/T$ gives a straight line of slope $\Delta H_I$ and intercept $I$. The advantage of the $\Sigma$ plot is that it can be used to cover a wider range of temperature than the integrated form of the van't Hoff equation, and is thus better for checking the consistency of equilibrium data. The values of $\Delta H_I$ and $I$ obtained from the $\Sigma$ plot should, of course, agree with those obtained from thermal data.

## The Free-energy Function

Although Eq. (2-41) can be used to calculate the free energy and hence the equilibrium constant at any temperature within the range of validity of the heat-capacity equations, such a calculation is tedious, especially where $\Delta F^\circ$ is changing rapidly with temperature. For this reason, a tabular method is now commonly used to determine free energies. If we consider a particular chemical reaction, the quantity $(\Delta F_T^\circ - \Delta H_0^\circ)/T$ is a slowly varying function of temperature, and is known as the free-energy function. From tabulated values of the free-energy function, it is possible to accurately extrapolate to any intermediate value of temperature and obtain the value of the free energy from the equation

$$\frac{\Delta F_T^\circ}{T} = \frac{(\Delta F_T^\circ - \Delta H_0^\circ)}{T} + \frac{\Delta H_0^\circ}{T} \tag{2-47}$$

Tables of the free-energy function may be given in terms of the standard heats of reaction at absolute zero $\Delta H_0^\circ$ or standard heats of reaction at room temperature $\Delta H_{298}^\circ$. Note also that if a material is formed from its elements, the free-energy function is given in terms of the standard free energy of formation $F_T^\circ$ and standard heat of formation $H_0^\circ$ or $H_{298}^\circ$.

## Electrochemical Processes

Suppose that we allow zinc and sulfuric acid to react at constant pressure in a thermostat. This process will be highly irreversible, and the only work done will be the small amount resulting from the pressure of the evolved hydrogen against the atmosphere. However, it is also possible to carry out the same reaction in a galvanic cell using zinc as one electrode, a second electrode consisting of hydrogen in contact with a platinized electrode and the two electrodes connected to a motor or some suitable electrical system to utilize the electrical energy produced by the cell. Furthermore, if the external electrical system is arranged in such a manner as to balance the cell voltage with a counter emf, the reaction between the zinc and the sulfuric acid can be carried out reversibly and the work thus obtained will be a maximum.

The total work done by such a cell is the sum of the electrical work and the mechanical work $P\ dV$. From the first law for a reversible process

$$dE = dQ - dW = T\,dS - dW \qquad (2\text{-}48)$$

where $dW$ includes both the electrical and mechanical work done by the system. By definition

$$F = H - TS = E + PV - TS$$

However, for a process carried out at constant pressure and constant temperature,

$$dF = dE + P\,dV - T\,dS \qquad (2\text{-}49)$$

Eliminating $dE$ between Eqs. (2-48) and (2-49)

$$-dF = dW - P\,dV \qquad (2\text{-}50)$$

Thus, the decrease in free energy represents the maximum amount of work other than expansion work which can be done by a system in a reversible process at constant temperature and pressure. This is the reason for referring to $F$ as the "free" energy.

If a particular reaction takes place reversibly in an electrical cell, the electrical work done is

$$\Delta W = \Delta F = -n\mathfrak{F}E \qquad (2\text{-}51)$$

where $\mathfrak{F}$ is the Faraday constant 23,062 cal/volt equivalent, $E$ is the cell voltage, and $n$ is the number of equivalents passing through the cell when the particular chemical reaction occurs. From Eqs. (2-39) and (2-51), we can obtain the Gibbs-Helmholtz equation for the temperature coefficient of the emf of a reversible cell, namely,

$$-n\mathfrak{F}\frac{dE}{dT} = -\Delta S = \frac{-n\mathfrak{F}E - \Delta H}{T} \qquad (2\text{-}52)$$

or

$$E + \frac{\Delta H}{n\mathfrak{F}} = T\frac{dE}{dT} \qquad (2\text{-}53)$$

## CHEMICAL KINETICS

Thermodynamics is a very powerful tool for determining the maximum possible yield from a given chemical reaction assuming equilibrium is established. However, the actual yield will always be smaller and will be determined by the kinetics of the particular reaction. For example, ethylene is an extremely important raw material for the petrochemical industry, yet the free energy of formation of ethylene at room temperature is strongly positive. Thus, from the standpoint of thermodynamics, ethylene should immediately dissociate practically 100 per cent into carbon and hydrogen; however, the rate of dissociation is fortunately virtually zero under all practical conditions of temperature and pressure, and ethylene is usually considered to be a completely stable material in chemical reactions.

In actual plant practice, it is always necessary to select rates of flow of material to the various processing vessels which are low enough to permit approximate attainment of equilibrium (theoretically only at zero flow), yet high enough to permit a reasonable production of product. Many industrial processes involve the use of a catalyst. It is important to remember that a catalyst can have no influence on the point of equilibrium as determined by thermodynamics, but can only increase the rate at which equilibrium is attained. Thus, from a practical standpoint, a catalyst permits the use of a smaller processing vessel and often permits operation at a lower temperature where the yield is higher if the reaction is exothermic. Another great advantage of a catalyst is that it can direct the reaction in one particular direction. This is particularly important in the case of organic reactions where side reactions are almost always possible; the use of a proper catalyst can strongly favor one particular reaction, and side reactions can sometimes be hindered by the use of an inhibitor or anticatalyst.

### Reaction Rates

The rate[1] of a reaction can be given in terms of the concentration of any one of the reactants or the products. In the case of liquids, concentrations are normally expressed in moles/liter; however, in the case of gases, concentrations are more commonly given in atmospheres pressure. Thus, if $P_A$ is the concentration of a reactant at any time $t$, the reaction rate is $-dP_A/dt$. Similarly, if $P_B$ is the concentration of a product at time $t$, the reaction rate is $+dP_B/dt$. In some cases it makes a difference which reactant or product is chosen, and this should be clearly specified to avoid confusion. From its definition, reaction rates have the dimensions of concentration divided by time.

Usually, the rate of a reaction varies with the concentration of the reacting substances. The way in which the rate varies with concentration is defined in terms of the order of the reaction. For example, a reaction which is proportional to the first power of one reactant is called a first-order reaction, one which is proportional to the product of two reactant concentrations is a second-order reaction, etc. Thus, in general, if

$$\text{Rate} = kP_A^\alpha P_B^\beta \cdots \tag{2-54}$$

[1] K. J. Laidler, "Chemical Kinetics," New York, McGraw-Hill Book Co., Inc., 1950; P. G. Ashmore, "Catalysis and Inhibition of Chemical Reactions," London, Butterworth and Sons, Ltd., 1963; P. H. Emmett, "Catalysis," New York, Reinhold Publishing Corp., 1954.

the reaction is said to be of the $\alpha$th order with respect to A, etc., and the over-all order of the reaction $n$ is simply $n = \alpha + \beta + \dots$.

If $P_A$, $P_B$, ... in Eq. (2-54) are equal to unity, the reaction rate becomes equal to the constant $k$. For this reason, $k$ is known as the specific reaction rate or the rate constant. The dimensions of $k$ depend on the order of the reaction and the dimensions used for concentration. Obviously, the higher the value of $k$, the faster will be the particular reaction. Note that $k$ is constant only if the temperature is constant; for most reactions, $k$ increases sharply with temperature.

The use of concentration as a measure of reaction rate may lead to some confusion when the rate equations are applied to actual processes, since the quantity of material which has reacted is not always directly proportional to the change in concentration. In these cases, the calculations may be simplified by first carrying out a material balance based on 1 mole of reactant, then changing over to concentration when substituting in the rate equations. Often there is no difference, regardless of which method is used, as in the case of reactions in dilute solution or for reactions of ideal gases at constant pressure where there is no change in the total number of moles. However, in the important industrial case of a gas reaction at constant pressure where there is a change in the total moles, there will be a change in concentration as a result of the change in the total volume, and this change in concentration will be in addition to the change caused by the reaction. The integrated rate equations as normally written are not valid under these conditions, and a different method of calculation is required.

For convenience, let us summarize some of the typical types of kinetic reactions which may be encountered:

(1) **Zero-order, Single Reactant** ($A \xrightarrow{k} B + C + \dots$). In a zero-order reaction, the rate is independent of concentration. This type of reaction is sometimes encountered in surface reactions, for example, the decomposition of ammonia on tungsten, where the diffusion of ammonia from the gas phase to the surface of the tungsten is so rapid in comparison with the other steps in the decomposition that the surface is always saturated and hence the ammonia pressure has essentially no effect on the over-all rate. If $n_A$ is the number of moles of reactant present at any time, then

$$-\frac{dn_A}{dt} = \text{Constant} \tag{2-55}$$

If the gases are ideal, $n_A = P_A V / RT$, where $V$ is the total volume and $P_A$ the partial pressure of the reactant. For a constant volume process or for a constant pressure process where there is no change in the total number of moles, $n_A$ is directly proportional to $P_A$. Under these circumstances Eq. (2-55) becomes

$$-\frac{dP_A}{dt} = k \tag{2-56}$$

This is the customary way of writing a zero-order reaction. On integration

$$P - P_A = kt \tag{2-57}$$

where $P$ is the total pressure, and it is assumed that only the reactant is present at zero time.

Note that Eq. (2-55) is valid for any reaction of this type at constant temperature, even if there is a change in the total number of moles present. However, Eqs. (2-56) and (2-57) would not be valid since $P_A$ would no longer be proportional to $n_A$.

(2) First-order, Single Reactant. This is a very common type of reaction where rate is proportional to concentration and

$$-\frac{dP_A}{dt} = kP_A \tag{2-58}$$

For a constant volume reaction or where there is no change in the total number of moles,

$$\int -\frac{dP_A}{P_A} = k \int dt \qquad \text{or} \qquad P_A = Pe^{-kt} \tag{2-59}$$

where again it is assumed that only the reactant is present at zero time.

But if $P_A$ is expressed in terms of the ideal gas law, substituting into Eq. (2-58) gives

$$\frac{RT}{V}\left(-\frac{dn_A}{dt}\right) = \frac{kn_A RT}{V}$$

or

$$-\frac{dn_A}{dt} = kn_A \qquad \text{and} \qquad n_A = n_{A0}e^{-kt} \tag{2-60}$$

where $n_{A0}$ is the number of moles present at zero time. Thus, for a first-order reaction, the total number of moles present decreases exponentially with time, even if there is a change in the pressure or the volume of the system. The reason for this is that if, for example, the volume is suddenly doubled, the rate of reaction will be only half as great, but the product of the reaction rate and the volume over which the reaction occurs remains unchanged.

(3) Single Reactant, General Order. In the general case

$$-\frac{dP_A}{dt} = kP_A^n \tag{2-61}$$

which for a constant volume process or where there is no change in the total number of moles gives

$$P^{(1-n)} - P_A^{(1-n)} = (1-n)kt \qquad n \neq 1 \qquad (2\text{-}62)$$

In practice, many examples exist where $n$ is not an integer, and values such as $n = 0.5, 1.5$, etc., are quite common for the more complex reactions, especially those involving a complex mechanism.

(4) Second-order, Single Reactant, Change in Volume. To illustrate the calculations when there is a change in the number of moles, consider a constant pressure process where 1 mole of reactant goes to 2 moles of product. The kinetic equation is

$$-\frac{dP_A}{dt} = kP_A^2 \qquad (2\text{-}63)$$

Starting with 1 mole of reactant at zero time, and if $n_A$ is the number of moles of reactant left at any time $t$, then the total number of moles present is $n_A + 2(1 - n_A) = 2 - n_A$. From the ideal gas law,

$$P_A = \frac{n_A RT}{V}$$

$$-\frac{dP_A}{dt} = -\frac{RT}{V}\frac{dn_A}{dt} + \frac{n_A RT}{V^2}\frac{dV}{dt} \qquad (2\text{-}64)$$

The first term on the right of Eq. (2-64) is the decrease of pressure resulting from the loss of reactant. The second term is the decrease of pressure from the increase in volume; this term would be zero if there were no change in the total number of moles present. However, the rate of loss of reactant is given by Eq. (2-63), and hence,

$$-\frac{RT}{V}\frac{dn_A}{dt} = kP_A^2 \qquad (2\text{-}65)$$

The volume from the ideal gas law is

$$V = \frac{(2 - n_A)RT}{P} \qquad \text{or} \qquad \frac{dV}{dt} = -\frac{RT}{P}\frac{dn_A}{dt} \qquad (2\text{-}66)$$

Substituting Eqs. (2-65) and (2-66) into Eq. (2-64)

$$-\frac{dP_A}{dt} = kP_A^2 + \frac{k}{P}P_A^3 \qquad (2\text{-}67)$$

$$-\frac{dP_A}{PP_A^2 + P_A^3} = \frac{k\,dt}{P} \qquad (2\text{-}68)$$

which can be rewritten

$$\frac{dP_A}{P^2 P_A} - \frac{dP_A}{PP_A^2} - \frac{dP_A}{P^2(P + P_A)} = \frac{k \, dt}{P}$$

Integrating between the limits $P$ to $P_A$ and 0 to $t$ gives

$$\frac{1}{P^2} \ln \frac{P_A}{P} + \frac{1}{P} \left( \frac{1}{P_A} - \frac{1}{P} \right) - \frac{1}{P^2} \ln \frac{2P_A}{P + P_A} = \frac{kt}{P} \qquad (2\text{-}69)$$

Thus, even in a simple case, the integrated equation is fairly complex. For a more detailed treatment of reaction rates, the reader is referred to the standard texts.[1]

## Reverse Reactions

If the products of a reaction are much more stable than the reactants, corresponding to a large negative change in $\Delta F°$, then the reaction will proceed essentially in one direction to completion. However, in most practical cases an equilibrium is established which differs appreciably from completion. Under these circumstances there is an increasingly important reverse reaction, and the equation must be written

$$A \underset{k_{-1}}{\overset{k_1}{\rightleftharpoons}} B$$

where $k_{-1}$ is the rate constant in the reverse direction.

The existence of a reverse reaction complicates the kinetic equations. For example, if we have a simple case such as Eq. (2-58) where both reactions are first-order, then

$$+\frac{dP_A}{dt} = -k_1 P_A + k_{-1} P_B = -k_1 P_A + k_{-1}(P - P_A) \qquad (2\text{-}70)$$

where for this very simple reaction, the first term on the right represents the loss of A by the forward reaction and the second term represents the production of A by the reverse reaction. Rewriting Eq. (2-70)

$$\frac{dP_A}{dt} + (k_1 + k_{-1})P_A = k_{-1}P \qquad (2\text{-}71)$$

Multiplying both sides of Eq. (2-71) by the integrating factor $e^{(k_1+k_{-1})t}$ $dt$

$$d[P_A e^{(k_1+k_{-1})t}] = k_{-1} P e^{(k_1+k_{-1})t} \, dt$$

Integrating between the limits $P_A = P$ when $t = 0$ and $P_A = P_A$ when $t = t$,

---

[1] For example, the integrated equations for both batch and flow systems are given by O. A. Hougen and K. M. Watson, "Chemical Process Principles-Part 3," New York, John Wiley & Sons, Inc., 1947.

$$P_A = \frac{P}{k_1 + k_{-1}} \left[ k_{-1} + k_1 e^{-(k_1 + k_{-1})t} \right] \qquad (2\text{-}72)$$

The rate constants in the forward and reverse directions are related to the equilibrium constant $K$ for the reaction. From Eq. (2-70), at equilibrium $dP_A/dt = 0$, and

$$\frac{k_1}{k_{-1}} = \frac{P_B}{P_A} = K \qquad (2\text{-}73)$$

The same result would have been obtained by letting $t$ go to infinity in Eq. (2-72).

It is also possible to simplify the rate equations by substituting the concentration at equilibrium. Thus, the equilibrium pressure of the reactant can be found by setting $t$ equal to infinity in Eq. (2-72) to obtain

$$P_A - P_{Ae} = \frac{Pk_1}{k_1 + k_{-1}} e^{-(k_1 + k_{-1})t} \qquad (2\text{-}74)$$

where $P_{Ae}$ is the equilibrium concentration of the reactant.

### Effect of Temperature

The rate of most chemical reactions increases with temperature. If Eq. (2-73) is substituted into the van't Hoff equation for the variation of equilibrium constant with temperature, then

$$\frac{d(\ln K)}{dT} = \frac{d(\ln k_1)}{dT} - \frac{d(\ln k_{-1})}{dT} = \frac{\Delta H}{RT^2} \qquad (2\text{-}75)$$

which can be split into two equations

$$\frac{d(\ln k_1)}{dT} = \frac{\Delta H_1}{RT^2} + \text{Const.} \qquad \text{and} \qquad \frac{d(\ln k_{-1})}{dT} = \frac{\Delta H_{-1}}{RT^2} + \text{Const.} \qquad (2\text{-}76)$$

where $\Delta H = \Delta H_1 - \Delta H_{-1}$. However, it has been found experimentally that the constant in Eq. (2-76) is zero. Thus,

$$\frac{d(\ln k_1)}{dT} = \frac{\Delta H_1}{RT^2}$$

If $\Delta H_1$ is independent of temperature,

$$k_1 = A e^{-\Delta H_1/RT} \qquad (2\text{-}77)$$

This is the general form of the Arrhenius equation.

The constant $\Delta H_1$ is known as the activation energy for the particular reaction. This corresponds to the minimum energy which must be given the reactants to cause them to react chemically. For example, suppose that two different types of molecules are reacting in the gas phase at a given temperature and pressure. It is known from kinetic theory that the molecules of a gas are in a continual state of motion involving collisions with each other and with the walls of the container. The energy of the individual molecules follows the maxwellian distribution law

$$dn = \frac{2\pi n_0}{(\pi \mathbf{k} T)^{3/2}} E^{1/2} e^{-E/\mathbf{k}T} \, dE \qquad (2\text{-}78)$$

where $dn$ is the number of molecules having an energy between $E$ and $E + dE$, $n_0$ is the total number of molecules, $T$ is the absolute temperature, and $\mathbf{k}$ is Boltzmann's constant $3.30 \times 10^{-24}$ cal/(molecule) (°K). This equation is plotted in Fig. 2-1.

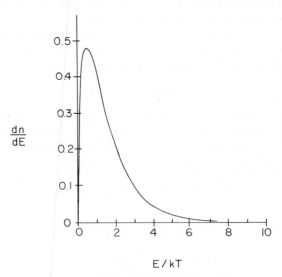

Fɪɢ. 2-1. Maxwellian distribution law.

If the quantity $E \, dn/n_0$ from Eq. (2-78) is integrated from zero to infinity, it is found that the average energy of a molecule is $3\mathbf{k}T/2$. Thus, if we have 1 mole of a gas at a temperature of 1000°K., the energy possessed by these molecules is only about 3000 cal/mole. Yet many common reactions involve activation energies of tens of thousands of calories per mole. How can these reactions take place at any reasonable temperature? The answer is that although the average energy of a molecule is $3\mathbf{k}T/2$, there is a finite probability that a molecule will possess energies of several times the average value. These molecules under the tail of the maxwellian distribution are those which have sufficient energy to react chemically, so that it is perhaps no exaggeration to say that in this case it is the tail that wags the dog. If the temperature is raised, the entire maxwellian distribution curve shifts higher in energy. This is the reason why most reactions have such a strong temperature dependence, since an increase of temperature increases the relative number of active molecules.

The constant $A$ in the Arrhenius equation is called the frequency factor of the reaction. According to simple collision theory, for reactions of higher order than the first, $A$ is proportional to the number of collisions between the reacting molecules.

Although many elementary reactions follow the Arrhenius law and collision theory has been quite successful in explaining such reactions, it must be emphasized that many chemical processes do not, in fact, occur by a simple rearrangement of the molecules in a single step. These more complex reactions take place in a series of steps involving the formation of intermediate compounds which may be present only in very small concentrations. As a specific example, consider the reaction

$$2NO + 2H_2 \xrightarrow{k} N_2 + 2H_2O \tag{2-79}$$

From the stoichiometry of the reaction, it would be expected that the rate should be proportional to the square of both the nitric oxide and the hydrogen concentrations. However, for a homogeneous gas-phase reaction, the rate is proportional to the square of the nitric oxide concentration but only the first power of the hydrogen concentration.[1]

The explanation is that Eq. (2-79) actually takes place in two steps, namely,

$$2NO + H_2 \xrightarrow{k_2} N_2 + H_2O_2 \tag{2-80}$$

$$H_2O_2 + H_2 \xrightarrow{k_3} 2H_2O \tag{2-81}$$

Presumably, the second reaction between hydrogen peroxide and hydrogen is so fast that the over-all reaction is controlled entirely by Eq. (2-80), and hence the reaction rate is dependent on only the first power of the hydrogen concentration.

Many reactions also appear to take place through the formation of intermediate atoms or free radicals. These chain reactions may involve several intermediate steps, and the reaction mechanism may be quite complex. The over-all kinetics of such reactions may be very complicated, involving fractional orders or sometimes an apparent inhibition of the reaction by one of the products.

[1] C. N. Hinshelwood, and T. E. Green, *J. Chem. Soc.*, **129**, 730 (1926).

## CATALYSIS

The rate of a chemical reaction can be greatly increased by the use of a suitable catalyst. In practice, catalysts are used for most exothermic processes where the equilibrium is not virtually 100 per cent to the right. In addition, catalysts are frequently used to direct a reaction in one particular way or to inhibit undesired side reactions. Most industrial catalytic processes involve the use of a heterogeneous gas-phase catalyst consisting of either a high-boiling liquid or, more commonly, a porous bed of solid pellets through which the reacting gases are passed.

Since a catalyst is unchanged during the course of the chemical reaction, it can have no effect on the point of equilibrium. However, the catalyst does enter into the reaction, presumably by forming intermediate compounds with the reactants which then break down to give the products of the reaction and simultaneously regenerate the catalyst. Since the intermediate compounds have lower activation energies, the over-all reaction is thus faster in the presence of the catalyst.

In the case of a solid catalyst, the reaction is assumed to take place in the following way: (1) diffusion of the reactants to the surface of the catalyst; (2) adsorption of the reactants on the surface; (3) reaction on the surface; (4) desorption of the products; (5) diffusion of the products away from the surface. The over-all rate of reaction depends on the rate of each individual step, and it is apparent that one or more of the steps may be controlling. For a nonporous catalyst, the diffusion steps are usually unimportant, and the reaction depends on the adsorption and desorption steps. However, diffusion is often important for a porous catalyst, in which case all five steps must be considered.

### Solid Catalysts

The success of a solid catalyst is dependent on the adsorption and desorption of gases on its surface. Two different types of adsorption may be encountered, depending on the temperature and on the nature of the catalyst and the gas. In the first type, the adsorption is fairly weak and results from the weak Van der Waals forces between the surface and the molecules. The energy involved in this type of adsorption is much too small to materially affect the rate of reaction, and hence Van der Waals adsorption is unimportant in all commercial catalysts.

In the second type of adsorption, the adsorbed molecules are bound to the surface by valence forces of the same magnitude as those occurring in chemical compounds. This type is sometimes called chemisorption, and has been extensively studied by Langmuir. At low pressures, the fraction of the surface covered by the adsorbed molecules is roughly proportional to the absolute pressure; this is equivalent to a first-order kinetic reaction where the rate is proportional to concentration. However, as the pressure is increased, the surface eventually becomes completely covered by a single layer of adsorbed molecules and is thus saturated. The rate of reaction now depends only on the rate of desorption of the products from the surface, and is hence zero-order. Intermediate values of pressure will exhibit a fractional-order reaction.

In practice, these elementary concepts have to be considerably modified. For example, much evidence now indicates that the surface of a catalyst is nonuniform, even in the case of the metal catalysts. There appear to be certain active centers where the heat of adsorption is higher and where the reaction is much more favorable. These active centers appear to be associated with certain types of lattice defects on the surface of the catalyst, and it has been found that the addition of small quantities of "promoter" to the catalyst can increase lattice defects and thereby increase catalytic action.

### Preparation of Catalysts

The preparation of solid catalysts is still very much of an art, and only a few very general rules can be given. Catalysts are usually prepared by precipitation, gel formation, impregnation of an inactive support, or wet mixing of the catalyst components. These are then dried under very carefully controlled conditions, and the dried material ground and screened to obtain the desired particle size. In some cases the catalyst is extruded in the form of tablets or raschig rings. The catalyst is converted to the active state by slow heating to a fairly high temperature; often the heating is done in a special atmosphere such as a reducing, oxidizing or inert atmosphere. Some catalysts require a special further treatment to show maximum activity.

Frequently, some form of carrier is used to act as a base for the catalytic component and give better mechanical properties. Carriers also increase the surface area, increase porosity and decrease the amount of active material which must be used. Common carriers include "Alundum," diatomaceous earth, charcoal, silicon carbide, silica gel, aluminum gel, etc. Usually, the carrier is simply impregnated with a solution of the active material, and then heated to decompose the salt and deposit the catalyst on the surface of the carrier.

The activity of a catalyst can also be increased by the use of a suitable promoter. This consists of the addition of a relatively small quantity of another component to the catalyst in order to increase its effectiveness. The following types of promotion have been observed: (1) Structural promoters increase the surface area of the active component by inhibiting loss of surface during use. An example is the addition of alumina to iron synthetic-ammonia catalyst. (2) The active centers in many oxide catalysts appear to be associated with lattice defects. The addition of small amounts of impurity atoms can greatly increase defects and in some cases increase catalytic activity. (3) A selectivity promoter is commonly used in those cases where more than one reaction is possible. This often involves the poisoning of the sites which are active for the undesired side reaction. An example is the addition of potassium to a Fischer-Tropsch catalyst to poison those sites which are active in cracking the hydrocarbons. (4) Some reactions on metallic surfaces are strongly affected by the electronic character of the surface. An electronic promoter may be added to increase the number of electron "holes" in the metal, and thereby increase catalytic activity.

It has also been found that certain impurities in the processing streams can poison a catalyst. The most common type of poisoning involves the adsorption of the poison on the surface to convert the active sites into an inactive surface. For example, compounds of sulfur and arsenic will poison many of the common catalysts. A second type of poison includes those which influence the selectivity by gradually poisoning the active sites for the desired reaction. The best example of this is heavy metals in gas oils used for catalytic cracking. A third type of poison includes those which mechanically affect the catalyst. For example, steam poisons silica and aluminum gel catalysts as a result of a gradual sintering process which fills the pores of the catalyst and thereby reduces the surface area. A fourth type of poison includes those which block diffusion of reactants to the active centers of the catalyst. An example is the deposition of entrained solids on the surface of a porous catalyst to mechanically prevent the reactants from reaching the internal surfaces.

## Engineering Design

The amount of catalyst required in a given process can be calculated if the reaction rates are known as a function of temperature and pressure. However, in practice, the design calculations are usually based on the space velocity, namely, the rate of gas flow measured at standard conditions which can be used for each cubic foot of catalyst. This is, of course, equal to the reciprocal of the catalyst contact time. The method is more or less empirical, since allowable space velocities vary with temperature, pressure and concentration of reactants. However, the method is widely used because of its simplicity and because it is so easy to scale up laboratory experiments to actual commercial design.

# CHAPTER 3

# Natural Salts

The naturally occurring salts include the following: (1) Common salt, sodium chloride, occurs in many areas as rock salt, salt brines, and in sea water. (2) Salt cake, sodium sulfate, is present in western semidry lake beds. (3) Soda ash, sodium carbonate, is prepared from the mineral trona, a hydrated sodium sesquicarbonate. (4) Potassium chloride occurs as the mineral sylvinite in the Carlsbad region of New Mexico and in the complex mixture of salts present in Searles Lake, California. (5) Bromine and iodine occur in sea water and in natural brines on the Michigan Peninsula.

The importance of natural salts can perhaps be appreciated from the fact that they serve as the ultimate source of essentially all compounds of sodium, potassium, bromine, chlorine and iodine. The early location of the chemical industry was based largely on the availability of common salt as a raw material, and this is still a determining factor in the location of much of our heavy chemical industry.

## COMMON SALT

Table 3-1 gives the chief uses of salt in the United States. About 39 per cent of the total production goes to the manufacture of chlorine and caustic, about 21 per cent is used to manufacture soda ash and 13 per cent goes for highway snow and ice removal, smaller amounts being used in chemical manufacture of various kinds, animal feeds, meatpacking, as table salt, etc. Note that over half the salt produced is in the form of brine for the manufacture of chlorine and soda ash.

Sodium chloride is one of the most widely distributed of our chemical raw materials.[1] An inexhaustible supply of salt is available from sea

[1] "Sodium Chloride," D. W. Kaufmann, Editor, New York, Reinhold Publishing Corp., 1960.

water in the form of a solution varying from about 1-5 per cent of total dissolved solids (salinity), with an average of 3.5 per cent. The composition of the dissolved solids is quite uniform, namely, 55 per cent chlorine, 31 per cent sodium, 8 per cent sulfate ion, 4 per cent magnesium and about 1 per cent each of calcium and potassium. At one time it was believed that the oceans were originally fresh water, and the salt content gradually built up as a result of the leaching of the continental rocks by rain water with the transport of soluble minerals to the ocean. However,

TABLE 3-1.  SALT SOLD OR USED IN THE UNITED STATES IN 1963
(From Minerals Yearbook, 1963; figures are in thousands of short tons)

| Use | Evaporated | Rock | Brine | Total |
|---|---|---|---|---|
| Chlorine and caustic | (1) | (1) | 10,121 | 11,985 |
| Soda ash | (1) | (1) | 6,508 | 6,513 |
| States and counties (snow removal) | (1) | 3707 | (1) | 3,909 |
| Misc. chemical manufacture | (1) | (1) | 733 | 1,418 |
| Feed dealers | 615 | 415 | — | 1,030 |
| Grocery stores (table salt) | 576 | 286 | — | 862 |
| Meatpackers, tanners, casing manufacturers | 333 | 414 | — | 747 |
| Water softening | (1) | 293 | (1) | 507 |
| Other | (1) | (1) | (1) | 3,673 |
| Total | 4774 | 8345 | 17,525 | 30,644 |

(1) Figures withheld to avoid disclosing individual company confidential data. Included in total figures.

all geologic and biologic evidence is opposed to this theory, and it is now believed that the composition of the ocean has been essentially unchanged since the earliest forms of life appeared on the earth.

Although sea water is an important source of salt in many regions of the world, in recent years it has accounted for only a small fraction of the production of salt in the United States. Substantial quantities of salt are produced by solar evaporation of sea water in the San Francisco Bay area. This region is favored because the evaporation rate is several times the annual rainfall, large areas of low tidelands having essentially no other value are available, and there is proximity to markets and low-cost shipping facilities, important considerations for a low-price material. Sea water is simply pumped to large ponds where solar evaporation increases the density from 3 to about 20°Bé. The solution is then transferred to "lime" ponds where further evaporation increases the density to about 26°Bé and deposits most of the calcium sulfate present in the sea water. The concentrated brine is then transferred to the crystallizing or harvesting ponds where most of the salt is deposited from solution. Salt production is about 550 ton/(year)(acre), based on the total pond area.

### Rock Salt

Deposits of salt occur in the United States in three major basins: (1) The Eastern Basin includes the important salt-producing states of Michigan, Ohio and New York. Here the salt occurs as beds up to several hundred feet in thickness and at depths ranging from several hundred to several thousand feet. (2) The Gulf Coast salt basin includes the coastal regions of Texas, Louisiana and Mississippi. Here the salt occurs most commonly in the form of salt domes in which salt under high pressure and temperature has been forced upward through the earth by plastic flow to form a vertical cylinder of very pure salt. These domes are up to 4 miles in diameter and 6 miles in depth, and are covered by a relatively thin cap consisting largely of calcite, gypsum, and anhydrite. (3) The Southwest or Permian Basin underlies thousands of square miles of Texas, Oklahoma, New Mexico, Colorado and Kansas. These deposits have not been worked extensively for salt, chiefly because of the relatively large distance from markets. However, this basin does serve as an important source of potassium which was deposited after the deposition of the sodium chloride.

Rock salt is mined in very much the same way as coal, namely, by deep shaft and room-and-pillar systems. Usually, primary crushing is done underground, the salt is loaded into a mine car and transported to a skip hoist which carries it to the surface. The crude rock salt is further crushed and screened, and can be used directly for such purposes as highway snow removal. When a more pure salt is required, the rock salt can be dissolved in water, treated with such materials as soda ash and caustic to precipitate impurities, filtered, and the purified salt crystallized by multiple-effect evaporation in conventional cast iron evaporators fitted with copper, "Monel," or stainless steel heating elements.

### Natural Brines

Depending on the source, ground waters vary in salinity from practically pure water to saturated solutions. Although salt is the most common dissolved mineral in ground water, calcium, magnesium, potassium, bromine and iodine may also be present. Natural brines have been an important source of salt since prehistoric time. In some cases the brines reach the surface as a salt spring; usually, however, a well must be drilled directly into the reservoir rock and the brine obtained by pumping. Michigan, Ohio and West Virginia produce large quantities of salt from natural brines.

When salt is used as a raw material for chemical manufacture, the salt is normally used in the form of a solution in water. Here natural brines have a considerable economic advantage, since they can be used directly without the need for evaporation and crystallization of pure product. Although natural brines are still used to some extent for chemical manufacture, it is now more common to produce an artificial brine by direct injection of water into an underground salt deposit.

## Salt Lakes

Water tends to accumulate in any topographic depression which occurs on the earth. If the climate is sufficiently dry so that evaporation balances inflow of water, and if the floor of the depression is sufficiently impervious to water, then the water will eventually become mineralized because the inflowing streams carry in minerals in solution whereas only pure water evaporates. The composition of the water depends, of course, on the composition of the rocks that make up the watershed. The sodium chloride lakes are either bodies of sea water which have been cut off from the oceans, or else they are created by the leaching of salt from the rocks of the watershed. Because of the low rainfall and high evaporation, many salt lakes occur in the western United States. The mineral content ranges from practically pure salt to complicated mixtures of salt, potassium, magnesium, boron, etc.

The most important salt sake in the United States is Great Salt Lake in Utah. This lake is only the remnant of a much larger fresh water lake, Lake Bonneville, which formerly covered this region and discharged north into the Snake River. Great Salt Lake varies considerably in size, depending on the precipitation and evaporation. The water is so close to saturation with sodium chloride that salt crystals are often precipitated on the floor of the lake. In spite of the unlimited quantities of salt which are available in a fairly concentrated solution, only a relatively small amount is produced by solar evaporation. This can be attributed to the limited markets in the vicinity of Salt Lake City and high shipping costs that make it uneconomic to ship a cheap product over large distances.

## Brine Wells

As illustrated in Fig. 3-1, most of the salt used for chemical manufacture comes directly from brine wells. An artificial brine well consists essentially of a well drilled directly into a layer of salt with an 8- or 10-in. steel casing extending from the ground level down to the top of the salt layer. Within the casing is a central pipe of about 4-6 in. diameter which extends down into the salt layer below the end of the casing. By a valve arrangement at the top known as a "christmas tree," means are provided for pumping water down through the annular space into the stratum and withdrawing brine through the central pipe. Sometimes it is necessary to reverse the flow of water and brine in order to

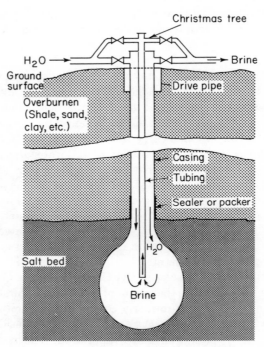

Fig. 3-1. Typical brine well (see D. W. Kaufmann, *op. cit.*).

unplug the central pipe or to modify the shape of the underground cavity.

As the well continues to operate, an enormous cavity is gradually formed within the salt bed. Eventually, this may become large enough to cause a cave-in of the roof and resultant failure of the well. However, experience has shown that brine wells are most likely to fail shortly after they are placed in service, and the chances of failure become less once they survive their "childhood diseases."

Hydraulic fracturing[1] is now commonly used to increase the output of brine wells. This is done by drilling a series of wells to the base of a salt formation, and then injecting water under high pressure into one of the wells and continuing to pump until a fracture occurs to a nearby

[1] U.S. Bureau of Mines, "Minerals Yearbook," 1963.

well. After the fracture, which is indicated by a pressure increase in the opposing well, the pumping is continued until the channel becomes large enough for a flow of about 300 gal/min, which is considered to be a satisfactory production rate. Although several weeks or months may be necessary to complete this "wash in" phase, conventional brine wells often require several years to achieve maximum production.

## NATURAL SODA ASH

The word "soda ash" goes back to very early days when primitive people burned the stalks of certain plants to ashes which were leached with hot water to obtain a brown-colored lye for domestic laundering. Natural sodium carbonate is produced from the brines of Searles Lake and Owens Lake in California, and from trona in southwestern Wyoming. The trona production is by far the most important. Figure 3-2 illustrates the production of both natural and manufactured soda ash in recent years. It can be seen that essentially all the increase has been in the natural product. This is discussed in a recent survey[1] which estimates that the cost to construct a 1000 ton/day plant to produce soda ash by the ammonia-soda process (this is the smallest plant that can be operated profitably in the United States) is approximately 40 million dollars, whereas the cost of a comparable plant to produce natural soda ash is only about half as great. Although about 80 per cent of the soda ash is consumed in eastern markets, recently reduced freight rates and the introduction of high-capacity 95-ton cars have benefitted the natural product. There is essentially no difference in quality between the natural and manufactured products. Table 3-2 gives estimated capacities for soda ash in the United States.

The trona which occurs in the Green River Basin of Wyoming is a hard, greyish white mineral consisting of sodium sesquicarbonate, $Na_2CO_3 \cdot NaHCO_3 \cdot 2H_2O$. About 50 million years ago, this region was covered by a large fresh water lake. Later the climate became more arid, the lake started to shrink, and gradually became an alkaline lake containing appreciable quantities of sodium carbonate and sodium bicarbonate which was in equilibrium with the carbon dioxide of the air. When the lake reached its smallest size, the trona was deposited in the form of beds 10-20 ft in thickness. In subsequent years the lake expanded in size, and the trona became overlaid with layers of shale and other sediments until the trona was buried to a depth of about a mile. Millions of years later the entire region was uplifted and partially eroded, exposing the lake beds and permitting economic mining of the trona.

[1] "Soda Ash on Parade," *Oil Paint Drug Reporter,* **182**(16), 3 (1962).

The crude ore contains more than 90 per cent trona, about 7 per cent insoluble shale, and 0.3 per cent organic. Commercially, the trona is mined using conventional room-and-pillar mining by either blasting the ore or cutting it out by means of a continuous boring machine. The ore

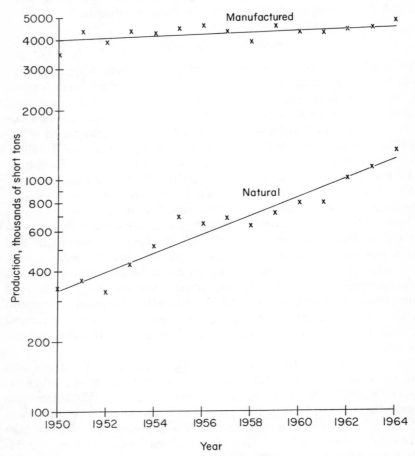

Fig. 3-2. United States production of soda ash in recent years (Bureau of The Census Reports).

is transported to the surface by conveyors and a skip hoist, where it is crushed and dissolved in water. Insolubles are allowed to settle, the solution is filtered, cooled under vacuum to crystallize purified trona, and the crystals separated from the mother liquor by centrifugation. Both light and dense soda ash are made by calcining the purified trona.

TABLE 3-2.  SODA ASH ANNUAL PRODUCTION CAPACITY
[Survey by *Chem.* and *Eng. News*, *41* (34), 19 (1963)]

| Manufactured Soda* | Plant Location | Process | Annual Capacity (thousands of short tons) |
|---|---|---|---|
| Allied Chemical | Baton Rouge, La. | Ammonia-soda | 875 |
| Allied Chemical | Detroit, Mich. | Ammonia-soda | 800 |
| Allied Chemical | Syracuse, N.Y. | Ammonia-soda | 900 |
| Diamond Alkali | Painesville, Ohio | Ammonia-soda | 700 |
| Dow Chemical | Freeport, Texas | Caustic carbonation | 180 |
| Olin Mathieson | Lake Charles, La. | Ammonia-soda | 375 |
| Olin Mathieson | Saltville, Va. | Ammonia-soda | 360 |
| Pittsburgh Plate Glass | Barberton, Ohio | Ammonia-soda | 600 |
| Pittsburgh Plate Glass | Corpus Christi, Texas | Ammonia-soda | 240 |
| Wyandotte | Wyandotte, Mich. | Ammonia-soda | 700 |
| Total | | | 5730 |
| *Natural Soda* | | | |
| American Potash and Chem. | Trona, Calif. | Lake brine evaporation | 150 |
| FMC Corp. | Green River, Wyo. | Trona mining | 750 |
| Pittsburgh Plate Glass | Bartlett, Calif. | Lake brine evaporation | 70 |
| Stauffer Chem. Co. | Green River, Wyo. | Trona mining | 200 |
| Stauffer Chem. Co. | Westend, Calif. | Lake brine evaporation | 150 |
| Total | | | 1320 |

* Note that the capacity is about 25 per cent greater than the total 1963 production of soda ash.

## SALT CAKE

Crude sodium sulfate was referred to as "salt cake" because it represented the final residue from the Mannheim furnace reaction between salt and sulfuric acid to generate hydrogen chloride. Natural sodium sulfate is produced from natural brines occurring near Monahans and Brownfield, Texas, and as a by-product in the working of the brines at Searles Lake, California. Table 3-3 gives the 1963 production of salt cake. Note that the natural product represents about 35 per cent of the total production, and that most of the manufactured salt cake is produced as a by-product. The manufacture of kraft paper accounts for about 70 per cent of the end use of salt cake. In addition to the United States production, substantial quantities of natural salt cake are also produced in Canada where the material is recovered from lake beds in Saskatchewan.

The solubility of sodium sulfate in water is shown in Fig. 3-3. Note

TABLE 3-3.  SODIUM SULFATE PRODUCTION IN THE
UNITED STATES* FOR 1963

| Process | Production (thousands of short tons) |
|---|---|
| Mannheim and Hargreaves | 201 |
| Viscose rayon | 378 |
| Sodium dichromate | 92 |
| Phenol, boric acid, formic acid, etc. | 127 |
| Total manufactured and by-product | 798 |
| Natural salt cake | 435 |
| Grand total | 1233 |

* Bureau of Census reports, Bureau of Mines, "Minerals Yearbook 1963."

the steep solubility for the Glauber's salt and the transition point to the anhydrous form at well below the boiling point of the saturated solution.

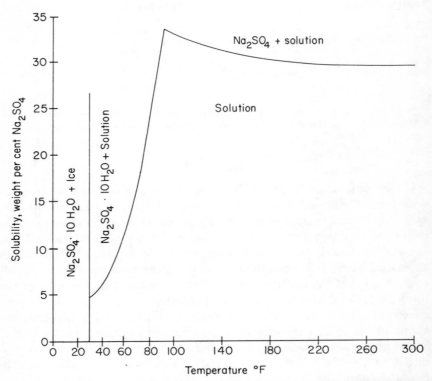

FIG. 3-3. Solubility of sodium sulfate in water (data from A. Seidell, "Solubilities of Inorganic and Metal Organic Compounds," D. Van Nostrand, 1941).

Commercially,[1] sodium sulfate is recovered by crystallizing Glauber's salt at about 30°F, filtering, washing, and evaporating the water of crystallization by means of a submerged combustion evaporator.

## POTASH

The word "potash" goes back to the early days of the United States when potassium salts were produced by burning hardwoods and leaching the ashes with water to recover crude potassium carbonate. In principle, the word potash should refer only to potassium carbonate; however, in the fertilizer industry the word potash is used to refer to any potassium salt, the potassium content of which is usually given in terms of the oxide $K_2O$.

About 94 per cent of the potash which is produced in the United States[2] goes into the manufacture of fertilizers, usually in the form of potassium chloride. About 6 per cent of the total potash goes for industrial use, the soap industry taking the greatest share for the manu-

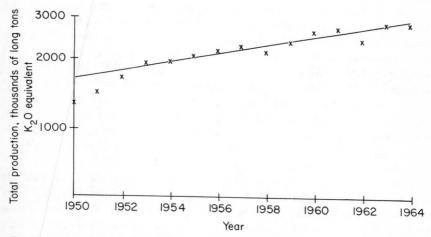

Fig. 3-4. United States production of potash in recent years (Bureau of Mines "Minerals Yearbook").

facture of soaps and synthetic detergents. Figure 3-4 shows the total production of potash in recent years. It can be seen that there is a

---

[1] W. I. Weisman, "Sodium Sulfate from Brine," *Chem. Eng. Progr.,* **60**(11), 47 (1964).

[2] George Sweeney and James Bradley, "Potash Minerals in the West," paper presented at Las Vegas meeting of Amer. Inst. of Chem. Eng., Sept. 21, 1964.

strongly increasing demand, largely because of the population explosion which is increasing the demand for fertilizer.

## Occurrence of Potash

All deposits of potash presumably were produced by the evaporation of sea water or mineralized lake water. When sea water evaporates, the salts are deposited approximately in reverse order of their solubility, namely, calcium carbonate, gypsum, salt, magnesium chloride and sulfate, sodium bromide and potassium chloride. In practice, this must be considerably modified because there is always some overlap in the separations; double salts and eutectics may crystallize solids of mixed composition, interruptions of one type or another may occur during precipitation, and secondary changes may completely alter the nature of the deposits. In general, laboratory experiments can never duplicate actual conditions in nature, and geological studies have shown many differences between the theoretical and actual deposits of salt.

Up to World War I, practically the entire world's supply of potash was produced from the Stassfürt deposits in Germany. These deposits occur as the result of the evaporation during Permian time of a large sea which once covered northern Germany and the Netherlands. The potassium salts are contained in a layer several hundred feet thick which is overlaid and underlaid by layers of salt, anhydrite, clay, limestone and sandstone. Core drillings show that at least three cycles of evaporation occurred at Stassfürt, each one being ended by the influx of sea water which deposited a clay sediment that prevented the re-solution of the deposited salts. Only the first cycle, however, proceeded into the potash deposition stage. The potash reserves at Stassfürt are very large, estimates ranging from the tens to thousands of billions of tons. The most important potash mineral is carnallite, $KCl \cdot MgCl_2 \cdot 6H_2O$.

Table 3-4 gives information on potash production in the United States and Canada. The most important potash deposits in the United States are those in the Carlsbad region of New Mexico. In Permian time, a shallow sea covered large areas of Kansas, Colorado, Oklahoma, Texas and New Mexico. Since the lowest point of the basin was in southwestern New Mexico, the final precipitation of potassium from the mother liquor or "bittern" occurred in that region. The potash deposits in Carlsbad are at depths of 1200-1500 ft and occur in beds approximately 10-20 ft thick. The chief mineral mined at Carlsbad is sylvinite, a physical mixture of sylvite (KCl) and halite (NaCl). In addition, two producers mine langbeinite, $K_2SO_4 \cdot 2MgSO_4$.

Other producers of potash include American Potash and Chemical which has been recovering potash from the brines of Searles Lake, California since World War I. Searles Lake is the remnant of a former fresh-water lake that received alkaline drainage from the surrounding mountains. The potash is present in the form of a very complex mixture of salts. Also, Texas Gulf Sulfur has recently opened a mine near Moab,

TABLE 3-4.   UNITED STATES AND CANADIAN POTASH CAPACITY
(From Sweeney and Bradley, *op. cit.*)

| United States | Capacity (thousands of short tons $K_2O$) |
|---|---|
| *Carlsbad, New Mexico* | |
| United States Borax | 540 |
| Potash Corporation of America | 580 |
| International Minerals and Chemical | 425 |
| Duval | 450 |
| Southwest Potash | 495 |
| National Potash | 300 |
| Kermac | 300 |
| *California* | |
| American Potash and Chemical | 220 |
| *Utah* | |
| Bonneville, Ltd. | 110 |
| Texas Gulf Sulfur | 360 |
| Total United States | 3780 |
| *Canada* | |
| International Minerals and Chemical | 960 |
| Potash Corporation of America | 360 |
| Kalium Chemicals, Ltd. | 360 |
| Alwinsal Potash of Canada, Ltd. | 600 |
| United States Borax and Chemical | 600 |
| Total Canada | 2880 |

Utah to exploit a rich deposit of sylvinite. The Utah deposit is at a depth of about 3000 ft, but the richer ore will offset the greater depth from which it must be brought to the surface. In addition, a fairly small operation near Wendover, Utah recovers potash from salt brines.

Of considerable importance to the potash industry are the rich deposits discovered recently in Saskatchewan. The chief mineral is sylvinite having a composition of 25-35 per cent $K_2O$. The Canadian deposits are fairly deep, running from 3000-5000 ft in depth. Known reserves are in the order of billions of tons of potash, and it is possible these deposits may eventually exceed the present known world reserves.

### Separation of Potash

At Carlsbad, potash is recovered from sylvinite by flotation[1] of the potassium chloride. The ore is first ground to about 8-mesh, slurried in a saturated brine composed of the soluble constituents of the ore, and introduced to a flotation cell which is aerated at the bottom, froth being removed from the top. The collector reagent is a long-chain aliphatic amine containing 7-18 carbon atoms. Auxiliary reagents include alkyl-naphthalenes or alkyl sulfides. The recovery of KCl is better than 95 per cent. A similar flotation process is used by Texas Gulf Sulfur for the Utah ore.

Much of the high-grade sylvinite ore contains a clay slime which causes problems in the flotation since it tends to adsorb the flotation agent. When clay is present, the ground ore is sent to a classifier to separate coarse and fine fractions which are treated separately to remove the clay. The treatment consists of washing, desliming and a final addition of starch to act as a clay-blocking agent.

Two producers at Carlsbad are reported to mine langbeinite, $K_2SO_4 \cdot 2MgSO_4$, which often occurs as a mixture with sylvinite. International Minerals and Chem. Corp. has recently announced a new flotation process which separates sylvinite from langbeinite. This has essentially doubled the potash reserves at Carlsbad, since it permits the mining of mixed ores which could not previously be processed economically. Langbeinite is refined by adding KCl to produce a double decomposition with the formation of $K_2SO_4$ and $MgCl_2$, which are separated by crystallization.

The brines at Wendover, Utah are largely mixed chlorides of potassium, sodium and magnesium. These are solar evaporated to precipitate a mixture of potassium chloride and sodium chloride, and the potassium chloride is then separated by flotation.

The Searles Lake brine is a complex mixture of $NaCl$, $Na_2SO_4$, $Na_2CO_3$, $KCl$, $Na_2B_4O_7$ and smaller quantities of bromine, lithium, phosphate, iodine, etc. Figure 3-5 illustrates the processes used to separate these chemicals. The first step is a triple-effect evaporation with cycled mother liquors to precipitate sodium chloride and the double salt, burkeite, $Na_2CO_3 \cdot 2Na_2SO_4$. A relatively small amount of $Li_2NaPO_4$ also precipitates during this initial evaporation. The precipitate is classified in a salt removal system, the fines consisting chiefly of burkeite and entrained lithium values. The burkeite is leached free of NaCl and dissolved in water; the lithium-sodium phosphate remains in suspension and is re-

---

[1] Wilson, M., U.S. Patent 3,059,774; (assigned to U.S. Borax and Chemical) *Chem. Eng. News,* **37** (38), 46 (1959).

moved by froth flotation. The clarified burkeite is cooled to precipitate Glauber's salt, sodium chloride is added to precipitate any remaining sulfate as burkeite, and the solution sent to the carbonate process to recover soda ash. The hot concentrated liquor from the main evapora-

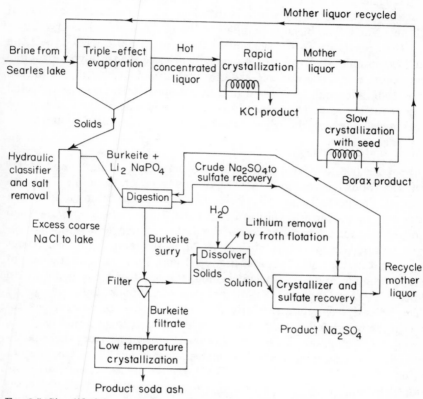

FIG. 3.5. Simplified Searles Lake separation process [J. V. Hightower, *Chem. Eng.*, **58** (8), 104 (1951)].

tors is cooled rapidly to crystallize potassium chloride while the borax remains in solution as a supersaturated solution. The mother liquor from the potash crystallization is then further cooled with the addition of borax seed crystals to precipitate crude borax.

The composition of the brine at Searles Lake varies considerably from point to point. The "lower brine" contains a much larger percentage of soda ash, which can be recovered by first carbonating the brine with $CO_2$ followed by crystallization of the soda ash.

The operation of Kalium Chemicals, Ltd., in Saskatchewan is of particular interest since solution mining will be used. The process[1] consists of first creating a cavity in the salt formation immediately below the potash layer by dissolving out the salt using a hydrocarbon layer to float on the injected water and prevent solution at the interface. After creating a sufficiently large cavity, the point of injection is then raised to the potash layer where the sylvinite is dissolved by a hot mixed solution of KCl and NaCl. The brine is pumped to the surface, cooled to crystallize KCl, then recycled. To be economical the process must recover as little NaCl as possible. By providing a cavity below the potash layer, insoluble components can settle out and thereby minimize blocking of the potash layer itself. Although the cost of potash obtained in this way is expected to be about the same as by the conventional methods, it does offer some advantages, particularly where deposits lie at substantial depths.

### Bromine and Iodine

About 200,000 tons/year of bromine are produced in the United States from the following sources: (a) Ethyl-Dow recovers bromine from sea water at Freeport, Texas. (b) FMC Corp. recovers bromine from sea water bittern at Newark, California. (c) American Potash and Chemical recovers by-product bromine at Searles Lake. (d) Several producers recover bromine from natural brines in Michigan and Arkansas. About 80 per cent of the total bromine produced goes into the manufacture of methyl bromide and ethylene dibromide, the chief end use being as an additive to tetraethyl or tetramethyl lead antiknock fluid.

The process[2] consists essentially of using chlorine to replace the bromine in the brine, followed by blowing with air to recover bromine. Thus, Michigan Chemical at El Dorado, Arkansas uses brine from the Smackover oil field containing 4200 ppm of bromine, about twice the concentration of the Michigan brines. The brine is treated to remove oil, pumped through brush-packed wooden towers to remove dissolved gases such as $H_2S$, and sent through a heat exchanger with stripped-end brine. The heated brine flows to ceramic packed towers where it is stripped of bromine by ascending steam and chlorine. Bromine vapors are condensed in a tantalum condenser, decanted from the water layer and purified by distillation and dehydration with sulfuric acid.

Iodine is recovered from well brines by Dow Chemical at Midland, Michigan. The hot brine containing 38 ppm of iodine is acidified with HCl and oxidized with chlorine to liberate iodine. The brine then passes

[1] J. B. Dahms and B. P. Edmonds, Canadian Patent 672,308 (1963).
[2] *Chem. Eng.*, **65**(11), 51 (1958).

down a packed tower where recycled air strips the iodine from solution. The iodine is absorbed in a tower fed with water and $SO_2$; the resulting $HI$-$H_2SO_4$ solution is then sent to a precipitator where gaseous chlorine precipitates elemental iodine which is removed by filtration.

# CHAPTER 4

# Manufactured Soda Ash
# and Chemical Caustic

About 40 per cent of the total soda ash production goes into the manu-facture of glass, 25 per cent goes for chemical manufacture and smaller amounts are used in the manufacture of pulp and paper, soaps and de-tergents, aluminum, in water treatment, etc. As was discussed briefly in Chapter 3, the manufactured soda ash industry has been essentially static in recent years. Some of the problems besetting the industry are as follows:

(1) Competition with Natural Soda Ash. A plant to produce natural soda ash can be constructed at about half the cost of an ammonia-soda plant. For this reason alone, any future growth will probably be in the natural product.

(2) Competition with Electrolytic Caustic. Because of the increasing demand for chlorine, there has been an equivalent increase in the pro-duction of the coproduct caustic soda. Thus, in the past 25 years, lime-soda caustic has decreased from about half the total caustic market to less than 5 per cent at present. In addition, caustic and soda ash are direct competitors in many applications. Even though caustic is more expensive on an equivalent $Na_2O$ basis, the increasing availability of caustic near the site of the consumer's operation and the cost of shipping soda ash often make the two alkalis comparable in price.

(3) The manufacturing plants that produce soda ash are old and plagued by rising costs of labor, materials, and repairs. The most recent plant to be constructed in the United States was completed in 1935.

## LE BLANC PROCESS

Although the Le Blanc process is now obsolete, it has considerable historical interest because it stimulated the development of our modern chemical industry. During the Napoleonic wars,[1] the French were cut off from their source of Spanish barilla (seaweed) which served as the source of natural soda. In 1775, the French Academy of Science offered a prize of 2400 livres for the development of a practical process to manufacture soda. The most promising method was one by Nicholas Le Blanc (1742-1806) which was based on common salt. Le Blanc obtained a patent in 1791, and received 200,000 livres from the Duke of Orleans to construct a plant near Paris to manufacture soda. However, the Duke was guillotined in 1793, Le Blanc was forced to make his patent public, but the manufacturing plant could not be operated because of a lack of working capital. Although it was promised him, the Academy of Science never awarded the prize to Le Blanc, and he was forced to spend his last years in an almshouse where he committed suicide in 1806.

The first commercial success of the Le Blanc process was in England where the repeal of a high tax on salt made available this raw material at a reasonable cost. The chemical reactions in the Le Blanc process are as follows:

$$2NaCl \text{ (s)} + H_2SO_4 \text{ (l)} \rightarrow Na_2SO_4 \text{ (s)} + 2HCl \text{ (g)} \qquad (4\text{-}1)$$

$$Na_2SO_4 + 4C \rightarrow Na_2S + 4CO \qquad (4\text{-}2)$$

$$Na_2S + CaCO_3 \rightarrow Na_2CO_3 + CaS \qquad (4\text{-}3)$$

The reaction between salt and sulfuric acid was first carried out in a reverberatory furnace; later, mechanical furnaces were used such as the Mannheim furnace which has mechanical scrapers to work the charge from the center of the furnace to the outside edge where the salt cake discharges. Originally, the evolved HCl gas was released to the atmosphere, but in later years it was recovered to make bleaching powder. The saltcake was then mixed with limestone and coal, and heated to 900-1000°C to fuse the saltcake and convert it to soda ash. The "black ash" was then leached with water, carbonated to remove impurities, and the soda ash crystallized from solution.

## AMMONIA-SODA PROCESS

The general chemical principles of the ammonia-soda process were developed in the first half of the nineteenth century, but all early attempts to commercialize the process failed. In 1861, Ernest Solvay, a Belgian, independently discovered the process and constructed a plant to manufacture soda ash. Following the success of his first plant, Solvay rapidly expanded operations until by the turn of the century the Solvay Syndi-

[1] T. P. Hou, "Manufacture of Soda," New York, Chemical Catalog Co., Inc., 1933.

cate controlled about 90 per cent of the world's production of soda ash. The development of the ammonia-soda process also rendered the Le Blanc process obsolete, and by the time of the first world war the Le Blanc process was extinct.

The success of Ernest Solvay was entirely dependent on efficient engineering, particularly methods for the recovery of the ammonia used in the process. Solvay had a central research organization which kept in close contact with the manufacturing plants. Any improvements in the process were immediately made available to all individual plants, and under these conditions the cost of manufactured soda ash rapidly decreased. In fact, the name of Solvay is so closely associated with the

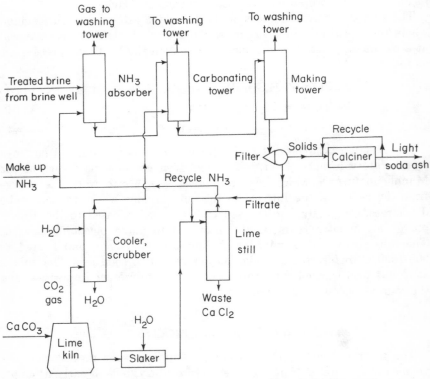

Fig. 4-1. Simplified flowsheet for ammonia-soda (Solvay) process.

growth of the industry that the ammonia-soda process is commonly referred to as the "Solvay process."

The ammonia-soda process for the manufacture of soda ash is illustrated in Fig. 4-1. The chief reactions are as follows:

$$NH_3 \text{ (sol'n)} + H_2O \text{ (l)} + CO_2 \text{ (g)} \rightleftharpoons NH_4HCO_3 \text{ (sol'n)} \qquad (4\text{-}4)$$

$$CaCO_3 \text{ (s)} \rightarrow CaO \text{ (s)} + CO_2 \text{ (g)} \qquad (4\text{-}5)$$

$$NH_4HCO_3 \text{ (sol'n)} + NaCl \text{ (sol'n)} \rightleftharpoons NaHCO_3 \text{ (s)} + NH_4Cl \text{ (sol'n)} \qquad (4\text{-}6)$$

$$2NaHCO_3 \text{ (s)} \rightarrow Na_2CO_3 \text{ (s)} + H_2O \text{ (g)} + CO_2 \text{ (g)} \qquad (4\text{-}7)$$

$$2NH_4Cl \text{ (sol'n)} + Ca(OH)_2 \text{ (s)} \rightarrow$$
$$CaCl_2 \text{ (sol'n)} + 2NH_3 \text{ (g)} + 2H_2O \text{ (l)} \qquad (4\text{-}8)$$

The over-all reaction is

$$CaCO_3 \text{ (s)} + 2NaCl \text{ (sol'n)} \rightarrow CaCl_2 \text{ (sol'n)} + Na_2CO_3 \text{ (s)} \qquad (4\text{-}9)$$

One severe disadvantage of the process is the production of large quantities of calcium chloride solution for which there is very little market. The most important economic consideration in the ammonia-soda process is the recovery of the ammonia which recirculates through the system, since the value of the circulating ammonia is greater than that of the product soda ash.

## CHEMICAL EQUILIBRIUM IN AMMONIA-SODA PROCESS

The basis of the ammonia-soda process is the reaction between salt and ammonium bicarbonate given by Eq. (4-6). Since one pair of salts is formed from the other by double decomposition, the two pairs of salts are known as reciprocal salt-pairs.[1] However, the four salts formed by two reciprocal salt-pairs constitute a system of only three components, not four. From the phase rule, the number of components is defined as the minimum necessary to express the composition of all phases present, and in the case of reciprocal salt-pairs one salt can always be expressed in terms of the other three. Thus, a system of two reciprocal salt-pairs in solution constitutes a four-component system, water being the fourth component.

The number of degrees of freedom for a system of reciprocal salt-pairs is $C + 2 - P = 6 - P$, where $P$ is the number of phases. Since there is always one solution phase, at a given temperature and pressure the system will have three degrees of freedom. Thus, up to three solid phases may exist in equilibrium with the solution.

Two methods are commonly employed for representing graphically the equilibrium in such systems, both of which use a three-dimensional model. The Löwenherz method uses a regular tetrahedral pyramid in which the four corners of the base represent the pure salts, and the compositions of the various solutions are traced off starting from the apex

[1] A. Findlay, "The Phase Rule and Its Applications," Seventh Edition, London, Longmans, Green, and Co., 1931.

of the pyramid. Usually only the vertical projection of the three-dimensional model on the base of the pyramid is used.

The method of Jänecke and Le Chatelier has the advantage that the compositions are expressed in terms of ions rather than salts, and is hence much easier to visualize. The four corners of a square represent the four pure salts, and a perpendicular is erected of length proportional to the number of moles of water present in the solution. Usually, however, only the plane diagram is used, the amounts of water being indicated, when desired, by numerals. Figure 4-2 illustrates the two diagrams for the

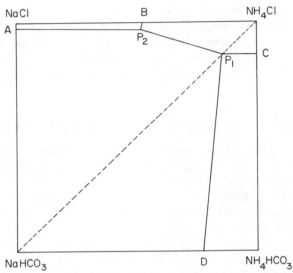

Fɪɢ. 4-2a. Ammonia-soda process; Jänecke-Le Chatelier diagram at 30°C.

sodium chloride + ammonium bicarbonate system. These data are taken from the paper by Fedotieff[1] and are for a temperature of 30°C which is close to the actual value used commercially. Note that when plotted on a Jänecke diagram, a vertical line corresponds to a constant ionic ratio of $Na:NH_4$ and a horizontal line corresponds to a constant ionic ratio of $Cl:HCO_3$.

Table 4-1 gives the solubilities of the various salts in water. Thus, point A on the diagrams represents the composition of a solution satu-

---

[1] P. P. Fedotieff, "Ammonia-Soda Process from the Standpoint of the Phase Rule," *Z. Physik. Chem.*, **49,** 162 (1904). This classical paper by Fedotieff has been ᴊpied and recopied so often, that many authors seem to be unfamiliar with the ᴊriginal reference.

rated with both NaCl and NaHCO₃, etc. If NH₄Cl is added to such a solution, the composition shifts along the line AP₂. The invariant points P₁ and P₂ represent solutions saturated with three salts simultaneously. The point P₁ is of particular interest since it represents an incongruently

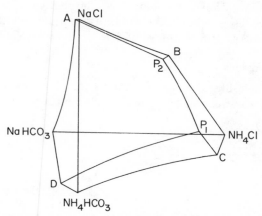

Fig. 4-2b. Ammonia-soda process; Löwenherz diagram at 30°C.

saturated solution. Thus, the solution at P₁ is in equilibrium with the solid phases NH₄Cl, NH₄HCO₃ and NaHCO₃, yet the composition of the solution lies in the triangular area representing solutions expressed in terms of the three salts NaHCO₃, NaCl and NH₄Cl.

It can be seen from the diagrams that both ammonium chloride and sodium bicarbonate are in equilibrium with saturated solution over the

TABLE 4-1. SOLUBILITIES AT 30°C

| Point | Solid Phases | Composition of Solution (g moles/1000 g water) | | | |
|---|---|---|---|---|---|
| | | NaHCO₃ | NaCl | NH₄HCO₃ | NH₄Cl |
| — | NaHCO₃ | 1.65 | — | — | — |
| — | NaCl | — | 6.16 | — | — |
| — | NH₄HCO₃ | — | — | 3.42 | — |
| — | NH₄Cl | — | — | — | 7.78 |
| A | NaHCO₃ + NaCl | 0.17 | 6.12 | — | — |
| B | NaCl + NH₄Cl | — | 4.26 | — | 4.77 |
| C | NH₄Cl + NH₄HCO₃ | — | — | 1.15 | 7.40 |
| D | NaHCO₃ + NH₄HCO₃ | 0.83 | — | 2.91 | — |
| P₁ | NaHCO₃ + NH₄HCO₃ + NH₄Cl | 1.20 | 0.08 | — | 7.62 |
| P₂ | NaHCO₃ + NaCl + NH₄Cl | 0.28 | 4.05 | — | 4.70 |

curve $P_1P_2$. However, in no part of the diagram can ammonium bicarbonate and sodium chloride both be in equilibrium with a solution. Hence, the combination $NaHCO_3 + NH_4Cl$ is known as the stable salt-pair, since this pair can coexist with solution. As was shown by van't Hoff, it is also possible to determine the stable salt-pair from the solubilities of the individual salts, since the stable pair has the smaller solubility product. Thus, for $NaHCO_3 + NH_4Cl$, the solubility product is $1.65 \times 7.78$, which is smaller than $3.42 \times 6.16$ the solubility product of $NaCl + NH_4HCO_3$.

### Operating Conditions

Let us now consider the best conditions for plant operation. As shown in Fig. 4-3, if solutions of sodium chloride and ammonium bicarbonate

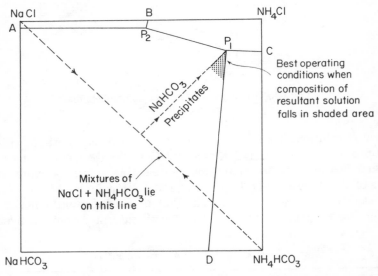

FIG. 4-3. Best conditions for plant operation in ammonia-soda process.

are mixed, the composition of the resultant system will lie somewhere on a line connecting the two pure components. Commercially, the concentrations must be adjusted so that sodium bicarbonate precipitates; hence, the resultant solution will lie somewhere inside the area $AP_2P_1D$. As shown in Table 4-2, the highest yield is obtained when the composition of the resultant solution approaches line $P_1P_2$. The highest conversion of ammonia is for point $P_2$, but the highest conversion of sodium is for point $P_1$. However, the conversion of sodium falls off more rapidly than the conversion of ammonia along $P_1P_2$, so that optimum plant conditions exist when the composition of the resultant solution falls within the shaded area near point $P_1$. However, precautions must be taken that ammonium chloride does not precipitate with the sodium bicarbonate, since this would contaminate the product with sodium chloride when the

TABLE 4-2. THEORETICAL YIELD OF SODIUM BICARBONATE AT 30°C

| Point | Initial Composition (moles/1000 g water) | | Composition of Final Solution (moles/1000 g water) | | | Moles NaHCO₃ Prod. | Sodium Yield (%) | Ammonia Yield (%) |
|---|---|---|---|---|---|---|---|---|
| | NaCl | NH₄HCO₃ | NaHCO₃ | NaCl | NH₄Cl | | | |
| $P_2$ | 8.75 | 4.70 | 0.28 | 4.05 | 4.70 | 4.42 | 50.5 | 94.1 |
| $P_1$ | 7.70 | 7.62 | 1.20 | 0.08 | 7.62 | 6.42 | 83.5 | 84.3 |

bicarbonate is calcined. Note that contamination with ammonium bicarbonate is not harmful, since this is completely decomposed on calcining.

In the commercial production of soda ash, the raw materials are salt, water, ammonia and carbon dioxide from limestone. Let us assume that these materials are combined in such a way as to produce solid sodium bicarbonate and a solution corresponding to point $P_1$ on the phase diagram. From a simple material balance:

$$\begin{array}{l} 7.70 \text{ moles NaCl} \\ 7.62 \text{ moles CO}_2 \\ 7.62 \text{ moles NH}_3 \\ 63.17 \text{ moles H}_2\text{O} \end{array} \rightarrow \left. \begin{array}{l} 1.20 \text{ moles NaHCO}_3 \\ 0.08 \text{ moles NaCl} \\ 7.62 \text{ moles NH}_4\text{Cl} \\ 55.55 \text{ moles H}_2\text{O} \end{array} \right\} \begin{array}{l} \text{Solution} \\ \text{at } P_1 \end{array}$$
$$6.42 \text{ moles NaHCO}_3 \text{ (s)}$$

corresponding to the equation

$$NaCl + H_2O + CO_2 + NH_3 \rightleftharpoons NaHCO_3 + NH_4Cl \qquad (4\text{-}10)$$

The ratio of salt to water to achieve stoichiometry is $7.70/18 \times 63.17 = 6.76$ moles/1000 grams water. This is somewhat higher than the concentration of salt in a saturated solution at 30°C. Thus, in practice point $P_1$ is not reached, and the solution in contact with the precipitated sodium bicarbonate will not be saturated with respect to ammonium chloride. In addition, the conversion of salt to sodium bicarbonate will be reduced from a maximum theoretical conversion of $6.42/7.70 = 83.5$ per cent down to a value of 70-75 per cent which is the maximum yield obtained commercially.

## Raw Materials

The ammonia-soda process is strongly dependent on the availability of cheap salt and limestone. Normally, the salt comes directly from a brine well, and may contain impurities such as calcium and magnesium which must be removed to prevent later precipitation in the carbonation towers. The brine is normally purified by the conventional lime-soda water treatment process, since both of these chemicals are plant products. Limestone comes either from rock or from oyster shells, and should have a low magnesium content. The limestone is burned to CaO in a conventional lime kiln. Gases from the kiln contain carbon dioxide as well as dust and combustion gases from the fuel. The kiln gases are passed through water sprays to cool them and remove dust, and are then sent directly to the carbonation towers.

### Ammoniating the Brine

Since ammonia has a high solubility in saturated brine solutions, the brine is first treated with ammonia and then with carbon dioxide to produce bicarbonate. Note that it would be impossible to reverse this order because of the very low solubility of carbon dioxide in brine. Also note that this method is much superior to a straight mixing of solutions of salt and ammonium bicarbonate, since the amount of water present is reduced and hence the yield of sodium bicarbonate correspondingly increased.

In commercial operation, the purified brine is first distributed to absorbers to recover small amounts of ammonia which may be present in off-gases from various points of the process. After picking up a small amount of ammonia, the brine then flows to the ammonia absorber. The absorber is commonly in the form of a cylindrical tank fitted with cooling coils to remove the heat of solution of ammonia in the concentrated brine; absorbers in the form of conventional bubble-plate columns have also been used. Cast iron is commonly used as a material of construction for handling ammonia solutions.

The introduction of ammonia into the brine decreases the density and reduces the solubility of salt in the resulting solution. However, in practice the ammoniated brine from the absorber is usually unsaturated with respect to salt because brine from the brine well is never completely saturated; some moisture is picked up in scrubbing the off-gases, the ammonia gases introduced to the absorber contain moisture, and the heat of solution raises the temperature which increases slightly the solubility of salt.

A small amount of carbon dioxide is also present in the ammonia sent to the absorber. This reacts to form ammonium bicarbonate, and if the brine has not been previously purified, calcium, magnesium and iron salts will precipitate at this time. These are allowed to settle, the clear solution is sent to the carbonation towers, and the precipitate sent to ammonia recovery. In practice, a small amount of magnesium in the brine is actually desirable since this forms a glass-like double salt with sodium chloride which coats the walls of the processing vessels and prevents iron contamination of the product soda ash.

## Carbonation

The carbonation of the ammoniated brine is commonly done using two towers. The first tower is fairly short, and is fed with sufficient carbon dioxide gas to convert the ammonia to the carbonate by the reaction

$$2NH_3 \text{ (sol'n)} + H_2O \text{ (l)} + CO_2 \text{ (g)} \rightarrow (NH_4)_2CO_3 \text{ (sol'n)} \quad (4\text{-}11)$$

Frequently, a more dilute carbon dioxide gas is used in the first tower, since the solubility is higher in the carbonate solution. The solution from the first tower is then pumped to the top of the taller "making" towers where additional carbon dioxide is introduced at a pressure of about 30 psig. Here the carbonate is converted to bicarbonate which reacts with salt according to the equations

$$(NH_4)_2CO_3 \text{ (sol'n)} + CO_2 \text{ (g)} + H_2O \text{ (l)} \rightleftharpoons 2NH_4HCO_3 \text{ (sol'n)} \quad (4\text{-}12)$$

$$NaCl \text{ (sol'n)} + NH_4HCO_3 \text{ (sol'n)} \rightleftharpoons NaHCO_3 \text{ (s)} + NH_4Cl \text{ (sol'n)} \quad (4\text{-}13)$$

A typical carbonation tower is illustrated in Fig. 4-4. These towers are from 5-9 ft in diameter and 70-90 ft high. The upper section of the tower consists of cast iron dome-shaped, slotted plates which deflect the ascending gas and redistribute the descending liquid in order to give better contact. The bottom section of the tower contains conventional tube-and-shell heat exchangers for cooling the liquid and favoring the precipitation of sodium bicarbonate. Temperature control is fairly critical to obtain an easily filtered precipitate. Because of the heat of the reaction, the temperature in the top section of the tower increases to about 150°F. This temperature is then gradually reduced in the lower section of the tower to about 80°F, which has been found to be the optimum temperature for crystallization. Off-gases from the top of the tower are scrubbed with fresh brine to recover any ammonia, and are then sent to the stack.

Since precipitation of sodium bicarbonate occurs throughout the tower, there is a gradual deposition of solid material on the cooling tubes and other internal surfaces. Thus, several making towers are operated in parallel, and when the deposits become excessive in one particular tower, the tower is taken out of service and the following procedure adopted: (1) All of the ammoniated brine is fed to the top of the tower. (2) A lean gas is fed to the bottom of the tower to partially carbonate the solution according to Eq. (4-11). (3) The temperature of the tower is allowed to increase to approximately 100°F. Since ammonium carbonate solutions are a good solvent for the bicarbonate, by operating the tower for about a day in this manner, the deposited bicarbonate is dissolved in the solution and the tower can be put back into service again. Thus, if there are a total of five making towers, each one would work on the average for four days and would be cleaned on the fifth day.

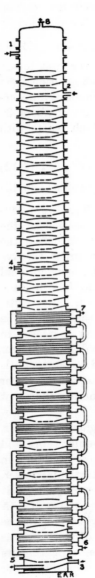

FIG. 4-4. A carbonating tower in the ammonia soda process (Solvay); it is 69 feet high and 6 feet in diameter. (*Modeled after Kirchner*) (From Riegel's Industrial Chemistry, J. A. Kent, Ed., p. 134, New York, Reinhold Publishing Corp., 1962)

1. Entry for ammoniated brine, used when the tower is being cleaned.

2. Entry for the ammoniated brine for the regular bicarbonate precipitation.

3. and 4. Carbon dioxide entries.

5. Outlet for the bicarbonate slurries.

6. Cooling water inlet.

7. Cooling water outlet.

8. Escape for uncondensed gases.

## Calcining Sodium Bicarbonate

The slurry from the bottom of the carbonation tower is filtered on a continuous vacuum filter of the drum or disk type. The filter cake is washed with water to remove ammonium chloride solution which would be converted back to salt on calcining. Approximately one-tenth of the bicarbonate is also lost during this washing. Air is sucked through the cake to partially dry it, and the bicarbonate is then sent to the calciners. All gases from the filter are scrubbed with fresh brine to recover any ammonia liberated from the decomposition of ammonium bicarbonate.

In the United States, the moist bicarbonate is converted to soda ash by calcining in an externally heated rotary kiln; the kiln is from 6-8 ft in diameter and 60-80 ft long, and is either externally fired or is heated with steam coils. Since the bicarbonate tends to stick to the walls of the kiln, from 20-50 per cent of the product is recycled with the fresh feed to prevent sticking and prevent the formation of large lumps which would be difficult to calcine. Temperatures in the calciner range from about 600-800°C maximum down to about 150°C at the discharge end. Gases from the calciner contain up to 90 per cent carbon dioxide plus small amounts of ammonia; these gases are passed directly to the carbonation towers.

The soda ash from the calciners is known as "light ash," since the material has a fairly low density. The light ash requires more packing space and is unsatisfactory for some purposes such as the manufacture of glass since it tends to be blown from the glass furnace. The density can be increased by adding water to the light ash and recalcining to obtain a density of about 60 lb/ft³. The total production of soda ash in the United States is divided about 50-50 between the light and the dense ash. A good grade of soda ash contains over 99 per cent $Na_2CO_3$, salt and moisture being the two chief impurities.

## Ammonia Recovery

The economic success of the ammonia-soda process is dependent on the virtually complete recovery of all ammonia used in the process. Most of the ammonia is present as $NH_4Cl$ in the filtrate and washings from the bicarbonate filtration, although smaller quantities of ammonia are present as carbonate, bicarbonate and carbamate. In addition, ammonia is present in the sludge which is formed on ammoniation of the brine, and other ammonia solutions may be recovered at various points in the process.

All solutions and slurries containing ammonia are sent to the ammonia recovery system. The solutions are first heated in an ammonia still to liberate ammonia from the decomposition of ammonium carbonate and bicarbonate. A lime slurry is then added to the solution to decompose ammonium chloride according to Eq. (4-8). The sludge from the ammoniated brine is also added at this point. The lime slurry plus the solution of ammonium chloride pass down the lime still, which is heated at the bottom by direct injection of steam. Excess lime must be used to prevent the discharge of undecomposed ammonium chloride (the plant operator refers to this as a "sour bottom"). The bottoms from the lime still contain about 8 per cent $CaCl_2$ in addition to about one-third of the original salt plus smaller amounts of $CaCO_3$, $CaSO_4$, $Ca(OH)_2$, etc. Because of the limited demand for calcium chloride, most of this material is simply wasted. The total ammonia losses are only a few pounds per ton of soda ash produced.

## CHEMICAL CAUSTIC

Because of the increasing availability of caustic from the electrolysis of brine, only relatively small quantities of soda ash now go into the manufacture of caustic. The reaction is as follows:

$$Na_2CO_3 \text{ (sol'n)} + Ca(OH)_2 \text{ (s)} \rightleftharpoons CaCO_3 \text{ (s)} + 2NaOH \text{ (sol'n)} \quad (4\text{-}14)$$

The values of $\Delta H°$ and $\Delta F°$ for the reaction depend on the concentration of the solution; under the conditions used commercially, both $\Delta H°$ and $\Delta F°$ are close to zero. Assuming ideal solutions, the equilibrium constant is

$$K_x = \frac{x^2_{NaOH}}{x_{Na_2CO_3}} = \frac{x^2_{OH^-}}{x_{CO_3^{--}}} \quad (4\text{-}15)$$

A similar equation is obtained merely from a consideration of the solubility products for lime and calcium carbonate. Thus, for the two solid phases, both of which are fairly insoluble,

$$K_1 = x_{Ca^{++}}x^2_{OH^-}$$

$$K_2 = x_{Ca^{++}}x_{CO_3^{--}}$$

$$K_x = \frac{K_1}{K_2} = \frac{x^2_{OH^-}}{x_{CO_3^{--}}} \quad (4\text{-}15)$$

However, these equations must be used with some caution, since for example, the solubility product for calcium carbonate in caustic solution will be different from the solubility product in pure water.

## Manufacture

From Eq. (4-15), it can be seen that the ratio of caustic to soda ash in the equilibrium solution depends on the concentration. The fraction of the original soda ash converted to caustic is

$$\text{Yield} = \frac{x_{\text{NaOH}}}{x_{\text{NaOH}} + 2x_{\text{Na}_2\text{CO}_3}} = \frac{1}{1 + \dfrac{2}{\sqrt{K_x}}\sqrt{x_{\text{Na}_2\text{CO}_3}}} \tag{4-16}$$

Thus, the yield is close to 100 per cent for very weak solutions, but falls off as the concentration increases. Figure 4-5 shows the equilibrium yield

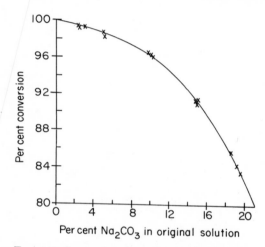

Fig. 4-5. Conversion in causticization of soda [data from J. C. Olsen and O. G. Direnga, *Ind. Eng. Chem.*, **33**, 304 (1941)].

as a function of the original concentration of soda ash. In practice, an economic balance must be made between the higher yield at low concentrations and the increased cost of concentrating dilute solutions.

Since the heat of reaction is very small, the equilibrium is virtually unaffected by temperature. However, in practice the reaction is carried out at 175-200°F to increase the rate of causticization, decrease the viscosity of the solution, and yield a calcium carbonate precipitate which is easier to filter. The lime and soda ash solution are simply mixed in a tank for about an hour, the caustic solution decanted, and the precipitated calcium carbonate washed with water to recover entrained caustic.

Continuous operation is also possible using classifiers and thickeners to purify the lime and separate the mud from the caustic liquor. A large fraction of chemical caustic production is for "captive" use, namely, it is used directly where it is produced, frequently in the form of a 10-12 per cent solution directly from the causticizer.

CHAPTER 5

# Electrolytic Chlorine and Caustic

The United States production of chlorine in recent years is illustrated in Fig. 5-1. Note the rapid growth rate since the end of the war, the result almost entirely of the increasing use of chlorine in chemical manufacture. It is now estimated [1] that approximately 80 per cent of the total production of chlorine goes for chemical use, some of the more important applications being the manufacture of chlorinated solvents, tetraethyl lead, ethylene oxide and glycol, plastics and resins such as vinyl chloride, insecticides such as benzene hexachloride and DDT, refrigerants, etc. About 16 per cent of chlorine production goes to the pulp and paper industry, about 3 per cent goes for sanitation and water treatment and small amounts go for hundreds of other uses.

Although the production of chlorine will probably continue to increase over the next few years, there are some problems faced by the industry. Probably the most important problem is the disposal of the coproduct caustic soda which is always produced in a fixed ratio. For economic success, there must be a balanced demand for both products. The inflation in construction costs has necessitated the construction of larger plants, and it is now felt that 100 tons/day of chlorine represents the smallest economic unit. A chlorine plant should supply a small geographic area since chlorine is sold commercially on a freight equalized basis. In addition chlorine suffers to some extent from process obsolescence, since new processes have been developed to manufacture such chemicals as ethylene oxide and glycerine without using chlorine.

[1] See J. S. Sconce, "Chlorine," New York, Reinhold Publishing Corp., 1962; H. A. Sommers, *Chem. Eng. Progr.*, 61(3), 94 (1965).

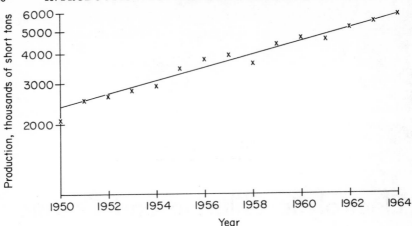

Fɪɢ. 5-1. United States production of chlorine in recent years (Bureau of the Census reports).

## ELECTROLYTIC CELLS

If an ionic material is placed in solution, a substantial fraction of the molecules will dissociate to form ions. Thus, if we have an aqueous solution of sodium chloride, there is an equilibrium

$$NaCl \rightleftharpoons Na^+ + Cl^-$$
5-1

Also, the water itself can ionize

$$2H_2O \rightleftharpoons H_3O^+ + OH^-$$
5-2

The relative fraction of the material which is ionized depends on the nature of the material and its concentration in the solution. For example, dilute solutions of strong electrolytes are almost 100 per cent ionized, whereas weak electrolytes, including water, are mostly in the molecular state.

If a metal is immersed in water, there is a tendency for the atoms of the metal to go into solution, thereby leaving the valence electrons on the metal and thus giving it a negative charge. This is known as the electrolytic solution pressure of the metal. However, if a metal is immersed in a solution of its own ions, there is also a tendency for the ions in solution to pass onto the metal surface giving it a positive charge. This tendency is known as the osmotic pressure of the solution.[1] Thus, in general, when a metal is placed in contact with a solution, an electro-

[1] H. J. Creighton and W. A. Koehler, "Principles and Applications of Electrochemistry," New York, John Wiley & Sons, Inc., 1935.

motive force will be produced of magnitude and direction dependent on the difference between the solution pressure of the metal and the osmotic pressure of the ions in solution.

The potential difference which is established between an electrode and a solution containing its own ions is known as the single-electrode potential. To measure this potential, it is necessary to have another metal-solution junction having a known potential difference. The combination of the two metal-solution junctions is known as a cell, and each half is known as a half-cell, half-element, or often simply an electrode. The two reference or standard electrodes which are most commonly used to measure electrolytic potentials are the calomel electrode which consists of mercury and mercurous chloride in contact with potassium chloride solution, and the hydrogen electrode which consists of hydrogen gas in contact with a 1 normal solution of hydrogen ions. If the standard electrolytic potentials of the chemical elements are arranged in order of their electromotive force, the familiar electromotive series is obtained.

## Decomposition Potential

The decomposition potential of a substance in solution is the smallest external electromotive force which must be applied to cause a continuous flow of current through the solution. If the electrodes are not polarized and if the solvent offers no resistance to the flow of current, the decomposition potential is slightly greater than the sum of the electrolytic potentials of the cation and the anion. The magnitude of the decomposition potential depends on temperature, concentration, and the nature of the solvent and solute.

The decomposition potential of an electrolyte also varies with the nature of the electrodes which are used for the electrolysis. Thus, for example, more work is required to liberate hydrogen from a graphite electrode than from a platinum electrode. These differences are caused by polarization on the surface of the electrode. The difference between the actual electrode potential required for the flow of the current and the equilibrium potential is known as the overvoltage for the particular electrode. The overvoltage is of considerable practical importance in electrolysis, since electrical power costs increase in direct proportion to the overvoltage.

Overvoltage has been found to depend on many factors, some of which are not completely understood. However, the hydrogen overvoltage on metals is a function of the following: (1) In general, the overvoltage decreases with increase in temperature. (2) Overvoltage decreases with increase in pressure. (3) Overvoltage increases as current density increases, thus requiring a balance between power costs and plant capacity.

(4) Overvoltage appears to increase with time, and often does not reach its maximum value until long after the electrode was immersed in the solution. (5) Overvoltage can be reduced by superimposing an alternating current on a direct current.

## Deposition Potential

Although experimental measurements have been made of the standard electrolytic potential and overvoltage for many ions, tabulated values are usually based on 1 molar or 1 molal solutions of the ions. However, the voltage required to deposit a particular substance at an electrode is also dependent on the concentration of the ions in solution. The actual voltage required to deposit a material at an electrode under given conditions of concentration, current density, temperature, etc., is known as the deposition potential. Thus, for low concentrations of a particular ion, the deposition potential will be substantially greater than the standard electrolytic potential; however, for high concentrations of a particular ion, the deposition potential may be less than the standard electrolytic potential. When several different ions exist in solution, the one which will be deposited is the ion having the lowest deposition potential under the particular conditions which exist.

## Electrolysis of Brine

Let us consider now the basic principles involved in the electrolysis of brine to produce chlorine and caustic. As illustrated in Fig. 5-2, a typical brine cell consists of a suitable container to hold the brine, two nonreactive electrodes, and a permeable diaphragm which separates the solution which forms about the anode (the anolyte) from the solution which forms about the cathode (the catholyte). A direct current is passed through the cell to achieve electrolysis, the flow of electricity being from the anode to the cathode, opposite to the flow of electrons which is from the cathode to the anode.

The two chief anode reactions are as follows:

$$2Cl^- \text{ (sol'n)} \rightarrow Cl_2 \text{ (g)} + 2e \qquad (5\text{-}3)$$

$$4OH^- \text{ (sol'n)} \rightarrow O_2 \text{ (g)} + 2H_2O \text{ (l)} + 4e \qquad (5\text{-}4)$$

where the symbol e refers to a negative electron. The standard electrolytic potential of the chloride ion is 1.36 volts in comparison with a value of only 0.40 volt for the hydroxyl ion. However, the hydroxyl ion concentration is very small in comparison with the chloride ion concentration in a strong brine solution, so that the decomposition potential of the chloride ion is less than that of the hydroxyl ion and with good operating conditions, chlorine will constitute approximately 97 per cent of the total anode discharge.

However, some side reactions do occur at the anode which affect the purity of the product and the operating life of the anode and the dia-

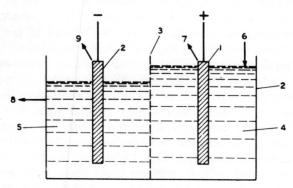

1. Anode
2. Cathode
3. Diaphragm
4. Anolyte-chlorine container for anolyte and chlorine
5. Catholyte hydrogen container for catholyte and hydrogen
6. Brine inlet
7. Chlorine outlet
8. Caustic outlet
9. Hydrogen outlet

FIG. 5-2. Diaphragm of percolating diaphragm chlor-alkali cell.

phragm. With graphite electrodes, there is some oxidation according to the equation

$$4OH^- \text{ (sol'n)} + C \text{ (s)} \rightarrow CO_2 \text{ (g)} + 2H_2O \text{ (l)} + 4e \qquad (5\text{-}5)$$

In addition, chlorine has a certain solubility in the anolyte and an equilibrium is established

$$Cl_2 \text{ (g)} + H_2O \text{ (l)} \rightleftharpoons HCl \text{ (sol'n)} + HOCl \text{ (sol'n)} \qquad (5\text{-}6)$$

Both products of this reaction are acidic, and ionize according to the equations

$$HCl + H_2O \rightleftharpoons H_3O^+ + Cl^- \qquad (5\text{-}7)$$

$$HOCl + H_2O \rightleftharpoons H_3O^+ + OCl^- \qquad (5\text{-}8)$$

Because of these reactions, the pH of the anolyte is in the range of 3.0-4.0 during normal operation.

The two chief reactions taking place at the cathode are as follows:

$$2H_3O^+ \text{ (sol'n)} + 2e \rightarrow H_2 \text{ (g)} + 2H_2O \text{ (l)} \qquad (5\text{-}9)$$

$$Na^+ \text{ (sol'n)} + e \rightarrow Na \text{ (s)} \qquad (5\text{-}10)$$

The standard electrolytic potential of sodium is 2.72 volts in comparison with a standard value of zero for hydrogen. During normal operation, the cell liquor contains about 12 per cent NaOH and 15 per cent NaCl. The decomposition potential of sodium in such a solution will be lowered and the decomposition potential of hydrogen will be increased. However, even with a hydrogen overvoltage of 0.8 volt, which is typical for a steel cathode at the current densities used commercially, the decomposition potential of hydrogen will still be smaller than that of sodium. Hence, the hydrogen discharges first, and in normal operation represents almost 100 per cent of the cathode discharge. In practice, it is very difficult to differentiate between Eqs. (5-9) and (5-10), since if sodium is deposited on a steel cathode, it reacts immediately with water to form hydrogen gas and caustic, and hence the end result is the same.

The over-all cell reaction is

$$2NaCl \text{ (sol'n)} + 2H_2O \text{ (l)} \rightarrow H_2 \text{ (g)} + Cl_2 \text{ (g)} + 2NaOH \text{ (sol'n)} \qquad (5\text{-}11)$$

Thus, if there is no mixing and no side reactions, the products of the electrolysis are chlorine, caustic and by-product hydrogen.

### Use of a Diaphragm

The cell reactions can be summarized as follows:

| *Cathode* $(-)$ | *Anode* $(+)$ |
|---|---|
| Removal of positive charge; catholyte becomes basic. | Removal of negative charge; anolyte becomes acidic. |
| $2H_3O^+ + 2e \rightarrow H_2$ (g)  $\xleftarrow{\text{diffusion}}$ $H_3O^+$ | |
| $Na^+$  $\xleftarrow{\text{diffusion}}$ $Na^+$ | |
| $Cl^- \xrightarrow{\text{diffusion}}$ | $2Cl^- \rightarrow Cl_2$ (g) $+ 2e$ |
| $OH^- \xrightarrow{\text{diffusion}}$ | $OH^-$ |

At the cathode, the evolution of hydrogen is equivalent to a loss of positive charge; hence, the catholyte tends to become basic and acquire a net negative charge. At the anode, the evolution of chlorine is equivalent to a loss of negative charge; hence, the anolyte tends to become acidic and acquire a net positive charge. If there were no separation of the anode and cathode solutions, this difference in acidity and difference in net charge would tend to be neutralized by the diffusion of negative ions from the cathode to the anode and of positive ions from the anode to the cathode.

However, the over-all reaction from Eq. (5-11) results in the formation of a caustic solution. Thus, if the cathode and anode solutions are not separated, in a short time the anolyte will become basic. However, from Eq. (5-6), the solubility of chlorine is much higher in a basic solution, and under these conditions an appreciable fraction of the chlorine would continually dissolve to form sodium hypochlorite, which at temperatures greater than 40°C is rapidly converted to sodium chlorate.

To reduce the diffusion of hydroxyl ions to the anode, a permeable diaphragm separates the anolyte from the catholyte, and the brine feed is introduced into the anolyte so that there is a continuous net flow of solution from the anode to the cathode. Under optimum conditions, this flow of solution through the diaphragm is just sufficient to balance the back diffusion of hydroxyl ions from the cathode to the anode, and the balance of charge in the cell is achieved by a transfer of positively charged sodium ions from the anode to the cathode. The diaphragm thus separates a strongly alkaline solution from a weakly acidic solution. Furthermore, the diaphragm is essentially self-regulating, since the amount of back diffusion depends on the difference between the pH of the catholyte and the pH of the anolyte. Suppose, for example, the pH of the anolyte starts increasing; this decreases back diffusion, increases the flow from anode to cathode, and thus tends to reduce the pH of the anolyte back to the normal value.

## Cell Efficiencies

Several types of efficiency are used in describing the operation of a cell. The voltage efficiency is the ratio of the theoretical decomposition voltage to the actual voltage drop across the cell. In the electrolysis of brine, the theoretical decomposition voltage is calculated from the Gibbs-Helmholtz equation for the over-all reaction given by Eq. (5-12). For the concentration used commercially, this theoretical decomposition voltage is commonly taken as 2.25 volts. The actual voltage required in a well designed cell is approximately 3.5-4.5 volts, so that the voltage efficiency ranges from about 50-65 per cent, depending on the type of cell, current density, etc.

The current efficiency is usually based on the cathode reaction, and is defined as the ratio of the amount of caustic actually produced to the amount which theoretically should have been produced from the number of coulombs (ampere hours) of electricity passing through the cell. Current efficiencies as high as 96 per cent are often achieved commercially. The current efficiency is most strongly affected by the uniformity of the diaphragm and the relative fraction of the entering brine which is converted to caustic.

Since power is the product of voltage and current, the power efficiency or energy efficiency of a cell is simply the product of the voltage efficiency and the current efficiency. The magnitude of the power efficiency is a direct measure of the yield of product per kilowatt-hour of electricity.

### Diaphragm Cells

In recent years, all new diaphragm cells have been of two basic types, the Hooker cell and the Dow cell. Both of these cells have vertical graphite anodes, steel screen cathodes and deposited asbestos diaphragms. The essential difference between the two cells is the arrangement of the units. The Hooker cell consists of individual units which are connected together by external metal conductors, whereas the Dow bipolar cell incorporates many individual cell units in a box-like "filter press" which provides a compact unit with reduced floor area.

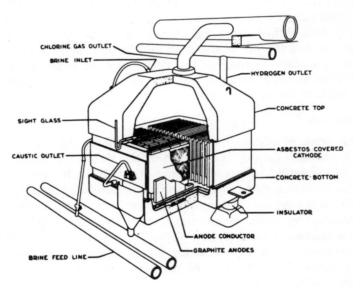

CHLORINE GAS OUTLET
BRINE INLET
HYDROGEN OUTLET
CONCRETE TOP
SIGHT GLASS
ASBESTOS COVERED CATHODE
CAUSTIC OUTLET
CONCRETE BOTTOM
INSULATOR
ANODE CONDUCTOR
GRAPHITE ANODES
BRINE FEED LINE

FIG. 5-3. Sectional diagram of Hooker Type S-3C cell.

Figure 5-3 illustrates the Hooker Type S-3C cell, and Table 5-1 gives typical operating data. The cell is roughly cubical in shape with a dimension of about 5 ft on a side. It consists of top and bottom sections of concrete and a middle cathode section of steel. The bottom section contains a lead casting which is sealed to the concrete and which is fitted with 128 vertical graphite anodes 1-1/4 in. × 6-1/4 in. × 25 in. long. The cathode section consists of a steel frame having steel screens which are so spaced that they alternate with the anodes. The cathode is

TABLE 5-1. TYPICAL OPERATING DATA FOR HOOKER CHLORINE CELLS
(Courtesy Hooker Chemical Corp.)*

| Cell | S-1 | S-3C | S-3D | | S-4 | |
|---|---|---|---|---|---|---|
| Current, amperes | 10,000 | 30,000 | 30,000 | 40,000 | 40,000 | 55,000 |
| Current efficiency, per cent | 96.0 | 96.2 | 95.7 | 96.2 | 95.6 | 96.2 |
| Cell voltage, average | 3.75 | 3.95 | 3.67 | 3.96 | 3.66 | 3.97 |
| Power, dc kw-hr/ton $Cl_2$ | 2,650 | 2,810 | 2,640 | 2,810 | 2,620 | 2,830 |
| Chlorine, ton/day | 0.34 | 1.01 | 1.00 | 1.35 | 1.34 | 1.85 |
| Caustic, ton/day | 0.38 | 1.14 | 1.13 | 1.52 | 1.51 | 2.09 |
| Caustic, per cent NaOH | 10.9 | 11.6 | 11.1 | 11.6 | 11.1 | 11.7 |
| Steam, lb/ton $Cl_2$ | 7,900 | 7,300 | 7,800 | 7,300 | 7,800 | 7,200 |
| Graphite oxidized, lb/ton $Cl_2$ | 6.7 | 6.0 | 6.4 | 6.0 | 6.5 | 6.0 |
| Anode life, days | 338 | 248 | 313 | 247 | 310 | 244 |
| Diaphragm life, days | 110-170 | 80-120 | 100-160 | 80-120 | 90-130 | 80-120 |
| Approximate cell dimensions, in.: | | | | | | |
|   Along row, center to center | 72 | 72 | 90 | | 90 | |
|   Across row, center to center | 95 | 110 | 112 | | 112 | |
|   Cell height above pad | 61 | 73 | 74 | | 83 | |
| Typical analyses: | | | | | | |

Chlorine: 97.5% $Cl_2$, 0.3% $H_2$, 1% $CO_2$, 0.5% $O_2$.
Hydrogen: 99 8-99.9% $H_2$.
Cell liquor: 11.6% NaOH, 16.2% NaCl, 71.8% $H_2O$, 0.4% $Na_2SO_4$, 0.01% $NaClO_3$.

* Also see J. S. Sconce, *op. cit.*

a wire mesh made of 1/16-in. steel wires with about 6 wires to the inch, which is supported by steel fingers welded to the steel frame. The diaphragm is applied to the steel screen section by immersing the cathode in a bath of asbestos slurried in cell liquor (approximately 12 per cent NaOH and 15 per cent NaCl), and applying a vacuum over an appropriate time interval. When the cathode is lowered into place, the anodes line up so that each vertical cathode face is close to a similar graphite face.

The brine normally comes directly from a brine well, and is treated with soda ash to remove calcium and magnesium. Treated brine is preheated to 140-160°F and is introduced into the top of the cell through a tantalum orifice. The head of brine on the orifice is controlled for the entire cell-bank, and is varied, depending on the current load and the strength of caustic which is desired. The brine drips into the cell to prevent any electrical short circuiting between cells. The level of the anolyte depends on the porosity of the diaphragm. The brine level is about 5 in. above the top of the cathode for a cell having a new diaphragm; as the cell operates, impurities will reduce the porosity of the diaphragm and the brine level will rise. When the level reaches about 17 in., the cell is shorted out and the diaphragm replaced.

In the Hooker cell the electrodes do not extend completely across the cell, and a central gap is left to permit circulation. During operation, evolved chlorine gas causes the brine to rise between the electrodes, and the central gap permits the brine to descend back to the bottom of the cell. Up to 4 per cent higher current efficiency is obtained in a cell having this central circulation space.

Chlorine gas leaves the top of the cell through a ceramic or plastic pipe to a central header. Hydrogen is withdrawn from the top of the cathode chamber through a steel pipe. Caustic flows by gravity from the bottom of the cathode chamber through a steel pipe which discharges into the caustic header; the caustic discharge can be adjusted to maintain the proper caustic level in the chamber. A fairly high cell operating temperature is desired, since this lowers the electrical resistance of the solution and decreases the solubility of chlorine in the brine; however, this must be balanced against the increased corrosion as the temperature is raised. The voltage of a cell gradually increases with time; when it reaches a value of about 4.5 volts after perhaps a year of operation, the cell is shorted and the anode section replaced.

## MERCURY CELLS

Although diaphragm cells have accounted for most of the chlorine production in the United States, mercury cells are gaining in favor and now account for about 20 per cent of the total production. The chief advantages of the mercury cell are that they are simpler in design, they operate at high current densities, and they produce a concentrated caustic of high purity. The chief disadvantages are the 10-20 per cent higher power costs, and the costs associated with the high inventory of mercury plus the inevitable mercury losses. Mercury cells have been favored in Europe for many years, but their use in the United States has been held back to some extent by the fact that the technology has only been available here for about the last 20 years.

In the mercury cell, the cathode consists of a pool of mercury and no diaphragm is used. The cathode reaction is

$$Na^+ \text{ (sol'n)} + e \rightarrow Na \text{ (Hg amalgam)} \qquad (5\text{-}12)$$

Instead of liberating hydrogen at the cathode, the sodium is liberated to form an amalgam with the mercury. The reasons for liberating sodium rather than hydrogen are as follows: (1) Hydrogen has a much higher overvoltage on mercury than on steel. (2) The hydrogen overvoltage is increased still more by using high current densities. (3) The electrolytic solution pressure of sodium is much smaller in an amalgam than in the free state, and hence it is much easier to discharge sodium under these conditions.

## The Decomposer

The sodium amalgam which forms at the cathode must be continually removed, or else hydrogen will start to be liberated when the sodium concentration becomes excessive. In the older cells mercury was removed by rocking the cell, but this is now usually done by pumping the mercury. Although the sodium can be used for chemical purposes, normally it is decomposed with water to form caustic according to the reaction

$$\text{Na (Hg)} + \text{H}_2\text{O (l)} \rightarrow \text{NaOH (sol'n)} + \tfrac{1}{2}\text{H}_2 \text{ (g)} + \text{Hg (l)} \quad (5\text{-}13)$$

The decomposer consists of a tank of caustic solution containing packing or grids of graphite. The combination of the liquid mercury, graphite, and caustic solution acts as an internally shorted battery, although no attempt is made to recover energy from the system. However, there is a flow of current from the graphite to the mercury which causes a rapid interaction between the sodium and the solution. Hydrogen is liberated, and a strong solution of very pure caustic is produced.

## Cell Design

A typical mercury cell is illustrated in Fig. 5-4, and Table 5-2 gives typical operating data. The electrolyzer consists of a box-like vessel hav-

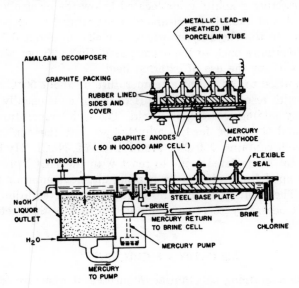

Fig. 5-4. Olin-Mathieson E-11 mercury cell.

TABLE 5-2. TYPICAL OPERATING DATA FOR
SOLVAY MERCURY CELLS*

|  | V-100 Cell | V-200 Cell |
|---|---|---|
| Rated current, kiloamps | 96 | 160 |
| Maximum current, kiloamps | 110 | 190 |
| Max. cathode current density, amps/cm$^2$ | 0.61 | 0.60 |
| Average rated cell voltage | 4.34 | 4.34 |
| Cell voltage at maximum amps | 4.52 | 4.56 |
| Current efficiency, per cent | 96+ | 96+ |
| Kw-hr/ton chlorine (rated) | 3130 | 3130 |
| Kw-hr/ton chlorine (maximum amps) | 3260 | 3280 |
| Cathode width, meters | 1.29 | 1.29 |
| Cathode length, meters | 13.36 | 23.26 |
| Total number of anodes | 108 | 180 |
| Weight of anodes, lb | 4560 | 8150 |
| Anode life, months | 17 | 24 |
| Weight of mercury, lb | 4850 | 8150 |
| Mercury losses, lb/ton chlorine | 0.3 | 0.3 |
| Graphite losses, lb/ton chlorine | 3-4 | 3-4 |

* J. S. Sconce, *op. cit.*, p. 182.

ing a bare steel bottom with sides and top lined with hard rubber to prevent attack by chlorine gas. Graphite anodes extend down into the electrolyzer from the bus bars, and a pool of mercury at the bottom of the electrolyzer serves as a cathode. The decomposer is a rectangular steel tank containing graphite grids located below the electrolyzer. Mercury is pumped continuously by means of a centrifugal sump pump from the decomposer to the electrolyzer where it picks up about 0.5 per cent Na before it overflows back to the decomposer. Up to 73 per cent NaOH can be made without the use of external heat.

Brine is admitted to the cell at a temperature of about 50°C and close to saturation with respect to salt. The pH of the brine is usually adjusted to about 4.0 by adding hydrochloric acid. The cell temperature is kept below 85°C, and the brine feed is adjusted so that the depleted brine leaving the cell contains 260-280 grams/liter of NaCl. Hydrochloric acid is added to the depleted brine to react with the HOCl present, and chlorine is stripped from solution by heating under vacuum or by blowing with air. The solution is then resaturated by the addition of solid salt, treated if necessary to remove impurities, and is then returned to the cells.

## RECOVERY OF CHLORINE

Chlorine gas containing substantial quantities of moisture leaves the cells at about 80-90°C. Under these conditions chlorine is extremely corrosive and must be handled in ceramic, plastic or rubber-lined equipment. The gas is first scrubbed with cold water to remove moisture and any traces of HCl which may be present. The gas is then dried with strong sulfuric acid and compressed to 25-60 psig. Formerly, sulfuric acid ring compressors such as the Nash Hytor were used; these do an excellent job but have a low power efficiency, and thus high-speed two- or three-stage centrifugal compressors with intercooling appear to be favored for modern plants. Dried chlorine is then condensed using conventional refrigeration equipment and is sent to storage. The dry chlorine can be handled in steel equipment. The off-gases (known as "blow gas" or "sniff gas") from the chlorine liquefier consist of noncondensibles plus up to 5 per cent of the chlorine produced; this chlorine may be recovered by absorption in water, absorption in carbon tetrachloride or by absorption in alkali to make hypochlorite or bleaching powder.

Liquid chlorine is commonly shipped in steel 100- and 150-lb cylinders, in 1-ton containers, in multi-unit tank cars and in single-unit tank cars with up to 55-ton capacity. Larger quantities are often shipped in tank barges with from 550-1100 tons capacity. Much of the chlorine going into chemical manufacture is also simply pumped by pipe line directly to the consumer whose plant is often adjacent to the manufacturer.

Hydrogen gas from the cells is scrubbed with water and is then compressed for chemical use or for use as a fuel. Special precautions are taken to prevent mixing of hydrogen and chlorine, since these two gases can form explosive mixtures over a wide range of concentration.

## RECOVERY OF CAUSTIC

The chief uses of caustic include chemical manufacture where a stronger alkali than soda ash is required, rayon and film, pulp and paper, petroleum refining, soap and detergents, textiles, etc. Since caustic is obtained as a coproduct of the electrolysis, the growth rate of caustic obviously parallels the growth rate of chlorine now that chemical caustic is relatively unimportant. Although chlorine has been the chief product of the electrolysis in recent years, the disposal of the caustic is essential for the economic success of the operation.

Caustic from the cells contains about 12 per cent NaOH and 15 per cent NaCl. This solution is concentrated to 50 per cent NaOH in double- or triple-effect evaporators, often using forced circulation to improve heat transfer to the viscous solution. The salt is less soluble in concentrated caustic and crystallizes out of solution. The crystals are separated by decantation and filtering, are washed to remove caustic and are then recycled to the brine system. Standard 50 per cent caustic contains about

1 per cent salt, which is not harmful for most purposes. Much caustic is sold as a 50 per cent solution; some is also concentrated to about 73 per cent solution in single-effect evaporators, the savings in shipping costs offsetting the cost of evaporation. For some purposes such as the manufacture of rayon, the salt concentration must be reduced to about 0.1 per cent NaCl. The most widely used process to further desalt caustic is the Columbia-Southern process which uses liquid ammonia to extract impurities.

Fused caustic is made by heating the solution to about 500°C in a direct-fired cast iron or nickel-lined pot. The anhydrous caustic can then be pumped directly into steel shipping drums or sent to a water-cooled flaker to produce a flake form which can be handled more easily. Modern plants are now tending to use forced-circulation evaporators for the production of both the 73 per cent and the anhydrous caustic. These are commonly of nickel tubes heated with a high-temperature fluid such as "Dowtherm" or a fused salt.

Iron and steel equipment have been commonly used in the past to handle caustic solutions. Although corrosion is not excessive, there is some iron pickup which renders the caustic unsuited for rayon manufacture. For this reason, it is now becoming increasingly common to use nickel and nickel-lined equipment to handle caustic solutions.

## OTHER CHLORINE PROCESSES

The first large-scale production of chlorine was by the Deacon process,

$$4HCl \text{ (g)} + O_2 \text{ (g)} \rightleftharpoons 2Cl_2 \text{ (g)} + 2H_2O \text{ (g)} \qquad (5\text{-}14)$$

$$\Delta H^\circ_{298} = -27,344 \qquad \Delta F^\circ_{298} = -18,194$$

The reaction was carried out at 450-650°C, using a cupric chloride catalyst. The HCl was obtained as a by-product from the manufacture of salt cake, and air was used for the oxidation. The chlorine was produced as a fairly dilute gas which was often absorbed in lime to form bleaching powder. Under the conditions used commercially, only about 65 per cent of the HCl was converted to chlorine. The Deacon process is now obsolete, since it could not compete with electrolytic chlorine.

The salt process[1] for the manufacture of chlorine has been operated commercially by Allied Chemical Corp. at Hopewell, Virginia. The overall reaction is

$$3NaCl \text{ (s)} + 4HNO_3 \text{ (sol'n)} \rightarrow$$
$$3NaNO_3 \text{ (sol'n)} + Cl_2 \text{ (g)} + NOCl \text{ (g)} + 2H_2O \text{ (l)} \quad (5\text{-}15)$$

[1] See chapter by M. F. Fogler in Sconce, *op. cit.*

Salt and strong nitric acid are slurried together and pass to a heated digester which completes the solution of the salt. Nitrosyl chloride and chlorine are stripped from the solution with steam, unconverted nitric acid is neutralized with soda ash, and sodium nitrate is recovered by crystallization. The gaseous mixture from the digester is scrubbed with refrigerated nitric acid to remove moisture, and the chlorine and nitrosyl chloride separated by distillation.

Originally, the nitrosyl chloride was treated with soda ash to convert it to salt and sodium nitrate. At present, nitrosyl chloride is oxidized with 95 per cent oxygen according to the reaction

$$2NOCl \text{ (g)} + O_2 \text{ (g)} \rightarrow N_2O_4 \text{ (g)} + Cl_2 \text{ (g)} \qquad (5\text{-}16)$$

The nitrogen tetroxide is separated by distillation, and can be recycled to produce strong nitric acid or else sold as such, since there is a limited demand for $N_2O_4$ as an oxidizer for rocket fuels. In addition, there is an increasing demand for nitrosyl chloride which is shipped in cylinders as a liquefied gas.

Obviously the chief problem in the salt process is corrosion. The mixture of salt and nitric acid forms aqua regia, which is powerful enough to dissolve gold. Brick-lined stainless steel is used for the salt digestor, and a special "mantling liquid" is used in the space between the shell and brick lining to neutralize any leakage through the brick.

## ELECTROLYSIS OF FUSED SALTS

Fused salts are good conductors of electricity and hence can be electrolyzed directly. Commercially, the most important chemical process is the electrolysis of fused sodium chloride to produce metallic sodium and byproduct chlorine. The electrolysis is carried out in the Downs cell [1] which consists of a steel tank lined with firebrick and containing a eutectic mixture of about 33 per cent NaCl and 67 per cent $CaCl_2$. This mixture has a melting point of 505°C in comparison with 803°C for pure NaCl. A graphite anode projects vertically from the bottom of the cell and steel cathodes enter from the side. The normal operating temperature is about 600°C.

Although the decomposition voltages of both fused sodium chloride and calcium chloride are less than 3 volts, the Downs cell is operated at about 8-9 volts with a current efficiency of about 75 per cent. The power requirements are approximately 13,500 kw-hr/short ton of sodium produced. Chlorine gas is taken off through a collecting dome and is compressed, cooled, and sent to storage. Sodium liberated at the cathode

[1] J. C. Downs, U.S. Patent 1,501,756 (July 15, 1924).

overflows to a sodium collector; small amounts of liberated calcium are frozen out of the molten sodium and returned to the electrolyzer where the calcium is converted back to calcium chloride.

About 126,000 tons of metallic sodium were produced in the United States in 1963, corresponding to almost 200,000 tons of by-product chlorine. The chief use of sodium is in the manufacture of tetraethyl lead by the reaction between ethyl chloride and a lead-sodium alloy.

## HYDROCHLORIC ACID

Hydrochloric acid, sometimes called muriatic acid, is used for pickling iron and steel, as an acidulator in oil wells to increase the flow of petroleum, and for many chemical uses such as the manufacture of chlorides, dyes, plastics, etc. Most of the acid is shipped as a solution in glass carboys or in rubber-lined wooden or steel tanks. The commercial acid is sold in several strengths ranging from 16°Bé (24.5 per cent HCl) to 22°Bé (36 per cent HCl). In addition, some anhydrous HCl is shipped as a compressed gas in high-pressure steel cylinders. In 1963, about 155,000 tons were produced in the United States from salt, 134,000 tons from chlorine and 791,000 tons from by-product HCl.

The oldest method for the manufacture of hydrochloric acid is the salt + sulfuric acid process already briefly discussed in connection with the Le Blanc process. At one time, virtually all the hydrochloric acid was made in this way, but the process has become of less importance now that large quantities of by-product acid are available. In this older salt process, the gases from the Mannheim furnace are cooled, passed through packing to remove sulfuric acid, and sent to the absorption towers. The towers are normally ceramic packed with coke or stoneware, 3-5 towers being required, depending on the temperature and the concentration of HCl in the entering gases. Absorbing acid is continually recirculated through coolers to the top of each tower, using either a rubber-lined pump or an air lift. Product acid is often yellow colored due to impurities which carry over from the furnace.

The direct process for the manufacture of HCl involves the reaction

$$H_2 \text{ (g)} + Cl_2 \text{ (g)} \rightarrow 2HCl \text{ (g)} \tag{5-17}$$

$$\Delta H^\circ_{298} = -44,126 \qquad \Delta F^\circ_{298} = -45,538$$

Although both reactants are available from the electrolysis of brine, the economics of the process depend on the relative costs and demands for chlorine and hydrochloric acid. The reaction is strongly exothermic; the explosive limits for mixtures of hydrogen and chlorine range from about 10-93 per cent $Cl_2$. Commercially, the gas mixture is commonly burned in a brick-lined furnace, using a water-cooled iron nozzle to introduce the gases. A small excess of hydrogen is usually used to minimize corrosion. A rupture disk is used on the top of the furnace, since every plant usually experiences at least one explosion. Gases from the furnace are absorbed in water, often using a tantalum absorber.

By-product acid from organic chlorinations is now the chief source of hydrochloric acid, and at times this has been literally a drug on the market. Gases from the chlorinators are simply scrubbed with a suitable solvent to remove any organic vapors, and are then sent to a tantalum absorber to produce hydrochloric acid. Thus, in 1963, almost three-fourths of the total hydrochloric acid produced in the United States was by-product acid.

## PHOSGENE

Phosgene has had a rapid growth in recent years because of its use in the manufacture of polyurethanes and polycarbonates. The total production of phosgene in 1963 was 212 million pounds, and 1964 production increased to 245 million pounds. Polyurethanes account for about two-thirds of the end use of phosgene, smaller quantities going into polycarbonate resins and other miscellaneous uses.

Phosgene is produced by the direct reaction of chlorine with excess carbon monoxide according to the equation

$$Cl_2 \text{ (g)} + CO \text{ (g)} \rightarrow COCl_2 \text{ (g)}$$
$$\Delta H^\circ_{298} = -26,880 \qquad \Delta F^\circ_{298} = -17,500$$

The reaction has been shown to be a typical chain reaction in which chlorine atoms serve as the chain carriers according to the equation

$$Cl_2 \rightarrow 2Cl^\bullet$$
$$Cl^\bullet + CO \rightarrow COCl^\bullet$$
$$COCl^\bullet + Cl_2 \rightarrow COCl_2 + Cl^\bullet \quad \text{etc.}$$

There is general agreement that the reaction at moderate temperatures is first-order with respect to chlorine and half-order with respect to carbon monoxide.

Commercially, phosgene is easily prepared simply by passing a carefully dried mixture of carbon monoxide and chlorine over activated carbon at temperatures of 400-500°F. Since the reaction is exothermic, the reactor commonly consists of tubes of about 2-in. diameter filled with carbon catalyst and externally cooled with water. Liquid phosgene is obtained merely by cooling the effluent gases. Mild steel is used as a material of construction, and is quite satisfactory as long as the gases are dry.

The carbon monoxide required for phosgene manufacture frequently comes from synthesis gas such as the carbon monoxide-hydrogen mixture used for synthetic methanol. In other cases, the carbon monoxide may be a by-product of some other plant operation or may be recovered from flue gas. In any case, water, hydrogen, and hydrocarbons must be removed from the carbon monoxide since these cause hydrolysis of phosgene to form hydrochloric acid and also may poison the catalyst. Purification of carbon monoxide is frequently carried out by low-temperature refrigeration to condense all gases except hydrogen, followed by fractionation to obtain pure carbon monoxide.

Substantially all phosgene production is for captive use. The phosgene process is extremely simple, and hence it is cheaper to ship the chlorine and manufacture the phosgene where it is needed. Also, since phosgene is extremely toxic, there is a natural reluctance to ship large quantities by common carrier.

## BLEACHING AGENTS

A bleaching agent has the property of whitening materials by removing color. A "true bleach" accomplishes this by a chemical reaction with the colored constituents in the material. True bleaches normally work by oxidation, although some chemical bleaching is by reduction.

An "optical bleach" is a substance which converts part of the ultraviolet radiation into blue or blue-green light, and thereby changes the apparent color of a material. Optical bleaches or "brighteners" are commonly added to household detergents to permit simultaneous cleaning and bleaching of fabrics.

Chlorine is an important chemical bleaching agent, although it is too strong for many purposes. In solution, chlorine reacts with water to form hypochlorous acid, which in turn releases oxygen to permit bleaching of materials. However some of the chlorine may also be present as elemental chlorine which can add directly across double bonds. The chief commercial use of chlorine as a bleach is in the preliminary bleaching of wood pulp in the paper industry.

Sodium hypochlorite is an important household bleach, and also finds some use in commercial laundries. It is produced by the direct reaction of chlorine and caustic

$$Cl_2 + 2NaOH \rightarrow NaOCl + NaCl + H_2O$$

Sodium hypochlorite is normally sold as a 12-15 per cent solution containing equimolar quantities of salt and hypochlorite. It is stable in alkaline solution, but must be handled carefully since impurities such as traces of metals will cause decomposition. In practice two types of decomposition may occur, either to elemental oxygen or to the chlorate ion by oxidation-reduction.

Commercially, an extremely important bleach is chlorine dioxide $ClO_2$ which is widely used in the bleaching of textiles and in the pulp industry. Direct use of chlorine dioxide as a bleach was at first held up because of problems encountered in the use of sodium chlorite as a raw material. However these problems have now been eliminated by the use of chlorine dioxide generators which produce the material directly from readily available sodium chlorate. The first step is the production of sodium chlorate by electrolysis of brine using a cell without a diaphragm

$$NaCl + 3H_2O + 6e \rightarrow NaClO_3 + 3H_2$$

The reaction proceeds through the intermediate formation of sodium hypochlorite. Chlorine dioxide is then produced in a reactor using sodium chlorate, acid, and a reducing substance such as methanol or sulfur dioxide. Chlorine dioxide generators are widely used in the pulp industry to produce chlorine dioxide directly where it is needed.

Reducing bleaches include such materials as sulfur dioxide and the sulfites. In addition to their use as a bleach, these materials also find use as an antichlor to eliminate final traces of chlorine compounds or other oxidizing agents from materials.

## Hydrogen Peroxide

Hydrogen peroxide is widely used as a mild bleaching agent for textiles, wood pulp, and other materials, as a rocket fuel, and in the manufacture of peroxides and other chemicals. Hydrogen peroxide is unstable, the rate of decomposition depending on temperature, concentration, and the presence or absence of impurities such as suspended material or metallic cations such as iron, copper, or nickel. Finely divided metals or activated charcoal will decompose hydrogen peroxide rapidly and completely. Commercially, hydrogen peroxide is commonly produced as a 30 per cent solution having a pH of about 4.0. An anticatalyst such as sodium stannate may be added to stabilize the solution.

Hydrogen peroxide may be produced by electrolysis of a solution of sulfuric acid or a salt such as ammonium or potassium sulfate. The electrolysis produces persulfates, which are then hydrolyzed to yield hydrogen peroxide. However the process which now appears to be favored for the production of hydrogen peroxide involves the oxidation of a substituted hydroquinone according to the typical equation

2-Ethyl anthrahydroquinone    2-Ethyl anthraquinone

This process was first used commercially in Germany during the second world war,* and has substantial advantages over the older electrochemical processes.

From patents, the hydroquinone is dissolved in a solvent such as octanol or methylnaphthalene, and air is passed through the solution at a moderate temperature. The choice of solvent is extremely important, since it must resist oxidation, must be insoluble in water, and must have an appreciable solubility for both the quinone and hydroquinone forms of the oxidizable substance. To meet these requirements, it has sometimes been necessary to use mixtures of solvents. Following oxidation, the hydrogen peroxide is recovered by countercurrent extraction with water in a packed tower to yield a 20-25 per cent solution of $H_2O_2$. The anthraquinone solution is then treated to remove water and oxidized organic materials, and is converted back to the hydroquinone form by direct reduction with hydrogen at moderate temperature and pressure using a fixed catalyst of platinum, palladium, or Raney nickel.

* W. C. Schumb et al, "Hydrogen Peroxide," New York, Reinhold Publishing Corp., 1955. The 2-ethyl anthraquinone was prepared by a Friedel-Crafts condensation of ethyl benzene and phthalic anhydride, followed by dehydration and ring closure with fuming sulfuric acid.

# CHAPTER 6

# Sulfuric Acid

Sulfuric acid is the work horse of the chemical industry. In 1963, almost 21 million tons of sulfuric acid (100 per cent basis) were produced in the United States, 92 per cent of this acid coming from the contact process and only 8 per cent coming from the chamber process. About 32 per cent of this acid was used for the manufacture of phosphate fertilizers, 8 per cent for chemical manufacture, 8 per cent for the manufacture of paints and pigments, 6.5 per cent for synthetic and coke oven ammonium sulfate, 5 per cent for pickling iron and steel, and smaller quantities for petroleum refining, manufacture of rayon, aluminum sulfate, and thousands of other uses.

The production of sulfuric acid in the United States in recent years is illustrated in Fig. 6-1. The growth rate has been modest in comparison to many other chemicals such as ammonia, chlorine, and the organics.

As shown in Table 6-1, sulfuric acid is sold commercially in several grades. The weaker acids are sold on the basis of the specific gravity referred to the standard Baumé scale. However, the specific gravity changes very little above about 93 per cent $H_2SO_4$ and, in fact, goes through a maximum at about 97.5 per cent $H_2SO_4$. Thus, the stronger acids are sold on the basis of the acid content. Fuming sulfuric acid or oleum is always sold on the basis of the percentage of free $SO_3$.

In the manufacture of contact acid, the strength of the acid in the absorption towers is 98-99 per cent during normal operation. Thus, on an $H_2SO_4$ basis, this acid is no more expensive than the weaker grades. Since shipping costs represent an appreciable fraction of the total delivered cost of sulfuric acid, many customers would save money by purchasing contact acid rather than one of the weaker grades.

## Raw Materials

Sulfuric acid is manufactured from elemental sulfur, pyrites, hydrogen sulfide, and sulfur-containing gases from the roasting of sulfide ores such

79

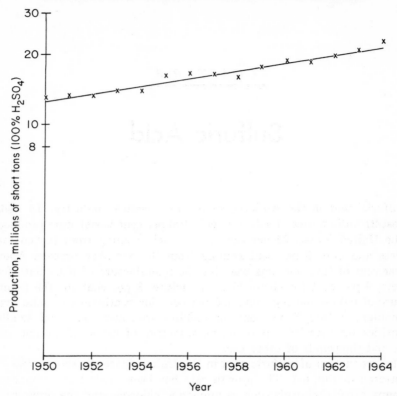

FIG. 6-1. United States production of sulfuric acid in recent years (Bureau of The Census reports).

TABLE 6-1.  STANDARD GRADES OF SULFURIC ACID ADOPTED
BY THE MANUFACTURING CHEMISTS' ASSOCIATION

| Common Name | °Bé | H₂SO₄ (%) | Specific Gravity (60°F/60°F) |
|---|---|---|---|
| — | 52 | 65.13 | 1.5591 |
| — | 58 | 74.36 | 1.6667 |
| Tower acid | 60 | 77.67 | 1.7059 |
| Oil of vitriol | 66 | 93.19 | 1.8354 |
| Contact acid | | 98.00 | 1.8437 |
| Monohydrate | | 100.00 | 1.8391 |
| 20% Oleum | | 104.50 | 1.915 |
| 30% Oleum | | 106.75 | 1.952 |
| 40% Oleum | | 109.00 | 1.983 |
| 65% Oleum | | 114.63 | 1.992 |
| Stabilized sulfur trioxide | | 122.28 | — |

as zinc and copper sulfide. Table 6-2 gives the consumption of sulfur in the United States for 1963. Approximately 87 per cent of the sulfuric acid manufactured in the United States comes from elemental sulfur (brimstone). This fraction has been increasing in recent years, since

TABLE 6-2. APPARENT CONSUMPTION OF SULFUR
IN THE UNITED STATES IN 1963
(From Minerals Yearbook, 1963)

| Source of Sulfur | Consumption (thousands of short tons) |
|---|---|
| Native sulfur (Frasch) | 4905 |
| Recovered sulfur | |
| Sales | 1041 |
| Imports | 546 |
| Pyrites | |
| Production | 385 |
| Imports | 104 |
| Smelter acid | 376 |
| Other ($H_2S$, liquid $SO_2$) | 130 |
| Total | 7487 |

practically all new construction has been based on brimstone as a raw material.

In the United States the chief deposits of sulfur occur in the coastal plain of Louisiana and Texas. The deposits are at depths up to 2000 ft and average about 125 ft in thickness. Early conventional mining attempts were unsuccessful, and it was not until the development of the Frasch process in 1894 that these deposits were exploited. In this process, a well is drilled down to the sulfur layer, and a casing is set and cemented into the cap rock to maintain pressure and to prevent contamination by cold surface water. Three concentric pipes are then run down into the sulfur layer, a central 1-in. air line, a 3-in. sulfur line, and an external 6- or 8-in. water line. During normal operation, water at a pressure of 100-125 psig and a temperature of 320-340°F is pumped down the outer pipe to melt the sulfur which collects in a pool at the base of the well. Air at about 500 psig is forced down the central pipe, and the mixture of air and molten sulfur is brought to the surface in the annular space between the 1-in. and 3-in. pipes. Molten sulfur is distributed to enormous vats containing hundreds of thousands of tons, where the sulfur solidifies and can be later broken up and handled by mechanical loaders.

Temperature control is extremely important in the Frasch process. The stable high-temperature form of sulfur is the monoclinic which has a melting point of about 246°F. However, at a temperature of 320°F, liquid sulfur changes to an extremely viscous liquid which cannot be handled by conventional means. Thus, the water pumped down the well must be hot enough to melt the sulfur, but not sufficiently hot to change the sulfur to the viscous form.

There is also the problem of disposing of the several million gallons a day of hot water that are pumped down into each well. This can be done by the use of either "bleeder wells" or else exhausted sulfur wells to withdraw some of the cooled water from underground.

Crude sulfur mined by the Frasch process is 99.0-99.9 per cent pure. Chief impurities are ash, moisture, sulfuric acid and often oil or other carbonaceous material. Formerly, bulk sulfur was shipped in open railroad cars and barges. However, now most sulfur is being shipped as liquid sulfur in insulated tank cars, barges and larger ocean vessels. Such shipments have the advantage that the sulfur is not contaminated during shipment, and it can be unloaded quickly and economically by means of pumps.

### Other Sources of Sulfur

The name "pyrites" is used to refer to several iron sulfide minerals.[1] These include pyrite and marcasite ($FeS_2$), and pyrrhotite (approximate formula $Fe_7S_8$) which is a solid solution of sulfur in FeS. Commercial pyrites contains 35-52 per cent sulfur and 40-50 per cent iron. The most important zinc mineral is sphalerite (ZnS) which contains 28-32 per cent sulfur and 50-58 per cent zinc. Copper sulfide concentrates usually contain more than 30 per cent sulfur; in addition, small quantities of acid are made from lead sulfide ores. All of the above sulfide minerals are usually obtained as concentrates by flotation from the crude ore.

In the past, the chief problem with the sulfide ores has been the fact that much of the mineral industry is located at a considerable distance from potential markets. Sulfuric acid is such a cheap chemical that it cannot be shipped over large distances because the shipping costs would be more than the value of the acid. Thus, large quantities of sulfur have been and still are being wasted in the refining of ores. However, more of this sulfur will probably be recovered in the future because of anti-pollution laws, if not for economic reasons.

Hydrogen sulfide is a contaminant of natural gas, refining gas and coke-oven gas. Small amounts of sulfuric acid are made by burning hydrogen sulfide, and in addition some hydrogen sulfide is converted to elemental sulfur. Substantial quantities of sulfuric acid are recovered from

---

[1] See chapter by E. M. Jones in "Manufacture of Sulfuric Acid," edited by W. W. Duecker and J. R. West, New York, Reinhold Publishing Corp., 1959.

acid sludges and other acid wastes from the refining of petroleum. In Europe, sulfuric acid is made as a by-product in the manufacture of cement. Gypsum is used in place of limestone in a cement kiln, coke is added to reduce the gypsum, and sulfur dioxide in the kiln gases is converted to acid by the conventional contact process.

## CHAMBER PROCESS

The chamber process for the manufacture of sulfuric acid is rapidly becoming obsolete in the United States. Fifty years ago, the chamber process accounted for most of the production. By 1940, the contact process had overtaken the chamber process, and today only about 5 per cent of the total production is chamber acid. No new chamber plants have been built since the war, and those plants still in operation are gradually being replaced with contact plants.

There are several reasons for the gradual disappearance of the chamber process. After World War I, there was an increasing demand for strong acid and oleum which could not be supplied by the chamber process. When new contact plants were built to supply this demand, it was found that these plants could be constructed at less cost, required less floor space and produced a pure and concentrated acid. With the development of improved catalysts, efficient heat recovery and simplified equipment, contact plants have been even further improved. Thus, contact acid is now substantially cheaper than chamber acid, even for those uses such as the manufacture of fertilizer which do not require a strong acid.

A flow sheet of the chamber process is shown in Fig. 6-2. Sulfur dioxide from the combustion of brimstone or pyrites enters the base of the Glover tower and passes countercurrent to chamber acid which is pumped to the top of the tower. The Glover tower is of masonry or acid-proof brick; its purpose is to cool the combustion gases and denitrate and concentrate the acid from the chambers. In addition, a substantial production of acid occurs in this tower. Exit gas from the Glover tower enters the lead chambers where sulfur dioxide is converted to sulfuric acid using oxides of nitrogen as a catalyst. Gases from the final chamber pass to the Gay-Lussac tower countercurrent to cold 60°Bé sulfuric acid which recovers oxides of nitrogen before discharging the gases to the stack.

The high investment costs in the chamber process are largely determined by the required volume of the lead chambers. These are often simply large box-like rooms of volume up to 500,000 ft³ each which are cooled only by air circulation. In more modern plants, the chambers are

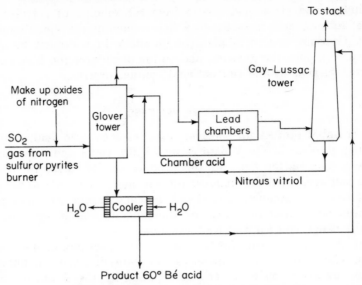

FIG. 6-2. Simplified flow sheet for chamber process.

in the form of a truncated cone, and water is sprayed on the outside to provide cooling. If cooling is provided, approximately 6-7 ft$^3$ of chamber volume is required per pounds/day of sulfur burned.

### Theory of Chamber Process

There is still considerable question as to the mechanism of the reactions occurring in the chamber process. The over-all reaction is the conversion of sulfur dioxide to sulfuric acid according to the equation

$$SO_2 \text{ (g)} + \tfrac{1}{2}O_2 \text{ (g)} + H_2O \text{ (l)} \xrightarrow{NO_2} H_2SO_4 \text{ (sol'n)} \qquad (6\text{-}1)$$

Oxides of nitrogen act as a catalyst in the oxidation. In the gas phase, the following homogeneous reaction takes place:

$$2NO \text{ (g)} + O_2 \text{ (g)} \rightarrow 2NO_2 \text{ (g)} \qquad (6\text{-}2)$$

At the gas-liquid interface, the following heterogeneous reactions occur:

$$SO_2 \text{ (g)} + H_2O \text{ (l)} \rightleftharpoons H_2SO_3 \text{ (sol'n)} \qquad (6\text{-}3)$$

$$H_2SO_3 \text{ (sol'n)} + NO_2 \text{ (g)} \rightleftharpoons H_2SO_4 \cdot NO \text{ (sol'n)} \qquad (6\text{-}4)$$

$$NO \text{ (g)} + NO_2 \text{ (g)} + 2H_2SO_4 \text{ (sol'n)} \rightleftharpoons$$
$$2HO\!-\!SO_2\!-\!ONO \text{ (sol'n)} + H_2O \text{ (l)} \qquad (6\text{-}5)$$

The compound $H_2SO_4 \cdot NO$ is known as sulfonitronic acid or violet acid; it is a very loose molecular compound which is present in very small concentrations in the chamber acid. Nitrosylsulfuric acid, HO—SO$_2$—ONO, is a stable compound which can be prepared in the crystalline form. The solubility of nitrosylsulfuric acid in sulfuric acid solutions increases as the acid strength increases. For acid strengths below about 80 per cent, an appreciable fraction of the nitrosylsulfuric acid is hydrolyzed to regenerate the oxides of nitrogen.

There is still some uncertainty as to the particular reactions in solution which result in the formation of sulfuric acid. However, there is good evidence to show that the rate-controlling step in the chamber process is the oxidation of NO to NO$_2$ according to Eq. (6-2). Thus, it is known from plant experience that the production from a chamber plant is greater in the winter because of the lower operating temperature. It has also been shown experimentally that the capacity of a chamber plant varies directly as the square of the absolute pressure. Yet it is a well-known fact that the oxidation of nitric oxide according to Eq. (6-2) is a relatively slow homogeneous gas reaction in which the rate of oxidation decreases with temperature and is proportional to the square of the absolute pressure. These facts clearly indicate that this reaction is the rate-controlling step in the chamber process.

## THE CONTACT PROCESS

The success of the contact process is dependent on the catalytic oxidation of sulfur dioxide according to the equation

$$2SO_2 \text{ (g)} + O_2 \text{ (g)} \rightleftharpoons 2SO_3 \text{ (g)} \tag{6-6}$$

$$\Delta H^\circ_{298} = -46,980 \qquad \Delta F^\circ_{298} = -33,460$$

Since the reaction is exothermic, the conversion is favored by low temperature. However, a catalyst is required to obtain a satisfactory rate of reaction at a reasonable temperature. Because there is a decrease in the total number of moles, the conversion is also favored by pressure; however, in practice, the reaction is always carried out at atmospheric pressure. The equilibrium constant $K_p$ for the reaction in atm$^{-1}$ is

$$K_p = \frac{P^2_{SO_3}}{P^2_{SO_2}P_{O_2}} \tag{6-7}$$

Values of the equilibrium constant have been determined by many investigators.[1] Data are plotted in Fig. 6-3. A fairly good straight line is

[1] Bodenstein and Pohl, *Z. Elektrochem.*, **11**, 373 (1905); Kapustinskii and Shamovskii, *Acta Physicochimica U.S.S.R.*, **4**, 791 (1936); Knietsch, *Angew. Chem.*, **1**, 617 (1903); Lunge and Reinhardt, *Angew. Chem.*, **45**, 1041 (1904); Taylor and Lehner, *Z. Physik. Chem. (Bodenstein-Festband)*, p. 30 (1931). For a discussion of the probable error made by other investigators, see the paper by Kapustinskii and Shamovskii.

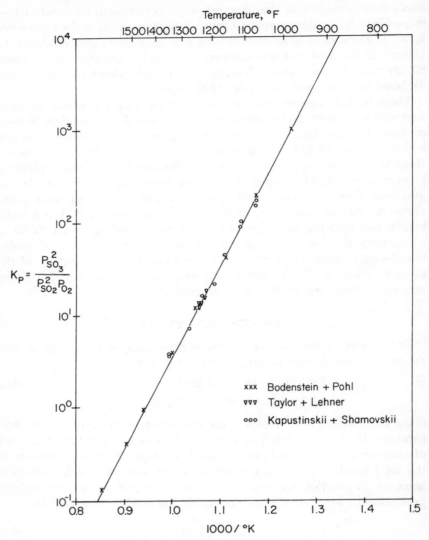

FIG. 6-3. Equilibrium constant for $2SO_2 + O_2 \rightarrow 2SO_3$

obtained in which the logarithm of the equilibrium constant (to the base 10) is given by the equation

$$\log K_p = \frac{9910}{T} - 9.36 \qquad (6\text{-}8)$$

The equilibrium yield of sulfur trioxide may be determined in the following way. Take a basis of 100 moles of gas fed to the converters and let $P$ = total pressure in atm, $2a$ = initial moles $SO_2$, $b$ = initial moles $O_2$, and $2x$ = moles $SO_3$ present at equilibrium. Then a material balance gives

| Feed | At Equilibrium |
|---|---|
| Moles $SO_2$ to converter = $2a$ | Moles $SO_3$ = $2x$ |
| Moles $O_2$ to converter = $b$ | Moles $SO_2$ = $2a - 2x$ |
| Moles inert = $100 - 2a - b$ | Moles $O_2$ = $b - x$ |
| Total moles = $100$ | Moles inert = $100 - 2a - b$ |
| | Total moles = $100 - x$ |

In practice, the oxygen is always in excess, and hence $b > a$. At equilibrium

$$P_{SO_3} = \frac{2x}{100 - x} P$$

$$P_{SO_2} = \frac{2(a - x)}{100 - x} P$$

$$P_{O_2} = \frac{b - x}{100 - x} P$$

$$K_p = \frac{x^2(100 - x)}{P(a - x)^2(b - x)}$$

Values of the equilibrium conversion of $SO_2$ to $SO_3$ for brimstone gas are plotted in Fig. 6-4. Note that the conversion is close to 100 per cent at temperatures below about 800°F.

## Oxidation Catalysts

The three materials which have been used commercially as catalysts for the oxidation of sulfur dioxide are iron oxide, platinum, and vanadium pentoxide. Iron oxide is a relatively poor catalyst. It was used at one time in a preliminary high temperature converter with platinum used to finish the oxidation; however, iron oxide has not been used commercially since the development of the vanadium catalysts.

Platinum is an excellent catalyst since it has a low kindling temperature and high space velocities can be used. However, platinum is very

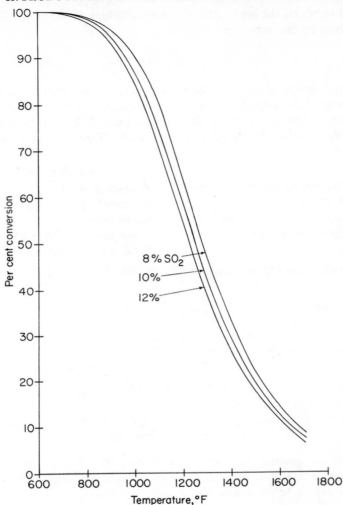

FIG. 6-4. Equilibrium conversion $SO_2$ to $SO_3$—brimstone gas at 1 atm.

susceptible to poisoning, especially by metals such as arsenic. In addition, platinum has a high cost per unit weight and losses of active material are hence more important.

Vanadium pentoxide activated with potassium is now used almost exclusively for the commercial oxidation of sulfuric dioxide.[1] The cat-

_____
[1] See chapter by J. P. Donovan in "Manufacture of Sulfuric Acid," edited by W. W. Duecker and J. P. West, New York, Reinhold Publishing Corp., 1959.

alyst is made by mixing together vanadic acid, caustic potash, sulfur, and a physical support such as kieselguhr or diatomaceous earth until the mixture has the consistency of damp earth. It is then extruded in the form of $\frac{1}{8}$-$\frac{3}{8}$ in. cylinders which are dried and screened before being placed in service. The final catalyst has about 5 per cent $V_2O_5$ and a molar ratio of potassium to vanadium of about 3:1. The installed catalyst has a packing density of about 40 lb/ft.$^3$

Vanadium catalysts are very resistant to poisoning, and reduced activity is almost always the result of physical coating or choking of the catalyst by foreign dust. For this reason and to avoid increased pressure drop through the converter, it may be necessary to periodically screen the top section of the catalyst bed to remove dust. The catalyst is damaged by the condensation of free sulfuric acid which may occur during plant startup or shutdown. Also extremely high temperatures (over 1100°F) may decrease the activity of the catalyst. However, in normal plant operation, vanadium catalysts have been used for 20 years or longer without significant decrease in activity. The total volume of catalyst required is usually based on the production rate, and varies from about 5-9 ft$^3$/daily ton 100 per cent $H_2SO_4$. In practice the conversion is accomplished in three or four stages, most of the catalyst being required for the final stage because of the lower temperature and hence smaller rate of reaction.

## Kinetics

Although the kinetics[1] of the oxidation have been quite widely studied, there is still some uncertainty as to the exact mechanism and the kinetic equation for the reaction. There appears to be general agreement that in the oxidation on a platinum catalyst, the rate is proportional to the sulfur dioxide pressure, inversely proportional to the square root of the sulfur trioxide pressure, and independent of the oxygen pressure. The activation energy on platinum is about 10,000 cal/mole $SO_2$.

In the case of vanadium catalysts, the rate is strongly dependent on the oxygen pressure and less strongly dependent on the sulfur dioxide pressure. The activation energy for a promoted vanadium catalyst is 23,000-31,000 cal/mole, in comparison with a higher value of 34,000-38,000 cal/mole for pure vanadium pentoxide. The limiting reaction on vanadium has been variously attributed to the rate of chemisorption of sulfur dioxide and oxygen on the catalyst, the reaction between chemisorbed sulfur dioxide and gaseous oxygen and the rate of desorption of sulfur trioxide. The situation is particularly complex because the surface

[1] For a recent survey, see P. G. Ashmore, "Catalysis and Inhibition of Chemical Reactions," London, Butterworth and Co. Ltd., 1963.

of the promoted catalyst may exist as a "melt," and the oxidation may involve a series of reactions between the gas, catalyst, promoter and supports.

## PLANT CONSTRUCTION

The design of sulfuric acid plants has become more or less standardized.[1] All plants must perform the following operations: (1) produce sulfur dioxide from a suitable raw material; (2) cool, purify, and dry the sulfur dioxide gases; (3) preheat the gases to the kindling temperature for conversion to sulfur trioxide; (4) catalytically oxidize the sulfur trioxide; (5) cool the converted gases; (6) absorb the sulfur trioxide in strong sulfuric acid.

Contact sulfuric acid plants fall into two general categories, "hot-gas-purification" plants and "cold-gas-purification" or "metallurgical" plants. The first type includes those plants operating on Frasch or recovered sulfur. These are the cheapest, easiest to operate, and by far the most common. In these plants, the air for combustion is usually predried, and the only purification of the burner gases consists of a filtration at temperatures of 800-850°F. The second type of plant includes those operating on metallurgical gases, pyrites and acid sludges. Here the sulfur dioxide is contaminated with water, dust, sulfuric acid mist, and other impurities which must be removed by cooling the gases to about room temperature, condensing out moisture, filtering, and drying before sending the purified gas to the converters. Although the initial and operating costs are higher for such plants, the cost of the product sulfuric acid may be lower if the sulfur dioxide is available as a by-product or waste product from some other operation.

Figure 6-5 illustrates a typical hot-gas-purification plant. Atmospheric air is compressed to 1.5-3.0 psig by a blower located either before or after the drying tower. Centrifugal blowers are now almost always used, although positive-displacement blowers were used in many of the older plants. Note that all equipment after the blower operates under a slight positive pressure, which prevents leakage of moisture into the system. Atmospheric air is dried in a packed column with 93-98 per cent sulfuric acid. The drying tower is of steel lined with acid-resistant brick; sometimes a mastic membrane is used between the steel shell and the brick lining. Packing is raschig rings and quartz supported on a tile grid.

Sulfur is melted and burned with the predried air in a sulfur burner consisting of a horizontal or vertical steel cylinder lined with firebrick

[1] For descriptions of modern plants, see W. W. Duecker and J. P. West, *op. cit.*

and insulating brick. The molten sulfur is either sprayed into the furnace (Chemico type), or is vaporized as it flows down a brick chequer (Monsanto type). Combustion gases leave the furnace at about 1600°F and are cooled to 800°F in a waste-heat boiler of either the water-tube or

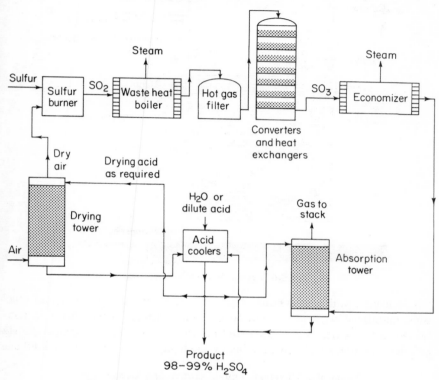

FIG. 6-5. Typical "hot-gas" purification contact plant.

fire-tube type. The steam pressure is normally at least 200 psig to maintain the skin temperature of the boiler tubes above the dew point of sulfuric acid in the gases, since condensation of acid would increase corrosion. A hot-gas filter may or may not be used after the boiler; it is now more common to filter the sulfur admitted to the furnace rather than to filter the gases.

### Converter Design

Although converters are now more or less standardized, they are still designed largely on the basis of experience rather than theory. Figure 6-6 gives details of the Monsanto converter and Table 6-3 gives typical

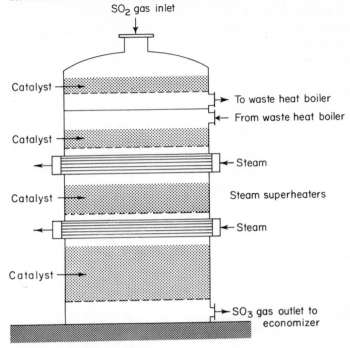

Fɪɢ. 6-6. Typical four-pass converter.

temperatures and conversions. The converter consists of a vertical steel shell metalized with aluminum to prevent scaling. The catalyst is contained in trays which are supported on triangular cast-iron grids. Quartz pebbles are placed above and below each layer of catalyst to increase

Tᴀʙʟᴇ 6-3.   Tʏᴘɪᴄᴀʟ Tᴇᴍᴘᴇʀᴀᴛᴜʀᴇꜱ ᴀɴᴅ Cᴏɴᴠᴇʀꜱɪᴏɴꜱ
ɪɴ Bʀɪᴍꜱᴛᴏɴᴇ Pʟᴀɴᴛ*

| Location | Temperature (°F) | Total Conversion (%) |
|---|---|---|
| Gas entering first pass | 770 | |
| Gas leaving first pass | 1115 | 74 |
| Gas entering second pass | 820 | |
| Gas leaving second pass | 906 | 92.4 |
| Gas entering third pass | 810 | |
| Gas leaving third pass | 830 | 96.7 |
| Gas entering fourth pass | 800 | |
| Gas leaving fourth pass | 806 | 98.0 |

* W. W. Duecker and J. P. West, *op. cit.*

the heat capacity of the converter and thereby lengthen the time the converter can be shut down without cooling below the kindling temperature of the catalyst.

The sulfur dioxide is converted to sulfur trioxide in four passes through the catalyst, most of the conversion taking place in the first pass. Cooling after the first pass is by a waste-heat boiler; cooling after the second and third passes is by steam superheaters using saturated steam from the steam drum. Gases from the final pass are cooled in an economizer which either preheats the boiler feed water or preheats the dried air going to the sulfur burner. In normal operation, the sulfur dioxide concentration in the burner gas is about 9 per cent. This can be increased to about 10.0-10.5 per cent for overload conditions at some sacrifice in the over-all conversion.

## Absorption of Sulfur Trioxide

Sulfur trioxide is absorbed in strong sulfuric acid in an absorbing tower similar to the drying tower. Operating experience has shown that an acid strength of 98.3-98.5 per cent gives best results. Absorbing acid is continually recirculated through an external cooler, water or dilute acid being added to maintain the concentration. Exit gases from the absorber usually pass directly to the stack.

It may at first seem strange that concentrated sulfuric acid is a much better absorbant than weaker acid or water. The reason for this is the relative mobility of water vapor and sulfur trioxide vapor. Thus, if a dry gas containing sulfur trioxide is brought into contact with water or dilute sulfuric acid, there is a tendency for the sulfur trioxide to diffuse into the liquid phase and there is also a tendency for water vapor to back-diffuse into the gas phase. However, because of the lower molecular weight, the rate of diffusion of water will be much greater. Furthermore, the water diffusing into the gas phase will react with sulfur trioxide to form molecules of sulfuric acid. Because of the extremely low vapor pressure of sulfuric acid, these molecules will coalesce to form a colloidal fog or mist of sulfuric acid which is very difficult to remove. The reason that the 98.3-98.5 per cent acid is optimum is that the vapor pressure of sulfuric acid goes through a minimum at this concentration, and hence the tendency to form sulfuric acid mist is also a minimum.

## Treatment of Tail Gases

Even though commercially the contact process has a conversion efficiency of 96-98 per cent, in a good sized plant as much as several tons a day of unconverted sulfur dioxide may be discharged up the stack. In addition, smaller quantities of sulfuric acid may be present as a mist.

Unfortunately, sulfur dioxide concentrations above about 0.25 ppm are injurious to growing plants. Thus, many manufacturers of sulfuric acid have been forced to take steps to reduce the pollution by the tail gases.

The only process which has been used to any extent in the United States to reduce sulfur dioxide concentrations in the tail gases is that developed by Consolidated Mining and Smelting Co. at Trail, British Columbia. The reactions are as follows:

$$NH_4OH \text{ (sol'n)} + SO_2 \text{ (g)} \rightarrow NH_4HSO_3 \text{ (sol'n)}$$

$$2NH_4HSO_3 \text{ (sol'n)} + H_2SO_4 \text{ (l)} \rightarrow (NH_4)_2SO_4 \text{ (sol'n)} + 2SO_2 \text{ (g)} + 2H_2O \text{ (l)}$$

The tail gases are scrubbed with a solution containing ammonia to produce a mixture of ammonium sulfite and ammonium bisulfite. The mixture is then treated with sulfuric acid to form ammonium sulfate which is recovered and sold as a fertilizer. The sulfur dioxide liberated by the acid treatment is returned to the drying tower of the contact plant to be converted to sulfuric acid. A two-stage tail-gas absorption system of this kind will remove up to 90 per cent of the sulfur dioxide in the tail gas.

Another method of reducing the sulfur dioxide in the tail gas is through the use of the double-contact sulfuric acid process[1] used in Germany. In this process the sulfur dioxide passes through three catalyst stages, the sulfur trioxide is absorbed in sulfuric acid, and the exit gases are then reheated, passed through a fourth catalyst stage and the sulfur trioxide again absorbed in sulfuric acid. By the double removal of the reaction product, the over-all yield is increased to about 99.7 per cent with a corresponding reduction in the sulfur dioxide sent to the stack.

## METALLURGICAL PLANTS

Although the United States is blessed with an abundant supply of elemental sulfur, this is not true in the rest of the world where pyrites is the major source of sulfuric acid. When a sulfide ore is used to produce sulfuric acid, the roasting of the ore may be carried out in two general ways. If the sulfur dioxide is the chief product, the purpose of the roasting will be to produce a concentrated gas for acid manufacture and the nature of the cinder or calcine produced from the roasting will be secondary. However, if the metallic value of the calcine is of chief importance, then the quality of the sulfur dioxide will be secondary and any acid produced will be a by-product.

When pyrites is burned in air, the product depends on the temperature

[1] *Chem. Eng. News,* Dec. 21, 1964, p. 42.

and the relative amount of air supplied. If insufficient air is supplied, the calcine will consist of a mixture of FeS and $Fe_3O_4$ and the exhaust gases will contain about 12-15 per cent of sulfur dioxide. If 100-105 per cent[1] of theoretical air is used at temperatures of about 1650°F, the calcine will consist almost entirely of black $Fe_3O_4$. If the excess air is increased still further, the calcine will consist almost entirely of red $Fe_2O_3$. The concentration of sulfur dioxide in the gas will of course decrease as the excess air increases.

If the sulfur-containing gases are to be used to manufacture sulfuric acid, it is necessary to have at least a 1:1 ratio of oxygen to sulfur dioxide in the gases sent to the converter. This can be achieved either by using a substantial excess of air in the combustion of the ore or, more commonly, by adding secondary air at some later part of the process. If pure $FeS_2$ is roasted to $Fe_2O_3$, the resultant gas will contain a maximum of 9.2 per cent sulfur dioxide if the oxygen ratio is at least 1:1. Since there are always some losses of sulfur, the actual gas concentration obtained commercially will be smaller. If pyrrhotite is used as a source of sulfur, the sulfur dioxide concentration will be still smaller because of the higher fraction of iron in the ore. Thus, in metallurgical plants, the gases sent to the converters contain about 7-9 per cent $SO_2$. However, metallurgical plants have successfully handled sulfur dioxide concentrations as low as 3 per cent without having to use auxiliary fuel to achieve proper temperatures for conversion.

Several types of roaster have been used for pyrites ore. The oldest type was the lump burner which consisted of a series of individual ovens operated on a batch basis. A large amount of hand labor was required, and this roaster is now obsolete. Rotary kilns have been successfully used in Germany, but have never been used to any extent in the United States. One of the most widely used roasters has been the multiple-hearth shelf roaster such as the Herreshoff or Wedge roaster which consists of a number of superimposed circular hearths. An air-cooled rotating shaft is located in the center of the furnace which contains arms carrying rabble blades or plows which work the ore across each hearth. Air is admitted at the bottom of the furnace, ore is admitted at the top and gradually works its way down the furnace, the calcine being discharged from the bottom hearth.

Two types of roaster have also been developed to burn powdered ore. In the flash roaster, the feed is blown into a cylindrical combustion chamber and the calcine is discharged through the bottom by a conveyor. The feed must be dry and finely ground. The fluidized roaster

[1] See chapter by R. B. Thompson and W. W. Jukkola in Duecker and West, *op. cit.*

is based on the suspension of solid particles in a rising gas stream. This roaster consists of a vertical cylindrical brick-lined vessel in which air is supplied at the bottom to maintain a fluidized bed of solid particles. The feed is introduced into the side of the vessel as a slurry containing about 80 per cent of solids. The calcine is removed at the bottom of the vessel through an overflow pipe; a substantial fraction of the calcine also carries over with the burner gases, and is recovered in cyclone separators.

### Purification of Metallurgical Gases

Metallurgical gases will contain large quantities of suspended solids, water vapor and possibly metallic vapors such as arsenic, lead or zinc. In addition, these gases will always contain some sulfur trioxide resulting from the oxidation of sulfur dioxide catalyzed by the iron oxide present in the calcine. The sulfur trioxide is particularly harmful because it forms a sulfuric acid mist when the gases are cooled. This mist is extremely difficult to remove, and sometimes carries over into the conversion system where it can cause increased corrosion in the cool parts of the system.

The treatment of metallurgical gases depends to some extent on the nature of the ore which is burned. Figure 6-7 illustrates a typical puri-

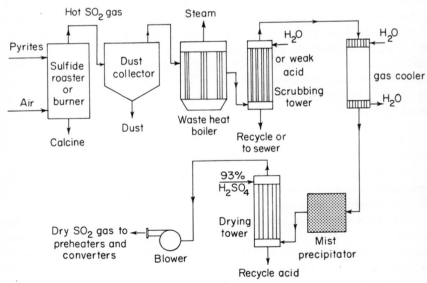

FIG. 6-7. Typical metallurgical wet-gas purification system (Duecker and West, *op. cit.*).

fication system. Usually the combustion gases first pass through cyclone separators to remove most of the entrained dust. If the calcine has substantial metallurgical value, a hot electrostatic precipitator may be used after the cyclone separators. The hot gases are then cooled in a waste-heat boiler to about 700°F; because these gases still contain some abrasive dust, care must be taken in the design of the boiler to minimize erosion of the boiler tubes. The gases then pass to a spray tower or packed tower where they are cooled to the adiabatic saturation temperature by direct contact with recirculated dilute sulfuric acid solution. The saturated gas at about 160°F then passes to a graphite shell-and-tube heat exchanger where the gases are further cooled to about 100°F with the condensation of a substantial quantity of water. Sulfuric acid mist is removed in an electrostatic precipitator, and the purified gas is then dried with 93-98 per cent sulfuric acid before passing to the converters.

In a metallurgical plant, the blower is usually located after the drying tower. In this way, the roaster and purification system are under a negative pressure so that any leakage will be into the system. Secondary air is introduced before the drying tower to bring the ratio of oxygen to sulfur dioxide up to a value of about 1.3:1.

When hydrogen sulfide is used as a raw material, the combustion gases contain large quantities of water. Often the gases are handled in the same way as metallurgical gases except that usually there is no dust removal problem. It is also possible to partially cool the combustion gases from hydrogen sulfide and then pass the wet gases directly to the converters. However, only weak acid can be produced in this way, and there is also the problem of mist removal from the converted gases. Acid sludges from petroleum refining can be burned to sulfur dioxide in a furnace, and then converted to acid by the conventional metallurgical process. In some cases supplementary fuel must be added to the furnace to obtain a sufficiently high temperature to decompose the acid sludge.

## MANUFACTURE OF OLEUM

Fuming sulfuric acid, or oleum, is widely used in organic sulfonations and nitrations where the free sulfur trioxide reacts with any water formed in the process. Oleum can be made directly from the contact process merely by installing an oleum tower before the sulfuric acid absorbing tower. The maximum strength of oleum which can be produced depends on the partial pressure of sulfur trioxide in the converter gas and the temperature of absorption. Figure 6-8 gives the vapor pressure of sulfur trioxide over solutions of oleum; strengths up to 40 per cent oleum can easily be made directly from converter gas. Higher strengths of up to

100 per cent oleum can be made by boiling a weak oleum to produce essentially pure sulfur trioxide gas which can be liquefied and collected as such or diluted to produce a strong oleum of the desired concentration.

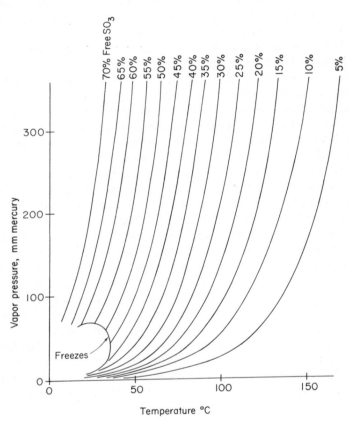

Fig. 6-8. Vapor pressure $SO_3$ over oleum [Miles, Niblock and Wilson, *Trans. Faraday Soc.*, **36**, 345 (1943)].

However, as illustrated in Fig. 6-9, the freezing point of oleum is in some cases above room temperature. For this reason, the 20 and 65 per cent grades have been more popular than the 30 and 40 per cent grades. Of particular interest is the 100 per cent oleum, or pure liquid sulfur trioxide.[1] The freshly prepared material (γ form) freezes at about 62°F and boils at about 113°F. However, over the period of a few hours or

[1] A. T. Royle, *Chem. Ind.*, 1140 (1959).

days, the liquid polymerizes to the undesirable $\alpha$ and $\beta$ forms which are solids at room temperature and which may require temperatures greater than 200°F to remelt. Recently, Allied Chemical has introduced a stabilized sulfur trioxide known as "Sulfan" which contains about 0.1 per

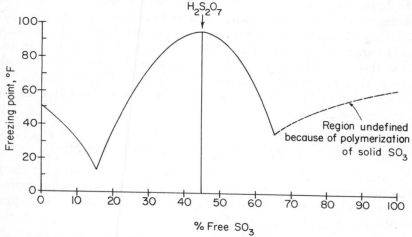

FIG. 6-9. Freezing point of oleum [C. M. Gable *et al.*, *Jour. Am. Chem. Soc.*, **72,** 1445 (1950)].

cent of a stabilizing agent such as boric oxide, methyl borate or boron trifluoride dimethyl etherate. The stabilized material can be kept indefinitely at room temperature without freezing and has substantial advantages in comparison with the other grades of oleum.

## MATERIALS OF CONSTRUCTION

Sulfuric acid of strengths greater than about 54°Bé and at moderate temperatures can be handled in ordinary cast iron and steel equipment. Pumps and valves are commonly of FA-20 alloy (such as Carpenter 20) which contains about 20 per cent chromium, 29 per cent nickel, and smaller amounts of molybdenum, copper, and silicon. Weak sulfuric acid up to about 60°Bé is handled normally in chemical lead equipment; pumps and valves are commonly of FA-20 alloy. In addition, high-silicon cast iron can be used for all strengths of sulfuric acid up to 98.5 per cent, but has the disadvantages of being expensive and quite brittle.

Oleum is handled in steel equipment with pumps and valves of FA-20 alloy. Cast iron and high-silicon irons must not be used with oleum.

Note that the corrosion resistance of steel is the result of the formation of a sulfate film on the surface which protects the metal from further attack. In pumping and handling oleum, care must be taken not to have excessively high flow rates or turbulence, or else the protective film may be washed off with a resultant marked increase in the rate of corrosion.

In brimstone plants, ordinary steel is used for the heat exchangers, converters and other equipment used in handling the dry gases. In metallurgical plants, corrosion is more of a problem because the gases are wet and contain traces of sulfuric acid. Carbon steel can be used as long as the gases are above about 600°F where there is little chance of acid condensation. At lower temperatures, lead, FA-20 alloy, type 316 stainless steel, rubber-lined steel and plastics are used, depending on the particular conditions.

## OTHER PRODUCTS FROM THE CONTACT PROCESS

Several manufacturers of sulfuric acid use the sulfur dioxide available from the contact plant as a raw material for chemical manufacture. Thus, if sulfur dioxide is absorbed in a solution of soda ash, sodium bisulfite is produced by the reaction

$$Na_2CO_3 + H_2O + 2SO_2 \rightarrow 2NaHSO_3 + CO_2$$

If the sodium bisulfite is crystallized and dried, two molecules react to split off water and yield the commercial sodium bisulfite $Na_2S_2O_5$ which is really sodium metabisulfite or sodium pyrosulfite.

If a solution of sodium bisulfite is treated with additional soda ash, the neutral sodium sulfite is formed by the reaction

$$2NaHSO_3 + Na_2CO_3 \rightarrow 2Na_2SO_3 + H_2O + CO_2$$

The market for sodium sulfite is quite limited, however, because large quantities of sodium sulfite are also produced as a by-product in the caustic fusion process for the manufacture of phenol. If a solution of sodium sulfite is heated with powdered sulfur, sodium thiosulfate is formed by the reaction

$$Na_2SO_3 + S \rightarrow Na_2S_2O_3$$

The sodium thiosulfate (hypo) finds considerable use in the photographic industry.

The sulfuric acid product can, of course, be used as a raw material for further chemical manufacture. In fact about half the total production of sulfuric acid in the United States is for captive use where the acid is consumed in the producing plant. Most captive acid goes into the manufacture of superphosphate fertilizers, but substantial quantities also go to other types of chemical manufacture such as wet-process phosphoric acid, aluminum sulfate, salt cake and hydrochloric acid, hydrofluoric acid, etc.

# CHAPTER 7

# Fixed Nitrogen

Since the atmosphere serves as an inexhaustible source of nitrogen, it is perhaps surprising that severe shortages of nitrogen should exist in many regions of the world. However, atmospheric nitrogen is extremely inert chemically; to make this nitrogen available for chemical and biological purposes, it is necessary to "fix" atmospheric nitrogen, i.e., cause it to combine with some other element. Of course, a certain amount of nitrogen is continually being fixed in the soil as a result of natural processes involving the legumes and other types of plants. However, this natural fixation of nitrogen is now entirely inadequate to supply the world's needs for nitrogenous fertilizer, and in recent years it has been necessary to supply increasing quantities of chemically fixed nitrogen to supply food for an exploding population. This is illustrated graphically in Fig. 7-1 which shows the rapidly increasing demand for fixed nitrogen in recent years.

There are only two important natural sources of fixed nitrogen, namely, ammonium salts from by-product coke manufacture and the Chilean deposits of sodium nitrate. The three important chemical processes for fixing nitrogen are the electric arc process, the cyanamide process and synthetic ammonia. Of these three processes, synthetic ammonia now accounts for practically all the nitrogen which is fixed chemically. The electric arc process has never been important in the United States, but will be discussed briefly because of its historical and theoretical interest. The cyanamide process is of some importance in the manufacture of organic nitrogen compounds, and is thus described in Chapter 13.

### Arc Process

The electric arc process for fixing nitrogen is based on the direct synthesis of nitric oxide according to the equation

$$N_2 + O_2 \underset{k_2}{\overset{k_1}{\rightleftharpoons}} 2NO \qquad \Delta H^\circ_{298} = 43,200 \qquad \Delta F^\circ_{298} = 41,400 \qquad (7\text{-}1)$$

all three components being, of course, in the gas phase. Since the reaction is strongly endothermic, it is apparent that extremely high temperatures are required to obtain any significant yield of nitric oxide. It is

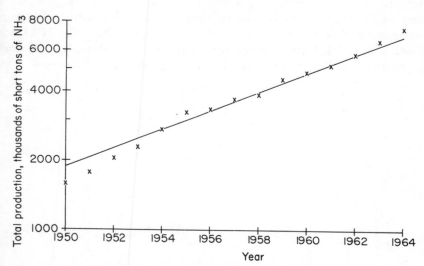

Fig. 7-1. United States production of synthetic ammonia in recent years (Bureau of the Census Reports).

also apparent that there is no advantage in operating under pressure since there is no change in volume. Thus, at atmospheric pressure the gases may be assumed to be ideal and

$$K_p = \frac{P^2_{NO}}{P_{O_2}P_{N_2}} = \frac{x^2_{NO}}{x_{O_2}x_{N_2}} \qquad (7\text{-}2)$$

The free energy at higher temperatures can be calculated from Eq. (2-41). From the heat capacities, $\Delta a = 0.07$, $\Delta b = -0.06 \times 10^{-3}$, and $\Delta c = 0.24 \times 10^5$. Also from Eqs. (2-10) and (2-42)

$$\Delta H_I = 43,200 - 21 + 3 + 81 = 43,263$$

$$I = \frac{41,400 - 43,200}{298} + (6.697)(0.07) + (298)(-0.06 \times 10^{-3})$$

$$- (5.63 \times 10^{-6})(0.24 \times 10^5) = -5.73$$

Thus, from Eq. (2-45),

$$-R \ln K_p = \frac{43,263}{T} - 0.07 \ln T + 0.03 \times 10^{-3}T$$

$$- \frac{0.12 \times 10^5}{T^2} - 5.73 \quad (7\text{-}3)$$

$$(298 < T < 2500)$$

Because of the fact that $\Delta C_p$ is small for this reaction, the integrated form of the van't Hoff equation could have been used with little error. Percentages of NO in air at equilibrium calculated from Eq. (7-3) are shown in Fig. 7-2. Only at temperatures greater than about 2000°K does the equilibrium concentration reach a value greater than 1 per cent.

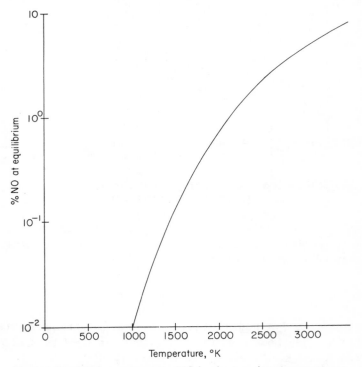

Fɪɢ. 7-2. Equilibrium percentage NO in air at various temperatures.

In addition to the problem of establishing equilibrium, there is also the problem of the kinetics. Recent experiments[1] have shown that the formation and decomposition of nitric oxide occurs in several steps, but

[1] H. S. Glick, J. J. Klein, and W. Squire, *J. Chem. Phys.*, **27,** 850 (1957); E. Freedman and J. W. Daiber, *Ibid.* **34,** 1271 (1961).

that the over-all reaction can be approximated by a bimolecular kinetic equation

$$\frac{dP_{NO}}{dt} = k_1 P_{N_2} P_{O_2} - k_2 P_{NO}^2 \tag{7-4}$$

where $k_1$ and $k_2$ are the rate constants for the forward and reverse reactions. At equilibrium the net rate must be zero and

$$K = \frac{k_1}{k_2} = \frac{P_{NO}^2}{P_{N_2} P_{O_2}} \tag{7-5}$$

where $K$ is the equilibrium constant.

The problem in the synthesis of nitric oxide is that the rate constant $k_1$ for the formation of NO has an activation energy of 135,000 cal/mole whereas the rate constant $k_2$ for the decomposition has an activation energy of only 92,000 cal/mole. Thus, the decomposition reaction is much more rapid than the formation reaction, and the reaction products must be rapidly quenched below the kindling temperature for the decomposition, or else the equilibrium will gradually shift to lower conversions if the reaction products are slowly cooled.

Commercially the arc process has been successful only in Norway[1] where large quantities of cheap hydroelectric power were available. Air was passed through a stabilized electric arc to obtain 1-2 per cent NO, the reaction products were rapidly cooled to freeze the equilibrium, passed to a waste-heat boiler to recover sensible heat, and then to absorption towers. Some plants produced nitric acid by absorption of the oxides of nitrogen in water; however, because of the low concentration of NO, the maximum strength which could be produced was about 30 per cent $HNO_3$. In other cases the nitric oxides were absorbed in a solution of soda ash to produce $NaNO_2$ for the dye industry. Much of the nitric acid produced was reacted with limestone to produce calcium nitrate (Norwegian saltpeter) and sold as fertilizer.

Although the arc process has never been commercially important, periodically someone announces an improvement which might make the process economical. For example, the rapid cooling necessary to freeze the equilibrium can be accomplished by adiabatic expansion from nozzles as the gases leave the arc. Recently, considerable work has been done on the possibility of using natural gas to obtain the necessary temperatures by preheating the reacting gas and air in a pebble-bed preheater. There is also the possibility that a nuclear reactor could be used to obtain the required temperature directly. Certainly, the arc process remains as a tantalizing possibility, and it is not entirely out of the question that some

[1] For a historical discussion of the arc process, see H. C. Curtis, "Fixed Nitrogen," New York, Chemical Catalog Co., Inc., 1932.

new breakthrough may eventually make the process commercially successful.

## SYNTHETIC AMMONIA

The synthesis of ammonia is of considerable historical importance in the chemical industry because it represents the first important application of thermodynamic principles to the solution of a difficult commercial process. For more than 100 years following the discovery of ammonia, attempts were made[1] to synthesize it directly from the elements. The first encouraging results were obtained by Ramsey and Young in 1884 when they showed that in the decomposition of ammonia over materials such as asbestos, glass and iron, detectable quantities of undecomposed ammonia were present in the hydrogen-nitrogen mixture up to temperatures as high as 800°C. In 1904, Perman and Atkinson passed a hydrogen-nitrogen mixture through a heated tube containing iron nails, and obtained enough ammonia in the exit gases to give a positive test with Nessler's reagent. Meanwhile, the basic principles of chemical equilibrium were becoming more firmly established, and shortly after the turn of the century three great physical chemists, Wilhelm Ostwald, Walter Nernst, and Fritz Haber, started active work on the ammonia synthesis.

In 1905, Haber showed that approximately 0.005 per cent ammonia is in equilibrium with a stoichiometric hydrogen-nitrogen mixture at 1000°C and atmospheric pressure. Using the equation of van't Hoff, Haber then calculated that 8 per cent ammonia should be obtained if equilibrium could be established at 327°C. In 1907, Nernst showed that the equilibrium concentration of ammonia could be increased by going to higher pressures. As a result of these preliminary experiments, Haber then started a series of decomposition and synthesis experiments to determine more accurately the value of the equilibrium constant as a function of temperature. In 1908, Haber entered into an agreement with the Badische Anilin and Soda Fabrik which resulted several years later in the first commercial synthesis of ammonia.

### Equilibrium Constant

Consider the reaction

$$\tfrac{1}{2}N_2 \text{ (g)} + \tfrac{3}{2}H_2 \text{ (g)} \rightleftharpoons NH_3 \text{ (g)} \tag{7-6}$$

$$\Delta H^\circ_{298} = -11,040 \qquad \Delta F^\circ_{298} = -4000$$

Since the reaction is exothermic, the yield of ammonia will be increased

[1] W. G. Frankenburg, "Catalysts, Vol. III," edited by Paul H. Emmett, New York, Reinhold Publishing Corp., 1955.

by establishing equilibrium at as low a temperature as possible. Also, since there is a decrease in volume, pressure will favor the conversion. For ideal gases, the highest yield would be obtained for a stoichiometric mixture of reactants; however, because of nonideal behavior, there is some evidence to show that at high pressure the maximum yield occurs at a ratio slightly different than 3:1.

Commercially, the ammonia synthesis is carried out at pressures as high as 1000 atm. The gases would certainly not be expected to be ideal under these conditions, especially the ammonia gas. Although P-V-T data are available for the pure components, no experimental data have been determined for mixtures of hydrogen, nitrogen, and ammonia. Thus, the fugacities of an equilibrium mixture cannot be determined, and this complicates any theoretical treatment of the ammonia equilibrium.

However, considerable experimental data are available[1] on the amount of ammonia present at equilibrium at various temperatures and pressures. From these experimental data, it is possible to calculate values for an equilibrium constant

$$K_p = \frac{P_{NH_3}}{P_{N_2}^{1/2} P_{H_2}^{3/2}} \tag{7-7}$$

assuming the three components are present as an ideal gas at the given temperature and pressure. These data are summarized in Table 7-1. The value of $K_p$ defined in this way can perhaps be called an "engineering" equilibrium constant, since it permits the calculation of the yield of ammonia under any given conditions, even though the partial pressures used in Eq. (7-7) are probably not the true pressures existing in the equilibrium mixture because of deviations from the ideal gas law.

It is very interesting to note the effect of pressure on the equilibrium constant. If the gases were ideal, $K_p$ would be constant at a given temperature. From Table 7-1 it can be seen that $K_p$ is essentially constant up to 50 atm. However, the values at 100 atm are slightly higher, and there is a marked increase in the value of $K_p$ at 300 atm and above. This is shown graphically in Fig. 7-3 where $\ln K_p$ is plotted as a function of the reciprocal of the absolute temperature. All values of $K_p$ measured at 50 atm or less fall on the same straight line corresponding presumably to the ideal gas state. However, at higher pressures there is a continuous increase in the value of $K_p$ at a given temperature, showing that the conversion is greater under these conditions than would be predicted, assuming perfect gases.

[1] Haber and Le Rossignol, *Berichte*, **40**, 2144 (1907); Haber, Tamaru and Ponnaz, *Z. Elektrochem.*, **21**, 89 (1915); A. T. Larson, *J. Am. Chem. Soc.*, **46**, 367 (1924); A. T. Larson and R. L. Dodge, *J. Am. Chem. Soc.*, **45**, 2918 (1923); B. F. Dodge and L. J. Winchester, *Amer. Inst. Chem. Eng. J.*, **2**, 431 (1956).

TABLE 7-1. EQUILIBRIUM CONSTANT $K_p$ FOR THE AMMONIA SYNTHESIS
(All experimental values multiplied by 1000)

| °C | 1 | 10 | 30 | 50 | 100 | Pressure in Atmospheres 300 | 600 | 1000 | 1500 | 2000 | 2500 | 3000 | 3500 |
|---|---|---|---|---|---|---|---|---|---|---|---|---|---|
| 325 | | 40.1 | | | | | | | | | | | |
| 350 | | 26.6 | 27.3 | 27.8 | | | | | | | | | |
| 375 | | 18.1 | 18.4 | 18.6 | 20.2 | | | | | | | | |
| 400 | | 12.9 | 12.9 | 13.0 | 13.7 | 18.9 (at 260 atm) | 29.4 (at 650 atm) | 61.4 | 138.4 | 297.7 | 786.4 | 1254 | 1628 |
| 425 | | 9.19 | 9.19 | 9.32 | 9.87 | | | | | | | | |
| 450 | | 6.59 | 6.76 | 6.90 | 7.25 | 8.84 | 12.9 | 25.0 23.3 | 69.62 | 133.7 | | | 1075 |
| 475 | | 5.16 | 5.15 | 5.13 | 5.32 | 6.74 | 8.95 | 14.9 | | | | | |
| 500 | | 3.81 | 3.86 | 3.88 | 4.02 | 4.98 | 6.51 | | | | | | |
| 561 | | 2.11 | | | | | | | | | | | |
| 607 | | 1.34 | | | | | | | | | | | |
| 620 | | 1.25 | | | | | | | | | | | |
| 631 | | 1.13 | | | | | | | | | | | |
| 700 | 0.68 | | | | | | | | | | | | |
| 704 | | 0.652 | | | | | | | | | | | |
| 710 | | 0.641 | | | | | | | | | | | |
| 722 | | 0.580 | | | | | | | | | | | |
| 750 | 0.468 | | | | | | | | | | | | |
| 800 | 0.333 | | | | | | | | | | | | |
| 812 | | 0.336 | | | | | | | | | | | |
| 850 | 0.279 | | | | | | | | | | | | |
| 914 | | 0.198 | | | | | | | | | | | |
| 930 | 0.200 | | | | | | | | | | | | |
| 952 | | 0.167 | | | | | | | | | | | |
| 1000 | 0.148 | | | | | | | | | | | | |

This deviation of $K_p$ from the ideal gas law is discussed by Gillespie and Beattie[1] who show that other similar cases are known. Thus, when a vapor is condensed from a gaseous mixture, more of the vapor remains in the gas phase than would be expected from the ideal gas law. Examples are the removal of ammonia from synthesis gas, removal of carbon monoxide from water gas, etc. Dodge and Winchester (op. cit.) also discuss this problem of the variation of $K_p$ with pressure and attempt to correct the ideal gas laws by five different methods.

It is of interest to note that the slope of the curve for the low-pressure equilibrium data in Fig. 7-3 corresponds to $\Delta H° = -12,700$ cal/mole. This value is the same as that given by thermal data for a temperature of about 450°C. It is unusual that the curve is linear over such a wide range of temperature, especially since $\Delta H°$ changes from $-11,040$ at 298°K to $-13,750$ at 1300°K.

### Lewis and Randall Rule

If we have an equilibrium mixture of gases, the fugacity of any component in the mixture may be expressed by the equation

$$f = \gamma x f^* \tag{7-8}$$

[1] L. J. Gillespie and J. A. Beattie, Phys. Rev., 36, 743 (1930).

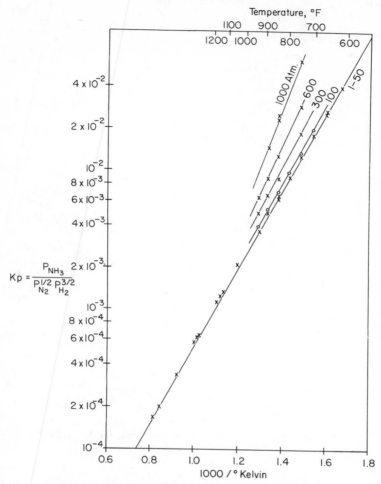

Fig. 7-3. Equilibrium constant in ammonia synthesis.

where $f^*$ is the fugacity of the pure component at the temperature and pressure of the mixture, $x$ is its mole fraction in the mixture, and $\gamma$ is the activity coefficient. For the ammonia synthesis, the equilibrium constant can thus be written

$$K_f = \frac{\gamma_{NH_3} x_{NH_3} f^*_{NH_3}}{\gamma_{N_2}^{1/2} x_{N_2}^{1/2} f^{*1/2}_{N_2} \gamma_{H_2}^{3/2} x_{H_2}^{3/2} f^{*3/2}_{H_2}} \tag{7-9}$$

which may be written

$$K_f = K_x K_\gamma \frac{f^*_{NH_3}}{f^{*1/2}_{N_2} f^{*3/2}_{H_2}} \tag{7-10}$$

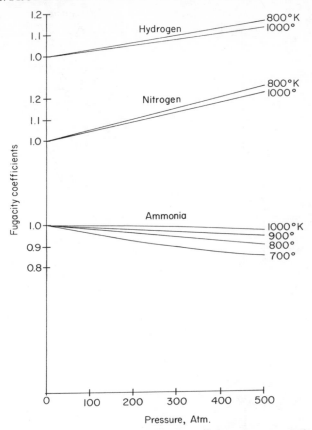

FIG. 7-4. Fugacity coefficients of hydrogen, nitrogen, and ammonia (data from C. E. Holley *et. al.*, LA-2271).

where

$$K_\gamma = \frac{\gamma_{NH_3}}{\gamma_{N_2}^{1/2}\gamma_{H_2}^{3/2}} \qquad (7\text{-}11)$$

Lewis and Randall found that many gaseous mixtures act as ideal gaseous solutions, i.e., the fugacity coefficients are unity for all components of the mixture. If this assumption is made for the ammonia synthesis, the equilibrium constant may be evaluated using known values of the fugacities for the pure components. For example, the fugacities of hydrogen, nitrogen and ammonia have been calculated [1] at Los Alamos Scientific Laboratory, using the Beattie-Bridgeman equation of state for

[1] C. E. Holley, Jr., *et al.*, U. S. Atomic Energy Commission Report LA-2271 (1958).

pressures up to 500 atm. The data are plotted in Fig. 7-4. If these data are then used to reevaluate the equilibrium constant in the ammonia synthesis using Eq. (7-10) and assuming $K_\gamma$ is unity, the resulting curve of ln $K_f$ as a function of the reciprocal temperature is given in Fig. 7-5. Note that all data points up to 650 atm pressure fall on the same straight line, indicating either that the gaseous mixtures are ideal or else the ratio of the activity coefficients given by Eq. (7-11) is close to unity.

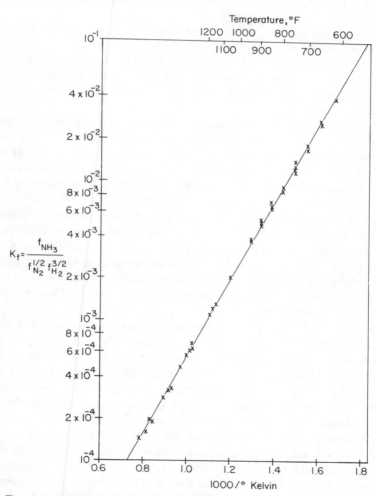

Fig. 7-5. Equilibrium constant in ammonia synthesis (experimental data for pressures to 650 atm).

### Ammonia Catalysts

Even though a reasonable percentage of ammonia is present at equilibrium, the commercial success of the synthesis reaction is dependent on the use of a suitable catalyst to speed up the reaction. The mechanism of the ammonia synthesis has been widely studied both because of its industrial significance and because there are no important side reactions to complicate the theoretical analysis. In selecting a catalyst, the following facts must be kept in mind:

(1) All attempts to combine nitrogen and hydrogen directly in a homogeneous gas phase reaction have been unsuccessful.

(2) It has been impossible to produce ammonia by a homogeneous gas phase reaction between atomic hydrogen and molecular nitrogen.

(3) Hydrogenation catalysts such as platinum are ineffective in synthesizing ammonia.

(4) Ammonia can be produced in a homogeneous gas phase reaction between atomic nitrogen and molecular hydrogen.

These facts clearly show that the reason ammonia cannot be produced in a homogeneous gas phase reaction is the extreme chemical inertness of the nitrogen molecule. The heat of dissociation of nitrogen is about 171,000 cal/mole in comparison with values of 118,000 cal/mole for oxygen and 104,000 cal/mole for hydrogen. At any reasonable temperature, the thermal energy of motion of the molecules is not sufficiently great to overcome the bond energy of the nitrogen molecule and the reaction rate is thus negligible. If an attempt is made to speed up the rate by increasing the temperature, then the equilibrium becomes so unfavorable that almost no ammonia is present even if a reasonable rate of reaction could be established.

From the above, it is obvious that ammonia synthesis can be achieved only by the use of a catalyst which will lower the energy required for the activation of the nitrogen molecule. This can be done if the catalyst has sufficient affinity for the nitrogen molecule to form an active complex on the surface of the catalyst with a minimum expenditure of energy. However, there must be a very delicate balance of the chemical affinity of the catalyst toward nitrogen, since if the affinity is too strong, the nitrogen cannot be released by the catalyst. For example, active metals such as lithium, calcium and aluminum react readily with nitrogen to form ionic nitrides, yet these metals are completely ineffective ammonia catalysts. In general, the metals suitable as ammonia catalysts are those elements which are incapable of forming nitrides at the temperatures and pressures of the synthesis reaction.

The early work of Haber showed that several metals such as iron and nickel can be used as ammonia catalysts, although the pure metals are not very effective and often lose their catalytic action after a short time. It was recognized that an improved catalyst was essential for the commercial success of the ammonia synthesis, and active work was started by Mittasch in Germany and later at the Fixed Nitrogen Research Laboratory in the United States to determine other possible catalysts. This work showed that, with the exception of cerium which is a relatively poor catalyst, all the catalytically active base metals can be found in the transition metals lying in the sixth, seventh and eighth groups of the periodic table. The data are summarized in Table 7-2.

TABLE 7-2. EFFICIENCY OF PURE METALS AS AMMONIA CATALYSTS[1]

| Metal | Yield of $NH_3$ under Test Conditions[2] (%) | Change of Activity with Time | Poisoning Effects Reversible | Irreversible | Composition under Test Conditions |
|---|---|---|---|---|---|
| Iron | 2.0 | Rapid decrease to about 10% of initial activity | $H_2O$, $O_2$, $CO_2$ | S, Se, Te, As, P, CO | Metal |
| Cobalt | 0.2 | Slow decline of activity | $H_2O$, $O_2$, $CO_2$ | S, Se, Te, As, P, CO | Metal |
| Nickel | 0-0.1 | Soon becomes completely inactive | $H_2O$, $O_2$, $CO_2$ | S, Se, Te, As, P, CO | Metal |
| Molybdenum | 1.5 | Retains initial activity over long period | Less susceptible than iron, cobalt, and nickel | | Metal-metal nitride mixture |
| Tungsten | 0.4 | Retains initial activity over long period | Less susceptible than iron, cobalt, and nickel | | Metal-metal nitride mixture |
| Manganese | 0.8 | Rapid decrease due to high susceptibility to poisons | | $H_2O$, $O_2$, S, Se, Te, As, P, CO | Metal-metal nitride mixture |
| Uranium | 1.0-2.5 | Slow decrease | | $H_2O$, $O_2$, S, Se, Te, As, P, CO | Metal-metal nitride mixture |
| Cerium | 0.3-1.0 | Slow decrease | | $H_2O$, $O_2$, S, Se, Te, As | Metal-metal nitride mixture |
| Osmium | 2.0 | Remains fairly constant | $H_2O$, $O_2$, CO | As, P | Metal |
| Ruthenium | Probably 1.0 | | $H_2O$, $O_2$, CO | As, P | Metal |

[1] Reprinted with permission from W. G. Frankenburg, "Catalysis Vol. III," P. H. Emmett, Editor, New York, Reinhold Publishing Corp., 1955.
[2] The standard test was 2 grams of catalyst in a small tube, 550°C, 100 atm pressure, 1:1 ratio of hydrogen to ammonia, space velocity = 30,000-50,000, 5 per cent $NH_3$ at equilibrium.

It can be seen that the pure metals are not very good catalysts under the standard conditions of the test. Uranium, osmium and iron show the highest activity, but even here the yield is only about half theoretical. All metal catalysts are also susceptible to poisoning, which must be considered in the purification of the synthesis gas. Of particular importance is poisoning by compounds of oxygen and sulfur, both of which may be present in the synthesis gas. Note that some of the metals are converted to a metal-metal nitride mixture by the synthesis gas, although the nitrogen is probably present as a loose complex and is not chemically bound to the metal.

In order to increase the effectiveness of the metal catalysts, various promoters have been investigated. These data are summarized in Table 7-3. Of particular importance is the effect of various oxides including

TABLE 7-3.    PROMOTER EFFECTS ON METALS AS AMMONIA CATALYSTS*

| Metal | Promoting Oxides and Oxide Combinations | Promoting Metals | Effect on Activity of Unpromoted Metal |
|---|---|---|---|
| Iron | $Al_2O_3$, CaO, $Cr_2O_3$, rare earth oxides, $Al_2O_3$ + $K_2O$, $Cr_2O_3$ + MnO | Mo, W | $2\% \rightarrow 4\% \rightarrow 5\%$ Greatly prolonged useful lifetime |
| Cobalt | $Al_2O_3$ | Mo, W | $0.2\% \rightarrow 1.5\%$ Smaller effect of promoters than with Fe |
| Nickel | | Mo, W | $0.1\% \rightarrow 0.3\%$ |
| Molybdenum | No promoter effects by oxides | Ni, Pd, Co, Pt, Fe | $1.5\% \rightarrow 4\%$ |
| Tungsten | No promoter effects by oxides | Ni, Pd, Co, Pt, Fe | $0.4\% \rightarrow 1.2\%$ |
| Osmium | $Li_2O$, $Na_2O$, $K_2O$, $ThO_2$ | Mn | $2\% \rightarrow 4\%$ |
| Manganese | $Al_2O_3$, CaO, $V_2O_5$ | Os | $0.8\% \rightarrow 2.5\%$ |
| Uranium | MgO, ZrO | | $1.0\% \rightarrow 2.5\%$ |
| Cerium | MgO | | $0.3\% \rightarrow 1.0\%$ |

* Reprinted with permission from W. G. Frankenburg, "Catalysis Vol. III," P. H. Emmett, Editor, New York, Reinhold Publishing Corp., 1955.

the alkaline oxides such as $K_2O$, the alkaline earth oxides such as CaO, and the amphoteric oxides such as $Al_2O_3$. Thus, the standard yield of ammonia is doubled by the use of a singly promoted iron catalyst, and the yield is close to theoretical for a doubly promoted iron catalyst.

Commercially, the promoted iron catalysts are the cheapest and most suited for industrial use. The catalyst is normally produced by fusion of an iron oxide such as magnetite ($Fe_3O_4$) containing 0.6-2.0 per cent $Al_2O_3$ and 0.3-1.5 per cent $K_2O$, followed by reduction of the oxide catalyst with synthesis gas. The reduction is usually done *in situ* by very slow heating of the catalyst; care must be taken during the reduction process that the evolved water vapor does not poison the catalyst as it is formed. The reduced catalyst is pyrophoric. Commercial catalysts are usually supplied as a mixture of coarse pellets approximately

6-10 mm in diameter. Both triply and quadruply promoted iron catalysts[1] have also been used in an attempt to increase further the activity.

## Kinetics of the Ammonia Synthesis

From the previous discussion of the ammonia synthesis, it is apparent
that the rate-controlling step is the chemisorption of nitrogen on the
surface of the catalyst. Although this step requires a considerable activation energy, the subsequent steps of hydrogenation on the surface of
the catalyst and desorption of the ammonia require only small amounts
of activation energy and thus occur at a fast rate. Similarly, in the decomposition of ammonia, the rapid adsorption and dehydrogenation of
ammonia on the surface of the catalyst is followed by the slow desorption of nitrogen molecules from the surface of the catalyst. Recent studies have shown that with doubly promoted iron catalysts, the adsorption
of nitrogen in the synthesis reaction and the desorption of nitrogen in
the decomposition reaction are rate-controlling over a very wide range
of pressure, temperature, and composition.

The kinetics of the synthesis and decomposition of ammonia have
been studied by many investigators.[2] In the case of a doubly promoted
iron catalyst, the experimental data show good agreement with the
following equation proposed by Temkin and Pyzhev,

$$\frac{dP_{NH_3}}{dt} = k_1 P_{N_2} \left( \frac{P_{H_2}^3}{P_{NH_3}^2} \right)^n - k_2 \left( \frac{P_{NH_3}^2}{P_{H_2}^3} \right)^{1-n} \tag{7-12}$$

where $k_1$ and $k_2$ are the rate constants for the synthesis and decomposition reactions, and $n$ is a constant. The numerical value of the constant
$n$ depends on the heat of adsorption of nitrogen on the catalyst and the
activation energies for adsorption and desorption of nitrogen molecules.
Temkin and Pyzhev used a value of $n = 0.5$, although other investigators
have found better agreement with experimental data with $n = 0.6$ or
0.7. At equilibrium the synthesis and decomposition reactions are the
same and

$$\frac{k_1}{k_2} = K = \frac{P_{NH_3}^2}{P_{H_2}^3 P_{N_2}} \tag{7-13}$$

where $K$ is the equilibrium constant.

In the derivation of Eq. (7-12), Temkin and Pyzhev recognized that

---

[1] Anders Nielsen, "An Investigation on Promoted Iron Catalysts for the Synthesis of Ammonia," Copenhagen, Jul. Gjellerups Forlag, 1956.

[2] Recent publications include: R. Brill and S. Tauster, *J. Chem. Phys.*, **36**, 2100
(1962); A. K. Mills and C. O. Bennett, *Am. Inst. Chem. Engrs. J.*, **5**, 539 (1959);
A. Ozaki, *et al.*, *Proc. Roy. Soc.*, **258**, 47 (1960); Peters and Krabetz, *Z. Elektrochem.*, **60**, 859 (1956); M. Temkin and U. Pyzhev, *Acta Physicochim. USSR*, **12**,
327 (1940).

nitrogen adsorption and desorption by the catalyst are the rate-controlling steps. They assumed that the nitrogen adsorbed on the catalyst is in equilibrium, not with the actual nitrogen pressure in the gas phase, but with a fictitious nitrogen pressure that would exist in the gas phase if complete equilibrium were established between nitrogen and the actually existing partial pressures of hydrogen and ammonia. This fictitious nitrogen pressure is, of course, that given by Eq. (7-13), using the actual pressures of hydrogen and ammonia in the gas phase and the value of $K$ for the temperature of the reaction.

Calculated values for the activation energy in the ammonia synthesis have ranged from about 17,000-53,000 cal/mole. Similarly, there has been considerable variation in the experimental values for the rate constants. These deviations can be attributed to several factors such as differences in the activity of the catalysts which were used, possible wall effects, nonisothermal conditions in several cases, and the fact that most values are obtained by an integration of the rate equations which gives only an average value for the rate constant. Also, Mills and Bennett have shown that the rate constants appear to have a strong pressure dependence.

In view of these facts, it can be seen that the design of an ammonia converter is still more or less of an art. There have been several publications[1] describing the design of converters. Also, some information is available on allowable space velocities; for example, Fig. 7-6 gives experimental values for the ammonia yield as a function of space velocity. Low space velocities achieve a high yield but require a large converter; high space velocities permit a smaller converter but increase the cost of the recovery and recycle system. In practice, a space velocity must be chosen which gives an economic balance between these two opposing factors.

## PREPARATION OF SYNTHESIS GAS

The success of the synthetic ammonia process is, of course, dependent on the availability of the required 3:1 mixture of hydrogen and nitrogen known as "synthesis gas." Not only is the synthesis gas required in tremendous quantities, but it also must be extremely pure. Thus, sulfur, phosphorus, carbon monoxide and arsenic are irreversible catalyst poisons and can only be present in the order of parts per million in the synthesis gas. Water, oxygen and carbon dioxide are reversible poisons

---

[1] For example, a very detailed analysis of converter design is given by J. Kjaer, "Measurement and Calculation of Temperature and Conversion in Fixed-Bed Catalytic Reactors," Copenhagen, Julian Gjellerups Forlag, 1958.

which can be removed by heating the catalyst; however, even here there is some permanent damage, so these gases also must be present in very low concentrations.

Various sources of synthesis gas have been used commercially. The

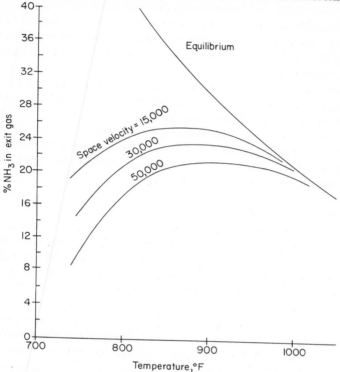

Fɪɢ. 7-6. Ammonia yield as function of space velocity—triply promoted iron catalyst, 315 atm (see A. Nielsen, *op. cit.*).

early plants were usually based on water gas obtained from the reaction between steam and incandescent coke. The reactions are as follows:

$$C\ (s) + O_2\ (g) \rightarrow CO_2 \quad \text{``blow''} \tag{7-14}$$
$$\Delta H^{\circ}_{298} = -94,052$$

$$2C\ (s) + O_2\ (g) \rightarrow 2CO\ (g) \quad \text{``blow-run''} \tag{7-15}$$
$$\Delta H^{\circ}_{298} = -52,832$$

$$C\ (s) + H_2O\ (g) \rightarrow CO\ (g) + H_2\ (g) \quad \text{``run''} \tag{7-16}$$
$$\Delta H^{\circ}_{298} = +31,382$$

Since the water-gas reaction is endothermic, it is necessary to first blow air through the coke for about 2 minutes to heat it to 1000-1100°C. As the coke heats up, the exit gases contain increasing amounts of carbon monoxide, and a fraction of the blow-run gas is used to provide nitrogen for the synthesis gas. The blow run is then followed by a steam run of 5-6 minutes until the temperature of the coke falls to about 900°C when the cycle is repeated. In practice the reactions are more complicated than given above since the exit gases contain an equilibrium mixture of $CO + CO_2$, and there is always some mixing of the gases when the cycle reverses.

Synthesis gas has also been produced using coke-oven gas as a source of hydrogen, using electrolytic hydrogen from water, and by-product hydrogen from refinery off-gases or chemical manufacture; in these cases, the nitrogen is supplied from liquid air. However, virtually all the synthetic ammonia plants built in the past 25 years have used either natural gas or a petroleum fraction to produce the synthesis gas, and hence this process will be discussed in more detail.

### Reforming of Hydrocarbons

In the United States, natural gas is the basic raw material for the manufacture of about 80 per cent of the synthetic ammonia. A typical flow sheet is illustrated in Fig. 7-7. The process consists essentially of converting a mixture of natural gas, air, and steam to $CO_2$, $H_2$ and $N_2$, followed by absorption of the $CO_2$ and purification of the 3:1 mixture of hydrogen and nitrogen.

Starting with a hydrocarbon of a given composition, the quantities of air and steam which are used must be determined from the stoichiometry. Thus, if we start with pure methane, the over-all reaction must be

$$\begin{array}{ll} 1 \text{ mole } CH_4 & 1 \text{ mole } CO_2 \\ 1.13 \text{ moles } N_2 + 0.30 \text{ moles } O_2 \text{ (air)} \rightarrow 3.40 \text{ moles } H_2 \\ 1.40 \text{ moles steam} & 1.13 \text{ moles } N_2 \end{array}$$

$$\Delta H^\circ_{298} = +4754$$

Since the over-all reaction is endothermic, heat must be supplied in order to bring it about. In practice this material balance must be modified, since excess steam is used in order to push the reaction to the right and to prevent carbon formation, natural gas contains nitrogen as well as ethane and some higher hydrocarbons, and a small amount of carbon monoxide is left in the gases sent to the purification system because of the equilibrium in the water gas shift reaction.

The reforming of natural gas is done in two steps. In the first, a mixture of steam and purified hydrocarbon reacts according to the equations

$$CH_4 \ (g) + H_2O \ (g) \rightleftharpoons CO \ (g) + 3H_2 \ (g) \qquad (7\text{-}17)$$

$$\Delta H^\circ_{298} = +49,271 \qquad \Delta F^\circ_{298} = +33,967$$

$$CO \ (g) + H_2O \ (g) \rightleftharpoons CO_2 \ (g) + H_2 \ (g) \qquad (7\text{-}18)$$

$$\Delta H^\circ_{298} = -9838 \qquad \Delta F^\circ_{298} = -6817$$

$$2CO \ (g) \rightleftharpoons CO_2 \ (g) + C \ (s) \qquad (7\text{-}19)$$

$$\Delta H^\circ_{298} = -41,220 \qquad \Delta F^\circ_{298} = -28,644$$

The first reaction is known as the reforming reaction, the second is the shift reaction, and the third is the carbon reaction.

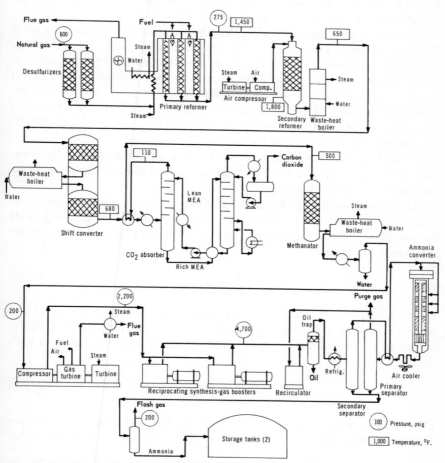

FIG. 7-7. Typical flow sheet for synthetic ammonia. [E. P. Wells *et al.*, *Oil and Gas J.*, **62** (29), 92 (1964)].

The reforming reaction is strongly endothermic, and must be carried out at temperatures of 1400°F or greater to obtain a high degree of reforming. The reaction is obviously less favorable at higher pressures; however, despite this fact, present practice is to carry out the primary reforming at pressures of about 200-300 lb/in.[2] gage. Since the gases are ultimately required at a high pressure and since the volume of the feed is much smaller than the volume of the reformed gases, it is easier and cheaper to compress the gases before they are reformed. Also, the higher pressure favors several of the succeeding steps of the process. These advantages must be balanced against the higher steam ratio which must be used and the problems of high-pressure operation, especially the design of the catalyst tubes for the primary reformer.

Figure 7-8 gives typical values for the percentage of reforming as a function of temperature, assuming equilibrium in both the reforming and shift reactions.[1] Little is known of the kinetics of the reforming reaction. There is some evidence[2] to show that with reforming on a nickel catalyst at temperatures of over 1400°F, the reforming reaction is first-order with respect to the methane concentration and has an activation energy of about 14,000 cal/mole. At temperatures above about 1800°F the reaction becomes autocatalytic.

The shift reaction is moderately exothermic and is unaffected by pressure if the gases are ideal. The reaction is beneficial since it converts additional steam to hydrogen.

The carbon reaction is definitely unwanted since it wastes carbon, increases the pressure drop through the reformer, and coats the surface of the catalyst, thereby rendering it inactive. The equilibrium constant for the carbon reaction is

$$K_p = \frac{P_{CO_2}}{P_{CO}^2} = \frac{x_{CO_2}}{P x_{CO}^2} \qquad (7\text{-}20)$$

Values of $K_p$ as a function of temperature are plotted in Fig. 7-9. The requirements for the carbon reaction to occur are quite clear, namely, carbon will deposit on the catalyst if the composition of the gases is such that

$$\frac{x_{CO_2}}{x_{CO}^2} \gtrless P K_p \qquad (7\text{-}21)$$

Thus, carbon deposition can be prevented in the following ways: (1) reducing the pressure; (2) increasing the temperature to reduce the value

[1] P. Wellman and S. Katell, *Hydro. Proc. Petrol. Refiner,* **42** (6), 135 (1963).
[2] R. D. Obolentsev and V. P. Rozhdestvenskii, *J. Appl. Chem. USSR,* **29,** 1999 (1956).

of $K_p$; (3) increasing the ratio of steam to hydrocarbon in order to shift more carbon monoxide over to carbon dioxide; (4) reducing the molecular weight of the feedstock to reduce the relative amount of carbon oxides in the gas.

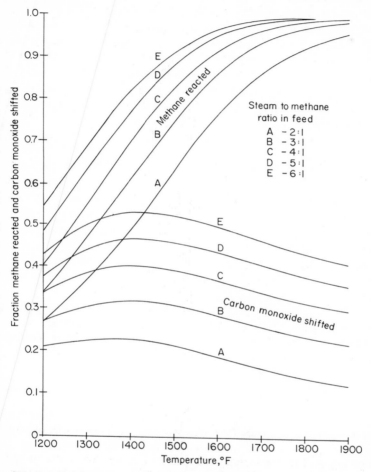

FIG. 7-8. Reforming of methane [P. Wellman, S. Katell, *Hydro. Proc. Petrol. Refiner,* **42** (6), 135 (1963)].

## Primary Reforming

Depending on the composition of the natural gas, the first step in the process is desulfurization since the reforming catalyst is poisoned by sulfur. This can be done by the use of activated carbon to adsorb hydrogen sulfide and mercaptans, by the use of iron oxide, or by the use of "yellow oxide" containing[1] about 95 per cent ZnO to remove $H_2S$, COS, $CS_2$, and mercaptans at temperatures of 400-420°C. Acid treatment may be required for naphtha feedstocks, and hydrodesulfurization may be required for feedstocks containing refractory sulfur compounds.

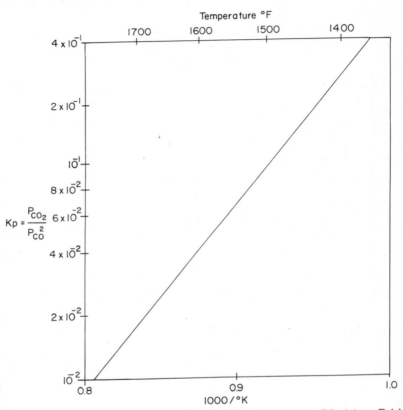

Fig. 7-9. Equilibrium constant for carbon reaction: $2 CO (g) \rightarrow CO_2 (g) + C (s)$.

Following sulfur treatment, the purified gases are then mixed with steam and sent to the primary reformer. The ratio of steam to natural gas varies from about 2-5, depending on the reforming pressure and the amount of nitrogen in the natural gas. For low-pressure reforming, the steam ratio is about 2.5; however, at the higher pressures now commonly used, the steam ratio must be increased because of the less favor-

---

[1] D. J. Borgars and G. W. Bridger, "Catalysts Used in the Manufacture of Ammonia," *Chem. Ind.*, **1960**, 1426; L. C. Axelrod and T. E. O'Hare, "Fertilizer Nitrogen," edited by V. Sauchelli, New York, Reinhold Publishing Corp., 1964.

able equilibrium conditions and to prevent carbon deposition on the catalyst. Table 7-4 gives typical compositions of the gas entering and leaving the primary and secondary reformers.

The primary reformer consists of vertical stainless steel tubes up to

TABLE 7-4.   TYPICAL OPERATING DATA FOR STEAM-HYDROCARBON
REFORMING PROCESSES*

|  | Low Pressure, Low Nitrogen | Intermediate Pressure, High Nitrogen | Intermediate Pressure, Low Nitrogen |
|---|---|---|---|
| Ammonia capacity, tons/day | 300 | 300 | 300 |
| Composition of feed, % | | | |
| $CO_2$ | 0.17 | 0.01 | 0.05 |
| $N_2$ | 0.10 | 3.3 | 0.62 |
| $C_1$ | 28.0 | 14.5 | 18.8 |
| $C_2$ | 1.25 | 1.28 | 1.83 |
| $C_3$ | 0.24 | 0.70 | 0.24 |
| $C_4$ | 0.06 | 0.20 | 0.01 |
| $C_5$ and higher | 0.06 | 0.01 | 0.05 |
| $H_2O$ | 70.0 | 80.0 | 79.0 |
| Total moles/hr of feed | 2290.8 | 3892.39 | 3435.15 |
| Gas from primary reformer, % | | | |
| $H_2$ | 49.9 | 41.0 | 43.0 |
| CO | 9.8 | 6.2 | 6.6 |
| $N_2$ | 0.07 | 2.5 | 0.37 |
| $CO_2$ | 5.66 | 6.25 | 6.2 |
| $C_1$ | 6.80 | 2.62 | 3.9 |
| $H_2O$ | 27.8 | 41.5 | 39.8 |
| Total moles/hr effluent | 3301.4 | 5177.7 | 4615.8 |
| Primary outlet pressure, psig | 125 | 220 | 220 |
| Primary outlet temperature, °F | 1470 | 1491 | 1481 |
| Moles/hr air to secondary reformer | 1004 | 884 | 1011 |
| Gas from secondary reformer, % | | | |
| $H_2$ | 41.7 | 34.9 | 36.4 |
| CO | 11.7 | 7.2 | 8.1 |
| $N_2$ | 17.3 | 13.2 | 13.9 |
| A | 0.22 | 0.25 | 0.19 |
| $CO_2$ | 4.35 | 5.4 | 5.2 |
| $C_1$ | 0.14 | 0.12 | 0.13 |
| $H_2O$ | 24.5 | 38.9 | 36.0 |
| Total moles/hr secondary effluent | 4531 | 6133 | 5762 |
| Secondary outlet temperature, °F | 1760 | 1729 | 1754 |

* Data courtesy of the M. W. Kellogg Co. Reprinted from V. Sauchelli, "Fertilizer Nitrogen," New York, Reinhold Publishing Corp., 1964, with permission.

10 in. in diameter and 20-30 ft long, which are mounted in a refractory-lined furnace. Since the tubes expand considerably in heating up to the operating temperature, the tubes must be suspended in such a manner as to accommodate this expansion. This can be done by the use of counter-weights with flexible tubing at the gas inlet. The operating conditions in the primary reformer are quite severe, and the catalyst tubes are made of a high-alloy stainless steel such as type 310 containing 25 per cent chromium and 20 per cent nickel. The catalyst is contained within the tubes, and the tubes are externally fired with a mixture of natural gas and purge gas from the ammonia synthesis system. The outer wall temperature of the tubes may be as high as 1800°F, which is close to the metallurgical limit. The feed to the primary reformer is heated to about 950°F by convective heat transfer with the exhaust gases from the reformer, and then passes downward through the catalyst tubes. Waste heat from the reformer is used to preheat the feed and to generate process steam.

The reforming catalyst contains from about 15-35 per cent nickel in the reduced state on a refractory support consisting of calcium and aluminum oxides. When first placed in use, the nickel is in the form of the oxide which is reduced to elemental nickel by gradual heating in an atmosphere of steam and hydrogen at a maximum rate of 200°F per hour. Standard catalysts can be used to a maximum temperature of about 1800°F, and special catalysts will go as high as 2400°F. With a clean gas, catalyst lifetimes of 20 years have been reported. Figure 7-10 illu-

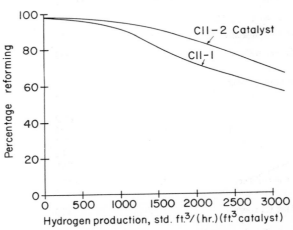

Fig. 7-10. Typical efficiencies of reforming catalysts
(*Courtesy Catalysts & Chemicals, Inc.*).

strates the efficiency of these catalysts as a function of the space velocity. The C11-1 catalyst contains 22-25 per cent nickel oxide in the unreduced state, and the more efficient C11-2 catalyst contains 32-35 per cent nickel oxide. Sulfur is the main poison, although there may be a tendency to deposit carbon on the catalyst if unsaturates or substantial quantities of heavy hydrocarbons are present in the feedstock. The catalyst is supplied commercially in the form of ½-in. and ¾-in. pellets and ¾-in. and ⅝-in. raschig rings.

### Secondary Reforming

The secondary reformer consists of a vertical cylindrical brick-lined vessel containing a bed of nickel catalyst. The exit gases from the primary reformer are mixed with sufficient air to establish the necessary nitrogen stoichiometry and are then sent directly to the secondary reformer. Heat liberated by the partial oxidation of the hydrogen and methane raises the temperature to 1700-1800°F, which essentially completes the reforming of the natural gas. Exit gases from the secondary reformer are cooled to about 650°F in a waste-heat boiler to recover sensible heat and reduce the temperature to the proper value for shift conversion.

### Water-gas Shift Converter

Exit gases from the secondary reformer contain appreciable quantities of carbon monoxide which are converted to hydrogen by the catalytic shift reaction

$$CO\ (g) + H_2O\ (g) \rightleftharpoons CO_2\ (g) + H_2\ (g) \tag{7-22}$$

$$\Delta H^{\circ}_{298} = -9838 \qquad \Delta F^{\circ}_{298} = -6817$$

The reaction is exothermic and hence favored by a low operating temperature. Pressure has no effect on the equilibrium as long as the gases are ideal. Figure 7-11 gives the conversion of carbon monoxide to hydrogen as a function of temperature.

The kinetics of the reaction have been studied [1] by several investigators. Bohlbro found the rate in the forward direction could be correlated by an equation of the type

$$-\frac{dP_{CO}}{dt} = k \frac{P_{CO}^a P_{H_2O}^b}{P_{CO_2}^c} \tag{7-23}$$

where $a = 0.80$-$1.00$, $b = 0.20$-$0.35$, and $c = 0.50$-$0.65$. The equation was obtained using a conventional iron oxide-chromium oxide catalyst for temperatures of 330-500°C and pressures to 20 atm. The activation en-

[1] For example, see H. Bohlbro, *Acta Chem. Scand.*, **15**, 502 (1961); **16**, 431 (1962).

ergy for the reaction is 27,400. The rate-determining step is probably the reaction between gaseous CO and oxidized surface sites on the catalyst, or possibly just the chemisorption of CO. It is of interest to note that the reaction is independent of the hydrogen pressure.

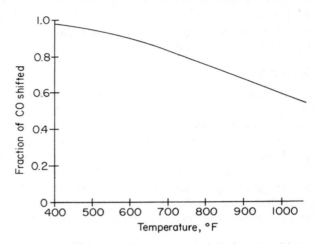

Fɪɢ. 7-11. Water-gas shift reaction—initial composition of feed = 1 mole CO, 2 moles $H_2O$, 3 moles $H_2$.

The catalyst is prepared by coprecipitating iron oxide and chromium oxide. It is supplied commercially in the form of $\frac{1}{4}$-$\frac{3}{8}$-in. pellets having a composition of about 10 per cent $Cr_2O_3$, 80 per cent $Fe_2O_3$ and 3-4 per cent graphite. At atmospheric pressure the catalyst has sufficient activity to permit commercial use at temperatures as low as 750°F; at higher pressures the catalyst is even more efficient, and can be used down to 650°F at 100 psig. Gas velocities of about 1000 standard $ft^3/(hr)(ft^3$ catalyst) are commonly used with about 98 per cent approach to equilibrium.

In practice, two stages of shift conversion are commonly required. The effluent gases from the secondary reformer are sent to the first stage of the shift converter at a temperature of about 650°F. Since most of the conversion takes place in the first stage, considerable heat is evolved which prevents the attainment of a high conversion. Thus, gases from the first stage are sent to a waste-heat boiler where they are cooled back to about 650°F and returned to the second stage of shift conversion which they leave at about 680°F. Frequently, the same vessel is used to achieve both stages of shift conversion, an internal head serving to divide the vessel into top and bottom sections.

Recently, an improved shift catalyst has become commercially available[1] which can be used as low as 400°F provided the pressure is greater than about 100 psig. This catalyst has a fairly short life and is very susceptible to poisoning, particularly to sulfur compounds. However, the lower kindling temperature permits operation with only one stage of shift conversion and also has the great advantage of allowing a reduction in the ratio of steam to carbon monoxide, and hence a corresponding reduction in the size of equipment. The catalyst is reported to be essentially the same as that disclosed in the Larson patent, namely, copper promoted by oxides of W, Mo, Ce, V, Mn or Mg.

## Carbon Dioxide Absorption

Exit gases from the shift converter pass to a heat exchanger to cool them, condense water vapor and recover sensible heat. Carbon dioxide can then be removed by absorption in solvents such as water, hot potassium carbonate, or 20 per cent monoethanolamine in conventional absorption towers with regeneration of the absorbent. Often the first absorber is hot potassium carbonate with monoethanolamine for the second absorber. Note that when monoethanolamine is used, there is gradual decomposition to form products which may cause foaming and which increase corrosion. Thus, a portion of the circulating solution is sent to a still to remove impurities.

## Carbon Monoxide Removal

Since carbon monoxide is an irreversible poison to the synthesis catalyst, it must be reduced to a few parts per million in the synthesis gas. Carbon monoxide can be removed in the following ways: (a) scrubbing with a solution of cuprous ammonium acetate, cuprous ammonium formate or a combination of the two at pressures of about 100-300 atm; (b) scrubbing with liquid nitrogen; (c) catalytic methanation.

Scrubbing with copper liquor is one of the oldest processes for carbon monoxide removal, and has been used very little in new construction. Scrubbing with nitrogen is economic only in conjunction with partial oxidation plants, since the nitrogen is available from the liquid air plant. In this process the gases are first dried and then washed directly with liquid nitrogen to remove carbon monoxide, methane and argon. The overhead gases contain about 90 per cent hydrogen and 10 per cent nitrogen, so that additional nitrogen must be provided to reestablish

[1] R. Habermehl and K. Atwood, "Low Temperature Carbon Monoxide Conversion Catalysis," paper presented to the Division of Fuel Chemistry, American Chemical Society, Philadelphia, Pa., April 5-10, 1964. See also U.S. Patent 1,889,672 (Nov. 29, 1933), issued to A. T. Larson.

stoichiometry. A very pure gas is obtained for ammonia synthesis, but low-temperature operation requires the use of considerable heat exchange equipment to make the process economical.

Most new construction in the United States uses catalytic methanation to remove carbon monoxide, carbon dioxide and oxygen. If we consider the reactions

$$CO\ (g) + 3H_2\ (g) \rightarrow CH_4\ (g) + H_2O\ (g) \tag{7-24}$$
$$\Delta H^{\circ}_{298} = -49,271 \qquad \Delta F^{\circ}_{298} = -33,967$$

$$CO_2\ (g) + 4H_2\ (g) \rightarrow CH_4\ (g) + 2H_2O\ (g) \tag{7-25}$$
$$\Delta H^{\circ}_{298} = -133,485 \qquad \Delta F^{\circ}_{298} = -121,410$$

$$O_2\ (g) + 2H_2\ (g) \rightarrow 2H_2O\ (g) \tag{7-26}$$
$$\Delta H^{\circ}_{298} = -115,596 \qquad \Delta F^{\circ}_{298} = -109,270$$

All three reactions are strongly exothermic with the equilibrium virtually 100 per cent to the right. The success of the process is obviously dependent on the use of a catalyst to achieve equilibrium at a moderate temperature. The methanation catalyst consists of nickel on a refractory support consisting largely of alumina. The catalyst as originally compounded contains from 45-70 per cent nickel oxide, which is reduced to elemental nickel by heating slowly in a hydrogen atmosphere. The catalyst is normally used in the form of pellets about $\frac{1}{4}$-in. diameter.

The methanator is simply a vertical cylindrical vessel containing a bed of catalyst. Gases enter at a temperature of about 500°F, and pass downward through the catalyst. At a pressure of about 200 psig, the space velocity is approximately 3000 ft³/(hr)(ft³ catalyst); this space velocity must be reduced to about 1000 for operation at atmospheric pressure. Oxygen and oxides of carbon present in concentrations from a few parts per million to several per cent can be hydrogenated over the catalyst to less than 5 ppm. Either dry or wet gases may be used, and pressures may vary from atmospheric to several thousand pounds.

### Ammonia Synthesis

Table 7-5 lists some of the more important ammonia-synthesis processes which have been used, and Fig. 7-12 shows how the theoretical yield is affected by pressure and temperature. It is apparent that there has been considerable variation in the operating conditions which have been used. In general, increasing the pressure increases the conversion to ammonia and helps the recovery of ammonia from the exit converter gases. However, higher pressure reduces the approach to equilibrium and increases the horsepower requirements for compression. Increasing the

TABLE 7-5 COMPARISON OF AMMONIA-SYNTHESIS PROCESSES*

| System | Converter Features | Pressure (psig) | Peak Temp. Range (°F) | Hydrogen Conversion | NH₃ Concen. mole % in | mole % out |
|---|---|---|---|---|---|---|
| Haber-Bosch (original) | Single catalyst charge with feed preheat. | 3000 | 930-1100 | 9-18 | 0 | 5-10 |
| Claude (original) | Single catalyst charge with pre-heat of feed in converter annulus. Series-parallel operated converters. | 15,000 | 930-1200 | 80 (over-all) | 0 | 25 |
| Claude (present) Grande Paroisse | Single catalyst charge with heat exchange in catalyst bed. | 5000-9500 | 1000-1100 | 30-34 | 3-4.5 | 20 |
| Casale | Single catalyst charge with pre-heat via internal heat exchange. Use of special catalyst. | 9000 | 850-1000 | 30 | 3-5 | 23 |
| Mont Cenis | Internal heat ex-change in catalyst bed. Use of high-activity low-temperature catalyst. | 1500-2400 | 750-800 | 9-20 | 0 | 5-12 |
| TVA | Single catalyst charge with countercurrent cooling tubes. Interchanger to preheat feed. | 3700-5200 | 900-1000 | 25 | 5 | 17.5 |
| Chemico | Single catalyst charge with co-current cooling tubes. Interchanger to pre-heat feed. | 3700-5200 | 900-950 | 25 | 3 | 17 |
| Fauser-Montecatini | Interchanger to preheat feed. Catalyst temperature controlled by steam generation between catalyst beds. | 4000-5000 | 950 | 30 | 1.5 | 20 |
| Kellogg | Interchanger to preheat feed. Catalyst temperatures controlled by introduction of cold feed between catalyst beds. | 3500-4700 | 900-950 | 25 | 3 | 17 |
| UHDE | Interchanger to preheat feed. Catalyst temperatures controlled by introduction of cold feed between catalyst beds. | 4600-6400 | 950 | 25-30 | 3 | 17-20 |
| Lummus | Interchanger to preheat feed. Single catalyst charge with countercurrent cooling tubes. | 4000-5000 | 930-950 | 25 | 3 | 14-18 |

* L. C. Axelrod and T. E. O'Hare, "Fertilizer Nitrogen," edited by V. Sauchelli, New York, Reinhold Publishing Corp., 1964.

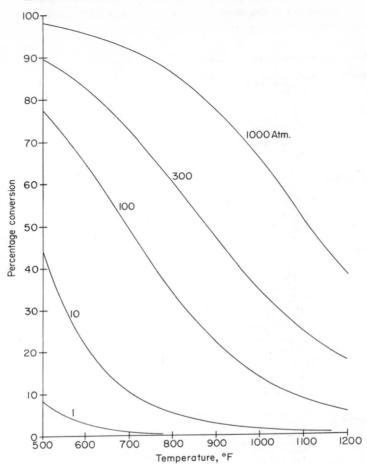

Fig. 7-12. Theoretical conversion of 3:1 ammonia synthesis gas.

temperature increases the reaction rate but reduces the theoretical conversion, reduces the life of the catalyst, and increases corrosion of equipment. Present practice favors the intermediate pressure process of 250-360 atm and operating temperatures of 900-1050°F in the catalyst bed.

Synthesis gas from the methanator is cooled, condensed water is removed, and the gas is then compressed to the final synthesis pressure. In the past reciprocating compressors were used for the high pressure compression; however, there now appears to be a trend toward the use of centrifugal compressors for at least part of the final compression. The high-pressure synthesis gas is mixed with recycle gas from the ammonia converter, passes through an oil trap to remove any entrained oil from the reciprocating compressors, and is sent to an ammonia refrigeration exchanger which condenses out ammonia from the recycle gas and removes nearly all traces of water from the synthesis gas. The purified synthesis gas passes to a separator and heat exchanger before entering the ammonia converter.

The design of the converter is quite critical since fairly large quantities of heat are given off during the synthesis reaction. The converter consists essentially of a vertical cylindrical steel vessel clad with stainless steel and containing one or more stainless steel baskets of catalyst. Promoted iron catalyst in the form of 6-10 mm particles is contained within the baskets. Usually an annular space is left between the inside of the converter and the outside of the catalyst bed; the entering synthesis gas first passes down through this annular gap to cool the shell of the vessel and protect it from hydrogen embrittlement. In some converter designs such as TVA and Chemico, cooling tubes are placed within the catalyst bed to partially preheat the synthesis gas and to reduce the temperature of the catalyst. Figure 7-13 illustrates several types of converters. A particularly interesting design is the Kellogg "quench" converter. In this converter, an internal heat exchanger is used to heat the gas to about 730°F before passing through the catalyst. Several beds of catalyst are used with mixing chambers before each bed; bypass tubes are provided so that the cold feed gas can be introduced before each catalyst section in order to maintain the optimum temperature.

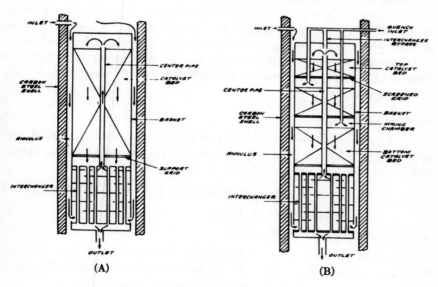

(A)          (B)

Fig. 7-13. Synthesis converter design.

Exit gases from the converter are normally cooled by heat exchange with water to condense out most of the ammonia. Note, however, that the amount of ammonia remaining in the gas phase is greater than that predicted by the ideal gas law because of nonideal behavior. The stripped gas then passes to a booster compressor which recycles it back to the ammonia converter. Since the purified synthesis gas contains up to 2 per cent of inerts consisting of methane, argon from the air, and any helium which may be present in the feedstock, a fraction of the recycle gas is purged to remove inerts. Even though the inerts act only as a diluent, they reduce the partial pressures of the reacting gases and also decrease the velocity of the synthesis reaction by tending to blanket the surface of the catalyst.

## ALTERNATE FEEDSTOCKS

Although natural gas is the most common feedstock for the manufacture of synthesis gas in the United States, this is not true in the rest of the world. Other possible feedstocks include hydrogen-rich refinery gases, cracked refinery gases, liquefied petroleum gas containing mostly propane and butane, gasoline and naphtha fractions and crude and residual oils. Steam reforming can be used for hydrocarbon fractions as heavy as the light naphthas, although special sulfur treatment may be required in some cases. Also, in general, the higher the ratio of carbon to hydrogen in the feedstock, the greater is the cost of reforming. This can be seen from a straight material balance, since as the C:H ratio increases, there is a corresponding increase in the relative amount of carbon dioxide which must be removed, the reforming reaction becomes more endothermic, smaller quantities of air can be used in the secondary reformer, and there is increased tendency for carbon deposition on the reforming catalyst.

### Naphtha Reforming

Light petroleum fractions having distillates up to about 400°F end point can be reformed at pressures up to 300 psig without carbon deposition.[1] The reactions are as follows:

$$C_nH_{2m} \text{ (g)} + nH_2O \text{ (g)} \rightleftharpoons nCO \text{ (g)} + (n + m)H_2 \text{ (g)} \qquad (7\text{-}27)$$

$$CO + 3H_2 \rightleftharpoons CH_4 + H_2O \qquad (7\text{-}28)$$

$$CO + H_2O \rightleftharpoons CO_2 + H_2 \qquad (7\text{-}29)$$

The naphtha contains many hydrocarbons ranging from $C_4$ to $C_{10}$ which react according to Eq. (7-27). All of these reactions are strongly endo-

---

[1] J. Voogd and J. Tielrooy, *Hydro. Proc. Petrol. Refiner,* **42**(3), 144 (1963).

thermic. Methane will be produced from the reaction products, the concentration of methane being close to the equilibrium value. In addition, equilibrium will be established in the shift reaction.

The essential differences between naphtha reforming and methane reforming are as follows: (1) Because of the higher sulfur content (up to 0.1 per cent), a preliminary acid treatment is required to remove most of the sulfur. (2) More unsaturates and aromatics will be present, thereby increasing the tendency for carbon deposition. (3) A naphtha vaporizer must be added. (4) Additional carbon dioxide removal capacity is required because of the higher ratio of carbon to hydrogen in the feedstock. (5) A special reforming catalyst must be used which contains a promoter to inhibit carbon formation.

### Partial Oxidation

The partial oxidation process can be used for feedstocks ranging from natural gas to heavy fuel oils. Thus, the process has great flexibility and can be used where natural gas is unavailable. However, it does require a source of oxygen which is normally obtained from a liquid air plant. A diagrammatic flow sheet is given in Fig. 7-14, and Table 7-6 gives typical operating data.

The chief reactions taking place are as follows:

$$C_nH_{2m} \text{ (g)} + \frac{n}{2} O_2 \text{ (g)} \rightarrow nCO \text{ (g)} + mH_2 \text{ (g)} \tag{7-30}$$

$$2CO \text{ (g)} \rightleftharpoons CO_2 \text{ (g)} + C \text{ (s)} \tag{7-31}$$

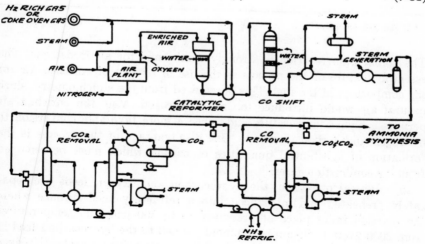

Fig. 7-14. Partial oxidation process flow sheet.

TABLE 7-6. TYPICAL PERFORMANCE DATA FOR THE TEXACO
PARTIAL OXIDATION SYSTEM*

| | Natural Gas | 64° api Naphtha | 9.7° api Fuel Oil |
|---|---|---|---|
| Feed composition, wt % | | | |
| Carbon | 73.40 | 83.8 | 87.2 |
| Hydrogen | 22.76 | 16.2 | 9.9 |
| Oxygen | 0.76 | — | 0.8 |
| Nitrogen | 3.08 | — | 0.7 |
| Sulfur | — | — | 1.4 |
| Gross heating value, Btu/lb | 22,630 | 20,300 | 18,200 |
| Product gas composition, mole % | | | |
| Hydrogen | 61.1 | 51.2 | 45.8 |
| Carbon monoxide | 35.0 | 45.3 | 47.5 |
| Carbon dioxide | 2.6 | 2.7 | 5.7 |
| Nitrogen | 1.0 | 0.1 | 0.2 |
| Methane | 0.3 | 0.7 | 0.5 |
| Hydrogen sulfide | — | — | 0.3 |
| Operating conditions | | | |
| Pressure, psig | 340 | 350 | 350 |
| Fuel and steam preheat, °F | 900 | 665 | 630 |
| Oxygen feed temperature, °F | 260 | 105 | 72 |
| Flow rates per million standard ft³ of dry-product gas | | | |
| Fuel, lb | 16,354 | 18,524 | 19,486 |
| Steam, lb | none | 4625 | 11,043 |
| Oxygen, millions of ft³ | 248 | 239 | 240 |
| Net carbon produced, lb | none | 112 | none (1034 lb recycled) |

* V. Sauchelli, *op. cit.*, p. 71.

The combustion reaction is strongly exothermic for all feedstocks. The essential feature of the process is the use of oxygen or enriched air for the combustion of the fuel. This is required from the stoichiometry, since natural air would introduce too much nitrogen. Also, the enriched air permits a higher temperature and hence a more favorable conversion to hydrogen and carbon monoxide. One disadvantage of the process is the formation of substantial quantities of carbon which must be removed from the combustion gases.

In a typical operation, the hydrocarbon and oxygen feeds are separately preheated and introduced into a refractory-lined furnace where the reaction takes place at pressures up to 500 psig and temperatures from 2000-2700°F. Steam is commonly added to the hydrocarbon feed in order to maintain flow velocity, inhibit cracking during preheat, reduce carbon formation, reduce the flame temperature, and increase the amount of hydrogen in the combustion gases. When fuel oil is used as feedstock, as much as 2-4 per cent of the carbon is deposited in the combustion gases. The carbon is removed by scrubbing with water, and is recycled to recover thermal values. The scrubbed gases may then be used for the production of synthetic ammonia, synthetic methanol, or to produce aldehydes by the oxo synthesis.

## NITRIC ACID

The production of nitric acid in recent years is illustrated in Fig. 7-15. The chief use of nitric acid is in the manufacture of fertilizers such as

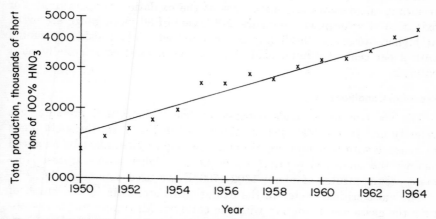

FIG. 7-15. United States production of nitric acid in recent years (Bureau of the Census Reports).

ammonium nitrate. About 15 per cent of the acid produced goes into the manufacture of explosives, and smaller amounts go into synthetic fibers, films, dyes, plastics, etc.

At one time, substantial quantities of nitric acid were made by the reaction between sodium nitrate and sulfuric acid. However, with the improvements in the manufacture of synthetic ammonia, most nitric acid is now made by ammonia oxidation. The two chief reactions are as follows:

$$NH_3 \ (g) + \tfrac{5}{4}O_2 \ (g) \rightarrow NO \ (g) + \tfrac{3}{2}H_2O \ (g) \qquad (7\text{-}32)$$
$$\Delta H^\circ_{298} = -54{,}057 \qquad \Delta F^\circ_{298} = -57{,}257$$

$$NH_3 \ (g) + \tfrac{3}{4}O_2 \ (g) \rightarrow \tfrac{1}{2}N_2 \ (g) + \tfrac{3}{2}H_2O \ (g) \qquad (7\text{-}33)$$
$$\Delta H^\circ_{298} = -75{,}657 \qquad \Delta F^\circ_{298} = -77{,}976$$

Other possible reactions such as the formation of $N_2O$ and $NO_2$ do not occur to any appreciable extent at the temperatures used commercially for the ammonia oxidation. Also the dissociation of ammonia, although thermodynamically possible, does not occur in the absence of a suitable catalyst.

It can be seen that the equilibrium in both Eqs. (7-32) and (7-33) is virtually 100 per cent to the right. Thus, the commercial success is dependent entirely on the use of a catalyst to direct the oxidation to the formation of nitric oxide as a reaction product rather than the more thermodynamically stable nitrogen. Commercially, platinum gauze is normally used as catalyst for the oxidation; by alloying the platinum with about 10 per cent of rhodium, the yield can be improved and the resultant alloy shows less metal loss at the oxidation temperatures. For oxidation at atmospheric pressure, 2-3 layers of 80-mesh gauze are used; at higher pressures, 16-20 layers are required. Cobalt oxide promoted with 9 per cent aluminum oxide has also been used commercially as a catalyst.

### Reaction Conditions

The yield of nitric oxide depends on the temperature, pressure, gas velocity and type of catalyst. As illustrated in Fig. 7-16, the yield tends to increase with temperature, although the higher yield must be balanced against the increased catalyst losses at the higher temperatures. Normally, temperatures of about 1600-1700°F are used commercially.

The most critical factor in the oxidation of ammonia is the length of time the gases are in contact with the catalyst. Maximum yields are obtained when this contact time is of the order of $10^{-4}$ sec. This increases the rates of transport of oxygen to the surface of the catalyst and of desorption of the reaction products. However, of probably greater importance is the fact that the nitric oxide which is produced can react with ammonia according to the equation

$$NH_3 \text{ (g)} + \tfrac{3}{2}NO \text{ (g)} \rightarrow \tfrac{5}{4}N_2 \text{ (g)} + \tfrac{3}{2}H_2O \text{ (g)} \qquad (7\text{-}34)$$

$$\Delta H^\circ_{298} = -108{,}057 \qquad \Delta F^\circ_{298} = -109{,}055$$

This strongly exothermic reaction can occur if, for example, the reaction products mix with the reactants by back diffusion. A short contact time will sweep away the nitric oxide as fast as it is formed, and prevent any interaction with undecomposed ammonia.

There is some evidence that higher operating pressures will reduce the yield of nitric oxide, although the effect is quite small. Higher pressures will, of course, increase the throughput and hence the production from a given volume of catalyst. In addition, pressure strongly favors the subsequent oxidation and absorption of the nitric oxide to form nitric acid.

Under some conditions, air and ammonia can form an explosive mixture. This is not a serious problem when ordinary air is used for the oxidation, since in this case the lower limit of the explosive mixture is about

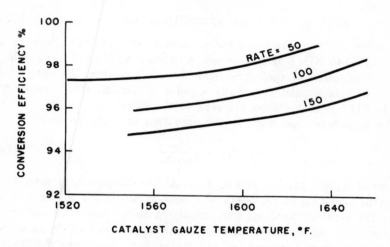

RATE = LBS. NH₃/TROY OUNCE/DAY
PRESSURE – ATMOSPHERIC
CATALYST 98% PLATINUM - 2% RHODIUM
80 MESH GAUZE - 0.003 INCH WIRE
NH₃ CONC. 10.8 - 11.2 VOLUME %

FIG. 7-16. Effect of temperature and gas flow rate on ammonia conversion efficiency.

20 per cent $NH_3$, which is much greater than the concentrations normally used in the oxidation step. Explosive mixtures may be a problem, however, when enriched air or oxygen is used for the oxidation.

### Reaction Mechanism

Since the over-all reaction is so rapid, it is obvious that each individual step in the catalytic oxidation of ammonia must also be very rapid. Presumably, the reaction requires preliminary chemisorption of oxygen by the catalyst, since the ammonia must be oxidized on the surface of the catalyst as rapidly as it is adsorbed. There is still considerable uncertainty as to the exact mechanism of the reaction. Several investigators have postulated the formation of intermediates such as hydroxylamine or nitrous acid, but the extreme rapidity of the reaction makes it very difficult to carry out any meaningful experimental studies.

## OXIDATION OF NITRIC OXIDE

The production of nitric acid is dependent on the oxidation of nitric oxide according to the equation

$$2NO \text{ (g)} + O_2 \text{ (g)} \rightleftharpoons 2NO_2 \text{ (g)} \tag{7-35}$$

$$\Delta H^\circ_{298} = -27,118 \qquad \Delta F^\circ_{298} = -16,658$$

followed by the absorption of nitrogen dioxide in water according to the reaction

$$3NO_2 \text{ (g)} + H_2O \text{ (sol'n)} \rightleftharpoons 2HNO_3 \text{ (sol'n)} + NO \text{ (g)} \tag{7-36}$$

The nitric oxide generated in the absorption reaction must then be oxidized again to $NO_2$ and reabsorbed to produce additional nitric acid. As the concentration of the nitric oxide becomes smaller, the rate of oxidation decreases until eventually a point is reached where recovery is not justified and the gases are sent to the stack.

The equilibrium constant in the oxidation of nitric oxide is

$$K_p = \frac{P^2_{NO_2}}{P^2_{NO}P_{O_2}} \tag{7-37}$$

Values of $K_p$ are plotted in Fig. 7-17. At the temperatures used in the catalytic oxidation of ammonia, the equilibrium is far to the left and hence the reaction products are considered to be essentially all in the form of nitric oxide. However, the absorption towers operate at slightly greater than room temperature, and under these conditions the thermodynamic equilibrium is almost 100 per cent to the right.

However, the oxidation of nitric oxide is strongly limited by the kinetics of the reaction. The rate of oxidation is

$$-\frac{dP_{NO}}{dt} = k_1 P^2_{NO} P_{O_2} - k_2 P^2_{NO_2} \tag{7-38}$$

where $k_1$ and $k_2$ are the rate constants in the forward and reverse directions. The reaction has been widely studied [1] because of its technical importance and its unique features. It is one of the few examples of a third-order homogeneous reaction. Furthermore, as shown in Fig. 7-18, the rate constant in the forward direction $k_1$ decreases with increasing temperature.

There is still considerable uncertainty as to the mechanism of the oxi-

[1] M. Bodenstein, Z. Elektrochem., 24, 183 (1918); M. Bodenstein and P. Z. Lindner, Z. Physik. Chem., 100, 105 (1922); R. L. Hasche and W. A. Patrick, J. Am. Chem. Soc., 47, 1207 (1925); G. Kornfield and E. Klinger, Z. Physik. Chem., 4B, 37 (1929); M. N. Rao and O. A. Hougen, Chem. Eng. Prog. Symposium Series, 48, No. 4 (1952).

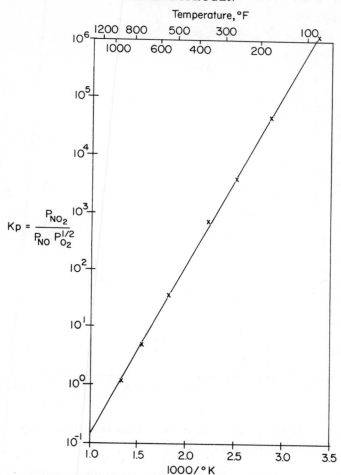

Fig. 7-17. Equilibrium constant for reaction $NO + \frac{1}{2}O_2 \rightleftharpoons NO_2$
(Experimental points from Sauchelli).

dation of nitric oxide, especially the reason for the negative temperature coefficient. Presumably, the limiting reaction is the formation of some intermediate complex which is more stable at a lower temperature. Thus, reactions have been postulated which involve intermediate formation of complexes such as $NO_3$ or $(NO)_2$ which then react further or give $NO_2$. However, these suggestions are only hypothetical, and there is even some question as to whether the reaction is truly homogeneous, or whether it may be affected by the walls of the confining vessel or by the presence of water vapor in the gas. Some attempts have been made to speed up

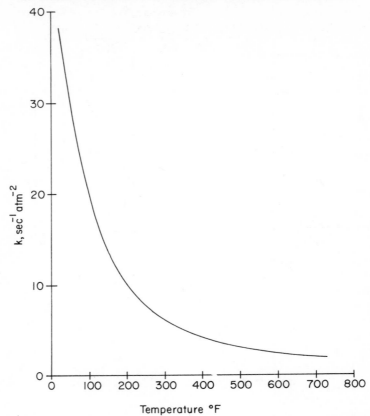

Fɪɢ. 7-18. Rate constant for oxidation of nitric oxide (data of Bodenstein).

the reaction by the use of catalysts, but the results are inconclusive as to whether any catalyst significantly affects the rate.

A reaction following immediately after the formation of nitrogen dioxide is the polymerization to nitrogen tetroxide according to the equation

$$2NO_2 \text{ (g)} \rightleftharpoons N_2O_4 \text{ (g)} \tag{7-39}$$

$$\Delta H^\circ_{298} = -13{,}773 \qquad \Delta F^\circ_{298} = -1289$$

This equilibrium is established very rapidly. At room temperature and atmospheric pressure, a substantial fraction of the nitrogen dioxide polymerizes, and at higher pressures most of the nitrogen dioxide polymerizes. However, in practice, this polymerization reaction is often simply ignored, and all chemical reactions are considered to take place with the nitrogen dioxide.

## Calculation of Oxidation Rates

In the commercial manufacture of nitric acid, the gases sent to the absorption towers contain about 11 per cent oxides of nitrogen and about 7 per cent oxygen with the balance nitrogen. An important consideration is the time required to oxidize the NO to $NO_2$. At room temperature the equilibrium is almost 100 per cent to the right; under these conditions the reverse reaction can be ignored and the rate equation becomes

$$-\frac{dP_{NO}}{dt} = kP_{NO}^2 P_{O_2}$$ (7-40)

This equation has been integrated for oxidation at both constant pressure and constant volume.[1] When ordinary air is used for the oxidation of the ammonia, there is little difference between the constant pressure and constant volume cases because of the large amount of nitrogen present. Since the calculations are easier, let us integrate Eq. (7-40) at constant volume.

Suppose we start with a mixture of nitric oxide and oxygen with no nitrogen dioxide present at zero time. Assume the oxygen is present in excess. Let $2a =$ initial pressure of the NO in atm, $ma =$ initial pressure of oxygen in atm, and $2ay =$ pressure of $NO_2$ at any time $t$, where $y$ is the fraction of nitric oxide converted. Then at constant volume, the pressure of NO at any time is $P_{NO} = 2a(1 - y)$ and the pressure of the oxygen at any time is $P_{O_2} = a(m - y)$, where $m \gtrless 1$. Substituting in the rate equation

$$\frac{dy}{(1 - y)^2(m - y)} = 2ka^2 \, dt$$ (7-41)

If a stoichiometric quantity of oxygen is present, $m = 1$ and Eq. (7-41) can be integrated directly to give

$$\frac{1}{(1 - y)^2} - 1 = 4ka^2t$$ (7-42)

If $m \neq 1$, Eq. (7-41) can be written

$$\frac{-dy}{(m - 1)^2(1 - y)} + \frac{dy}{(m - 1)(1 - y)^2} + \frac{dy}{(m - 1)^2(m - y)} = 2ka^2 \, dt$$

Integration between the limits of $y = 0$ at $t = 0$ and $y = y$ at $t = t$ gives

$$\frac{1}{(m - 1)^2} \ln \frac{m(1 - y)}{m - y} + \frac{y}{(m - 1)(1 - y)} = 2ka^2t$$ (7-43)

[1] Todd, *Phil. Mag.*, **35**, 281,435 (1918).

Figure 7-19 gives the conversion to $NO_2$ as a function of the parameter $ka^2t$. The time required to convert a given fraction of NO to $NO_2$ at a given temperature and pressure may be calculated from data plotted in Figs. 7-18 and 7-19. Because of the factor $a^2$ in Eqs. (7-42) and

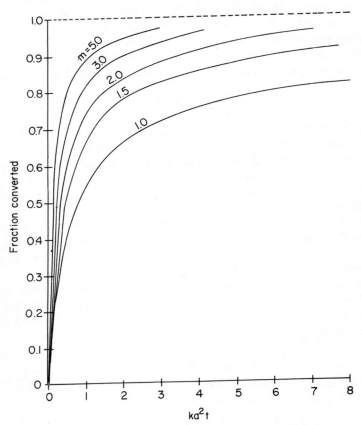

FIG. 7-19. Conversion of NO to $NO_2$ as function of $ka^2t$.

(7-43), the time of oxidation is inversely proportional to the square of the absolute pressure.

### Absorption of Nitrogen Dioxide

The absorption of nitrogen dioxide in nitric acid solutions presumably takes place through the intermediate formation of nitrous acid. However, the equilibrium concentration of nitrous acid is very small, and Eq. (7-36) gives the over-all reaction. The equilibrium constant is

$$K = \frac{P_{HNO_2}^2 P_{NO}}{P_{H_2O} P_{NO_2}^3} \tag{7-44}$$

which is commonly broken down into the two constants

$$K_1 = \frac{P_{NO}}{P_{NO_2}^3} \quad \text{and} \quad K_2 = \frac{P_{HNO_2}^2}{P_{H_2O}} \tag{7-45}$$

where $K = K_1 K_2$. The value of $K_1$ is determined by the composition of the gases and the total pressure; the value of $K_2$ is determined by the partial pressures of $H_2O$ and $HNO_3$ over nitric acid solutions.

There is still considerable uncertainty as to the exact value of the equilibrium constant for the absorption of oxides of nitrogen to form nitric acid. The value of $K$ could be calculated if the free energies were known, but since nitric acid dissociates in the vapor phase, it is very difficult to measure $K$ directly. Several investigators[1] have eliminated this problem by measuring the equilibrium pressures of NO and $NO_2$ over nitric acid solutions, thereby obtaining values for $K_1$. These data are plotted in Fig. 7-20; it can be seen that there is considerable scatter.

However, the situation is even worse when these data are combined with the vapor pressures of $HNO_3$ and $H_2O$ over nitric acid solutions to obtain values for $K$ defined by Eq. (7-44). Figure 7-21 shows how these values agree with values for $K$ calculated from thermal data. The inconsistencies are discussed by Forsythe and Giaque[2] who show that the available vapor pressure data are wrong and other errors also may exist.

Even with the admittedly unsatisfactory data available, certain conclusions may be drawn from the values of $K_1$. For nitric acid strengths less than about 20 per cent, the value of $K_1$ is large and the equilibrium pressure of $NO_2$ is correspondingly small. Under these conditions most of the $NO_2$ is absorbed, and the chief problem in this part of the absorption system will be providing sufficient time for NO to oxidize. However, for nitric acid strengths greater than about 40 per cent, the equilibrium pressure of $NO_2$ is so large that very little will be absorbed in passing through concentrated acid. Thus, the problem in this part of the absorption system will be to provide sufficient cooling to produce acid of the desired strength.

Several investigators have studied the mechanism of the absorption reaction with various conclusions. In view of the uncertainties about the

---

[1] E. Abel, *et al.*, *Z. Elektrochem.* **36**, 692 (1930); F. S. Chambers and T. K. Sherwood, *J. Am. Chem. Soc.*, **59**, 316 (1937); K. G. Denbigh and A. J. Prince, *J. Chem. Soc.* (London), 790 (1947); D. A. Epshtein, *Dokl. Akad. Nauk* SSSR, **74**, 1101 (1950); the data of Burdick and Freed, *J. Am. Chem. Soc.*, **43**, 518 (1921) are inconsistent with the other measurements, and hence are omitted.

[2] N. R. Forsythe and W. F. Giaque, *J. Am. Chem. Soc.*, **64**, 48 (1942).

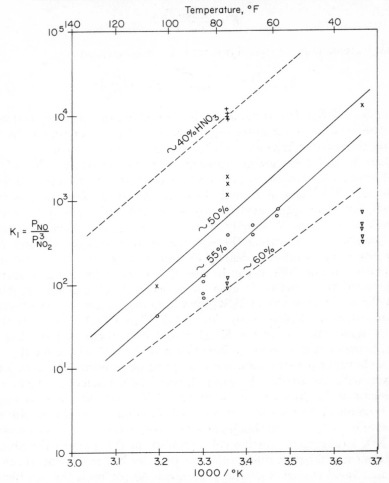

FIG. 7-20. Equilibrium pressures of NO and NO₂ over nitric acid solutions.
(V. Sauchelli, *op. cit.*).

equilibrium relationships, any detailed discussion of mechanisms is un-
justified. In practice, the absorption reaction is so rapid in comparison
with the NO oxidation that the gases in contact with nitric acid solutions are normally considered to be in complete equilibrium.

### Effect of Temperature and Pressure

Low temperatures increase the rate of oxidation of nitric oxide to
nitrogen dioxide, and reduce the equilibrium pressure of nitrogen dioxide

over nitric acid solutions. High pressures increase the partial pressures of nitric oxide and oxygen in the gases and thus decrease the time required for oxidation of the nitric oxide, since the rate of oxidation is proportional to the square of the nitric oxide pressure. Also, high pressures favor the absorption reaction since 3 moles of $NO_2$ react to regenerate only 1 mole of NO. Thus, low temperatures and high pressures favor the production of a stronger acid with smaller losses of nitric oxide in the tail gases.

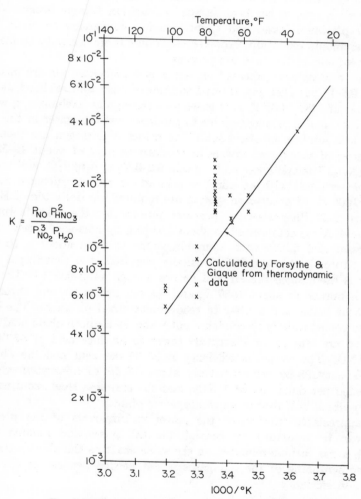

FIG. 7-21. Equilibrium constant in absorption of $NO_2$.

## MANUFACTURING PROCESSES FOR NITRIC ACID

The three general processes for the manufacture of nitric acid are as follows: (1) oxidation and absorption at atmospheric pressure; (2) oxidation and absorption at elevated pressure; (3) oxidation at atmospheric pressure but absorption at elevated pressure. Because of the greater absorption efficiency and smaller physical size, the pressure plant has been used in the United States for practically all recent construction. The combination process has been favored in western Europe because of the smaller platinum losses and slightly higher conversion to nitric oxide in the ammonia oxidation; however, even here there seems to be increasing acceptance of the pressure process.

In the atmospheric process,[1] ammonia and preheated air are mixed to give a 9.5-11 per cent gas, filtered to remove dust, and oxidized at temperatures of 1380-1470°F. Exit gases pass through an exchanger, a waste-heat boiler, and a primary cooler to condense out the water in the form of a dilute solution of nitric acid. The oxides of nitrogen are then sent to a series of absorption towers to produce an acid of about 45-52 per cent $HNO_3$. The tail gases still contain 0.2-0.3 per cent NO, and usually must be scrubbed with an alkaline solution to recover nitrogen values. About 1000 ft³ of absorption system are required per daily ton of $HNO_3$.

Figure 7-22 illustrates the pressure process for the manufacture of nitric acid. Air is compressed to about 110 psig by means of a centrifugal compressor and mixed with ammonia vapor to form about a 10.5 per cent mixture. Preheating is not usually required if a centrifugal compressor is used, since the air will be hot enough (450-500°F). The ammonia is burned at about 1650°F, and the hot exit gases sent through a waste-heat boiler and a filter to recover entrained platinum. The gases are then cooled rapidly to condense out water as a dilute nitric acid solution, and are sent to an absorption tower to produce acid of 57-60 per cent $HNO_3$. The oxidation efficiency is 95-96 per cent and the absorption efficiency 98-99 per cent. Only about 17 ft³ of absorption volume are needed per daily ton of $HNO_3$, and the stainless steel requirements are only about half that of an atmospheric plant.

An appreciable fraction of the power requirements of the pressure plant can be recovered by heating the tail gases and passing them through a gas turbine mounted on the same shaft as the air compressor. Alkaline scrubbing of the tail gases is not needed because of the high absorption efficiency.

---

[1] For a discussion of the three processes, see S. Strelzoff, *Chem. Eng.*, 63(5), 170 (1956).

Considerable heat is evolved in the absorption tower as a result of the oxidation of NO to $NO_2$ and the reaction to form nitric acid with water. The heat is removed by cooling the acid as it passes downward through the tower. Since $N_2O_4$ has an appreciable solubility in strong nitric acid, it is necessary to "bleach" the product acid by stripping out

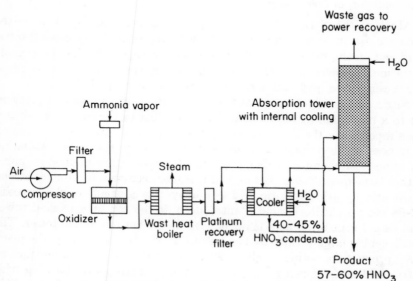

Fig. 7-22. Typical pressure process for nitric acid.

the dissolved oxides of nitrogen. In the atmospheric system, this is done by blowing air through the acid; in the pressure system, the bleaching is done in the main tower. Platinum losses in the pressure process are 0.005–0.010 troy oz/ton $HNO_3$ produced, about double the loss in an atmospheric plant. However, the pressure process produces a stronger acid from a less expensive plant with higher absorption efficiency.

## Materials of Construction

At one time, nitric acid was handled chiefly in ceramic or brick-lined vessels. However, at present, stainless steel is used almost exclusively as a material of construction; in fact, it was the development of stainless steel that made possible the pressure process. For weak acids at room temperature, the straight chrome stainless steels are satisfactory; for stronger acids or higher temperatures, the conventional 18-8 type may be used. The resistance of stainless steel to attack by nitric acid is the result of the formation of a tight oxide film on the surface of the metal which protects it from further attack. Cold working or welding of stainless steel may increase the susceptibility to corrosion; hence, for severe conditions, vessels should be annealed or fabricated of stabilized stainless steel. Note that stainless steel is very susceptible to corrosion by impurities, particularly chlorides.

### Concentration of Nitric Acid

Much of the nitric acid produced goes into the manufacure of mixed acid for use in organic nitrations. Mixed acid is made by mixing nitric acid and oleum, the latter serving as a dehydrating agent for the organic nitration. However, the nitric acid from the absorption towers is too dilute for use in mixed acid and hence must first be concentrated.

Nitric acid can be concentrated by distillation at atmospheric pressure up to a maximum of 68 per cent, corresponding to the nitric acid-water azeotrope. Since the composition of the azeotrope varies with pressure, it is possible to produce anhydrous nitric acid by alternate distillation at atmospheric and elevated pressure. However, this method requires rather large quantities of steam, and it is more common to produce strong nitric acid by using sulfuric acid as a dehydrating agent. In this process, 93-98 per cent sulfuric acid is introduced at the top of a packed tower and 68 per cent nitric acid is introduced at the bottom of the tower. The nitric acid is largely vaporized as a result of the heat of mixing, the overhead product consisting of about 98 per cent $HNO_3$. Small quantities of nitric acid are stripped from the sulfuric acid bottoms by blowing with steam, the final bottoms product being about 70 per cent $H_2SO_4$. This process is normally operated in conjunction with a sulfuric acid contact plant which can refortify the dilute sulfuric acid in the $SO_3$ absorption towers.

Considerable work has also been carried out on the direct production of strong nitric acid. This can be done by refrigerating the ammonia oxidation products to condense out nitrogen tetroxide, which is then heated in an autoclave with oxygen and dilute nitric acid at about 50 atm to produce 98 per cent $HNO_3$. It is also possible to use oxygen rather than air for the initial ammonia oxidation, and thereby produce 98-99 per cent acid directly.

## AMMONIUM NITRATE

The most important use of nitric acid is in the manufacture of ammonium nitrate by direct interaction with anhydrous ammonia. The production of ammonium nitrate in the United States has been increasing rapidly in recent years, the annual production increasing from 1.56

million tons in 1953 to 3.94 million tons in 1963. Most of the material goes into fertilizer use, since the available nitrogen in ammonium nitrate is 35 per cent. However, increasing amounts are being used for other purposes such as in explosives.

Precaution must be taken in the handling of solid ammonium nitrate because of the possible explosive reaction

$$NH_4NO_3 \text{ (s)} \rightarrow N_2 \text{ (g)} + 2H_2O \text{ (g)} + \tfrac{1}{2}O_2 \text{ (g)} \tag{7-46}$$
$$\Delta H_{298}^\circ = -28,326$$

This exothermic reaction will take place only at fairly high temperatures, especially in the presence of organic material which can react with the liberated oxygen. Thus, in the Texas City disaster, a ship loaded with ammonium nitrate caught fire and exploded, killing almost 600 people and destroying about 33 million dollars' worth of property.

## UREA

Urea is of considerable historical interest because it was the first organic compound to be synthesized from inorganic materials. The presence of urea had been noted as early as 1773 in the urine of animals, but it was not until 1824 that the empirical formula was determined. In 1828, Wöhler performed his classical experiment of heating ammonium cyanate to give urea according to the equation

$$NH_4CNO \rightarrow NH_2—CO—NH_2$$

Until this time, many chemists thought that organic compounds could be produced only by living organisms. Thus, urea represented the first synthetic organic chemical.

In recent years, urea has become an extremely important fertilizer because it contains about 46 per cent available nitrogen. Figure 7-23 illustrates the rapid growth, which can be attributed to the increasing demand for fertilizers, general availability of the two raw materials ammonia and carbon dioxide, and the development of more economic processes to manufacture urea. In addition to the direct use of urea as a fertilizer, a complex between urea and formaldehyde known as "ureaform" is also commonly used. The advantage of the urea-form is that it releases the nitrogen slowly, and hence is effective over the entire growing season.

Although about 80 per cent of the urea in the United States goes into fertilizers, about 11 per cent now goes into animal feeds where the urea serves as a protein substitute. Urea is also used in the manufacture of urea-formaldehyde and other synthetic resins, as a softening agent for

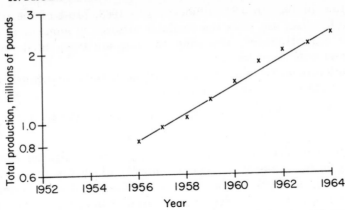

Fig. 7-23. Total United States production of urea in recent years (United States Tariff Commission, "Synthetic Organic Chemicals").

wood products, has limited use in the petroleum industry, and is used as a raw material for a wide variety of drugs and medicinals.

## MANUFACTURE OF UREA

At one time substantial quantities of urea were made by the hydrolysis of cyanamide produced from calcium carbide. However, at present, virtually all urea in the United States is made from ammonium carbamate according to the reactions

$$2NH_3 \text{ (g)} + CO_2 \text{ (g)} \rightleftharpoons NH_2{-}\overset{\overset{\displaystyle O}{\|}}{C}{-}ONH_4 \text{ (s)} \tag{7-47}$$

$$\Delta H^\circ_{298} = -38{,}078 \qquad \Delta F^\circ_{298} = -7258$$

$$NH_2{-}\overset{\overset{\displaystyle O}{\|}}{C}{-}ONH_4 \text{ (s)} \rightleftharpoons H_2O \text{ (l)} + H_2N{-}\overset{\overset{\displaystyle O}{\|}}{C}{-}NH_2 \text{ (s)} \tag{7-48}$$

$$\Delta H^\circ_{298} = +6259 \qquad \Delta F^\circ_{298} = +5660$$

with the possible side reaction

$$NH_2COONH_4 + H_2O \rightleftharpoons (NH_4)_2CO_3 \tag{7-49}$$

Most urea is manufactured in conjunction with synthetic ammonia plants since the necessary carbon dioxide is available from the synthesis gas purification system at essentially no cost. The equilibrium constant for Eq. (7-47) is

$$K_p = \frac{1}{P^2_{NH_3}P_{CO_2}} \tag{7-50}$$

If the reactants are present in stoichiometric quantities,

$$P_{NH_3} = \frac{2P}{3}, \qquad P_{CO_2} = \frac{P}{3}, \qquad \text{and} \qquad K_p = \frac{27}{4P^3}$$

where $P$ is the total pressure. Since $K_p$ is a function of temperature only, the equilibrium pressure or decomposition pressure $P$ is also a function only of temperature, provided the gases are ideal. Values of $P$ are plotted in Fig. 7-24. Ammonium carbamate will be produced if the two

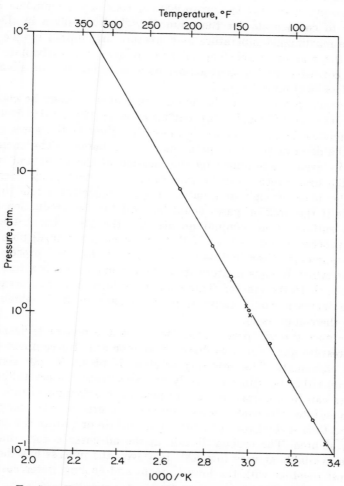

Fig. 7-24. Equilibrium vapor pressure of ammonium carbamate [R. N. Bennett *et al.*, *Trans. Faraday Soc.*, **49**, 925 (1953)].

reactants are passed into a cooled vessel at a pressure greater than the decomposition pressure.

Commercially, the ammonia and carbon dioxide are passed into a reactor which is maintained at a temperature of 175-220°C and a pressure of 170-400 atm. A melt is formed which consists of ammonium carbamate, urea, water and unreacted excess ammonia. At the temperature of the reactor, an equilibrium is established according to Eq. (7-48) in which about half the carbamate is converted to urea. The yield of urea is favored by high temperature, high pressure and a stoichiometric ratio of the reactants. In practice, up to 200 per cent excess ammonia is used in order to compensate for the ammonia which dissolves in the melt. Also, the maximum temperature and pressure are limited by the corrosion of the reactor vessel. The mixture of urea and carbamate is extremely corrosive, and a special liner of a material such as silver, lead or stainless steel must be used.

The various processes for the manufacture of urea[1] may be classed as follows: (1) once-through; (2) partial-recycle; (3) total-recycle. The only difference in the processes is in the handling of the gases evolved during the decomposition of the ammonium carbamate. The choice of a process is largely determined by the location of the plant and whether or not the urea process can be integrated with other plant operations. Thus, the once-through and partial-recycle processes might be most economic if the urea off-gases could be used for the production of ammonium sulfate or ammonium nitrate. On the other hand, the total-recycle process would be used if there were no place to dispose of the off-gas, ammonia. Note in this connection that the ideal process would be one in which the gas mixture from the decomposition is recompressed and fed back to the reactor. This cannot be done, however, because the pressure increase would cause solid carbamate to form which would damage the compressors.

In the once-through process, the melt from the reactor is flashed to a lower pressure and heated to drive off ammonia and decompose the unreacted carbamate. The resulting solution is about 80 per cent urea, which can either be utilized directly or concentrated to crystalline urea. Off-gases can be absorbed in acid to produce ammonium nitrate or ammonium sulfate. The conversion of ammonia to urea is only about 32 per cent, and thus several tons of ammonium sulfate or nitrate are produced per ton of urea. The carbon dioxide in the off-gases is lost, and hence must be available at very low cost. However, the process has the lowest plant cost together with the lowest steam and cooling water costs.

[1] See chapter by R. F. Church in V. Sauchelli, "Fertilizer Nitrogen," *op. cit.*; S. Strelzoff and S. Vasan, *Chem. Eng. Progr.*, **59**(11), 60 (1963).

In the partial-recycle process, the carbamate is first decomposed at about 350 psig to give a gas consisting chiefly of ammonia which is recycled back to the reactor. The second-stage decomposer is at about 30 psig, and gives a mixture of ammonia and carbon dioxide which can be used to manufacture fertilizer.

Several types of total-recycle processes have been developed. For example, the ammonia and carbon dioxide can be separated by absorption in a suitable solvent and recycled individually back to the reactor. In another process, the carbamate is recycled as a slurry in an oil medium. A significant recent development is the liquid recycle process where the gas mixture is totally absorbed in water and recycled to the reactor. Although the total-recycle processes have the highest investment costs, this is offset by the fact that there are no by-products. With continued improvement of the total-recycle processes, it is likely that they will gradually replace the other two types of processes.

## HYDROGEN CYANIDE

Hydrogen cyanide is widely used as a raw material for the manufacture of petrochemicals such as acrylonitrile and the methacrylates. In 1963, total U.S. production of HCN was 293 million pounds. Commercially, hydrogen cyanide is produced by the direct reaction between ammonia and a hydrocarbon according to the typical equations

$$NH_3 + CH_4 + \tfrac{3}{2}O_2 \rightleftharpoons HCN + 3H_2O$$

$$\Delta H^\circ_{1300} = -112{,}800 \qquad \Delta F^\circ_{1300} = -141{,}500$$

$$NH_3 + CH_4 \rightleftharpoons HCN + 3H_2$$

$$\Delta H^\circ_{1300} = +66{,}090 \qquad \Delta F^\circ_{1300} = -15{,}350$$

The equilibrium is favorable for both reactions, and by using about one-third of the stoichiometric quantity of oxygen, the heat of reaction becomes roughly equal to zero. The chief side reactions are the oxidation of the hydrocarbon to carbon monoxide and water, and the thermal decomposition of ammonia and methane, both of which are thermodynamically unstable at the temperatures used in the reaction.

The success of the process is dependent on the use of a catalyst. This is normally either platinum or platinum alloyed with rhodium to reduce catalyst losses by volatilization. The reaction is carried out at pressures of about 10 psig and temperatures of 1800-2200°F. Effluent gases are rapidly quenched in a waste-heat boiler to prevent decomposition of the HCN, are scrubbed with dilute sulfuric acid to recover unreacted ammonia in the form of ammonium sulfate, and the HCN is recovered by conventional absorption-desorption in water. Product HCN is purified by distillation. The yield based on ammonia is 60-70 per cent, and about half the unconverted ammonia is recovered as by-product ammonium sulfate.

One annoying problem in the manufacture of HCN is the tendency for the material to polymerize to form tarry polymers which can foul up the processing equipment. The product is stabilized by the addition of about 0.3 per cent acetic acid, and inhibitors are also added to certain of the liquid and vapor streams to minimize polymerization. Substantially all production of HCN is for captive use, since the material is extremely toxic and for this reason difficult to ship.

### Metal Cyanides

Sodium cyanide is the most important of the metal cyanides, and finds considerable use in electroplating, in heat treatment and case hardening of metals, in the extraction of precious metals, in ore flotation, and as a raw material for the synthesis of various organic chemicals. Before the war, the Castner process accounted for most of the production of sodium cyanide. This process involves the reaction between metallic sodium, charcoal, and ammonia at temperatures above the melting point of sodium (207.5°F) according to the equation

$$2Na + 2C + 2NH_3 \rightarrow 2NaCN + 3H_2$$

The reaction occurs in three steps, with the intermediate formation of sodamide and sodium cyanamide. The yield is over 90 per cent.

At present the Castner process is obsolete and has been replaced by the neutralization process which involves the direct absorption of HCN in caustic. Many problems were encountered in the first use of this process because of the unstable nature of sodium cyanide solutions. Thus HCN may be regenerated by hydrolysis, there may be a decomposition into ammonia and sodium formate, and if impurities are present these may cause trouble in the crystallization of the sodium cyanide. However, these problems have now been overcome. Commercially, HCN is simply absorbed in caustic solution using excess alkali to stabilize the solution and prevent polymerization of the HCN. Sodium cyanide is then prepared by careful evaporation under vacuum.

Limited quantities of potassium cyanide are made in a similar way by absorbing HCN in potassium hydroxide. The material finds some use in electroplating, for fused salt baths, and in the electrolytic refining of platinum.

Calcium cyanide is made commercially by the cyanamide process, which is discussed in Chapter 13. This process involves the heating of crude calcium cyanamide (which contains carbon) in an electric furnace to temperatures of over 1800°F in the presence of sodium chloride. The reaction is

$$CaCN_2 + C \xrightarrow{NaCl} Ca(CN)_2$$

The reaction product must be cooled rapidly to prevent a reversion back to calcium cyanamide. Calcium cyanide finds limited use as a flotation agent and in the recovery of gold and silver.

# CHAPTER 8

# Inorganic Phosphorus and Fluorine Compounds

Phosphorus is an essential element for both plant and animal metabolism. The total $P_2O_5$ content of the adult human body is about 1600 grams, most of which is contained within the bones. Phosphorus is also the chief active component in commercial fertilizer, and larger quantities are continually being used because of the world's population explosion. Total production of phosphorus in recent years is illustrated in Fig. 8-1; note the rapid increase, chiefly because of increasing agricultural requirements.

Small amounts of phosphorus are available from crushed bones and from guano deposits in arid regions such as the famous Peruvian deposits. However, commercially, phosphate rock serves as the source of essentially all phosphorus chemicals. The phosphorus occurs as the mineral apatite, which when pure contains about 40-42 per cent $P_2O_5$. Two varieties of apatite occur in nature, namely, chloroapatite, $Ca_5(PO_4)_3Cl$, and fluorapatite, $Ca_5(PO_4)_3F$. The fluorapatite is the commercial mineral in the United States.

The chief U.S. deposits of phosphate rock occur in Florida, Tennessee, North Carolina and western states such as Utah, Idaho, Wyoming and Montana. In recent years, the Florida deposits have accounted for over 80 per cent of the total U.S. production of phosphate rock. These deposits occur close to the surface and are thus easy to mine; in addition, the deposits are conveniently located with respect to cheap ocean transportation facilities, and eastern markets account for about half the consumption of fertilizer.

Outside the United States, the chief deposits of phosphate rock are in Morocco, Tunisia, Algeria, Egypt, the Soviet Union and certain islands in the Pacific and Indian Oceans such as Christmas, Nauru and Ocean Islands.

Florida rock is mined by conventional open-pit techniques. The phosphate rock matrix from the mines is washed, screened, and classified to

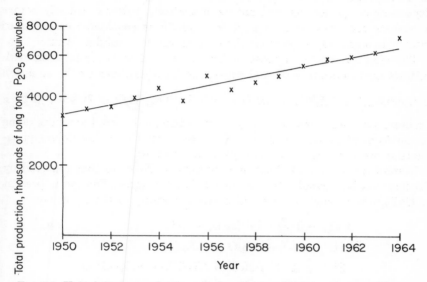

Fig. 8-1. United States production of phosphate rock in recent years (Bureau of Mines "Minerals Yearbook").

yield a $-20$ $+35$ mesh fraction which is sent to the flotation plant. Concentrates are produced by froth flotation, using separation agents such as caustic, fuel oil and fatty acids. A second flotation removes silica by the use of cationic surfactants such as an amine of a higher fatty acid. The final concentrate contains roughly 68-74 per cent BPL,* and may be used directly for the manufacture of superphosphates, elemental phosphorus or phosphoric acid.

In 1963, the total U.S. mine production of phosphate rock was about 69 million short tons, 88 per cent of which came from Florida deposits. The total U.S. production of phosphate fertilizers was 3.23 million short tons (100 per cent $P_2O_5$ basis), normal and enriched superphosphate accounting for 38 per cent of the production, concentrated superphosphate accounting for 34 per cent of the production and the balance going into ammonium phosphates and other special fertilizers.

---

* Phosphate rock is sold on the basis of the percentage of calcium phosphate or "bone phosphate of lime" (BPL) which is present.

### Normal Superphosphate Fertilizer

Phosphate rock is insoluble in water, and thus the phosphorus is not available for agricultural use. If finely ground rock is applied directly to the soil, there is a slow conversion of the phosphorus to a soluble form, depending on the acidity and nature of the soil. However, usually before phosphate rock can be used as a fertilizer, it is considered essential to treat it in some way to convert the phosphorus to a soluble form.

The classical and still most widely used method is acidulation with sulfuric acid to produce normal superphosphate fertilizer by the equation

$$2Ca_5(PO_4)_3F + 7H_2SO_4 + 3H_2O \rightarrow 3CaH_4(PO_4)_2 \cdot H_2O + 7CaSO_4 + 2HF$$

Calcium sulfate is present largely as anhydrite, only small amounts being in the form of gypsum, $CaSO_4 \cdot 2H_2O$. However, the monocalcium phosphate is present largely as the crystalline hydrate.

In most domestic rock, fluorine is present in excess of that required by the fluorapatite formula. It is assumed that the excess fluorine is present as $CaF_2$, which reacts with sulfuric acid according to the equations

$$CaF_2 + H_2SO_4 \rightarrow CaSO_4 + 2HF$$

$$4HF + SiO_2 \rightarrow 2H_2O + SiF_4 \text{ (g)}$$

$$3SiF_4 + (2 + n)H_2O \rightarrow 2H_2SiF_6 + SiO_2 \cdot nH_2O$$

Hydrofluoric acid produced by the acidulation reacts with silica impurity to form volatile silicon tetrafluoride. This is scrubbed from the exit gases using water to form fluosilicic acid and hydrated gelatinous silica; the fluosilicic acid is either wasted or recovered as fluosilicate salts. In practice, only about half the fluorine present in the rock is evolved, the balance remaining in the superphosphate fertilizer.

Economic production of superphosphate fertilizer[1] is dependent on the use of the minimum amount of acid consistent with the use of the material. Since dicalcium phosphate ($CaHPO_4 \cdot 2H_2O$) is insoluble in water, it is necessary to use sufficient acid to convert the BPL to monocalcium phosphate plus excess acid to react with the $CaF_2$ and other impurities such as limestone which may be present. The rate of reaction is dependent on the fineness to which the rock is ground and the strength of acid which is used. If the acid is too strong, it is hard to mix uniformly

---

[1] V. Sauchelli, Editor, "Chemistry and Technology of Fertilizers," New York, Reinhold Publishing Corp., 1960; W. H. Waggaman, "Phosphoric Acid, Phosphates, and Phosphatic Fertilizers," Second Edition, New York, Reinhold Publishing Corp., 1952; W. C. Weber, "Phosphoric Acid Production Technology," paper presented at Washington, D. C. Fertilizer Round Table, November 1964 (preprint available from Dorr-Oliver, Inc.).

with the rock and there is a tendency to coat the particles with calcium sulfate, which prevents complete reaction of rock with acid. However, if the acid is too weak, the volume is large, the mass does not heat up sufficiently to complete the reaction, and the product has so much moisture that it is difficult to handle. In practice, the optimum strength of acid has been found to be about 55°Bé, corresponding to about 70 per cent $H_2SO_4$.

Commercially, most superphosphate fertilizer is made by the den process. Phosphate rock is ground to about 90 per cent through 100-mesh, and weighed amounts of acid and rock are mixed for 1-3 minutes in a pan mixer which is fitted with plows which rotate at several rpm. Depending on the composition of the rock and the strength of the acid, the ratio of acid to rock varies from about 0.82-0.95. Before the material sets up, a central plug is opened and a scraper discharges the soupy mass into the den which is located immediately below the pan. The exothermic reactions which started in the mixer are continued in the den, and the temperature of the material rises to 200-250°F. Carbon dioxide, steam and volatile fluorine compounds are evolved, and the superphosphate is left as a dry and fairly porous mass.

The den consists simply of a large concrete room or a cylindrical silo holding up to several hundred tons of product. Although the first dens were fairly crude, modern plants are usually fitted with automatic handling equipment for loading, aerating and discharging the superphosphate. The material stays in the den for a period of time ranging from 15 minutes to several hours until it sets up; however, the product still contains an appreciable percentage of free acid and unconverted BPL. Thus, to convert the maximum amount of phosphorus to an available form, the material is conveyed to huge storage piles where the final curing requires 2-4 weeks, depending on the acid to rock ratio and the manufacturing conditions.

## Triple Superphosphate

Although sulfuric acid is the cheapest acid which can be used for acidulating rock, it has two substantial disadvantages. First, the available $P_2O_5$ in the product is only about 20 per cent because of the large quantities of calcium sulfate which are formed in the reaction. Second, many parts of the world do not have available sulfur deposits, and thus sulfuric acid is much more expensive than in the United States.

A much more concentrated product can be obtained by acidulating the rock with phosphoric acid to produce triple superphosphate (the product has also been called double or concentrated superphosphate, but these terms are falling into disuse). The reaction is as follows:

$$Ca_5(PO_4)_3F + 7H_3PO_4 + 5H_2O \rightarrow 5CaH_4(PO_4)_2 \cdot H_2O + HF$$

As in the case of normal superphosphate, about half the fluorine is evolved as $SiF_4$ which is absorbed in water and either wasted or converted to fluosilicates.

Most triple superphosphate is made by the use of wet-process phosphoric acid because it is cheaper than the electric-furnace acid. The theoretical acid strength required for triple superphosphate is about 88 per cent $H_3PO_4$. However, the use of acid of this strength causes undesirable side reactions and also gives a reduced yield of monocalcium phosphate because some some water must be present to permit the reaction to approach completion at a reasonable rate. If the triple superphosphate is not artificially dried, the acid strength is normally about 70-78 per cent $H_3PO_4$. This introduces some moisture into the final product, but not enough to cause problems in handling. However, if the triple superphosphate is dried before shipment or if it is to be subsequently ammoniated and/or incorporated into mixed fertilizers, the acid strength may be as low as 34 per cent $H_3PO_4$.

Commercially, there is little difference between the manufacture of triple and normal superphosphate, except that the triple superphosphate sets up much faster. Although pan mixers have been used, most modern plants use continuous mixers in which the rock and acid are fed continuously either to a mechanical mixer or to a mixing bowl which produces a slurry of rock and acid. Temperatures of about 200°F are commonly used to favor the acidulation of the rock. The slurry then flows either to a den or to a conveyer system which provides time for the material to set up. The product is then crushed and sent to storage for several weeks to permit the final curing of the material. The entire operation is quite rapid; thus, the mixing requires less than a minute, and the product goes into the storage pile within 15-30 minutes from the time of mixing.

Depending on the grade of rock and the strength of phosphoric acid used, the triple superphosphate product contains from 40-49 per cent available $P_2O_5$. This is over twice the concentration in normal superphosphate. Thus, when the product must be shipped over large distances, there is little question that triple superphosphate is more economical from the standpoint of both manufacturer and consumer. At present, there appears to be a definite trend toward the use of the more concentrated fertilizers.

### Ammoniated Phosphates

Since ammonia is the cheapest source of fixed nitrogen, considerable work has been carried out on the production of ammoniated phosphates.

Thus, anhydrous ammonia may be passed directly into phosphoric acid to produce either mono- or diammonium phosphate. The product may then be obtained by cooling, centrifuging and drying. If wet-process phosphoric acid is used, impurities such as iron, aluminum and magnesium will first precipitate as a gelatinous sludge which may be removed by a preliminary filtration. The diammonium phosphate has a higher nitrogen content, but is less stable than the monoammonium phosphate.

It is also possible to ammoniate superphosphate to increase the plant-food value of the material. In practice, a maximum of 30-40 lb of anhydrous ammonia can be used for 1000 lb of superphosphate; however, even larger quantities of other nitrogen compounds such as ammonium nitrate or urea can be used. When ammonia is used, the chemical reactions are fairly complex. Any free sulfuric acid will be neutralized to form ammonium sulfate; this is beneficial, since it reduces the chemical attack on the shipping bags. There is also some conversion of monocalcium phosphate to dicalcium phosphate, and perhaps some adsorption of ammonia by the material.

## PHOSPHORIC ACID

Phosphoric acid is made by two processes, the wet-process and the electric-furnace or thermal process. Wet-process acid is cheaper, but is quite impure; it is used chiefly for the manufacture of fertilizer and chemicals where purity is not important. Electric-furnace acid is more expensive, but is quite pure and can be produced from a lower grade of phosphate rock. The chief use of the electric-furnace acid is for the manufacture of chemicals, particularly phosphate chemicals for the food and detergent industries.

The total U.S. production of wet-process phosphoric acid for 1963 was 1.96 million short tons (100 per cent $P_2O_5$ basis), over 90 per cent of the acid going into fertilizer use. Total production of electric-furnace acid was 0.95 million short tons with only about 20 per cent going into fertilizer use. Phosphoric acid has shown quite a respectable growth in recent years, chiefly because of the increasing production of triple superphosphate fertilizer.

### Wet-Process Phosphoric Acid

Phosphoric acid can be made by the complete acidulation of phosphate rock, using a strong acid such as hydrochloric, nitric or sulfuric. However, sulfuric acid is the only one now used commercially in the United States because of its cheapness and the fact that the reaction products can be easily separated by filtration. Hydrochloric and nitric acids have been used at times in the past, but these acids are more expensive and there is the problem of separating soluble calcium salts from the phosphoric acid product. However, it is possible that this situation may change as the result of a new process developed by Dow Chemical of Canada. This process involves the use of hydrochloric acid to digest the rock, tributyl phosphate being used to extract the phosphoric acid from the acid solution. It is claimed that the added cost of the hydrochloric acid is compensated for by the shorter leaching time, the fact that the rock can be used directly without grinding, and savings in filtration and evaporation costs.

In practice, the reaction between sulfuric acid and phosphate rock is carried out continuously according to the equation

$$Ca_5(PO_4)_3F + 5H_2SO_4 + 10H_2O \rightarrow 3H_3PO_4 + HF + 5CaSO_4 \cdot 2H_2O$$

The purity of the sulfuric acid is relatively unimportant, and contact acid, chamber acid and even spent acid from petroleum refining may be used, as long as there is not an appreciable amount of organic sludge, chlorides or metallic impurities present. However, a fairly good grade of rock is required, since carbonates will consume sulfuric acid and cause foaming, iron and aluminum are soluble in phosphoric acid and may produce water-insoluble phosphates in a fertilizer, etc. It is also necessary to have some silica present to react with the HF and thereby reduce corrosion. Typical rock for wet-process acid contains 31-35 per cent $P_2O_5$, 1.5-4.0 per cent $Al_2O_3 + Fe_2O_3$ and 2-10 per cent $SiO_2$.

The most important side reactions are as follows: (1) Any carbonates present in the rock will react to evolve carbon dioxide and form the corresponding sulfate. (2) Iron and aluminum will form phosphates which are soluble in phosphoric acid. These reduce the strength of the acid, and may appear as a heavy sludge when the acid is concentrated. These impurities usually have to be removed if the acid is used for other than fertilizer purposes. (3) Most of the HF will react with silica to form volatile $SiF_4$. However, there is some moisture in the effluent gases, and thus hydrated silica will be deposited in the gas ducts and scrubbing system of the plant. (4) Chlorides should be kept out of the system as much as possible because chloride ions in acid solution greatly increase the rate of corrosion. (5) Organic impurities or residual flotation reagents may give rise to a dirty acid, foaming and reduced filtration rates. Such rocks may require a preliminary calcining to remove organics.

## Acidulation of Rock

A successful process for the manufacture of phosphoric acid will extract the maximum amount of $P_2O_5$ from the rock, precipitate a calcium sulfate which filters rapidly and washes easily, and produce a phosphoric acid having as high a $P_2O_5$ content as possible. In practice, there must always be some compromise, since not all of these objectives can be achieved simultaneously.

In general, losses of $P_2O_5$ are caused by the presence of undecomposed rock, the formation of insoluble phosphate compounds, and any loss of phosphoric acid from spillage, leakage, vapor entrainment or washings passed to the sewer. The first type of loss can be reduced by fine grinding of the rock and providing sufficient time for the reaction to take place. However, another factor which must be considered is the possible formation of a layer of insoluble calcium sulfate on the surface of the rock particles which prevents complete reaction. This effect is caused by high acid concentrations, and usually becomes noticeable at concentrations of about 4 per cent $H_2SO_4$ or greater.

The possible formation of insoluble phosphate compounds results from the fact that both gypsum and dicalcium phosphate ($CaHPO_4 \cdot 2H_2O$) form monoclinic crystals. Thus, under some conditions, it is possible for phosphate ions to replace sulfate ions in the gypsum lattice. The magnitude of this effect depends on the concentration of phosphate and sulfate ions in the solution from which the gypsum is crystallizing. In practice, losses become excessive when the sulfate concentration falls below about 1 per cent.

The other types of losses can be reduced simply by good housekeeping. However, a matter of critical importance in determining $P_2O_5$ losses in the filter cake is the nature of the gypsum which is produced. Thus, a high sulfate concentration will produce needle-like clusters of gypsum which are easy to filter but hard to wash. Lower concentrations produce rhombic crystals which are easy to filter and wash. Still lower concentrations produce plate-like crystals that are hard to filter and wash. In practice, the best gypsum crystals are obtained at a sulfate concentration of about 2 per cent. Fortunately, this is also about optimum for decomposition of rock and for minimizing phosphate losses in the crystals.

A typical flow sheet for the production of wet-process phosphoric acid is illustrated in Fig. 8-2. The feed consists of phosphate rock (50-55 per cent through 200-mesh) and dilute sulfuric acid made by mixing fresh acid with washings from the gypsum filters and any other recovered $P_2O_5$-containing solutions. The rock is first mixed with a recycle slurry consisting of phosphoric acid carrying gypsum in suspension. This recycle is extremely important in promoting an easily filterable gypsum, since it provides nuclei for crystal growth and prevents the formation of a supersaturated solution of gypsum. Sulfuric acid is then added, and the mixture of acid, rock and recycle gypsum passes through several agitated digesters which provide time for the reaction to occur. Slurry from the final digester is filtered to obtain product acid, the gypsum is washed, and is then normally sent to waste disposal. Under good operating conditions, the yield of phosphoric acid is 95 per cent or greater, based on the $P_2O_5$ content of the rock.

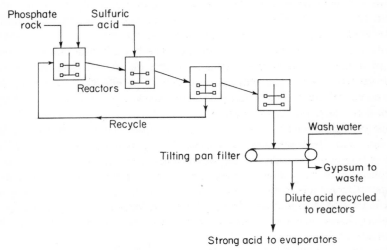

Fig. 8-2. Typical flow sheet for wet-process phosphoric acid.

Since the reactions are exothermic (under typical plant conditions, about 280 Btu/lb of rock), air is commonly blown over or through the slurry to remove the heat of reaction. The air passes to a fume exhaust system where volatile fluorine compounds are removed by absorption in water. The digestion of the rock has often been carried out in a series of agitated tanks. However, a single-tank reactor has been recently introduced which is divided into a series of compartments by means of baffles, and this type of reactor appears to be favored for new construction. Operating conditions are very severe, and resistance to both corrosion and erosion must be provided. The digesters are usually lined with carbon brick (ordinary silica brick would be attacked by fluorine), with rubber- or plastic-lined steel used for the cover, piping and fume exhaust system. Filters, pumps and agitators are usually made of stainless steel; types 316 and 317 are commonly used, although higher alloys may be required under some conditions.

The filtration of the gypsum is a particularly critical operation since this affects the losses of $P_2O_5$ in the filter cake and the strength of the phosphoric acid which is produced. Various types of filter have been used over the years, but practically all large plants now use the tilting pan filter such as the Eimco or Prayon. This filter consists of a series of rectangular shallow pans mounted on a rubber belt. The bottoms of the pans are ribbed to support a filter cloth, and a narrow vacuum box applies suction to the pans. As the belt rotates, slurry flows into the pans, the cake is sucked dry, washed and the gypsum either blown or washed out of the pans when they are in the reverse position on the belt.

## Concentration of Phosphoric Acid

Most wet-process phosphoric acid is used for the manufacture of triple superphosphate where a strength of about 54 per cent $P_2O_5$ is normally required. However, the usual wet-process acid has a strength of only about 30-32 per cent $P_2O_5$. The factors which limit the maximum strength of the acid are as follows: (a) Gypsum crystals precipitated from solutions containing more than 33 per cent $P_2O_5$ are fine and hard to wash. (b) Stronger acids require lower operating temperatures, and the cooling requirements become excessive at temperatures below about 150°F. (c) The higher viscosity and density of stronger acid adds to filtration and washing problems. (d) Stronger acids limit the amount of water that can be used for washing, and this tends to decrease the yield.

For these reasons, wet-process acid must be concentrated by evaporation to a strength of 38-55 per cent $P_2O_5$, depending on the use of the material. This evaporation is difficult and expensive because of the corrosive nature of the acid and the presence of iron, aluminum, fluorine and other impurities in the acid. Various types of direct heat and submerged combustion evaporators have been used, but forced-circulation vacuum evaporation is now used almost universally. The exchanger consists of externally heated Karbate tubes cemented into Karbate tube sheets. Acid solution is recirculated through the tubes at a high velocity to minimize scaling, and passes to a rubber-lined flash chamber where water is evaporated by means of a steam-jet ejector with a barometric leg. The boiling point of commercial acid containing 55 per cent $P_2O_5$ is about 193°F at 3 in. Hg absolute.

A substantial fraction of the fluorine from the rock is evolved during the concentration of the acid. This fluorine may be recovered as fluosilicic acid, provided there is any market for the material. Iron and aluminum impurities present in the acid are less soluble in the strong acid, and hence precipitate during concentration. Because of scaling, the evaporator units must be boiled out (cleaned) on a regular schedule, and on-stream time is usually figured at about 85 per cent. If the plant capacity is greater than that obtainable from a single unit, several units in series may be used. Note that series operation is more efficient than

parallel operation because the early stages operate at a low acid concentration.

## ELECTRIC-FURNACE PROCESS

The electric-furnace process had a very rapid growth in past years,
particularly over the period from about 1945-55. However, the growth
has been quite modest in recent years, chiefly because of the fact that
essentially all new fertilizer phosphoric acid has come from the wet
process.

The electric-furnace process for the manufacture of phosphorus and
phosphoric acid is based on the fact that silica assumes the properties of
a strong acid at elevated temperatures. Thus, if a mixture of phosphate
rock, silica and carbon is heated to a high enough temperature, the
silica can replace the phosphate radical to form a calcium silicate, and
elemental phosphorus can be distilled out of the reaction mixture. Although various reactions occur, the over-all reaction is often expressed
by the simple equation

$$Ca_3(PO_4)_2 + 3SiO_2 + 5C \rightarrow 3CaSiO_3 + P_2 + 5CO \qquad (8\text{-}1)$$

$$\Delta H^{\circ}_{298} = +338,000 \qquad \Delta F^{\circ}_{298} = +271,000$$

About 20 per cent of the fluorine present in the rock will also react according to the equation

$$2CaF_2 + 3SiO_2 \rightarrow SiF_4 + 2CaSiO_3 \qquad (8\text{-}2)$$

$$\Delta H^{\circ}_{298} = +72,000 \qquad \Delta F^{\circ}_{298} = +58,000$$

Any iron and aluminum present in the rock will be converted to the corresponding silicate; in addition, about 0.09 ton of by-product ferrophosphorus will be produced per ton of phosphorus product.

The phosphate rock used in the electric-furnace process normally contains less than 68 per cent BPL. There is no need to use a high-grade
rock since silica is required anyway in the reaction. However, the rock
does have to be in lump form, which means that the flotation product
must be agglomerated in some way such as by pelletizing, nodulizing or
sintering. In practice, the $CaO:SiO_2$ ratio is about 1.2:1, corresponding
to less silica than called for by Eq. (8-1). Under these conditions, the
calcium silicate is partly in the form of $3CaO \cdot 2SiO_2$; however, heats of
reaction are about the same as long as the $CaO:SiO_2$ ratio is less than
1.5:1.

A typical electric furnace consists of a water-cooled shell roughly 32
ft long, 15 ft wide and 12 ft high. The bottom of the furnace contains

about a 4-ft thick monolithic lining of carbon brick, and the carbon lining extends up the walls to a point well above the slag pool. The upper walls and domed top are lined with firebrick. Three carbon electrodes of about 40-in. diameter extend down into the furnace through water-cooled glands which are packed with asbestos to prevent escape of phosphorus to the room or entrance of air into the furnace. The electrodes are automatically raised or lowered during operation to maintain a constant energy input to the charge. The larger furnaces are operated at about 42,000 kVA, using 3-phase alternating current.

For one ton of product, the typical charge consists of 7.25 tons of phosphate rock, 2.66 tons of silica pebbles and 1.43 tons of coke. Silica reacts with the rock at temperatures over 2200°F to liberate phosphorus pentoxide, which is reduced to elemental phosphorus by the incandescent coke. Slag and ferrophosphorus collect in the furnace hearth, and are removed periodically by tapping the furnace. Furnace gases pass through two hot electrostatic precipitators at temperatures of about 700°F or greater to remove dust; electrical heating units maintain the temperature above the dew point of phosphorus. Gases then pass to an unlined steel tower in which water sprays condense the phosphorus to a heavy liquid which settles out and is pumped directly to storage by a submerged pump. Off-gases from the spray tower consist chiefly of carbon monoxide, and may be used for chemical purposes or burned for fuel.

The yield of phosphorus is about 92 per cent of that present in the rock. Over half the remaining phosphorus combines with iron to form ferrophosphorus, a valuable by-product. Under some conditions, the calcium silicate slag may also be marketed as a by-product. The power consumption is about 12,000-13,000 kw hr/ton of phosphorus produced. This is the largest single cost in the process, and hence a cheap source of electricity is essential if the process is to be economic.

## Conversion to Phosphoric Acid

Phosphoric acid may be produced by the one-step process which involves direct combustion of the furnace gases followed by absorption of the phosphorus pentoxide in water. However for various reasons, the two-step process is now more common. Here liquid phosphorus is produced as described above, and is sprayed into a graphite combustion chamber by means of a water-cooled burner. Combustion gases leave at about 1450°F, and enter a hydrator where water sprays convert slightly over half the $P_2O_5$ to 75-95 per cent $H_3PO_4$. Effluent gases then pass to three electrostatic precipitators where acid mist and the remaining $P_2O_5$ are recovered as strong phosphoric acid.

### Superphosphoric Acid

Two or more molecules of phosphoric acid can split off water to form low molecular weight polymers according to the equation

$$\underset{\text{orthophosphoric acid}}{HO-\overset{\displaystyle O}{\overset{\|}{\underset{\underset{OH}{|}}{P}}}-OH + HO-\overset{\displaystyle O}{\overset{\|}{\underset{\underset{OH}{|}}{P}}}-OH} \rightleftharpoons \underset{\text{pyrophosphoric acid}}{HO-\overset{\displaystyle O}{\overset{\|}{\underset{\underset{OH}{|}}{P}}}-O-\overset{\displaystyle O}{\overset{\|}{\underset{\underset{OH}{|}}{P}}}-OH + H_2O} \quad \text{etc.}$$

Even at acid strengths less than 100 per cent $H_3PO_4$, some of the higher polymers are present in equilibrium amounts in concentrated solutions. For example, at 95 per cent $H_3PO_4$ about one-third of the orthophosphoric acid is converted to a nonortho-form. This mixture of orthophosphoric acid, pyrophosphoric acid, and higher polymers is known as "superphosphoric acid."

Superphosphoric acid can be easily prepared from elemental phosphorus because it is necessary only to limit the amount of water added to the $P_2O_5$. However, recently considerable interest has been shown in the possible production of superphosphoric acid from wet-process acid. This can be done either by the use of a submerged combustion process or by the use of conventional vacuum evaporation at temperatures of about 350°F to produce acid of 95-100 per cent $H_3PO_4$.

The superphosphoric acid has three advantages over the dilute acid. First is the obvious saving in shipping costs. Second, the trend to higher analysis fertilizers has created a demand for stronger acids. Third, the polymers of phosphoric acid have the ability to "sequester" solids which would otherwise precipitate from solution. This, of course, is the basis for the use of phosphates in the detergent industry to soften hard water. Thus, by concentrating wet-process acid to the superacid range, the iron, aluminum and other such impurities do not precipitate, even under ammoniation; therefore, this acid can be used directly for liquid fertilizer applications and other uses where only the more expensive electric-furnace acid could be used in the past.

### SALTS OF PHOSPHORIC ACID

Various salts of phosphoric acid can be easily made by neutralization of one or more of the hydrogen atoms. Commercially, the most important are the sodium salts. Thus, one or two of the hydrogens can be neutralized with soda ash according to the equations

$$H_3PO_4 + Na_2CO_3 \begin{cases} \rightarrow NaH_2PO_4 \xrightarrow{heat} H_2O + NaPO_3 \\ \qquad\qquad\qquad\qquad\qquad meta \\ \rightarrow Na_2HPO_4 \xrightarrow{heat} H_2O + Na_4P_2O_7 \quad etc. \\ \qquad\qquad\qquad\qquad\qquad pyro\ or\ tetrabasic \end{cases}$$

Sodium tripolyphosphate is made by heating a 1:2 mixture of the mono- and disodium phosphates

$$NaH_2PO_4 + 2Na_2HPO_4 \xrightarrow{heat} Na_5P_3O_{10} + 2H_2O$$

If the tribasic phosphate (TSP) is required, since soda ash is too weak to neutralize the third hydrogen, caustic must be used according to the equation

$$Na_2HPO_4 + NaOH \rightarrow Na_3PO_4 + H_2O$$

The chief use of the sodium phosphates is in various types of water treatment. For example, sodium phosphates are often added directly to boiler feed water to prevent the formation of scale and permit the removal of suspended solids during blowdown. The polyphosphates have the ability to sequester ions such as $Ca^{++}$ and $Mg^{++}$, and are thus widely used as "builders" in synthetic detergents to increase the cleaning ability of the material. In 1963, total U.S. production was 818 thousand short tons of sodium tripolyphosphate, 109 thousand short tons of pyrophosphate, and 65 thousand short tons of metaphosphate. It can thus be seen that the water-treatment and detergent industries account for over 80 per cent of the total nonfertilizer use of phosphoric acid.

Substantial quantities of phosphoric acid also go into the manufacture of calcium phosphates. These may be produced merely by mixing appropriate quantities of the acid and lime to produce either the mono-calcium phosphate, $CaH_4(PO_4)_2 \cdot H_2O$, or the dicalcium phosphate, $CaHPO_4 \cdot 2H_2O$. These are used in animal feeds, in baking powders and as a polishing agent in dentifrice. In 1963, the total U.S. production of dibasic calcium phosphate was 240 thousand short tons (100 per cent $CaHPO_4$ basis).

## FLUORINE CHEMICALS

Essentially all fluorine chemicals come from the following three sources: (a) natural cryolite; (b) phosphate rock; (c) fluorspar. Cryolite, $Na_3AlF_6$, occurs naturally in Greenland where it has been mined commercially for many years. In 1963, 21 thousand short tons were imported for use as a solvent in the electrolysis of aluminum. In addition, substantial quantities of synthetic cryolite were also required by the aluminum industry.

We have already discussed the formation of by-product fluosilicic acid from the manufacture of phosphate fertilizers. Although much of the material is wasted, it can be converted to sodium silicofluoride by the addition of salt or soda ash. Thus, in 1963, about 40 thousand short tons of sodium silicofluoride were produced in the U.S. It is used as an insecticide and in the fluoridating of municipal water supplies.

However, the chief source of fluorine chemicals has been fluorspar rock. Although fluorspar occurs naturally in certain regions of the Southwest, most of the material is imported. Thus, in 1963, total U.S. production was only 188 thousand short tons as contrasted with imports of 555 thousand short tons, chiefly from Mexico, Italy and Spain. About 56 per cent of the fluorspar consumption goes into the manufacture of hydrofluoric acid. This requires an "acid grade" of rock which is low in silica to minimize the amount of fluorine appearing as $SiF_4$. About 37 per cent of the fluorspar is sold as a metallurgical grade which is used as a flux in the steel industry. About 5 per cent of the fluorspar goes into the manufacture of ceramics, and small quantities are used for welding rods, enamels, and in the glass industries.

### Hydrofluoric Acid

Before the war, most hydrofluoric acid was produced as a 60 per cent solution which was used largely for the manufacture of chemicals, pickling of metals, etching glass, etc. However, the development of the HF alkylation process for aviation gasoline, the production of uranium hexafluoride by the Atomic Energy Commission, and the increased use of fluorocarbons has resulted in an increasing demand for the anhydrous acid. Thus, in 1963, the total U.S. production of anhydrous HF was 117 thousand short tons as compared with only about 12 thousand short tons of the dilute acid (100 per cent basis). Almost 40 per cent of the acid goes into the manufacture of fluorocarbons, the aluminum industry takes about the same amount in the form of aluminum fluoride and synthetic cryolite, and smaller amounts go into the manufacture of uranium hexafluoride, pickling of stainless steel, petroleum alkylation, manufacture of fluorine chemicals, etc. Most of the hydrofluoric acid production is for captive use, and less than one-quarter appears on the open market.

All production of hydrofluoric acid is by one process, namely, the reaction of sulfuric acid with fluorspar rock according to the equation

$$CaF_2 + H_2SO_4 \rightarrow HF + F\text{---}Ca\text{---}HSO_4 \rightarrow HF + CaSO_4$$
$$H_{298}^{\circ} = +13,400$$

In practice, finely ground 97-98 per cent fluorspar containing less than 1 per cent silica is fed with a slight excess of strong sulfuric acid to one end of a direct-fired rotary kiln. The first fluorine atom comes off fairly easily, but heating to about 400°F is required to evolve the second fluorine atom. Under good operating conditions, the gas leaving the kiln contains over 90 per cent HF, 1-3 per cent impurities such as $SiF_4$, $H_2O$, $CO_2$, $SO_2$ and $H_2SO_4$, the balance being air. The solid residue, primarily calcium sulfate, discharges from the opposite end of the kiln. Normally, the material is wasted, which introduces a disposal problem since about 4 tons are produced per ton of HF.

Although the treatment of the kiln gases is subject to some variation, normally, the first step is a precooling to knock out moisture, sulfuric acid mist, and entrained solids. A 98-99 per cent acid can then be obtained by refrigeration at temperatures of 10-30°F. Uncondensed gases can then be scrubbed either with strong sulfuric acid to recover residual HF or with water to form a 40-60 per cent dilute acid. Product acid is made by distillation to remove impurities and produce about a 99.9 per cent HF product.

One of the chief problems in commercial operation is to prevent excessive dilution of the kiln gases with air, since this causes problems in the recovery of a strong acid. At least one plant is reported to use a special kneader to premix the acid and rock before it is fed to the furnace, and thereby permit better control of the reaction. Materials of construction are a problem, since hydrofluoric acid is extremely corrosive. Mild steel can be used as long as the acid strength is about 70 per cent or greater; in fact, mild steel tank cars are used for shipping acid as low as 60 per cent HF, provided the surface of the steel has been properly passivated. "Monel" can be used for handling all strengths of acid from anhydrous down to the constant boiling mixture. Distillation towers are fabricated of steel if the weakest acid is about 70 per cent; for dilute acids, "Monel" is used as a material of construction. Lead was commonly used in the past for handling weak acid; however, lead cannot be used with strong acid, and thus has become of less importance with the present trend toward the anhydrous grades.

## Fluorine Salts

The chief fluorine salts are aluminum fluoride and synthetic cryolite, both of which are used in the electrolysis of aluminum. These are made by direct absorption of the HF kiln gases by alumina or a mixture of alumina and soda ash. In 1963, total U.S. production of aluminum fluoride was 81 thousand short tons.

A relatively small amount of hydrofluoric acid is also converted to other salts such as sodium fluoride, sodium bifluoride, ammonium bifluoride, fluoboric acid, etc. These find some use in the manufacture of metals, electroplating, water fluoridation, etc. These uses are quite minor, and have changed relatively little in recent years. One potentially important fluorine salt is boron trifluoride, which is an extremely active catalyst for many organic reactions. This is best prepared by first reacting anhydrous HF with $SO_3$ to form fluosulfonic acid, followed by reaction with boric acid according to the equation

$$3HFSO_3 + H_3BO_3 \rightarrow BF_3 + 3H_2SO_4$$

Boron trifluoride is available either as a compressed gas or as an organic complex such as the boron trifluoride etherate. However, large-scale applications of boron trifluoride have not developed to any appreciable extent, and no spectacular growth is predicted for the immediate future.

# CHAPTER 9

# Organic Raw Materials

Raw materials for the commercial manufacture of organic chemicals include the following: (1) petroleum; (2) natural gas; (3) coal; (4) wood; (5) animal and vegetable oils, fats, and waxes; (6) carbohydrates such as sugar, starch, and molasses. In the United States, practically all synthetic organic chemicals are now being manufactured from petroleum or natural gas. Coal serves as an important source of aromatics, particularly benzene and naphthalene; however, even here, coal is becoming of less importance with the increasing production of aromatics from petroleum. The other three types of raw materials are relatively unimportant on a tonnage basis. Wood is a source of charcoal and small amounts of by-product methanol and acetic acid. Oils and fats are used by the soap industry, although synthetic detergents are now far more important. Carbohydrates serve as a source of drugs, medicinals and beverage ethanol; at one time, most industrial ethanol was produced from molasses, but this also now comes chiefly from petroleum.

## COAL CHEMICALS

Chemicals based on coal include calcium carbide and carbon bisulfide which are made from coke, by-product ammonium sulfate, coke-oven gas, benzene, toluene, xylenes, naphthalene, pyridine, phenol and other aromatics present in the light oil and tars from by-product coke manufacture. Table 9-1 gives the production of coke and coal chemicals for the year 1963. In comparing the production of aromatics from coal and petroleum, in 1963 approximately 17 per cent of the benzene, 7 per cent of the toluene, 2 per cent of the xylenes and 54 per cent of the naphthalene came from coal. These fractions have been decreasing in recent years, and this trend will probably continue as increased demand causes further expansion of petroleum-based aromatics.

TABLE 9-1.  PRODUCTION OF COKE AND COAL CHEMICALS
IN THE UNITED STATES FOR 1963
(Data from U.S. Tariff Commission and Minerals Yearbook 1963)

| | |
|---|---:|
| Total coal carbonized | 78,082,619 short tons |
| Total production of coke | 54,278,307 short tons |
| Total ammonia produced (ammonium sulfate basis) | 718,778 short tons |
| Total crude tar | 671,875,628 gal |
| Total light oil | 218,165,707 gal |
| Total coke oven gas | 800,582 million ft$^3$ |
| Light oil derivatives | |
|     Benzene, total | 121,525,000 gallons |
|     Toluene | 28,998,000 gallons |
|     Xylenes | 7,397,000 gallons |
|     Solvent naphtha | 9,090,000 gallons |
|     Other light oil derivatives | 11,444,000 gallons |
| Tar derivatives | |
|     Naphthalene, crude | 338,715,000 lbs |
|     Crude tar-acid oils | 25,696,000 gal |
|     Creosote oil | 98,110,000 gal |
|     All other distillate products | 31,793,000 gal |
|     Tar, road | 58,042,000 gal |
|     Tar, other | 18,228,000 gal |
|     Pitch of tar | 1,788,000 short tons |

## CARBONIZATION OF COAL

When a bituminous coal is heated in the absence of air, it fuses to form
a pasty mass. As the temperature is increased, the volatile matter in the
coal is evolved to leave a solid porous residue consisting of carbon plus
the mineral matter in the original coal. The chief purpose in the carbonization of coal is to produce coke, and any chemicals produced are of
secondary importance. This was a serious disadvantage when coal chemicals served as the sole source of aromatics for the chemical industry,
since anything affecting the demand for coke would also affect the supply
of the chemical raw materials. Most coke produced in the United States
is used in blast furnaces for the reduction of iron ore; smaller quantities
are used in foundries, as a domestic fuel, for the manufacture of water
gas and producer gas and for chemical purposes such as the manufacture
of graphite, calcium carbide and carbon bisulfide. Essentially all coke
is now made in by-product coke ovens. The wasteful beehive ovens were
important at one time, but they are now used only to augment the production if there is a sudden and temporary demand which cannot be met
by the by-product ovens.

The first problem in the carbonization of coal is the selection of a suitable "coking" coal.[1] If the coal softens and eventually solidifies into a more or less solid cake, it is classed as a coking coal. If the coal crumbles on heating or forms a weakly coherent mass, it is classed as a noncoking coal. However, not every coal classed as coking yields a merchantable coke, and it is hard to find a single coal which possesses all the desired characteristics. For this reason, it is customary to blend two or more bituminous coals into a mix which experience has shown produces a satisfactory coke. Unfortunately, there is no method of analysis which will show whether or not a given coal is a satisfactory coking coal, so that most work is still largely empirical in nature.

Figure 9-1 illustrates a typical by-product coke oven. A single oven consists of a narrow vertical chamber of silica brick 37-45 ft long, 9-15 ft high, and 14-24 in. in average width. To facilitate the pushing out of the coke, the ovens taper in width by 2-4 in.; hence, a 20-in. oven might have a width of 18 in. at the pusher end and 22 in. at the coke end. The average oven will hold from 15-20 tons of coal. The ovens are heated by the combustion of gas in flues located in silica brick walls parallel to the oven. To conserve heat and space, by-product coke ovens are built in batteries containing up to 100 ovens, the ovens and heating flues alternating from one end to the other.

Each end of the oven is fitted with a removable door to permit pushing out the coke. The older doors were sealed with mud to prevent leakage, but self-sealing doors are used on all modern ovens. Several openings are located in the top of the oven which are fitted with removable lids; a "larry car" runs on rails above the battery of ovens and charges each oven with a weighed quantity of coal. The coking temperature ranges from 1600-2000°F, and 12-18 hours are required to complete the coking, depending on the temperature and the width of the oven. When coking is completed, the oven doors are removed and a pusher machine containing a powerful ram pushes the red hot coke out into a quenching car. As soon as the oven is empty, the quenching car is run under water sprays and up to 10,000 gal of water are sprayed on the coke over a period of 1 or 2 minutes.

## Recovery of By-products

Volatile material produced by the carbonization of coal includes hydrogen, methane, hydrogen sulfide, carbon monoxide, ammonia, pyridines, thiophenes, phenols and all types of aliphatic and aromatic hydrocarbons ranging from gases to heavy tars. The volatile materials normally leave

[1] P. J. Wilson, Jr. and J. H. Wells, "Coal, Coke, and Coal Chemicals," New York, McGraw-Hill Book Co., Inc., 1950.

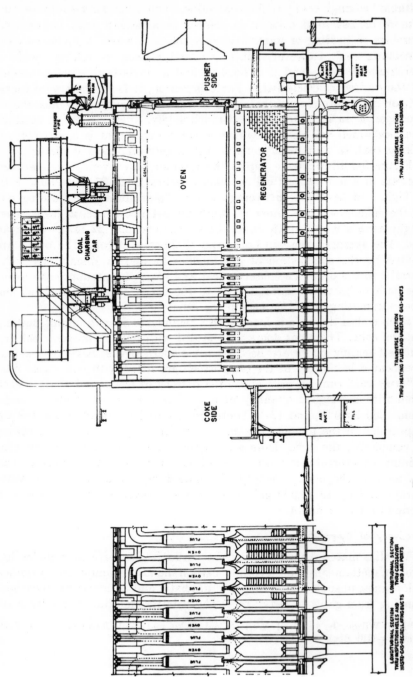

Fig. 9-1. Koppers-Becker coke oven. (*Courtesy Koppers Co., Inc.*)

the oven through a standpipe located on top of the oven at the pusher end (in some cases, two standpipes have been used). A gooseneck at the top of the standpipe conducts the hot gas into a common collecting main. The gas from the oven is cooled by direct contact with a spray of aqueous ammonia liquor known as "flushing liquor" which is recirculated through an external cooler. The flushing liquor condenses out most of the tar from the gas and dissolves ammonium salts and part of the free ammonia in the gas. The mixture of tar and liquor passes to a decanter which separates a lower layer of tar which runs to tar storage and an upper layer of liquor which is recycled to the collecting main. The noncondensible gases leave the collecting main through a crossover main to primary coolers which further reduce the temperature and condense additional water and tar fractions. Any tar fog remaining in the gases is then removed by either an impingement tar extractor or an electrostatic precipitator.

Ammonia in the coke oven gas is usually recovered by absorption in dilute sulfuric acid to form ammonium sulfate. Some ammonia also dissolves in the flushing liquor; this is recovered by distillation in an ammonia still, using lime to free the "fixed" ammonia present as the chloride, sulfate, etc. The coke-oven gas is then scrubbed with a high-boiling petroleum fraction ("wash oil") to recover aromatics; steam distillation of the wash oil produces the light oil fraction which contains about 62 per cent benzene, 14 per cent toluene, 4 per cent xylenes and smaller amounts of other materials. Hydrogen sulfide is removed from the coke-oven gas by absorption in a weak alkaline solution such as sodium carbonate. In some plants the hydrogen sulfide is converted to sulfuric acid; in other plants the hydrogen sulfide is converted to elemental sulfur by the Thylox process which involves absorption in a solution of sodium thioarsenate containing under 1 per cent $As_2O_5$ at a pH of 7.5-8.0. The solution is regenerated by blowing with air. The chief reactions are

$$Na_4As_2S_5O_2 + H_2S \rightarrow Na_4As_2S_6O + H_2O$$

$$Na_4As_2S_6O + \tfrac{1}{2}O_2 \rightarrow Na_4As_2S_5O_2 + S$$

The finely divided sulfur is filtered on a continuous filter, and can be used either as a fungicide or for acid manufacture.

Although the purified coke-oven gas has a fairly high heating value, there is essentially no market for it in the United States because of the wide use of natural gas for domestic heating. For this reason, most coke-oven gas is used as a fuel in steel mills which are often located adjacent to the coke plants.

The light oil is subjected to a preliminary distillation, and the various fractions washed with strong sulfuric acid to remove olefins and other impurities. A final distillation then produces benzene, toluene, xylenes and solvent naphtha. However, even the final fractions are still relatively impure in comparison with the petroleum-based aromatics. For example, a particularly troublesome contaminant is thiophene ($C_4H_4S$) which boils at 84°C in comparison with the boiling point of 79.6°C for pure benzene. Because of the competition with petroleum-based aromatics, the coke plants have been forced to introduce processes such as hydrogenation to remove thiophene and other impurities from the aromatics.

The tar produced from by-product coke ovens may be refined by the coke-oven operator or may be sold to a tar distiller. Usually the tar is first distilled to produce the following crude fractions:

(1) Light Oil Fraction. This is usually simply combined with the main light oil stream from the gas scrubbers.

(2) Tar Acid Oil. Modern plants use solvent extraction to first extract the phenol, cresols, and other tar acids. Pyridine bases are then removed by acidifying with sulfuric acid, followed by neutralization and distillation. Naphthalene is recovered from the resulting "neutral oil" by distillation or crystallization.

(3) Creosote Oil. Only a limited market exists in the United States for creosote, although it does find some use as a wood preservative. Much of the creosote oil is simply burned to recover the fuel value.

(4) Pitch. The pitch is now one of the most valuable constituents of the coal tar. It is marketed on the basis of the melting point and the percentage of free carbon present. It finds a ready market as roofing pitch, in highway construction, as a binder in the manufacture of electrodes, etc.

The only pure chemicals produced in any quantity from coal tar are naphthalene and some anthracene. However, coal tar represents a rich reservoir of the higher aromatics.[1] Some of these present to at least 1 per cent include phenanthrene, fluoranthene, pyrene, fluorene, chrysene, carbazole, 2-methyl-naphthalene, etc. Although tens of thousands of tons of these chemicals are produced each year, at present they are simply wasted because there is no market for them.

## NATURAL GAS AND NATURAL GAS LIQUIDS

In 1963, 14,746,663 million cubic feet of natural gas were produced in the United States. The natural gas accompanying crude oil or separated from it is known as "wet" gas. This gas contains small quantities of propane, butanes, pentanes, etc., as determined by the partial pressures

[1] See article by Heinz-Gerhard Franck, "The Challenge in Coal Tar Chemicals," *Ind. Eng. Chem.*, **55**(5), 39 (1963).

of the various components of the crude oil. Since these materials have a market value which is considerably greater than their fuel value, they are usually removed from the natural gas to obtain what is known as "natural gas liquids." Thus, in 1963, a total of 16,837 million gallons of natural gas liquids were recovered from natural gas. Over half this material was sold for heating use as low-pressure gas (LPG) which consists chiefly of propane and butane. The remainder was used chiefly for blending with petroleum fractions and as a source of hydrocarbons for chemical use. The relatively poor gasoline obtained from the natural gas liquids is known as "casinghead" gasoline.

Three general processes are used for the recovery of the natural gas liquids. The most common is to scrub the natural gas with a heavy petroleum fraction such as straw oil, followed by distillation of the straw oil to recover absorbed liquids. The second process uses a straight compression and cooling of the natural gas to condense out the heavier hydrocarbons. The third process involves recycling whereby the heavier hydrocarbons are removed and the natural gas is then pumped back into the ground through an injection well where it can pick up more of the heavy components.

## REFINING OF PETROLEUM

Table 9-2 gives the production of petroleum products in the United States for 1963. From the standpoint of the chemical industry, two im-

TABLE 9-2.   PETROLEUM PRODUCTION IN THE UNITED STATES FOR 1963
(Data from Minerals Yearbook, 1963)

| Material | Production (thousands of 42-gal barrels) |
|---|---|
| Crude petroleum | 2,752,723 |
| Imports | 412,660 |
| Total new supply | 3,165,383 |
| Gasoline and naphtha, from crude | 1,413,081 |
| From natural gas liquids | 214,814 |
| Benzol blended | 80 |
| Total | 1,627,975 |
| Kerosine, from crude | 164,705 |
| From natural gas liquids | 1,141 |
| Total | 165,846 |
| Distillate fuel oil, total | 764,953 |
| Residual fuel oil | 276,766 |
| Military jet fuel | 99,360 |
| Lubricants | 63,086 |
| Wax (1 barrel = 280 lb) | 5,126 |
| Petroleum coke (5 barrels = 1 short ton) | 80,268 |

portant facts must be kept in mind. First, the total production of petroleum is extremely large; for example, the tonnage of crude petroleum is over 20 times that of sulfuric acid, the most important of the "heavy" chemicals. Thus, even a material present in petroleum in small quantities may constitute an abundant raw material for chemical use. Second, the value of petroleum fractions to the refiner is approximately 1-2 cent/lb. If these can be upgraded to chemicals, the potential profit becomes very large.

At one time, refiners of crude petroleum were willing to sell raw materials to the chemical industry at a fairly low cost. However, today there is an increasing trend toward vertical integration in which the refiners carry out all processing operations starting with the crude petroleum and ending up with finished plastics and chemical products. In fact, the former petroleum refiners now refer to their business as the "hydrocarbon processing industries" (HPI). It is a fact that the HPI are accounting for an increasingly large fraction of the total chemical production in the United States, and this fraction will probably continue to increase over the near future. This is partly the result of the availability of the raw materials, and the fact that these raw materials can be converted into more valuable products. However, a more important reason is the increasing competition in the petrochemical industry whereby profit margins can be maintained only by carrying out all processing steps from crude to final product.

**Nature of Petroleum.** The word petroleum comes from the Latin *petra* (rock) and *oleum* (oil). There is still considerable uncertainty as to the exact origin of petroleum. It is found only in sedimentary rocks[1] where it is derived from marine animal organisms and plant life which accumulated along the seashore. As a result of the deposition of sediments, the oil and gas were squeezed out of the source mud and migrated into a reservoir rock, usually a porous sandstone, limestone or dolomite. The transformation of the animal and vegetable material into petroleum has been variously attributed to heat, pressure, time, radioactivity, bacterial action or some type of low-temperature catalysis. However, laboratory attempts to synthesize crude petroleum from animal or vegetable matter have been unsuccessful, and the question of the origin of petroleum is still unanswered.

Crude oils vary considerably in appearance; some are black, some are lighter colored, some are viscous, some are fairly fluid and some carry paraffin wax in suspension. However, regardless of the appearance and origin of crude oil, the empirical composition is remarkably uniform. Thus, all crudes consist chiefly of hydrocarbons, the composition being

[1] G. Sell, "The Petroleum Industry," London, Oxford University Press, 1963.

approximately 85 per cent carbon, 13 per cent hydrogen and smaller quantities of organic sulfur, nitrogen, oxygen and ash. The hydrocarbons present in crude oil are of the following three types: (a) Paraffinic hydrocarbons have the general formula $C_nH_{2n+2}$. These range from methane to heavy paraffin wax, including thousands of different isomers. It is of interest to note that the olefins are almost nonexistent in crude petroleum, although they are produced in very large quantities in subsequent refining operations. (b) Naphthenic hydrocarbons are those present as a saturated ring structure. These consist almost entirely of derivatives of cyclopentane and cyclohexane in which various side chains may be attached, two or more rings may combine to form a honeycomb structure, etc. The heaviest members of the naphthene series are solids similar to asphalt. (c) Aromatic hydrocarbons are characterized by the six-carbon-atom benzene ring. The aromatics are present in only small amounts in crude oil as compared to the paraffins and naphthenes. However, substantial quantities of aromatics are produced in certain of the refining operations, and the aromatics are particularly valuable components of gasoline since they have very good antiknock properties.

The sulfur in crude oil ranges from under 0.2 per cent up to as much as 5 or 6 per cent. Sulfur is in general undesirable since it may cause trouble in subsequent refining operations. Sulfur may be present as elemental sulfur, hydrogen sulfide, mercaptans, organic sulfides, thiophenes, etc. Nitrogen in crude oil is usually less than 0.1 per cent, and is believed to be present chiefly as complex aromatics. Oxygen in crude oil consists chiefly of phenolic compounds. The ash from crude oil may contain many different elements, depending on the source of the particular crude. Strangely enough, practically every crude contains vanadium and nickel. It is believed that these two elements were essential to the growth of the animal or vegetable organisms from which the crude was originally formed.

## Distillation

Although the particular refining operations carried out on crude oil differ from one refinery to another, certain general statements can be made. Figure 9-2 illustrates a typical flow sheet for a modern refinery. Crude oil as it comes from the ground is always accompanied by substantial quantities of natural gas. Much of this gas is separated at the well head, although some will be present in solution in the crude sent to the refinery. Usually the first refinery operation is to wash the crude with water to remove salt and other water-soluble impurities which might cause problems of corrosion or plugging of the equipment. The treated crude at a pressure of about 50 psig is then sent through heat exchangers with hot products from the distillation, and is flashed at a temperature of about 300°F to a primary flash column which separates most of the methane, ethane, propane and butane from the crude (note that in the petroleum industry, the word "gas" refers to those materials

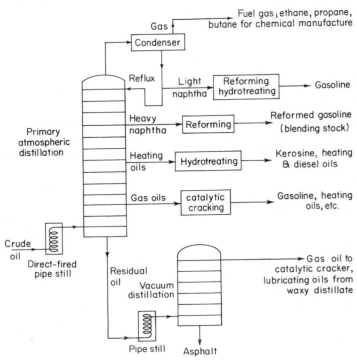

FIG. 9-2. Typical flow sheet for petroleum refinery.

which are gases at room temperature and atmospheric pressure; the liquid needed to make an automobile go is known as "gasoline").

After the removal of most of the gas, the crude oil is heated to 600-800°F in a direct-fired pipe still and sent to a large bubble-plate distillation column operating at slightly above atmospheric pressure. This primary distillation column separates the crude oil purely on the basis of boiling point into an overhead fraction consisting of methane, ethane and other gases, a bottoms fraction consisting of heavy residual oil, and up to a dozen side streams which are withdrawn from various plates on the column. Each side stream is run through a smaller "stripper column" to remove the lower-boiling materials or "light ends." Thus, he primary distillation separates the crude into the following rough ractions:

(1) Gas. Gases from the top of the column consist chiefly of methane, thane, propane, butane, isobutane and hydrogen sulfide. In addition, mall quantities of unsaturates such as ethylene and propylene may be present as a result of some cracking of the crude oil as it is heated in the pipe still. The methane is usually of no value except as a fuel. Ethane has onsiderable market value as a raw material for the manufacture of thylene and other petrochemicals. Propane may be used for the manu-acture of propylene, or the propane and butane may be compressed und sold as LPG. Some butane is also used for chemical purposes, and he isobutane is commonly separated and used as a raw material for lkylation.

(2) Gasoline or Light Naphtha. The overhead liquid constitutes the owest boiling liquid fraction, and is commonly called the gasoline or ight naphtha fraction. The boiling range is approximately 80-400°F, und the liquid consists of a mixture of paraffins, naphthenes, and aro-natic hydrocarbons plus mercaptans and other sulfur compounds. In the United States, this fraction is almost always further refined and blended vith other stocks to produce engine gasoline.

(3) Heavy Naphtha. The heavy naphtha fraction has a boiling range of approximately 200-450°F. In the United States, this fraction is usually catalytically reformed and blended with the finished gasoline.

(4) Kerosine. The kerosine fraction has a boiling range of about 300-550°F. After treatment, this fraction can be used directly as a light fuel oil for domestic heating, as a jet fuel for aircraft, and as an illumi-nating oil for oil lamps.

(5) Middle Distillates. The middle distillates include the gas oils, light fuel oil, heavy fuel oil and diesel oils. The over-all boiling range is roughly 400-700°F. Depending on the demand, these fractions are mar-keted as domestic fuel oil, industrial fuel oil, and diesel fuel. Surplus amounts are sent to the catalytic cracker to be converted to gasoline and light fuel oil.

(6) Residual Oil. The residual oil fraction from the still bottoms is usually redistilled under vacuum to produce lubricating oils and asphalt.

### Products from Primary Distillation

The relative quantities of the various products obtained from the primary distillation of crude petroleum depend only on the boiling range of the various components present in the crude oil. This distribution inevitably differs, in one way or another, from the market demand for the various products. Thus, in order to operate economically, petroleum fractions which are present in surplus amounts must be converted to more marketable materials. In the United States, the chief petroleum product is gasoline; thus, the middle distillates such as the gas oils are usually cracked in order to increase the yield of gasoline, and lighter fractions such as the $C_3$-$C_5$ hydrocarbons are polymerized to form polymer gasoline or "alkylate." In the rest of the world, usually the fuel oils and diesel oils are the products having the largest demand. Here the light fractions such as the naphtha may be literally a drug on the market, and are sometimes burned for their fuel value or used as a raw material for the manufacture of ethylene or synthesis gas.

There is a similar situation with respect to the petrochemical raw materials. In the United States, the greatest demand has been for ethylene, benzene, and synthesis gas. Most ethylene has been produced from ethane and propane from petroleum refineries plus additional ethane and propane recovered from natural gas. Large quantities of benzene are produced from petroleum, and synthesis gas usually comes from cheap and abundant natural gas. In the rest of the world, the demand for benzene has been largely supplied by coke-oven benzene, although some benzene is being produced from petroleum in western Europe. Because of the fact that natural gas has not been available to any extent outside of the United States, both ethylene and synthesis gas have usually been produced from naphtha.

These economic factors must be clearly kept in mind, since they determine the raw materials which are available for the manufacture of petrochemicals.

### Separation of Pure Hydrocarbons from Petroleum

The individual fractions available from the distillation of petroleum consist of mixtures of various hydrocarbons as determined by their boiling points. Although these mixtures are perfectly satisfactory for most purposes, the chemical industry frequently requires pure components to use as chemical raw materials. To illustrate the problems involved in the separation of pure hydrocarbons from petroleum, Table 9-2A gives the boiling points and relative abundances of the hydrocarbons present in one particular reference petroleum.

From a consideration of the boiling points of the individual components, it is evident that pure hydrocarbons from methane to *n*-pentane can be readily obtained by conventional fractionation. Cyclopentane and 2,2-dimethylbutane cannot be separated by conventional fractionation; however, these can be separated by extractive or azeotropic distillation using a third component to emphasize the paraffinic-naphthenic differences between them. However, above this point, the mixtures be-

TABLE 9-2A. HYDROCARBONS ISOLATED FROM ONE REFERENCE PETROLEUM*

| Hydrocarbon | Boiling Point (°C) | Volume Per Cent in Petroleum |
|---|---|---|
| Methane | −161.49 | — |
| Ethane | −88.63 | 0.06 |
| Propane | −42.07 | 0.11 |
| Isobutane | −11.73 | 0.14 |
| *n*-Butane | −0.50 | 0.79 |
| 2-Methylbutane | 27.85 | 0.77 |
| *n*-Pentane | 36.07 | 1.43 |
| Cyclopentane | 49.26 | 0.05 |
| 2,2-Dimethylbutane | 49.74 | 0.04 |
| 2,3-Dimethylbutane | 57.99 | 0.08 |
| 2-Methylpentane | 60.27 | 0.37 |
| 3-Methylpentane | 63.28 | 0.35 |
| *n*-Hexane | 68.74 | 1.80 |
| Methylcyclopentane | 71.81 | 0.87 |
| 2,2-Dimethylpentane | 79.20 | 0.02 |
| Benzene | 80.10 | 0.15 |
| 2,4-Dimethylpentane | 80.50 | 0.08 |
| Cyclohexane | 80.74 | 0.71 |
| 1,1-Dimethylcyclopentane | 87.85 | 0.16 |
| 2,3-Dimethylpentane | 89.78 | 0.15 |
| 2-Methylhexane | 90.05 | 0.73 |
| 1,*cis*-3-Dimethylcyclopentane | 90.77 | 0.87 |
| 1,*trans*-3-Dimethylcyclopentane | 91.72 | 0.21 |
| 3-Methylhexane | 91.85 | 0.51 |
| 1,*trans*-2-Dimethylcyclopentane | 91.87 | 0.48 |
| 3-Ethylpentane | 93.48 | 0.06 |
| *n*-Heptane | 98.43 | 2.3 |
| Methylcyclohexane | 100.93 | 1.6 |
| Ethylcyclopentane | 103.47 | 0.16 |
| 1,1,3-Trimethylcyclopentane | 104.89 | 0.30 |
| 2,2-Dimethylhexane | 106.84 | 0.01 |
| 2,5-Dimethylhexane | 109.10 | 0.06 |
| 1,*trans*-2,*cis*-4-Trimethylcyclopentane | 109.29 | 0.22 |
| 2,4-Dimethylhexane | 109.43 | 0.06 |
| 2,2,3-Trimethylpentane | 109.84 | 0.004 |
| 1,*trans*-2,*cis*-3-Trimethylcyclopentane | 110.2 | 0.26 |
| Toluene | 110.62 | 0.51 |

* B. J. Mair, *Oil Gas J.*, **62**, 130 (Sept. 14, 1964). The above table gives the first 37 from a total of 234 compounds isolated to date by the API Research Project 6.

come so complex that separation of pure components becomes very difficult and expensive. If there were sufficient demand, relatively pure $C_6$ and $C_7$ hydrocarbons could be prepared using combinations of super-fractionation, extractive and azeotropic distillation, solvent extraction, molecular sieves, etc. This would of course be very expensive, since it would involve the separation of mixtures of various paraffinic, naphthenic and aromatic hydrocarbons having very close boiling points.

In practice, the only important chemical raw materials recovered from petroleum are ethane, propane, butane, benzene and cyclohexane. Ethane, propane and butane are used as cracking stock for the manufacture of ethylene; in addition, butane is used to produce butadiene. Benzene is recovered by solvent extraction of reformed gasoline using a material such as diethylene glycol to extract aromatics. Cyclohexane is recovered from natural-gas liquids by a complex process involving catalytic reforming, hydrogenation and final product separation by superfractionation.

### Refining Operations

In general, each fraction from the primary distillation of crude oil must be further refined before it can be marketed. Thus, all fractions normally must be "sweetened" or desulfurized, and unsaturates must often be removed to prevent gum formation. For those fractions going into gasoline, the most important refining operation is to improve the knock rating or octane number* of the gasoline. This depends on the composition of the hydrocarbons; thus, the aromatics have the highest octane numbers, the straight-chain paraffins have the lowest octane numbers, and the branched-chain paraffins and the naphthenes are in between. For this reason, the refining operations carried out on gasoline fractions have the purpose of converting straight chains to branched chains and naphthenes to aromatics.

Although the particular refining operations which are carried out do vary considerably from plant to plant, there are some operations which are more or less standard. Let us briefly discuss some of the most important of these.

### Catalytic Cracking

Modern catalytic cracking plants are of two general types, the fluid bed and the moving bed. In the fluid bed, which is the most common, a powdered catalyst is used which is physically suspended in the moving stream of hydrocarbon vapor. In the moving bed, a pelleted catalyst is used which circulates continuously by means of elevators or a gas lift.

---

* The octane number of a gasoline is based upon two reference fuels, n-heptane which is arbitrarily assigned an octane number of zero and isooctane (2,2,4-trimethylpentane) which is assigned an octane number of 100. Thus, if a given gasoline has the same knock characteristics as a mixture of 90 per cent isooctane and 10 per cent n-heptane, the octane number is equal to 90. Unfortunately, there are two standard methods of testing the fuel, and hence two types of octane number are commonly used, namely the research octane number (RON) and motor octane number (MON), the latter normally being lower. In addition it has been necessary to extrapolate to octane numbers above 100, so that there is still some confusion about the use of many of the terms.

Ail commercial plants now use catalysts of the silica-alumina type.[1] These may be either natural, synthetic or a mixture of natural and synthetic materials. The early types contained about 12 per cent $Al_2O_3$, but it has been found that increasing the alumina to about 25 per cent gives better performance. The fluid catalysts consist chiefly of particles less than 150 microns in diameter; they are extremely porous, and have surface areas up to several hundred square meters per gram of catalyst.

Figure 9-3 illustrates a typical fluid catalytic cracker. The feedstock

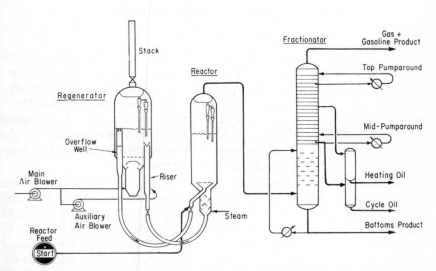

FIG. 9-3. Typical fluid catalytic cracker. [Esso Research and Engineering Co., *Hydroc. Proc. Petrol. Refiner*, **43** (9), 151 (1964)]

is usually a gas oil or wax distillate, although other fractions may also be used. The preheated feed enters the reactor at a pressure of about 10 psig where it is mixed with recycle oil and the powdered catalyst from the regenerator. The temperature in the reactor is usually held at about 850-950°F. Gases leave the reactor through cyclones to remove the powdered catalyst, and enter a distillation column which separates the various fractions in the cracked hydrocarbons. There is always a

[1] C. H. Reisz and F. L. Morritz, "Catalysts for Petroleum Refining," chapter in "Advances in Petroleum Chemistry and Refining," edited by J. J. McKetta, Jr., New York, Interscience Publishers, Inc., 1961; for a description of the various commercial processes, see the "Refining Process Handbook," issued annually by the *Hydrocarbon Processing and Petroleum Refiner*.

certain amount of coke formation because of cracking and dehydrogenation of some of the materials in the feedstock. This coke coats the catalyst and renders it inactive; for this reason, a portion of the catalyst is continually withdrawn from the bottom of the reactor, hydrocarbons are stripped from it by blowing with steam, and the catalyst is regenerated by burning off the carbon at a temperature of about 1100°F by blowing with air.

The chemical reactions taking place during catalytic cracking are quite complex. The primary reactions are considered to be as follows:

$$\text{Paraffin} \rightarrow \text{paraffin} + \text{olefin}$$

$$\text{Alkyl naphthene} \rightarrow \text{naphthene} + \text{olefin}$$

$$\text{Alkyl aromatic} \rightarrow \text{aromatic} + \text{olefin}$$

The aliphatics produced by catalytic cracking are chiefly $C_3$-$C_6$ hydrocarbons, and few olefins are formed above $C_4$. There is a substantial production of aromatics from naphthenes, and considerable skeletal isomerization whereby straight chains are converted to branched chains. However, the primary products may be modified as a result of secondary reactions. Although the products of the cracking process range all the way from hydrogen to coke, commercially up to 40 per cent of the feedstock can be converted to debutanized gasoline.

It is now common practice to use two stages of catalytic cracking either by using recycle or by using two separate crackers. The first stage involves a fairly short contact time with the catalyst; the light ends are then removed by distillation, and the heavier fraction sent to the second cracking stage. Yields as high as 75 per cent are obtained in this way. The octane number of the gasoline produced is about 90-95. Catalytic cracking also produces substantial quantities of butanes, butylenes, propane, propylene, ethane and ethylene which may be used for chemical purposes. Catalytic crackers are among the largest pieces of equipment used in the chemical industry; some units are 200 ft or more in height and circulate 50-100 tons/min of catalyst.

### Catalytic Reforming

Catalytic reforming is widely used to upgrade the octane number of straight-run gasoline, naphtha and other feedstocks. The process goes under various names such as Platforming (Universal Oil Products Co.), Powerforming (Esso Research and Engineering Co.), Ultraforming (Standard Oil Co. of Indiana), etc. Most reforming processes use a platinum catalyst having about 0.6 per cent platinum deposited on a base of alumina or silica-alumina; fluoride or chloride may be added as an acid promoter. The chief competitor of platinum has been a molybdena-alumina catalyst containing about 10 per cent $MoO_3$. However, the platinum catalyst has higher efficiency, and thus has found most favor. An efficient catalyst must be dual-function, namely, contain an acid function ($Al_2O_3$) to promote isomerization and an electron defect structure (Pt) to promote dehydrogenation.

Catalytic reforming is carried out by passing a mixture of hydrogen plus feedstock over the catalyst at pressures of 200-800 psig and temperatures of 850-1000°F. However, it must be emphasized that reforming is not a hydrogenation, but a dehydrogenation. The upgrading of the octane number is accomplished by dehydrogenation of naphthenes to aromatics, isomerization, hydrocracking and dehydrocyclization. Some typical desirable reactions are as follows:

$\Delta H^\circ_{298} = +49,250 \qquad \Delta F^\circ_{298} = +23,399 \qquad \Delta F^\circ_{800} = -23,122$

$n$-hexane $\rightarrow$ 2-methylpentane

$\Delta H^\circ_{298} = -1700 \qquad \Delta F^\circ_{298} = -1160 \qquad \Delta F^\circ_{800} = -230$

$n$-hexane $\rightarrow$ benzene + $4H_2$

$\Delta H^\circ_{298} = +59,780 \qquad \Delta F^\circ_{298} = +31,059 \qquad \Delta F^\circ_{800} = -20,372$

$\Delta H^\circ_{298} = -62,460 \qquad \Delta F^\circ_{298} = -42,130 \qquad \Delta F^\circ_{800} = -4170$

$\Delta H^\circ_{298} = +45,320 \qquad \Delta F^\circ_{298} = +22,439 \qquad \Delta F^\circ_{800} = -19,092$

Free energies are given for a temperature of 800°K since this is approximately the temperature used commercially. Note that the equilibria are favorable at this temperature for all the examples given above.

During operation, the reforming catalyst is gradually fouled by coke produced from a small amount of cracking of the hydrocarbons. In most processes, the catalyst can be regenerated by very cautious combustion, using a low-oxygen gas. Catalytic reformers are usually built in pairs so that one can operate while the other is being regenerated. Several cycles of regeneration are possible before the activity of the catalyst is reduced to the point where it must be replaced. The platinum catalysts are, of course, very susceptible to poisoning, especially by metals such as arsenic. Note that catalytic reforming produces large quantities of hydrogen which can be used as a raw material for other refinery operations.

### Other Refining Operations

Distillation, catalytic cracking and reforming are the three most important refining operations in the United States. Others of less importance include the following:

(1) Alkylation. Whereas the purpose of catalytic cracking is to make little ones from big ones, the purpose of alkylation is to make big ones from little ones. Alkylation is second to reforming as a means of obtaining high-octane blending stocks. Alkylation also offers an economic way of using the lighter hydrocarbons such as the $C_3$-$C_5$ fractions.

The process of alkylation involves the reaction of an isoparaffin, usually isobutane, with olefins such as propylene, butylenes and amylenes according to the typical reaction

$$CH_3-CH-CH_3 + CH_3-C=CH_2 \rightarrow CH_3-\overset{\overset{\displaystyle CH_3}{|}}{C}-CH_2-\overset{\overset{\displaystyle CH_3}{|}}{CH}-CH_3$$

$$\underset{\text{isobutane}}{\overset{|}{CH_3}} \qquad \underset{\text{isobutylene}}{\overset{|}{CH_3}} \qquad \underset{\text{isooctane}}{\overset{|}{CH_3}}$$

$$\Delta H^{\circ}_{298} = -18{,}775 \qquad \Delta F^{\circ}_{298} = -7156$$

Catalysts used commercially for alkylation include aluminum chloride, sulfuric acid and anhydrous hydrogen fluoride. The reactions are strongly exothermic, and temperature control is extremely important. For example, when sulfuric acid is used as catalyst, temperatures over 70°F result in substantial oxidation of the hydrocarbons. Aluminum chloride and anhydrous HF will permit higher temperatures, although the octane number of the alkylate decreases with increasing temperature of alkylation.

Commercially, the catalyst, olefin and a substantial excess of isobutane are pumped under pressure to a reactor which thoroughly mixes the catalyst and the liquid hydrocarbons. The catalyst is then separated in a settler, the hydrocarbon layer is distilled in a deisobutanizer, the isobutane is recycled to the reactor, and the alkylate further distilled and treated to produce a stabilized alkylate. The octane number of the product is of the order of 100 or more, depending on the relative fraction of propylene and butylene in the feed.

(2) Isomerization. Isomerization is a fairly recent method of improving the octane number of gasoline. The process consists essentially of passing a mixture of straight-chain paraffins over a catalyst to produce the corresponding isoparaffins. The catalysts which have been used include platinum and aluminum chloride activated with HCl. Both liquid and vapor phase processes are used, temperatures ranging from 150-900°F and pressures from 150-1000 psig.

(3) Hydrotreating. Hydrotreating is a hydrogenation process which is of increasing importance because of the availability of by-product hydrogen from catalytic reforming. The process is usually carried out in the vapor phase, using a platinum catalyst. Operating conditions vary considerably, temperatures ranging up to 850°F and pressures ranging from 50-3000 psig. Although straight-run naphtha has been the most common feedstock, the process can be used for fractions ranging from gas to heavy residual oils. The chief purposes of hydrotreating are for desulfurization, denitration, to saturate olefins to prevent gum formation, and improve odor, color and stability.

(4) Refining of Lubricating Oils. Although lubricants constitute only about 2 per cent of finished petroleum products, they are a fairly high-profit item. One of the chief requirements of a lubricating oil is that it must have a small change in viscosity with temperature as measured by the viscosity index. Most lubricating oils are now made by solvent extraction of a feedstock having the proper viscosity and lubricating oil components. Furfural and phenol are the two solvents most commonly used to separate the undesirable sulfur, aromatic and naphthenic components from the charge stock. The resulting oil is then dewaxed by extraction with a solvent such as methyl ethyl ketone to remove the heavy paraffin wax which would cause the oil to set at low temperatures.

(5) Molecular Sieves. Although not usually classed as a refining operation, the use of molecular sieves to produce chemical raw materials has become increasingly important in the HPI. A molecular sieve[1] is a synthetic crystalline zeolite consisting of hydrated sodium aluminum silicate or calcium aluminum silicate. The zeolites are commercially available in the form of a crystalline powder which has been pelletized to tablets of 1/16 to 1/8-in. diameter. The remarkable feature of the molecular sieves is the fact that they contain extremely uniform pores of molecular dimensions which can be controlled to a diameter of 4, 5 or 10 Angstroms. A molecule can be adsorbed in these pores or holes only if the molecule has the proper size and polarity. Thus, molecular

---

[1] See chapter by R. A. Jones in "Advances in Petroleum Chemistry and Refining," edited by J. J. McKetta, Jr., Vol. 4, New York, Interscience Publishers, Inc., 1961.

sieves can be used to separate materials which are extremely difficult to separate by more conventional techniques.

Examples of the use of molecular sieves are as follows: (1) Drying of liquid or gas streams. Molecular sieves have a strong affinity for the polar water molecule, and can be used to remove moisture from hydrocarbons and from chemical liquids. Thus, process streams containing several thousand ppm of moisture can be dried to approximately 1-30 ppm. (2) Removal of carbon dioxide and sulfur compounds. Molecular sieves have a strong affinity for carbon dioxide, hydrogen sulfide and sulfur dioxide, and can be used to remove these materials from process streams. (3) Separation of normal paraffins from branched chains. Molecular sieves can be used to adsorb normal paraffins from a mixture of paraffins, naphthenes, and aromatics. Thus, Universal Oil Products Co. has developed the Molex process for increasing the octane number of gasoline by adsorbing out the straight chains which have poor knock qualities. Of even more importance to the chemical industry is the use of molecular sieves to separate normal paraffins for the manufacture of "soft" detergents which are based on straight chain paraffins.

Molecular sieves are used commercially in conventional fixed-bed adsorption-desorption systems. The feed is passed through the zeolite until it is saturated, and the zeolite is then regenerated by heating to 350-600°F and blowing with purge gas to remove the adsorbed material. Heat may be supplied either by heating the purge gas in an external heater or by the use of heaters which are placed directly in the beds themselves.

## AROMATICS FROM PETROLEUM

We have already seen that the continually increasing demand for benzene has resulted in the recovery of substantial quantities of aromatics from petroleum. Although straight-run naphtha may contain 10 per cent or more aromatics, catalytic reforming and catalytic cracking greatly increase the quantity of aromatics present, and cracked or reformed cycle stocks may contain 40-60 per cent aromatics. However, even with the increased production of aromatics from petroleum, only a fairly small percentage of the total aromatics present are now recovered for chemical purposes, and most simply go into the blended gasoline to improve the octane number. Thus, if necessary, the HPI could fairly easily expand the production of aromatics to several times the present rate.

However, there is one major problem in the production of aromatics from petroleum. We have seen that in the production of by-product coke, the temperatures are so high that benzene is the chief component of the light oil, the toluene and xylenes being present in smaller amounts. This distribution is fortunately very close to the market demand for these aromatics. However, petroleum aromatization is carried out at such a low temperature that the product distribution is about 10 per cent benzene, 40 per cent toluene and 50 per cent xylenes, which is entirely different from the market demand. Thus, it is economic to convert toluene and possibly also xylenes to benzene by dealkylation in order to increase the supply of benzene. Also the rerun bottoms from catalytic reforming may contain 60 per cent or more naphthalene plus methylnaphthalenes, and these also may be dealkylated to produce naphthalene.

At the present time,[1] only the virgin aromatics and those produced from catalytic reforming are recovered to any appreciable extent by the HPI. Although substantial quantities of aromatics are present in naphthas from catalytic cracking, these have not been recovered because of the presence of large quantities of olefins and sulfur compounds which make the separation of the aromatics more difficult and cause problems in the use of these materials as feedstocks for dealkylation.

## Thermodynamics and Kinetics

Let us consider now in more detail the reactions involved in the cyclization and aromatization of hydrocarbons. Consider the following types of reactions: (1) paraffins to naphthenes; (2) paraffins to olefins + hydrogen; (3) olefins to aromatics + hydrogen; (4) naphthenes to aromatics + hydrogen; (5) paraffins to olefin + paraffin; (6) alkyl cyclopentanes to cyclohexanes. Free energies as a function of temperature are plotted in Fig. 9-4. The following general conclusions may be drawn:

(1) Although benzene and other aromatics are extremely unstable at room temperature, at temperatures greater than about 500°F the aromatics become the most stable hydrocarbons. At temperatures greater than about 800°F, the aromatics become so stable that even the presence of substantial quantities of hydrogen has little effect on the conversion of naphthenes to aromatics.

(2) There is little tendency for paraffins to be converted to olefins below about 1000°F.

(3) Thermal cracking of the paraffins becomes increasingly favorable as temperature increases. In practice, the amount of cracking can be controlled by the use of the proper catalyst.

(4) Even though the aromatization of the naphthenes goes virtually to

[1] See chapter by J. L. Edgar in H. Steiner, "Introduction to Petroleum Chemicals," Oxford, Pergamon Press, Inc., 1961; "Hydrodealkylation Processes," *Ind. Eng. Chem.*, 54(2), 28 (1962); chapter by H. Steiner in P. H. Emmett, "Catalysis, Vol. IV," New York, Rheinhold Publishing Corp., 1956; chapter by P. D. Meek in "Advances in Petroleum Chemistry and Refining," edited by J. J. McKetta, New York, Interscience Publishers, Inc., 1961.

completion at the temperatures used commercially, these reactions are strongly endothermic.

The production of aromatics during catalytic reforming results from two general types of reaction. The first involves isomerization and de-

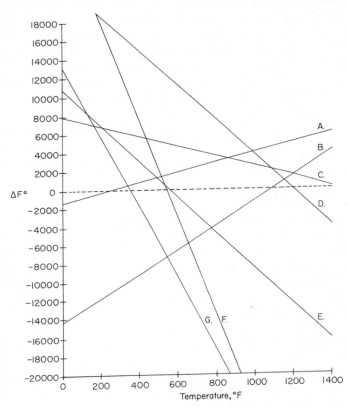

Fig. 9-4. Thermodynamics of hydrocarbon reactions. (From A.P.I. Project 44)

A— Methylcyclopentane →
    Cyclohexane
B— 1-Hexene → Cyclohexane
C— n-Hexane → Cyclohexane
    + $H_2$
D— n-Hexane → 1-Hexene
    + $H_2$

E— n-Hexane → 1-Butylene
    + Ethylene
F— Cyclohexane → Benzene
    +$3H_2$
G— 1-Hexene → Benzene
    + $3H_2$

hydrogenation of naphthenes present in the feedstock. These reactions are fairly rapid; thus, the relative quantities of benzene and cyclohexane in the product are very close to the equilibrium value. The dehydrogenation of cyclohexane has been studied recently by Bridges[1] who

[1] J. M. Bridges, *et al., J. Phys. Chem.*, **66**, 871 (1962).

found that the rate of dehydrogenation on a chromia catalyst is approximately first-order with an activation energy of about 30,000. The dehydrogenation reaction is strongly dependent on the use of the proper catalyst; thus, Bridges found that aluminum oxide, an acid catalyst, produced no benzene but merely cracked the cyclohexane.

The cyclization reactions of the paraffins are much more complex, and equilibrium is not attained during commercial operations. There appears to be good evidence that olefins are intermediates in the cyclization. Thus, in the conversion of *n*-heptane to toluene, it has been postulated that the reaction mechanism is as follows:

$$\text{heptane} \rightarrow \text{adsorbed heptane} \rightarrow \text{adsorbed heptene} \rightarrow \text{toluene}$$
$$\uparrow \qquad \qquad \downarrow$$
$$\text{heptene in gas phase}$$

The limiting reaction appears to be the conversion of heptane to heptene; once this is accomplished, there is fairly rapid conversion of heptene to toluene.

However, the situation is even more complex because it has been shown that the rate of cyclization also depends on the position of the double bond. Thus, olefins with a double bond located in the center of the molecule are less reactive than those with the double bond near the end of the molecule. Evidently the molecule attaches itself to the catalyst by a two-point contact across the double bond, and cyclization occurs only if the tail of the molecule bends around to form a closed ring. Thus, *n*-hexene-1 can be cyclized directly; however, *n*-hexene-2 can be cyclized only after isomerization to *n*-hexene-1.

The rate of dehydrocyclization of paraffins[1] depends strongly on the molecular weight of the paraffin. Thus, a $C_6$ paraffin will not be converted to a naphthene under normal reforming conditions. The rate of cyclization of a $C_7$ paraffin is small, but a $C_8$ paraffin will cyclize at more than twice the rate of the $C_7$ paraffin, and a $C_{10}$ paraffin will cyclize at about five times the rate of the $C_7$ paraffin.

## Recovery of Aromatics

If reforming is carried out primarily for aromatics production, a feedstock is selected which has any benzene, toluene and xylene which were present in the original crude oil plus naphthenes which yield aromatics on dehydrogenation plus $C_7$ to $C_{10}$ paraffins which can be cyclized to aromatics. A typical feed for aromatics production might contain on a volume basis 50 per cent paraffins, 40-45 per cent naphthenes and 5-10 per cent aromatics. Catalytic reforming will convert this to about 53

[1] A. B. Groh, *et al.,* Fifth World Petroleum Congress, May 30, 1959.

per cent paraffins, 0-5 per cent naphthenes and 42-47 per cent aromatics. Normally the conversion of naphthenes to aromatics is of the order of 90 per cent or more; the conversion of paraffins to aromatics is fairly small, but may increase the total yield of aromatics by the order of 10 per cent or more.

Different processes may be used to recover the aromatics from the reformer product including distillation, solvent extraction, adsorption and crystallization. Straight fractional distillation is unsatisfactory because benzene forms azeotropes with several naphthenes and paraffins; in addition, there are so many other compounds present which have boiling points close to those of the aromatics that the relative volatilities are too small to effectively separate them. However, by the addition of a third component, the relative volatilities of the aromatics can be increased sufficiently to permit a separation by distillation. Thus azeotropic distillation using a methyl ethyl ketone-water solution has been used to separate toluene, and extractive distillation using phenol has been used to separate benzene and toluene.

However, the process which is now used almost exclusively for the separation of aromatics from reformed gasoline is solvent extraction using

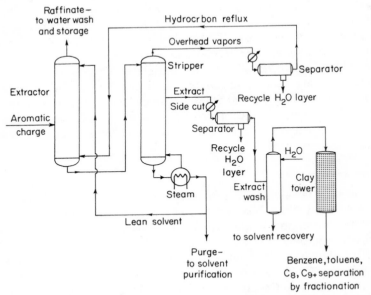

FIG. 9-5. Udex extraction process. (*Courtesy Universal Oil Products Co.*)

either liquid sulfur dioxide or aqueous diethylene glycol as a selective solvent. The sulfur dioxide double-extraction process was used during the war for the production of toluene for explosives manufacture.[1] The product from catalytic reforming containing 21-28 per cent toluene was extracted with liquid sulfur dioxide at $-32°C$ to yield an extract containing 65-70 per cent toluene. The extract was then washed with a heavy petroleum fraction which had a high selectivity for nonaromatics, and thus further concentrated the toluene in the extract. Toluene was recovered by distillation, and the sulfur dioxide recycled to the extraction unit.

In the case of toluene and the xylenes, the sulfur dioxide process has certain advantages, particularly in recovery. However, the Udex process is most commonly used to extract benzene. This process is illustrated in Fig. 9-5 and Table 9-3 gives typical analyses before and after extraction.

TABLE 9-3.  AROMATICS FROM WEST TEXAS CRUDE OIL REFINING*
(All Compositions in Volume Per Cent)

| Component | Sour West Texas Naphtha (%) | Sweet West Texas Naphtha (%) | Typical Reformate (%) | Typical Aromatic Concentrate (%) |
|---|---|---|---|---|
| Initial boil. pt., 149°F | 5.96 | 2.90 | Depentized | Trace |
| $C_6$ Paraffins | 5.16 | 4.29 | 5.89 | — |
| Methylcyclopentane | 3.43 | 1.48 | 2.35 | Trace |
| Cyclohexane | 3.52 | 2.15 | 0.41 | — |
| Benzene | 1.97 | 0.70 | 6.51 | 12.50 |
| $C_7$ Naphthenes | 16.05 | 17.27 | 1.87 | — |
| $C_7$ Paraffins | 11.58 | 15.94 | 13.23 | — |
| Toluene | 4.39 | 2.35 | 18.63 | 35.72 |
| $C_8$ Naphthenes | 15.18 | 14.06 | — | — |
| $C_8$ Paraffins | 13.45 | 10.09 | 15.37 | — |
| $C_8$ Aromatics | 4.64 | 4.57 | 20.08 | 38.50 |
| $C_{9+}$ | 14.67 | 24.20 | 15.66 | 13.28 |

* Data from P. D. Meek, "Advances in Petroleum Chemistry and Refining," edited by J. J. McKetta, Jr., New York, Interscience Publishers. Inc., 1961.

Note that the aromaticity of the extract is almost 100 per cent. The process consists essentially of extracting the aromatics with a diethylene glycol-water solution containing about 8-10 per cent $H_2O$ at a temperature of about 300°F, using a solvent weight ratio from 8:1 to as high as 15:1. Aromatics are stripped from the solvent by distillation, treated with clay to remove olefins and improve color and separated into pure fractions by distillation. Although the selectivity of the solvent is in-

[1] C. H. Marshall, *Chem. Eng. Progr.*, **46**, 313 (1950).

creased by the addition of water, this decreases the solubility of the aromatics so that in practice a balance must be made between better selectivity and higher distillation costs resulting from an increase in the required solvent ratio. During commercial operation,[1] benzene recovery of 99 per cent or more, toluene recovery of 96-99 per cent, xylene recovery of 85-93 per cent, and $C_9$ recovery of about 70 per cent have been reported. Nitration-grade benzene (1°C boiling range) can be made by the Udex process whereas sulfur dioxide extraction does not yield nitration-grade benzene because too many nonaromatics boiling in the benzene range are left in the extract.

### Purification of Aromatics

Benzene and toluene are separated from the aromatics extract by conventional fractional distillation. However, as illustrated in Table 9-4, the $C_8$ aromatics are much harder to separate because there are

TABLE 9-4. PHYSICAL PROPERTIES OF AROMATICS

| Compound | Boiling Point (°F) | Freezing Point (°F) |
|---|---|---|
| Benzene | 176.2 | +42.0 |
| Toluene | 231.1 | −139.0 |
| o-Xylene | 291.9 | −13.3 |
| m-Xylene | 282.4 | −54.2 |
| p-Xylene | 281.0 | +55.9 |
| Ethylbenzene | 277.1 | −138.9 |

four isomers having similar properties. All of these isomers are produced in large quantities by catalytic reforming; a limited market exists for all of them, provided they can be separated in sufficient purity.

The one isomer for which there is virtually an unlimited market is ethylbenzene which serves as a raw material for the manufacture of styrene. Although most ethylbenzene has been produced by the alkylation of benzene, in recent years it has also been recovered from mixed xylenes. Although there is only about a 4°F difference between the boiling point of ethylbenzene and the lowest boiling xylene, the ethylbenzene can be separated by superfractionation using 300-350 trays and a reflux ratio ranging from 60:1 to 80:1. The fractionating column is split into three 200-ft sections connected in series. The purity of the product is better than 99 per cent, and ethylbenzene in the bottoms ranges from 1-5 per cent, depending on operating conditions. Because of the high reflux ratio and the fact that the relative volatility is very close to unity, the operation of the distillation column has several unique features. Thus,

[1] H. W. Grote, *Chem. Eng. Progr.*, **54**(8), 43 (1958).

the holdup or inventory of liquid in the column is equivalent to several days' production of product, and the column responds very slowly to any change in the operating conditions. For example, even a minor change in temperature, pressure, feed rate or feed composition may require several days of operation before steady-state conditions are reestablished.

The other isomer which has a substantial market is $o$-xylene which can be oxidized to phthalic anhydride. The $o$-xylene is the highest boiling isomer, and can be separated by fractional distillation to give a purity of 95 per cent or better. From 100-150 trays are required, with a reflux ratio of from 15:1 to 20:1. It was first produced commercially in 1945 by Oronite Chem. Co., and is now available from many manufacturers.

The $p$-xylene is almost impossible to separate by distillation, but can be separated by fractional crystallization since the freezing point is substantially higher than that of the other isomers. The chief disadvantage of crystallization is the fairly low recovery of about 70 per cent, which prevents the production of high-purity $m$-xylene from the mother liquor. However the yield of $p$-xylene can be increased by combining crystallization with isomerization. Thus if the $p$-xylene mother liquor is passed over an isomerization catalyst ($Al_2O_3$-$SiO_2$ containing 0.5-1.5% Pt) at 900°F and 175 psig in the presence of hydrogen, a substantial fraction of the ortho and meta xylenes will be converted to the para form. In fact, with recycle the $o$-xylene and $m$-xylene can be isomerized practically to extinction to produce a $p$-xylene product of 99 per cent purity. The chief use of $p$-xylene is in the manufacture of terephthalic acid, an important intermediate for the manufacture of polymers such as "Dacron" and "Mylar."

The $m$-xylene is produced commercially only by Oronite Chem. Co., which uses the material to produce isophthalic acid. However, no details have been released about the process used by Oronite. Because of the very limited chemical market for $m$-xylene, most of the material is not recovered but simply goes into solvents or gasoline blending stocks.

Many $C_9$, $C_{10}$ and heavier aromatics are also present in the reformate. The only $C_9$ isomer to receive much attention is pseudocumene (1,2,4-trimethylbenzene) which can be separated by fractional distillation of the $C_9$ fraction, using about 130 trays and a 13:1 reflux ratio. The $C_{10}$ isomer of most interest is durene (1,2,4,5-tetramethylbenzene) which can be separated by crystallization because of its high melting point of 175°F. At present, the demand for the heavier aromatics is so small that large-scale recovery is not warranted. However, these aromatics do serve as an enormous potential source of chemical raw materials if the markets ever should develop.

## HYDRODEALKYLATION

As was discussed previously, aromatization of petroleum to produce benzene yields large quantities of toluene, xylenes and heavier aromatics for which there is a limited market except as a solvent or gasoline additive. Hydrodealkylation[1] can be used to convert toluene and xylenes to benzene and to convert methylnaphthalenes to naphthalene. Various processes have been developed which permit a variety of feeds including toluene, xylenes, alkyl benzenes, reformate and aromatic stock from catalytic cracking. The reactions are carried out at temperatures of 1000-1400°F, pressures up to 1000 psig, and in the presence of hydrogen gas. From 60-90 per cent conversion of the alkyl aromatics to the parent aromatic compound is obtained per pass, and both catalytic and non-catalytic processes have been developed. Although the type of catalyst used commercially for dealkylation has not been disclosed, it is known that this type of reaction is catalyzed by acid catalysts. Recent patents indicate that the catalyst is probably either alumina-silica or alumina-chromia, which may be activated with small amounts of chloride.

If the dealkylation is carried out thermally without using a catalyst and in the absence of hydrogen, the dealkylation is a first-order homogeneous reaction having an activation energy of 77,500 cal/mole for the removal of a methyl group from the ring. The products are fairly complex, including substantial quantities of both lighter and heavier molecules. Thermal dealkylation in the presence of hydrogen but without the use of a catalyst is also a first-order reaction, but has an activation energy of only about 50,000. Here the rate-controlling step appears to be the dissociation of the hydrogen molecule, which would imply an activation energy of 54,000. If the dealkylation is carried out catalytically in the presence of hydrogen, the rate equations for toluene, xylenes and methylnaphthalenes all have the same form. Thus, they are all first-order with respect to the aromatic and half-order with respect to hydrogen. The activation energy for the removal of a methyl group is in each case equal to 35,400 cal. The reaction always occurs at the aromatic-aliphatic bond. Thus, xylene is first dealkylated to toluene and then to benzene; ethylbenzene is dealkylated directly to benzene.

[1] A recent survey is given in *Ind. Eng. Chem.*, **54**(2), 28 (1962); also see A. H. Weiss, *et al.*, *Hydro. Proc. Petrol. Refiner*, **41**(6), 185 (1962); A. H. Weiss and L. C. Doelp, *Ind. Eng. Chem. Process Design Develop.*, **3**(1), 73 (1964); W. D. Betts and F. Popper, *J. Appl. Chem.*, **8**, 509 (1958); G. F. Asselin, chapter in "Advances in Petroleum Chemistry and Refining," edited by J. J. McKetta, Jr., Vol. 9, New York Interscience Publishers, Inc., 1964.

## Thermodynamics

All the dealkylation reactions are exothermic with the equilibrium lying far to the right at the temperatures used commercially. The reaction is unaffected by pressure if the gases are ideal. Thus, in the dealkylation of toluene

$$\text{C}_6\text{H}_5\text{—CH}_3 + \text{H}_2 \rightarrow \text{CH}_4 + \text{C}_6\text{H}_6$$

$$\Delta H^\circ_{1000} = -12{,}508 \qquad \Delta F^\circ_{1000} = -9440$$

For example, in the Houdry DETOL process, the conversion of toluene to benzene is reported to be as high as 96 per cent. The purity of the benzene is about 99.95 per cent $C_6H_6$ with only 0.2 ppm of thiophene. Only equilibrium quantities (0.01–0.05 mole per cent) of cyclohexane are observed in the product benzene. There is some condensation of benzene to biphenyl and some coke formation, although this is inhibited by the presence of hydrogen. The catalyst will last approximately a year before it must be regenerated.

Actually, the use of a catalyst in dealkylation is of marginal value. Better yields and higher selectivity are presumably obtained with a catalyst, but this must be balanced against the additional cost of the catalyst plus the regeneration costs. It is of interest to note that about half the commercial processes are catalytic and half are noncatalytic.

*CHAPTER 10*

# Manufacture of Olefins

Most of the synthetic organic chemicals produced commercially in the United States are based on ethylene and propylene. These two petrochemical raw materials are usually made by thermal dehydrogenation of ethane and propane. Although the production of olefins is in some ways more or less of an empirical art, sufficient information has been released to discuss the basic features of the various processes which are used commercially.

### PRODUCTION OF ETHYLENE

Ethylene is by far the most important petrochemical raw material. Thus, Fig. 10-1 illustrates the rapid growth of ethylene in the United States in recent years. Ethylene is made commercially by dehydrogenating ethane according to the reaction

$$C_2H_6 \text{ (g)} \rightleftharpoons C_2H_4 \text{ (g)} + H_2 \text{ (g)}$$

$$\Delta H^{\circ}_{298} = +32{,}822 \qquad \Delta F^{\circ}_{298} = +24{,}142 \qquad (10\text{-}1)$$

$$\Delta H^{\circ}_{1100} = +34{,}520 \qquad \Delta F^{\circ}_{1100} = -1120$$

The reaction is strongly endothermic, and must be carried out at temperatures of the order of 1500°F (1090°K) to obtain any substantial conversion to ethylene. The reaction is favored by low pressure. The equilibrium constant in atmospheres is

$$K_p = \frac{P_{C_2H_4}P_{H_2}}{P_{C_2H_6}} \qquad (10\text{-}2)$$

Values of $K_p$ calculated from thermal data are plotted in Fig. 10-2 with

202

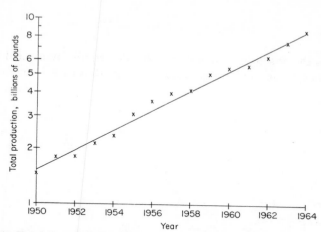

FIG. 10-1. Total United States production of ethylene in recent years. (United States Tariff Commission, "Synthetic Organic Chemicals.")

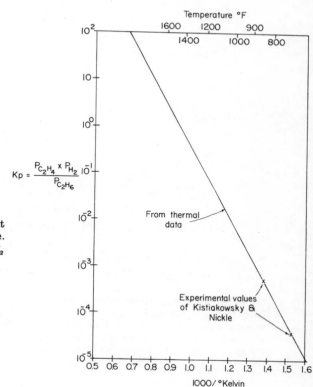

FIG. 10-2. Equilibrium constant for dehydrogenation of ethane.

$$C_2H_6 \rightarrow C_2H_4 + H_2$$

experimental data of Kistiakowsky and Nickle.* A straight line is obtained in which the logarithm of $K_p$ to the base 10 is given by the equation

$$\log K_p = 7.046 - \frac{7495}{T} \tag{10-3}$$

where $T$ is the absolute temperature, °K. The equilibrium yield of ethylene at atmospheric pressure is plotted in Fig. 10-3 as a function of tem-

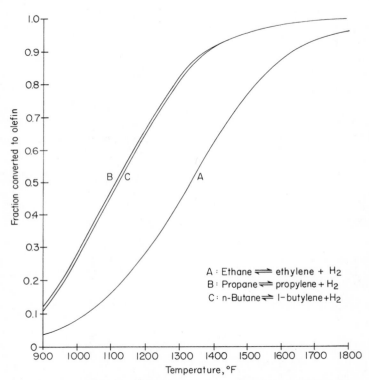

Fɪɢ. 10-3. Equilibrium yields of ethylene, propylene, and butylene.

perature. Similar data are also given for other olefins. Note that the equilibrium is least favorable in the case of ethylene.

* Values of $K_p$ are calculated from free energies tabulated by the American Petroleum Institute, Research Project 44. Experimental values of $K_p$ are from B. Kistiakowsky and A. G. Nickle, *Discussions Faraday Soc.*, **10**, 175 (1951). According to Kistiakowsky, there is some question as to the accuracy of the other experimental values of $K_p$ reported in the literature.

If propane is used as feedstock, the principal reaction at 1500°F is

$$C_3H_8 \rightarrow CH_4 + C_2H_4$$

$$\Delta H^{\circ}_{298} = +19,427 \qquad \Delta F^{\circ}_{298} = +9756 \qquad \Delta F^{\circ}_{1100} = -15,960$$

with the competing reaction

$$C_3H_8 \rightleftharpoons H_2 + C_3H_6$$

$$\Delta H^{\circ}_{298} = +29,699 \qquad \Delta F^{\circ}_{298} = +20,604 \qquad \Delta F^{\circ}_{1100} = -5560$$

If butane is used as feedstock, the chief reaction is probably a cracking to ethane and ethylene, followed by further dehydrogenation of the ethane. However, methane, propane, propylene and higher hydrocarbons are also produced. If naphtha is used as feedstock, the reactions obviously become even more complex. However, by proper control of the temperature and time of cracking, butane and naphtha may be cracked to yield a gas containing 25 per cent or more of ethylene.

Note that only small amounts of acetylene are formed at the temperatures employed for the manufacture of ethylene. Possible reactions are as follows:

$$C_2H_4 \rightleftharpoons H_2 + C_2H_2$$

$$\Delta H^{\circ}_{298} = +41,698 \qquad \Delta F^{\circ}_{298} = +33,718 \qquad \Delta F^{\circ}_{1100} = +9179$$

$$C_3H_6 \rightleftharpoons H_2 + CH_3-C{\equiv}CH$$

$$\Delta H^{\circ}_{298} = +39,440 \qquad \Delta F^{\circ}_{298} = +31,323 \qquad \Delta F^{\circ}_{1100} = +7420$$

The acetylene reactions are strongly endothermic, and the yield of acetylene is not significant below temperatures of about 2000°F.

## Side Reactions

Numerous side reactions are possible, some of which act to reduce the yield of ethylene. Examples are

$$C_2H_6 + H_2 \rightarrow 2CH_4$$

$$\Delta H^{\circ}_{298} = -15,542 \qquad \Delta F^{\circ}_{298} = -16,420 \qquad \Delta F^{\circ}_{1100} = -16,840$$

$$C_2H_4 + C_2H_6 \rightarrow C_3H_6 + CH_4$$

$$\Delta H^{\circ}_{298} = -5270 \qquad \Delta F^{\circ}_{298} = -5572 \qquad \Delta F^{\circ}_{1100} = -6440$$

In practice, the dehydrogenation of ethane is carried out at a temperature of about 1500°F which is equal to approximately 1100°K. Under these conditions, the equilibrium is favorable for the production of methane, propane, propylene, etc., by side reactions. Thus, the success of the industrial dehydrogenation of ethane is dependent on the achievement of partial equilibrium in the ethane-ethylene reaction, but without any substantial equilibrium in any of the side reactions of ethane and ethylene.

Usually a problem such as this could be solved by the use of the proper catalyst to promote the desired reaction and inhibit side reactions. Considerable work has been carried out on the catalytic dehydrogenation of paraffins, and catalysts such as alumina-chromia have been found to favor most of the reactions. However, in the case of ethane, the temperatures required from equilibrium considerations are so high that the rate of the dehydrogenation reaction is not a problem. Although a catalyst could conceivably cut down on side reactions, the catalysts which have been investigated have not been found to appreciably reduce side reactions. In view of the fact that a catalyst is expensive, increases the size and cost of equipment, and would have to be periodically regenerated because substantial quantities of coke are formed during the dehydrogenation of ethane, the use of a catalyst commercially has not been warranted.

Table 10-1 gives typical compositions obtained when ethane, propane and butane are cracked thermally to produce ethylene. Note that the

TABLE 10-1. TYPICAL COMPOSITIONS OF CRACKED GASES*

| Furnace feed, mole % | | | | | | |
|---|---|---|---|---|---|---|
| $C_2H_4$ | 0.6 | 0.6 | 1.5 | 1.8 | — | — |
| $C_2H_6$ | 99.3 | 99.2 | 96.8 | 96.4 | 0.5 | — |
| $C_3H_6$ | 0.1 | 0.2 | 1.4 | 1.4 | — | — |
| $C_3H_8$ | — | — | 0.3 | 0.4 | 98.1 | 0.1 |
| $n\text{-}C_4H_{10}$ | — | — | — | — | 1.4 | 97.2 |
| iso-$C_4H_{10}$ | — | — | — | — | — | 2.5 |
| $C_5H_{12}$ | — | — | — | — | — | 0.2 |
| Moles $H_2O$/100 moles feed | 15.0 | 40.3 | 30.0 | 94.0 | 45 | 32 |
| Outlet pressure, psig | 8.5 | 8.3 | 27.5 | 27.5 | 8.5 | 9.1 |
| Outlet temperature, °F | 1496 | 1532 | 1490 | 1525 | 1495 | 1500 |
| Conversion products | | | | | | |
| $H_2$ | 31.8 | 37.8 | 29.8 | 36.9 | 13.1 | 11.4 |
| $CH_4$ | 3.8 | 6.5 | 5.8 | 10.9 | 37.4 | 37.5 |
| $C_2H_2$ | 0.2 | 0.3 | 0.2 | 0.3 | 0.3 | 0.4 |
| $C_2H_4$ | 30.5 | 35.8 | 30.1 | 33.8 | 28.9 | 28.6 |
| $C_2H_6$ | 32.6 | 18.0 | 32.8 | 16.6 | 7.0 | 6.4 |
| $C_3H_6$ | 0.6 | 0.9 | 0.7 | 0.7 | 6.8 | 11.1 |
| $C_3H_8$ | 0.2 | 0.2 | 0.2 | 0.1 | 5.4 | 0.6 |
| $C_4H_{10}$ | | | | | 0.2 | 2.2 |
| $C_4H_8 + C_4H_6$ | } 0.3 | 0.5 | 0.4 | 0.7 | 0.9 | 1.8 |
| Moles/100 moles feed | 147.4 | 162.5 | 144.8 | 160.1 | 176.3 | 215.2 |
| $C_{5+}$ liquid and carbon, wt. % of feed | 1.0 | 2.0 | 1.9 | 5.9 | 10.3 | 13.0 |
| Conversion, % of feed | 51.7 | 70.5 | 50.9 | 72.8 | 90.2 | 95.0 |
| Equilibrium approach | 0.324 | 0.541 | 0.49 | 0.78 | 0.49 | 0.51 |

* Data from H. C. Schutt, *Chem. Eng. Progr.*, **55**(1), 68 (1959).

products range from hydrogen to $C_5$ and greater. These data are commonly analyzed in terms of what is referred to as the "equilibrium approach." This is obtained by dividing the apparent equilibrium constant calculated from the total pressure and the composition of the gas by the theoretical value of $K_p$ at the given temperature. The equilibrium approach is a measure of the plausibility of the yield data and also indicates the extent to which side reactions have occurred.

### Kinetics

The kinetics of the dehydrogenation of paraffins have been widely studied [1] because the reactions are of both theoretical and commercial interest. The decomposition of ethane is a chain reaction in which the chain carriers are hydrogen atoms and ethyl radicals. Thus, the decomposition chain is as follows:

$$H^{\bullet} + C_2H_6 \rightarrow H_2 + C_2H_5^{\bullet}$$
$$C_2H_5^{\bullet} \rightarrow H^{\bullet} + C_2H_4 \quad \text{etc.}$$

The decomposition is first-order with an over-all activation energy of about 75,000 cal/mole. However, in practice, the cracking of a hydrocarbon feedstock to ethylene is deliberately controlled so that equilibrium is not attained in the ethane dehydrogenation reaction. This is done to prevent excessive side reactions which decrease the yield of ethylene and increase the deposition of coke in the cracking furnaces.

## COMMERCIAL PRODUCTION OF ETHYLENE

In the United States, it is customary to manufacture ethylene by a straight thermal cracking of hydrocarbons such as ethane, propane and butane. A typical process[2] is illustrated in Fig. 10-4. Refinery off-gases consisting chiefly of methane, ethane, ethylene, propane and propylene are mixed with cracked gas from the cracking furnaces and compressed to 100-200 psig by means of a multistage centrifugal compressor equipped with interstage coolers and liquid separators. The compressed gas is scrubbed with ethanolamine to remove acidic impurities such as $H_2S$, COS and $CO_2$, and a caustic scrubber acts as a cleanup unit to remove the last traces of sulfur. If the acid gas concentration in the feed is low, sometimes the ethanolamine absorber is omitted and the entire job done by caustic.

[1] For example, see C. Hinshelwood, *et al., Proc. Roy. Soc. (London)*, **A214, 471** (1952); **A271,** 34 (1963); E. W. R. Steacie, "Atomic and Free Radical Reactions," 2'nd Edition, New York, Reinhold Publishing Corp., 1954.
[2] C. H. Davenport, *Hydrocarbon Proc. Petrol. Refiner,* **39** (3), **125** (1960).

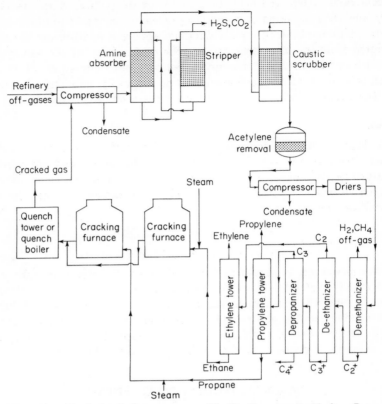

FIG. 10-4. Typical ethylene process. [C. H. Davenport, *Hydro. Proc. Petrol. Refiner,* **39** (3), 125 (1960)].

If the ethylene product is to be used for the manufacture of poly-ethylene, acetylenic compounds must be reduced to about 20 ppm or less in the finished olefin. This can be accomplished in two general ways. If it is desired to recover the acetylene, the product ethylene stream can be scrubbed with a solvent such as dimethyl formamide and the acetylene recovered by a conventional absorption-desorption technique. In this case the acetylene becomes a by-product for credit. However, in most cases the acetylene is present in such small amounts that it is not worth recovering, but is simply destroyed by means of catalytic hydrogena-tion of the diolefins and acetylenes to monoolefins. Under these condi-tions, the purification unit is placed rather early in the process to take advantage of the hydrogen already present in the gas stream and to permit the subsequent recovery of any ethylene or propylene produced by the hydrogenation. Although various types of catalyst have been used, the best[1] appears to be a combination of nickel, cobalt and chromium on a rugged refractory base of alumina-silica. The preferred temperature range is 300-400°F for greatest selectivity; pressures have ranged from 50-500 psig and standard space velocities are normally from 1000-3000 ft$^3$/ (hr)(ft$^3$ catalyst). The concentration of acetylenic compounds can be reduced from several per cent to less than 5 ppm, with less than 1 per cent loss of ethylene by hydrogenation. Although the catalyst does have to be regenerated periodically, cycles of up to two years have been obtained in commercial operation.

After acetylene removal, the gas is further compressed to 400-600 psig, refrigerated to condense out moisture and heavier hydrocarbons, and sent through a battery of driers to reduce the moisture content to a very low level. Moisture removal is extremely important to prevent the formation of ice or solid hydrocarbon hydrates in the subsequent low-temperature fractionation towers. Activated alumina and silica gel are commonly used to remove moisture; in some modern plants, molecular sieves are also being used. A two-stage system has been used in some plants, a liquid such as triethylene glycol being used in the first stage to remove the bulk of the water, followed by activated alumina to act as final cleanup.

## Demethanizer

Hydrogen and methane are separated from the process gases and usually simply burned for fuel after heat exchange to recover their refrigeration value. This demethanization is the most critical operation in the recovery of ethylene, since any $C_2$ or higher hydrocarbons carrying over with the $H_2-CH_4$ mixture will be lost. Three general methods have been used to achieve this separation, namely, absorption in oil, hypersorption and low-temperature fractionation.

Oil absorption involves the use of a highly aromatic oil as a selective solvent to remove $C_2$ and higher paraffins, the hydrogen and methane passing through essentially unabsorbed. The absorption takes place at room temperature and at 450-500 psig, followed by desorption of the gases from the solvent at 430-460°F. The second method for demethanization was developed by Union Oil Co. of Calif., and is known as "hypersorption." This process involves the use of a moving bed of activated carbon to adsorb the $C_{2+}$ fraction from the mixed gas. Esso Research and Engineering Co. has slightly modified the process by the substitution of a fluid adsorbent; the modified process is known as the "fluid char adsorption" process (FCA).

[1] R. E. Reitmeier and H. W. Fleming, *Chem. Eng. Progr.*, **54**(12), 48 (1958).

Although both oil absorption and hypersorption have operated successfully, the process now used commercially for practically all new construction involves low temperature fractionation. In this process, the gas at a pressure of 400-600 psig is heat exchanged with various process streams and further refrigerated using propylene and ethylene refrigerants to condense most of the $C_{2+}$ hydrocarbons. The mixture of liquid and vapor then enters the demethanizer which maintains an overhead temperature of $-90$ to $-140°F$. By fractionation, using a fairly low reflux ratio and 20-30 trays, most of the methane and hydrogen are stripped from the liquid, and only small amounts of ethylene are present in the overhead product. Thus, in modern plants, the loss of ethylene in the overhead from the demethanizer is only about 4-5 per cent of the ethylene produced in the cracking furnaces.

The bottoms from the demethanizer pass to a second fractionator which separates the $C_2$ fraction from the $C_{3+}$ at a pressure of 200-400 psig, using 30-40 trays with an overhead temperature of 0 to $-10°F$. The $C_2$ overhead is then split into product ethylene and recycle ethane, using 50-60 trays with an overhead temperature of about $0°F$. If no acetylene removal facilities are employed, most of the acetylene appears in the ethylene stream. Any methane carrying through the demethanizer will also be present as a diluent in the product ethylene. However, under good operating conditions, the purity of the product ethylene may be as high as 99.9 per cent $C_2H_4$.

The $C_{3+}$ bottoms from the de-ethanizer may be handled in several ways. Depending on demand, the simplest method is to simply sell this fraction as LPG for fuel. A second alternative is to recycle this material through a cracking furnace to produce more ethylene. This is not particularly good practice since propylene is not the best ethylene feedstock. A third alternative is to pass this fraction through a catalytic polymerization unit to produce low molecular-weight polymers of propylene which may be used as a gasoline blending stock or as chemical raw materials. The fourth alternative is the one illustrated in Fig. 10-4, namely, to use two additional fractionators to separate propylene for use as a chemical raw material, propane for recycling to the cracking furnace, and a $C_{4+}$ fraction which can be used as a fuel.

Carbon steel is normally used as a material of construction for all equipment in the purification system except the demethanizer, which operates at such a low temperature that an impact-resistant material such as nickel or stainless steel must be used. Note that the simplified flow sheet illustrated in Fig. 10-4 omits all intermediate heat exchangers. The economic success of the low-temperature fractionation process is dependent on efficient recovery of refrigeration values from all process streams. Thus, in practice, elaborate heat exchange between the feeds and product streams is essential to reduce the power costs for the various refrigeration units.

## Cracking Furnaces

The cracking furnaces are normally of the tubular type in which the hydrocarbons are heated externally by direct firing of a suitable fuel gas. For maximum yield of ethylene, certain rather restrictive conditions must be met. First, the residence time in the furnace must be approximately 0.6-1.3 sec to maximize ethylene production while holding side reactions to a reasonable value. Second, the temperature must be carefully controlled to a value of about 1500°F for the cracked gas leaving the furnaces. Third, since the dehydrogenation of ethane is reversible, the cracked gases must be rapidly quenched to prevent a reduction in yield as a result of the back reaction. Fourth, there is always some carbon formation which coats the inside surface of the furnace tubes and thereby reduces the coefficient of heat transfer.

The yield of ethylene in the furnaces can be increased and carbon formation decreased by the addition of steam to the hydrocarbon feed to the furnaces. The weight ratio of steam to hydrocarbon varies from about 0.2:1 for cracking ethane and propane up to about 1:1 for cracking naphthas or gas oils. The four beneficial effects of steam are as follows: (1) The steam reduces the partial pressures of all gases present, and hence increases the conversion to ethylene since the dehydrogenation is favored by low pressures. (2) By increasing the volume of the gas, the residence time in the furnace is reduced. (3) Steam helps to keep the furnace tubes clean by reacting chemically with carbon to form carbon monoxide and hydrogen. (4) When naphthas or heavier feedstocks are used, any liquid hydrocarbon present in the feed to the furnace will greatly increase carbon deposition. Steam helps to achieve complete vaporization of these feedstocks, and thus reduces carbon formation.

The dehydrogenation of paraffins is a strongly endothermic reaction. In addition, the short residence time in the furnace plus the rapid quench of the reaction products require a high heat flux and steep temperature gradients. Cracking furnaces are usually designed with a convection section in the flue gas area to preheat (and also vaporize if naphtha is used) the feed, and with a radiation section to finish the heating of the hydrocarbon to the desired temperature and to supply the heat of reaction. The design of a cracking furnace is quite complicated because of the large number of simultaneous reactions which occur. Calculations are often made by a point-to-point determination of the temperature, pressure, and composition of the hydrocarbons as they pass through the tubes. The calculations can be simplified by the use of an analog computer[1] to simulate the conditions existing within the furnace; thus, Lichtenstein describes the design of a propane cracking furnace in which a computer was used to simulate 10 simultaneous chemical reactions and 14 material balances.

Cracking furnaces are commonly fabricated of seamless tubing, using 18-8 stainless steel as a material of construction.[2] Since the tubes in the radiant section of the furnace are exposed to the most severe conditions, these may be of a higher alloy such as "Incoloy," 21 per cent Cr and 34 per cent Ni. Coke deposits on the inside surface of the tubes during operation; this increases the pressure drop through the furnace and reduces the thermal conductivity of the tube wall with the danger that a "hot spot" may cause burnout of the tube. The deposited coke must be removed at intervals of one to several months by taking the unit out of service and blowing with steam or a mixture of air and steam at a temperature of about 1600°F to burn off the coke.

In addition to the conventional tubular furnace, other designs have been used in an effort to improve heat transfer to the hydrocarbons. Thus, Mobil Oil Co. and Phillips Petroleum have developed pebble heaters in which the hydrocarbons are cracked by direct contact with preheated pebbles which are cycled mechanically between the reactor and a pebble heater. This process has the advantage that extremely heavy feedstocks can be used, and the temperature can be increased to the point where both ethylene and acetylene are produced by the pyrolysis of the hydrocarbons. Fluidized sand and fluidized coke have also been used as a thermal cracking medium. Monsanto Chemical Co. uses a particularly novel method at Texas City, Texas to crack propane; here the cracking is achieved by bubbling propane gas through molten lead, which permits precise control of the cracking temperature.

### Quenchers

Hydrocarbons leaving the cracking furnace must be cooled rapidly to prevent reversal of the ethylene equilibrium. This is often accomplished simply by passing the hydrocarbons directly to a spray tower which cools the hot gas by direct contact with water or oil sprays. This also condenses out most of the steam plus any heavy hydrocarbons present in the cracked gas. In most modern plants, a "quench boiler" is used between the furnace and the spray tower to generate by-product steam.

---

[1] For example, I. Lichtenstein, "Design Cracking Furnaces by Computer," *Chem. Eng. Progr.*, **60**(12), 64 (1964).

[2] R. P. Schindelka, "Ethylene Manufacture at C-I-L Edmonton Works," paper presented at Canadian Natural Gas Processing Association meeting, Calgary, Dec. 5, 1963.

Also in some plants "in-line" quenchers have been used with or without a spray tower. In these plants, water or oil is sprayed directly into the hot cracked gas as it leaves the furnace, followed by a separator to separate the water, oil and gas phases.

## CRACKING OF HEAVIER HYDROCARBONS

Although ethane, propane and butane have served as the principal feedstocks in the United States, it is becoming increasingly common to use heavier fractions for the manufacture of ethylene. Thus, light distillates, naphthas, gas oils, fuel oils, crude oil and residual oils may be used, the most economical feedstock being determined by the availability of the particular hydrocarbon and the market for any by-products which may be produced.

The chief modification which must be made in the process to accommodate a heavier feedstock is in the design of the cracking furnaces. Thus, even though naphthas and gas oils are usually cracked in tubular furnaces, the design of the furnace will be different from one used to crack ethane. Very heavy feedstocks may require a preliminary distillation to remove nonvaporizable heavy ends. In some cases, complex feedstocks are split into several different fractions which are fed to separate cracking furnaces. This permits better control of the furnaces, since each operates on a more homogeneous feed. Coke deposition is more severe with the heavier feedstocks; for this reason, the steam to hydrocarbon ratio is increased to a weight ratio of about 1:1 for a gas oil or heavy naphtha. Table 10-2 gives typical results for the cracking of naphthas and light distillates.

In addition to the boiling point of the feedstock, the types of hydrocarbons present also affect the nature of the cracking pattern. Thus, aromatics are, in general, very difficult to crack and usually pass through the furnaces unchanged. Naphthenes can be cracked under special conditions, but have a strong tendency to dehydrogenate to aromatics rather than crack to olefins. Paraffins are by far the best cracking stock, especially the normal paraffins which tend to split near the middle of the molecule to give an olefin plus a lower-weight paraffin. The isoparaffins are not as good since they tend to split off methyl groups, which results in excessive production of methane.

The second modification which must be made when cracking a heavy feedstock is in the product recovery section. Because of the increased quantities of $C_3$ and heavier hydrocarbons in the cracked gases, additional fractionators are required to separate the $C_3$, $C_4$ and $C_{5+}$ fractions. The $C_4$ fraction is a particularly valuable by-product stream since it

TABLE 10-2. TYPICAL GAS COMPOSITIONS FROM CRACKING NAPHTHAS AND LIGHT DISTILLATES*

| | Light Distillate (89-215°F boiling range) | | Naphtha (215-430°F boiling range) | |
|---|---|---|---|---|
| Outlet temperature, °F | 1365 | 1410 | 1340 | 1405 |
| Pressure, psig | 12.5 | 15.3 | 13.6 | 15.0 |
| Steam/feed molar ratio | 3.05 | 7.5 | 3.5 | 8.2 |
| Composition of products, mole % | | | | |
| $H_2$ | 11.2 | 14.6 | 10.5 | 15.5 |
| $CH_4$ | 31.4 | 29.5 | 28.3 | 28.7 |
| $C_2H_2$ | 0.2 | 0.6 | 0.1 | 0.6 |
| $C_2H_4$ | 25.0 | 32.4 | 26.7 | 32.4 |
| $C_2H_6$ | 8.5 | 5.7 | 9.1 | 3.4 |
| $C_3H_6$ | 14.3 | 10.5 | 15.1 | 11.7 |
| $C_3H_8$ | 1.2 | 0.7 | 1.1 | 0.4 |
| $C_4H_6$ | 2.5 | 2.5 | 2.4 | 3.2 |
| $C_4H_8$ | 5.5 | 4.3 | 5.8 | 3.9 |
| $C_4H_{10}$ | 0.2 | 0.2 | 0.3 | 0.2 |
| Cracked distillate, wt % | | | | |
| $C_5$ to 375°F end point | 24.1 | 17.8 | 35.2 | 30.5 |
| Fuel oil and carbon | 5.6 | 8.4 | 7.3 | 10.5 |

* Data from H. C. Schutt, *Oil Gas J.*, Feb. 13, p. 54, 1956.

contains 20-60 weight per cent butadiene, depending on the feedstock and cracking conditions. This stream is often sold to butadiene producers who extract the 1,3-butadiene and dehydrogenate the remaining butylenes to yield additional butadiene. The $C_{5+}$ fraction is a complex mixture of chiefly aromatics and olefins. Although this fraction has not been used to any great extent in the United States for chemical purposes, it does serve as a potential source of aromatics and other pure hydrocarbons.

To demonstrate the effect of feedstock, Table 10-3 gives typical yields

TABLE 10-3. YIELD OF ETHYLENE, PROPYLENE AND CRACKED OIL AS A FUNCTION OF FEEDSTOCK*

| Feedstock | Yield (% by wt of feedstock) | | |
|---|---|---|---|
| | Ethylene | Propylene | Cracked Oil |
| Ethane | 80-85 | 1-2 | nil |
| Propane | 44-45 | 15-20 | 5-15 |
| n-Butane | 32-35 | 17-22 | 6-9 |
| Natural gasoline | 27-30 | 12-16 | 25-30 |
| Kerosine | 24-28 | 12-15 | 30-35 |
| Field condensate | 20-25 | 10-12 | 35-40 |
| Crude oil | 6-17 | 6-12 | 30-40 |

* C. H. Davenport, *Hydro. Proc. Petrol. Refiner*, **39**(3), 125 (1960).

of ethylene, propylene and cracked oil. The yields for ethylene and propylene are based on complete recycle of all $C_2$ and $C_3$ products; the yields for butane and heavier feedstocks are based on recycle of any ethane produced, but with no recycle of $C_3$ or heavier fractions. Note that the yield of ethylene decreases and the yield of cracked oil increases as the average molecular weight of the feedstock increases.

## PROPYLENE

In spite of the fact that approximately 2710 million pounds of propylene were produced in the United States in 1963, essentially all this material was a by-product from ethylene manufacture or from other refinery operations. For example, enormous quantities of propylene are produced by catalytic cracking. However, approximately 90 per cent of this propylene is converted to polymer gasoline, and only a small fraction goes into chemical use.[1] Thus, from the standpoint of a chemical raw material, the HPI can easily supply as much propylene as may be needed for many years to come.

Present indications are that the production of propylene will increase faster than chemical markets develop for the material. Thus, catalytic cracking will continue to expand at the expense of thermal cracking, and tighter specifications on LPG may necessitate the removal of a larger fraction of the propylene which is currently left in this fuel. In addition, no spectacular growth is foreseen for the chemical derivatives of propylene. Thus, the survey by Lewis shows only four areas of good growth, three of modest growth, and one, the use of propylene trimer and tetramer in synthetic detergents, which will disappear entirely in 1965. It is apparent that the development of new chemical uses for propylene can be considered to be a challenge to the petrochemical industries.

## C₄ DERIVATIVES

In 1963, approximately 6325 million pounds of $C_4$ hydrocarbons were recovered for chemical use from petroleum and natural gas in the United States. Butadiene for the manufacture of synthetic rubber represented about 37 per cent of this total and $n$-butane represented about 23 per cent of the total.

Table 10-4 gives the boiling points of the most important $C_4$ hydrocarbons. The only ones present to any appreciable extent in crude petroleum are $n$-butane and isobutane which total roughly 1 per cent in crude petroleum. These are commonly separated in the primary distilla-

---

[1] N. J. Lewis, *Chem. Eng. Progr.*, **59**(2), 32 (1963).

TABLE 10-4. BOILING POINTS OF $C_4$ HYDROCARBONS

| Hydrocarbon | Boiling Point (°F) |
|---|---|
| n-Butane | 31.1 |
| Isobutane | 10.9 |
| 1-Butylene (butene-1) | 20.7 |
| 2-Butylene, cis (butene-2, cis) | 38.7 |
| 2-Butylene, trans (butene-2, trans) | 33.6 |
| Isobutylene (isobutene or 2-methylpropene) | 19.6 |
| 1,3-Butadiene (divinyl) | 24.1 |
| 1,2-Butadiene (methylallene) | 51.5 |

tion of the crude petroleum, and are then blended into the gasoline fraction to control the volatility. However, tremendous quantities of $C_4$ hydrocarbons are also produced from catalytic cracking. Thus, in the catalytic cracking of a typical gas oil, the $C_4$ fraction ranges from 15-20 volume per cent of the cracked product, and consists chiefly of n-butane, isobutane and the four butylenes; note that butadiene is not usually produced to any appreciable extent in catalytic cracking. Of the total quantity of $C_4$'s available in petroleum,[1] approximately **48** per cent is used for the manufacture of alkylate, **27** per cent goes into the blending of gasoline, **12** per cent goes into LPG and **8** per cent is unrecovered and simply goes into light fuel gases. Thus, only about **5** per cent of the $C_4$'s go into chemicals, although even this small percentage represents a sizable industry. Under these conditions, it is not surprising that increasing amounts of cheap and readily available n-butane are being used for the manufacture of ethylene and other petrochemicals.

### Separation of $C_4$ Hydrocarbons

The methods used to separate the $C_4$ hydrocarbons are strongly dependent on the proposed use of the individual components. Thus, if it is desired to recover all the $C_4$ hydrocarbons produced by cracking, usually the first step in the separation is a fractional distillation to separate an overhead fraction containing isobutane, isobutylene, and 1-butylene, and a bottoms fraction containing n-butane, together with cis- and trans-2-butylene. These fractions may then be treated as follows to separate the individual hydrocarbons:

(1) The n-butane can be separated from the 2-butylenes by extractive distillation, using furfural or aqueous acetone as a selective solvent.

(2) Isobutylene is readily removed from the overhead fraction, since

---

[1] W. H. Davis, "Market Prospects of $C_4$ Chemicals," *Chem. Eng. Progr.*, **59**(2), 28 (1963); chapter by E. B. Evans in H. Steiner, "Introduction to Petroleum Chemicals," London, Pergamon Press, 1961.

it reacts with 60-65 per cent sulfuric acid at room temperature to give *tert*-butyl alcohol. This may be either recovered as such, may be converted back to isobutylene by dilution and heating of the acid, or may be polymerized to an isobutylene dimer by heating the acid solution. Frequently the isobutylene is removed from the original $C_4$ fraction before distillation, since this reduces the heat load on the primary fractionator.

(3) The isobutane can then be separated from the 1-butylene by extractive distillation using furfural. The three normal butylenes may then be combined and used as feed for the production of butadiene. An alternate method of separating isobutane and 1-butylene is to treat the mixture with 70-80 per cent sulfuric acid at room temperature to convert the 1-butylene to *sec*-butyl alcohol, which can be dehydrogenated to the important solvent, methyl ethyl ketone.

## Isomerization of *n*-Butane

The *n*-butane is the least valuable $C_4$ hydrocarbon, and for this reason is frequently upgraded to a more useful material. Thus, one major chemical use of *n*-butane is as a feedstock for the manufacture of butadiene. However, an important refinery use of *n*-butane is in the manufacture of isobutane which is in great demand for alkylation. The reaction is

$$CH_3-CH_2-CH_2-CH_3 \rightleftharpoons CH_3-\underset{\underset{\displaystyle CH_3}{|}}{CH}-CH_3$$

$$\Delta H^\circ_{298} = -1640 \qquad \Delta F^\circ_{298} = -542$$

This reaction was of great importance during the war because of the large demand for aviation gasoline which was obtained partly from alkylate. The isomerization is favored by low temperature. Commercially, the reaction is carried out by passing *n*-butane vapor at 200-250°F over a catalyst containing 15-22 per cent aluminum chloride adsorbed on a granular bauxite support. Small quantities of HCl are used to activate the catalyst.

The isobutylene required for alkylation is normally recovered from various refinery streams, particularly the $C_4$ fraction from catalytic cracking. Isobutylene can also be produced readily by dehydrogenation of isobutane

$$(CH_3)_3CH \rightleftharpoons H_2 + (CH_3)_2-C=CH_2$$

$$\Delta H^\circ_{298} = +28{,}109 \qquad \Delta F^\circ_{298} = +18{,}878 \qquad \Delta F^\circ_{1000} = -4370$$

However, present requirements for isobutylene are adequately met by the by-product material. Note that in addition to the manufacture of alkylate, substantial quantities of isobutylene are used to produce butyl rubber.

## BUTADIENE

The most important $C_4$ hydrocarbon for the chemical industry is 1,3-butadiene, which is used chiefly for the manufacture of synthetic rubber and latex. The great demand for butadiene started during the war when the United States was cut off from the supplies of natural rubber. The first plants to produce butadiene used either ethyl alcohol or $n$-butylenes as raw materials.[1] However, at present the use of ethyl alcohol has stopped, and most of the new butadiene plants have used $n$-butane as a raw material since the cost is less than half that of the mixed butylenes.

### Manufacture from Butylenes

Because of the fact that most of the wartime plants were based on butylenes as a raw material, this process still accounts for a majority of the butadiene which is produced in the United States. The reactions are

$$\left.\begin{array}{l} \text{1-butylene} \\ cis\text{-2-butylene} \\ trans\text{-2-butylene} \end{array}\right\} \rightarrow H_2 + CH_2{=}CH{-}CH{=}CH_2$$

$$\Delta H^\circ_{298} = +26{,}050\text{-}28{,}735 \qquad \Delta F^\circ_{298} = +18{,}920\text{-}20{,}960$$

$$\Delta F^\circ_{1000} = -300 \text{ to } -990$$

From the standpoint of the thermodynamic equilibrium, there is little difference between the three normal butylenes, and usually a mixed feed is used for butadiene manufacture. The reaction is strongly endothermic, and the yield is favored by low pressure and high temperature.

In addition to the familiar 1,3-butadiene, there is also the relatively unstable compound 1,2-butadiene or methylallene. However, the free energy of formation of the 1,2-butadiene is roughly 10,000 cal/mole greater than that of the 1,3-butadiene. Thus, the formation of 1,2-butadiene is normally ignored in thermodynamic calculations since it is present in only trace amounts.

In practice, the temperature of the dehydrogenation must be carefully controlled. Below 1100°F, the equilibrium is so unfavorable that only a small conversion can be obtained. However, above about 1250°F, there is excessive cracking of the $C_4$ hydrocarbons and polymerization of the butadiene can occur. The reaction is favored by the use of a catalyst.

[1] See chapter by G. F. Hornaday, *et al.*, in "Advances in Petroleum Chemistry and Refining," Vol. IV, edited by J. J. McKetta, Jr., New York, Interscience Pub., Inc., 1961.

Although alumina-chromia is the best dehydrogenation catalyst for converting paraffins to olefins, this catalyst cannot be used in the presence of large quantities of steam. The original catalyst used in the wartime plants consisted of 72.4 per cent MgO, 18.4 per cent $Fe_2O_3$, 4.6 per cent CuO, and 4.6 per cent $K_2O$. This catalyst roughly doubled the conversion at 1200°F and increased selectivity from 65 to 85 per cent. The iron oxide was the active ingredient, the magnesia served as a support, potassium was a promoter and the copper was a stabilizer and helped to prevent volatilization of the catalyst. However, a major disadvantage of the catalyst was that it required regeneration by steaming after a run of only an hour or two. For this reason, the original catalyst has been replaced by one patented by Shell Development Co. which consists chiefly of $Fe_2O_3$ containing 5 per cent $Cr_2O_3$ and promoted by 2-5 per cent $K_2O$. This catalyst also must be regenerated with steam for approximately one hour in each 24-hour operating period, but still represents considerable improvement over the original. In addition, Dow Chemical Co. has developed a calcium nickel phosphate catalyst which reportedly has higher selectivity than the other two catalysts; however, the Dow catalyst is more expensive, and existing plants would have to be modified since this catalyst must be regenerated with air.

In the commercial manufacture of butadiene from butylenes, the mixed butylenes at a pressure of about 10 psig are preheated to about 1000°F, mixed with from 10-20 moles of steam/mole butylene, and sent to the fixed-bed catalytic converter at a temperature of 1150-1250°F. The high steam ratio favors the dehydrogenation by reducing the partial pressure of the butylenes and keeps the catalyst clean by reacting chemically with any carbon deposited as a result of cracking. The standard space velocity through the catalyst is 200-800 $ft^3$/(hr)($ft^3$ catalyst). Exit gases from the converter are quenched to about 900°F by direct injection of steam or water, pass through a waste-heat boiler, are further cooled in an oil quench tower and a water quench tower, and are then compressed to separate a liquid fraction containing most of the $C_{4+}$ and a gas fraction consisting of hydrogen and light hydrocarbons produced from side reactions. The gas fraction is washed with naphtha to recover $C_4$ values, and the hydrogen then used for fuel purposes. The liquid is then fractionated to produce a crude butadiene stream containing about 18 per cent butadiene and 65 per cent normal butylenes. Commercially, the yield of butadiene from butylenes is 20-25 per cent per pass.

## Separation of Butadiene

Processes which have been used commercially for the separation of butadiene include azeotropic distillation with ammonia, extractive distillation with furfural and absorption in copper liquor as a butadiene complex.[1] The third process accounted for most of the wartime production of butadiene. In this process, the $C_4$ mixture is contacted with a cuprous ammonium acetate solution containing 3.0-3.5 moles cuprous ion/liter in either a packed tower or a series of agitated vessels. Butadiene is absorbed as a complex with copper; the butadiene is then desorbed by heating the solution in a packed tower, the butadiene is washed with water to remove ammonia, and is then redistilled. Unabsorbed $C_4$'s from the butadiene absorber are scrubbed with water to recover ammonia, and are recycled back to the cracking furnaces.

Azeotropic distillation with ammonia was used during the war to treat $C_4$ fractions containing more than about 40 per cent butadiene. This process involves a distillation at about 240 psig in the presence of ammonia. An interesting feature of the process is that most of the $C_4$ hydrocarbons form azeotropes with ammonia under these conditions, and these azeotropes all boil at about the same temperature. However, the butadiene azeotrope has the lowest volatility, and hence can be separated from the others by fractionation.

The separation process which appears to be most favored for new construction is extractive distillation using furfural. As can be seen from Table 10-5, this process is based on the change in the relative volatility

TABLE 10-5.   RELATIVE VOLATILITIES OF $C_4$ HYDROCARBONS

| *Normal Order, Decreasing Volatility* | *In Furfural Solution* |
|---|---|
| Isobutane | Isobutane |
| Isobutylene | *n*-Butane |
| 1-Butylene | Isobutylene |
| Butadiene | 1-Butylene |
| *n*-Butane | 2-Butylene, *trans* |
| 2-Butylene, *trans* | 2-Butylene, *cis* |
| 2-Butylene, *cis* | Butadiene |

of the $C_4$ hydrocarbons when they are present as a solution in furfural. A typical flow sheet is illustrated in Fig. 10-5. The purified $C_4$ fraction is first sent to the butylene tower where most of the 2-butylenes are removed as bottoms. The overhead from this tower consists chiefly of butadiene, 1-butylene and any *n*-butane or isobutane which may be

---

[1] E. T. Borrows and W. L. Sedden, "Separation and Utilization of $C_4$ Hydrocarbons," *Chem. Ind.* (*London*), Aug. 10, page S57 (1953); for a description of the furfural process, see J. Happel, *et al., Amer. Inst. Chem. Engrs. Trans.*, **42**, 189 (1946).

present in the feed. This butadiene fraction is introduced at the middle of the butadiene solvent tower, and furfural is introduced near the top of the tower at a temperature of 140°F and leaves the bottom of the tower at about 350°F. The tower contains about 100 plates and must

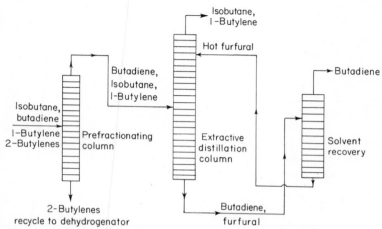

FIG. 10-5. Furfural extractive distillation of butadiene. (E. T. Borrows and W. L. Seddon, *Chem. & Ind.,* pp. 5-57 (Aug. 10, 1953)

handle a high heat load since the furfural feed rate is of the order of 10-20 times the $C_4$ feed rate. The overhead consists chiefly of 1-butylene which is recycled to the cracking furnaces, and the bottoms consist of a solution of butadiene and furfural which is separated in a 20-plate fractionator. The chief disadvantage of the process is the low thermal efficiency which results from the high solvent ratio in the butadiene solvent tower.

## Manufacture of Butadiene from Butane

Most butadiene plants built in the United States since the war have used *n*-butane as a raw material because of its cheapness and availability. The process involves passing *n*-butane over a catalyst to dehydrogenate to *n*-butylenes, followed by separation and recycle of the $C_4$ fraction to convert the *n*-butylenes to butadiene. The over-all reaction is

$$CH_3—CH_2—CH_2—CH_3 \rightarrow 2H_2 + CH_2{=}CH—CH{=}CH_2$$

$$\Delta H^\circ_{298} = +56,480 \qquad \Delta F^\circ_{298} = +40,110 \qquad \Delta F^\circ_{900} = +4065$$

The reaction is quite unfavorable even at a temperature of 900°K (1160°F), which is close to the upper limit of the temperatures used commercially. However, the yield of butadiene can be increased by operation at reduced pressure. Thus, Fig. 10-6 shows the equilibrium between the normal $C_4$ hydrocarbons at an absolute pressure of 5 in. Hg. Note that the equilibrium composition of butadiene is over 50 per cent at a temperature of 1200°F.

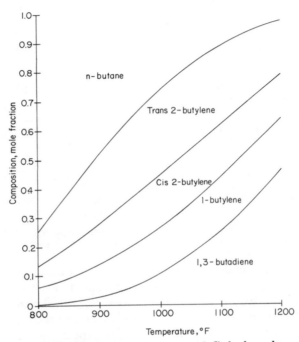

FIG. 10-6. Equilibrium between normal $C_4$ hydrocarbons at 5 in. Hg (G. F. Hornaday *et al.*, "Advances in Petroleum and Refining," Vol. 4, New York, Interscience Publishers, 1961)

The most widely used process for the production of butadiene from *n*-butane is the Houdry "one-step" process (see G. F. Hornaday, *et al.*, *op. cit.*) which is illustrated in Fig. 10-7. The essential feature of this process is the adiabatic dehydrogenation in which the heat of reaction during the on-stream cycle is supplied by the burning off of coke during the regeneration cycle. The *n*-butane feed is preheated to 1000-1200°F and is passed through a brick-lined reactor containing a fixed bed pelletized alumina-chromia catalyst having about 18 per cent $Cr_2O_3$. The absolute pressure in the reactor is about 5-7 in. Hg; the active catalyst is mixed with about a 2:1 volume ratio of alumina to increase the heat capacity of the reactors and thereby permit a longer on-stream run.

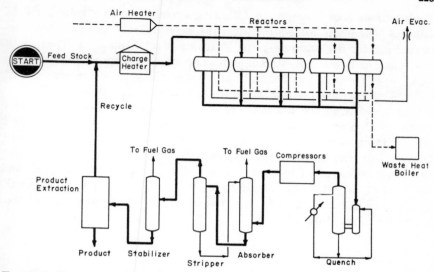

FIG. 10-7. Houdry Butadiene Process [*Hydro. Proc. Petrol. Refiner,* **42** (11), 160 (1963)]. (Copyright 1954, Gulf Publishing Co., Houston, Texas)

TABLE 10-6. DEHYDROGENATION OF *n*-BUTANE TO MAXIMIZE BUTADIENE PRODUCTION*

| Component (wt %) | Fresh Feed | Total Feed, Fresh + Recycle | Reactor Effluent | Fuel Gas | Butadiene Product | Unre-covered |
|---|---|---|---|---|---|---|
| Hydrogen | | | 1.1 | 5.5 | | |
| Methane | | | 1.3 | 6.5 | | |
| Ethylene | | | 0.8 | 4.0 | | |
| Ethane | | | 0.8 | 4.0 | | |
| Propylene | | | 1.4 | 6.9 | | |
| Propane | | | 0.7 | 3.4 | | |
| Isobutane | 1.5 | 3.9 | 3.6 | | | |
| Isobutylenes | | 6.8 | 6.9 | 0.5 | | |
| *n*-Butylenes | | 24.7 | 25.0 | 0.5 | 1.0 | |
| *n*-Butane | 98.5 | 64.3 | 44.7 | 1.0 | | |
| Butadiene | | 0.3 | 11.8 | 0.5 | 56.7 | |
| C₅₊ | | | 0.3 | 1.5 | | |
| Coke | | | 1.3 | | | 6.5 |
| Other | | | 0.3 | | | 1.5 |
| Total | 100.0 | 100.0 | 100.0 | 34.3 | 57.7 | 8.0 |

Selectivity of butadiene from *n*-butane consumed
| | | | | | | |
|---|---|---|---|---|---|---|
| Wt % | | | 59.9 | | 57.6 | |
| Mole % | | | 64.3 | | 61.9 | |

* G. H. Hornaday, *et al.* "Advances in Petroleum Chemistry and Refining," Vol. 4 New York, Inter-science Publishers, Inc., 1961.

Each reactor goes through the following cycles: (a) on-stream for 5-15 minutes; (b) purge for 1-3 minutes; (c) regenerate by blowing with pre-heated air for 5-15 minutes; (d) evacuate for 1-3 minutes. Thus, with five reactors, two are on-stream simultaneously, two are on regeneration, and one is on purge, evacuation, and valve changes. A catalyst life of over 18 months has been obtained in commercial operation.

Exit gases from the reactors are cooled in a quench tower by direct contact with a circulating oil. The gases are then compressed, cooled, and the $C_4$ fraction separated by conventional absorption and distillation. If there is no demand for them as such, the butylenes are recycled along with any unconverted $n$-butane. Table 10-6 gives typical compositions for total $C_4$ recycle to maximize butadiene production. The process can be modified to maximize butylene production, and it can also be modified to handle other feedstocks.

# CHAPTER 11

# Products from Ethylene

Over the period from 1950-60, the production of ethylene in the United States increased [1] at an average annual growth rate of about 14 per cent. Figure 11-1 illustrates the chief products which are based on ethylene. About 30 per cent of the ethylene is used for the manufacture of polyethylene, 24 per cent for ethylene oxide, 17 per cent for synthetic ethanol, 8 per cent for ethylbenzene and 7 per cent for ethylene dichloride. Although the production of ethylene will probably continue to grow at a healthy rate over the near future, there will probably be a gradual decrease in the growth rate. Thus, much of the growth of synthetic ethanol has been through displacement of fermentation alcohol, much of the growth of ethylene glycol has been the result of the displacement of methanol as an automobile antifreeze, and polyethylene is facing increased competition from polypropylene and possibly other polyolefins. Thus, the survey by King shows that the ethylene producing industries will gradually assume the following characteristics: (a) an annual growth rate of about 5 per cent; (b) increased competition and a trend to larger-sized units; (c) extensive ethylene pipeline systems to better service customers; (d) use of LPG as the major feedstock; (e) most of the capacity concentrated in the Gulf Coast area.

## SYNTHETIC ETHANOL

Over 90 per cent of the total ethanol production in the United States now comes from petroleum. The first process used commercially[2] was the sulfuric acid process, which is similar to that used since 1920 for the manufacture of isopropanol from propylene. The reactions are as follows:

[1] W. C. King, "Ethylene Chemicals—the Dicennial Outlook," *Chem. Eng. Progr.*, 59(2), 22 (1963).
[2] T. C. Carle and D. M. Stewart, "Synthetic Ethanol Production," *Chem. Ind.*, p. 830 (1962).

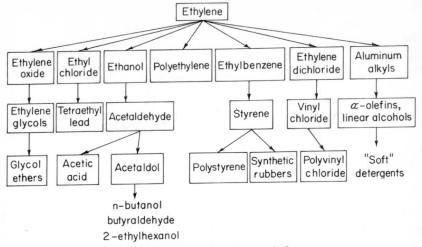

Fɪɢ. 11-1. Chief products from ethylene.

$$C_2H_4 \text{ (g)} + H_2SO_4 \text{ (l)} \rightarrow C_2H_5HSO_4 \text{ (sol'n)} \tag{11-1}$$

$$C_2H_5HSO_4 + C_2H_4 \rightarrow (C_2H_5)_2SO_4$$

$$C_2H_5HSO_4 + H_2O \rightarrow C_2H_5OH + H_2SO_4 \tag{11-2}$$

$$(C_2H_5)_2SO_4 + 2H_2O \rightarrow 2C_2H_5OH + H_2SO_4$$

The chief side reaction is the formation of diethyl ether according to the equation

$$C_2H_5HSO_4 + C_2H_5OH \rightarrow C_2H_5OC_2H_5 + H_2SO_4$$

The essential features of the process are the absorption of ethylene gas in 90-98 per cent sulfuric acid to form a mixture of ethyl hydrogen sulfate and diethyl sulfate. This mixture is then hydrolyzed to give ethanol plus about 45 per cent sulfuric acid. Thus, the over-all reaction is equivalent to an indirect hydration of ethylene. However, the chief advantage of the process is that the yield is not limited thermodynamically to low conversions as in the case of the direct hydration, and in fact yields up to 95 per cent can be achieved during commercial operation. A second advantage is that a dilute ethylene gas can be used as feed as long as it is free from higher olefins. The major disadvantage of the process is the large amount of dilute sulfuric acid which must be reconcentrated or disposed of in some way.

The rate of absorption of ethylene in sulfuric acid is strongly affected by the acid concentration. For example, increasing the acid strength from 93 to 96 per cent causes a 75 per cent increase in the rate of absorption. Actually, ethylene is not very soluble in free sulfuric acid, but the solubility increases as ethyl hydrogen sulfate is formed. Thus, the rate of reaction increases to a maximum, then falls off as the concentration of free sulfuric acid decreases. In practice, an acid strength of about 96 per cent is used since it is difficult and expensive to reconcentrate to a higher strength than this. Temperatures are in the range of 130-170°F and pressures about 350 psig, depending on the concentration of ethylene in the feed. The molar ratio of ethylene to sulfuric acid in the liquid leaving the absorbers is normally 1:1 or higher to limit the amount of acid which must be reconcentrated.

Commercially, the sulfuric acid and ethylene gas flow countercurrently through packed absorption towers which are cooled by recirculating acid through external heat exchangers. If a concentrated ethylene feed is used, the absorption efficiency is about 97 per cent. Unreacted ethylene from the final absorber is scrubbed with caustic and either used as fuel or returned to the ethylene plant for upgrading. The ester solution from the absorption towers passes to a flash drum where the pressure is dropped to about 25 psig to flash off dissolved ethylene, and is then sent to the hydrolyzer. Since the hydrolysis of diethyl sulfate is a slow reaction, the residence time in the hydrolyzer is about 2 hours for a temperature of 160°F. Although the rate of the hydrolysis can be speeded up by raising the temperature, this is undesirable since more by-product ether and polymer oils are formed at higher temperatures. The hydrolyzed products are fed to the top of a stripping column where alcohol and ether are stripped from the 45 per cent sulfuric acid by open steam. A 50-tray fractionator is used to separate diethyl ether, which may be either taken as product or dissolved in sulfuric acid and recycled. The aqueous bottoms from the ether column are then distilled to produce the 95 per cent ethanol-water azeotrope.

If anhydrous ethanol is required, this can be prepared by two general methods. Since the composition of the azeotrope varies with pressure, alternate distillation at atmospheric and elevated pressures can be used to produce anhydrous ethanol. In the second method, benzene is added to carry off the water as a ternary azeotrope which on condensation yields two liquid layers. The benzene layer is recycled, and the aqueous layer is fractionated to remove water and recover ethanol values.

### Direct Hydration Process

Practically all new construction now uses the direct hydration process based on the reaction

$$C_2H_4 \text{ (g)} + H_2O \text{ (g)} \rightleftharpoons C_2H_5OH \text{ (g)} \qquad (11\text{-}3)$$

$$\Delta H^\circ_{298} = -10{,}938 \qquad \Delta F^\circ_{298} = -1947$$

The equilibrium constant is

$$K_p = \frac{P_{C_2H_5OH}}{P_{C_2H_4}P_{H_2O}} \qquad (11\text{-}4)$$

Values of $K_p$ as a function of reciprocal temperature are plotted in Fig. 11-2. A fairly good straight line is obtained, having the equation

$$\log K_p = \frac{2130}{T} - 6.25 \qquad (11\text{-}5)$$

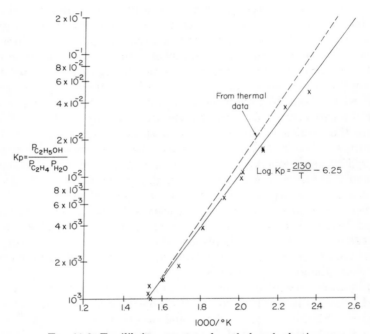

FIG. 11-2. Equilibrium constant for ethylene hydration.

From a consideration of the thermodynamics of the reaction, it is apparent that the commercial success of the process is dependent on achieving the following three conditions: (a) A catalyst is required to bring about the reaction at as low a temperature as is possible. (b) Since there is a decrease in volume, high pressures must be used to favor the conversion. (c) High-purity ethylene is required to permit recycle of unconverted ethylene without excessive buildup of inerts.

In 1945, Shell Development Co. found that phosphoric acid is an active catalyst for the reaction. To permit the use of a bed of solid catalyst, the phosphoric acid is adsorbed on pellets of a siliceous carrier such as diatomaceous earth or "Celite." The only major disadvantages of phosphoric acid are that it is volatile and has a strong affinity for water. Hence, the reaction conditions must be chosen in accordance with the vapor-pressure characteristics of the acid. Thus, if the partial pressure of water in the gas is too high, the acid will become diluted, the activity of the catalyst will be decreased, and there may be excessive losses of acid by "weeping." Conversely, if the partial pressure of water is too low, the acid becomes more concentrated and there is an increase in undesirable side reactions.

The hydration of ethylene over phosphoric acid has been investigated theoretically both in the United States and in the Soviet Union.[1] Thus, Gel'bshtein found that the hydration is zero-order with respect to $H_2O$ under commercial conditions. The limiting step is a conversion of a $\pi$-complex of $H^+$ and $C_2H_4$ into the carbonium ion $H_3CC^+H_2$. Since the gases are not ideal at the pressures used commercially, the equilibrium yield must be determined from the fugacities. These calculations are discussed in the paper by Cope and Dodge. Unfortunately, in the case of ethanol and water, it is necessary to extrapolate to a region where neither can exist as a gas; thus, there is some question as to the accuracy of the calculated conversions.

Cope and Dodge also show that a substantial fraction of the ethanol should be converted to diethyl ether by the side reaction

$$2C_2H_5OH \text{ (g)} \rightleftharpoons (C_2H_5)_2O \text{ (g)} + H_2O \text{ (g)} \qquad (11\text{-}6)$$

Although this reaction does occur to some extent, the quantities formed are much less than those predicted theoretically, thus indicating that equilibrium is not attained in this reaction under commercial operating conditions.

### Commercial Production

A flow sheet for the commercial production of synthetic ethanol is illustrated in Fig. 11-3. Based on plant operating experience, the optimum conditions for the hydration of ethylene are as follows: (a) pressure = 960 psig; (b) temperature = 570°F; (c) molar ratio $H_2O/C_2H_4$ = 0.68:1; (d) space velocity = 1500-2000 standard $ft^3/(hr)(ft^3$ cat-

[1] C. S. Cope and B. F. Dodge, "Equilibria in the Hydration of Ethylene," *Amer. Inst. Chem. Engrs. J.*, **5**(1), 10 (1959); A. I. Gel'bshtein, *et al.*, "Kinetics for the Vapor Phase Hydration of Ethylene," *Doklady Akad. Nauk SSSR*, **132**, 384 (1960); Yu. M. Bakshi *et al., Ibid.*, **132**, 157 (1960).

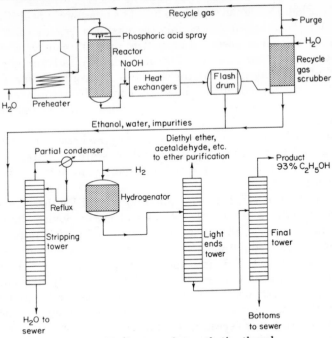

FIG. 11-3. Shell process for synthetic ethanol.

alyst); (e) purity of hydrocarbon feed = 85 per cent $C_2H_4$ in recycle + fresh feed. Approximately 5 per cent conversion of ethylene per pass is obtained under these conditions, which is roughly half the theoretical yield. About 1 per cent of the unreacted ethylene in the product stream is purged, the remainder being recycled with fresh ethylene of at least 96 per cent purity.

In practice, the reactor feed is first heat exchanged with reactor product, is then preheated to about 550°F, and is passed downward through the catalyst bed. The reactor consists of a cylindrical copper-lined vessel packed with $\frac{1}{4} \times \frac{1}{4}$-in. pellets of diatomaceous earth or "Celite" which are impregnated with phosphoric acid. To replace losses, phosphoric acid is continually injected onto the surface of the catalyst bed. Product gases from the reactor are cooled, phosphoric acid is neutralized by the direct injection of caustic solution, crude ethanol is separated by condensation in a high pressure flash drum, and the remainder of the ethanol in the recycle gases is removed by scrubbing with water. The crude ethanol is concentrated by distillation and sent to the hydrogenation system where aldehydes and other unsaturates are hydrogenated over a nickel-kieselguhr catalyst. Purified ethanol and by-product diethyl ether are then separated by conventional fractionation.

The chief side reaction is the formation of diethyl ether according to Eq. (11-6). The ether may be either sold as a by-product for credit, or recycled back to the reactor to be hydrolyzed to ethanol. The chief aldehyde impurity is acetaldehyde produced from the hydration of acetylene which may be present in the ethylene feed. There is also some polymerization of ethylene to form higher olefins such as butylene; when these are recycled back to the reactor, they can be hydrated to form the corresponding alcohol such as *sec*-butyl alcohol, etc.

## ACETALDEHYDE

Over half the ethanol produced in the United States is converted to acetaldehyde, which itself is an intermediate for the manufacture of acetic acid, $n$-butanol, and 2-ethylhexanol. The process normally used is a dehydrogenation according to the reaction

$$C_2H_5OH \text{ (g)} \rightarrow H_2 \text{ (g)} + CH_3CHO \text{ (g)} \qquad (11\text{-}7)$$
$$\Delta H^\circ_{298} = +16,480 \qquad \Delta F^\circ_{298} = +8340$$

The reaction is favored by low pressure and high temperature. The equilibrium constant for the reaction is approximately

$$\log K_p = 5.96 - \frac{3610}{T} \qquad (11\text{-}8)$$

The reaction is reported to be first-order[1] in the forward direction with an activation energy of 19,720.

Commercially, the dehydrogenation is carried out by passing ethanol vapors at 500-575°F and about atmospheric pressure over a copper catalyst activated with chromium. Yields up to about 50 per cent are obtained per pass. Exit gases are cooled to condense out acetaldehyde and unreacted ethanol, and the by-product hydrogen is scrubbed with water to remove the last traces of organics. The product is separated by distillation and the ethanol recycled. The hydrogen has a purity of about 99 per cent, and represents a useful by-product.

An alternate process for the manufacture of acetaldehyde is air oxidation of ethanol according to the reaction

$$C_2H_5OH \text{ (g)} + \tfrac{1}{2}O_2 \text{ (g)} \rightarrow CH_3CHO \text{ (g)} + H_2O \text{ (g)} \qquad (11\text{-}9)$$
$$\Delta H^\circ_{298} = -41,318 \qquad \Delta F^\circ_{298} = -46,295$$

[1] S. Hada and Y. Mihara, Kagaku Kogaku, **25**, 518 (1961).

The reaction is carried out at about 850°F, using a silver gauze catalyst. Although the equilibrium is very favorable, this is a mixed blessing since the high heat of reaction may cause degradation of the acetaldehyde through side reactions. It is also possible to use insufficient air, and thereby carry out the oxidation and dehydrogenation reactions simultaneously so that the endothermic dehydrogenation will balance the exothermic oxidation.

Recently considerable interest has been taken in the Wacker process,[1] developed in Germany, which produces acetaldehyde directly from ethylene without going through ethanol. The process is now being used commercially by Celanese Chemical Corp. at Bay City, Texas. The reactions are

$$C_2H_4 + PdCl_2 + H_2O \rightarrow CH_3CHO + Pd + 2HCl$$

$$Pd + 2CuCl_2 \rightarrow PdCl_2 + 2CuCl$$

$$2CuCl + \tfrac{1}{2}O_2 + 2HCl \rightarrow 2CuCl_2 + H_2O$$

Adding the three equations gives the over-all reaction

$$C_2H_4 \text{ (g)} + \tfrac{1}{2}O_2 \text{ (g)} \rightarrow CH_3CHO \text{ (g)}$$

$$\Delta H^\circ_{298} = -52{,}256 \qquad \Delta F^\circ_{298} = -48{,}242$$

In the first step of the process, ethylene gas at moderately superatmospheric pressure is passed into a solution of palladium chloride containing cupric chloride as an oxidizing agent. The ethylene forms a $\pi$-complex with palladium chloride which then breaks down to give acetaldehyde and elemental palladium; the reaction is strongly exothermic with better than 99 per cent of the ethylene reacting. Acetaldehyde is distilled off by reducing the pressure and taking advantage of the heat of reaction. As long as cupric chloride is present, the precipitated palladium is immediately re-oxidized back to palladium chloride.

In the second step of the process, the solution after removal of acetaldehyde is blown with air to re-oxidize the copper to cupric state. This reaction is so complete that the exit gas from the oxidizer can be used as an inert atmosphere.

The chief problem in the Wacker process was the development of suitable materials of construction to handle the corrosive chloride solutions. This has been solved by the use of titanium and titanium-lined equipment. There are some disadvantages in a two-step process, and it is possible to combine all the reactions into a continuous one-step process which also has been developed in Germany. However, the one-step proc-

[1] J. Smidt, "Oxidation of Olefins with Palladium Chloride Catalysts," *Chem. Ind.* (*London*), Jan. 13, p. 54 (1962).

ess has not been used commercially in the United States, although commercial units are in operation in Canada and in western Europe.

## Acetic Acid

Approximately 40 per cent of the acetaldehyde produced in the United States is converted to acetic acid and acetic anhydride. The reaction is normally carried out in the liquid phase according to the equations

$$CH_3CHO + O_2 \text{ (g)} \rightarrow CH_3COOOH$$
peracetic acid

$$CH_3COOOH + CH_3CHO \rightarrow 2CH_3COOH$$

which is equivalent to the over-all reaction

$$CH_3CHO \text{ (l)} + \tfrac{1}{2}O_2 \text{ (g)} \rightarrow CH_3COOH \text{ (l)}$$

$$\Delta H^\circ_{298} \cong -70,000 \qquad \Delta F^\circ_{298} \cong -61,000$$

The equilibrium is virtually 100 per cent to the right near room temperature. Either air or oxygen may be used at a temperature of about 160°F and a high enough pressure to keep the acetaldehyde liquid. A manganese acetate or cobalt acetate catalyst is used to prevent the formation of explosive amounts of peracetic acid.

It is also possible to modify the oxidation process to obtain acetic anhydride directly.[1] This discovery was evidently made simultaneously in Germany and in Canada. The modified process involves the removal of water by the use of an ester such as ethyl acetate, methyl acetate, or dibutyl phthalate which forms an azeotrope with water but not with acetic acid or acetic anhydride. It is also necessary to use a different catalyst such as the acetates of nickel + manganese, copper + manganese, or copper + cobalt. Although the reactions are fairly complex, the over-all reaction can be written

$$2CH_3CHO \text{ (l)} + O_2 \text{ (g)} \rightarrow (CH_3CO)_2O \text{ (l)} + H_2O \text{ (l)}$$
acetic anhydride

$$\Delta H^\circ_{298} = -126,092$$

The ratio of acetic anhydride to acetic acid which is produced depends on the relative quantity of ester which is used. For example, by starting with a 1:1 ratio of ethyl acetate to acetaldehyde, a final product containing more than 50 per cent acetic anhydride can be prepared. The oxidation is carried out at temperatures of 100-120°F and pressures of about 80 psig, using a catalyst of approximately 0.1 per cent mixed copper-cobalt or copper-manganese acetates. Since there is a much greater

---

[1] R. F. Goldstein, "The Petroleum Chemicals Industry," New York, John Wiley & Sons, Inc., 1950.

industrial demand for acetic anhydride than for acetic acid, the importance of the process is that it produces acetic anhydride directly and thus eliminates the need for a costly dehydration of acetic acid.

A second method for the production of acetic anhydride involves the thermal decomposition of acetic acid to form ketene according to the equations

$$CH_3COOH \ (g) \rightarrow \underset{ketene}{CH_2=C=O} \ (g) + H_2O \ (g)$$

$$\Delta H^\circ_{298} = +38,220$$

$$CH_2CO \ (g) + CH_3COOH \ (l) \rightarrow (CH_3CO)_2O \ (l)$$

$$\Delta H^\circ_{298} = -19,760$$

Acetic acid is cracked thermally by heating to temperatures of about 1400°F at an absolute pressure of about 1 psig, using triethylphosphate as a catalyst. The furnace gases are quenched to room temperature or below to condense out dilute acetic acid, and the ketene is absorbed in acetic acid to give acetic anhydride. Product acetic anhydride is concentrated to about 95 per cent by vacuum distillation in copper equipment. The yield is about 90 per cent, based on the acetic acid reacted. Most acetic anhydride goes into the manufacture of cellulose acetate resins and plastics.

### n-Butanol

Approximately 27 per cent of the acetaldehyde produced in the United States is converted to n-butanol by the aldol condensation. The chief use of n-butanol is as a lacquer solvent in the surface coatings industry; other uses are in the manufacture of butyl acetate, in synthetic resins and in plasticizers. The chief competing route for the manufacture of n-butanol is via the Oxo process, which will probably gain in relative importance over the near future. Note that although substantial quantities of butanol are produced by the hydration of n-butylenes, this process always yields the secondary butanol which has found only limited use as a solvent.

The first step in the production of n-butanol from acetaldehyde is a condensation at room temperature in the presence of dilute alkali to form acetaldol by the reaction

$$2CH_3CHO \rightarrow CH_3\!-\!\underset{\underset{OH}{|}}{CH}\!-\!CH_2\!-\!CHO$$

$$\Delta H^\circ_{298} = -11,400$$

Actually, the acetaldol can exist (see R. F. Goldstein, *op. cit.*) either as an open chain aldehyde or as a cyclic hemi-acetal according to the equilibrium

$$CH_3-CH-CH_2-CHO \rightleftharpoons CH_3-CH-CH_2-CHOH$$
$$\quad\quad\; | \quad\quad\quad\quad\quad\quad\quad\quad\quad |$$
$$\quad\quad OH \quad\quad\quad\quad\quad\quad\quad\quad\quad O$$

In addition, acetaldol can condense with another molecule of acetaldehyde to give a dioxane according to the reaction

$$CH_3-CHO + \quad\begin{array}{c} HOCHCH_3 \\ \backslash \\ CH_2 \\ | \\ CHO \end{array} \rightarrow \quad CH_3CH \begin{array}{c} O-CHCH_3 \\ / \quad\quad \backslash \\ \quad\quad\quad CH_2 \\ \backslash \quad\quad / \\ O-CHOH \end{array}$$

*4-hydroxy-2,6-dimethyl-1,3-dioxane*

This compound is the chief component of crude technical acetaldol.

If *n*-butanol is the desired product, the aldol condensation is allowed to run to about 60 per cent conversion corresponding to 90 per cent formation of the dioxane. Either batch or continuous reactors can be used; in either case, the reaction time is several hours and cooling must be provided to remove the heat of reaction. The alkali is then neutralized with a slight excess of acetic or phosphoric acid, and the solution is immediately distilled. On distillation, the dioxane splits to give 1 mole of acetaldehyde and 1 mole of acetaldol; thus, the first distillation yields an overhead consisting of unreacted acetaldehyde plus that liberated from the splitting of the dioxane. In a second distillation, acetaldol is dehydrated to crotonaldehyde according to the reaction

$$CH_3-CH(OH)-CH_2-CHO \rightarrow H_2O + CH_3-CH=CH-CHO$$

The crotonaldehyde is taken as the overhead product, since it forms an azeotrope with water containing about 90 per cent crotonaldehyde. The yield is 80-90 per cent, based on the acetaldehyde consumed in the process.

By the use of the proper catalyst[1], the crotonaldehyde can be either hydrogenated across the double bond, hydrogenated at the carbonyl group, or both simultaneously. In the production of *n*-butanol, the reaction is

$$CH_3-CH=CH-CHO + 2H_2 \rightarrow CH_3-CH_2-CH_2-CH_2OH$$

The hydrogenation is normally carried out in the vapor phase at temperatures of about 400°F and at pressures slightly above atmospheric. Catalysts which may be used include nickel, nickel promoted with

[1] J. E. Fernandez and T. W. G. Solomons, "Crotonaldehyde," *Chem. Rev.,* **62,** 485 (1962).

chromium, and copper or copper-nickel supported on silica. There is always some formation of $n$-butyraldehyde as a by-product.

If it is desired to produce $n$-butyraldehyde as the chief product, the hydrogenation of the crotonaldehyde is carried out in the liquid phase at a temperature of about 200°F, using a nickel catalyst. The reaction is

$$CH_3-CH=CH-CHO \text{ (l)} + H_2 \text{ (g)} \rightarrow CH_3-CH_2-CH_2-CHO \text{ (l)}$$

The butyraldehyde is then separated by distillation.

## Manufacture of 2-Ethylhexanol

The manufacture of 2-ethylhexanol accounts for about 15 per cent of the total end use of acetaldehyde. The 2-ethylhexanol is a useful high-boiling solvent which finds considerable application as a defoaming and wetting agent and as an intermediate for the manufacture of plasticizers. It is made by an aldol condensation of butyraldehyde in the presence of dilute alkali followed by acidification, splitting off of water, and hydrogenation. The reactions are as follows:

$$2CH_3-CH_2-CH_2-CHO \rightarrow CH_3-CH_2-CH_2-\underset{\underset{OH}{|}}{CH}-\underset{\underset{C_2H_5}{|}}{CH}-CHO$$

$$CH_3-CH_2-CH_2-CH=\underset{\underset{C_2H_5}{|}}{C}-CHO \xrightarrow{+2H_2}$$

$$\xleftarrow{-H_2O}$$

$$CH_3-CH_2-CH_2-CH_2-\underset{\underset{C_2H_5}{|}}{CH}-CH_2OH$$

## ETHYLENE OXIDE

Approximately 1889 million pounds of ethylene oxide were produced in the United States in 1963, over half of which was converted to ethylene glycol. Two general methods are used commercially for the manufacture of ethylene oxide. In the older method, ethylene is reacted with water and chlorine gas to form ethylene chlorohydrin according to the reactions

$$Cl_2 \text{ (g)} + H_2O \text{ (l)} \rightleftharpoons HOCl \text{ (sol'n)} + HCl \text{ (sol'n)} \qquad (11\text{-}10)$$

$$C_2H_4 \text{ (g)} + HOCl \rightarrow \underset{\underset{CH_2Cl}{|}}{CH_2OH} \qquad (11\text{-}11)$$

A possible side reaction is

$$C_2H_4 + Cl_2 \rightarrow C_2H_4Cl_2 \qquad (11\text{-}12)$$

Commercially, ethylene, chlorine and water are introduced into either an open or packed tower at temperatures of 120°F or lower. Although the equilibrium concentration of hypochlorous acid in water is very small, the rate of addition of hypochlorous acid to ethylene is so much faster than the addition of chlorine across the double bond that ethylene chlorohydrin is the chief product of the reaction. By maintaining a slight excess of ethylene, the concentration of chlorohydrin can reach a value of 6-8 per cent before an appreciable amount of ethylene dichloride is formed. The solution is extremely corrosive, and must be handled in ceramic, plastic, or rubber-lined equipment.

Although the chlorohydrin can be separated by distillation, in most cases the chlorohydrin is simply converted to ethylene oxide by reacting the solution with lime or caustic according to the equation

$$2CH_2(OH)CH_2Cl + Ca(OH)_2 \rightarrow 2CH_2\underset{\diagdown O \diagup}{\phantom{x}}CH_2 + CaCl_2 + 2H_2O$$

The solution is heated with live steam, and the ethylene oxide product is rapidly removed to prevent hydration to ethylene glycol. Ethylene oxide is condensed, and separated by fractional distillation from water and chlorinated by-products. The two chief by-products are ethylene dichloride produced by direct chlorination of ethylene, and dichloro-ethyl ether produced by splitting off water from two molecules of ethylene chlorohydrin according to the reaction

$$2Cl—CH_2—CH_2—OH \rightarrow Cl—CH_2—CH_2—O—CH_2—CH_2—Cl + H_2O$$

Both by-products are of value, since the ether is widely used as a solvent and ethylene dichloride is used as a gasoline additive and as an intermediate for the manufacture of vinyl chloride.

The chief disadvantage of the chlorohydrin process is that the over-all reaction involves the conversion of valuable chlorine into waste calcium chloride. Thus, the chemical costs for the process are fairly high. In the direct oxidation process for the production of ethylene oxide, the chemical costs are low and the yield is about the same as in the chlorohydrin process. Since all recent construction has used direct oxidation, it is apparent that the chlorohydrin process is gradually becoming obsolete for ethylene oxide manufacture.

### Direct Oxidation Process

The direct oxidation process now accounts for about 85 per cent of the total ethylene oxide production in the United States. The reaction involves the direct addition of oxygen across a $\pi$-bond by the reaction

$$C_2H_4 \text{ (g)} + \tfrac{1}{2}O_2 \rightarrow C_2H_4O \text{ (g)} \qquad\qquad (11\text{-}13)$$

$$\Delta H^\circ_{298} = -24,696 \qquad \Delta F^\circ_{298} = -19,072$$

with the competing reaction

$$C_2H_4 + 3O_2 \rightarrow 2CO_2 + 2H_2O \text{ (g)} \qquad\qquad (11\text{-}14)$$

$$\Delta H^\circ_{298} = -316,196 \qquad \Delta F^\circ_{298} = -314,072$$

The success of the process is dependent on the use of a selective catalyst to direct the reaction to the formation of ethylene oxide and to inhibit the strongly exothermic combustion to carbon dioxide and water. Although many catalysts have been investigated, the best is silver promoted with gold, copper, iron, manganese or alkaline earth oxides. In practice, the silver is usually supported on pellets of alumina. This catalyst has been very satisfactory for commercial operation; thus, some ethylene oxide plants have operated continuously for 6 years without showing any measurable change in pressure drop, activity or selectivity of the catalyst.

There is still some uncertainty as to the mechanism[1] of the oxidation on a silver catalyst. It has been shown that the chemisorption of oxygen by silver is slow and activated; ethylene shows very little chemisorption on silver. Several investigators have concluded that the chemisorption of oxygen is the rate-determining step in the oxidation to ethylene oxide. Various rate laws have been proposed, and activation energies ranging from 10,000-19,000 have been reported. Very little has been disclosed in the literature about the mechanism of promoters, although it is known that the selectivity of the original catalyst has been increased considerably by the addition of suitable promoters. Thus, the maximum yield which can be achieved with pure silver is about 50 per cent, but the promoted catalysts now used commercially show yields of 70 per cent or better. Recent patents indicate that the catalysts are produced by heating a silver salt with an organic reducing agent such as sucrose or lactose. Sodium and barium may be added as promoters. The finished catalyst contains 10-20 per cent Ag on an $Al_2O_3$ support. An interesting feature is that side reactions can be reduced by the addition of small amounts of an inhibitor to the ethylene before it passes over the catalyst; thus, one patent describes the addition of 6 ppm of ethylene dichloride to increase selectivity.

A typical flow sheet for the production of ethylene oxide is shown in Fig. 11-4. Ethylene of commercial purity (up to 10 per cent of inerts is permissible) and air or oxygen are mixed with recycle gas and passed

---

[1] P. G. Ashmore, "Catalysis and Inhibition of Chemical Reactions," London, Butterworth and Co., Ltd., 1963.

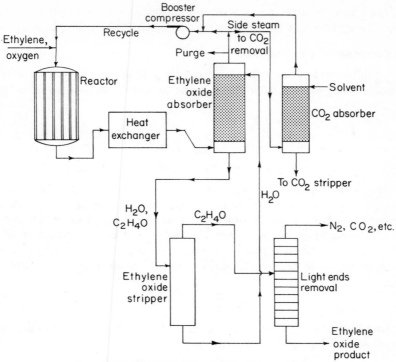

FIG. 11-4. Typical flowsheet for ethylene oxide.

over the silver catalyst at temperatures of 460-570°F and pressures ranging from atmospheric up to 450 psig. The ratio of oxygen to ethylene is adjusted so that only a fairly small conversion occurs per pass through the catalyst. This limits the temperature rise and thereby minimizes the combustion of ethylene to carbon dioxide. The catalyst is contained within tubes, and an organic coolant is circulated outside the tubes to maintain precise temperature control. When pure oxygen is used, the temperature is held at about 450°F; when air is used, temperatures of 500-550°F are more common. During normal operation, the yield of ethylene oxide is about 70 per cent, based on total ethylene reacted.

Exit gases from the reactor are cooled and the ethylene oxide is absorbed in water. Product ethylene oxide is stripped by heating the solution, and is purified by conventional fractionation. When oxygen is used, the residual gases are compressed and recycled; a side stream of the recycle gas is scrubbed with a solvent such as ethanolamine to absorb carbon dioxide, and a very small fraction of the residual gas is purged to remove inerts. If air is used as oxidant, a substantial fraction of the residual gases is diverted to a second catalytic reactor to purge nitrogen from the system and to recover ethylene remaining in the purge gas.

## Isomerization of Ethylene Oxide

A subject which has been discussed very little in the literature is the possible isomerization of ethylene oxide to acetaldehyde according to the equation

$$\underset{CH_2 \overline{\quad\quad} CH_2}{\overset{\displaystyle O}{\diagup \diagdown}} \rightarrow CH_3\text{---}CHO$$

$$\Delta H^\circ_{298} = -27,570 \qquad \Delta F^\circ_{298} = -29,170$$

Although the equilibrium is virtually 100 per cent to the right at the temperatures used commercially, it has been stated that acetaldehyde formation is not a problem during normal operation of an ethylene oxide plant. Presumably the silver catalyst is specific to the formation of the oxide, and the temperatures are not high enough to permit any substantial degree of thermal isomerization of ethylene oxide to acetaldehyde.

## Ethylene Glycol

Over half the ethylene oxide produced in the United States is converted to ethylene glycol by the reaction

$$C_2H_4O \ (l) + H_2O \ (l) \rightarrow HO\text{---}CH_2\text{---}CH_2\text{---}OH \ (l)$$

The hydration is carried out in the liquid phase at temperatures of 300-400°F and at pressures of 300-350 psig. A trace of acid may be used to initiate the reaction. Commercially, the reactants are heated to about 200°F to start the reaction, and are then passed through a reaction vessel where the exothermic reaction is allowed to continue at a higher temperature until all the ethylene oxide has reacted. A substantial excess of water is used, since higher glycols can be produced as byproducts according to the reactions

$$HOCH_2CH_2OH + C_2H_4O \rightarrow$$

$$\underset{\textit{diethylene glycol}}{HO\text{---}CH_2\text{---}CH_2\text{---}O\text{---}CH_2\text{---}CH_2\text{---}OH} \quad \downarrow +C_2H_4O$$

$$\underset{\textit{triethylene glycol, etc.}}{HO\text{---}CH_2\text{---}CH_2\text{---}O\text{---}CH_2\text{---}CH_2\text{---}O\text{---}CH_2\text{---}CH_2\text{---}OH}$$

Normally the mono-, di- and triethylene glycols are produced in a ratio of about 100:10:1, although this can be varied over a wide range by adjusting the reaction conditions. The glycols are concentrated by multiple-effect evaporation, and are purified by distillation at an absolute pressure of 1-1.5 in. Hg absolute, since there is some decomposition if they are distilled at atmospheric pressure. The yield is close to 100 per cent, based on total ethylene oxide which is hydrated.

The chief use of ethylene glycol is as an automobile antifreeze. In addition, ethylene glycol finds some use as a chemical intermediate for the manufacture of polyester resins, plasticizers, etc. The polyethylene glycols are used as gas dehydrants, as a selective aromatic-aliphatic solvent in the petroleum industry, and as intermediates for the manufacture of emulsifiers, plasticizers, lubricants, etc.

### Glycol-Ethers

One or more molecules of ethylene oxide will react with the hydroxyl group of an alcohol in the same manner as the reaction with water. For example, the reaction with ethanol is

$$C_2H_5OH + C_2H_4O \rightarrow C_2H_5\!-\!O\!-\!CH_2\!-\!CH_2\!-\!OH$$
ethylene glycol ethyl ether
$$\downarrow C_2H_4O$$
$$C_2H_5\!-\!O\!-\!CH_2\!-\!CH_2\!-\!O\!-\!CH_2\!-\!CH_2\!-\!OH$$
diethylene glycol ethyl ether, etc.

The reaction conditions vary, depending on the particular alcohol which is used. In general, the reactions are slower than in the case of water, and a catalyst such as boron trifluoride may be required. Normally temperatures of about 350°F and pressures of about 200 psig are used; the reaction is carried out using excess alcohol to reduce the formation of polyethers. About 9 per cent of the total production of ethylene oxide goes into glycol-ethers.

The chief uses of the glycol-ethers are as solvents for cellulose esters, lacquers, varnishes, and enamels, as mutual solvents for soluble oils and insecticides, as plasticizer intermediates, and in hydraulic fluids. A large number of different glycol-ethers are commercially available, but the most important are the methyl, ethyl, and *n*-butyl monoethers. It is also possible to esterify the hydroxyl group to obtain an ether-ester; thus, if the ethylene ether is treated with acetic acid,

$$C_2H_5OC_2H_4OH + CH_3COOH \rightleftharpoons$$
$$H_2O + C_2H_5\!-\!O\!-\!CH_2\!-\!CH_2\!-\!O\!-\!\overset{\displaystyle O}{\overset{\|}{C}}\!-\!CH_3$$
ethylene glycol ethyl ether acetate

The chief use of the esters is as solvents for lacquers, cellulose acetate, etc.

## Ethanolamines

The production of ethanolamine accounts for about **7** per cent of the total consumption of ethylene oxide. The process involves a direct addition of ethylene oxide to ammonia, the three hydrogen atoms of ammonia being more reactive than those which are part of the hydroxyl groups formed by the reaction. The equations are

$$NH_3 + 1, 2, \text{ or } 3C_2H_4O \begin{cases} \rightarrow NH_2CH_2CH_2OH & \text{(monoethanolamine)} \\ \rightarrow NH(CH_2CH_2OH)_2 & \text{(diethanolamine)} \\ \rightarrow N(CH_2CH_2OH)_3 & \text{(triethanolamine)} \end{cases}$$

The rate of addition of ethylene oxide to each hydrogen atom in ammonia is about the same. Thus, a mixture of all three ethanolamines is always obtained, although the relative proportions of the di- and triethanolamines can be reduced by using excess ammonia.

Commercially, the reaction is carried out in the liquid phase by mixing ethylene oxide and aqueous ammonia in a reactor at pressures up to several hundred psig and at temperatures of 100°F or higher. The reaction is strongly exothermic, so that the feed rate to the reactor is adjusted to the amount of cooling which is available. The products are separated by fractionation, and excess ammonia is recycled to the reactor. If the ratio of ammonia to ethylene oxide in the feed is about 10:1, monoethanolamine is the chief product. If this ratio is about 5:1, diethanolamine is the chief product, and if the ratio is reduced to about 2:1, triethanolamine becomes the chief product. It is also, of course, possible to recycle some of the product in order to increase the production of the di- and triethanolamines. The yield based on both ammonia and ethylene oxide is better than 95 per cent.

The chief uses of the ethanolamines are as acid-gas absorbents, corrosion inhibitors, and as intermediates for the manufacture of soaps, emulsifiers, foaming agents, cosmetics, and detergents such as "Thrill," "Gain" and "Joy." Diethanolamine can be dehydrated with sulfuric acid to give the cyclic derivative, morpholine:

$$\begin{array}{c} CH_2-CH_2-OH \\ / \\ NH \\ \backslash \\ CH_2-CH_2-OH \end{array} \xrightarrow{-H_2O} \begin{array}{c} CH_2-CH_2 \\ / \quad\quad \backslash \\ NH \quad\quad\quad O \\ \backslash \quad\quad / \\ CH_2-CH_2 \end{array}$$

Morpholine finds considerable use as a solvent, corrosion inhibitor and intermediate for pharmaceuticals and rubber chemicals.

## ETHYLBENZENE AND STYRENE

In 1942, the annual production of styrene in the United States was about 8400 tons. Three years later, the production rate had risen to about 216 thousand tons, and in 1963 over a million tons of styrene were produced. This fantastic growth is the result of two factors, the decision to base the wartime production of synthetic rubber on a styrene-butadiene copolymer (SBR), and the increasing use of styrene in the manufacture of polystyrene and other types of plastic. Although there are several processes which can be used to manufacture styrene, most production in the United States now comes from the dehydrogenation of ethylbenzene.

As we have already seen, a limited amount of ethylbenzene is produced by superdistillation of petroleum aromatics, but this is literally a drop in the bucket when it comes to supplying the demand for styrene. For this reason, most ethylbenzene is produced by the alkylation of benzene with ethylene according to the equation

$$\text{(l)} + C_2H_4 \text{ (g)} \rightarrow \text{(l)} \quad (11\text{-}15)$$

$$\Delta H^\circ_{298} = -27{,}203 \qquad \Delta F^\circ_{298} = -16{,}063 \text{ (gas-phase reaction)}$$

The equilibrium is essentially 100 per cent to the right near room temperature. The reaction may be carried out in either the vapor phase or the liquid phase. The vapor phase process operates at about 570°F and 6000 psig with a ratio of ethylene to benzene of about 0.2:1. A catalyst of either silica-alumina or phosphoric acid supported on diatomaceous earth can be used. However, the liquid phase process using an aluminum chloride catalyst is much more common.

The alkylation of benzene with aluminum chloride is a classic example of the Friedel-Crafts reaction. The mechanism[1] of the reaction is as follows:

$$CH_2{=}CH_2 + HCl \rightarrow CH_3{-}CH_2{-}Cl$$

$$CH_3{-}CH_2{-}Cl + AlCl_3 \rightarrow CH_3{-}C^+H_2 + AlCl_4^-$$

$$\text{(l)} + CH_3C^+H_2 \rightarrow \rightarrow + H^+$$

[1] R. M. Roberts, *Chem. Eng. News*, Jan. 25, 1965, p. 96.

A carbonium ion is produced by the interaction between ethyl chloride and aluminum chloride. This attaches itself to the benzene ring, followed by decomposition of the complex to give ethylbenzene and a proton. All reactions are extremely rapid, even at room temperature. Note that both the HCl and the AlCl₃ are regenerated over the course of the reactions.

Although there have been minor modifications, the process used commercially is still essentially the one[1] developed simultaneously by Dow Chemical Co. in the United States and I. G. Farben in Germany in the early 1930's. The process is illustrated in Fig. 11-5. Benzene of 1°C

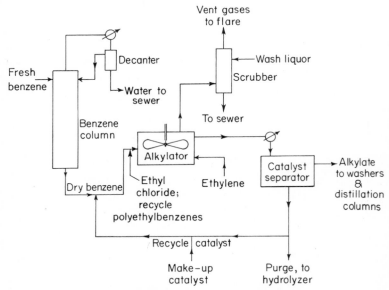

Fig. 11-5. Alkylation of benzene to ethylbenzene.

boiling range and low in sulfur is fractionated to remove water and is then fed to the alkylator. It is important to first dry the benzene to less than 30 ppm of water, since water increases the consumption of catalyst and promotes sludge formation. The alkylator consists of a jacketed glass-lined or "Hastelloy"-lined vessel with side-stream coolers to remove the heat of reaction. The alkylation is carried out continu-

[1] See chapter by S. H. Dawson in H. Steiner, *op. cit.*; J. N. Hornibrook, "Manufacture of Styrene," *Chem. Ind.* (*London*), p. 872 (1962); R. H. Boundy and R. F. Boyer, "Styrene, Its Polymers, Copolymers, and Derivatives," New York, Reinhold Publishing Corp., 1952.

ously at a temperature of 185-200°F and a pressure of about 5 psig. Ethylene of 90 per cent or greater purity is bubbled through the benzene in the presence of the catalyst. The purity of the ethylene is not critical as long as it is free from other unsaturates such as acetylenes and higher olefins.

The aluminum chloride catalyst is in the form of a liquid complex having the following approximate composition: combined $AlCl_3 = 26$ per cent; free $AlCl_3 = 1$ per cent; high molecular-weight hydrocarbons = 25 per cent; and benzene and ethylbenzene = 48 per cent. This complex plays a vital part in the reaction mechanism; it is reddish brown in color, has a specific gravity slightly greater than unity, and is virtually insoluble in the hydrocarbon layer. The catalyst is activated by anhydrous HCl. This is usually done by vaporizing a small quantity of ethyl chloride continuously into the ethylene feed to the reactor; the ethyl chloride reacts to give HCl, and this is more convenient than handling anhydrous HCl gas. The absorption of ethylene in the alkylator is almost quantitative. Exit gases from the alkylator are scrubbed with water and caustic to remove HCl and entrained hydrocarbons, and are then either burned or sent to the stack.

The liquid products overflowing from the alkylator are cooled and passed to a decanter which separates the catalyst from the hydrocarbon layer and recycles catalyst back to the alkylator. Catalyst activity is maintained by continuously purging a small fraction of the recycled catalyst and replacing with fresh catalyst. The alkylated product stream consists of approximately 40-55 per cent benzene, 35-45 per cent ethylbenzene, and 10-20 per cent polyethylbenzenes plus tar and other high-boiling impurities. A fraction of this product stream is normally recycled to the alkylator, and the remainder washed with caustic and water to remove traces of HCl and $AlCl_3$. This hydrocarbon mixture is then fractionated in three distillation columns to produce benzene, ethylbenzene, polyethylbenzenes and a tar residue. The first column produces pure benzene as overhead product, which is recycled to the alkylator. This column contains about 20 plates and operates at atmospheric pressure. The second column contains 60 plates, operates at an absolute pressure of about 8 in. Hg, and produces pure ethylbenzene as overhead product. The third column contains 10 plates, operates at an absolute pressure of about 1.5 in. Hg, and produces an overhead product consisting of polyethylbenzenes and a bottoms product consisting of high-boiling tars. It is essential that the polyethylbenzenes be reduced to less than 0.02 per cent in the finished ethylbenzene, since dehydrogenation converts these materials to divinylbenzene which readily polymerizes to form insoluble polymers in the styrene plant.

The polyethylbenzenes have no market value, and hence every effort is made to prevent their formation. Usually they are simply recycled to the alkylator where they can be dealkylated back to ethylbenzene and where they will suppress the formation of new polyethylbenzenes. Some operators prefer to use a separate higher temperature dealkylation system to treat the polyethylbenzenes. Over-all yields in the process are very high, normally being about 96 per cent for benzene to ethylbenzene and 97 per cent for ethylene to ethylbenzene. About 75-100 lb of ethylbenzene are produced per lb of aluminum chloride consumed in the process.

Although aluminum chloride alkylation accounts for most of the production of ethylbenzene, recently there has been considerable interest shown in the phosphoric acid process developed by Universal Oil Products Co. This process uses a solid catalyst of phosphoric acid adsorbed on kieselguhr. A mixture of benzene and ethylene is passed over the catalyst at temperatures of 350-435°F and pressures of 400-1000 psig. Although the U. O. P. process has been used largely for the production of cumene and propylene polymers, it can be used to produce ethylbenzene efficiently, particularly from a low-concentration ethylene feedstock.

**Manufacture of Styrene**

Ethylbenzene is converted to styrene by the dehydrogenation reaction

$$\Delta H^{\circ}_{298} = +28{,}100 \qquad \Delta F^{\circ}_{298} = +19{,}892$$

$$\Delta H^{\circ}_{900} = +29{,}824 \qquad \Delta F^{\circ}_{900} = +1751$$

In spite of the large amount of experimental work which has been carried out on this reaction, there is still considerable uncertainty as to the kinetics and mechanism of the dehydrogenation. Experimental values of the equilibrium constant are hard to measure because of side reactions. Boundy and Boyer (*op. cit.*) have calculated $K_p$ on the basis of thermal data. Over the temperature range of commercial interest, the equilibrium constant is given by the equation

$$\log K_p = 6.82 - \frac{6520}{T}$$

where $T$ is in degrees Kelvin. This equation checks fairly well with conversions obtained during actual commercial operation.

Although an increase of temperature favors the conversion, in practice the maximum temperature is limited because of thermal cracking of hylbenzene to toluene, benzene and other degradation products. Comercially, the reaction is carried out at temperatures of 1100-1200°F in ıe presence of a catalyst. Several metallic oxides have been found to ıtalyze the reaction such as alumina, chromia, magnesia, ferric oxide ıd zinc oxide. The practice in the United States has been to use the ıme catalyst that is used in the dehydrogenation of butylenes, namely ther the Standard Oil catalyst (18.4 per cent $Fe_2O_3$, 4.6 per cent $K_2O$, 2.4 per cent MgO and 4.6 per cent CuO) or the Shell catalyst ($Fe_2O_3$ romoted with about 5 per cent $Cr_2O_3$ and 7 per cent $K_2CO_3$). The Gerıan plants have used zinc oxide as catalyst activated with 7.6 per cent l$_2O_3$, 9.4 per cent CaO, 2.8 per cent $K_2CrO_4$ and 2.8 per cent $K_2SO_4$. 'he catalysts are nonregenerative, and have an operating life of about year. A conversion of 35-40 per cent is obtained per pass, with an ultiıate yield with recycle of 90-92 per cent.

Since the dehydrogenation is favored by a reduction in pressure, aproximately 2.6 lb of steam/lb ethylbenzene are added to the reactor eed. In addition to reducing all partial pressures, the steam helps to revent side reactions, removes carbon which is deposited on the surface f the catalyst, and supplies part of the endothermic heat of reaction by ncreasing the heat capacity of the gases.

In practice, the ethylbenzene is preheated to about 930°F and mixed vith steam which has been preheated to about 1300°F. The mixture eners the base of the reactor at 1100-1140°F, and the dehydrogenated mixure leaves the top of the reactor at about 1040°F. Since the catalyst oses activity as it ages, the steam temperature is gradually raised until he inlet temperature to the reactor reaches a value of about 1220°F ıfter about a year of operation. The reactor consists of an unheated ·ylindrical vessel fabricated of either stainless steel or brick-lined car-)on steel. The catalyst is in the form of hard nonfriable pellets which ıre contained within a catalyst basket. The Germans have used gas-ıeated tubular reactors, with the tubes filled with catalyst. However, :his increases the cost of the reactor, and leads to possible corrosion problems with the catalyst tubes.

Exit gases from the reactor are heat exchanged with fresh feed, are :ooled with water in a spray tower, and are then condensed in a tubular ıeat exchanger. Noncondensible gases containing hydrogen, carbon mon-)xide and carbon dioxide are compressed, refrigerated to recover aroıatics, and may then be used as fuel. The hydrocarbon and water layers from the spray tower are separated by decantation, and a portion of the water recycled to the tower. The crude styrene has the following approxiınate composition: 37 per cent styrene, 61 per cent ethylbenzene, 1-2 per cent toluene, 0.5-2.0 per cent benzene and 0.2-0.5 per cent tar.

**Styrene Distillation**

The chief problem in the commercial production of styrene was the purification of the final product. Since the normal boiling points of styrene and ethylbenzene differ by about 16°F, at first glance the separation would not be considered very difficult. However, the distillation of styrene is complicated by the fact that the material can undergo an exothermic polymerization to form polystyrene. The rate of polymerization depends on temperature. Thus, at the normal boiling point of styrene, 293.4°F, the rate of polymerization is about 30 per cent/hr, which is obviously much too high. By reducing the temperature to about 194°F, the rate of polymerization of pure styrene is reduced to about 1 per cent/hr which is tolerable. However, the rate of polymerization is strongly affected by the presence of even a few ppm of impurities which can either inhibit or catalyze the polymerization. For this reason, the commercial production of styrene is dependent on achieving the following two conditions: (a) The distillation of pure styrene must be under vacuum to limit the maximum temperature to 194°F. (b) A polymerization inhibitor is added to allow styrene monomer to be held for short periods at elevated temperatures without excessive polymerization.

Figure 11-6 illustrates the process used to purify styrene. Crude styrene from the dehydrogenation unit is first passed through a vessel containing sulfur which acts as a polymerization inhibitor. The styrene is then purified by means of six distillation towers operating as follows:

(1) Splitting Column. The splitting column has about 30 plates, and makes a rough separation into an overhead consisting of benzene, toluene and some ethylbenzene, and a bottoms consisting of ethylbenzene, styrene and tar. The overhead pressure is about 7 in. Hg absolute, and the bottoms temperature is 205°F. Since the styrene is diluted with ethylbenzene and tar, there is less danger of polymerization at this point.

(2) The overhead fraction from the splitter passes to a conventional benzene tower containing 40 plates and operating at atmospheric pressure. Benzene is recycled to the ethylbenzene plant for alkylation.

(3) The bottoms from the benzene tower are fractionated at atmospheric pressure in a conventional 35-plate toluene tower to produce nitration grade toluene.

(4) The bottoms from both the toluene tower and the splitting column are combined and fed to the primary ethylbenzene column. The separation of the ethylbenzene is in two stages, since a single tower would have such a high pressure drop that it would be difficult to hold the bottoms temperature below 194°F. The primary ethylbenzene column contains about 38 plates and operates with a top pressure of about 1.5 in. Hg

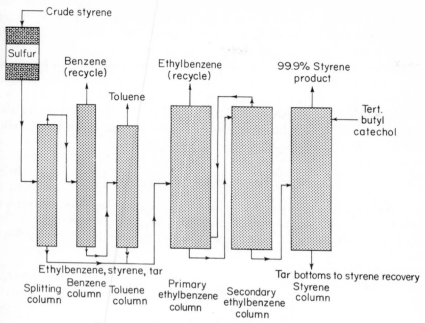

FIG. 11-6. Flowsheet for distillation of styrene.

absolute, a top temperature of 122°F and a bottoms temperature of 194°F. The column is designed for minimum pressure drop, and the reboiler operates with a low temperature difference to prevent high skin temperatures.

(5) The bottoms from the primary ethylbenzene column are pumped to the top of the secondary column which contains about 32 plates and maintains essentially the same conditions as the primary column.

(6) The final styrene tower produces an overhead of pure styrene and a bottoms consisting of tar plus some styrene. This tower may be either a bubble plate or a packed tower, the latter having the advantage of a lower pressure drop. The pressure at the top of the tower is about 1.5 in. Hg absolute, the top temperature is about 140°F and the bottoms temperature about 165°F. The tar bottoms from the styrene tower are quite viscous; these may be mixed with alkylation residues and sent to a styrene recovery unit where styrene is taken overhead. The residues from the recovery unit are usually burned for fuel.

Product styrene from the final distillation is cooled to 60-70°F before being sent to product storage. Since there is little sulfur present in the styrene above the feed plate of the final column, *tert*-butyl catechol is added to the reflux of the styrene column as a low-temperature polymerization inhibitor. Under normal conditions, over-all styrene recovery is better than 99 per cent. The styrene product has a purity of 99.9 per cent or greater, ethylbenzene being the chief impurity.

The fact that over one million tons of styrene are produced annually in the United States is certainly a tribute to the success of the original Dow process. However, the penalty for a mistake is severe, and the punishment truly "fits the crime." Thus, the plant operator who allows the temperature of a styrene tower to get out of hand can spend many months cleaning out a plugged column.

## OTHER DERIVATIVES OF ETHYLENE

In addition to the uses of ethylene discussed above, large quantities also go into the manufacture of polyethylene, halogenated derivatives and surface-active agents. These uses will be discussed in future chapters of the book.

# CHAPTER 12

# Products from Propylene
# and Butylene

We have already discussed the availability of propylene and butylenes as chemical raw materials. The chief products of propylene are illustrated in Fig. 12-1. Of the total quantity of propylene used for chemical purposes, about 37 per cent goes into the manufacture of isopropanol, 23 per cent goes into propylene trimer and tetramer, 13 per cent goes into polypropylene, 12 per cent goes into propylene oxide, 6.5 per cent goes into cumene and smaller amounts go into the manufacture of synthetic glycerol, acrylonitrile, etc.

## ISOPROPANOL

Isopropanol is one of the oldest petrochemicals. It was first produced commercially by Standard Oil Co. at Bayway, New Jersey in 1920 and by Carbide and Carbon Chem. Corp. at South Charleston, West Virginia at about the same time. The process which was used involved the absorption of propylene in sulfuric acid, followed by dilution with water to form the isopropanol. This process is still used for the manufacture of most of the isopropanol produced in the United States.

The hydration of the lower olefins[1] becomes increasingly easier as the molecular weight increases. Thus, 96 per cent sulfuric acid gives optimum results with ethylene, 80-90 per cent is adequate for propylene, 75-85 per cent for n-butylenes, and 60-65 per cent for isobutylene. Therefore, the problems and costs of acid recovery are less, and a more dilute olefin stream can be used. However, it should be noted that hydration of an olefin always gives a secondary or tertiary alcohol, except in the case of

---

[1] See chapter by F. E. Salt in H. Steiner, *op. cit.*

251

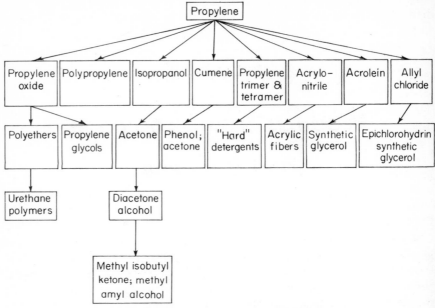

F<small>IG</small>. 12-1. Chief products from propylene.

ethylene where only the primary alcohol exists. Thus, propylene gives isopropanol, *n*-butylenes give *sec*-butanol, etc. When primary alcohols are required, these are usually produced by hydrogenation of the corresponding aldehyde.

Commercially, propylene is absorbed in sulfuric acid to form isopropyl hydrogen sulfate, followed by dilution to obtain isopropanol. The reactions are

$$CH_3—CH\!=\!\!CH_2 \text{ (g)} + H_2SO_4 \rightarrow CH_3CH(OSO_3H)CH_3 \xrightarrow{H_2O}$$
$$CH_3CH(OH)CH_3 + H_2SO_4$$

The absorption of propylene is carried out at temperatures below 100°F, using 70-90 per cent sulfuric acid. The propylene is usually a $C_3$ off-gas from some refinery operation which contains 30-85 per cent propylene mixed with propane. Pressures up to several hundred psig are used to favor the absorption. The acid liquors containing isopropyl hydrogen sulfate pass to a dilution tank where water is added to reduce the acid concentration to 35-40 per cent. Following hydrolysis, isopropanol is stripped from the dilute acid by blowing with open steam and the 87.7 per cent isopropanol azeotrope obtained by fractional distillation. If anhydrous isopropanol is required, this can be obtained by azeotropic distillation using toluene, xylene or ethylene dichloride to remove the water.

The direct hydration of propylene is possible according to the reaction

$$CH_3—CH=CH_2 \text{ (g)} + H_2O \text{ (g)} \rightarrow CH_3—CH(OH)—CH_3 \text{ (g)}$$

$$\Delta H_{298}^\circ = -12,481 \qquad \Delta F_{298}^\circ = +4875$$

This process is used commercially by Imperial Chemical Industries, Ltd., in England and by Montecatini in Italy; however, it is not used commercially in the United States. Propylene and water are preheated and reacted over a tungsten oxide catalyst at a pressure of about 3600 psig, a temperature of 480-550°F, and using a ratio of water to propylene of about 2.5:1. The chief reasons this process has not found favor in the United States are as follows: (a) At a given temperature and pressure, the hydration of propylene is less favorable than the hydration of ethylene. (b) Propylene shows a strong tendency to polymerize to undesirable polymers, particularly at high temperature and pressure. (c) The competing sulfuric acid process for the manufacture of isopropanol is cheaper than in the case of ethanol because lower-strength acid can be used.

The total production of isopropanol in the United States for 1963 was 1466 million pounds. Over half of this material was converted to acetone. In addition, the anhydrous isopropanol finds considerable use as a solvent, as a gasoline additive, and for conversion to esters.

## ACETONE

Future markets for acetone are strongly affected by the increasing availability of by-product acetone from the manufacture of synthetic phenol by the cumene process. Thus, in 1963, by-product acetone accounted for almost one-fourth of the 943 million pound total acetone production in the United States. In addition, a new process now under development for the manufacture of synthetic glycerol produces acetone as a by-product. Note, however, that these new processes do not change the demand for propylene, but merely change the way in which the propylene is converted to acetone.

The production of acetone from isopropanol is usually carried out by dehydrogenation in the vapor phase

$$CH_3CH(OH)CH_3 \rightarrow (CH_3)_2CO + H_2$$

$$\Delta H_{298}^\circ = +13,680 \qquad \Delta F_{298}^\circ = -1530$$

The equilibrium is more favorable than the dehydrogenation of ethanol.

Thus, recent data[1] show that the equilibrium constant $K_p$ for the dehydrogenation has a value of about $10^4$ at a temperature of 260°F and becomes even more favorable at higher temperatures. Commercially, the dehydrogenation is carried out by passing vapors of isopropanol over a catalyst at temperatures of 600-700°F and pressures of 50-100 psig. In the United States, brass or copper is usually used as catalyst; in Germany, zinc oxide has been used. The catalyst gradually loses activity as a result of the deposition of carbon and tar on the surface, and must be periodically regenerated by blowing with air. Exit gases from the catalytic converter are cooled to condense out acetone, and washed with water to recover organics from the by-product hydrogen. The product is purified by conventional distillation. The yield is about 98 per cent, based on the isopropanol feed to the converter.

It is also possible to oxidize isopropanol to acetone using air or oxygen and a metallic catalyst such as silver, nickel, copper or platinum. However, dehydrogenation is more common since it is easier to control and yields a valuable by-product.

### Derivatives of Acetone

Acetone is widely used in the manufacture of drugs and miscellaneous chemicals, and as a solvent for cellulose acetate, paints, varnishes and lacquers. In addition, over half the acetone produced in the United States is converted to other chemicals. For example, acetone will undergo an aldol condensation to form diacetone alcohol (4-hydroxy-4-methylpentanone-2) according to the reaction

$$2(CH_3)_2CO \rightarrow CH_3-\underset{\underset{CH_3}{|}}{\overset{\overset{OH}{|}}{C}}-CH_2-\overset{\overset{O}{\|}}{C}-CH_3$$

The condensation is carried out at room temperature or below, using about 1 per cent caustic solution as a catalyst. Several hours are required to complete the reaction. If diacetone alcohol is desired as product, the caustic is then carefully neutralized with phosphoric acid, the precipitated phosphates allowed to settle, and the diacetone alcohol recovered by distillation. The neutralization of the caustic must be carefully controlled, since excess caustic will catalyze the dissociation back to acetone and excess acid will cause the diacetone alcohol to dehydrate to mesityl oxide.

However, the chief use of diacetone alcohol is as an intermediate for the manufacture of methyl isobutyl ketone and methyl amyl alcohol.

[1] K. A. Kobe and H. R. Crawford, *Hydro. Proc. Petrol. Refiner,* 37(7), 125 (1958).

Thus, if the solution after the aldol condensation is acidified with a weak acid such as phosphoric or oxalic acid, heating to about 250°F will dehydrate the diacetone alcohol according to the reaction

$$(CH_3)_2C(OH)CH_2COCH_3 \xrightarrow{\text{acid}} H_2O + CH_3-\overset{\overset{\displaystyle CH_3}{|}}{C}=CH-\overset{\overset{\displaystyle O}{\|}}{C}-CH_3$$

mesityl oxide

The vapors consist chiefly of water and unreacted acetone which are separated by fractionation and the acetone recycled. The mesityl oxide boils at about 266°F. It finds limited use as a solvent and as a chemical intermediate.

If mesityl oxide is hydrogenated under mild conditions, only the double bond is attacked according to the reaction

$$CH_3-\overset{\overset{\displaystyle CH_3}{|}}{C}=CH-\overset{\overset{\displaystyle O}{\|}}{C}-CH_3 + H_2 \to CH_3-\overset{\overset{\displaystyle CH_3}{|}}{CH}-CH_2-\overset{\overset{\displaystyle O}{\|}}{C}-CH_3$$

methyl isobutyl ketone or<br>4-methylpentanone-2

Methyl isobutyl ketone boils at 241°F, and is an important solvent for resins, esters, lacquers, etc. Approximately 158 million pounds were produced in the United States in 1963, corresponding to a consumption of about 20 per cent of the total acetone production. If mesityl oxide is hydrogenated under vigorous conditions, the carbonyl group is also attacked to form methyl amyl alcohol by the reaction

$$CH_3-\overset{\overset{\displaystyle CH_3}{|}}{C}=CH-\overset{\overset{\displaystyle O}{\|}}{C}-CH_3 + 2H_2 \to CH_3-\overset{\overset{\displaystyle CH_3}{|}}{CH}-CH_2-\overset{\overset{\displaystyle OH}{|}}{CH}-CH_3$$

methyl amyl alcohol, methyl isobutyl<br>carbinol, or 4-methylpentanol-2

The methyl amyl alcohol has a boiling point of 269°F, and finds moderate use as a medium boiling solvent, as a frother in ore flotation, and for the manufacture of xanthates and organic esters.

If acetone is condensed under more drastic conditions using catalysts such as sodium amide or sodium alkoxide, three molecules condense to form the cyclic ketone isophorone. The reaction is

$$3CH_3COCH_3 \to 2H_2O + \begin{array}{c} \text{CO} \\ \diagup \quad \diagdown \\ \text{CH} \qquad \text{CH}_2 \\ \| \qquad\qquad | \\ \text{C} \qquad\quad \text{C(CH}_3)_2 \\ \diagup \quad \diagdown \\ \text{CH}_3 \qquad \text{CH}_2 \end{array}$$

In practice, acetone is heated in the liquid phase in the presence of the catalyst, water and unreacted acetone are taken as an overhead product, and acetone is recycled to the reactor. Isophorone boils at 419°F, and finds limited use as a high-boiling solvent for paints and vinyl resins.

## PROPYLENE OXIDE

Although considerable work has been carried out on the direct oxidation of propylene to propylene oxide, the yields are much smaller than in the oxidation of ethylene. The chief problem appears to be that the methyl group next to the double bond can also be attacked, and this causes a substantial reduction in yield through side reactions. It is possible that someone will eventually discover a catalyst which will direct the reaction primarily to the formation of propylene oxide. However, direct oxidation is not economical with present technology, and thus propylene oxide is produced commercially by the chlorohydrin process. The chief reactions are

$$Cl_2 + H_2O \rightleftharpoons HCl + HOCl$$

$$CH_3-CH{=}CH_2 + HOCl
\begin{cases}
\xrightarrow{90\%} CH_3\overset{\overset{\displaystyle OH}{|}}{-}CH\overset{\overset{\displaystyle Cl}{|}}{-}CH_2 \\[2ex]
\xrightarrow{10\%} CH_3\overset{\overset{\displaystyle Cl}{|}}{-}CH\overset{\overset{\displaystyle OH}{|}}{-}CH_2
\end{cases}
\begin{array}{c}
\searrow^{Ca(OH)_2} \\
\\
\nearrow_{Ca(OH)_2}
\end{array}
CH_3-CH\underset{\diagdown O \diagup}{-\!\!-\!\!-}CH_2$$

with the chief side reaction

$$CH_3-CH{=}CH_2 + Cl_2 \rightarrow CH_3-CHCl-CH_2Cl$$

A typical flow sheet for the manufacture of propylene oxide[1] is illustrated in Fig. 12-2. Water, chlorine and propylene are mixed in the chlorohydrin tower at slightly greater than atmospheric pressure and at a temperature of about 95°F, which is the natural temperature of the system. The liquid solution in the chlorohydrin tower is recirculated by means of an air lift, overflow solution passing by gravity to the saponifier. Best results are obtained when the propylene chlorohydrin concentration is maintained at about 4 per cent by weight. Exit gases are scrubbed with cold caustic solution to remove propylene dichloride and traces of chlorine, and a small fraction of the gas is purged and replaced with fresh propylene before being recycled to the chlorohydrin tower. The chlorine feed rate must be adjusted so that only small quantities

[1] A. C. Fyvie, "Propylene Oxide and its Derivatives," *Chem. Ind. (London)*, **384** (1964).

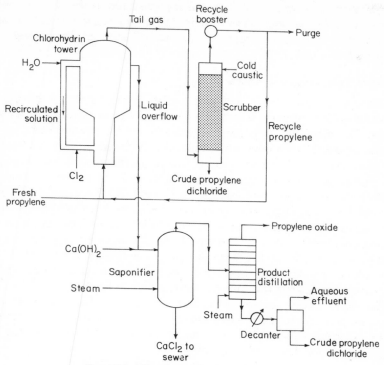

FIG. 12-2. Flowsheet for propylene oxide.

are present in the recycle gas; larger quantities would represent a significant loss of chlorine and, in addition, there is the danger of an explosion if the chlorine concentration becomes greater than 20 per cent.

The chlorohydrin solution is mixed with a slurry of lime in the saponifier and heated with open steam to distill off the propylene oxide. It is necessary to complete the saponification reaction fairly rapidly, since propylene chlorohydrin is itself volatile and may appear in the overhead product or, if unconverted, may be lost in the aqueous effluent from the saponifier. The saponifier may be a multi-compartment chamber, a simple pipe reactor followed by a stripper, or only a stripping column. Mild steel is used as a material of construction for all equipment after the point of mixing of the lime and chlorohydrin solution. Excess lime is recovered from the stripped solution by a conventional thickener and clarifier, and the aqueous solution containing 5-6 per cent $CaCl_2$ sent to the sewer. The distillate from the saponifier contains water, propylene oxide, and propylene dichloride. This is condensed, washed with soda ash solution to remove any traces of chlorine, and is distilled to produce propylene oxide as overhead product and a two-phase bottoms which is separated by decantation into an aqueous effluent and by-product crude propylene dichloride.

### Products from Propylene Oxide

The total production of propylene oxide in the United States in 1963 was 497 million pounds, about one-fourth of the production of ethylene oxide. The chief use of propylene oxide is for the manufacture of propylene glycol. The process used commercially is completely analogous to the manufacture of ethylene glycol, namely, an uncatalyzed high-pressure liquid phase hydration using a high ratio of water to propylene oxide, followed by vacuum distillation to separate the individual glycols. The chief uses of propylene glycol are as a solvent, as antifreeze, and as a humectant for tobacco and foodstuffs where propylene glycol is non-toxic as contrasted to ethylene glycol. An increasingly important use of propylene glycol is in the manufacture of polyester resins; thus, it is anticipated that this use alone will account for most of the growth of propylene glycol over the immediate future.

The other major use of propylene oxide is in the manufacture of urethane polyethers. If present trends continue, this use of propylene oxide will more than double over the period from 1963-68. The urethane polymers will be discussed in Chapter 19.

## PROPYLENE TRIMER AND TETRAMER

Propylene can be polymerized to form various low molecular-weight polymers of which the trimer (nonene) and the tetramer (dodecene) are the most important. Thus, in 1963, propylene trimer and tetramer accounted for about 23 per cent of the total chemical use of propylene. The chief chemical use of these two chemicals has been in the manufacture of detergents such as the alkyl benzene sulfonates (ABS). However, this use in the United States is scheduled to disappear in 1965 as the detergent manufacturers shift to the production of the "soft" detergents which are based on straight-chain paraffins. The other chemical uses of the trimer and tetramer are relatively minor, so that these minor uses plus the export market will be all that is left for these chemicals by the late 1960's.

The older process for the manufacture of propylene trimer and tetramer involved absorption of propylene in sulfuric acid, followed by dilution and controlled polymerization. However, Fig. 12-3 illustrates

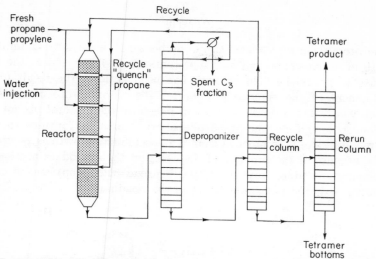

Fig. 12-3. Phosphoric acid process for propylene trimer or tetramer (E. K. Jones, "Advances in Catalysis," Vol. 8, Academic Press, Inc., New York, 1956).

the phosphoric acid [1] process which is now most commonly used. In this process, propylene at temperatures of 350-435°F and pressures of 400-1200 psig is passed through beds of solid catalyst to polymerize the propylene to the dimer, trimer, tetramer, etc. The catalyst consists of phosphoric acid adsorbed on kieselguhr. The reactions are exothermic, and cooling is provided by using a quench of cold reactor effluent between catalyst beds. The reaction products include thousands of different isomers of $C_6$, $C_9$, $C_{12}$, etc., polypropylenes, although conditions can be adjusted to yield chiefly the trimer or the tetramer.

In the case of a tetramer unit, the reactor effluent is cooled and fractionated in a depropanizer to produce a $C_3$ fraction consisting largely of propane which can be used as fuel. A second column produces an overhead $C_6$ and $C_9$ mixture which is recycled, and a bottoms which is fractionated in a third column to produce tetramer and a heavy polymer bottoms. The tetramer product has a standard boiling range of about 353-450°F. With recycle, the conversion of propylene is better than 90 per cent.

[1] E. K. Jones, "Polymerization of Olefins from Cracked Gases," Advances in Catalysis, Vol. VIII, New York, Academic Press, Inc., 1956.

## CUMENE

The production of cumene (isopropylbenzene) has shown a fantastic growth in recent years, and now represents about 7 per cent of the total end use of propylene. This growth has been entirely the result of the development of the cumene process for the manufacture of synthetic phenol, which now accounts for about one-third of the total phenol production. Although cumene-based phenol will probably continue to grow at a modest rate, it is obvious that the spectacular growth is now over, chiefly because of the problem of disposing of the coproduct acetone.

Cumene is produced by alkylating benzene with propylene in either the vapor or liquid phase according to the reaction

$$\Delta H^{\circ}_{298} = -23{,}759 \qquad \Delta F^{\circ}_{298} = -13{,}241$$

The alkylation proceeds much more easily than in the case of ethylene. Catalysts which may be used include sulfuric acid, aluminum chloride and phosphoric acid. However, the process which has been used for most new construction is the Universal Oil Products Co. direct alkylation, using a solid catalyst of phosphoric acid adsorbed on kieselguhr. In practice, the process is virtually identical with the one used to produce propylene trimer and tetramer. Thus, a mixture of benzene and propylene at 400-600°F and 400-900 psig is passed over the catalyst, using a quench of recycle benzene between stages. The reactor effluent is cooled, fractionated to remove $C_3$'s, fractionated to remove benzene, and fractionated to produce product cumene and a bottoms consisting chiefly of polyisopropylbenzenes. The yield of cumene is about 95 per cent, based on benzene consumed.

## SYNTHETIC GLYCEROL

At one time, all glycerol came as a by-product from the manufacture of soap. However, in 1936, Shell Development Co. found that the reaction of chlorine and propylene at high temperatures led not to addition, but to interaction with the methyl group to give allyl chloride. This discovery led to the development of the "hot chlorination process" for the manufacture of synthetic glycerol.[1] At about this same period of time, the introduction of synthetic detergents led to a gradual decrease in the production of old-fashioned soap, with a resultant decrease in the availability of byproduct glycerol. For these reasons, Shell Chemical Co. in 1948 started the manufacture of synthetic glycerol at Houston, Texas with an initial design capacity of 50 million pounds/year. By 1963, the production of synthetic glycerol in the United States had risen to 162 million pounds/year, whereas the production of natural glycerol had decreased to about 130 million pounds/year.

The manufacture of synthetic glycerol represents about 2.5 per cent of the total end use of propylene. However, in spite of the availability of the synthetic material and several recent price cuts, the demand for glycerol has changed relatively little in the past 10 years. The chief uses of glycerol are in the manufacture of cellophane and alkyd resins, and as a humectant in drugs, cosmetics, tobacco and foodstuffs. These have shown little growth in recent years, and no other large markets are in sight.

The initial Shell synthesis is illustrated in Fig. 12-4. Propylene is chlorinated noncatalytically at a temperature of 930-950°F and a pressure of about 15 psig to give allyl chloride according to the equation

$$CH_3—CH{=}CH_2 + Cl_2 \rightarrow CH_2Cl—CH{=}CH_2 + HCl$$

The reaction involves a direct substitution of chlorine, not an addition of $Cl_2$ across the double bond followed by a splitting off of HCl. The chief side reaction is the formation of *cis* and *trans*-1,3-dichloropropene by the further chlorination of allyl chloride

$$CH_2Cl—CH{=}CH_2 + Cl_2 \rightarrow CH_2Cl—CH{=}CHCl + HCl$$

There is also some direct addition of chlorine across the double bond to form 1,2-dichloropropane, and many other chlorinated by-products are also formed in fairly small amounts.

Commercially, the reaction is carried out using a propylene to chlorine ratio of 3:1 or 4:1 to reduce side reactions. The engineering design of the chlorinator is of critical importance, since this can cause the yield of allyl chloride to vary from 75 per cent with good design down to perhaps 25 per cent with poor design. In practice, the residence time in the chlorinator is about 1.8 seconds and the gases are carefully mixed to prevent any local concentration of chlorine. Because of carbon formation, the chlorinator must be cleaned about every two weeks. Exit gases from the

[1] F. C. Williams, *Amer. Inst. Chem. Engrs. Trans.*, **37**, 157 (1941); A. W. Fairbairn, *et al.*, *Chem. Eng. Progr.*, **43**(6), 280 (1947).

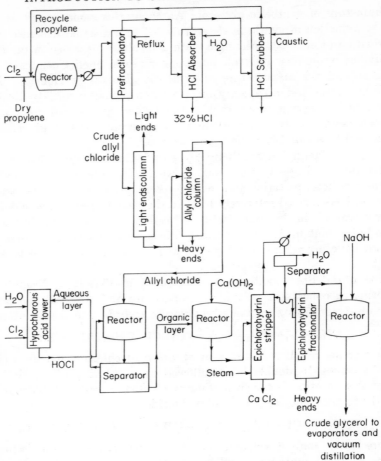

Fig. 12-4. Synthetic glycerol process [*Hydro. Proc. Petrol. Refiner,* **38** (11), **253** (1959)]. (Copyright 1959, Gulf Publishing Co., Houston, Texas)

chlorinator are rapidly cooled and sent to a prefractionator which uses liquid propylene from storage as reflux. The overhead from the prefractionator consists of propylene and HCl; the HCl is absorbed in water, and the propylene is washed with caustic and recycled to the chlorinator. The bottoms from the prefractionator consist chiefly of chlorinated hydrocarbons; these are further distilled to yield 20-25 per cent high-boiling material or "heavy ends," 3-4 per cent low-boiling material or "light ends," the balance being allyl chloride.

In the manufacture of glycerol, the allyl chloride is next converted to the dichlorohydrin by reaction with hypochlorous acid. However, this reaction cannot be carried out using free chlorine because of the possible direct addition of chlorine to allyl chloride (note that 1,2,3-trichloropropane cannot be saponified by the usual methods). Thus, a solution of hypochlorous acid is first made from sodium hypochlorite

$$NaOCl + Cl_2 + H_2O \rightarrow NaCl + 2HOCl$$

This is then mixed continuously with allyl chloride at room temperature to form the dichlorohydrin

$$CH_2Cl—CH{=}CH_2 + HOCl \rightarrow CH_2Cl—CH(OH)—CH_2Cl$$

The upper aqueous layer is treated and recycled; the lower organic layer contains about 5 per cent trichloropropane, 2.5 per cent high-boiling impurities and 91 per cent dichlorohydrin chiefly as the 1,3-isomer.

The dichlorohydrin can be saponified directly to glycerol with caustic solution, but not with lime since hot calcium chloride solutions will decompose glycerol. However, it is possible to use lime for the saponification of one of the chlorines by distilling off epichlorohydrin according to the reaction

$$2CH_2Cl—CH(OH)—CH_2Cl + Ca(OH)_2 \rightarrow$$

$$\overset{\displaystyle O}{\overset{\displaystyle \diagup \diagdown}{2CH_2Cl—CH{—}CH_2}} + CaCl_2 + 2H_2O$$

The epichlorohydrin has a normal boiling point of 239.4°F. A mixture of water and epichlorohydrin can be distilled from solution, and the epichlorohydrin recovered in a stripping column. The epichlorohydrin itself has a substantial market for the production of epoxy resins. It can be easily hydrated and saponified to glycerol by the reaction

$$\overset{\displaystyle O}{\overset{\displaystyle \diagup \diagdown}{CH_2Cl—CH{—}CH_2}} + NaOH + H_2O \rightarrow NaCl + \overset{\displaystyle OH \quad OH \quad OH}{\overset{\displaystyle |\qquad |\qquad |}{CH_2—CH—CH_2}}$$

The dilute glycerol is then concentrated and purified by multiple-effect evaporation.

It must be emphasized that there are several alternate methods for the production of glycerol from allyl chloride. The one described here is a possible one but not necessarily the one used commercially. For competitive reasons, Shell Chemical has not as yet disclosed the process which is most economical for commercial operations.

### Acrolein

Acrolein can be made by the direct oxidation of propylene at temperatures of 550-750°F according to the equation

$$CH_2{=}CH—CH_3 + O_2 \rightarrow CH_2{=}CH—CHO + H_2O$$

The oxidation is carried out over a solid copper oxide or bismuth molybdate catalyst using a mixture of propylene, steam and oxygen. Acrolein is obtained in yields of over 80 per cent, based on the propylene consumed. The kinetics of the reaction are quite interesting: thus, over cuprous oxide the reaction is first-order in oxygen and independent of propylene, whereas over bismuth molybdate the reaction is first-order in propylene and independent of oxygen.

At one time, high hopes were held for the future of this unsaturated aldehyde. However, even with the commercial availability of acrolein, its growth has been quite limited. Only about 5 million pounds/year are sold in the United States, the chief use being for the production of methionine, a protein supplement for animal feed. However, there is now renewed interest in acrolein because Shell Chemical has started the commercial production of synthetic glycerol by a new route which uses acrolein as an intermediate. The first step of the process is an oxidation of isopropanol with pure oxygen according to the equation

$$(CH_3)_2CH(OH) + O_2 \rightarrow (CH_3)_2CO + H_2O_2$$

The oxidation takes place in the liquid phase at 200-280°F and a pressure of about 40 psig. The reaction mixture is then diluted with water and distilled to obtain a hydrogen peroxide solution, product acetone, and recycle isopropanol. In the second step of the process, acrolein is reacted with isopropanol to obtain more acetone by the reaction

$$CH_2{=}CH{-}CHO + (CH_3)_2CH(OH) \rightarrow$$
$$CH_2{=}CH{-}CH_2(OH) + (CH_3)_2CO$$

This reaction takes place in the gas phase at about 750°F over a magnesium oxide-zinc oxide catalyst using a molar ratio of isopropanol to acrolein of from 2:1 to 3:1. The yield of allyl alcohol is reported to be 77 per cent, based on acrolein. In the final step of the process, allyl alcohol reacts with hydrogen peroxide to form glycerol by the reaction

$$CH_2{=}CH{-}CH_2OH + H_2O_2 \rightarrow CH_2(OH)CH(OH)CH_2(OH)$$

This reaction is carried out in the liquid phase at 140-160°F, using a tungstic oxide catalyst. A yield of over 80 per cent is reported, based on allyl alcohol.

If all intermediate products are neglected, the over-all reaction is

$$3CH_2{=}CH{-}CH_3 + 2O_2 + H_2O \rightarrow$$
$$CH_2OH{-}CHOH{-}CH_2OH + 2(CH_3)_2CO$$

The chief advantage of this synthetic glycerol process is that it eliminates the need for caustic and chlorine which are required in the traditional allyl chloride process. The chief disadvantage of the process is the large number of complex interlocking processes which must be operated. Thus, it is rumored that Shell Chemical has encountered some problems in bringing the over-all process into commercial operation.

## ACRYLONITRILE

The manufacture of acrylonitrile will require rapidly increasing quantities of propylene over the immediate future. The chief use of acrylonitrile is in the manufacture of acrylic fibers which have shown a very rapid growth. Thus, in 1950 the production of acrylonitrile in the United States was essentially zero; in 1960 the production was about 200 million pounds, and by 1963 this had increased to 455 million pounds. The older processes were based on either the direct addition of HCN to acetylene or the addition of HCN to ethylene oxide, followed by the splitting off of a molecule of water. However, the propylene-based process uses relatively cheap raw materials, and hence appears to have completely replaced the older processes for new construction.

The new route to acrylonitrile was developed by Standard Oil Co. of Ohio,[1] which is licensing plants for construction throughout the world. The process involves a direct vapor-phase reaction of propylene, ammonia and oxygen according to the equation

$$CH_2 \!\!=\!\! CH\!\!-\!\!CH_3 + NH_3 + \tfrac{3}{2}O_2 \rightarrow CH_2 \!\!=\!\! CH\!\!-\!\!C \!\!\equiv\!\! N + 3H_2O$$

The process is illustrated in Fig. 12-5. The reaction is carried out at temperatures of 750-925°F and pressures of 5-30 psig, using a bismuth molybdate fluid catalyst. Silica is used as a catalyst support. The feed contains 10 per cent propylene, 70 per cent air, 10 per cent ammonia and 10 per cent water by volume. A fairly long catalyst contact time of several seconds is required. The conversion to acrylonitrile is 60-65 per cent, based on propylene, and there is a 2-10 per cent conversion to acetonitrile ($CH_3 - C \equiv N$). In addition, substantial quantities of acrolein and HCN are produced, which may be recovered as by-products. The reaction products are recovered by absorption in water at atmospheric pressure and at temperatures below 75°F to prevent the reaction of acrylonitrile with aqueous ammonia. Acrylonitrile and acetonitrile product are separated by conventional and azeotropic distillation; if desired, the final product distillation can be under vacuum to minimize

---

[1] F. Veatch, et al., "New Route to Acrylonitrile," *Chem. Eng. Progr.*, **56**(10), 65 (1960); J. D. Idol, Jr. (assigned to Standard Oil Co., Ohio), U.S. Patent 2,904,580 (Sept. 15, 1959).

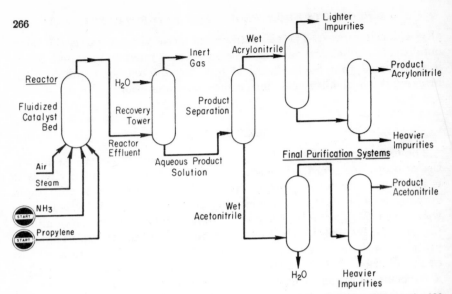

Fig. 12-5. Acrylonitrile from propylene [*Hydro. Proc. Petrol. Refiner,* **42** (11), 139 (1963)]. (Copyright 1962, Gulf Publishing Co., Houston, Texas)

thermal degradation of the heavy ends. A small amount of oxalic acid is added to the final column to stabilize impurities.

Reportedly, the conversion of ammonia and propylene to acrylonitrile is accomplished by the oxygen atoms of the catalyst through a single discrete reaction sequence not going through acrolein as an intermediate.[1] Thus, catalysts are known which produce acrylonitrile from propylene in the presence of ammonia but produce no acrolein in its absence. Also, acetonitrile is not mechanistically necessary since catalysts are known which produce high yields of acrylonitrile without acetonitrile. Recent Soviet work reports an activation energy of about 21,000 for the reaction. The reaction over a bismuth molybdate catalyst is first-order with respect to propylene and independent of oxygen. The effect of water is more than that of a diluent, and probably helps in adsorption or desorption on the surface of the catalyst. Certainly the reaction is an extremely interesting one, although it is obvious that the reaction mechanism has not as yet been fully explained.

## PRODUCTS FROM $C_4$ HYDROCARBONS

With the exception of butadiene, the chemical uses of the $C_4$ and higher hydrocarbons are very limited. Considerable *n*-butane is used as

[1] F. Veatch, *et al., Hydro. Proc. Petrol. Refiner,* **41**(11), 187 (1962); M. A. Dalin, *et al., Doklady Akad. Nauk SSSR,* **145,** 1058 (1962); C. R. Adams and T. J. Jennings, *J. Catalysis,* **3,** 549 (1964).

a raw material for the production of butadiene, ethylene, and a variety of alcohols, aldehydes, and acids by direct oxidation. Isobutylene is used to produce tertiary butyl alcohol, di- and triisobutylene, and butyl rubber. The *n*-butylenes are used to produce secondary butanol, which is an intermediate for the manufacture of methyl ethyl ketone. With the growing interest in stereo rubber, the production of isoprene from a $C_5$ fraction is now under commercial development, although there is some question as to how the process will compare economically with other processes used to produce isoprene.

### Isobutylene

We have seen that the first step in the separation of $C_4$ hydrocarbons is usually a scrubbing with cold 50-60 per cent sulfuric acid to absorb isobutylene. This acid solution may then be treated in different ways to obtain various products. If the temperature is kept low, little polymerization occurs, and the isobutylene is hydrated to *tert*-butyl alcohol. Since this alcohol is easily dehydrated, it must be recovered by considerable dilution or by extraction with a solvent such as cresol. Unfortunately, the *tert*-butyl alcohol is a relatively poor solvent, and hence finds only a very limited market.

If the acid solution of isobutylene is heated to about 175°F, the isobutylene readily polymerizes to the dimer, trimer, etc. A typical reaction for the dimer is

$$2(CH_3)_2C\!\!=\!\!CH_2 \rightarrow CH_3\!-\!\underset{\underset{CH_3}{|}}{\overset{\overset{CH_3}{|}}{C}}\!-\!CH_2\!-\!\overset{\overset{CH_3}{|}}{C}\!\!=\!\!CH_2$$

These polymers separate out as an oily layer which can be withdrawn and purified. Diisobutylene is sold as a uniform mixture of two specific isomers of trimethyl pentene, and is used mainly to produce octyl phenol. The triisobutylene has a very limited market because it cannot compete economically with propylene tetramer.

However, the most important use of isobutylene is in the manufacture of butyl rubber where a 99 per cent purity is required. A typical process for the recovery of isobutylene is illustrated in Fig. 12-6. A feedstock containing 10-40 weight per cent isobutylene is contacted with 50 per cent sulfuric acid at a pressure of 120-180 psig in a series of reactors. The temperature varies from about 120°F in the first stage to room temperature or slight refrigeration in the final stage. The rich liquid passes to a settler to separate the acid and hydrocarbon phases. The hydrocarbon polymer consists of a mixture of about 97 per cent dimer and 3

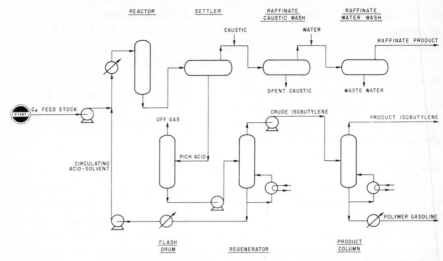

FIG. 12-6. Recovery of isobutylene [*Hydro. Proc. Petrol. Refiner,* **42** (11), 186 (1963)].
(Copyright 1962, Gulf Publishing Co., Houston, Texas)

per cent trimer. It is washed with caustic and water, and can then either
be separated for chemical use or used as a gasoline blending stock. The
acid layer is flashed to atmospheric pressure to remove dissolved hydrocarbon impurities, and is then heated to 250-260°F at about 1-2
psig to drive off isobutylene vapor. The isobutylene is fractionated to
obtain a purity of 99 per cent or better. About 90 per cent of the isobutylene in the feedstock is recovered as product, and about 5 per cent
is recovered as by-product polymer gasoline.

### Secondary Butanol

After removal of the isobutylene, the mixed *n*-butylenes present in the
$C_4$ fraction may then be converted to *sec*-butanol by the reaction

$$CH_3-CH_2-CH=CH_2$$

$$\text{or} \qquad + H_2O \rightarrow CH_3-CH_2-\overset{\displaystyle OH}{\underset{|}{C}}H-CH_3$$

$$CH_3-CH=CH-CH_3$$

Note that both *n*-butylenes give the same alcohol. The process involves
the usual absorption in 70-85 per cent sulfuric acid at temperatures below
about 100°F, followed by dilution with water to 20-40 per cent $H_2SO_4$.
Low temperatures and rather extensive dilution are required because

there is much more polymer formation than in the case of ethylene or propylene. The *sec*-butanol is stripped from the acid solution by blowing with open steam, and the product purified by distillation. The *sec*-butanol forms an azeotrope with water which boils at 190°F and contains 68 per cent *sec*-butanol. If the anhydrous alcohol is required, this can be obtained by extraction or by azeotropic distillation using a suitable water entrainer.

The direct hydration of *n*-butylene in the vapor phase is possible, but the equilibrium is even less favorable than the hydration of propylene. For this reason, direct hydration is not used commercially.

### Methyl Ethyl Ketone

Although *sec*-butanol has a limited market as a solvent and as an intermediate for the manufacture of *sec*-butyl esters, the chief use of *sec*-butanol is in the production of the important solvent, methyl ethyl ketone. The process used commercially is a dehydrogenation according to the reaction

$$CH_3—CH_2—CH(OH)—CH_3 \rightarrow H_2 + C_2H_5—\overset{\overset{\displaystyle O}{\|}}{C}—CH_3$$

A brass catalyst is commonly used, although other catalysts such as ZnO activated with $Na_2CO_3$, Cu-Ni on kieselguhr and Raney[*] copper may be used. The dehydrogenation of *sec*-butanol is slightly easier than in the case of isopropanol; temperatures of about 600-650°F are commonly used at about atmospheric pressure. Exit gases are cooled and scrubbed with water to recover organics from the byproduct hydrogen. Methyl ethyl ketone is purified by distillation and unreacted *sec*-butanol recycled to the reactor. The yield is about 94 per cent or better, based on the *sec*-butanol reacting.

The chief use of methyl ethyl ketone is as a solvent where a lower vapor pressure than acetone is desired. In addition to the manufacture from *sec*-butanol, substantial quantities of methyl ethyl ketone are also produced by the direct oxidation of propane and butane.

[*] In 1925, Murray Raney patented a method of preparing catalysts which consisted of reacting an alloy such as nickel-aluminum with aqueous caustic, followed by reduction to elemental nickel. Catalysts produced in this way show much greater activity than the usual base metals. A substantial fraction of the catalysts used commercially are manufactured according to the method developed by Raney.

# CHAPTER 13

# Acetylene and Its Products

Acetylene is an extremely versatile chemical raw material. In some countries such as Japan, West and East Germany, the Soviet Union and France, acetylene serves as the basis for a substantial fraction of the entire petrochemical industry. However, in the United States, only a relatively small fraction of the petrochemicals is produced from acetylene. The reason for this is entirely economic, namely, that the cost of acetylene is about twice the cost of ethylene and four times the cost of propylene. Since any given chemical product can usually be made in several different ways, a process based on acetylene can be justified only when the higher cost of acetylene can be offset by a more direct process, a higher yield or a savings in the cost of other chemical raw materials.

Table 13-1 lists the major producers of acetylene in the United States for chemical purposes, and Fig. 13-1 illustrates the principal uses of acetylene. Approximately 850 million pounds of acetylene were used in 1963 for the manufacture of petrochemicals; an exact figure is hard to determine because much of the production is for captive use, and there is the question as to what fraction of the carbide acetylene goes into fuel gas. About 33 per cent of the chemical use of acetylene was for the production of vinyl chloride, 26 per cent for neoprene rubber, 16 per cent for acrylonitrile, 11 per cent for vinyl acetate and 9 per cent for trichloroethylene.

## MANUFACTURE OF ACETYLENE

The manufacture of acetylene from calcium carbide still accounts for most of the world's production, although hydrocarbon-based acetylene is rapidly taking over in the United States.[1] The carbide process goes

---

[1] For recent reviews, see S. A. Miller, "Chemicals from Acetylene," *Chem. Ind.* (*London*), p. 4 (1963); J. W. Haworth and W. J. Grant, "Acetylene from Hydrocarbons," chapter in H. Steiner, *op. cit.*, p. 134; W. B. Howard, "The Manufacture of Petrochemical Acetylene," chapter in J. J. McKetta, Jr., Vol. 3, *op. cit.*

TABLE 13-1. PRODUCTION OF ACETYLENE IN THE UNITED STATES*

I. Hydrocarbon-based Acetylene

| Company | Location | Process | Capacity (million lbs/yr) |
|---------|----------|---------|---------------------------|
| American Cyanamid | Fortier, La. | BASF | 100 |
| Diamond | Deer Park, Texas | Montecatini | 40 |
| Dow | Freeport, Texas | Dow | 15 |
| du Pont | Montague, Mich. | du Pont modified arc | 50 |
| Monochem | Geismar, La. | BASF | 80 |
| Monsanto | Texas City, Texas | BASF | 80 |
| Rohm and Haas | Deer Park, Texas | BASF | 35 |
| Tenneco | Pasadena, Texas | SBA | 100 |
| Union Carbide | Institute, W. Va. | Wulff | 10 |
| | Texas City, Texas | Union Carbide | 75 |
| Total hydrocarbon-based | | | 585 |

II. Carbide-based Acetylene

| Company | Location | Carbide source | Capacity (million lbs/yr) |
|---------|----------|----------------|---------------------------|
| Air Reduction | Calvert City, Ky. | Own, same location | 100 |
| | Louisville, Ky. | Own, Ivanhoe, Va.; Calvert City, Ky. | 200 |
| duPont (to be replaced by arc process) | Montague, Mich. | Union Carbide, Sault St. Marie, Mich. | 50 |
| Union Carbide | Ashtabula, Ohio | Own, same location | 150 |
| | Memphis, Tenn. | Own, Sheffield, Ala. | 40 |
| | Moundsville, W. Va. | Own | 50 |
| | Niagara Falls, N.Y. | Own, same location | 150 |
| | S. Charleston, W. Va. | Own, various locations | 15 |
| Total carbide-based | | | 755 |

* Estimates by *Chem. Eng. News*, p. 54, July 22, 1963.

back to 1892 when T. L. Willson, a Canadian electrical engineer, produced the first substantial quantities of calcium carbide from lime and coke in an electric furnace at Spray, North Carolina. Moissan in France also independently produced calcium carbide the same year, but on a much smaller scale. Within a few years, calcium carbide had become an important industrial chemical.

Although many engineering improvements have been made in carbide furnaces, the basic process is still the same, namely, the heating of lime and coke in an electric furnace to give calcium carbide by the reaction

$$CaO \ (s) + 3C \ (s) \rightarrow CaC_2 \ (s) + CO \ (g) \qquad (13\text{-}1)$$

$$\Delta H^{\circ}_{298} = +110{,}500 \qquad \Delta F^{\circ}_{298} = +95{,}400$$

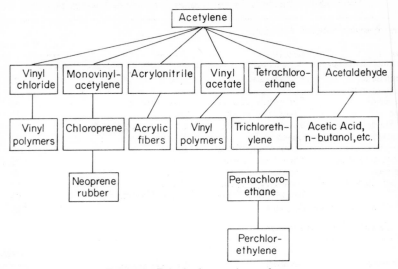

FIG. 13-1. Principal uses of acetylene.

The reaction is strongly endothermic, and must be carried out at temperatures of 3300-3600°F to obtain a satisfactory rate of reaction. The success of the process is dependent on the removal of the gaseous reaction product carbon monoxide. In commercial practice, the total electrical energy consumed is about 5 kw-hr/lb of acetylene generated from the calcium carbide. Modern carbide furnaces consist of a closed bricklined vessel; carbon monoxide is recovered, and may be used in the burning of the limestone. The lime should be at least 95 per cent CaO and low in magnesium and phosphorus; carbon is in the form of coke which may be mixed with anthracite coal. The electrodes consist of mixtures of tar, pitch, ground coke, and anthracite which are encased in metal and baked *in situ*. Continuous operation is achieved by gradually adding new material on top as the electrodes are consumed below. Although the melting point of pure calcium carbide is about 4180°F, a eutectic is formed with lime which melts at about 3180°F and contains 69.4 per cent $CaC_2$. Liquid carbide is usually tapped from the furnace at about 3600°F, the furnace product containing 80-84 per cent $CaC_2$, 10-14 per cent CaO, 0.4-3.0 per cent C, 2-3 per cent MgO, and smaller amounts of other impurities such as $SiO_2$, $Fe_2O_3$, $Al_2O_3$, etc.

One substantial advantage of carbide as a source of acetylene is that the reaction with water immediately yields acetylene of about 99.5 per cent purity. The equation is

$$CaC_2 \text{ (s) } + 2H_2O \text{ (l) } \rightarrow Ca(OH)_2 \text{ (s) } + C_2H_2 \text{ (g)}$$

$$\Delta H^{\circ}_{298} = -30,000 \qquad \Delta F^{\circ}_{298} = -34,800$$

The generation of the acetylene may be either "wet" or "dry." The wet process uses excess water which permits easier temperature control and purification; the dry process uses limited water, and thus produces a more easily handled by-product lime. The chief impurities in the acetylene are $NH_3$, $H_2S$, $PH_3$ and $AsH_3$, which can be easily removed by conventional chemical absorption.

It is obvious that the economical production of calcium carbide is dependent on a cheap source of electricity, but this may not necessarily represent the best location for a petrochemical complex. Shipping calcium carbide is not very feasible, since it involves the handling of a bulk solid and since 2 lb of dead weight must be handled per lb of acetylene equivalent. It is certainly significant that in 1963 only about one-quarter of the calcium carbide produced in the United States was shipped commercially, and most of this was probably used to generate acetylene for fuel purposes. The other three-quarters of the carbide production was for captive use, chiefly to produce acetylene for chemical purposes. However it should be noted that many companies make acetylene from carbide or from hydrocarbons and sell the acetylene through pipelines to other concerns. Thus the acetylene itself is not captive, since the carbide manufacturer does not always use it himself to make acetylene chemicals.

## Other Uses of Calcium Carbide

In addition to serving as a source of acetylene, at one time substantial quantities of calcium carbide were used for the manufacture of fertilizer. The old cyanamide process involves the direct reaction between nitrogen and calcium carbide according to the equation

$$CaC_2 + N_2 \rightarrow Ca{=}N{-}C{\equiv}N + C$$
$$\textit{calcium cyanamide}$$

$$\Delta H^{\circ}_{298} = -69,000$$

This process represented one of the first methods of fixing nitrogen. The reaction is carried out at 1850-2000°F and about atmospheric pressure, using a catalyst such as calcium fluoride. The crude calcium cyanamide product contains about 25 per cent nitrogen, and is an excellent fertilizer. However, calcium cyanamide cannot compete economically with synthetic ammonia for fertilizer purposes; thus, although relatively small quantities of calcium cyanamide are used for agricultural purposes as a defoliant, the fertilizer use of calcium cyanamide in the United States has now essentially ended.

However, the American Cyanamid Corp. has been very successful in developing new products from cyanamide which are noncompetitive with those from ammonia. For example, if calcium cyanamide is dissolved in water, it is hydrolyzed to the acid salt. If the solution is acidified with sulfuric or carbonic acid, the hydrolysis is completed according to the equation

$$CaCN_2 + H_2O + CO_2 \rightarrow CaCO_3 + \underset{cyanamide}{H_2N—C\equiv N}$$

If the pH of the cyanamide solution is adjusted to 8.5 by the addition of calcium cyanamide, heating to about 180°F for 2-3 hr causes the cyanamide to polymerize to the dimer

$$2H_2NCN \rightarrow \underset{dicyandiamide}{H_2N—\overset{\overset{\displaystyle NH}{\|}}{C}—NH—CN}$$

The dicyandiamide can be crystallized by slow cooling to about 45°F. Heating dicyandiamide under pressure with anhydrous ammonia at several hundred degrees F produces melamine according to the reaction

$$3H_2N—\overset{\overset{\displaystyle NH}{\|}}{C}—NH—CN \rightarrow 2 \quad \text{melamine}$$

$$\Delta H^{\circ}_{298} = -52,140$$

$$\Delta F^{\circ}_{298} = -45,840$$

Melamine is an important intermediate for the manufacture of resins. It is also possible to produce melamine by dehydration of urea, and it is probable that urea-based melamine will become increasingly important over the immediate future.

## ACETYLENE FROM HYDROCARBONS

In order to reduce the cost of acetylene, considerable work has been carried out on possible methods of producing acetylene directly from hydrocarbons such as natural gas, naphtha, or refinery off-gases. The free energies of formation of various hydrocarbons are plotted in Fig. 13-2 in terms of the number of calories per carbon atom in the molecule. The following conclusions can be drawn from these data: (a) At low temperatures, acetylene is the least stable common hydrocarbon. (b) The stability of acetylene increases with temperature whereas the stability of the other hydrocarbons decreases with temperature. At temperatures greater than about 1500°K, acetylene becomes the most stable common hydrocarbon. (c) Light hydrocarbons may be converted to acetylene at

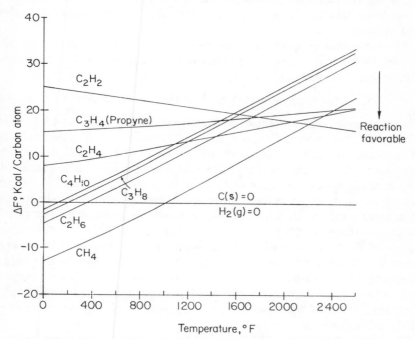

Fig. 13-2. Free energies of formation of hydrocarbons. (Data from A.P.I. Project 44)

temperatures greater than about 1200°K; however, methane requires temperatures in excess of about 1500°K. (d) All hydrocarbons including acetylene are unstable with respect to the elements at temperatures over 800°K.

Thus, to produce acetylene from hydrocarbons, we must consider reactions of the type

$$2CH_4 \rightarrow C_2H_2 + 3H_2 \tag{13-2}$$

$$\Delta H^\circ_{1500} = +96{,}668 \qquad \Delta F^\circ_{1500} = -1170$$

$$C_2H_6 \rightarrow C_2H_2 + 2H_2 \tag{13-3}$$

$$\Delta H^\circ_{1300} = +78{,}571 \qquad \Delta F^\circ_{1300} = -4766$$

with the competing reaction

$$C_2H_2 \rightarrow 2C + H_2 \tag{13-4}$$

$$\Delta H^\circ_{1300} = -52,851 \qquad \Delta F^\circ_{1300} = -36,854 \qquad \Delta F^\circ_{1500} = -34,410$$

The formation of acetylene is strongly endothermic at all temperatures. The yield of acetylene is favored by high temperature and low pressure. However, the reactions cannot be carried out under equilibrium conditions, since this would result only in complete decomposition to carbon and hydrogen.

The successful production of acetylene from hydrocarbons is dependent on the kinetics of the various reactions. Consider the following reaction chain:

$$\text{methane} \xrightarrow{k_1} \text{acetylene} \xrightarrow{k_2} \text{carbon} + \text{hydrogen} \tag{13-5}$$

The exact reaction mechanism whereby paraffins are converted to acetylene is not yet known. However, it is highly unlikely that the conversion of methane to acetylene is as simple as Eq. (13-2) would imply. The reaction probably involves first a thermal decomposition of methane into free radicals such as methine $CH\equiv$, followed by a combination to form acetylene. If steam or oxygen is present, the reactions obviously become even more complex. However, on the basis of a large amount of empirical work over the past 30 years, it has been found that the reaction constant $k_2$ for the decomposition of acetylene is appreciably smaller than the constant $k_1$ for the formation of acetylene. Thus, it is possible to produce acetylene commercially by heating a hydrocarbon to a high temperature, and holding for a very short period of time to permit the formation of acetylene, followed by rapid cooling to prevent excessive decomposition of the acetylene which is produced.

The yield of acetylene is determined by the nature of the hydrocarbon feed, the absolute pressure, the maximum reaction temperature, and the time-temperature relationship during the heating of the reactants and cooling of the products. In practice, the maximum yield of acetylene is obtained under the following conditions:

(1) The reaction temperature is in the range of 2200-2800°F, the higher temperature being required for methane and lower temperatures for heavier feedstocks such as naphtha.

(2) The total heating time at the reaction temperature must be limited to about 0.01 second.

(3) The products must be immediately quenched to below 800°F to prevent decomposition of the acetylene which is produced.

(4) Reduced pressure increases the yield of acetylene; this can be achieved either by a reduction of the total pressure or by the use of diluents such as steam, hydrogen or carbon dioxide.

(5) The product gas contains at most 25 per cent acetylene which must be separated from a large number of different impurities.

## Electric Arc Process

One obvious way to achieve directly the high temperatures required for acetylene production is by the use of an electric arc. This process was first used commercially by I. G. Farben at Hüls, Germany starting about 1940. The feedstock was chiefly methane from a mixture of coke oven gas and natural gas which was heated to a peak temperature of about 2900°F and was then quenched by water sprays. A dc arc was struck between a water-cooled copper cathode and a grounded water-cooled anode; the voltage was about 8000 volts and the current about 850 amp/tube. The acetylene concentration in the effluent gas was 13-16 per cent by volume, with a power consumption of about 5.5 kw-hr/lb acetylene. The product was recovered by low-temperature fractionation. The plant production was about 60,000 ton/yr of acetylene, with 8000 ton/yr of carbon black, 13,000 ton/yr of ethylene and 13,000 ton/yr of hydrogen as by-products.

A silent-discharge arc process has been developed by Schoch at the University of Texas; this process was recently sold to Standard Oil Co. of New Jersey, although it has not as yet been commercialized. In addition, improved arc processes have reportedly been developed in Japan, Czechoslovakia and the Soviet Union. E. I. du Pont is operating a 25,000 ton/yr modified arc process at Montague, Michigan, but no engineering details have been released. Reportedly, the du Pont process uses a magnetic field to rotate the arc, and thereby increase the volume of hydrocarbon which is subject to the arc temperatures.

Recently, announcements have been made concerning the development of electric arc plasma processes for the manufacture of acetylene. One such process is now in the pilot plant stage; this uses a plasma jet capable of reaching temperatures of 50,000°F in a small region of the arc. Yields of acetylene up to 80 per cent are claimed. However, there are obviously many engineering problems which will have to be worked out before the process can be used commercially.

The chief problem with the arc process is the cost of electricity. The power consumption is at least as great as in the calcium carbide process, and there is the additional cost of acetylene recovery from a dilute gas. Thus, it is hard to see any future for the arc process unless the efficiency can be substantially increased. From the heat of reaction given by Eq. (13-2), the minimum power requirement to convert methane to acetylene is about 2 kw-hr/lb. Since there are other heat losses such as in sensible heat, by-products, etc., it can be seen that the power requirements for the arc process can be reduced by at most a factor of 2. Presumably, the du Pont process has a higher efficiency than previous arc processes, and it will be interesting to see how the process works out in commercial operation.

### Regenerative Thermal Pyrolysis Processes

The thermal pyrolysis or regenerative process is best exemplified by the Wulff process which has been under development since before the war. The essential feature of this process is the use of a pair of furnaces containing refractory brick. In one furnace, the hydrocarbon feed is cracked at a temperature of about 2100°F to yield a gas containing 7-15 per cent acetylene. In the second furnace, air and fuel gas are burned to reheat the refractory brick up to about 2650°F. The process is operated on about a 1 minute cycle so that each furnace is alternately on "make" and "reheat." The pyrolysis step is carried out at about 0.5 atm pressure, and steam diluent further reduces the hydrocarbon partial pressure to about 0.15 atm. Residence time in the furnace at peak temperature is about 0.03 second.

One advantage of the regenerative process is the fact that there is no mixing of the combustion gas and the cracked gas; hence, there is no dilution of the cracked gas by combustion products, acetylene recovery is thus easier, and ordinary air can be used for combustion (no oxygen plant). A substantial disadvantage of the regenerative process is the fairly low temperature, which almost eliminates methane as an economic feedstock. However, the economics of the regenerative process may be considerably altered as the result of recent work in Japan which has shown that dilution of the feedstock with hydrogen instead of steam improves the yield and permits operation at atmospheric pressure. A Wulff pilot plant has been in operation for some time, and a small commercial unit is now being operated by Union Carbide at Institute, West Virginia.

### Partial Combustion Processes

Most of the acetylene produced from hydrocarbons is by means of the partial combustion process. In this process, the energy required for the endothermic conversion to acetylene is supplied by burning a fraction of the hydrocarbon feed with pure oxygen. Thus, taking natural gas as an example, the following two reactions occur simultaneously:

$$CH_4 + \tfrac{1}{2}O_2 \rightarrow CO + 2H_2 \tag{13-5}$$
$$\Delta H^\circ_{1500} = -5485 \qquad \Delta F^\circ_{1500} = -76{,}160$$

$$2CH_4 \rightarrow C_2H_2 + 3H_2 \tag{13-6}$$

$$\Delta H^{\circ}_{1500} = +96,668 \qquad \Delta F^{\circ}_{1500} = -1170$$

Note that at 1500°K, carbon monoxide is more stable than carbon dioxide or water. Thus, the combustion is largely to the formation of CO, although some $H_2O$ will also be formed in small amounts, depending on the ratio of oxygen to hydrocarbon which is used. The great advantage of the partial combustion process is that the energy is supplied *in situ*, and there is no need to transfer heat to the hydrocarbons by radiation or convection. The fact that oxygen, not air, must be used for the combustion does add to the cost of the acetylene. However, the use of oxygen increases the yield of acetylene, the nitrogen by-product from the liquid air plant can be used for ammonia manufacture, and the plant off-gases after removal of the acetylene consist chiefly of hydrogen and carbon monoxide, and thus can be used as synthesis gas for the manufacture of methanol or synthetic ammonia.

The development of the partial combustion process is largely based on the work of Sachsse at the Badische Anilin and Soda Fabrik (BASF) in Germany. The hydrocarbon and oxygen feeds are separately preheated, and are then mixed, burned and quenched in a burner or converter which produces an effluent gas containing 7-10 per cent acetylene. The degree of preheat is limited to about 1300°F maximum to prevent preignition in the mixing plenum of the burner. The commercial success of the process is largely dependent on the design of the burner. Figure 13-3 illustrates the BASF burner[1]. The hydrocarbon and oxygen are introduced through separate feed lines, are mixed in a diverging nozzle, and pass through orifices on a burner block which prevents the flame from striking back into the mixing section. If preignition of the feed occurs, the increased pressure activates a solenoid which causes nitrogen to be introduced for several seconds to restore normal flame conditions. The reaction temperature of 2700-2800°F is reached in 0.001-0.01 second, and the products are immediately quenched by water or oil sprays which also scrub most of the carbon out of the effluent gases. When an oil quench is used, the hot oil can be recirculated to a waste-heat boiler to generate steam. The BASF burner will convert up to 30 per cent of the feedstock into acetylene.

Heavier feedstocks such as naphtha can also be used by modifying the design of the burner. It is also possible to use a two-stage burner for heavier feedstocks in which a fuel such as coke oven gas or residual gas from the acetylene plant is burned, and the hydrocarbon feedstock is in-

[1] E. Bartholome, U.S. Patent 2,862,984 (Dec. 2, 1958).

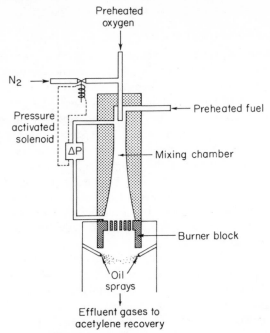

Fɪɢ. 13-3. B.A.S.F. burner for acetylene.

jected directly into the hot combustion gases. Such a two-stage process permits the use of a fuel which is different from the reactant hydrocarbon. Another modification which can be made in the process is to adjust the conditions so that both ethylene and acetylene are produced by the combustion. For example, the Hoechst high temperature pyrolysis process produces a mixture of acetylene and ethylene which can be varied from 80:20 to less than 30:70 merely by changing the operating conditions.

## RECOVERY OF ACETYLENE FROM CRACKED GAS

Table 13-2 gives typical compositions for the cracked gases from the various processes. The cost of recovering acetylene from the product gas is about the same as the cost of operating the cracking stages. The reason for this high cost is the fact that the acetylene is present in a fairly low concentration as a complex mixture of gases. Separation processes which have been investigated include the following:

(a) Partial or total condensation of the gas, followed by low-temperature fractionation. This method was used in the original Hüls plant. Dis-

TABLE 13-2. TYPICAL COMPOSITION OF CRACKED GASES
FOR ACETYLENE PRODUCTION*

| Feedstock Composition, vol. % | Arc Process | | Regenerative Process | | Partial Combustion Process | |
|---|---|---|---|---|---|---|
| | Process Gas | Natural Gas | Methane | Propane | Methane | Naphtha |
| $C_2H_2$ | 16.2 | 13.3 | 7.0 | 10.0 | 8.1 | 10.4 |
| Higher acetylenes | | | 0.6 | 0.9 | 0.3 | 0.7 |
| CO | 1.0 | 2.9 | 8.0 | 7.0 | 25.3 | 20.4 |
| $CO_2$ | 0.0 | 0.0 | 1.4 | 1.2 | 3.6 | 11.1 |
| $H_2$ | 50.5 | 46.0 | 49.1 | 54.4 | 57.1 | 42.8 |
| $O_2$ | 0.2 | 0.2 | — | — | — | — |
| $N_2$ | 3.4 | 8.9 | 4.1 | 5.4 | 0.5 | 3.3 |
| $CH_4$ | 25.1 | 27.8 | 28.1 | 17.9 | 4.8 | 7.4 |
| Olefins | 3.6 | 0.9 | 1.1 | 3.0 | 0.3 | 3.2 |
| $C_3 + C_4$ | — | — | 0.5 | — | — | 0.6 |

* Data from *Hydro. Proc. Petrol. Refiner*, **32**(5), 151 (1953); **37**(11), 180 (1958); data on the German arc process from post-war intelligence reports C. I. O. S. 22/21 and 30/83.

advantages include the cost of low-temperature refrigeration and the hazards in handling acetylene under high pressure.

(b) Selective adsorption and desorption by a solid adsorbent. The new Japanese regenerative process expects to recover acetylene by adsorption on charcoal, using a fluid bed. The chief disadvantage of this process is the low selectivity of solid adsorbents and the large quantity of solids which must be handled.

(c) Chemical reaction of acetylene to form a loose chemical compound, followed by regeneration of acetylene by heating. This process has been very successful for the recovery of butadiene. In principal, it could be equally successful for the recovery of acetylene, except that no satisfactory chemical reagent has yet been discovered.

(d) Selective absorption of acetylene in a suitable solvent, using a combination of heat and pressure to separate acetylene from the other components present. This process is being used for essentially all new construction.

The ideal solvent for the recovery of acetylene should have the following characteristics: (1) It should dissolve large quantities of acetylene at moderate temperature and pressure. (2) None of the other gases present should dissolve under these conditions. (3) The solubility of acetylene should rapidly decrease with temperature to permit easy recovery of the acetylene and regeneration of the solvent. (4) The solvent should have a low vapor pressure, low viscosity, low freezing point, good thermal stability and should not react chemically with any component present in the gas. (5) The solvent should be cheap, readily available, noncorrosive and nontoxic.

No single solvent meets all the above conditions, so that in practice the choice of a solvent involves many compromises. Probably the most important requirement is the selectivity of the solvent, namely, the ratio of the solubility of acetylene to the solubility of the other components present in the gas. Some components such as hydrogen, carbon monoxide and methane are relatively insoluble in all acetylene solvents, and hence are easily removed. Fortunately, these represent the bulk of the cracked gas. However, olefins such as ethylene have a moderate solubility in acetylene solvents, carbon dioxide has a moderate solubility, and higher acetylenes such as vinyl acetylene and diacetylene are even more soluble than acetylene itself. In addition, many of the higher unsaturated hydrocarbons polymerize easily, and can thereby contaminate the solvent and foul the processing equipment. It can thus be seen that a fairly complicated, and hence expensive, purification system is required.

Usually the first step in the recovery of acetylene is the removal of tar and soot which are produced in the partial combustion and arc processes. These are normally removed by the use of cyclone separators, water scrubbers, filters and electrostatic precipitators. The second step is usually the removal of the higher acetylenes which can polymerize and cause trouble later in the process. Diacetylene is a particularly troublesome component, since it is very unstable and liable to explosion if it accumulates in the system. Following this preliminary purification, the next step is the recovery of the acetylene itself. Solvents which have been used or proposed for the recovery of acetylene include water, ammonia, methanol, acetone, γ-butyrolactone, dimethylformamide, N-methylpyrrolidine, and dimethylsulfoxide. In some cases, two or three different solvents are used to selectively remove different components from the gas. Because of limited operating experience, it is hard at this time to evaluate the various recovery processes which have been developed. To illustrate the complexity of the process, Fig. 13-4 gives the BASF acetylene process which accounts for over half the hydrocarbon-based acetylene produced in the United States.

## PRODUCTS FROM ACETYLENE

The hydration of acetylene has been known since 1881 when Kutscherov showed that mercuric salts in sulfuric acid catalyze the direct reaction

$$HC\equiv CH + H_2O \rightarrow CH_3CHO$$

$$\Delta H^\circ_{298} = -36,156 \qquad \Delta F^\circ_{298} = -27,325$$

This process came into importance during World War I, and has been operated on a large scale in Germany since that time. The reaction is car-

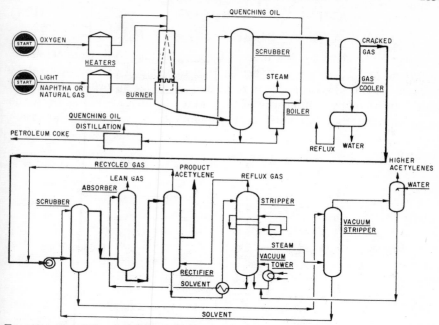

Fig. 13-4. B.A.S.F. acetylene process [*Hydro. Proc. Petrol. Refiner,* **42** (11), 132 (1963)]. (Copyright 1963, Gulf Publishing Co., Houston, Texas)

ried out by passing acetylene countercurrent to an acid solution in a packed tower at a temperature of about 200°F. Manganese dioxide or ferric salts are added to prevent reduction of the catalyst to metallic mercury. Excess acetylene is used to sweep the acetaldehyde out of solution; product is recovered by cooling, scrubbing with water and recycle of the unreacted acetylene.

Although this process has never been of importance in the United States, it does illustrate the versatility of acetylene as a raw material. The acetaldehyde can, of course, be converted to *n*-butanol, butyric acid and other chemical derivatives. During World War II, the German synthetic rubber industry was dependent on butadiene produced largely by condensing acetaldehyde to acetaldol, hydrogenating to 1,3-butane diol and dehydration of the diol to 1,3-butadiene.

## VINYL CHLORIDE

In the United States, the chief use of acetylene is for the manufacture of vinyl chloride by the reaction

$$C_2H_2 + HCl \rightarrow CH_2{=}CHCl \qquad (13\text{-}7)$$

$$\Delta H^\circ_{298} = -24{,}631 \qquad \Delta F^\circ_{298} = -15{,}423$$

A typical flow sheet for the process is given in Fig. 13-5. Commercially, acetylene and 10-15 per cent excess HCl are passed over a catalyst at 220-350°F, and vinyl chloride is recovered either by absorption in a suitable solvent or by cooling the effluent gases to about −40°F. Both the acetylene and the HCl must be thoroughly dried to prevent corrosion

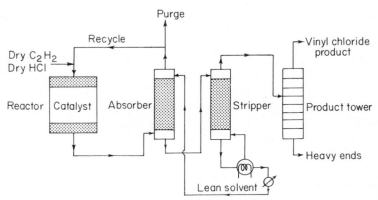

FIG. 13-5. Flowsheet for vinyl chloride.

and side reactions. The catalyst is activated charcoal containing either 10 per cent mercuric chloride or a mixture of barium and mercuric chlorides. The conversion per pass is 10-12 per cent, and the over-all yield about 95 per cent, based on acetylene consumed. The reaction is exothermic, and the equilibrium yield virtually 100 per cent to the right. Since some decomposition occurs, the catalyst gradually loses activity, and this must be compensated for by increasing the temperature until eventually the catalyst must be regenerated.

Although the acetylene route accounts for over half the vinyl chloride produced in the United States, there is a competing process based on ethylene. The reactions are

$$C_2H_4 + Cl_2 \rightarrow Cl{-}CH_2{-}CH_2{-}Cl \qquad (13\text{-}8)$$

$$\Delta H^\circ_{298} = -43{,}900 \qquad \Delta F^\circ_{298} = -34{,}375$$

$$(CH_2Cl)_2 \rightarrow HCl + CH_2{=}CHCl \qquad (13\text{-}9)$$

$$\Delta H^\circ_{298} = +16{,}800 \qquad \Delta F^\circ_{298} = +7115$$

The addition of chlorine to ethylene is highly exothermic. To prevent substitution, the reaction is normally carried out in the liquid phase at temperatures under 100°F. Metal chlorides such as $FeCl_3$ are catalysts for the reaction. The reaction is normally carried out using a solution of 0.1-0.5 per cent $FeCl_3$ in liquid ethylene dichloride at pressures of 20-75 psig. Chlorine and ethylene are passed into this solution, and the product separated from light and heavy ends by distillation. The yield of 1,2-dichloroethane is 96-98 per cent.

The dehydrochlorination of ethylene dichloride can be accomplished by heating the material with a solution of lime or caustic to split off a molecule of HCl. However, commercially, vinyl chloride is usually produced by thermal pyrolysis in a pipe still at temperatures of 600-1000°F and at pressures of about atmospheric or slightly above. The reaction is normally noncatalytic, although catalysts such as metallic chlorides have been described in patents. Effluent gases from the furnace are quenched with liquid ethylene dichloride, vinyl chloride separated by distillation, and ethylene dichloride recycled. Although conversions up to 90 per cent per pass have been reached, normally a lower conversion is taken to minimize side reactions. Pyrolysis conditions must be carefully controlled, since high temperatures, low pressures, or the presence of diluents may cause the loss of a second molecule of HCl to give acetylene.

The chief problem in the ethylene-based vinyl chloride has been the profitable disposal of the by-product HCl which accounts for half the chlorine consumption. Some plants have eliminated the problem by operating a combined process based on both acetylene and ethylene whereby the by-product HCl from Eq. (13-9) serves as the raw material for Eq. (13-7). Thus, the over-all reaction is

$$C_2H_2 + C_2H_4 + Cl_2 \rightarrow 2CH_2{=}CHCl$$

Although this gets rid of the by-product problem, it is not necessarily the most efficient process because it requires the operation of two small plants using different processes rather than one large plant.

Recently another ethylene-based process has been developed [1] which uses oxychlorination to utilize the by-product HCl. In this process, vinyl chloride is produced in the conventional way according to Eqs. (13-8) and (13-9). However, the by-product HCl is reacted with ethylene according to the equation

$$C_2H_4 + 2HCl + \tfrac{1}{2}O_2 \rightarrow CH_2Cl{-}CH_2Cl + H_2O$$
$$\Delta H_{298}^\circ = -57,500 \qquad \Delta F_{298}^\circ = -43,420$$

The reaction is carried out in the vapor phase at a "moderate" temperature and pressure, using a catalyst. From patents, the catalyst consists of

[1] E. F. Edwards and T. Weaver, *Chem. Eng. Progr.*, **61**(1), 21 (1965).

$CuCl_2$ on alumina or diatomaceous earth which contains about 10 per cent Cu and is promoted with KCl. Temperatures of 320-600°F are used, and yields of about 95 per cent, based on ethylene, are reported. The reactor effluent is refrigerated, the aqueous layer containing a small amount of unreacted HCl is separated by decantation, and the ethylene dichloride layer washed with caustic solution, then purified by distillation. Oxychlorination is being used commercially by B. F. Goodrich Chemical Co. at Calvert City, Kentucky. This plant changed from the acetylene to the ethylene-based process in 1964. It is probable that the trend toward the use of ethylene as a raw material for vinyl chloride manufacture will continue over the immediate future.

### Chloroprene

Under the influence of an acid solution of cuprous chloride, acetylene readily forms linear polymers such as the monovinylacetylene, divinylacetylene, etc. The most important is the dimer, monovinylacetylene, which serves as a raw material for the production of chloroprene. The reaction is as follows:

$$CH\equiv CH + CH\equiv CH \rightarrow CH\equiv C-CH=CH_2$$
*monovinylacetylene or 1-buten-3-yne*

The reaction can be carried out either in agitated reactors or in a packed tower in which acetylene passes countercurrent to an aqueous solution of cuprous chloride at about room temperature. From the patent literature, the catalyst consists of about 30 per cent CuCl, 25 per cent KCl, 0.5 per cent HCl and the balance water; ammonium chloride and sodium chloride may also be used in place of or in addition to the potassium chloride. The use of cuprous chloride + dimethyl amine + dimethylformamide is also disclosed. The conversion of acetylene per pass is limited to about 10 per cent to minimize the formation of higher polymers. The pure monovinylacetylene boils at 42°F, and is stripped from the catalyst solution by heating. The over-all yield is about 88 per cent, based on acetylene consumed.

Monovinylacetylene can be hydrochlorinated to chloroprene by the reaction

$$CH\equiv C-CH=CH_2 + HCl \rightarrow CH_2=\overset{\overset{\textstyle Cl}{\textstyle |}}{C}-CH=CH_2$$
*chloroprene or 2-chloro-1,3-butadiene*

The reaction is carried out at 85-140°F, using an aqueous solution containing 20-38 per cent HCl and 5-25 per cent CuCl as catalyst. Chloroprene is carried off by the unreacted monovinylacetylene, and is condensed and recovered. Approximately **300** million pounds of chloroprene were produced in the United States in **1963**, and were used for the manufacture of neoprene rubber.

## Acrylonitrile

As we have already discussed, propylene-based acrylonitrile will probably account for all future growth because of the cheapness of the raw materials and the simplicity of the process. The acetylene process for acrylonitrile is based on the direct reaction of HCN according to the equation

$$CH\equiv CH + HCN \rightarrow CH_2\!\!=\!\!CH\!\!-\!\!C\equiv N$$

The reaction is carried out at temperatures of about 150°F and pressures of atmospheric up to 15 psig using about a 10:1 ratio of acetylene to HCN. The catalyst is similar to those developed for the polymerization of acetylene, namely, an acidic cuprous chloride solution plus potassium, sodium or ammonium chloride. The catalyst requires regeneration after making 20 parts of product per part of copper. Acrylonitrile is carried away by the excess acetylene, and is absorbed by scrubbing with water. The crude product contains many impurities such as acetaldehyde, monovinylacetylene, vinyl chloride, chloroprene, etc. Final purification is by fractional distillation.

Another route to acrylonitrile is via ethylene oxide and HCN according to the reactions

$$C_2H_4O + HCN \rightarrow HO\!\!-\!\!CH_2\!\!-\!\!CH_2\!\!-\!\!C\equiv N \xrightarrow{-H_2O} CH_2\!\!=\!\!CH\!\!-\!\!C\equiv N$$

The production of ethylene cyanohydrin is exothermic, and is carried out in solution, using a basic catalyst such as diethylamine at temperatures of about 130°F. The solution is neutralized, and the ethylene cyanohydrin (boiling point 430°F) obtained by distillation. The dehydration is carried out in either the liquid phase at about 400°F using a dehydration catalyst such as magnesium carbonate, or in the vapor phase at about 550°F using an alumina catalyst.

## Vinyl Acetate

About 90 per cent of the total vinyl acetate production now comes from acetylene by the reaction

$$CH\equiv CH + CH_3COOH \rightarrow CH_2\!\!=\!\!CH\!\!-\!\!O\!\!-\!\!\overset{\displaystyle O}{\overset{\displaystyle \|}{C}}\!\!-\!\!CH_3$$

The reaction is carried out in the vapor phase at temperatures of 340-410°F and pressures slightly greater than atmospheric. The original catalyst developed in Germany was activated charcoal containing 15 per cent zinc as zinc acetate; other metals which catalyze the reaction include cadmium, bismuth and mercury. The reaction is exothermic, and is reported [1] to be first-order with respect to acetylene and independent of acetic acid and vinyl acetate at 350-400°F over a zinc acetate catalyst. Effluent gases from the reactor are refrigerated, vinyl acetate purified by distillation, and unreacted acetylene recycled. The conversion per pass is about 65 per cent, with an over-all yield of 92-95 per cent, based on acetylene, and 97-99 per cent, based on acetic acid.

A competing route to vinyl acetate is the reaction of acetaldehyde with acetic anhydride to form ethylidene diacetate, followed by cracking with a catalyst such as *p*-toluenesulfonic acid according to the equations

$$CH_3CHO + (CH_3CO)_2O \rightarrow \underset{\textit{ethylidene diacetate}}{CH_3CH(OCOCH_3)_2} \rightarrow$$

$$CH_3COOH + CH_2{=}CH{-}O{-}\overset{\displaystyle O}{\overset{\displaystyle \|}{C}}{-}CH_3$$

Reaction products are removed as overhead and are separated by distillation. A liquid stream is withdrawn from the bottom of the reactor and is flashed to recover acetaldehyde and acetic anhydride which are recycled. Any solids present in this stream are discarded. This process for vinyl acetate is used commercially by Celanese Corp. at one plant.

About 405 million pounds of vinyl acetate monomer were produced in the United States in 1963. The chief use is in the manufacture of poly-vinylacetate emulsions.

### Chlorinated Solvents

Substantial quantities of acetylene are used for the manufacture of trichlorethylene and perchlorethylene. This will be discussed in Chapter 14.

[1] I. B. Vasil'eva, *et al., Kinetika i Katiliz,* **5**(1), 144 (1963).

# CHAPTER 14

# Halogenated Paraffins

Chlorination is the only halogenation reaction carried out on a large scale commercially. Thus, even though large quantities of aliphatic fluorine compounds are produced such as $CCl_2F_2$, these are made by reacting the appropriate chlorine derivative with anhydrous HF. Chlorination may be carried out in either the vapor or liquid phase. Liquid-phase chlorination is more common when it is desired to add chlorine across a double bond; vapor-phase chlorination is more common when it is desired to substitute chlorine for hydrogen. Chlorination is strongly exothermic, and is normally carried out with a large excess of the organic reactant to give better temperature control, to prevent pyrolysis of the organic and to minimize the formation of polychlorides. Since most chlorinated organics are quite volatile, chlorination is often carried out under pressure to simplify the recovery of the products from a large excess of the organic reactant.

It is now generally accepted that chlorination occurs through a chain reaction involving free radicals. The reaction is initiated by chlorine atoms which are produced thermally or by a photochemical or radioactive process. Thus,

$$Cl_2 \rightarrow Cl^{\bullet} + Cl^{\bullet}$$
$$RH + Cl^{\bullet} \rightarrow R^{\bullet} + HCl$$
$$R^{\bullet} + Cl_2 \rightarrow RCl + Cl^{\bullet} \quad \text{etc.}$$

## CHLORINATION OF METHANE

Although methane is the most difficult paraffin to chlorinate, the reaction can be carried out with little difficulty at temperatures of 750-800°F according to the equations

$$CH_4 \text{ (g)} + Cl_2 \text{ (g)} \rightarrow CH_3Cl \text{ (g)} + HCl \text{ (g)} \tag{14-1}$$
$$\Delta H^{\circ}_{298} = -23,800 \qquad \Delta F^{\circ}_{298} = -24,700$$

$$CH_3Cl + Cl_2 \rightarrow CH_2Cl_2 + HCl \tag{14-2}$$

$$\Delta H^\circ_{298} = -23,500 \qquad \Delta F^\circ_{298} = -22,800$$

$$CH_2Cl_2 + Cl_2 \rightarrow CHCl_3 + HCl \tag{14-3}$$

$$\Delta H^\circ_{298} = -25,100 \qquad \Delta F^\circ_{298} = -24,800$$

$$CHCl_3 + Cl_2 \rightarrow CCl_4 + HCl \tag{14-4}$$

$$\Delta H^\circ_{298} = -23,600 \qquad \Delta F^\circ_{298} = -22,100$$

with the competing pyrolysis reaction

$$CH_4 + 2Cl_2 \rightarrow C + 4HCl$$

$$\Delta H^\circ_{298} = -70,500 \qquad \Delta F^\circ_{298} = -79,100$$

All chlorination reactions are reported [1] to be second-order with the rates proportional to the concentrations of both the chlorine and the hydrocarbon. Activation energies for Eqs. (14-1) through (14-4) are 28,100, 17,200, 15,600 and 14,100. As illustrated in Fig. 14-1, the composition of the products depends on the ratio of hydrocarbon to chlorine in the feed. If methyl chloride is desired, about a 5:1 ratio of methane to chlorine is used to minimize polysubstitution. If methylene dichloride is desired as the main product, a lower ratio of methane to chlorine is used and methyl chloride can be recycled up to a maximum of 20 per cent of the total organic feed; if recycle is increased above this figure, there is excessive carbon formation. Chloroform and carbon tetrachloride are produced by further decreasing the methane to chlorine ratio, and with recycle of methyl chloride and methylene dichloride. In addition, substantial amounts of carbon tetrachloride may also be recycled as diluent in order to regulate the reaction temperature.

Commercially, methane, chlorine and recycle organics are admitted to a chlorinator which may be a simple pipe reactor, chlorinated hydrocarbons are condensed by cooling the effluent gases, and product separated by distillation. The HCl is recovered by absorption in water, and unreacted methane may be compressed and recycled. The yield is about 95 per cent, based on methane, and is essentially quantitative, based on chlorine. Production figures in the United States for 1963 are as follows: (1) Methyl chloride—114 million pounds; chief uses are as a refrigerant, as a methylating agent and in the manufacture of silicones and butyl rubber. (2) Methylene dichloride—148 million pounds; chief uses are as a solvent, a paint remover, a diluent for insecticides and in the manufacture of plastics and plasticizers. (3) Chloroform—105 million pounds; about 88 per cent of the chloroform is used in the manufacture of fluorocarbon refrigerants and resins, and about 8 per cent is used in pharma-

[1] T. Arai, *et al.*, *Kogyo Kagaku Zasshi*, **61**, 1231 (1958).

ceuticals. (4) Carbon tetrachloride—519 million pounds; about 80 per cent goes into the manufacture of fluorocarbons, small amounts being used as a grain fumigant, as a solvent, for fire extinguishers, etc.

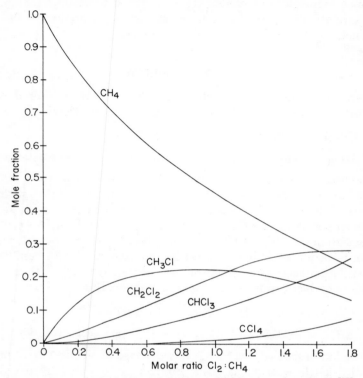

Fig. 14-1. Composition of products from chlorination of methane [W. Hirschkind, *Ind. Eng. Chem.*, **41**, 2749 (1949)].

At present, the direct chlorination of methane accounts for most of the production of these chlorinated hydrocarbons. The chief disadvantage of the process is the fact that half the chlorine ends up as by-product HCl. However, the development of hydrochlorination and oxychlorination reactions has permitted the use of much of this HCl for organic chlorinations. A competing process for the manufacture of methyl chloride is based on methanol, namely,

$$CH_3OH \text{ (g)} + HCl \text{ (g)} \rightarrow CH_3Cl \text{ (g)} + H_2O \text{ (g)}$$
$$\Delta H^\circ_{298} = -7200 \qquad \Delta F^\circ_{298} = -7200$$

The reaction is carried out in the vapor phase at atmospheric pressure and about 650°F, using a catalyst such as alumina gel. The yield is about 95 per cent. The chief advantage of the process is that it permits the use of by-product HCl which can be obtained from the further chlorination of the methyl chloride; the chief disadvantage of the process is the much higher cost of methanol as compared to methane. At present, only a relatively small fraction of the total production is based on methanol.

## CARBON DISULFIDE

Substantial quantities of carbon tetrachloride are still produced by chlorination of carbon disulfide according to the reaction

$$CS_2 \text{ (l)} + 3Cl_2 \text{ (g)} \rightarrow CCl_4 \text{ (l)} + S_2Cl_2 \text{ (l)}$$

$$\Delta H^\circ_{298} = -68,200 \qquad \Delta F^\circ_{298} = -45,180 \text{ (gas-phase reaction)}$$

The reaction is strongly exothermic, and is carried out at room temperature in the liquid phase, using a lead-lined chlorinator fitted with cooling coils. Chlorine gas is bubbled into a solution of $CS_2$ in $CCl_4$ at about room temperature, using finely divided iron as a catalyst. In some cases, sniff gas from chlorine manufacture has been used for the chlorination. Carbon tetrachloride is distilled, neutralized and dried. The residue from the distillation consists of about 85 per cent $S_2Cl_2$ which is then reacted with more carbon disulfide according to the equation

$$CS_2 \text{ (l)} + 2S_2Cl_2 \text{ (l)} \rightarrow 6S \text{ (s)} + CCl_4 \text{ (l)}$$

$$\Delta H^\circ_{298} = -26,500 \qquad \Delta F^\circ_{298} = -2190 \text{ (gas-phase reaction)}$$

The reaction is carried out in the liquid phase at about 140°F, using a lead lined kettle with an agitator. Product is separated by distillation, and by-product sulfur may be recycled to $CS_2$ manufacture.

Carbon disulfide itself is another interesting example of the penetration of the HPI into the chemical industry. The classical method of preparing carbon disulfide is by the direct interaction of sulfur and charcoal according to the equation

$$C \text{ (s)} + 2S \text{ (l)} \rightarrow CS_2 \text{ (g)}$$

$$\Delta H^\circ_{298} = +27,500 \qquad \Delta F^\circ_{298} = +15,500$$

Charcoal is used instead of coke because the velocity of the reaction is extremely small in the case of coke. The reaction is carried out in two ways, either by the use of an electric furnace or by the use of a direct-fired pot. The sulfur is liquified, reacts with the charcoal and carbon disulfide is distilled from the reactant mixture.

However, most carbon disulfide plants completed since the war[1] have used methane as a source of carbon. The reaction is

$$CH_4 \text{ (g)} + 2S_2 \text{ (g)} \rightleftharpoons CS_2 \text{ (g)} + 2H_2S \text{ (g)}$$

$$\Delta H^{\circ}_{298} = +35{,}870 \qquad \Delta F^{\circ}_{298} = +11{,}990$$

$$\Delta H^{\circ}_{900} = +2880 \qquad \Delta F^{\circ}_{900} = -26{,}770$$

The sulfur vapor is actually present as an equilibrium between $S_2$, $S_6$ and $S_8$ molecules. However, kinetic data show the reaction can be correlated in terms of a second-order reaction between methane and diatomic sulfur. Activation energies of 34,400 and 38,300 have been reported. At the temperatures used commercially, the equilibrium is virtually 100 per cent to the right.

In practice, liquid sulfur is vaporized, mixed with methane of over 99 per cent purity, superheated to 1200-1300°F, then passed down through a reactor containing a catalyst of synthetic activated clay. High-chrome steel is used for the sulfur vaporizer, superheater and reactor. The reactor operates adiabatically at about 1250°F, pressures of 15-25 psig and a standard space velocity of about 600 ft$^3$/(hr)(ft$^3$ catalyst). Approximately 5-10 per cent excess sulfur is used. The reactants are cooled and unconverted sulfur recovered by scrubbing with liquid sulfur. Carbon disulfide is recovered from by-product $H_2S$ by conventional absorption-desorption, using a mineral oil solvent, and the product purified by distillation in a steel column. The off-gas contains over 90 per cent $H_2S$, which is converted to elemental sulfur by controlled oxidation using a clay-type catalyst. The carbon disulfide yield is 85-90 per cent, based on methane, and 91-92 per cent, based on sulfur.

Total carbon disulfide production in the United States in 1963 was 652 million pounds. About 80 per cent of the production goes into the manufacture of regenerated cellulose such as viscose rayon and cellophane. However, carbon tetrachloride still takes about 15 per cent of the production.

### ETHYL CHLORIDE

Ethyl chloride can be produced by the direct chlorination of ethane

$$C_2H_6 + Cl_2 \rightarrow C_2H_5Cl + HCl \tag{14-5}$$

$$\Delta H^{\circ}_{298} = -27{,}000 \qquad \Delta F^{\circ}_{298} = -27{,}600$$

---

[1] H. W. Haines, Jr., "Carbon Disulfide," *Ind. Eng. Chem.*, **55**(6), 44 (1963); *Hydro. Proc. Petrol. Refiner*, "Petrochemical Handbook," November 1963.

The reaction is carried out at a temperature of 750-800°F and a pressure of about 80 psig, using a large excess of ethane. Product is recovered by cooling the effluent gases, and is purified by fractionation. Since ethyl chloride is much harder to chlorinate than ethane, by-product formation is not serious. The economics of the process are largely dependent on the disposal of the by-product HCl.

However, the competing process which has accounted for most of the production of ethyl chloride is the hydrochlorination of ethylene by the reaction

$$C_2H_4 + HCl \rightleftharpoons C_2H_5Cl \tag{14-6}$$

$$\Delta H^\circ_{298} = -15,500 \qquad \Delta F^\circ_{298} = -6200$$

The reaction is reversible and equilibrium controlled. The equilibrium constant is reported [1] to be equal to

$$\log K_p = \frac{2925}{T} - 4.96 \tag{14-7}$$

However, it should be noted that this equation is inconsistent with data given in NBS Circular 500. Commercially, the reaction may be carried out in either the vapor or liquid phase. The vapor-phase hydrochlorination is carried out at about 350°F, using a catalyst such as copper chloride. The reaction is, of course, favored by high pressure and low temperature. The liquid-phase hydrochlorination is carried out under pressure at a temperature of about 100°F, using an aluminum chloride catalyst.

Figure 14-2 illustrates the Shell process[2] for the production of ethyl chloride which eliminates the by-product problem by combining both chlorination and hydrochlorination in the same process. Ethane and chlorine react according to Eq. (14-5) at 800°F and 80 psig in a reactor having a residence time of about 3 seconds. The reaction occurs in the presence of recycle ethylene which is essentially inert under the reaction conditions. Effluent gases are cooled to separate most of the ethyl chloride, are mixed with fresh ethylene feed, and are compressed to 250 psig. The hydrochlorination reaction takes place at 350°F in a reactor containing tubes filled with a catalyst consisting of $CuCl_2$ promoted with $ZnCl_2$. Temperature control is critical, and is achieved by recirculating oil on the outside of the catalyst tubes. The effluent gases are cooled to separate ethyl chloride, and are then recycled. Product is separated from light and heavy ends by conventional fractionation. The yield of ethyl

[1] Rudkovskii, et al., Ukr. Khim. Zhr., **10**, 277 (1935).
[2] U.S. Patent 2,807,656 (Sept. 24, 1957).

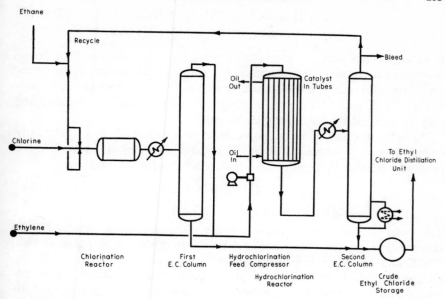

FIG. 14-2. Shell process for ethyl chloride [*Hydro. Proc. Petrol. Refiner,* **42** (11), 241 (1961)]. (Copyright 1961, Gulf Publishing Co., Houston, Texas)

chloride is about 90 per cent over-all, based on $C_2H_6 + C_2H_4$, and about 95 per cent, based on chlorine.

Total production of ethyl chloride in the United States for 1963 was 592 million pounds. The chief use is for the manufacture of tetraethyl lead according to the equation

$$4PbNa + 4C_2H_5Cl \rightarrow Pb(C_2H_5)_4 + 3Pb + 4NaCl$$

In practice, ethyl chloride reacts under pressure with a lead-sodium alloy at a temperature of about 120°F, and product is separated by distillation. The tetraethyl lead is used as a gasoline antiknock additive, although it is now facing increased competition from tetramethyl lead.

## TRICHLOROETHYLENE

Commercial production of trichloroethylene began in Germany in 1910, and helped launch acetylene as the basis for so much of the German chemical industry. In the first step of the process, acetylene is chlorinated to tetrachloroethane according to the equation

$$CH \equiv CH + 2Cl_2 \rightarrow CHCl_2 - CHCl_2 \tag{14-8}$$

$$\Delta H^\circ_{298} = -92,200 \qquad \Delta F^\circ_{298} \cong -72,000$$

A catalyst consisting of about 0.01 per cent $FeCl_3$ dissolved in tetra-chloroethane is used. Commercially, the reactants are simply passed continuously into a reactor maintained at atmospheric pressure and 160-185°F. Product is withdrawn continuously to intermediate storage, and may be purified by distillation if desired.

However, the use of tetrachloroethane as a solvent has now virtually ended since it is extremely toxic (it causes jaundice). However, it can be easily dehydrochlorinated to trichlorethylene by the reaction

$$CHCl_2 - CHCl_2 \rightarrow CHCl \equiv CCl_2 + HCl \tag{14-9}$$

$$\Delta H^\circ_{298} = +13,700 \qquad \Delta F^\circ_{298} \cong +4000$$

The reaction may be carried out using a lime slurry at about 220°F. However, in practice, it is usually carried out in the vapor phase at 480-570°F and atmospheric pressure, using a catalyst of 30 per cent $BaCl_2$ on charcoal. The conversion is about 90 per cent. Effluent gases are cooled and refrigerated to condense out the organics, and HCl sent to by-product recovery. Trichlorethylene is produced by fractionation, washed with caustic to remove traces of HCl, dried, and sent to product storage. The over-all yield based on acetylene or chlorine is about 90 per cent.

A competing process which accounts for about one-tenth of the total trichlorethylene production is based on ethylene. Chlorine is first added to ethylene, two hydrogens are substituted to give tetrachloroethane, followed by dehydrochlorination to trichlorethylene. Although ethylene is a cheaper raw material than acetylene, the ethylene-based process requires one additional molecule of chlorine, has more steps, and has a lower yield because of side reactions.

About 368 million pounds of trichlorethylene were produced in the United States in 1963. The chief use of trichlorethylene is as a degreasing agent for metal, glass and some plastics, since painting, enameling and electroplating can only be done on a dry and clean surface. Since trichlorethylene does undergo some decomposition, a stabilizing agent is usually added to the commercial material.

## PERCHLORETHYLENE

Perchlorethylene (tetrachloroethylene) can be produced from trichlorethylene by the reactions

$$CHCl \equiv CCl_2 + Cl_2 \rightarrow CHCl_2 - CCl_3 \rightarrow CCl_2 \equiv CCl_2 + HCl$$

The chlorination reaction is carried out at about 185°F and atmospheric pressure, using about 0.2 per cent $FeCl_3$ as catalyst. The pentachloroethane can then be dehydrochlorinated by milk of lime at 230°F to give perchlorethylene.

However, it is now more common to produce perchlorethylene by chlorination of a hydrocarbon such as propane or propylene. Thus, if propane[1] is chlorinated under pyrolysis conditions, the chief over-all reaction is

$$C_3H_8 + 8Cl_2 \rightarrow CCl_4 + CCl_2{=}CCl_2 + 8HCl$$

$$\Delta H^\circ_{298} = -181,200 \qquad \Delta F^\circ_{298} = -187,100$$

The reaction takes place at about 1100°F and 10 psig with a feed consisting of 1 mole of propane, 11.5 moles of chlorine and 4.2 moles of a recycled 1:1 mixture of $CCl_4 + C_2Cl_4$. Effluent gases are cooled, refrigerated to condense out chlorinated organics, and the products purified by distillation. The off-gases are scrubbed with water to remove HCl, and unreacted chlorine is recycled. The products consist of about 56 per cent carbon tetrachloride, 44 per cent perchlorethylene and 0.2 per cent hexachloroethane.

It is obvious that the reaction is more complex than the above equation would indicate. Thus, in this particular case, the ratio of carbon tetrachloride to perchlorethylene shows that there has been some cracking of $C_2$ to $C_1$. However, at higher temperatures, two molecules of carbon tetrachloride can split off chlorine to form perchlorethylene. In practice, it is possible to vary the ratio of carbon tetrachloride to perchlorethylene from about 70:30 to 35:65 by changing the operating conditions.

Total production of perchlorethylene in the United States in 1963 was 325 million pounds. The chief use of perchlorethylene is as a dry-cleaning solvent. Only limited amounts are used for degreasing since the material is slightly more expensive than trichlorethylene.

## Toxicity of Chlorinated Hydrocarbons

The chlorinated hydrocarbons are widely used as solvents because they are nonflammable. In practice, the choice of a suitable solvent must often be made on the basis of the toxicity of the various materials available. Toxicity is measured in terms of the maximum average concentration (MAC) in air for repeated daily exposure under normal working conditions without adverse affect on health, and is measured in parts of vapor per million parts of air by volume. Table 14-1 gives values for the important chlorinated solvents.

---

[1] For example, see U.S. Patent 2,857,438 (assigned to Stauffer Chem. Co.).

TABLE 14-1. PROPERTIES OF CHLORINATED HYDROCARBONS*

| Material | MAC (ppm) | Vapor Pressure (mm at 20°C) | Relative Standing |
|---|---|---|---|
| Perchlorethylene | 200 | 18.8 | 1 |
| Trichlorethylene | 200 | 58.6 | 4 |
| Methylene dichloride | 500 | 350 | 15 |
| Chloroform | 100 | 159 | 24 |
| Carbon tetrachloride | 25 | 92.1 | 42 |

* Data courtesy Stauffer Chemical Co.

Although the MAC can be used as a rough guide, the hazard associated with a given solvent depends also on other factors, particularly the vapor pressure and molecular weight. These are taken into consideration in the "relative standing" of the solvents listed in Table 14-1. On this basis, perchlorethylene is the least hazardous and carbon tetrachloride the most hazardous. Unfortunately perchlorethylene is also the most expensive; thus, although it finds considerable use in dry cleaning, industrial users of degreasing solvents usually select the slightly cheaper trichlorethylene.

## FLUOROCARBONS

The chlorofluoro derivatives of methane and ethane form a very important group of halogenated hydrocarbons. The most important are listed in Table 14-2. Like the chlorinated hydrocarbons, these compounds are nonflammable; however, in addition, the chlorofluoro hydrocarbons are also essentially nontoxic. When first introduced in 1931, they were used chiefly as a refrigerant in place of the flammable and toxic refrigerants then being used. However, since the war, they have found considerable use as a propellant for aerosols such as shaving cream, insecticides, etc. Thus, at present, fluorocarbons propel over 90 per cent of all nonfood aerosols,[1] and research is under way to find a fluorocarbon which is stable and odorless which could be used for food aerosols. Approximately 90 per cent of all new industrial and commercial refrigeration uses fluorocarbon refrigerants. Of the total production of fluorocarbons, about 50 per cent are used for propellants, 30 per cent as refrigerants, 10 per cent for resins and 10 per cent for the manufacture of film, plastics, lubricants, etc.

One important disadvantage of the fluorocarbons is their cost of 20 cent/lb and up. This is the reason they have found little use as solvents and degreasing agents. In addition, manufactures of aerosols have been

[1] *Chem. Eng. News,* July 18, 1960, p. 92; Sept. 7, 1964, p. 29.

TABLE 14-2. PROPERTIES OF FLUOROCARBONS

| Fluorocarbon | Formula | Boiling Point (°F) | Total 1963 Production (millions of lb) | Uses |
|---|---|---|---|---|
| 12 | $CCl_2F_2$ | −21.6 | 217 | Most widely used; aerosol propellant, household and commercial refrigeration. |
| 11 | $CCl_3F$ | 74.8 | 140 | Low-pressure aerosols; commercial air conditioning. |
| 22 | $CHClF_2$ | −41.4 | 36 (sales) | Air conditioning and refrigeration; raw material for tetrafluoroethylene. |
| 113 | $CCl_2F—CClF_2$ | 117.6 | — | Mixture with others; raw material for chlorotrifluoroethylene. |
| 114 | $CClF_2—CClF_2$ | 38.4 | 12 | Stable and odorless; propellant in cosmetics; industrial air conditioning. |

gradually replacing fluorocarbons with cheaper propellants such as carbon dioxide, propane and butane. Thus, it is entirely possible that the rapid growth of fluorocarbons has ended unless important new markets can be developed.

## Manufacture of Fluorocarbons

All chlorofluoro hydrocarbons are produced in the same general way, namely, by reacting[1] the appropriate chlorinated hydrocarbon with anhydrous HF according to the typical equation

$$CCl_4 \text{ (l)} + 2HF \text{ (l)} \rightarrow CCl_2F_2 \text{ (g)} + 2HCl \text{ (g)}$$

The reaction is carried out in the liquid phase at temperatures ranging from about 40°F for the lower-boiling compounds up to about 300°F for the higher-boiling compounds. Pressures range from atmospheric to about 100 psig, depending on the temperature and the nature of the fluorocarbon produced.

Catalysts which can be used to bring about the halogen exchange include silver, mercury and antimony. Commercially, antimony is normally

[1] See U.S. Patents 2,005,705; 2,005,706; 2,058,453; 2,062,743.

used, either in the trivalent or pentavalent state. The pentavalent antimony is a more active catalyst, but it does result in more side reactions. Thus, trivalent antimony may be used for the easier exchange reactions, and pentavalent antimony only when needed for the more difficult reactions. The antimony is probably the actual fluorinating agent, and the reaction proceeds in the following typical manner:

$$CCl_4 + SbF_3 \rightarrow CCl_3F + SbClF_2$$

$$SbClF_2 + HF \rightarrow HCl + SbF_3 \quad \text{etc.}$$

For the manufacture of fluorocarbons 11 and 12, anhydrous HF and $CCl_4$ are charged to a mild-steel reactor at atmospheric pressure and about 40°F. The catalyst consists of $SbF_3$ to which has been added a small amount of elemental chlorine to oxidize part of the antimony to the pentavalent state. The solution is allowed to react at about room temperature, and the vapors are passed to a fractionator. Since the fluorocarbon always has a much lower boiling point than the chlorinated hydrocarbon, the desired product can be obtained merely by holding the pressure and temperature of the overhead vapors at the proper values. Effluent gases from the fractionator are scrubbed with a hydrofluoric acid solution in which HCl is relatively insoluble, and the HCl then recovered by absorption in water. The fluorocarbons are washed with alkali to remove traces of acid, and are separated by conventional distillation. The yield is 95 per cent or better.

For the fluorocarbons 113 and 114, the appropriate chlorinated ethane is reacted with anhydrous HF, using a catalyst of $SbCl_2F_3$. Temperatures of about 300°F and pressures of 100 psig or more are required. The yield is about 90 per cent.

CHAPTER 15

# Products from Carbon Monoxide
# and Hydrogen

The three important reactions based on a carbon monoxide-hydrogen synthesis gas are as follows: (a) the synthesis of methanol; (b) the oxo process; (c) the Fischer-Tropsch process. In the past, the methanol synthesis has been the most important of these reactions, since it serves as a source of formaldehyde which is widely used in resins and plastics. However, the oxo process is rapidly gaining in importance since it serves as the basis for the production of many different aldehydes and primary alcohols. Although the Fischer-Tropsch synthesis was of importance in Germany during the war, it cannot compete economically under free-market conditions, and attempts to commercialize the process in the United States have been unsuccessful.

### FISCHER-TROPSCH SYNTHESIS

Although the Fischer-Tropsch synthesis[1] is not economic in the United States at present, the reaction is of considerable historical interest because it has led directly to the synthesis of methanol and the synthesis of aldehydes and alcohols by the oxo process. As early as 1902, it had been shown by Sabatier and Senderens that methane could be produced by the hydrogenation of carbon monoxide and carbon dioxide on reduced nickel and cobalt catalysts at atmospheric pressure and temperatures of about 500°F. In 1913 and 1914, patents were issued to the Badische Analin and Soda Fabrik describing the production of a mixture of alcohols, acids, aldehydes, ketones and aliphatic hydrocarbons by the

[1] B. H. Weil and J. C. Lane, "The Technology of the Fischer-Tropsch Process," London, Constable and Co., Ltd., 1949; H. H. Storch, et al., "The Fischer-Tropsch and Related Syntheses," New York, John Wiley & Sons, Inc., 1951.

hydrogenation of carbon monoxide at 100-200 atm pressure and temperatures of about 650°F over catalysts such as cobalt or osmium oxide activated with alkali. In 1923, Franz Fischer and Hans Tropsch described the production of organics by the hydrogenation of carbon monoxide over a catalyst of iron turnings activated with alkali.[1] This process was given the name "Synthol" (synthetic oil) and the product "Synthin." At 100-150 atm and about 800°F, the product consisted chiefly of oxygenated compounds plus small amounts of hydrocarbons. When the pressure was reduced to about 7 atm, the product consisted chiefly of olefinic and paraffinic hydrocarbons with only small quantities of oxygenated compounds. However, at the lower pressures, the catalyst had a low efficiency and rapidly lost activity with time. For about the next 10 years, an intensive search was made for more active and longer-lived catalysts.

The Fischer-Tropsch process is designed primarily for the production of synthetic fuels, and was actively studied in Germany because of the desire to obtain liquid fuels from coal which could be used to replace petroleum. The specific reactions which take place in the synthesis depend on the ratio of hydrogen to carbon monoxide, the temperature, pressure and catalyst which is used. The reactions for the synthesis of paraffins and olefins are as follows:

$$(2n + 1)H_2 + nCO \rightarrow C_nH_{2n+2} + nH_2O \qquad (15\text{-}1)$$

$$(n + 1)H_2 + 2nCO \rightarrow C_nH_{2n+2} + nCO_2 \qquad (15\text{-}2)$$

$$2nH_2 + nCO \rightarrow C_nH_{2n} + nH_2O \qquad (15\text{-}3)$$

$$nH_2 + 2nCO \rightarrow C_nH_{2n} + nCO_2 \qquad (15\text{-}4)$$

Free energies for those reactions leading to the formation of $CO_2$ are negative at all temperatures below about 800°F; the reactions leading to the formation of $H_2O$ are less favorable, but have negative free energies of up to about 680°F. This in itself is only part of the story, since the reactions to form the higher hydrocarbons certainly do not occur in one step. However, if we consider the intermediate reactions such as

$$CH_4 + CO + 2H_2 \rightarrow C_2H_6 + H_2O \qquad (15\text{-}5)$$

$$C_2H_6 + CO + 2H_2 \rightarrow C_3H_8 + H_2O \qquad (15\text{-}6)$$

Eq. (15-5) has a negative free energy up to about 625°F and Eq. (15-6) up to about 700°F. Also since high pressure favors the reactions, it is apparent that there is no thermodynamic limit to the maximum molecular weight of the hydrocarbons which are produced.

[1] Franz Fischer and Hans Tropsch, *Brennstoff-Chem.*, **4,** 276 (1923); **5,** 201,217 (1924).

## Catalysts

All active catalysts for the Fischer-Tropsch synthesis are found in Group VIII of the periodic table. Thus, iron, nickel, cobalt and ruthenium have been found to catalyze the synthesis; it is significant that all four of these metals form metal carbonyls at the temperatures and pressures used in the synthesis. The original iron catalyst used by Fischer and Tropsch rapidly lost activity as a result of the deposition of carbon and heavy hydrocarbons on the surface. For this reason, and because of the fact that most of the early work was carried out at atmospheric pressure, iron catalysts were more or less ignored for the next 10 years. However, in 1936, it was found that the yield over an iron catalyst could be doubled and the operating life increased several-fold by raising the pressure to about 15 atm. This renewed interest in this type of catalyst, and over the next few years sintered iron catalysts activated with alkali were developed which had operating lives of several months.

Meanwhile, it had been found that nickel and cobalt are active catalysts at atmospheric pressure, but rapidly lose activity during operation. However, the life of the catalysts could be increased by the use of a kieselguhr support and by the addition of promoters such as alumina, magnesia and thoria. Several satisfactory catalysts based on nickel and cobalt were developed. Thus, the standard catalyst used in the commercial synthesis in Germany during the war had the composition Co: $ThO_2:MgO:kieselguhr = 100:5:8:200$.

## Commercialization of the Fischer-Tropsch Process

The German work on the Fischer-Tropsch process was based on the need for synthetic fuels to replace petroleum. Thus, by the start of the war, nine plants had been erected in Germany with a rated output of 740,000 ton/yr. Synthesis gas was made from coke in standard water gas generators, using the shift reaction to obtain a 2:1 ratio of hydrogen to carbon monoxide. Since sulfur is a permanent catalyst poison, it was removed by passing the synthesis gas over hydrated iron oxide. All plants operated with the standard cobalt catalyst, with about 75 per cent of the production at atmospheric pressure and 25 per cent at medium pressure (7-20 atm). The atmospheric process produced mostly light oil with a fairly high olefin content; the medium-pressure process produced larger quantities of wax and less olefins.

In spite of the successful operation of these plants, no major increase in capacity was made during the war. By the end of the war, the Fischer-Tropsch process accounted for less than 20 per cent of the German production of synthetic oil, with coal-hydrogenation accounting for the remainder.

Following the war, it was felt that the Fischer-Tropsch synthesis might be economic in the United States where cheap natural gas could be used as a source of synthesis gas. A commercial unit was constructed by Carthage Hydrocol at Brownsville, Texas with initial operation in 1949. Natural gas was oxidized with oxygen at about 450 psig, purified, and sent to a fluidized catalytic reactor containing a promoted iron catalyst. Many operating difficulties were encountered, although little detailed information has been released except the fact that the plant never achieved over 30 per cent of the design capacity. In 1953 the plant was shut down, and a later attempt to resume commercial operation was also unsuccessful.

It is thus apparent that the Fischer-Tropsch process cannot at present compete with petroleum. The German experience also indicates that the hydrogenation of coal is a preferred method to the production of synthetic fuels. However, it is impossible to predict the future of these processes, and the economics of the Fischer-Tropsch process would be radically changed if an improved catalyst were discovered. The only present commercial operation of the Fischer-Tropsch process is in South Africa where a plant has been in operation since 1955, using sub-bituminous coal available locally. Here the economic success is dependent on the remoteness from sources of petroleum.

## METHANOL SYNTHESIS

The synthesis of methanol [1] is similar in many ways to the synthesis of ammonia, since the pressure, temperature and thermodynamic considerations are all very similar. However, there is one essential difference, namely, the possibility of side reactions. Thus, in the synthesis of ammonia, the interaction of elemental hydrogen and nitrogen can yield only ammonia as a reaction product; in the reaction of carbon monoxide and hydrogen, many products are possible of which methanol is thermodynamically one of the least favorable. Thus, the methanol synthesis is possible only by the use of a selective catalyst which will promote the desired reaction and inhibit side reactions.

The methanol synthesis is based on early studies made by the Badische Analin and Soda Fabrik of the reaction between carbon monoxide and hydrogen. This work showed that a complex liquid product could be ob-

---

[1] See chapter by G. Natta, "Synthesis of Methanol," in P. H. Emmett, Vol. III, . *cit.*

tained which consisted of acids, aldehydes, ketones, etc., methanol being present only in fairly small amounts. However, in 1923, it was found that methanol becomes the chief product of the reaction when a ZnO-$Cr_2O_3$ catalyst was used and when the reacting gases were not exposed to iron or iron alloys which give iron pentacarbonyl by reaction with carbon monoxide. In the following years, extensive work was carried out throughout the world to develop suitable catalysts and to determine the optimum experimental conditions for the commercial synthesis of methanol.

## Thermodynamic Considerations

The synthesis of methanol is based on the reaction

$$CO \text{ (g)} + 2H_2 \text{ (g)} \rightleftharpoons CH_3OH \text{ (g)} \tag{15-7}$$

$$\Delta H^\circ_{600} = -24,020 \qquad \Delta F^\circ_{600} = +11,130 \qquad \Delta F^\circ_{700} = +17,030$$

In practice, temperatures of 600-800°F (approximately 600-700°K) are used. The over-all reaction occurs in two steps with the intermediate formation of formaldehyde which is then hydrogenated to methanol according to the reactions

$$CO + H_2 \rightleftharpoons HCHO \tag{15-8}$$

$$\Delta H^\circ_{600} = -2520 \qquad \Delta F^\circ_{600} = +15,140 \qquad \Delta F^\circ_{700} = +18,110$$

$$HCHO + H_2 \rightleftharpoons CH_3OH \tag{15-9}$$

$$\Delta H^\circ_{600} = -21,500 \qquad \Delta F^\circ_{600} = -4010 \qquad \Delta F^\circ_{700} = -1080$$

Important side reactions are as follows:

$$CO + 3H_2 \rightleftharpoons CH_4 + H_2O \tag{15-10}$$

$$\Delta H^\circ_{600} = -52,060 \qquad \Delta F^\circ_{600} = -17,290 \qquad \Delta F^\circ_{700} = -11,440$$

$$2CO \rightleftharpoons CO_2 + C \text{ (s)} \tag{15-11}$$

$$\Delta H^\circ_{600} = -41,463 \qquad \Delta F^\circ_{600} = -15,728 \qquad \Delta F^\circ_{700} = -11,445$$

$$CO + H_2O \rightleftharpoons CO_2 + H_2 \tag{15-12}$$

$$\Delta H^\circ_{600} = -9294 \qquad \Delta F^\circ_{600} = -3930 \qquad \Delta F^\circ_{700} = -3059$$

In addition, other possible side reactions include the following: (a) Further reaction of methanol and CO may produce higher alcohols and acids. (b) Two molecules of methanol may split off water to form dimethyl ether. (c) Dehydration of higher alcohols will produce olefins. (d) Alcohols and acids may form esters, etc. Thus, a very complex mixture of organics is possible, depending on the catalyst and the reaction conditions.

**Equilibrium Constant**

The equilibrium constant for the methanol synthesis is

$$K_f = \frac{f_{CH_3OH}}{f_{CO}f_{H_2}^2} \tag{15-13}$$

where fugacities must be used instead of partial pressures because of the high pressures used commercially. Over the temperature range of commercial interest, the equilibrium constant based on thermal data is given by the equation

$$\log K = \frac{5304}{T} - 12.89$$

where $T$ is the absolute temperature in degrees Kelvin. Equilibrium data are plotted in Fig. 15-1. Experimental values are based on measurements of Newton and Dodge[1] at about 3 atm plus measurements by other investigators at pressures of up to 200 atm which are corrected for pressure by the use of calculated values of $K_\gamma$. Note that there is considerable scatter in the data, which largely results from the problem of obtaining equilibrium in the methanol reaction while simultaneously inhibiting all side reactions.

**Catalysts**

Many different catalysts for the synthesis of methanol are described in the patent literature. However, in practice, only two types of catalyst are important, those based on ZnO and those based on CuO. Pure ZnO is a relatively poor catalyst, but the activity can be increased by the addition of a promoter in the form of a difficulty-reducible oxide. Promoters which have been studied include $Cr_2O_3$, MgO, CdO, $Al_2O_3$, $ThO_2$, etc. However, the most important catalyst is ZnO promoted with $Cr_2O_3$; the activity of such a catalyst is highest for a 25-30 per cent $Cr_2O_3$ mixture, but the composition used commercially is about 11 per cent $Cr_2O_3$, since this has better selectivity than the higher chromia catalysts. Such a catalyst may be prepared by coprecipitation of the mixed hydroxides, reduction of zinc chromate or simply by mechanically mixing together ZnO and $Cr_2O_3$. However, the preparation of an efficient catalyst is very much of an art, since both the activity and operating life are strongly affected by the methods used to prepare and activate the catalyst.

The other important type of methanol catalyst is that based on CuO. Although pure cupric oxide is a poor catalyst, the activity can be increased by the addition of promoters such as $Cr_2O_3$, ZnO, $Al_2O_3$ or traces

[1] R. H. Newton and B. F. Dodge, *Ind. Eng. Chem.*, **27**, 577 (1935); *J. Am. Chem. Soc.*, **56**, 1287 (1934).

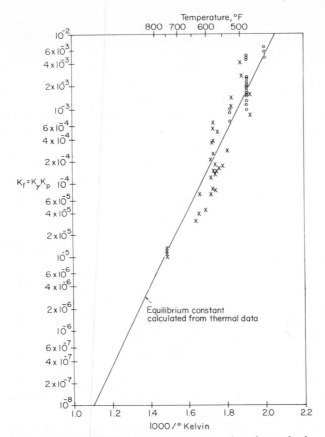

FIG. 15-1. Equilibrium constant for methanol synthesis.
[000 Data from R. H. Newton and B. F. Dodge, *J. Am.
Chem. Soc.,* **56,** 1287 (1934) xxx other investigations]

of alkali. A ternary $CuO$-$ZnO$-$Cr_2O_3$ catalyst is also very active. The
copper-based catalysts are active at temperatures below 570°F, where
the $ZnO$-$Cr_2O_3$ catalysts do not have any appreciable activity. However,
the copper catalysts are very susceptible to poisoning, are easily deac-
tivated by overheating, and are thus less suited for commercial use.

The selectivity of a methanol catalyst is strongly affected by the
presence of small traces of impurities. Thus, any metallic iron or nickel
promotes the formation of methane, while strongly alkaline substances
inhibit methane formation but promote the synthesis of higher alcohols.
The rate of the methane reaction is appreciable only at temperatures

over 750°F; below this temperature, small amounts of iron may be tolerated in the catalyst. The synthesis of methane is particularly favored by the presence of finely divided iron or nickel which may be produced by thermal decomposition of volatile iron or nickel carbonyl. Thus, iron and nickel alloys can be used in a methanol converter only if they are resistant to attack by carbon monoxide.

The catalysts based on ZnO are not very sensitive to the typical catalyst poisons such as $H_2S$, $PH_3$, As, etc. However, the copper-based catalysts are rapidly and permanently poisoned by sulfur compounds. It is of interest to note that nitrogen acts as an inert in the methanol synthesis, and does not form ammonia. This is not surprising since ZnO is not an active ammonia catalyst, and carbon monoxide is a very effective poison for the ammonia synthesis.

### Kinetics

The kinetics of the synthesis reaction are fairly complicated. The limiting reaction in the synthesis appears to be the reaction between the adsorbed molecules on the surface of the catalyst. Natta (*op. cit.*) has shown that the existing experimental data can be correlated in terms of a catalytic trimolecular surface reaction. The activation energy for a zinc oxide catalyst is 27,000-30,000; for the copper-based catalyst, lower values of 14,000-18,000 have been reported.

It has been observed that when a synthesis gas contains more CO than the stoichiometric value, the yield of methanol is reduced more than would be predicted on the basis of thermodynamics. Similarly, when $H_2$ is in excess of the stoichiometric value, there may be an actual increase in the yield of methanol. The explanation seems to be that carbon monoxide is more strongly adsorbed than hydrogen, so that in order to obtain a stoichiometric $H_2$:CO ratio on the catalyst, the ratio in the gas phase must be increased. It has also been observed that small quantities of $CO_2$ in the gas favor the conversion to methanol at high space velocities. Evidently the presence of $CO_2$ decreases the formation of dimethyl ether, retards the decomposition of CO into $CO_2$ and permits better temperature control of the synthesis gas.

## MANUFACTURE OF METHANOL

A typical process for the manufacture of methanol is illustrated in Fig. 15-2. Synthesis gas is produced in the same general manner as in the manufacture of synthetic ammonia; thus, in the United States, natural gas is the usual feedstock. For methanol synthesis, a lower reformer pressure is used, there is no secondary reformer and no shift conversion is required. The stoichiometric ratio of $H_2$:$CO$ is 2:1, but in practice the ratio is usually increased to about 2.25:1. However, in the reforming of natural gas, the theoretical $H_2$:$CO$ ratio is 3:1 for pure $CH_4$. Thus, it is necessary to add $CO_2$ to the gas before reforming in order to reduce the $H_2$:$CO$ ratio to the desired value. If the $CO_2$ is not available from an

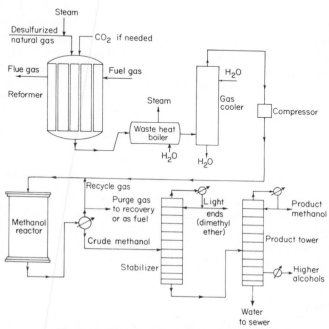

Fig. 15-2. Flowsheet for methanol synthesis.

outside source, it may be obtained by scrubbing the flue gas from the reformer with ethanolamine solution.

Reformed gases are quenched with water, cooled, condensed water separated, and the synthesis gas compressed to 4600-5500 psig by a reciprocating compressor. The methanol converter consists of a pressure vessel provided with an internal heat exchanger to preheat the feed and to control the heat of reaction. The general design is very similar to that of the ammonia converter. Gases enter the catalyst beds at about 615°F at a standard space velocity of about 25,000 ft³/(hr) (ft³ catalyst). Crude methanol is condensed from the effluent converter gas, unreacted gas is recycled, and a small portion purged to remove inerts. Dissolved gases are removed by flashing the methanol to atmospheric pressure, and the product is purified by fractionation.

Carbon and low-alloy steels cannot be used for internal parts of the methanol converter since they are readily attacked by synthesis gas with the formation of iron carbonyl. At one time, it was customary to line the converter and process lines with copper or bronze to prevent carbon monoxide attack. This was not entirely satisfactory since these linings often ruptured during depressurizing because of gases trapped between the lining and the main vessel. Also, bronze and copper are not particularly heat resistant, and there have been cases where these materials have melted when the methanation reaction got out of hand. For these reasons, it is now customary to fabricate methanol converters of stainless steel or other alloys which are heat resistant, structurally strong and also chemically resistant to attack by carbon monoxide.

### Methanol from Carbon Dioxide

It is possible to produce methanol from carbon dioxide by the reaction

$$3H_2 + CO_2 \rightleftharpoons CH_3OH + H_2O$$

$$\Delta H^\circ_{600} = -14,490 \qquad \Delta F^\circ_{600} = +14,910 \qquad \Delta F^\circ_{700} = +19,880$$

The equilibrium is less favorable than in the case of the carbon monoxide reaction, and the hydrogen consumption is 50 per cent greater. Thus, the only conditions under which this process might be economic are where by-product hydrogen is available at essentially no cost, so that the cheaper raw materials would compensate for the lower yields which are obtained.

### Uses of Methanol

The total production of synthetic methanol in the United States for 1963 was 2333 million pounds. Approximately half the total production goes into the manufacture of formaldehyde. Other uses are as an antifreeze, as a methylating agent, in solvents and for miscellaneous chemical uses. The production of methanol in recent years has been fairly static because of the loss of several markets such as in automobile antifreeze, and because of the production of increasing quantities of formaldehyde by direct hydrocarbon oxidation. Much methanol production is associated with synthetic ammonia plants, and capacity can be shifted between the two products, depending on the relative demand.

## FORMALDEHYDE

Formaldehyde is manufactured from methanol by catalytic air oxidation according to the equation

$$CH_3OH + \tfrac{1}{2}O_2 \rightarrow HCHO + H_2O \text{ (g)} \tag{15-14}$$

$$\Delta H^\circ_{298} = -37,400 \qquad \Delta F^\circ_{298} = -42,140$$

$$CH_3OH \rightarrow HCHO + H_2 \tag{15-15}$$

$$\Delta H^\circ_{298} = +20,400 \qquad \Delta F^\circ_{298} = +12,500$$

with the possible side reaction

$$CH_3OH + \tfrac{3}{2}O_2 \rightarrow CO_2 + 2H_2O \tag{15-16}$$

$$\Delta H^\circ_{298} = -161,550 \qquad \Delta F^\circ_{298} = -164,830$$

The oxidation of methanol is strongly exothermic, and the equilibrium is very favorable. The oxidation is carried out at about atmospheric pressure and at temperatures of 900-1100°F. The catalyst consists of silver or copper, either in the form of a metal gauze or as a fixed catalyst on an inert support. In addition, metallic oxide catalysts such as vanadium pentoxide are also disclosed in the patent literature.

In practice, air and methanol vapors are mixed, preheated and passed over the catalyst. Formaldehyde is recovered by cooling the effluent gases, followed by absorption in water to form a 30-37 per cent solution. The yield is 85-90 per cent, based on methanol consumed. The oxidation may be carried out in two general ways. In the first, insufficient oxygen is used so that the over-all reaction is a combination of Eqs. (15-14) and (15-15). Some unreacted methanol is left in the product, which is desirable since it stabilizes the formaldehyde solution. Substantial quantities of hydrogen are obtained as a by-product.

In the second method, a large excess of oxygen is used with precise temperature control to minimize combustion to carbon dioxide. Practically all the methanol is oxidized in this case, but the costs are higher because a larger volume of gas must be handled.

Formaldehyde is sold commercially as a 37 per cent solution known as "formalin" which contains 6-15 per cent methanol to prevent polymerization. A low-methanol solution containing about 1 per cent methanol is also available. Pure formaldehyde is unstable at room temperature, and hydrates to form methylene glycol $CH_2(OH)_2$, which then polymerizes to polyoxymethylene glycols $H(CH_2O)_nOH$. The solid polymer of formaldehyde ($n = 8$ to $100$) is known as paraformaldehyde "paraform." Formaldehyde is also available as the solid cyclic trimer trioxane produced by the reaction

$$3HCHO \rightarrow O \begin{array}{c} CH_2 - O \\ \diagup \qquad \diagdown \\ \qquad\qquad CH_2 \\ \diagdown \qquad \diagup \\ CH_2 - O \end{array}$$

Most formaldehyde produced is for captive use where the material goes into the manufacture of phenolic, urea and melamine resins. Smaller amounts go into the manufacture of the two resin intermediates pentaerythritol and hexamethylenetetramine. About 300 million pounds/year of formaldehyde are used by du Pont at Belle, West Virginia for the manufacture of ethylene glycol. According to the patent literature, the process involves a condensation of aqueous formaldehyde with carbon monoxide at about 700 atm and 300-400°F, using a catalyst of sulfuric acid or boron trifluoride. Glycollic acid is produced by the reaction

$$HCHO + CO + H_2O \rightarrow HO—CH_2—COOH$$

The glycollic acid is easily esterified to methyl glycollate by the reaction

$$HOCH_2COOH + CH_3OH \rightleftharpoons H_2O + HOCH_2COOCH_3 \xrightarrow{2H_2}$$

$$HOCH_2CH_2OH + CH_3OH$$

The ester is hydrogenated with a large excess of hydrogen to give ethylene glycol and methyl alcohol which can be recycled. The hydrogenation is carried out at about 30 atm and 400-450°F, using a copper chromite catalyst. The over-all yield is about 75 per cent based on formaldehyde.

## THE OXO PROCESS

The oxo process involves the direct addition of carbon monoxide and hydrogen to an olefin according to the typical equation

$$R—CH{=}CH_2 + H_2 + CO \begin{array}{l} \rightarrow R—CH_2—CH_2—CHO \quad (15\text{-}17) \\ \rightarrow R—CH—CH_3 \quad\quad\quad\quad (15\text{-}18) \\ \phantom{\rightarrow R—}| \\ \phantom{\rightarrow R—}CHO \end{array}$$

The reaction is carried out in the liquid phase at high pressure and moderate temperature, using a cobalt catalyst. Normally the two aldehyde isomers are produced in about equal amounts. The synthesis was first carried out using ethylene, propionaldehyde and diethyl ketone being the chief products. Since each of these products contains a carbonyl group, the Germans chose the name "oxierung," meaning carbonylation or ketonization, for the synthesis. Since the reaction actually involves the addition of formaldehyde HCHO to the olefin, a better name for the process would be formylation or hydroformylation. However, the name "oxo" derived from the original German work is probably too deeply entrenched to be replaced at this time.

The oxo reaction was first noted by Smith[1] and his co-workers in experiments carried out to determine the mechanism of the Fischer-Tropsch synthesis. Thus, Smith reported that when a mixture of carbon monoxide, hydrogen and an olefin is subjected to the usual Fischer-Tropsch conditions, the resultant products contain 25-30 per cent of water-soluble organics. Otto Roelen of Ruhrchemie A. G., whose group had been investigating the Fischer-Tropsch synthesis for several years, later repeated the experiments of Smith and appreciated the practical significance of the work. Roelen believed that the oxygenated compounds came from the direct reaction with the olefin, and he then determined the conditions necessary to maximize the yield of the aldehyde products. In 1940, Ruhrchemie A. G. and I. G. Farben cooperated in the commercial development of the process, which resulted in the first production of oxo alcohols on a semiplant scale in Germany during the war.

The great advantage of the oxo process is that it permits the manufacture of a uniform product using readily available olefin feedstocks. Thus, although the synthol process can be used to produce large quantities of oxygenated products, these are obtained as a complex mixture of ketones, aldehydes, acids, esters, alcohols and hydrocarbons, which are very difficult to separate into pure components. In addition, the synthol process suffers from the usual handicap of any process producing a variety of products, namely, that the product distribution has no relationship to the market demand for the individual products.

**Thermodynamics**

The oxo reaction is strongly exothermic, with a standard heat of reaction of about 25,000 cal/mole, regardless of the olefin which is used. Free energies have been calculated[2] for the following two reactions:

$$C_2H_4 + CO + H_2 \rightarrow C_2H_5—CHO \qquad (15\text{-}19)$$

$$\Delta F^\circ = -34,787 + 58.1T$$

$$C_3H_6 + CO + H_2 \rightarrow (CH_3)_2CHCHO \qquad (15\text{-}20)$$

$$\Delta F^\circ = -31,140 + 61.4T$$

where $T$ is in degrees Kelvin. At the temperatures used commercially (about 350°K), both of the above reactions are favorable. However, in

[1] D. F. Smith, *et al., J. Am. Chem. Soc.*, **52**, 3221 (1930); Otto Roelen, German Patent 103,362 (filed Sept. 19, 1938) corresponding to U.S. Patent 2,327,066 (issued Aug. 17, 1943). For recent reviews, see V. N. Hurd and B. H. Gwynn, "Recent Developments in the Oxo Process," Fifth World Petroleum Congress, June 3, 1959; Chapter by A. Voorhies, *et al.,* in J. J. McKetta, Jr., Vol. I, *op. cit.*

[2] R. R. Wenner, *Chem. Eng. Progr.*, **45**, 194 (1949).

practice, a substantial yield is obtained only when the reaction is carried out at a high pressure.

Numerous side reactions are thermodynamically possible, of which the following are the most important:

$$C_2H_4 + H_2 \rightarrow C_2H_6 \tag{15-21}$$

$$\Delta H^\circ_{298} = -32,732 \qquad \Delta F^\circ_{298} = -24,142$$

$$C_2H_5CHO + H_2 \rightarrow C_3H_7OH \tag{15-22}$$

$$\Delta H^\circ_{298} = -16,690 \qquad \Delta F^\circ_{298} = -770$$

$$CH_2{=}CH{-}CH_2{-}CH_3 \rightarrow CH_3{-}CH{=}CH{-}CH_3 \;(trans) \tag{15-23}$$

$$\Delta H^\circ_{298} = -2685 \qquad \Delta F^\circ_{298} = -1902$$

$$2CH_3CH_2CHO \rightarrow CH_3CH_2CH(OH)CH(CH_3)CHO \rightarrow$$
$$H_2O + CH_3CH_2CH{=}C(CH_3)CHO$$

The hydrogenation of the olefin will always be strongly exothermic with the equilibrium virtually 100 per cent to the right. The fact that this reaction occurs to only a very small extent can be attributed to the lack of a hydrogenation catalyst and to the fact that carbon monoxide is a strong poison for the hydrogenation reaction. The hydrogenation of the aldehyde according to Eq. (15-22) always occurs to some extent, although here the high carbon monoxide pressure also tends to inhibit the reaction. Double-bond isomerization of the olefin also always occurs to some extent, and complicates the product distribution. Skeletal isomerization of the carbon chain, however, does not occur in the oxo synthesis. Isomerization is usually undesirable, since the normal products are more in demand than the branched products.

The aldol reaction is one of the most important of the side reactions. Depending on temperature and time, a substantial fraction of the aldol products will be hydrogenated to the corresponding saturated aldehyde or alcohol. In some cases the aldol condensation is desirable, and patents describe methods of increasing the yield of the aldol product. For example, formation of 2-ethylhexanol from propylene would certainly be considered a desirable reaction.

### Catalysts

Both cobalt and iron will catalyze the oxo synthesis, but cobalt is normally used since it is more effective. The actual catalyst in the oxo synthesis is a cobalt carbonyl. The three cobalt carbonyls which are known to exist are dicobalt octacarbonyl, $Co_2(CO)_8$, cobalt hydrocarbonyl, $HCo(CO)_4$, and tetracobalt dodecacarbonyl, $Co_4(CO)_{12}$. There is good evidence to show that the active catalyst is an equilibrium mixture of dicobalt octacarbonyl and cobalt hydrocarbonyl formed by the reactions

$$2Co + 8CO \rightleftharpoons Co_2(CO)_8 \overset{H_2}{\rightleftharpoons} 2HCo(CO)_4$$

The equilibrium for the formation of the carbonyls depends strongly on temperature. Thus, the dicobalt octacarbonyl is stable at room temperature and atmospheric pressure, but at 300°F the decomposition pressure is equal to 40 atm. This is presumably the reason the oxo reaction must be carried out at high pressure, since at the reaction temperatures used commercially, the cobalt carbonyls can only exist under a high CO partial pressure.

The original German oxo process used the standard Fischer-Tropsch catalyst. It is also possible to introduce the cobalt in other forms, for example, as finely divided cobalt metal, as cobalt salts, etc. At present, it is customary to introduce the cobalt as an organic salt such as cobalt oleate or naphthenate which is soluble in the olefin. An induction period is needed to convert the cobalt to the carbonyls. Note that the carbonyls are soluble in the liquid organics, and hence the cobalt acts as a homogeneous catalyst.

The oxo catalyst is not poisoned by the presence of sulfur, but the quality of the product is adversely affected if sulfur is present. Diolefins and acetylenic compounds are definitely undesirable, since they inhibit the oxo reaction. Such compounds should either be removed from the oxo feedstock, or else the catalyst concentration should be increased to compensate for their presence.

### Kinetics and Mechanism of Reaction

The kinetics of the oxo reaction have been studied[1] under a wide variety of conditions. The rate of the reaction is first-order with respect to the olefin, roughly first-order with respect to the hydrogen partial pressure, and roughly proportional to the amount of catalyst which is used. The rate increases with temperature, although side reactions also increase with temperature. However, the interesting feature of the reaction is the dependence on the carbon monoxide partial pressure. For a given temperature and hydrogen partial pressure, the rate of reaction first increases as the carbon monoxide pressure is increased. The rate then goes through a maximum at pressures of the order of 10-100 atm, then decreases as the carbon monoxide pressure is increased beyond this point. The position of the maximum depends on the temperature, the hydrogen pressure, and the olefin which is reacting.

The effect of the carbon monoxide pressure can be attributed directly

[1] See chapter by Irving Wender, *et al.*, in P. H. Emmett, Vol. V, *op. cit.*

to carbonyl formation. Thus, at low pressures, increasing the carbon monoxide pressure increases the concentration of the cobalt carbonyls and hence increases the rate of reaction. Eventually, most of the cobalt is converted to the active state, and beyond this point the carbon monoxide merely inhibits the reaction.

Various reaction mechanisms have been postulated for the oxo reaction. Since the rate varies inversely with the CO partial pressure under the conditions used in practice, it is obvious that the reaction involves more than a direct addition of carbon monoxide to the olefin. The oxo reaction takes place in the liquid phase, and thus the carbon monoxide in the gas phase must first be made available as a cobalt carbonyl which is soluble in the liquid. Also, the hydrogen must be transferred from the gas phase to the liquid phase, and the hydrogen molecule must be split. These facts clearly indicate that the cobalt hydrocarbonyl is the active catalyst for the reaction, since it can transfer both hydrogen and carbon monoxide to the olefin. It has been shown experimentally that cobalt hydrocarbonyl can exist at the temperatures and pressures used in the oxo synthesis; however, in the presence of an olefin, the cobalt hydrocarbonyl does not exist as such, but is converted almost 100 per cent to an olefin complex. This also strongly indicates that the cobalt hydrocarbonyl is the active catalyst.

Every simple olefin which has been investigated has been found to undergo the oxo synthesis. However, the rate of the reaction varies with the nature of the olefin. Experiments by Wender[1] have shown that the olefins can be divided into the following classes:

(1) Straight-chain Terminal Olefins. Olefins such as 1-heptene react most rapidly. Although there is a small decrease in the rate of reaction as the length of the carbon chain increases, the rate is fairly constant in going from $C_5$ to $C_{14}$.

(2) Straight-chain Internal Olefins. The rate of reaction of the internal olefins is approximately one-third that of the corresponding terminal olefins. The position of the double bond has little effect as long as it is internal.

(3) Branched Olefins. Branching always results in a decrease in the rate of reaction. The greatest decrease occurs when a side chain is attached to one of the carbon atoms of the double bond. The branched internal olefins have reaction rates as low as one-fiftieth that of the straight-chain terminal olefins.

(4) Cyclic Olefins. Since cyclic olefins are internal olefins, the rate of reaction is about the same as that of the straight-chain internal olefins.

---

[1] J. Wender, *et al.*, *J. Am. Chem. Soc.*, **78**, 5401 (1956).

However, there is a minimum at $C_6$, where cyclohexene shows a rate only about one-fourth that of cycloheptene or cyclopentene.

## COMMERCIAL USE OF OXO PROCESS

In the United States, the chief commercial use of the oxo process has been for the manufacture of alcohols for solvent, plasticizer and detergent use. The oxo process has two substantial advantages and one disadvantage in comparison with other processes. First, the oxo process always produces primary alcohols since it involves the hydrogenation of an aldehyde. Second, the oxo process can conveniently use feedstocks produced by the usual refining operations. One disadvantage of the oxo process is the fact that the product is almost always a mixture of many isomers, which may be a handicap if the material is to be used as a chemical intermediate. Oxo products now being produced commercially in the United States are listed in Table 15-1, and many others will un-

TABLE 15-1.   COMMERCIAL OXO PRODUCTS IN UNITED STATES*

| Oxo Product | Olefin Source | Principal Use |
|---|---|---|
| Propionic acid | Ethylene | Chemical intermediate |
| n-Butanol | Propylene | Solvent, solvent intermediate |
| Isobutanol | Propylene | Solvent, solvent intermediate |
| n-Butyraldehyde | Propylene | Chemical intermediate |
| Isobutyraldehyde | Propylene | Chemical intermediate |
| n-Amyl alcohol | n-Butylenes | Solvent, solvent intermediate |
| 3-Methylbutanol | n-Butylenes | Solvent, solvent intermediate |
| Isooctyl alcohol | Heptenes | Plasticizer intermediate |
| 2-Ethylhexanol | Propylene | Plasticizer intermediate |
| "Iso" 2-ethylhexanol | Propylene | Plasticizer intermediate |
| Decyl alcohol | Tripropylene | Plasticizer intermediate |
| Tridecyl alcohol | Tetrapropylene | Detergent intermediate |
| Neopentyl glycol | Propylene | Chemical intermediate |

* V. N. Hurd and B. H. Gwynn, *op. cit.*

doubtedly be introduced as markets develop. Thus, a recent estimate by *Chemical and Engineering News* shows eight United States manufacturers with a total oxo capacity of 785 million pounds/year, although much of this may not be fully utilized. However, it is obvious that the oxo process will have an increasingly important effect on the future development of the petrochemical industry.

Oxo feedstocks include ethylene, propylene, n-butylenes, propylene trimer and propylene tetramer produced in the usual way. In addition, substantial quantities of isooctyl alcohol are based on heptenes produced by polymerization of a mixture of propylene and *n*-butylenes. Synthesis gas required in the oxo process may come from partial oxidation of natural gas using $CO_2$ addition to increase the ratio of carbon monoxide to hydrogen. An alternative source of synthesis gas is by reforming of natural gas with carbon dioxide according to the equation

$$CH_4 + CO_2 \rightleftharpoons 2CO + 2H_2$$

$$\Delta H^\circ_{1000} = +62,212 \qquad \Delta F^\circ_{1000} = -5884$$

In practice, the ratio of hydrogen to carbon monoxide in the synthesis gas is 1.1-1.2, since there is always some hydrogenation of the aldehyde to the alcohol.

Practically nothing has been released on commercial operations except in the patent literature. In practice, temperatures are normally in the range of 300-400°F, pressures 2500-6500 psig, with a catalyst consumption based on cobalt equal to 0.5-1.0 per cent of the olefin feed. For the lower olefins, an inert solvent such as toluene is required. If the desired product is an aldehyde, it is necessary to operate at as low a temperature as possible to prevent excessive hydrogenation to the alcohol. Higher temperatures are needed for the more unreactive olefins such as heptene and the propylene polymers, which consist chiefly of branched internal olefins. The reaction rate is relatively insensitive to pressure, since the effects of hydrogen and carbon monoxide on the rate tend to cancel each other.

High-pressure reactors for the oxo synthesis may be of the packed type, the vertical tank type or the elongated tubular reactor. From the patent literature, the vertical tank reactor with agitation provided by the gas rising through the liquid appears to be favored. The reaction is strongly exothermic, and temperatures must be controlled by internal cooling coils or by recirculation of liquid through an external exchanger. Oxo reactors are usually fabricated of stainless steel which is resistant to attack by carbon monoxide.

The products from the oxo reaction will contain dissolved cobalt carbonyls plus smaller quantities of iron carbonyl. These must be removed to prevent poisoning of the catalyst in the subsequent hydrogenation stage and to recover cobalt values. The carbonyls are commonly removed by blowing with steam to decompose them to the metal, followed by filtration and water extraction to remove soluble cobalt compounds. A second method of cobalt removal involves extraction with a dilute acid such as formic or acetic acid. This is a very effective method of decobalting, and has the advantage that it permits the recovery of valuable cobalt salts.

Most commercial production involves the hydrogenation of the crude aldehyde product to the alcohol. This is a conventional operation using a catalyst such as nickel, cobalt, molybdenum sulfide, copper chromite, etc. Typical hydrogenation conditions include temperatures of 300-400°F and pressures of 500-1500 psig. Product is separated from light and heavy ends by fractionation; since hydrogenation can never in practice be carried to completion, a small amount of aldehyde in the product is recycled to the hydrogenator.

Figure 15-3 illustrates the Ruhrchemie A. G. oxo process. The oxo reactor operates at 340°F and 3700 psig, using a $H_2$:CO ratio of 1.2:1.0.

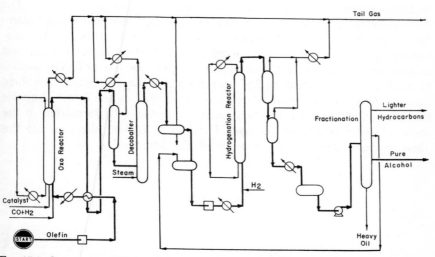

Fig. 15-3. Oxo process [*Hydro. Proc. Petrol. Refiner,* **40** (11), 278 (1961)]. (Copyright 1961, Gulf Publishing Co., Houston, Texas)

Olefin conversion is 95 per cent. Decobaltization is carried out at 350°F and 300 psig by blowing with steam. The aldehydes are hydrogenated at 300°F and 1500 psig, using a nickel catalyst, and separated by distillation into alcohol product, light ends, heavy ends and a recycle aldehyde fraction. The typical yield of isooctyl alcohol is 85-90 lb from 100 lb of heptene feed. Table 15-2 gives a typical composition for the isooctyl alcohol product.

In recent years, attempts have been made to control the isomeric distribution of the oxo products when a pure olefin is used as a feedstock. The chief use has been in the production of butyraldehyde from propylene, since the normal butyraldehyde, butanol and butyric acid are of more value than the corresponding iso-derivatives. The ratio of normal

TABLE 15-2. COMPOSITION OF
ISOOCTYL ALCOHOL*

| Component | Percentage |
| --- | --- |
| 4,5-Dimethylhexanol | 30-40 |
| 3,5-Dimethylhexanol | 25-30 |
| 5-Methylheptanol | 5-15 |
| 3,4-Dimethylhexanol | 15-20 |
| 5,5-Dimethylhexanol | 2-5 |
| 2,3-Dimethylhexanol | 2-5 |

* V. N. Hurd and B. H. Gwynn, *op. cit.*

to branched-chain aldehyde can be increased in three general ways. The first is by using very mild reaction conditions, since low temperatures favor the formation of the normal isomer. However, this has the disadvantage of reducing the production rate, and hence increasing the cost of production. The second method is to recycle the less desirable isomer to inhibit further formation by the principle of Le Chatelier. The third method involves the use of selective solvents such as the lower aliphatic ketones and alcohols which are claimed to increase the formation of the normal isomer. Of course, the second and third method also decrease the plant productivity, but not as much as the first method.

# CHAPTER 16

# Oxidation of Hydrocarbons

Many oxidation reactions have already been discussed such as the oxidation of ethylene, manufacture of synthesis gas, manufacture of acetylene, etc. This chapter will be concerned with those oxidation reactions which have not been covered previously, particularly the drastic oxidation of hydrocarbons to produce various oxygenated compounds such as formaldehyde, phthalic anhydride, adipic acid, etc.

## OXIDATION OF PARAFFINS

Oxidation of paraffins may be carried out using chemical oxidizing agents, using air or using pure oxygen. The oxidation may be carried out in either the liquid or vapor phase. Many practical problems are encountered in the commercial use of paraffin oxidation. First, it is highly desirable to stay outside the explosive limits of the hydrocarbon mixture; this requires the use of a large excess of paraffin, which involves a low conversion per pass and much recycle of unreacted paraffin. Second, the yield of useful products is fairly low because of the combustion of much of the paraffin to carbon monoxide and carbon dioxide. Third, a mixture of products is always obtained which is difficult and expensive to separate. In addition, the products are formed in an essentially constant ratio depending on the feedstock, and this product distribution may have no relationship to the market demand for the individual products.

The rate of oxidation of paraffins shows many very interesting and puzzling features.[1] Depending on the hydrocarbon and the experimental conditions, the rate of reaction has been found to vary from first- to third-order with respect to the hydrocarbon concentration and from first to inverse first-order with respect to the oxygen concentration. Also, the reaction orders often change with temperature. Often regions are en-

---

[1] For example, see M. Seakins and C. Hinshelwood, *Proc. Roy. Soc. (London)*, **A276,** 342 (1963); P. G. Ashmore, *op. cit.*

countered where the rate first increases with temperature to a maximum, then decreases to a minimum, and then increases again with further increase of temperature.

In the oxidation of a paraffin, the initial point of attack by the oxygen will usually be at the weakest C—H bond. Thus, carbon is attacked in the order tertiary > secondary > primary. Also, the difficulty of oxidation depends on the molecular weight. Methane is most difficult to oxidize, ethane less difficult, etc. When a paraffin is first mixed with oxygen, usually there is an induction period where the initial rate of reaction is very small. The rate then suddenly increases to a maximum value, and then decreases as the oxygen is consumed. This induction period can be reduced or eliminated entirely by the addition of small quantities of oxygenated compounds such as aldehydes or peroxides to the reactant gases.

The mechanism of the oxidation reactions has been carefully studied by Hinshelwood and his co-workers. There is general agreement that the reactions take place through a chain reaction involving the formation of peroxides and free radicals. The initial step in the chain is the formation of a hydrocarbon peroxide by the reactions

$$RH + O_2 \rightarrow R^{\bullet} + HO_2^{\bullet} \tag{16-1}$$

$$R^{\bullet} + O_2 \rightarrow RO_2^{\bullet} \tag{16-2}$$

$$RO_2^{\bullet} + RH \rightarrow R^{\bullet} + ROOH \tag{16-3}$$

$$RO_2^{\bullet} \text{ and } ROOH \rightarrow \text{aldehydes, ketones, acids, etc.} \tag{16-4}$$

The first step in the oxidation chain is a slow reaction which involves the abstraction of a hydrogen atom from the hydrocarbon according to Eq. (16-1). Although the $HO_2^{\bullet}$ radical is not very reactive, the hydrocarbon radical $R^{\bullet}$ readily forms peroxides which either continue the chain reaction or decompose to give oxygenated products.

All the essential characteristics of hydrocarbon oxidation are explained by the chain-reaction mechanism. Thus, the induction period is caused by the slow formation of intermediates which catalyze the reaction. Both the induction period and the initial rate of reaction can be strongly affected by the addition to the reactants of small quantities of either the intermediate products or other materials which readily form free radicals. The oxidation can be inhibited by the addition of any material which reacts with the free radicals that propagate the chain reaction. Since the stability of the intermediate reaction products is a function of temperature, it is not surprising that the rate constants and the reaction orders also vary with temperature.

## Oxidation of Methane and Ethane

The rate of oxidation of methane is appreciable only at temperatures greater than about 800°F. Methane oxidizes only by a high temperature mechanism, water and carbon dioxide being the chief products. The oxidation shows the typical induction period followed by a rapid reaction. The maximum rate of reaction at 800°F is second-order with respect to methane and first-order with respect to oxygen. There is general agreement that formaldehyde is the intermediate responsible for the autocatalysis of the oxidation. The chain reaction proceeds by the following mechanism:

$$CH_4 + O_2 \rightarrow CH_3^{\bullet} + HO_2^{\bullet}$$

$$CH_3^{\bullet} + O_2 \rightarrow HCHO + OH^{\bullet}$$

$$OH^{\bullet} + CH_4 \rightarrow CH_3^{\bullet} + H_2O \quad \text{etc.}$$

The induction period can be eliminated by the addition of formaldehyde to the reactants, and the oxidation can be accelerated by the addition of oxides of nitrogen which increase the formation of free radicals.

Extensive pilot plant work has been carried out in Germany on the production of formaldehyde by the direct oxidation of methane according to the equation

$$CH_4 + O_2 \rightarrow HCHO \text{ (g)} + H_2O \text{ (g)} \tag{16-5}$$
$$\Delta H^{\circ}_{298} = -67,610 \qquad \Delta F^{\circ}_{298} = -68,700$$

with the inevitable competing reaction

$$CH_4 + 2O_2 \rightarrow CO_2 + 2H_2O \text{ (g)} \tag{16-6}$$
$$\Delta H^{\circ}_{298} = -191,760 \qquad \Delta F^{\circ}_{298} = -191,390$$

One process involved the direct interaction at temperatures of 750-1100°F, using about 0.1 per cent NO as a gaseous catalyst. A second process involved the use of oxygen containing 1 per cent ozone at temperatures of 240-250°F, using a catalyst of barium peroxide promoted with silver oxide. However, in spite of the favorable thermodynamics, the yield in both cases was fairly low. Also, the oxidation of natural gas was carried out on a semicommercial scale in the United States by Cities Service Oil Co. for a short time starting in 1928, but the feedstock was later changed to LPG. However, Eq. (16-5) would certainly be of considerable commercial interest if a catalyst could ever be developed to direct the oxidation primarily to the formation of formaldehyde.

Ethane can be oxidized at temperatures of about 700°F or greater to form oxygenated compounds such as methanol, ethanol, formaldehyde, etc. The oxidation is a chain reaction involving ethyl radicals. However, the oxidation of ethane appears to be of less commercial interest than either methane or LPG.

### Oxidation of Propane and Butane

These two hydrocarbons are of most interest because of the use of LPG as a commercial oxidation feedstock.[1] The rate of oxidation of propane is illustrated in Fig. 16-1. The rate is small below about 550°F;

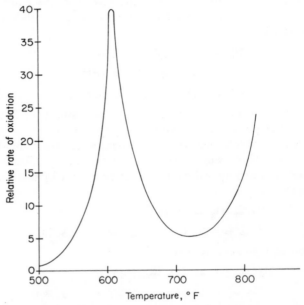

FIG. 16-1. Relative rate of oxidation of propane at low pressure. (M. Seakins and C. Hinshelwood, *op. cit.*)

the rate then increases with temperature to a maximum at about 600-700°F, depending on the pressure, and then decreases to a minimum before again increasing with temperature. Three temperature regions can be defined. Below 650°F, considerable oxygenated compounds are produced including methanol, formaldehyde, acetaldehyde, etc. From 650-850°F, the amount of oxygenated products decreases and the major products become propylene and hydrogen peroxide. Above about 850°F, the typical oxidative cracking products are formed such as propylene, ethylene, carbon dioxide, etc.

[1] F. B. Marcotte and R. L. Mitchell, "Encyclopedia of Chemical Technology," *op. cit.;* Chapter by H. D. Medley and S. D. Cooley in J. J. McKetta, Jr., Vol. III, *op. cit.;* P. G. Ashmore, *op. cit.*

The oxidation of butane is very similar to the oxidation of propane. Thus, at low temperatures, the chief products are acetaldehyde, formaldehyde, methanol, etc. At intermediate temperatures, the oxygenated compounds decrease and there is an increasing production of butylenes. Over about 750°F, the products are chiefly propylene and ethylene. In the oxidation of isobutane, the yield of oxygenated products also depends on the temperature. At low temperatures, the chief products are acetone and *tert*-butanol, resulting from the attack of the tertiary hydrogen atom. However, increasing amounts of acetaldehyde are produced at higher temperatures, thereby indicating an increasing attack of the primary hydrogen atoms.

The yield of oxygenated compounds is also affected by the pressure at which the oxidation occurs. Thus, moderate pressures will suppress olefin formation, extend the temperature range at which good yields of oxygenated products are obtained and minimize degradation of the carbon skeleton of the feedstock. However, an increase in pressure does cause the product distribution to shift from aldehydes to alcohols.

An interesting feature in the low-temperature oxidation of the higher paraffins is the formation of "cool flames" which are luminous because of the fluorescence of excited formaldehyde molecules. The cool flames propagate as waves throughout the reacting gases. In some cases, several cool flames may periodically arise and die out without materially affecting the composition of the products. In other cases, a cool flame may cause an autocatalytic increase in the rate of oxidation until a violent explosion occurs.

The products obtained in the low-temperature oxidation of propane and butane depend on the temperature, pressure, oxygen to hydrocarbon ratio, residence time, presence or absence of a catalyst and the rate of cooling of the reaction products. Typical results are given in Table 16-1.

TABLE 16-1. TYPICAL YIELDS FROM COMMERCIAL
VAPOR-PHASE OXIDATION*

| | Propane | Product distribution, lb/gal of fresh feed n-Butane | Isobutane |
|---|---|---|---|
| Acetaldehyde | 1.38 | 1.5 | 0.76 |
| Formaldehyde | 1.5 | 1.6 | 1.0 |
| Methanol | 1.2 | 0.98 | 0.62 |
| Mixed solvents | 0.36 | 0.60 | 0.61 |
| Acetone | 0.10 | 0.20 | 1.20 |
| Total | 4.54 | 4.88 | 4.19 |

* Data from R. E. Meyer, *Oil Gas J.*, **54**(7), 82 (1955).

For maximum yield of oxygenated products, the reaction temperature should be as low as possible and a moderate pressure should be used. Complete combustion of the hydrocarbon is minimized by the use of a low oxygen-to-hydrocarbon ratio, a fairly short residence time and rapid quench of the reaction products. Although the use of a catalyst could theoretically improve selectivity, effective catalysts have not been developed, and the commercial vapor-phase processes are noncatalytic.

## COMMERCIAL OPERATIONS

The commercial production of oxygenated compounds by hydrocarbon oxidation has had its ups and downs. The first commercial plant was operated by Cities Service Oil Co. at Tallant, Oklahoma in 1928. Later two additional plants were constructed at Oklahoma City and at Seminole, Oklahoma. These plants originally used natural gas as feedstock, but later changed to LPG. All three of these plants were fairly small, and all have now been shut down. In 1930, Hanlon-Buchanan constructed a plant at Goodhope, Louisiana, but this was unsuccessful and operation was ended in 1933. In 1949, a plant was constructed at Winnie, Texas by McCarthy Chemicals to oxidize residue gas from a natural gasoline plant with 95 per cent oxygen. However, the process was uneconomic, largely because more methane reacted than had been originally anticipated.

The first successful commercial operation is that of the Celanese Corp. of America at Bishop, Texas starting in 1945 and at Pampa, Texas starting in 1952. A simplified flow sheet of the Bishop plant is given in Fig. 16-2. The feedstock consists of propane and/or butane which is mixed with recycle gas and air or oxygen to produce a feed containing 3-10 per cent $O_2$. Initial operations used air for oxidation, but this has now been replaced with oxygen. Normally the oxygen concentration in the reactants is maintained below the explosive limits. The feed is preheated to 500-700°F and passed to a tubular reactor where the noncatalytic oxidation takes place at 800-1000°F and 100-300 psig with a residence time of 0.25-2.0 sec. Although the oxygen consumption is essentially complete, the conversion per pass is only about 10 per cent or less because of the large excess of hydrocarbon. It is possible that steam is used as a diluent to inhibit degradation of the products.

Effluent gases from the reactor are quickly quenched to about 200°F with cold 12-14 per cent formaldehyde solution which is recycled to the quench tower. Most new formaldehyde is removed at this point; the pH of the recycle formaldehyde solution is adjusted by the addition of caustic to minimize polymerization and other side reactions of the formalde-

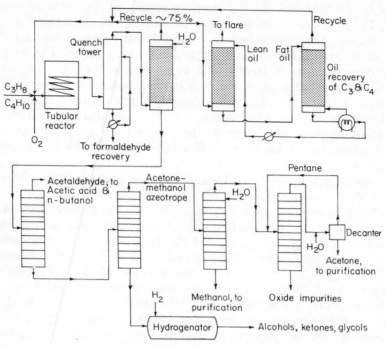

Fɪɢ. 16-2. Simplified flowsheet of oxidation plant.

hyde. Oxygenated compounds remaining in the quenched gases are removed by absorption in water in a second tower. About 75 per cent of the unreacted hydrocarbon gas is recycled and 25 per cent is purged to a conventional absorption-desorption system which recovers $C_3$ and heavier paraffins by oil absorption. Because of the large amount of recycle, the recovery system must be virtually 100 per cent efficient to prevent excessive losses in the purge gas.

The four chief products of the oxidation are formaldehyde, methanol, acetaldehyde and acetone; other products produced in smaller amounts include propanol, isobutanol, butanol, methyl ethyl ketone, mixtures of $C_4$-$C_7$ ketones, mixtures of $C_5$-$C_7$ alcohols, ethylene oxide, propylene oxide and butylene oxide. However, the typical product contains more than 40 components, which form more than 50 binary azeotropes and many ternary azeotropes. Product recovery[1] is by ordinary distillation, azeotropic distillation, extractive distillation and solvent extraction. In addition, hydrogenation is used to convert olefins to paraffins and alde-

[1] W. C. Hopkins and J. J. Fritsch, *Chem. Eng. Progr.,* **51,** 361 (1955).

hydes to alcohols, and thereby simplify certain of the recovery operations. The first step in the separation is the removal of acetaldehyde by fractionation; the acetaldehyde is then either oxidized to acetic anhydride or converted to *n*-butanol by the aldol condensation. The remaining aqueous mixture is fractionated to recover acetone and methanol. The acetone-methanol azeotrope is separated, using extractive distillation with water, followed by azeotropic distillation using pentane. The resulting material is then hydrogenated and fractionated into *n*-propanol, isopropanol, glycols, etc. Many of the products are not separated into pure components, but are simply sold as mixed solvents having a certain boiling range.

The economic success of the Celanese process is dependent on several factors. Precise temperature control is essential to minimize combustion of feedstock to carbon monoxide and carbon dioxide. Recycle costs must be minimized by the use of efficient heat exchangers, efficient gas compressors and high recovery of $C_3$ and $C_4$ paraffins from the purge gases. Product separation costs are high, and the product distribution is essentially determined by the nature of the feedstock. Much of the production by Celanese goes into captive use, thereby saving on shipping and distribution costs. The commercial success of the process is certainly a tribute to the chemists and engineers who overcame many practical problems, but direct hydrocarbon oxidation will probably continue to account for only a small fraction of the total production of oxygenated compounds unless greater selectivity can be obtained in the production of the various products.

### Liquid-phase Oxidation

Paraffins may be oxidized in the liquid phase, using air or oxygen. The reactions are similar to those occurring in the gas phase, except that the oxidation is more specific, there is less degradation of the oxygenated compounds and a smaller number of products is produced. For example, the liquid phase oxidation of *n*-butane gives chiefly acetic acid, isobutane gives acetone and methanol, and propane gives acetone or acetic acid. An interesting feature of the liquid-phase oxidation is that very little formaldehyde is produced.

The liquid-phase oxidation of *n*-butane has been carried out commercially by Celanese Corp. at Pampa, Texas since 1952. Air and liquid butane react at pressures of about 815 psig and a temperature of about 325°F in the presence of a catalyst such as 0.3 per cent cobalt acetate. Although this temperature is above the critical temperature of *n*-butane, the reaction is carried out in acetic acid solution. Presumably, the oxygen first attacks the second carbon atom in the butane molecule to form a hydroperoxide, which then decomposes to give chiefly acetic acid. The consumption of oxygen is essentially complete. The oxidized liquid is flashed to remove unreacted butane, the butane is recycled and the products separated by conventional fractionation. The principal product is acetic acid, with smaller quantities of acetone, acetaldehyde, methanol, methyl ethyl ketone, etc. However, the product distribution can be varied by changing the reaction conditions, although no details have been released as to commercial operations.

## OXIDATION OF AROMATICS

Phthalic anhydride, maleic anhydride and terephthalic acid are the most important products from the oxidation of aromatics. The oxidation of an aromatic may be carried out in two general ways. Under mild oxidizing conditions, the aromatic ring is not attacked and only the side chain will be oxidized. This is the general method used in the oxidation of xylenes to phthalic anhydride, isophthalic acid and terephthalic acid. Under more drastic oxidizing conditions, the aromatic ring can be attacked to produce acid anhydrides such as maleic anhydride from benzene and phthalic anhydride from naphthalene.

From the thermodynamic standpoint, complete combustion to carbon dioxide and water will always be more favored than partial oxidation to the desired product. Thus, as in the case of most oxidation reactions, the commercial success is dependent on the use of a suitable catalyst.

### Phthalic Anhydride

About 459 million pounds of phthalic anhydride were produced in the United States in 1963. The chief uses of phthalic anhydride are in the manufacture of plasticizers, alkyd resins for surface coatings, polyesters for reinforced plastics and as a chemical intermediate. The classical method of preparing phthalic anhydride is by the catalytic oxidation of naphthalene according to the equation

$$\text{naphthalene} + \tfrac{9}{2}O_2 \rightarrow \text{phthalic anhydride} + 2CO_2 + 2H_2O \text{ (g)} \quad (16\text{-}6)$$

$$\Delta H^\circ_{298} \cong -426,000$$

the chief side reaction being complete oxidation according to the equation

$$C_{10}H_8 + 12O_2 \rightarrow 10CO_2 + 4H_2O \text{ (g)} \qquad (16\text{-}7)$$

$$\Delta H^\circ_{298} \cong -1,202,000$$

The manufacture of phthalic anhydride by oxidation of naphthalene goes back to World War I when the United States was cut off from German sources of intermediates and dyestuffs. In 1916, H. D. Gibbs and C. Conover at the U.S. Dept. of Agriculture discovered the naphthalene oxidation process using a vanadium catalyst; patents were subsequently issued to them as a result of their work. At the end of the war, it was found that the process had been independently discovered in Germany by A. Wohl at I. G. Farben. The whole matter was taken to court, and the final judgment favored the Wohl patents because the date of "reduction to practice" was Sept. 4, 1916 in comparison with a date of Sept. 7, 1916 for the Gibbs and Conover work. This is certainly a good example of the necessity for all experimenters to keep accurate and complete notebooks of their experimental work, and to reduce an invention to practice as soon as possible.

Until after World War II, the standard catalyst used in the United States consisted of about 10 per cent $V_2O_5$ on an inert support such as alumina or silica. Furthermore, it was believed that the catalyst must be free of alkali metal oxides, since these were believed to cause a gradual decline in the activity of the catalyst. However, after the war, it was found that the catalyst used in Germany[1] consisted of about 10 per cent $V_2O_5$ and 20-30 per cent $K_2SO_4$ on a carrier of silica gel, and that this catalyst was markedly superior to those used in the United States. Thus, small amounts of alkali evidently decrease the activity of the vanadium, but large amounts are beneficial.

The oxidation of aromatics has been recently summarized by Dixon and Longfield.[2] The most important reactions in the oxidation of naphthalene are as follows: (1) oxidation of naphthalene to phthalic anhydride; (2) oxidation of naphthalene to 1,4-naphthoquinone; (3) oxidation of 1,4-naphthoquinone to phthalic anhydride; (4) oxidation of primary products to maleic anhydride; (5) complete combustion to carbon dioxide and water. Although reactions (1) and (2) occur at about equal rates, most of the naphthoquinone which is formed is re-oxidized to phthalic anhydride. The rate of oxidation to maleic anhydride is small in comparison with oxidation to phthalic anhydride. With the improved catalysts now available, only very small quantities of naphthoquinone and maleic anhydride are present in the product phthalic anhydride.

[1] R. F. Ruthruff, *Hydro. Proc. Petrol. Refiner,* **32**(10), 113 (1953).
[2] J. K. Dixon and J. E. Longfield, "Catalysis," Vol. VII, edited by P. H. Emmett, New York, Reinhold Publishing Corp., 1960.

The kinetics of the oxidation of naphthalene have been studied by several investigators using both differential and integrated rate equations. There is general agreement that the rate of oxidation depends on the partial pressures of both naphthalene and oxygen to an order intermediate between 0.5 and 1.0. However, the reaction is fairly complex, since there is some evidence that the reaction orders change with pressure and that the reaction products may inhibit the reaction. The best values for the activation energies for the oxidation of both naphthalene and naphthoquinone are about 26,000-30,000 cal/mole. The mechanism of the oxidation appears to be a direct interaction with the vanadium catalyst to form lower oxides such as $V_2O_4$ and $V_2O_3$, followed by a reoxidation of the catalyst to the +5 valence by oxygen.

Commercially, two general methods are used for the manufacture of phthalic anhydride. In the first, a fixed-bed reactor is used which consists of vertical tubes filled with catalyst which are cooled by recirculating a molten salt on the outside of the tubes. In the second method, a fluidized catalyst is used with cooling provided by cooling coils placed in the catalyst bed or by continuously withdrawing catalyst to an external cooler. Temperature control is extremely critical, since the side reactions are more exothermic than the desired reaction. The theoretical heat of reaction is about 6000 Btu/lb naphthalene consumed, but the actual heat evolution is about 8000 Btu/lb naphthalene because of side reactions. A typical flow sheet for the process is given in Fig. 16-3, and Table 16-2

TABLE 16-2.  TYPICAL PROCESSES FOR PHTHALIC ANHYDRIDE*

| Catalyst | Fixed Bed | | Fluidized | |
|---|---|---|---|---|
| | Conventional | German | Conventional | German |
| Temperature, °F | 750-885 | 645-705 | 680 | 700 |
| Pressure, psig | 25 | 7.5 | 15 | 15 |
| Contact time, sec | 0.6 | 4.2 | 19 | 19 |
| Lbs air/lb $C_{10}H_8$ | 25-30 | 30 | 15 | 15 |
| Lbs charge/(hr)(ft²) reactor cross section | 39 | 15 | 18 | 18 |
| Lbs charge/(hr)(ft³) reactor volume | 20 | 2 | 1 | 1 |
| Lbs catalyst per lb charge/hr | 5.9 | 13.4 | 37.5 | 37.5 |
| Yield, crude PA | 80 | 104 | 80 | 100 |

* Data from Ruthruff, *op. cit.* The quoted yields for the German processes appear to be high.

gives typical operating conditions and yields. Note that in accordance with standard practice, the yield is expressed as lb phthalic anhydride/100 lb naphthalene, not in terms of the stoichiometrical yield. Expressed in this way, the maximum possible yield is 115.6 lb phthalic anhydride/100 lb naphthalene.

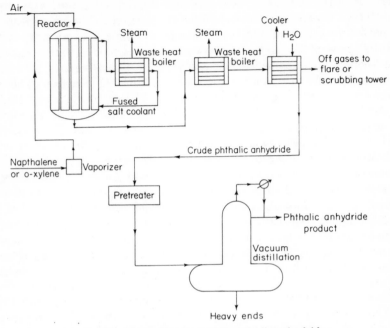

Fɪɢ. 16-3. Typical flowsheet for phthalic anhydride.

In practice, the feedstock (either naphthalene or *o*-xylene) is vaporized, mixed with air, passed over the catalyst and phthalic anhydride condensed from the effluent gases. Substantial excess air is used for the oxidation, ranging up to about 6 times theoretical; this favors the rapid and complete oxidation of the feedstock and permits operation below the explosive limits of the hydrocarbons. Final purification of the product is by vacuum distillation. The purified product analyzes 99.5 per cent phthalic anhydride or better, with about 0.1 per cent maleic anhydride and a trace of naphthoquinone. Commercially, yields range up to 94 lb/100 lb naphthalene.

With the recent availability of *o*-xylene from petroleum, increasing quantities of phthalic anhydride are now being produced by the reaction

$$\text{(o-xylene)} \quad \begin{array}{c} \text{—CH}_3 \\ \text{—CH}_3 \end{array} + 3\text{O}_2 \rightarrow \text{(phthalic anhydride)} + 3\text{H}_2\text{O} \qquad (16\text{-}8)$$

$$\Delta H^{\circ}_{298} = -269{,}580$$

The oxidation of *o*-xylene requires only minor modifications in the nature of the catalyst and the reaction conditions; in fact, some plants are now being built, using a combination catalyst which permits operation with either feedstock. The theoretical yield is 140 lb phthalic anhydride/100 lb of pure *o*-xylene. In practice, the weight yield from commercial *o*-xylene is about the same as in the oxidation of naphthalene, namely about 92.5 lb phthalic anhydride/100 lb of 95 per cent *o*-xylene feed.

## TEREPHTHALIC ACID

Terephthalic acid is an extremely important intermediate for the manufacture of synthetic fibers such as "Terylene," "Mylar," and "Dacron," which are made by the polymerization of ethylene glycol with dimethyl terephthalate. Commercial production started in 1951, and by 1963 the annual production of dimethyl terephthalate in the United States had reached 331 million pounds. Terephthalic acid is produced from *p*-xylene by the reactions

p-toluic acid      terephthalic acid

Note that in the case of both terephthalic and isophthalic acid, the acid anhydride does not exist because of the separation of the carboxyl groups.

The oxidation of *p*-xylene is considerably more difficult than the oxidation of *o*-xylene. Thus, vapor-phase oxidation over a vanadium catalyst produces mostly carbon dioxide with only trace amounts of terephthalic acid. The first step in the oxidation is to *p*-toluic acid; this oxidation is not too difficult, but the final oxidation to terephthalic acid requires strong oxidizing conditions. Relatively little has been published about the process used commercially to produce terephthalic acid. From the patent literature and from a recent survey by H. W. Earhart,[1] the following facts are known:

(1) The process used commercially by du Pont involves oxidation of *p*-xylene with nitric acid. Nitric acid oxidation is selective on the methyl

[1] H. W. Earhart, "Polymethylbenzenes," Kirk-Othmer Encyclopedia of Chemical Technology, New York, Interscience Publishers, Inc., 1960.

groups, and does not attack the aromatic ring. The reaction takes place at 400-450°F and about 400 psig, using 25-40 per cent nitric acid in an agitated autoclave fitted with cooling coils. The weight ratio of 100 per cent nitric acid to *p*-xylene is about 2.4:1. The strength of the nitric acid is not critical, but the proper ratio of nitric acid is important to maximize the yield of terephthalic acid. The yield is 85 per cent or better, based on *p*-xylene.

(2) Hercules produces terephthalic acid commercially at Burlington, New Jersey, using a two-stage oxidation process. In the first stage, *p*-xylene is oxidized to *p*-toluic acid at 300-500°F and 50-100 psig, using a manganese or cobalt catalyst. The toluic acid is esterified with methanol, which permits the second methyl group to be oxidized by air with good yield.

A second process studied on a pilot-plant scale by Hercules is based on toluene, a much cheaper raw material than *p*-xylene. Toluene is oxidized to benzoic acid and converted to the potassium salt, which is then heated to about 800°F under about 150 psig of $CO_2$ pressure in the presence of a Cd catalyst. The potassium benzoate disproportionates to benzene and potassium terephthalate (Henkel disproportionation). The yield is 90 per cent or better.

(3) Oronite (Standard Oil of California) is producing phthalic acids commercially by the oxidation of xylenes using a mixture of sulfur, ammonium sulfate and possibly aqueous ammonia as the oxidizing agent. The reaction is carried out at about 630°F and pressures of 2500-3000 psig. The oxidation is selective; the xylene goes first to toluic acid, the toluic acid is converted to the monoamide and a second oxidation produces the ammonium salt of the monoamide of the dicarboxylic acid. Evidently, the presence of the amide group facilitates the second oxidation. The yield is about 90 per cent, based on xylene.

(4) Standard of Indiana is producing terephthalic acid commercially using a one-stage process which can handle a feedstock of mixed xylenes. The oxidation takes place in acetic acid solution, using air or oxygen at a temperature of about 380°F and a pressure of 200-400 psig. Both manganese and bromine are used as catalysts. The process is extremely versatile, and can be used for feedstocks such as the xylenes, diphenyls, alkyl dicyclics and alkyl-substitute benzenes where the alkyl group is ethyl, propyl, etc.

(5) Various other processes are in the pilot-plant stage, and may eventually come into commercial operation. In view of the rapid developments which have occurred since 1951, it is difficult at this time to predict which process will eventually turn out to be most economic for the manufacture of terephthalic acid.

## Isophthalic Acid

Isophthalic acid can be produced from *m*-xylene in the same general way that terephthalic acid is produced from *p*-xylene. Although relatively small quantities of isophthalic acid have been produced by Oronite, the material has not as yet achieved commercial importance. However, isophthalic acid is potentially an important intermediate for the manufacture of polymers, and it is possible that future markets will develop now that semicommercial quantities are available.

## MALEIC ANHYDRIDE

Maleic anhydride is used for the manufacture of polyester resins, alkyd resins and as a chemical intermediate. Total production of maleic anhydride in the United States for 1963 was about 87 million pounds. The classical method of producing maleic anhydride is by vapor-phase oxidation of benzene according to the equation

$$\bigcirc + \tfrac{9}{2}O_2 \rightarrow \underset{\text{CH}}{\overset{\text{CH}}{\Vert}} \begin{array}{c} \text{C} \overset{O}{\diagup} \\ \diagdown \\ \text{C} \diagdown \\ \underset{O}{\diagdown} \end{array} O + 2H_2O + 2CO_2 \qquad (16\text{-}9)$$

$$\Delta H^\circ_{298} \cong -422{,}500$$

with, of course, the more exothermic side reaction corresponding to complete combustion to carbon dioxide and water. The oxidation of benzene to maleic anhydride is very similar to the oxidation of naphthalene to phthalic anhydride. Commercially, the oxidation is carried out at 750-850°F, using about 4 times the theoretical air to stay outside the explosive limits. A supported vanadium pentoxide catalyst promoted with $MoO_3$ and possibly other promoters is used. The catalyst is contained within tubes, with external recirculation of a fused salt to control the temperature. The contact time is about 0.1 second. Effluent gases are cooled in a waste-heat boiler, maleic anhydride absorbed in water to form a solution of maleic acid, and the solution is immediately pumped to a dehydrating tower which produces crude maleic anhydride before any substantial fraction of the maleic acid is converted to the fumaric acid isomer. Final product purification is by conventional fractionation.

The older catalysts gave a yield of about 50 per cent, but modern improved catalysts are reported to go as high as 65 per cent yield.

Maleic anhydride is also being produced commercially by the oxidation of mixed butylenes according to the typical equation

$$
\begin{array}{c}
CH_3 \\
| \\
CH \\
\| \\
CH \\
| \\
CH_3
\end{array}
\quad + \; 3O_2 \; \rightarrow \quad
\begin{array}{c}
CH-C \\
\| \quad\quad O \\
CH-C \\
\end{array}
\; O \; + \; 3H_2O
$$

$$\Delta H^\circ_{298} \cong -271,000$$

The oxidation takes place at 800-900°F and 10-15 psig, using a catalyst of vanadium pentoxide supported on alumina and activated with phosphorous pentoxide. The volume ratio of air to butylenes is about 75:1 in order to stay below the explosive limits. The converter consists of vertical tubes filled with catalyst which are externally cooled by recirculation of a fused salt. The yield is about 50 per cent of theory, based on the total $n$-butylene feed.

### Fumaric Acid

Fumaric acid is the *trans* isomer of maleic acid. The traditional process for the manufacture of fumaric acid was by fermentation of sugar. However, most fumaric acid is now being produced synthetically. Thus, about 24 million pounds of synthetic fumaric acid were produced in the United States in 1963, most of the material going into the manufacture of polyesters. Since fumaric acid is the lower energy form, it can be made by isomerization of maleic acid according to the equation

$$
\begin{array}{ccc}
HOOC \quad\quad COOH & & HOOC \\
\diagdown \quad\quad \diagup & \rightarrow & \diagdown \\
CH=CH & & CH=CH \\
& & \quad\quad \diagdown \\
& & \quad\quad COOH
\end{array}
$$

$$\Delta H^\circ_{298} = -6800 \quad\quad \Delta F^\circ_{298} = -7300$$

The reaction may be carried out simply by heating maleic acid or a mixture of maleic acid and maleic anhydride to a temperature of about 300°F in an inert atmosphere, and holding the material at the elevated temperature for a time long enough for the isomerization to occur. It is also possible to achieve the isomerization by heating a solution of maleic acid to a temperature of about 200°F, using a catalyst such as hydrogen peroxide. In addition to the direct production of fumaric acid, small quantities are also obtained as a by-product in the manufacture of maleic anhydride.

## ADIPIC ACID

Adipic acid is used for the manufacture of nylon by polymerization with hexamethylenediamine. The importance of this raw material can be appreciated from the fact that about 670 million pounds of adipic acid were produced in the United States in 1963. Adipic acid is used for the manufacture of the original nylon known as nylon 66 (the different types of nylon are named in terms of the number of carbon atoms in the monomers used in the polymerization). Recently, a new polymer known as nylon 6 has been developed, which is based on the single monomer caprolactam. Nylon 6 is already the leading form of nylon in Europe, and is becoming increasingly important in the United States. Thus, the future of adipic acid is very much in doubt, and there may be a gradual leveling off in production as other forms of nylon become more popular. Table 16-3 lists manufacturers of adipic acid in the United States. Note that there has been a substantial increase in capacity since these figures were published.

TABLE 16-3. MANUFACTURERS OF ADIPIC ACID*

| Manufacturer | Annual Capacity (millions of lb) | Raw Materials | Process |
|---|---|---|---|
| Allied Chemical, Hopewell, Va. | 20 | Phenol Cyclohexanol | Hydrogenation Nitric acid oxidation |
| Chemstrand, Pensacola, Fla. | 180-200 | Cyclohexane Cyclohexanol-cyclohexanone | Air oxidation Nitric acid oxidation |
| du Pont, Belle, W. Va. Orange, Texas | 105 105 | Cyclohexane Cyclohexanol-cyclohexanone | Air oxidation Nitric acid oxidation |
| Monsanto, Luling, La. | 30 | Phenol Cyclohexanol | Hydrogenation Nitric acid oxidation |
| Rohm and Haas, Louisville, Ky. | 20-25 | Cyclohexane Cyclohexanol-cyclohexanone | Air oxidation Air oxidation |

* Data from H. W. Haines, *Ind. Eng. Chem.*, **54**(7), 23 (1962). The Chemstrand production is captive use only; all other production is both captive and merchant.

Adipic acid is made by the oxidation of cyclohexane according to the reactions

Oxygen first reacts with cyclohexane to form the hydroperoxide, which then decomposes to a mixture of cyclohexanol and cyclohexanone. This mixture can then be oxidized to adipic acid, although this second step is more difficult. Except for the patent literature, practically nothing has been published on commercial operations. The oxidation of cyclohexane to cyclohexanol + cyclohexanone can be carried out using air at temperatures of about 300°F and pressures of 100-150 psig in the presence of a cobalt or manganese catalyst. Unreacted cyclohexane is separated by distillation, and a relatively small amount of adipic acid is recovered by cooling and filtering the bottoms product.

The residual oil consists of a mixture of cyclohexanol, cyclohexanone and other oxidation products. In the original du Pont process, this is oxidized to adipic acid in a stainless steel autoclave by the use of nitric acid at 140-240°F, using a copper-vanadium catalyst. However, in a recent process developed by Scientific Design Co., the oxidation to adipic acid is carried out in the liquid phase, using air or oxygen at temperatures of 200-400°F and pressures of 100 psig or more. The oxidation is carried out in acetic acid solution, using a catalyst of cobalt or manganese acetate. This process is being used commercially in a plant recently completed by Rohm and Haas.

A competing process for the manufacture of adipic acid uses phenol as a raw material in place of cyclohexane. The phenol is hydrogenated to cyclohexanol using a nickel or platinum catalyst and the cyclohexanol then oxidized to adipic acid using nitric acid. The over-all yield is higher since the hydrogenation of phenol is almost quantitative; however, phenol is a much more expensive raw material than cyclohexane, which more than compensates for the higher yield.

# CHAPTER 17

# Cyclic Intermediates

From a commercial standpoint, the most important cyclic intermediates are as follows: (a) ethylbenzene and styrene; (b) nitrobenzene and aniline; (c) phthalic anhydride and terephthalic acid; (d) phenol; (e) isocyanic acid derivatives such as toluene diisocyanate; (f) benzene, toluene, xylenes and naphthalene; (g) cyclohexane; (h) chlorobenzene. This chapter will discuss those which have not already been covered in previous chapters.

## CYCLOHEXANE

Total production of cyclohexane in the United States for 1963 was approximately 1079 million pounds. About 71 per cent of the cyclohexane[1] produced goes into the manufacture of adipic acid, 19 per cent goes into caprolactam and all other uses take only 10 per cent. Thus, most cyclohexane ends up as either nylon 66 or nylon 6. Cyclohexane is produced in two general ways, either by direct recovery from suitable petroleum fractions or by hydrogenation of benzene. Because of the much higher purity of the product, the second method is becoming increasingly favored.

Tremendous quantities of cyclohexane are potentially available from petroleum, and substantial amounts are recovered by fractionation of natural gas liquids. However, cyclohexane produced in this way has a purity of only about 85 per cent, since several other constituents of petroleum such as 2,2-dimethylpentane, benzene and 2,4-dimethylpentane have boiling points very close to that of cyclohexane. The purity of petroleum-based cyclohexane can be increased to about 98 per cent by superfractionation, but this is still relatively impure in comparison with benzene-based cyclohexane.

[1] For a recent review, see H. W. Haines, *Ind. Eng. Chem.*, **54**(7), 23 (1962).

The Phillips process (U.S. Patent 3,009,002) for the recovery of cyclohexane from natural-gas liquids involves a preliminary fractionation and reforming to give a mixture of dimethylpentanes, cyclohexane, $n$-hexane and other hydrocarbons boiling in this range. The mixture is then hydrogenated to convert any benzene present to cyclohexane, and the resultant mixture subject to an isomerization reaction to convert methylcyclopentane to cyclohexane. Superfractionation then produces a product of about 98 per cent purity.

Cyclohexane can also be produced by hydrogenation of benzene according to the reaction

$$\text{benzene} + 3H_2 \rightarrow \text{cyclohexane} \tag{17-1}$$

$$\Delta H^{\circ}_{298} = -49,250 \qquad \Delta F^{\circ}_{298} = -23,400$$

The hydrogenation becomes less favorable with increase of temperature, and $\Delta F^{\circ}$ becomes positive at a temperature of about 550°F, which represents the upper limit of the temperatures used commercially. However, even here the equilibrium benzene content is only about 0.01 per cent or less because of the high hydrogen pressures which are used. Commercially, the reaction is carried out in the liquid phase at temperatures of 300-500°F and pressures of 300-550 psig, using a catalyst. Although various metals including platinum, palladium, copper and cobalt are active catalysts for the hydrogenation, the usual commercial catalyst consists of 20-33 per cent nickel on a refractory oxide support. The benzene feed plus fresh and recycle hydrogen are preheated, charged to the catalytic reactor, the reactor effluent heat exchanged with cold feed and cyclohexane product separated in a flash drum. Part of the cyclohexane is recycled to control the temperature in the reactor. The reaction is stoichiometric, with a product purity of 99.8 per cent or better, as determined by the purity of the benzene feed. The chief problem in commercial operation is to avoid poisoning of the catalyst with sulfur compounds; thus, as little as 0.01 per cent of thiophene in benzene will rapidly inactivate the nickel.

The kinetics of the hydrogenation show an interesting relationship with temperature. Below about 230°F, the reaction in either the gas or liquid phase over a nickel catalyst is zero-order with respect to benzene and first-order with respect to hydrogen. However, above about 390°F, the reaction is first-order with respect to benzene and zero-order with respect to hydrogen. This change in order indicates that the benzene molecule is more strongly adsorbed than hydrogen at low temperatures, but at higher temperatures the relationship is reversed. In practice, the hydrogenation is so rapid and complete that the yield based on benzene is essentially quantitative.

## CHLOROBENZENE

Chlorobenzene is an example of a "mature" chemical, since the manufacturing technology has changed little in recent years. Approximately 519 million pounds of chlorobenzene were produced in the United States in 1963, with most production for captive use. The chief uses of chlorobenzene are as an intermediate for the manufacture of aniline, synthetic phenol, DDT, dyestuffs, etc. Small amounts also go into solvents. The classical process for the manufacture of chlorobenzene is a liquid-phase chlorination according to the equation

$$\bigcirc + Cl_2 \ (g) \rightarrow \bigcirc\!\!-Cl + HCl \ (g) \qquad (17\text{-}2)$$

$$\Delta H^{\circ}_{298} = -31{,}000 \qquad \Delta F^{\circ}_{298} = -15{,}100$$

The chlorination is carried out in either a batch or a continuous chlorinator at atmospheric pressure and at temperatures of about 100°F or less. A catalyst is used to prevent the accumulation of explosive quantities of unreacted chlorine in the solution. The usual catalyst is $FeCl_3$, although other chlorides such as $AlCl_3$, $SbCl_3$, etc., may also be used, and reportedly give smaller amounts of dichlorobenzenes. At room temperature, the rate of chlorination of monochlorobenzene is only about one-tenth the rate of chlorination of benzene, so that the production of dichlorobenzenes can be kept to a reasonable value.

Commercially, the reaction is carried out in cast iron or mild steel chlorinators of up to about 10,000-gal capacity. The benzene feed must be thoroughly dried to prevent corrosion. Chlorine gas is introduced at the bottom of the chlorinator through spargers, and the reaction is allowed to proceed until about 75 per cent of the benzene is chlorinated. Since the chlorination is strongly exothermic, cooling is provided by the use of cooling coils or by recirculating liquid through an external cooler. The HCl off-gases contain benzene vapor, which is recovered by cooling and scrubbing with refrigerated o-dichlorobenzene. Crude chlorobenzene product is washed with caustic solution to remove acids, and is then purified by fractionation. The yield of monochlorobenzene is about 75 per cent, based on benzene.

By-products include HCl, o-dichlorobenzene, and p-dichlorobenzene; however, essentially no m-dichlorobenzene is produced. The o-dichlorobenzene is nonflammable, and finds considerable use as degreasing solvent. The p-dichlorobenzene is used widely as a domestic moth killer.

In the continuous chlorination of benzene, the liquid from the chlorinator flows to a distillation column which separates the chlorinated products and recycles unreacted benzene. It is also possible to produce chlorobenzene by a vapor-phase oxychlorination of benzene. This process is one of the steps in the Raschig process for the manufacture of synthetic phenol, and will be discussed later in this chapter.

## NITROBENZENE AND ANILINE

The nitration of an organic compound is usually carried out by the use of "mixed acid" made by mixing nitric acid with sulfuric acid or oleum to produce a mixture ranging from 20 per cent $HNO_3$, 20 per cent $H_2O$ and 60 per cent $H_2SO_4$ up to about 55 per cent $HNO_3$ and 48 per cent $H_2SO_4$ with negative water. There is good evidence that the nitronium ion $NO_2^+$ is the actual nitrating agent, the general equation being

$$RH + HONO_2 \rightarrow H_2O + RNO_2$$

The sulfuric acid acts as a dehydrating agent, and prevents the nitrating acid from being excessively diluted by the water formed during the nitration. However, an even more important function of the sulfuric acid is to act as an acid medium which favors the formation of the nitronium ion by the equation

$$HONO_2 + H^+ \rightleftharpoons H_2O + NO_2^+$$

Sulfuric acid pushes this equilibrium to the right, and thus greatly increases the rate at which the nitration occurs.

Nitrobenzene and aniline are also examples of mature chemicals. Total production of nitrobenzene in the United States for 1963 was 220 million pounds, most of which was converted to aniline. In the batch process for the manufacture of nitrobenzene, the nitration is normally carried out in a cast iron or steel vessel fitted with an efficient agitator. The heat of reaction is about 800 Btu/lb of benzene nitrated; this heat is removed by the use of cooling coils in the nitrator or by recirculating liquid to an external heat exchanger. In practice, the nitrator is first charged with sufficient cycle acid from a previous run to cover the cooling coils. The benzene is then added, and mixed acid is fed to the nitrator at such a rate as to maintain the temperature at 100-140°F. After all the mixed acid is added, the temperature is raised to about 200°F to complete the nitration. The agitation is then stopped, and the upper nitrobenzene layer decanted from the spent acid. The crude nitrobenzene can then be used directly for the manufacture of aniline, or can be washed with water and caustic to remove acids and then distilled. The yield based on benzene is 95 per cent or more.

Nitration can be carried out continuously in two general ways. Two or more nitrators may be connected in series with benzene, and mixed acid fed continuously at one end and product withdrawn continuously at the other end. It is also possible to nitrate benzene continuously, using 60-65 per cent $HNO_3$ without any sulfuric acid. In this process, nitric acid and benzene are fed continuously to a distillation column, nitrobenzene is taken as bottoms product, and a mixture of benzene and water taken overhead. The overhead product is condensed, and benzene separated from the water by decantation and recycled to the column as reflux. Thus, the benzene acts as an entrainer which removes water from the system and thereby maintains the nitric acid at a strength sufficient to permit further nitration.

In the nitration of benzene, the mixed acid contains 55-65 per cent $H_2SO_4$, 35-40 per cent $HNO_3$, the balance being water. Polynitrations such as the manufacture of *m*-dinitrobenzene or trinitrotoluene require stronger acids and higher temperatures; these are usually carried out in more than one step. Weaker acids can be used for the nitration of substituted aromatics such as toluene and chlorobenzene, and for the higher aromatics such as naphthalene. It must be remembered that nitric acid is a strong oxidizing agent, which may cause problems in the nitration of compounds such as amines and phenols which are fairly easily oxidized.

## Aniline

About 155 million pounds of aniline were produced in the United States in 1963. Over half the aniline now goes into the manufacture of rubber-processing chemicals, such as derivatives of thiazole, which are used as rubber accelerators; other uses of aniline are as an intermediate for the manufacture of dyestuffs, drugs, photographic chemicals, etc.

Three processes are used commercially to produce aniline. The classical method is by the reduction of nitrobenzene according to the equation

$$\text{C}_6\text{H}_5-\text{NO}_2 + \tfrac{9}{4}\text{Fe} + \text{H}_2\text{O} \xrightarrow{\text{HCl}} \text{C}_6\text{H}_5-\text{NH}_2 + \tfrac{3}{4}\text{Fe}_3\text{O}_4 \quad (17\text{-}3)$$

$$\Delta H^{\circ}_{298} \cong -126,000 \qquad \Delta F^{\circ}_{298} \cong -126,000$$

The reduction is carried out using a hydrochloric acid catalyst which generates hydrogen by the reaction

$$\text{Fe} + 3\text{HCl} \rightarrow \text{FeCl}_3 + \tfrac{3}{2}\text{H}_2 \qquad (17\text{-}4)$$

However, the ferric chloride is hydrolyzed to regenerate HCl, so that in practice only about 3 lb of HCl are required to reduce 100 lb of nitrobenzene. The reduction is strongly exothermic. Commercially, crude nitrobenzene, water and catalyst are charged to a steam-jacketed cast iron reducer fitted with a reflux condenser, and 10-20 per cent of the iron is added to initiate the reaction. Best results are obtained with a clean, finely divided, grey cast iron; the ratio of iron to nitrobenzene is about 1.1:1, corresponding to about 10 per cent excess iron. The reaction mixture is heated to about 400°F with agitation, and the reduction allowed to proceed at reflux temperature while the remaining iron is added gradually over a period of several hours. Product is decanted from the iron oxide sludge, and is purified by vacuum distillation. Any aniline left in the sludge is recovered by steam distillation. The yield is about 95 per cent, based on nitrobenzene.

Aniline is also produced commercially[1] by a straight vapor-phase reduction of nitrobenzene with hydrogen gas according to the equation

$$\Delta H^\circ_{298} \cong -110,000 \qquad \Delta F^\circ_{298} \cong -110,000$$

A mixture of nitrobenzene and hydrogen containing about 3 times the theoretical hydrogen is passed at 520°F and 20 psig through a fluidized catalyst consisting of copper on silica gel. Effluent gases are filtered on a porous stainless steel filter and cooled to separate aniline and water from recycle hydrogen. Crude aniline is distilled to remove high boilers, and is redistilled in a finishing tower to produce pure product. The yield is about 98 per cent, based on nitrobenzene. The catalyst must be periodically regenerated by blowing with air to burn off organic deposits. However, careful control of the purity of the nitrobenzene feed will permit a catalyst life of about 1500 lb aniline/lb catalyst before regeneration is required.

Dow Chemical Co. produces aniline by ammination of chlorobenzene according to the equation

$$\Delta H^\circ_{298} \cong -48,000 \qquad \Delta F^\circ_{298} \cong -32,000$$

From the patent literature, 1 mole of chlorobenzene, 4-5 moles of aqueous ammonia, and 0.1 mole of cuprous oxide or cuprous chloride are reacted

[1] *Hydro. Proc. Petrol. Refiner,* **40**(11), 225 (1961).

in a rotating steel autoclave at temperatures of 350-480°F and pressures of 500-1500 psig. The active catalyst is cuprous chloride. The reaction mixture is cooled and separates into two layers, a lower aniline layer and an upper aqueous layer. The aniline layer is washed with caustic and fractionated to produce aniline; by-product diphenylamine is recovered by steam distillation of the aniline residue, and by-product phenol is recovered by acidification and distillation of the diphenylamine residue. The aqueous layer is treated with lime or caustic, and distilled to recover aniline and ammonia. The yield is 85-90 per cent, based on chlorobenzene.

## ISOCYANATES

Derivatives of isocyanic acid, $H-N=C=O$, are widely used in the manufacture of polyurethane resins. The polyurethanes have shown a very rapid growth in recent years. Thus in 1954, the production of isocyanic acid derivatives in the United States was essentially zero. In 1964, the total production of isocyanic acid derivatives was 138 million pounds, and this rapid growth is expected to continue over the near future. The most important derivative is toluene diisocyanate, which is normally produced as an 80/20 mixture of the 2,4- and 2,6-isomers.

A simplified flow sheet for the manufacture of toluene diisocyanate is given in Fig. 17-1. The first step is a nitration of toluene according to the equation

$$\text{Toluene} + 2HNO_3 \xrightarrow{H_2SO_4} \text{dinitrotoluene} + 2H_2O$$

The nitration is caried out continuously in a series of agitated cast iron nitrators, followed by separators. Nitration grade toluene flows continuously forward through the system; mixed acid is fed to the final nitrator, and is then fed in reverse flow back through the system countercurrent to the toluene. Nitric acid is introduced to each nitrator as required to maintain the proper strength of the nitrating acid. Since toluene is more easily oxidized than benzene because of the presence of the methyl group, the maximum nitration temperature is limited to about 120°F for mononitration and about 175°F for dinitration. The mononitration gives about 60 per cent *ortho* isomer, 36 per cent *para* and 4 per cent *meta*. The dinitration gives about a 4:1 ratio of the 2,4- and 2,6-

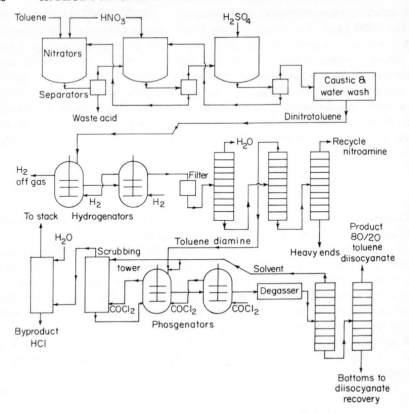

FIG. 17-1. Simplified flowsheet for toluene diisocyanate.

isomers. Toluene is more easily nitrated than benzene; thus, the mixed acid is about 56 per cent $H_2SO_4$ and 28 per cent $HNO_3$ for mononitration and about 75 per cent $H_2SO_4$ and 10-20 per cent $HNO_3$ for dinitration.

The organic layer from the final nitrator is separated by decantation, washed with water and dilute caustic solution, and fed continuously to the hydrogenator where the dinitrotoluene is reduced to toluene diamine by the reaction

The reduction is carried out in the liquid phase, using hydrogen gas at 150-250°F and 50-400 psig. A catalyst of about 0.02 per cent Pt, Pd, or Raney Ni is used. The hydrogenation is difficult in the presence of water because hydrogen and the dinitrotoluene are insoluble. Efficient agitation is essential to maintain the catalyst in suspension and to bring together the hydrogen and dinitrotoluene on the surface of the catalyst. Normally the reduction is carried out using two reactors in series with a controlled addition of the dinitrotoluene to prevent buildup of the material; excessive quantities of the nitro compound will wet the catalyst and render it inactive. In practice, temperatures under 200°F are favored since this permits operation at low pressure.

Catalyst is recovered by filtration of the effluent, and the solution fractionated to produce toluene diamine, recycle toluene nitroamine, and heavy ends which are burned. The diisocyanate is produced by phosgenation of the diamine according to the equations

The reaction occurs in two distinct steps. In the first, phosgene reacts with the diamine at low temperature to form the carbamyl chloride-hydrochloride derivative; smaller amounts of the dicarbamyl chloride and the dihydrochloride are also produced. The mixture is then heated in the presence of phosgene to convert it to the diisocyanate.

Commercially, the reactions are carried out in solution, using a liquid which is a good solvent for phosgene and toluene diamine. Solvents which have been patented include toluene, xylenes, chlorobenzene, o-dichlorobenzene, cyclohexane, etc. Toluene diamine and the solvent are first carefully dried to prevent the formation of highly corrosive dilute HCl. The amine is then dissolved in part of the solvent, and phosgene is dissolved in the remaining solvent, using a conventional bubble-plate absorption tower. The two solutions are mixed at 30-50°F to form the carbamyl chloride-hydrochloride mixture; in practice, about 1.4 moles of phosgene are used per mole of toluene diamine. The diisocyanate is then formed by heating to 200-320°F in the presence of additional phosgene. Off-gases are cooled, scrubbed with solvent to recover phosgene and organic vapors, and absorbed in water to produce by-product hydrochloric acid. The diisocyanate solution is filtered to remove impurities and degassed by blowing with nitrogen or methane, the bulk of the solvent is removed by atmospheric distillation, and product separated by vacuum distillation.

The above chemical equations have been written for the 2,4-isomer, but in practice the product is obtained as 80/20 toluene diisocyanate containing 20 per cent of the 2,6-isomer. A small amount of the *meta* isomer of diisocyanate is also formed, which is either burned or sold as a by-product if a market can be found for it. The over-all yield is about 75 per cent, based on toluene, and 85 per cent, based on hydrogen or phosgene.

## SYNTHETIC PHENOL

Phenol is an extremely important raw material for the manufacture of plastics and various chemical intermediates. Total production of phenol in the United States for 1963 was approximately 935 million pounds, including 51 million pounds of natural phenol, 325 million pounds of synthetic phenol from cumene and 559 million pounds of synthetic phenol from other processes. About 64 per cent of the total phenol produced goes into the manufacture of phenolic resins, 12 per cent is used for caprolactam, 9 per cent for detergents such as nonylphenol and octylphenol, 6 per cent for epoxy resins and the remainder for hundreds of miscellaneous small uses. Phenol capacity in the United States has been increasing rapidly in recent years, and is now substantially greater than current production. Table 17-1 gives a recent survey of phenol capacity by *Chemical and Engineering News;* note that the total capacity for synthetic phenol is substantially greater than the 1963 production.

Synthetic phenol represents an interesting example of the many factors which must be considered in the choice of the most economic process for the manufacture of a given material. Thus, in the case of phenol, six different manufacturing processes are used commercially. Some of the important factors which must be considered in comparing these processes are as follows: (a) The sulfonation and chlorobenzene processes consume large amounts of expensive raw materials. However, the chemistry of these processes is straightforward and the production plants are old and fully amortized. (b) The toluene process uses a cheaper aromatic raw material, but the reactions are fairly complex and not well suited to large-scale industrial use. (c) The Raschig and oxidation processes have very low raw-material costs, but involve much recycle and require elaborate control to prevent side reactions. (d) The cumene process has been used for most recent construction because of the favorable economics; however, the economic success is entirely dependent on the profitable disposal of the coproduct acetone.

TABLE 17-1.  UNITED STATES SYNTHETIC PHENOL CAPACITY*

| Company | Annual Capacity (millions of lb) | Process |
|---|---|---|
| Dow Chemical, | | |
| Midland, Mich. | 220 | Chlorobenzene |
| Kalama, Wash. | 36 | Toluene |
| Monsanto, | | |
| Monsanto, Ill. | 115 | Sulfonation |
| Chocolate Bayou, Texas | 75 | Cumene |
| Avon, Calif. | 30 | Sulfonation |
| Hooker Chemical, | | |
| Tonawanda, N.Y. | 60 | Modified Raschig |
| South Shore, Ky. | 60 | Modified Raschig |
| Allied Chemical, | | |
| Philadelphia, Pa. | 110 | Cumene |
| Union Carbide, | | |
| Marietta, Ohio | 110 | Modified Raschig |
| Reichhold Chemicals, | | |
| Tuscaloosa, Ala. | 90 | Sulfonation |
| California Chemical, | | |
| Richmond, Calif. | 50 | Cumene |
| Shell Chemical, | | |
| Houston, Texas | 50 | Cumene |
| Hercules Powder, | | |
| Gibbstown, N.J. | 30 | Cumene |
| Schenectady Chemical, | | |
| Rotterdam Jct., N.Y. | 20 | Benzene oxidation |
| Skelly Oil, | | |
| Eldorado, Kan. | 50 | Cumene |
| Clark Oil, | | |
| Chicago, Ill. | 30 | Cumene |
| Total | 1136 | |

* *Chem. Eng. News*, Feb. 4, 1963, p. 23.

## Sulfonation Process

The sulfonation process is the classical "brute force" method of synthesizing phenol. The first step in the process is a sulfonation of benzene according to the reaction

$$\text{C}_6\text{H}_6 + \text{H}_2\text{SO}_4 \rightarrow \text{C}_6\text{H}_5{-}\text{SO}_3\text{H} + \text{H}_2\text{O} \qquad (17\text{-}5)$$

The sulfonation can be carried out in a cast iron agitated vessel, using temperatures of 140-220°F. However, this requires a considerable excess of sulfuric acid since the sulfonation stops below about 78 per cent $H_2SO_4$, and the water formed by the reaction acts as a diluent. Thus, it is more common to carry out the sulfonation continuously by passing benzene vapors countercurrent to strong sulfuric acid in a sulfonation tower, the water being carried overhead and separated by decantation from the benzene reflux. In this case the sulfonation is carried out at about 300°F, the benzenesulfonic acid, which contains 3-4 per cent $H_2SO_4$, being continuously withdrawn as bottoms product.

The second step is a neutralization of the benzenesulfonic acid with sodium sulfite according to the equation

$$2\ \bigcirc\!\!-SO_3H + Na_2SO_3 \rightarrow 2\ \bigcirc\!\!-SO_3Na + SO_2 + H_2O \quad (17\text{-}6)$$

Because of the presence of free sulfuric acid, some sodium sulfate is also formed during the neutralization. Sodium sulfate is separated by a hot filtration, and the sodium benzenesulfonate solution pumped to a direct-fired cast iron fusion pot. Sodium phenate is formed by reaction with about 50 per cent excess caustic according to the equation

$$\bigcirc\!\!-SO_3Na + 2NaOH \rightarrow \bigcirc\!\!-ONa + Na_2SO_3 + H_2O \quad (17\text{-}7)$$

The caustic fusion is carried out at about 575°F over a period of several hours, with a final heating to about 700°F to complete the reaction. The mixture of sodium phenate, sodium sulfite and caustic is dissolved in water and neutralized with sulfur dioxide produced in Eq. (17-6),

$$2\ \bigcirc\!\!-ONa + SO_2 + H_2O \rightarrow 2\ \bigcirc\!\!-OH + Na_2SO_3 \quad (17\text{-}8)$$

A small amount of sulfuric acid is required to complete the neutralization. The phenol separates as an upper layer which is decanted and purified by vacuum distillation. Residual phenol in the aqueous layer is recovered by blowing with open steam. The yield of phenol is 85-90 per cent, based on benzene, by-product sodium sulfite and sodium sulfate also being made.

If all reactions were stoichiometric, the over-all reaction would be

$$C_6H_6 + H_2SO_4 + 2NaOH \rightarrow C_6H_5OH + Na_2SO_3 + 2H_2O \quad (17\text{-}9)$$

In practice, each mole of product requires about 1.3 moles of $H_2SO_4$ and 3 moles of caustic. Thus, the raw material consumption is quite large. In addition, there are many steps in the process, several of which involve expensive batch operations. Although sulfonation still accounts for an appreciable fraction of the total phenol production, it is probable that other processes will be used for all new construction.

## Chlorobenzene Process

The chlorobenzene process was developed by Dow Chemical Co. at Midland, Michigan. The process involves a direct liquid-phase reaction between chlorobenzene and caustic according to the equation

$$C_6H_5Cl + 2NaOH \rightarrow C_6H_5ONa + NaCl + H_2O \qquad (17\text{-}10)$$

with the side reaction

$$C_6H_5Cl + C_6H_5ONa \rightarrow C_6H_5OC_6H_5 + NaCl \qquad (17\text{-}11)$$

In practice, a mixture of chlorobenzene, caustic solution and diphenyl oxide is pumped through a steel pipe reactor at about 700°F and 4000 psig, with a residence time of several minutes. The purpose of the diphenyl oxide is to inhibit further formation through Le Chatelier's principle. The reaction products are cooled, the sodium phenate converted to phenol by the addition of hydrochloric acid and the phenol recovered by distillation. The yield is about 90 per cent, based on chlorobenzene, with some by-product diphenyl oxide also produced.

This process is economic only when operated in conjunction with an electrolytic chlorine-caustic plant, since in this case all necessary raw materials (except benzene) are available. It is possible to use soda ash instead of caustic for the saponification of the chlorobenzene; however, caustic is used commercially because it is available from the electrolytic plant and because the reaction proceeds better with caustic.

## Raschig Process

The regenerative or Raschig process involves two catalytic vapor-phase reactions. The first is an oxychlorination of benzene according to the equation

$$C_6H_6 + HCl + \tfrac{1}{2}O_2 \rightarrow C_6H_5Cl + H_2O \qquad (17\text{-}12)$$

$$\Delta H^\circ_{298} = -42{,}700 \qquad \Delta F^\circ_{298} = -38{,}700$$

followed by a hydrolysis of the chlorobenzene

$$C_6H_5Cl + H_2O \rightleftharpoons C_6H_5OH + HCl \qquad (17\text{-}13)$$

$$\Delta H^\circ_{298} \cong 0 \qquad \Delta F^\circ_{298} \cong 0$$

Thus, the over-all reaction in the Raschig process is simply a direct oxidation of benzene

$$C_6H_5 + \tfrac{1}{2}O_2 \rightarrow C_6H_5OH \tag{17-14}$$

$$\Delta H^\circ_{298} = -42,700 \qquad \Delta F^\circ_{298} = -38,700$$

The chief advantage of the process is the low consumption of raw materials, since the products from the first step become the reactants for the next. The chief disadvantage is the low conversion per pass, which requires extensive separation and recycle of intermediate products.

The Raschig process was developed in Germany by G. m. b. H., and a small commercial plant was operated near Ludwigshaven starting in 1935. Durez Plastics and Chem. Corp. acquired U.S. rights to the process, and have used the process commercially at North Tonawanda, New York since June 1940. Although both reactions used in the Raschig process had been known for some time, many practical problems had to be overcome before the process could be commercialized. For example, the oxychlorination of benzene according to Eq. (17-12) represents the first commercial application of oxychlorination. The reaction proceeds in two steps, namely,

$$2HCl + \tfrac{1}{2}O_2 \rightleftharpoons H_2O + Cl_2 \tag{17-15}$$

$$\Delta H^\circ_{298} = -13,700 \qquad \Delta F^\circ_{298} = -9100$$

$$Cl_2 + C_6H_6 \rightarrow C_6H_5Cl + HCl \tag{17-16}$$

$$\Delta H^\circ_{298} = -29,000 \qquad \Delta F^\circ_{298} = -29,600$$

Equation (17-15) is the old Deacon process for the manufacture of chlorine. The equilibrium constant is plotted in Fig. 17-2; note that the equilibrium is extremely favorable below about 600°F, but becomes less favorable at higher temperatures. The original Deacon process used a catalyst consisting of a porous material impregnated with copper chloride. Such a catalyst is active only at temperatures of 750-850°F, which are much too high for successful oxychlorination because of excessive decomposition and oxidation of the organics. Thus, the first job was to find a better catalyst for the oxidation of HCl.

As the result of the work of W. H. Prahl at G. m. b. H., catalysts were developed which were active as low as about 400°F. The improved catalysts are made by coprecipitating aluminum and copper hydroxides followed by heating in an atmosphere of HCl. Promoters consist of metals chosen from Groups III-VIII of the periodic table, particularly iron chloride. In plant practice, such a catalyst will make available as $Cl_2$ about **98** per cent of the HCl in the feed, with a monochlorobenzene yield of over 90 per cent, based on HCl feed.

The standard heat of reaction and change in free energy for the hydrolysis of chlorobenzene according to Eq. (17-13) are both roughly

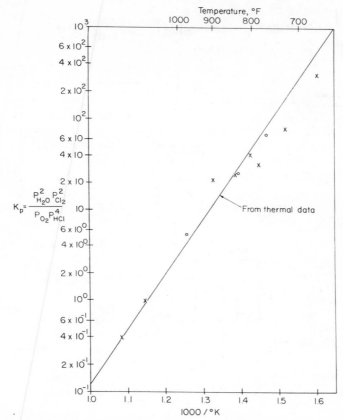

FIG. 17-2. Equilibrium constant in oxidation of HCl. xxx K. V. von Falckenstein, *Z. Physik. Chem.*, **59**, 313 (1907). ooo A. E. Korvezee, *Rec. Trav. Chim.* **50**, 1092 (1931).

zero (it is impossible to say more than this because of uncertainties in the thermodynamic properties of chlorobenzene vapor). In practice, the hydrolysis is carried out at temperatures up to about 930°F, the maximum temperature being limited by the decomposition of the organics. A catalyst of tricalcium phosphate is used. The conversion of chlorobenzene to phenol is about 12-15 per cent/pass.

A simplified flow sheet of the Raschig process is given in Fig. 17-3. Commercially, benzene at about 500°F and air at about 250°F are mixed with HCl vapors which are supplied by evaporation of aqueous acid with tantalum bayonet heaters in a brick-lined vessel. The catalyst chambers consist of steel cells which are alternately packed with cata-

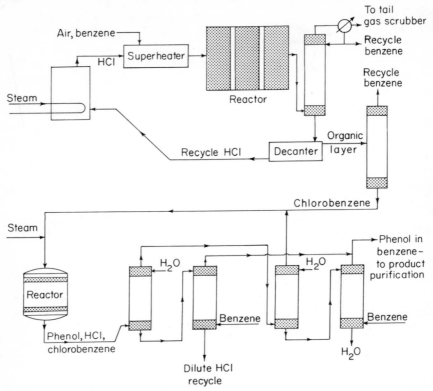

Fig. 17-3. Simplified flowsheet of Raschig process.

lyst; cooling is provided by air circulation between the catalyst beds. The ratio of benzene to HCl in the feed is about 8:1 to minimize polychlorination. The reactants enter the catalyst chamber at about 410°F with about a 10 per cent conversion to chlorobenzene, based on the total benzene feed. Product gases pass to a brick-lined packed column provided with a controlled reflux of benzene and water. The overhead consists of the benzene-water azeotrope plus nitrogen and unreacted oxygen from the air. Benzene is recovered by cooling the gases in an exchanger, followed by a scrubbing with a hydrocarbon oil before being discharged to the stack. The bottoms consist of a two-phase liquid having a lower phase of dilute HCl and an upper phase of chlorinated benzene in benzene solution. The organic bottoms are washed with caustic and fractionated, the chlorobenzene sent to the second step of the process and the benzene recycled.

The hydrolysis of the chlorobenzene is carried out at temperatures of

850-930°F, using excess steam. Effluent gases are scrubbed with water to remove HCl as a dilute acid containing a small amount of phenol which is recovered by extraction with benzene. The overhead consists of a mixture of water, phenol and chlorobenzene. Phenol is recovered by extraction with water, and chlorobenzene is recycled to the hydrolysis reactor. Product phenol is purified by benzene extraction from the aqueous solution, followed by distillation. The over-all yield is about 92 per cent, based on benzene, with about a 3 per cent loss of HCl.

The original Raschig process produced substantial quantities of by-products such as polychlorinated benzenes. In the "modified" process, an additional step has been added in which these polychlorinated benzenes are hydrolyzed back to monochlorobenzene, thereby increasing the yield of phenol.

## Cumene Process

The cumene process for the manufacture of phenol and acetone is at present the most favored process for new construction. This process is based on the two reactions

The cumene process is based upon work carried out during the war on the use of cumene hydroperoxide as an accelerator in the cold rubber process for the emulsion polymerization of butadiene-styrene mixtures. Although organic hydroperoxides were at one time considered unsuitable for commercial use because of the explosion hazard, it was found that some are quite stable. For example, cumene hydroperoxide can be readily formed in yields of 25 per cent or more, and the pure material can be isolated in the form of the sodium salt. This led to a further study of the reactions of the hydroperoxides, with the eventual development of the phenol process by the Distillers Co., Ltd., in England and by Allied Chemical and others in the United States.

It has been shown that the oxidation of cumene[1] according to Eq. (17-17) is a typical chain reaction involving free radicals, namely,

[1] G. P. Armstrong, *et al., J. Chem. Soc.,* p. 666 (1950).

$$R^{\bullet} + O_2 \rightarrow RO_2^{\bullet}$$

$$RO_2^{\bullet} + RH \rightarrow RO_2H + R^{\bullet} \quad \text{etc.}$$

where in this case, $R^{\bullet} = C_6H_5$—C—$(CH_3)_2$—. The second step is the rate-controlling step. The reaction is autocatalytic; thus, without a catalyst, there is an induction period of about 1.5 hours during which oxygen absorption is very small. The rate then increases to a maximum at a hydroperoxide concentration of about 20 per cent, and then decreases. In early stages of the oxidation, the yield of the hydroperoxide is almost quantitative. The induction period can be eliminated by the addition of either organic peroxides or the hydroperoxide itself. The oxidation is strongly inhibited by small traces of impurities such as copper or lead; phenol also inhibits the oxidation, and styrene derivatives tend to retard the oxidation.

In the Distillers' process, the cumene is present as an emulsion in water. Optimum conditions for the oxidation are at about 185°F and a pH of 8.5-10.5. Sodium stearate appears to be the best emulsifying agent. The rate of oxidation increases with increase in the water to oil ratio, although the oxygen absorption per unit volume decreases. The Allied process is essentially the same except that the oxidation is carried out using anhydrous cumene. In practice, the maximum concentration of the hydroperoxide is limited to about 25 per cent to prevent excessive side reactions.

The decomposition of the hydroperoxide is carried out using a solution of dilute acid. Since the reaction is strongly exothermic, a diluent such as acetone may be used to prevent excessive temperatures. The reaction products include phenol, acetone, unreacted cumene and by-products such as acetophenone, phenyl dimethyl carbinol and $\alpha$-methylstyrene formed by dehydration of the phenyl dimethyl carbinol. In practice, for each pound of phenol about 0.6 lb of acetone, 0.075 lb of acetophenone and 0.075 lb of $\alpha$-methylstyrene are produced. The $\alpha$-methylstyrene may be either sold as such or converted back to cumene by hydrogenation over Raney nickel.

Commercially, phenol is produced in a continuous process involving oxidation with air at temperatures of 185-260°F and at pressures slightly above atmospheric. The pH is maintained at 8.5-10.5 with a weak base such as soda ash; surfactants and other additives, including possible catalysts, are used to promote the rate of oxidation. The hydroperoxide is split using dilute sulfuric acid at temperatures of about 180°F. The oil layer is separated by decantation, washed with water and the resulting mixture of phenol, acetone, water, unreacted cumene, acetophenone and $\alpha$-methylstyrene separated by conventional fractionation. The over-all yield is about 93 per cent, based on the cumene reacting.

## Toluene Process

Dow Chemical Co. has recently completed a relatively small plant at Kalama, Washington to produce phenol by the oxidation of toluene.[1] The chief advantage of the process is, of course, the lower cost of toluene as compared to benzene. The first step of the process is an oxidation of toluene to benzoic acid according to the equation

$$C_6H_5\text{—}CH_3 + \tfrac{3}{2}O_2 \rightarrow C_6H_5COOH + H_2O \tag{17-18}$$

The oxidation is carried out in the liquid phase at about 300°F and 25-35 psig, using air as oxidant and cobalt naphthenate as catalyst. Toluene conversion is limited to about 40 per cent to prevent excessive side reactions. The yield of benzoic acid is about 90 per cent, based on toluene reacted. By-products include benzaldehyde, benzyl alcohol and benzyl benzoate; in addition, there is some oxidation to CO and $CO_2$.

Crude benzoic acid from the first reactor passes to a distillation column where toluene and benzaldehyde are taken overhead for recycle. Benzoic acid is separated from the bottoms by extraction with hot water followed by cooling, crystallization and filtration. The benzoic acid is melted and charged to a second reactor where it is oxidized to phenol according to the equation

$$C_6H_5COOH + \tfrac{1}{2}O_2 \rightarrow C_6H_5OH + CO_2 \tag{17-19}$$

The reaction is carried out in the liquid phase at about 450°F and 5-10 psig, using a homogeneous catalyst of cupric benzoate promoted with magnesium benzoate. A mixture of air and steam is sparged to the base of the reactor. As in the case of the Wacker process, the reaction occurs as a result of the oxidation-reduction of the copper catalyst. Thus, the cupric benzoate is first hydrolyzed to yield benzoic acid and salicylic acid, with the simultaneous reduction of the copper from the cupric to the cuprous state. The salicylic acid rapidly decarboxylates at the reactor conditions to form phenol and carbon dioxide. The copper is then re-oxidized to the active state by air.

Effluent gases from the second-stage reactor contain water, phenol and benzoic acid. The gases enter a primary distillation column which takes a mixture of water and phenol as overhead product and a bottoms of benzoic acid which is recycled. Product phenol is obtained by fractionation of the phenol layer from the primary column. The yield of

[1] *Hydro. Proc. Petrol. Refiner,* **40**(11), 280 (1961).

phenol is about 90 per cent, based on benzoic acid reacting, and the over-all process yield of phenol from toluene is about 80 per cent.

### Direct Oxidation Processes

Considerable work has been done on the possible direct oxidation of benzene to phenol according to Eq. (17-14). The thermodynamic equilibrium is virtually 100 per cent to the right at temperatures up to 1500°F or more. However, the problem is to direct the reaction to the formation of phenol rather than by-products such as diphenyl and decomposition products such as carbon dioxide and tar. Both catalytic and noncatalytic processes have been investigated. Some of the processes which have been described are as follows: (a) direct oxidation using an electric discharge; (b) noncatalytic oxidation at temperatures to 1500°F; (c) noncatalytic oxidation using $n$-hexene as a hydrogen donor; (d) vapor-phase using a fluidized vanadium catalyst; (e) vapor-phase using $SO_2$ and a metal catalyst; (f) liquid-phase using a fluoboric acid catalyst.

An interesting feature of the oxidation processes is the fact that impure benzene appears to give a higher yield of phenol than pure benzene. This strongly indicates some catalytic effect from the impurities, and offers the hope that a catalyst might exist which would increase the yield sufficiently to make direct oxidation economically feasible.

It has been reported [1] that the Solvay Process Co. (now Allied Chemical) used a vapor-phase noncatalytic process on a semicommercial scale. A 50 per cent yield of phenol from benzene was obtained; however, the process was abandoned because of excessive formation of diphenyl and other heavy polymers. Schenectady Chemical Co. is reported to be producing phenol commercially by direct oxidation of benzene, but no details of the process have been released. Scientific Design also has a proprietary direct-oxidation process based on cyclohexane. Although no technical details have been disclosed, the process presumably involves an oxidation of cyclohexane to a mixture of cyclohexanol and cyclohexanone, separation of unreacted cyclohexane and dehydrogenation of the cyclohexanol-cyclohexanone mixture over a nickel or platinum catalyst to yield phenol.

### BISPHENOL A

Bisphenol A (4,4'-isopropylidenediphenol) is an important intermediate for the manufacture of epoxy and polycarbonate resins. Total United States production was about 72 million pounds in 1963. Bisphenol

---

[1] L. F. Marek, *Ind. Eng. Chem.*, **40**, 1635 (1948).

A is produced by condensing phenol and acetone according to the equation

$$2 \ \langle \bigcirc \rangle -OH + (CH_3)_2CO \rightarrow HO-\langle \bigcirc \rangle -\overset{\overset{\displaystyle CH_3}{|}}{\underset{\underset{\displaystyle CH_3}{|}}{C}}-\langle \bigcirc \rangle -OH + H_2O$$

The condensation takes place readily at slightly over room temperature, using excess phenol and a catalyst of concentrated HCl. The reaction[1] is first order with acetone and second order with phenol; the activation energy is 19,000 at 77-113°F. Commercially, the reactants and catalyst are simply mixed at about 140°F in a series of agitated reactors, the products heated under vacuum to remove water, HCl and unreacted phenol, and the liquid bisphenol A sent to a flaker. The yield is 95 per cent or more, based on acetone.

Note that the manufacture of bisphenol A is particularly attractive to phenol producers using the cumene process, since both reactants are available. The bisphenol A process is very simple, requires little equipment and offers a means of disposing of some of the by-product acetone which is rapidly becoming a "drug on the market."

[1] T. Kato, *Nippon Kagaku Zasshi,* **84**(6), 458 (1963).

# CHAPTER 18

# Surface-active Agents

The total production of synthetic organic surface-active agents (surfactants) in the United States for 1963 was approximately 1981 million pounds. This represents a gradual transition over a period of about 30 years from the use of natural-based raw materials for the manufacture of soap to petroleum-based raw materials for the manufacture of synthetic detergents (syndets). Thus, it is obvious that the detergent industry now uses substantial quantities of petrochemicals, and any radical change in the detergent industry will have an appreciable effect on the chemical industry.

At present,[1] the entire detergent industry is in a transition period where the industry is being forced to discontinue the sale of some of the most successful synthetic detergents. This situation is the result of the fact that certain detergents, particularly the branched-chain alkylbenzene sulfonates (ABS), are alleged to be nonbiodegradable and hence largely responsible for the pollution of our rivers and surface waters. Although there is no question that the effects of detergents have been greatly exaggerated in the mind of the general public, industry is now substituting biodegradable (soft) detergents for the hard detergents formerly used. Since the soft detergents require different raw materials, this has resulted in a substantial change in the market for several of the important petrochemicals.

### Nature of Detergents

The characteristic feature of all surface-active agents or detergents is that they tend to concentrate at an interface, spreading and orienting to form a coherent film. This is the property which enables them to reduce surface tension, cause foaming and thereby emulsify and remove

[1] For recent reviews see L. F. Hatch, *Hydro. Proc. Petrol. Refiner,* **43**(3), 91 (1964); D. Justice and V. Lamberti, *Chem. Eng. Progr.,* **60**(12), 35 (1964); "Biodegradability of Detergents," *Chem. Eng. News,* March 18, 1963, p. 102.

dirt. The molecule of a surface-active agent contains two characteristic structures, a water-soluble (hydrophilic) group and an oil-soluble (lipophilic or hydrophobic) group. Thus, one end of the molecule wants to go into the oil phase and the other end wants to go into the water phase, with the net result that the material concentrates at the interface.

The lipophilic group in a detergent is usually supplied by a suitable $C_8$-$C_{22}$ hydrocarbon structure. The hydrophilic group can be supplied by many different ionic and polar groups. The following four general types of hydrophilic group can be used: (1) Anionic groups consist of any negatively charged radical such as the sulfonate, sulfate or carboxylate radicals. These are commercially the most important, since detergents of this type can be made from cheap and readily available sulfuric acid. (2) Cationic groups consist of any positively charged radical such as the amine salts or quaternary ammonium compounds. (3) Amphoteric groups contain both anionic and cationic groups in the same molecule; commercially these are relatively unimportant. (4) The nonionic type contains groups which are water soluble, yet do not ionize. Examples are the alcohols, glycols and ethers, which in practice are often used in multiples.

Examples of the most important detergents are given in Table 18-1.

## Biodegradability

At present, the biodegradability of a detergent is more important than the cost or cleaning efficiency of the detergent. The problem has come up in recent years because of the fact that small quantities of detergents may cause foaming in sewage-disposal plants, in river water and in fresh water from private wells. Most of the blame is placed on the branched-chain alkylbenzene sulfonates which have constituted about 80 per cent of the surfactant in household detergents. Because it is generally believed that branched-chain ABS is nonbiodegradable, proposals have been made to ban the sale of hard detergents. Thus, West Germany has already required that all detergents be at least 80 per cent biodegradable; several U.S. state legislatures have considered the possibility of banning hard detergents, and federal legislation has also been proposed. Because of this political pressure, the detergent industry in the United States has now voluntarily substituted soft detergents for the ABS-based hard detergents.

However, the situation is extremely complex, and it is questionable whether a satisfactory solution has yet been obtained. The facts seem to be that ABS detergents are nontoxic at the levels encountered, they do not impart taste or odor to water, and they do not interfere with conventional sewage-disposal treatments. However, the ABS detergents have

TABLE 18-1. TYPICAL DETERGENTS

| Detergent | Class | Biodegrad-ability* | Typical Formula |
|---|---|---|---|
| Soap | Anionic | 100% | $C_{17}H_{35}$—$COO^-Na^+$ |
| Alkylbenzene sulfonate (ABS) | Anionic | 50-60 | $CH_3$—$CH$—$(CH_2CH_2)_2$—$CH_2$—$CH$—$CH_3$ with $CH_3$ groups, benzene ring, $SO_3^-Na^+$ |
| Linear alkylbenzene sulfonate (LAS) | Anionic | 90 | $CH_3$—$(CH_2)_9$—$CH$—$CH_3$ with benzene ring, $SO_3^-Na^+$ |
| Nonylphenol, ethoxylated | Nonionic | 30 | $CH_3$—$CH$—$CH_2$—$C$—$CH_2$—$CH_2$—$CH_3$ with $CH_3$ groups, benzene ring, $(OCH_2CH_2)_6OH$ |
| Lauryl alcohol, sulfated | Anionic | 100 | $CH_3$—$(CH_2)_{11}$—$OSO_3^-Na^+$ |
| Secondary alcohol, ethoxylated and sulfated | Anionic | ~100 | $CH_3$—$(CH_2)_3$—$CH$—$(CH_2)_6$—$CH_3$ with $(OCH_2CH_2)_4OSO_3^-Na^+$ |

* Biodegradability expressed as the approximate decomposition occurring in a sewage plant of the activated sludge type.

two characteristics which have caused them to be blamed for most pollution, namely, they persist longer in water than most other organic pollutants and they foam at very low concentrations.

Actually, synthetic detergents account for only about 10 per cent of the total organic residue from a sewage-disposal plant. It has also been shown that ABS causes foaming only in the presence of protein material; thus, the ABS is not itself responsible for the pollution, but only gives a visible indication of pollution. Although the general public tends to blame synthetic detergents for most pollution, it is obvious that they are only a small part of the total pollution problem. However, the concern of the public is undoubtedly justified, since approximately 40 per cent of the population of the United States uses water that has been recycled at least once, and this percentage will undoubtedly increase over the years. In the words of L. F. Hatch, "More people than ever are using other peoples' effluent—and enjoying it less."

Another problem is to define what is meant by the word "biodegradable." Does it mean the complete decomposition of a material to carbon dioxide and water? If so, the linear alkylbenzene sulfonates are non-biodegradable because only the sidechain is attacked, and the benzene ring does not degrade. How is biodegradability to be measured? Thus, sewage-disposal plants involve aerobic degradation to dispose of organics whereas cesspools and septic tanks involve much anaerobic degradation. Figure 18-1 illustrates typical results based on the "die away" test which measures the time required for a detergent to degrade in river water. However, it is also possible to measure degradation in other ways, and the results are not necessarily comparable. It can be seen from Fig. 18-1 that even the hard detergents are to some extent degradable if given sufficient time, and the soft detergents which are eventually 100 per cent degradable still persist for an appreciable time in the water.

One additional point which should be noted concerning the biodegradable detergents is the fact that these materials may cause trouble by rapidly using up the oxygen present in river water. This can result in the reduction of sulfate ions present in the water, and thereby produce sulfide stinks which are just as annoying to the nose as foam is to the eyes.

## Soap

Before we discuss the synthetic detergents, let us first describe briefly the manufacture of the first important detergent, ordinary soap. Soap consists of the sodium or potassium salt of a fatty acid. It is made by exactly the same process Grandmother used, namely, the reaction of caustic and fat according to the typical equation

$$
3NaOH + \underset{\text{fat}}{\begin{array}{c} CH_2-\overset{\displaystyle O}{\overset{\|}{C}}-OR \\ | \\ CH-\overset{\displaystyle O}{\overset{\|}{C}}-OR \\ | \\ CH_2-\overset{\displaystyle O}{\overset{\|}{C}}-OR \end{array}} \rightarrow \underset{\text{glycerol}}{\begin{array}{c} CH_2-OH \\ | \\ CH-OH \\ | \\ CH_2-OH \end{array}} + \underset{\text{soap}}{3R-COONa}
$$

The fats and oils used in the manufacture of soap consist chiefly of glycerol esters of various fatty acids. In practice, a mixture of fats is always

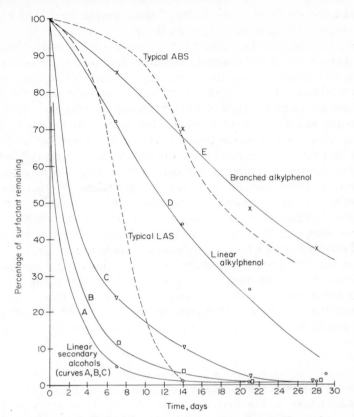

Fig. 18-1. Biodegradability of common detergents. (Data from
R. A. Conway and G. T. Waggy, paper presented at Delaware
Valley Section of the American Association of Textile Chemists
and Colorists, December 3, 1965).

Curve A = Linear secondary alcohol, sodium salt of the sulfated
3-mole ethylene-oxide adduct.
     B = Linear secondary alcohol, 7-mole ethylene oxide ad-
duct (nonionic).
     C = Linear secondary alcohol, 9-mole ethylene oxide ad-
duct (nonionic).
     D = Linear alkylphenol ethoxylate.
     E = Branched alkylphenol ethoxylate.

used to obtain a product with proper physical and detergent properties.
The most important fatty acids used include lauric ($R = C_{11}H_{23}$), myris-
tic ($C_{13}H_{27}$), palmitic ($C_{15}H_{31}$), stearic ($C_{17}H_{35}$), oleic ($C_{17}H_{33}$) and
linoleic ($C_{17}H_{31}$).

In the conventional batch process for the manufacture of soap, the fats are heated for several hours with about a 20°Bé caustic solution in a large steel tank with a conical bottom. Heat is supplied by direct injection of steam. The fats split to form glycerol and fatty acids which combine with caustic to form the sodium salt or soap. The process of hydrolyzing a fat is called "saponification" or "killing." After saponification is complete, salt is added and boiling continued to separate a lower aqueous layer called the "lye" and an upper layer known as "curd soap" which contains most of the soap. The lower layer is withdrawn and the glycerol recovered by vacuum distillation. The curd soap is further refined by boiling with caustic solution, boiling with water and the final "neat" soap dried and packaged for sale. In addition to the batch process, several continuous[1] processes have also been developed for the manufacture of soap.

Soap is an excellent detergent and is 100 per cent biodegradable. In view of these two facts, why has soap been largely replaced by the synthetics? The chief disadvantage of soap is the formation of an insoluble precipitate (the ring in the bathtub) when "hard" water is used. Hard water contains dissolved minerals such as calcium and magnesium which react chemically with the sodium soap to form insoluble calcium and magnesium soaps. Only after all the dissolved minerals have been removed can the soap again function as a cleaning agent. Thus, there is a considerable waste of soap, and the sticky precipitate may cause problems when soap is used for laundry purposes.

From an industrial standpoint, a second disadvantage of soap is that it cannot be used in acidic solutions. Strong acids will react with soap to precipitate fatty acids which closely resemble the precipitates formed in hard water. This is of particular importance in the textile industry where certain operations must be carried out in acid solution. In addition, the fatty acids may adhere to the fabric during processing, and prevent the even application of dyestuffs.

However, there is absolutely no reason why old-fashioned soap cannot be used for most household and commercial cleaning. Very seldom does cleaning have to be done in acid solution, and these few cases can be handled with other types of detergents with special waste-treatment facilities, if required. Soap can be used directly for household cleaning in all regions of the country having soft water. Even in hard water regions, it has been found that the addition of sequestering agents such as sodium tripolyphosphate will form a complex with calcium and magnesium ions, and thereby prevent them from interacting with the soap. Thus, if all other remedies fail, the biodegradability problem can always be solved simply by again using soap as the principal detergent.

[1] A. L. Schulerud, *J. Am. Oil Chemists Soc.*, **40**, 609 (1963).

## SYNTHETIC DETERGENTS

Active work to synthesize petroleum-based detergents started in Germany during World War I. Because of the Allied blockade, Germany was cut off from imported fats and oils, and the Badische Anilin and Soda Fabrik investigated the possibility of producing detergents from coal tar. As the result of this work, the first synthetic detergents were introduced in Germany in 1925 and in the United States starting in the early 1930's. The first synthetics were designed chiefly for industrial use, although small quantities went into household detergents. One of the first synthetics was "kerylbenzene" sulfonate made by chlorinating a kerosene fraction to form keryl chloride, alkylating with benzene and sulfonating to form the keryl-benzene sulfonate.

However, as illustrated in Fig. 18-2, it was not until after the second world war that the impact of the synthetics really began to be felt. By

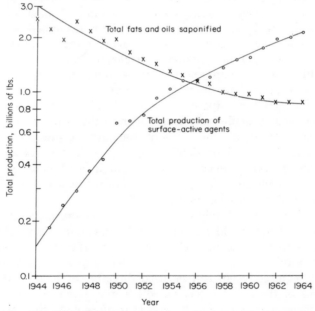

Fig. 18-2. United States production of soap and synthetic detergents. (Data from U.S. Tariff Commission and U.S. Dept. of Agriculture.)

*Note:* About 1.40 lb of soap are produced per lb of saponifiable material and 3-5 lb of detergent are produced per lb of surfactant.

1953, the synthetics had passed soap, and the relative production of soap has continued to decrease up to the present time. Before the biodegradability problem came up, the two most important synthetics were the alkylbenzene sulfonates and the ethoxylated alkylphenols. These are now being replaced by the linear alkylbenzene sulfonates and detergents based on the fatty alcohols. Because of the rapid changes now being made in the detergent industry, it is impossible at this time to predict which of the soft detergents will eventually be the most successful.

### Hard Detergents

The alkylbenzene sulfonates, especially dodecylbenzene sulfonate, have been the most important of the hard detergents. Thus, in 1964, ABS constituted about 80 per cent of the surfactant used in household detergents. Dodecylbenzene sulfonate is made by first carrying out a Friedel-Crafts condensation between benzene and propylene tetramer. Possible catalysts include sulfuric acid, anhydrous HF and aluminum chloride, the latter being most favored. The reaction is carried out at 95-115°F, using a considerable excess of benzene to minimize polymerization of the tetramer; aluminum chloride sludge is then separated by decantation and the products separated by conventional fractionation. The yield is about 80 per cent, based on the tetramer; the product consists of thousands of different branched isomers, the alkyl side chain consisting of about 40-55 per cent $C_{12}$, 12-28 per cent $C_{11}$ and 15-20 per cent $C_{13}$.

The dodecylbenzene is sulfonated in a type 316 stainless steel sulfonator, using oleum or liquid $SO_3$. The reaction is exothermic, the temperature being maintained at 75-100°F. In practice, lower temperatures increase the amount of acid required for sulfonation but produce a lighter colored product. After sulfonation is complete, the residual sulfuric acid is diluted to about 80 per cent to promote phase separation, and the organic layer is decanted and neutralized with caustic. The sodium dodecylbenzene sulfonate product is then mixed with various additives and spray dried for household use or drum dried for industrial use.

The second most important type of hard detergent is based on the alkyl phenols, particularly nonyl phenol. These nonionic detergents are made by a Friedel-Crafts condensation of phenol with propylene trimer or tetramer according to the typical equation

The hydrophilic properties are improved by ethoxylating the nonyl phenol with ethylene oxide according to the equation

$$C_9H_{19}\text{—}\langle\bigcirc\rangle\text{OH} + n\underset{\displaystyle CH_2\text{——}CH_2}{\overset{\displaystyle O}{\triangle}} \longrightarrow C_9H_{19}\langle\bigcirc\rangle(OCH_2CH_2)_nOH$$

where $n = 3\text{-}6$ moles of ethylene oxide/mole alkyl phenol.

## SOFT DETERGENTS

The "first generation" soft detergents will be largely based on linear alkylbenzene sulfonates (LAS) as a replacement for the branched-chain ABS. This change could be made rapidly and economically because facilities used to alkylate benzene with propylene tetramer could be easily converted to the use of raw materials such as linear olefins or linear monochloroparaffins. Also, in a similar way, linear chains can be substituted for branched chains in the alkyl phenols. However, there is considerable question as to whether or not this represents a long-range solution to the detergent problem. Even if the side chains degrade completely, this still leaves nonbiodegradable benzene and phenol to contaminate the water. When this fact is recognized by the general public, it is probable that the detergent industry will again come under pressure to produce detergents which are completely biodegradable.

One possible long-range solution is to go back to the use of soap as a household detergent. However, another possibility is to use linear alcohols as a source of detergents. This is not new, since alcohols from natural products (such as lauryl alcohol from coconut oil and tallow alcohol from fat) have been sulfated commercially for many years to produce anionic detergents. These sulfated alcohols are rapidly and completely biodegradable. The natural alcohols have had two major disadvantages, namely, they are not available in sufficient quantities to supply the entire demand for synthetic detergents and they are subject to wide fluctuations in price. However, straight-chain alcohols which are identical with the natural products are now available from petroleum at about the same price as the natural products. Thus, there is no reason why the straight-chain alcohols could not serve as a basis for most household detergents, and several companies appear to feel that linear alcohols represent a long-term solution to the problem of biodegradability.

## RAW MATERIALS

Raw materials which may be used for the manufacture of soft detergents include the linear olefins, the linear monochloroparaffins and the linear alcohols. With the rapid changes now going on in the detergent industry, it is impossible at this time to say what process or even what product will be most economical. However, all the raw materials now under consideration are based on straight-chain paraffins. These may be produced in the following ways: (a) from ethylene by Ziegler polymerization; (b) by thermal cracking of paraffin wax; (c) by direct recovery from suitable petroleum fractions using molecular sieves.

### Ziegler Polymerization

Polymerization using a Ziegler catalyst will be discussed in more detail in Chapter 19. For the manufacture of higher alcohols, the first step in the process is the manufacture of aluminum triethyl according to the equation

$$Al + \tfrac{3}{2}H_2 + 2C_2H_4 \rightarrow AlH(C_2H_5)_2 \xrightarrow{C_2H_4} Al(C_2H_5)_3$$

Commercially, high-purity aluminum, hydrogen, ethylene and recycle aluminum triethyl react in the presence of a solvent to form diethyl aluminum hydride. This is then reacted with additional ethylene under pressure to form aluminum triethyl. Although aluminum triethyl can be made in one step, the two-step process is more economical with respect to raw materials. Since the aluminum alkyls are extremely reactive (pyrophoric in air and react violently with water), they are usually handled as a solution in an inert liquid such as a paraffinic or aromatic hydrocarbon.

The second step in the process is the growth reaction whereby additional molecules of ethylene under high pressure add to the side chains according to the general equation

$$Al(C_2H_5)_3 + nC_2H_4 \rightarrow Al{\overset{\displaystyle CH_2R'}{\underset{\displaystyle CH_2R'''}{\diagup\!\!\!\!-CH_2R''}}}$$

Various even-numbered alkyls from $C_2$ to about $C_{22}$ are formed in a random manner, the relative amounts following a Poisson distribution. Approximately 58 per cent of the product alcohols are obtained in the desired $C_{12}$-$C_{18}$ detergent range when an average of about 5 ethylene groups is added to each alkyl group on the aluminum triethyl. The growth reaction is carried out at a pressure of 750-1500 psig and a temperature below 265°F to minimize side reactions. The heat of reaction is about equal to the heat of polymerization of ethylene; the temperature is controlled by cooling with an organic such as isopentane, since if water were used as coolant, there would be the danger of an explosion resulting from a leak.

For the manufacture of alcohols, the higher aluminum trialkyls are blown with dry air (dew point = −100°F) to form the corresponding alkoxides, which are distilled to remove the solvent and organic by-products, and are then hydrolyzed with sulfuric acid to form the alcohols. Equations are as follows:

$$Al \begin{matrix} \diagup CH_2R' \\ -CH_2R'' \\ \diagdown CH_2R''' \end{matrix} \xrightarrow{O_2} Al \begin{matrix} \diagup OCH_2R' \\ -OCH_2R'' \\ \diagdown OCH_2R''' \end{matrix} \xrightarrow{H_2SO_4}$$

$$R'CH_2OH + R''CH_2OH + R'''CH_2OH + Al_2(SO_4)_3$$

Excess sulfuric acid is neutralized with caustic, and the alcohols are dehydrated by fractionation to recover by-product ethanol and 1-butanol; in addition, by-product alum is obtained from the still bottoms. Final purification of the alcohols is by vacuum distillation.

The chief advantage of the Ziegler process is the fact that it gives straight-chain primary alcohols of high purity. Continental Oil Co. reportedly has a 100 million pound/year Ziegler alcohol plant already in operation, and other manufacturers also plan to use the Ziegler process. However, the Ziegler alcohols are expensive in comparison with linear alkylate produced by molecular sieves; thus, the Ziegler products will be favored only where high purity is required.

It is possible to produce $\alpha$-olefins by a slight modification of the Ziegler process. Thus, if the higher aluminum trialkyls are heated to about 570°F under a few atmospheres of ethylene partial pressure, there is a thermal displacement reaction whereby the side chains split off to regenerate aluminum triethyl with a high yield of $\alpha$-olefins. At one time it was expected that Ziegler olefins would find substantial use in the manufacture of the soft detergents; however, the high cost has just about eliminated them from the detergent market.

### Wax Cracking

Large quantities of paraffinic waxes are produced as a by-product in the refining of lubricating oils. These waxes can be converted to olefins by a straight thermal cracking process involving dehydrogenation and rupture of the skeletal chains. From patents, the process involves temperatures of 1000-1250°F, pressures under 100 psig, and a heating time of about 2-20 sec. Steam or nitrogen is used as a diluent to reduce the partial pressure of the hydrocarbons. Cracked gases are rapidly cooled, and products separated into fractions by distillation. Under optimum conditions, the conversion of wax to $C_{20}$ and lower olefins is reported to be about 80 per cent. The $\alpha$-olefin content of the product is about 95 per cent, with less than 2 per cent internal olefins and less than 3 per cent saturated paraffins.

Cracked-wax $\alpha$-olefins are a simple short-range answer to the detergent problem since they can be used as a direct substitute for propylene tetramer in the alkylation of benzene. However, these olefins are relatively impure in comparison with Ziegler olefins. In addition, the cost of the cracked-wax olefins is relatively high because of the following two factors: (a) A selected premium wax must be used as feedstock since this gives the highest conversion to $\alpha$-olefins in the $C_{11}$-$C_{14}$ detergent range. (b) A substantial fraction of the products from wax cracking fall outside the detergent range; since there is essentially no market for these nondetergent olefins, the cost of the detergent-grade product must be increased accordingly. Thus, the future use of cracked-wax olefins for the manufacture of linear alkylate is very much in doubt.

However, the cracked-wax olefins are very useful for the manufacture of other detergent raw materials. For example, they may be converted to primary alcohols by the oxo reaction. Also reaction with sulfuric acid followed by hydrolysis yields secondary alcohols which can be ethoxylated and then sulfated. Thus, there will probably continue to be a limited market for the $\alpha$-olefins, even though the market will not be as large as was originally anticipated.

## Molecular Sieves

The process which now appears to be most economic for the manufacture of soft detergent alkylate is the direct recovery of $n$-paraffins from kerosene fractions, using molecular sieves to separate the $n$-paraffins from the aromatics and naphthenes. The $n$-paraffins have cross-sectional diameters of about 4.9 Angstroms. Thus, these are readily adsorbed by a zeolite having a pore diameter of 5 Angstroms, whereas the branched paraffins, naphthenes and aromatics are rejected because of their larger diameters. The processes which are scheduled to be used commercially are as follows: (a) The Linde IsoSiv process is a vapor phase adsorption of the pressure-swing type. Adsorption takes place under pressure, and desorption is achieved by reducing the pressure.

This process is being used by Union Carbide at Texas City, Texas. (b)
The Molex process developed by Universal Oil Products is a liquid
phase displacement type. Desorption is achieved by flooding with an
adsorbable fluid to displace the previously adsorbed material. The process is being used by Continental Oil Co. at Lake Charles, Louisiana.
(c) The Esso process is a vapor phase thermal-swing type. Adsorption
takes place at a low temperature, and the adsorbed $n$-paraffins are desorbed by heating. (d) The British Petroleum Co. uses a vapor phase
displacement-type process. Reportedly, the process is now in operation
in West Germany.

An entirely different type of molecular sieve process is being used by
Shell in the Netherlands and also in the United States. This process
involves the use of crystalline urea to form a urea complex or "adduct"
with the $n$-paraffins. This is possible because the urea crystal contains
canals of about 5 Angstroms diameter inside the crystal lattice. Thus, i
solid urea plus a small amount of methanol is agitated with a petroleum
fraction at room temperature, the $n$-paraffins will penetrate the urea
lattice to form a crystalline complex. The adsorbed paraffins can then
be recovered merely by dissolving the urea in water. The urea process
has been widely studied by Shell and by Edeleanu G. m. b. H. in Germany; the cost is reported to be about the same as the zeolite processes,
namely in the range of 2-3 cents/lb of $n$-paraffin.

## MANUFACTURE OF SOFT DETERGENTS

The first soft detergents will be largely based on LAS manufactured
from $n$-paraffins. Two general processes may be used. In the first, the
$n$-paraffins are monochlorinated, using a considerable excess of paraffin
to minimize polychlorination. The monochloroparaffins can then be reacted directly with benzene by a Friedel-Crafts reaction

$$\langle\!\!\!\bigcirc\!\!\!\rangle + RCl \xrightarrow{\text{AlCl}_3} \langle\!\!\!\bigcirc\!\!\!\rangle\!\!-\!\!R + HCl$$

Sulfonation of the linear alkylbenzene with sulfuric acid or oleum then
yields the LAS.

In the second process, the monochloroparaffins are dehydrochlorinated
thermally according to the typical equation

$$RCl \rightarrow R'\!\!-\!\!CH\!\!=\!\!CH\!\!-\!\!R'' + HCl$$

The reaction occurs at about 500°F and atmospheric pressure, using a
heavy metal catalyst. This produces a mixture of random linear olefins

[1] W. J. Zimmerschied, et al., Ind. Eng. Chem., **42**, 1300 (1950).

which can then be used to alkylate benzene. This process appears to be favored at present because of the higher internal isomer content of the resultant alkybenzene. Thus it has been found that if the 1-phenyl, 2-phenyl, etc., isomers of LAS are compared with each other, the best foaming and end-use properties are associated with the internal isomers. Unfortunately, the internal isomers also have the poorest biodegradability, although they are still substantially better than ABS.

One problem which has not been solved is the profitable disposal of the large quantities of by-product HCl which will be available from LAS manufacture. Since this affects the cost of the alkylbenzene by as much as 20 per cent, it can be seen that this is an important factor in the economics of the process.

## Sulfated Alcohols

As we have already seen, anionic detergents have been produced for many years by the sulfation of lauryl alcohol and tallow alcohol according to the reactions

$$ROH + H_2SO_4 \rightarrow R{-}O{-}SO_3H + H_2O$$

$$R{-}O{-}SO_3H + NaOH \rightarrow R{-}O{-}SO_3^-Na^+ + H_2O$$

In general, sulfation is more difficult than sulfonation. The reaction is carried out using oleum at temperatures below 130°F. To minimize side reactions, it is essential that the sulfated product be quickly transferred to the neutralizer. Precise control of temperature and acid strength are essential, since oversulfation may produce olefins by dehydration, ethers by splitting off water between two alcohol molecules and aldehydes by oxidation.

The most promising sources of synthetic alcohols for detergent manufacture are as follows:

(a) Ziegler alcohols of high purity are readily available in various boiling ranges. These make excellent detergent feedstock, the only disadvantage being the relatively high cost.

(b) Olefins from cracked wax can be converted to primary alcohols by the oxo process. The product will consist chiefly of a 50:50 mixture of straight-chain and branched-chain alcohols. However, the branching is confined mainly to one end of the chain, and this does not significantly affect the biodegradability or performance of the resultant detergent.

(c) Secondary alcohols can be produced by sulfation and subsequent hydrolysis of olefins according to the reactions

$$R{-}CH{=}CH_2 + H_2SO_4 \rightarrow R{-}\overset{\displaystyle OSO_3H}{\underset{\displaystyle |}{C}}H{-}CH_3 \xrightarrow{H_2O} RCH(OH)CH_3 + H_2SO_4$$

The feedstock may consist of either cracked-wax olefins or olefins from dehydrochlorination of monochloroparaffins. It is interesting to note that the sulfation of higher olefins[1] is more difficult than the sulfation of lower olefins such as propylene and butylenes. The sulfation is carried out at about 32°F using 80-85 per cent $H_2SO_4$. The reaction is reported to be second-order, involving the formation of a carbonium-ion intermediate. The rate of the sulfation decreases as the length of the carbon chain increases, presumably because of steric hindrance. In practice, there is an upper limit to the temperature and acid strength which can be used because of the increasing tendency of the olefins to undergo polymerization and side reactions.

(d) Random linear secondary alcohols can also be produced by direct oxidation of $n$-paraffins, and it is reported that Union Carbide is producing 75 million pounds/year of secondary alcohols by this process. Practically no commercial information has been released. The process was developed in the Soviet Union,[2] and has been widely studied there. The oxidation is carried out in the liquid phase at about 330°F, using a gas containing 3-4.5 per cent $O_2$. A boric acid catalyst is used to esterify the alcohol as it is formed, and thereby inhibit further oxidation. If a reasonable yield can be achieved, this process should be the most economical for the manufacture of detergent alcohols.

## Ethoxylated Alcohols

Alcohols may be ethoxylated according to the equation

$$ROH + nCH_2\overset{O}{\overbrace{\qquad}}CH_2 \rightarrow R(OCH_2CH_2)_nOH$$

The reaction is carried out at temperatures of about 250°F and pressures of 20-50 psig, using either a basic catalyst such as sodium alkoxide or an acid catalyst such as HCl. The reaction is reported to be first-order with respect to ethylene oxide. In the case of a basic catalyst, the secondary and tertiary alcohols are much less reactive than the primary; however, in the case of an acid catalyst, there is little difference in the rates of reaction for the different types of alcohol.

Primary alcohols can either be sulfated to produce anionic detergents or ethoxylated to produce nonionic detergents. However, the sulfates of secondary alcohols are not very good detergents because of their undesirable physical properties and their tendency to hydrolyze. If the secondary alcohols are first ethoxylated with 3-9 moles ethylene

[1] K. L. Butcher and G. M. Nickson, *J. Appl. Chem.*, **10**, 65 (1960).

[2] A. N. Bashkirov and V. V. Kamzolkin, *World Petrol. Cong.*, 5th N.Y., **4**, 17 (1960).

oxide/mole of alcohol and are then sulfated, satisfactory detergents can be produced.

## SUMMARY

In conclusion, the author would like to make a few purely personal comments about the present detergent situation. First, there appears to be no question that hard detergents have been responsible for part of the pollution of our water supplies. Second, we have seen that perfectly satisfactory detergents can be made which are 100 per cent biodegradable. It is the opinion of the author that the manufacturers should change to these completely biodegradable detergents. Surely an extra penny or two for a box of soap flakes is a small price to pay for the solution of even 10 per cent of our water-pollution problem.

In addition, it must be remembered that the organic surfactant makes up only about 20 per cent of the material in a typical box of powdered household detergent. The remaining 80 per cent is made up of phosphate sequestering agents, sodium sulfate "builder", foam boosters, perfumes, optical brighteners, soil-suspending agents, etc. Some of these additives have no effect on the cleaning ability of the detergent. Although there appears to be no evidence that these materials act as water pollutants, it does seem that certain of these additives could be reduced or eliminated entirely without harm to anyone except possibly the gentlemen on Madison Avenue who have to think up TV commercials.

# CHAPTER 19

# Polymers

It is impossible to cover adequately the subject of high polymers i
one chapter in a book of this type. However, it is estimated that mor
than one-third of all chemists and chemical engineers in the Unite
States are employed in industries which are associated in one way o
another with polymeric materials. Thus, the polymer field is an ex
tremely important one, and it is hoped that the elementary treatmen
presented here will give some familiarity with the basic principles c
polymer science, and perhaps stimulate the reader to further study i
this area.[1]

The field of high polymers is extremely broad and extremely comple>
For example, if we consider just one important polymer such as poly
ethylene, literally hundreds of different grades of polyethylene can b
produced which range all the way from a high molecular-weight oil
liquid to a hard crystalline solid. Thus, it is meaningless to talk abou
the properties of polyethylene unless we specify exactly what grade o
polyethylene we are talking about.

At one time, the chief interest of the chemical engineers and chemist
employed in the polymer field was in the manufacture of the monomer
from which the finished polymeric materials were eventually mad
However, this is not true any more. At present, relatively large num
bers of chemical engineers and chemists are directly concerned wit'
problems of polymerization, manufacture of plastics and resins, prop
erties of polymeric materials, etc. Practically all the large industria
laboratories (although few university laboratories) are actively en
gaged in a study of high polymers which includes all problems fror
the manufacture of the monomers to the fabrication and uses of th
finished products. In fact, it is hard to find any segment of the chemic?

[1] For example, see W. Billmeyer, Jr., "Textbook of Polymer Science," New Yor<
Interscience Publishers, Inc., 1962; W. R. Moore, "An Introduction to Polyme
Chemistry," Chicago, Aldine Pub. Co., 1963.

istry which is not affected in one way or another by the recent de-
pments in the field of high polymers.

## NOMENCLATURE AND DEFINITIONS

{igh polymers are substances of very high molecular weight which
y be either natural or synthetic. The natural or biological polymers
ude such materials as rubber, wool, cellulose, starch and proteins.
hough these materials are extremely important in our daily lives,
y have the following two disadvantages: (a) Their physical prop-
es are fixed by the nature of the particular material, and cannot
mally be varied. (b) The supplies are limited by agricultural con-
erations, and thus the materials are often expensive and subject to
id fluctuations in price. The synthetic polymers are manufactured
m cheap and readily available petroleum fractions, and the physical
perties may be "tailor made" for almost any desired application.
Although the natural polymers have been known since prehistoric
ie, the industrial use of polymers is a fairly recent development.
us, rubberized fabrics were first used in the early nineteenth century,
d it is probable that other fabrics such as wool had been used in-
strially at an even earlier date. In 1839, Goodyear discovered the
lcanization of rubber, and in 1870, cellulose nitrate was first used in-
strially. The first purely synthetic polymer was the phenol-formalde-
de family of synthetic resins discovered by Baekeland in Germany
d first produced commercially in 1907. In 1930 polystyrene was first
anufactured in Germany, and research work starting at about this
me time throughout the world rapidly led to the development of
lon, polyvinyl chloride, polyethylene and most of the other synthetic
lymers now in common use.

### lymers

A high polymer or macromolecule is a large molecule built up by the
petition of small simple chemical units. The starting material from
hich the polymer is formed is known as the monomer. The repeating
iit in the polymer is usually equivalent to, or nearly equivalent to, the
onomer. However, some polymerizations involve the splitting off of a
nall molecule, usually water, during polymerization; in these cases the
peating unit will not be exactly equivalent to the monomer.

A linear polymer is one in which the repeating units are similar to the
nks in a very long chain. Such polymers are also sometimes known
s chain molecules or polymer chains. The length of a linear polymer
expressed in terms of the degree of polymerization, namely, the

number of repeating units in the chain. The molecular weight of a polymer is simply the product of the degree of polymerization and the molecular weight of the repeating unit. Most polymers of industrial importance have molecular weights between 10,000 and 1,000,000. In practice, a linear polymer usually has end groups which are different from the repeating unit because it is necessary in some way to terminate the polymerization. However, the polymers are usually so large that the effect of the end groups is negligible, and the composition is considered to be that of the repeating unit only. Although the end groups have no effect on the mechanical properties of a polymer, they may have a profound effect on the stability, solubility and adhesive properties of the polymers.

It is also possible to have a branched polymer in which some of the molecules are attached as side chains to the linear chains. However, note that in a branched polymer, the individual molecules are still discrete thus, regularly repeating side groups such as the methyl group in isoprene are not considered to be branches. If branched chains are joined together by cross-links, a three-dimensional cross-linked or network polymer is formed. The process of establishing a three-dimensional cross-linked structure in a polymer is known as "curing" or in the case of rubber, "vulcanization." Cross-linking tends to increase strength, increase hardness and decrease elasticity of a polymer.

Polymerizations are commonly divided into two general classes. In addition or chain-reaction polymerizations, the monomer polymerizes directly through a chain reaction in which the chain carriers are ions or free radicals. Reactions of this type involve the successive stages of initiation, propagation and termination common to chain reactions in general. Thus, in the polymerization of a monomer such as vinyl chloride, the free radical opens up the double bond of the monomer and initiates the polymerization reaction in the following manner:

$$R^\bullet + CH_2{=}CHCl \rightarrow R{-}CH_2{-}CHCl^\bullet \rightarrow R(CH_2{-}CHCl)_n^\bullet$$

The second class of polymerization is known as condensation or step reaction polymerization. These involve a condensation reaction between two polyfunctional molecules, usually with the elimination of a small molecule such as water. For example, the manufacture of nylon 66 involves the condensation of hexamethylene diamine and adipic acid according to the equation

$$H_2N{-}(CH_2)_6{-}NH_2 + HOOC{-}(CH_2)_4{-}COOH \rightarrow$$
$$H_2O + \cdots {-}NH{-}(CH_2)_6{-}NH{-}CO{-}(CH_2)_4{-}CO{-}\cdots$$

In this type of polymerization, the reaction continues until all of one reactant is used up. If one of the reactants contains more than two functional groups, a cross-linked network polymer will be obtained. Although condensation polymerization usually involves the elimination of a molecule such as water, there are cases such as in the polymerization of the polyurethanes which involve only a direct addition between two polyfunctional molecules. This type of condensation polymer is sometimes referred to as a polyadduct.

## Molecular Weight

The length of a polymer chain is determined by purely random events, and hence any polymeric material will contain molecules of many different chain lengths. Any experimental measurement of the molecular weight of a polymer will give only some average value for the molecular weight. Certain methods of determining molecular weight such as colligative experiments depend only on the number of molecules present. Such experiments give the number-average molecular weight of a polymer $\overline{M}_n$, defined by the equation

$$\overline{M}_n = \frac{w}{\Sigma N_i} = \frac{\Sigma M_i N_i}{\Sigma N_i}$$

where $w$ is the total weight of the sample, $M_i$ and $N_i$ are the molecular weights and number of moles of each species present, and the summation is for all values of $i$ from $1-\infty$. The number-average molecular weight is usually close to the value of the most probable molecular weight.

In other experiments such as sedimentation or light-scattering, the experimental results are also affected by the mass of the molecules which are present. Such experiments determine a weight-average molecular weight $\overline{M}_w$ defined by the equation

$$\overline{M}_w = \Sigma w_i M_i = \frac{\Sigma N_i M_i^2}{\Sigma N_i M_i}$$

where $w_i$ is the weight fraction of each species present. The weight-average molecular weight is particularly sensitive to the presence of even relatively small quantities of high molecular weight fractions. The numerical value of $\overline{M}_w$ is always equal to or greater than the value of $\overline{M}_n$. Values of $\overline{M}_w/\overline{M}_n$ for typical polymers range from about 1.5-50.

## Requirements of Monomers

To permit the formation of a high polymer by polymerization, a monomer must fulfill two requirements. First, it must be polyfunctional, namely, contain at least two reactive groups. This requirement is fairly obvious, since only in this way will the products of the polymerization still contain reactive groups to permit the further growth of the chain. However, a second requirement of a monomer is that it must not give cyclic products by intramolecular ring closure. Thus, if we consider the reaction of a dibasic acid with a glycol, the condensation may proceed in the following two ways:

$$HO—R'—OH + HOOC—R—COOH \rightarrow HO—R'—O—CO—R—COOH$$

$$\text{ring closure} \quad R' \overset{O—CO}{\underset{O—CO}{\diagup \diagdown}} R \quad H—(O—R'—O—CO—R—CO)_n—OH$$

$$\text{chain growth}$$

Since the cyclic product has no functional groups, it cannot react further with either the acid or alcohol molecules.

The chief factor determining whether rings or chains will be produced is the size of the ring which may be formed. Thus, five-membered rings are most stable and will usually be formed in preference to chains. Six- and seven-membered rings are moderately stable, and will usually compete with chain formation so that both products are formed. Higher nonplanar rings are possible, but are usually not formed to any appreciable extent under polymerization conditions used in practice; hence, chain growth is almost always observed for polymers containing 8 or more atoms in the repeating chain unit.

In chain-reaction polymers such as the derivatives of ethylene, the double bond acts as a polyfunctional group since it can be opened up to permit addition to each end of the molecule. Although six-membered rings could theoretically be formed from the polymerization of a material such as polyethylene, the formation of cyclic products is not usually observed in the case of the addition polymers.

### Plastics

Originally the word "plastic" was used only as an adjective to denote a degree of mobility or plasticity. With the introduction of the polymers such as "Bakelite," the word was used as a noun to refer to this type of material. The American Society for Testing Materials defines a plastic as "a material that contains as an essential ingredient an organic substance of large molecular weight, is solid in its finished state, and, at some stage in its manufacture or in its processing into finished articles, can be shaped by flow."

This is an extremely broad definition of a plastic, and includes essentially all the synthetic polymers. In practice, a plastic is usually considered to be an amorphous or crystalline polymer which is hard and brittle at ordinary temperatures. If crystalline regions are present, they are randomly oriented. A thermoplastic material is one which can be softened and molded on heating; a thermosetting material is one which involves considerable cross-linking, so that the finished plastic cannot be made to flow or melt. In the fabrication of plastic objects, additives such as colorants, fillers, plasticizers, lubricants and stabilizers are commonly added to modify the physical and mechanical properties of the material.

## Resins

The word "resin" originally referred to natural products of vegetable origin such as rosin, shellac, dammar, mastic, etc. In the plastics industry, a synthetic resin is considered to be the basic polymeric substance used in the fabrication of a plastic object. Similarly, in the surface coatings industry a resin is considered to be the basic binding material before it has been formulated into a paint, varnish or enamel. Thus, a resin may be considered to be the "active ingredient" in a polymer or a surface coating.

## Fibers

Fibers are linear polymers having relatively high tensile strength but low elasticity in the direction of the fiber axis. Often the linear chains are arranged in an orderly three-dimensional structure having strong interchain forces. Normally for a material to be classed as a fiber, its length must be at least 100 times its diameter. To be useful as a textile fiber, a polymer must have adequate tensile strength over a wide temperature range, a high softening point to permit ironing, solubility or meltability to permit spinning and good textile properties such as dyeability, stability, crease resistance, comfort, etc.

## Elastomers

The essential requirement of an elastomer is that it must be elastic, namely, that it must stretch rapidly under tension to several times its original length with little loss of energy as heat. All industrially important elastomers must also exhibit high tensile strength, a high modulus of elasticity when fully stretched, they must retract rapidly to their original dimensions and there must be very little permanent set after release of tension. Elastomers are amorphous polymers with considerable cross-linkage to prevent gross mobility of the linear chains. However, individual segments of the chains must have sufficient mobility to permit the extension and contraction of the chains without permanent change in the dimensions of the material.

## Summary

Since the properties of a polymer can be varied over wide limits, it is impossible to draw a sharp line between plastics, fibers and elastomers. In fact under different conditions, a given polymer may exhibit the properties of a plastic, a fiber or an elastomer. For example, polyamides such as nylon are widely used as both plastics and fibers, polyurethanes are used as both plastics and elastomers, etc. Thus, the classification of a given polymeric material is always more or less arbitrary, and is often done merely on the basis of the proposed use of the material in question.

## PHYSICAL PROPERTIES OF POLYMERS

The physical properties of a polymer are determined by the nature of the material, the molecular weight of the polymer and the arrangement of the chains in the bulk polymer. Since polymerization is determined by random events, the length of the chains in a given polymer will not be uniform, but will vary continuously over fairly wide limits. If the polymerization is entirely statistical, the molecular weight of the individual chains will show a maxwellian distribution about some average value. This average molecular weight can be determined in various ways such as by ultracentrifugation, by light scattering, or by measurement of colligative properties such as the elevation of the boiling point or osmotic pressure of a dilute solution.

Several physical properties of a polymer such as strength, hardness, elasticity and solubility are strongly affected by the average molecular weight of the polymer. Thus, for average molecular weights below about 1000, polymers usually consist of an oily viscous liquid. For molecular weights from 1000-10,000, amorphous polymers are usually soft, waxy solids. Above 10,000, amorphous polymers are either hard, brittle solids or else limp, flexible solids, depending on the nature of the polymer and the degree of cross-linking. Since the properties of a polymer are so strongly affected by the molecular weight, most industrial polymerization processes use chain transfer agents to control the average molecular weight of the product polymer.

### Crystallinity

A second factor which strongly affects the physical properties of a polymer is the degree of crystallinity which may be present in the material. A crystalline polymer is one which has an ordered structure both in the individual chains and in the three-dimensional configuration of polymer chains. In general, crystalline regions are fairly small, and no polymer is completely crystalline. Some polymers such as polyethylene show a highly developed crystallinity; others having bulky substituents such as polystyrene tend to show little crystallinity. However, as we shall see later, crystallinity can be favored by the use of certain catalysts which produce an ordered structure in the polymer chains. These stereospecific polymerizations are of considerable practical importance because they produce ordered polymers having unique physical properties.

Crystallinity tends to increase the strength, hardness and brittleness of a polymer. The degree of crystallinity can be determined by X-ray diffraction, by infrared absorption and by direct measurements of the density of the polymer. Experimental measurements show that most crystalline polymers are about 50-70 per cent crystalline. The crystallinity of linear polyethylene is as high as 80 per cent, and drawn fibers of polyamides and polyesters may show crystallinities in excess of 90 per cent.

## Melting Point

The melting point of a crystalline polymer is usually defined as the temperature at which all crystallinity disappears. In the case of a polymer, melting usually occurs over a range of 10-20°F because of preliminary melting of the less ordered structures in the polymer. The melting point of a given polymer is largely determined by the chain flexibility and the strength of interchain forces, since these determine the ease of separation of chains in the crystalline regions. Unless it is very low, molecular weight has little effect on the melting point. Melting points of the common crystalline polymers range from about 250-600°F.

Amorphous polymers and many finished plastics do not show a sharp melting point. When these materials are heated, eventually a temperature is reached at which the thermal energy of the molecules is sufficient to cause a decomposition of the polymer chains. This temperature is sometimes referred to as the degradation temperature of the material. The degradation temperature is more or less arbitrary, since the degree of degradation is a function of both temperature and time. Two types of degradation are encountered. In random degradation, the rupture occurs at random points along the chain, so that a mixture of degradation products is obtained. In chain depolymerization, the rupture involves the successive release of monomer units from one end of the chain. In some cases, both types of degradation occur simultaneously. Random degradation results in the formation of a mixture of decomposition products ranging in molecular weight up to several hundred; however, chain depolymerization may produce substantial quantities of the monomer.

### Glass Transition

At low temperatures, amorphous polymers are hard, glassy and brittle. This occurs because the thermal energy is too low to permit chain atoms to do more than vibrate about equilibrium positions. Thus, the individual chains are frozen in position, and the polymer is hard and brittle. However, as the temperature is raised, the increased thermal energy permits greater movement of segments of the polymer, and thus the material becomes flexible and less brittle. At still higher temperatures, sufficient energy is available to permit free movement of the chains, and the material becomes elastic. The temperature at which the material becomes soft and flexible is known as the glass-transition temperature.

The glass-transition temperature can be determined either from a direct measure of molecular motion or from measurements of the bulk properties of a material. For example, suppose the density of a material is measured as a function of temperature. Figure 19-1 illustrates typical results for the case of polystyrene. Note the sharp break in the curve at the glass temperature because of the increased mobility of the chains. The glass temperature of common polymers ranges from well below room temperature up to several hundred degrees Fahrenheit. In general, crystallinity, cross-linking and the addition of large rigid groups such as

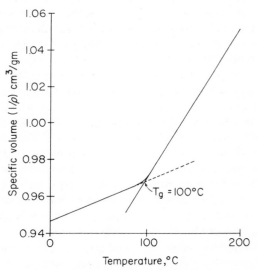

FIG. 19-1. Density of polystyrene as function of temperature [T. G. Fox and P. J. Flory, *J. Appl. Phys.*, **21**, 581 (1950). Average molecular weight = 85.000.]

benzene rings will raise the glass-transition temperature. Obviously, all elastomers must have glass temperatures below the minimum temperature at which the material is to be used.

## Solubility of Polymers

The solubility of a polymer is of considerable practical importance since polymerizations are frequently carried out in solution. Although the factors governing the solubility of a given polymer are more complex than those applying to the solubility of an ordinary chemical, several general rules have been found to apply to polymers. Thus, in general, like dissolves like, so that solution is favored by chemical and physical similarity between the polymer and the solvent. Polar polymers usually require polar solvents, and many polymers will dissolve in their own monomers if these are liquids, etc. Solubility decreases with increase in the molecular weight of the polymer, which is the basis for the fractionation of polymers according to their molecular weight. Crystalline polymers are usually relatively insoluble, and the solubility normally decreases with increase in the crystalline melting point. Highly cross-linked polymers are usually insoluble, although powerful solvents may cause swelling or chemical degradation of such polymers.

Solution of a polymer is usually a slow process which occurs in two stages. First, the solvent gradually penetrates the polymer to produce a swollen gel. The gel then gradually disintegrates to form a true solution. In the case of crystalline and cross-linked polymers, only the first stage may occur with the gradual disintegration of the polymer, but without ever forming a true solution.

## STEP-REACTION (CONDENSATION) POLYMERIZATION

W. H. Carothers in 1929 classified polymers into two groups, namely, condensation and addition polymers. The condensation polymers were considered to be those which were formed by a stepwise condensation of reactive groups whereas the addition polymers were considered to be those formed by chain reactions involving active centers. However, this original definition by Carothers has had to be modified, since condensation reactions are known which do not involve the splitting off of a small molecule. Thus, it is now more common to classify polymers in terms of the mechanism by which they are formed. In step polymerization, the polymerization proceeds through the direct interaction of the particular functional groups which are present. Usually step polymerization involves the splitting off of a small molecule such as water with the resultant formation of an interunit linkage. In chain polymerization, the polymerization proceeds through active centers, the growth reaction occurring only by the addition of individual molecules to the growing chains. Table 19-1 illustrates the distinguishing features of these two different mechanisms.

TABLE 19-1.  DISTINGUISHING FEATURES OF CHAIN- AND
STEP-POLYMERIZATION MECHANISMS*

| Chain Polymerization | Step Polymerization |
|---|---|
| Only growth reaction adds repeating units one at a time to the chain. | Any two molecular species present can react. |
| Monomer concentration decreases steadily throughout reaction. | Monomer disappears early in reaction: at degree of polymerization of 10, less than 1 per cent monomer remains. |
| High polymer is formed at once; polymer molecular weight changes little throughout reaction. | Polymer molecular weight rises steadily throughout reaction. |
| Long reaction times give high yields, but affect molecular weight little. | Long reaction times are essential to obtain high molecular weights. |
| Reaction mixture contains only monomer, high polymer and about $10^{-8}$ part of growing chains. | At any stage, all molecular species are present in a calculable distribution ranging from pure monomer to the highest polymer present. |

* F. W. Billmeyer, Jr., "Textbook of Polymer Science," New York, Interscience Pub., Inc., 1962.

## Mechanism of Step Polymerization

As an example of step polymerization, consider the condensation of a glycol with a dibasic acid to produce a polyester. If the two reactants are mixed in the liquid phase, polymerization will immediately occur throughout the entire material with the formation of dimers, trimers, etc. The growing chains will continue to react with monomer and with each other to form a polymer of increasing molecular weight, until eventually the polymerization will be terminated when all of one reactant is used up. A linear polymer will be formed if each monomer is bifunctional; if a trifunctional monomer such as glycerol is used, branched or cross-linked polymers will be formed.

In step polymerization, the degree of polymerization will be highest when the two reactants are present in exactly stoichiometric quantities. An excess of either reactant will lower the degree of polymerization and hence the molecular weight, since the polymer chains will tend to be terminated by the reactant present in excess. However, there are often cases where it is desired to limit the maximum degree of polymerization which is obtained. This can be done by the addition of a small quantity of a monofunctional reactant which will prevent further growth of the chains. Such a material is known as a "stabilizer."

The kinetics of step polymerization have been carefully studied by Flory.[1] An interesting feature is the fact that the kinetics appear to be essentially independent of both the molecular weight of the reactants and the number of functional groups present on the reactants. This, of course, considerably simplifies the kinetic equations, since the rates of reaction then depend only on the concentrations of the two functional groups, and the rate constants do not change with the degree of polymerization of the material.

In the polymerization of a glycol with a dibasic acid, the uncatalyzed reaction is quite slow, several hours being required to obtain a substantial degree of polymerization. However, the reaction proceeds readily in the presence of an acid catalyst such as toluene-$p$-sulfonic acid. The acid-catalyzed reaction is first-order with respect to both reactants and also first-order with respect to the catalyst concentration. Since the latter remains constant during the reaction, the kinetic equation for a given catalyst concentration is

$$-\frac{dC_1}{dt} = kC_1C_2 \tag{19-1}$$

where $C_1$ and $C_2$ are the concentrations of the hydroxyl and carboxyl groups in the solution. However, if stoichiometric quantities are used, $C_1 = C_2 = C$ and

$$-\frac{dC}{dt} = kC^2 \qquad \text{or} \qquad \frac{1}{C} - \frac{1}{C_0} = kt \tag{19-2}$$

where $C_0$ is the initial concentration of the reactants. If $p$ is the extent of polymerization, then $p = (C_0 - C)/C_0$, and substituting into Eq. (19-2),

$$ktC_0 = \frac{1}{1-p} - 1 = \frac{p}{1-p} \tag{19-3}$$

Thus, a plot of $p/(1-p)$ as a function of time should be linear. Typical data are given in Fig. 19-2; note the close agreement with theory.

## PHENOL-FORMALDEHYDE RESINS

The phenol-formaldehyde resins were the first synthetic polymers to be produced commercially. Theoretically, any aldehyde and any substituted

[1] P. J. Flory, "High Molecular Weight Organic Compounds," edited by R. E. Burk and O. Grummitt, New York, Interscience Pub., Inc., 1949.

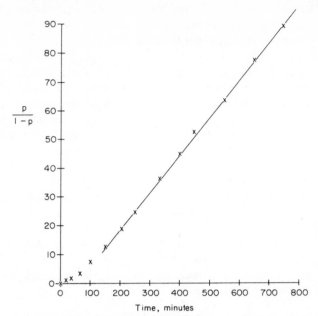

Fig. 19-2. Polymerization of diethylene glycol with adipic acid at 109°C catalyzed by *p*–toluenesulfonic acid [P. J. Flory, *Jour. Amer. Chem. Soc.* **61,** 3334 (1939)].

phenol can be used, as long as there are free positions on the benzene ring which are *ortho* and *para* to the phenolic hydroxyl group. However, formaldehyde is the most reactive aldehyde, and is thus used almost exclusively in practice. The total production of phenolic resins in the United States in 1963 was about 741 million pounds. The chief uses are as a molding powder for the manufacture of plastic objects, as a bonding resin for industrial laminants, in insulating varnishes, in bonding plywood, etc.

The reaction between phenol and formaldehyde is catalyzed either by acids or bases. The nature of the polymer depends on the type of catalyst that is used and the ratio of formaldehyde to phenol. The first step in the polymerization is the formation of methylol derivatives (phenol alcohols) by a direct condensation according to the reaction

The entrance of the methylol group is always either *ortho* or *para* to the hydroxyl group; one, two or three formaldehyde molecules may add to a phenol molecule, depending on the ratio of formaldehyde to phenol that is used.

With an acid catalyst and a molar ratio of formaldehyde to phenol less than 1:1, the methylol derivatives condense with phenol to form dihydroxydiphenyl methane with the splitting off of water. Further condensation produces linear low molecular-weight polymers known as novolaks according to the equation

etc.

The novolaks thus consist of phenol molecules linked by methylene bridges in random *ortho* and *para* positions. The polymers contain up to ten phenolic groups, corresponding to molecular weights up to about 1000. The novolaks are permanently fusible and soluble; however, they can be converted to a cross-linked resin by heating with an alkaline solution of formaldehyde to provide additional methylol groups for cross-linking.

If the ratio of formaldehyde to phenol is greater than 1:1 and if an alkaline catalyst is used, the phenol alcohols condense to form low molecular-weight polymers known as resols. Here the phenol molecules are linked either by methylene linkages or by ether linkages. Typical equations are as follows:

The essential difference between the novolaks and the resols is that the latter contain ether linkages and unreacted methylol groups. The resols are also fusible and soluble; however, by heating under pressure, they can be converted to a hard insoluble and infusible resin.

## Manufacture of Phenolic Resins

Phenolic resins are made by either a one-stage or two-stage process. In the one-stage process, phenol, aqueous formaldehyde or paraformaldehyde, and a basic catalyst such as ammonia or soda ash are charged to a jacketed agitated stainless steel kettle. The molar ratio of formaldehyde to phenol varies from about 1.1-1.5. The mixture is heated to about 200°F with agitation, and polymerization allowed to proceed until resols are formed. The reaction is exothermic. After most of the formaldehyde has reacted, the water is removed under vacuum. Polymerization is allowed to continue until the desired viscosity (and hence degree of polymerization) is obtained; the resin is then dumped into pans and allowed to cool. The cold resin is ground to a fine powder, mixed with fillers, colorants and lubricants, heated and fused on hot mill rolls and ground into molding powder.

With an alkaline catalyst and a formaldehyde to phenol ratio greater than unity, three not very well-defined stages in the polymerization can be distinguished. The first stage involves the formation of resols, the resols being soluble in the reaction mixture. The second stage involves the formation of longer chains known as "resitols" which are thermoplastic and soluble in solvents such as acetone. The third stage involves the production of considerable cross-linking and the formation of an insoluble and infusible resin known as a "resit." In the commercial manufacture of resins, the polymerization is always stopped at the second stage, the final cross-linking occurring during molding.

Two-stage resins are now used more commonly for the manufacture of molding powder. The condensation is carried out in essentially the same way except that an acid catalyst such as sulfuric acid is used and the ratio of formaldehyde to phenol is reduced to about 0.8:1. The rate of polymerization with an acid catalyst is about 3 times that with a basic catalyst. When the desired molecular weight is obtained, the acid is neutralized with lime or soda ash and the resin dumped and cooled. The resin is ground, mixed with hexamethylenetetramine (this serves as a source of additional formaldehyde) and converted to molding powder as described above.

Phenolic resins are cheap and have good heat resistance and good mechanical properties. They are widely used in compression or transfer molding to produce various plastic products (the phenolics are, of course, thermosetting resins since there is considerable cross-linking in the molding of the finished product). They also have good dielectric properties, and are widely used in the electronics industry. A substantial fraction of the one-stage resins is marketed as an alcoholic solution for laminating paper, wood, etc. Phenolic casting resins can be made by alkaline condensation using a high ratio of formaldehyde to phenol. Substantial quantities of phenolics also go into the manufacture of ion-exchange resins.

Although most phenolics are made using formaldehyde, other aldehydes have been used. The only one of commercial importance is furfural, which produces a resin having a high tensile and impact strength. Phenol-furfural resins find limited application in the molding of thick parts such as television cabinets, storage battery cases, etc. Other phenols can also be used for resin manufacture, but the only one of importance is resorcinol (*m*-dihydroxybenzene) which produces resins that cure rapidly at fairly low temperatures.

## AMINOPLAST RESINS

The aminoplast resins include urea-formaldehyde, melamine-formaldehyde, and others of limited importance such as guanidine-formaldehyde and aniline-formaldehyde. Total production in the United States in 1963 was about 368 million pounds of the urea-formaldehyde resins and 149 million pounds of the melamine-formaldehyde resins. The chief uses are as bonding and adhesive resins for laminating wood, in the production of decorative laminants such as table tops and for surface treatment of paper and textiles. As contrasted to the phenolics, the amino resins are clear and colorless. Thus, they are widely used for the manufacture of cosmetic containers, bathroom fixtures and similar molded objects; the largest single use of the melamine resins is in the manufacture of high-quality dinnerware.

To produce a thermosetting resin by reaction with formaldehyde, an amino-compound must meet the following two conditions: (a) It must possess at least two reactive primary amino groups. (b) The nitrogen atom of the amino group must be adjacent to a carbon atom having a double bond, so that tautomerism is possible. The urea-formaldehyde resins were first developed commercially in 1926. The condensation reactions are quite complex, and there is still some uncertainty as to the mechanism of the polymerization. The first stage in the condensation is presumably the formation of methylol groups through the reaction

$$HCHO + O=C\underset{\displaystyle NH_2}{\overset{\displaystyle NH_2}{\Big\langle}} \rightarrow O=C\underset{\displaystyle NH_2}{\overset{\displaystyle NH-CH_2OH}{\Big\langle}} \xrightarrow{\text{HCHO}}$$

monomethylolurea

$$O=C\underset{\displaystyle NH-CH_2OH}{\overset{\displaystyle NH-CH_2OH}{\Big\langle}}$$

dimethylolurea

The methylol groups then either react with each other to form ether linkages or react with $NH_2$ groups to form methylene linkages, both of these reactions involving the splitting off of water.

The commercial production of aminoplasts is similar to the production of phenolics. Thus, the condensation is catalyzed by acids or bases, and the same general stages in the condensation are observed. The ratio of formaldehyde to urea varies from about 1.3 to 1.8. The reactants are normally condensed under alkaline conditions to give a viscous resin which is commonly spray dried and mixed with fillers and other additives. The molding powder is then mixed with an acid catalyst, and plastic objects obtained by molding under heat and pressure to give a cross-linked thermosetting plastic.

The production of the melamine-formaldehyde resins is completely analogous to the production of the urea-formaldehyde type. However, since melamine has 6 reactive hydrogens, the ratio of formaldehyde to melamine is increased to about 2.5:1. Melamine forms methylol derivatives even more easily than urea, and these readily react with $NH_2$ groups to form a highly cross-linked plastic.

## ALKYD RESINS

The name alkyd is derived from *al*cohol + a*cid*, the two monomers used to produce these resins. The alkyds are produced by the polymerization of a polyhydric alcohol such as glycerol, glycol or pentaerythritol with a dibasic acid such as phthalic anhydride, maleic anhydride, isophthalic acid or sebacic acid. Originally, the alkyds included all polymers of polyhydric alcohols with polybasic acids; however, present practice uses the word "alkyd" only for polyesters made from polyhydric alcohols, polybasic acids and monobasic fatty acids. Total production of alkyd resins in the United States for 1963 was 606 million pounds. Most production is based on glycerol + phthalic anhydride to produce the so-called "Glyptal" resins. The only important use of the alkyd resins is in surface coatings where they are used widely in lacquers and varnishes.

The alkyds are produced by heating a mixture of fatty acids, polyhydric alcohols and dibasic acids to temperatures of about 425-535°F in an agitated reaction kettle. The fatty acid may be either a natural fatty acid derived from oils or a synthetic fatty acid from petroleum. In some cases an oil such as linseed, cottonseed or safflower is used as the fatty acid source, and a preliminary ester interchange carried out between the oil and the polyhydric alcohol. Water formed by the condensation is either vented or collected in a fume scrubber system. In most modern plants, an aromatic solvent is added to act as a water entrainer; the mixture of water and solvent is condensed in a reflux condenser, the water removed by decantation and the solvent returned to the kettle. Heating is commonly by a high-temperature fluid such as "Dowtherm." When the desired degree of polymerization has been obtained, the resin is discharged to a thinning tank where it is dissolved in the desired solvent for dilution to the finished product.

More than 90 per cent of the alkyds are blended with various resins and pigments to form different types of paint, varnish and lacquer for industrial or home consumption. In the "drying" alkyds, an unsaturated monobasic fatty acid is used so that the resin polymerizes on drying to give a strong coherent film. In the "nondrying" alkyds, the unsaturated acid is so low that little or no polymerization occurs on drying. The drying alkyds are often used alone whereas the nondrying alkyds are often blended with other polymers to give finished products. However, many different types of alkyd resin are produced commercially, so that any classification must be more or less arbitrary.

### EPOXY RESINS

The epoxy resins or epoxides are polymers of epoxy compounds with dihydric phenols. Theoretically, the epoxy resins are polyethers; however, the name "epoxy" is normally used to describe these polymers since it designates the starting material and also the fact that epoxide groups are present in the polymer before cross-linking.

The epoxies were introduced in Germany just before the war. The commercial development in the United States was slow until epichlorohydrin became available from the manufacture of synthetic glycerol. Since then there has been a fairly rapid growth, with a total production of over 81 million pounds in 1963. A survey by *Chemical and Engineering News* estimates that the total U.S. capacity for epoxy resins will be roughly 150 million pounds/year by 1965. The chief use of the epoxies is in surface coatings such as floor coatings, tank linings, etc., where they

combine toughness, flexibility and excellent chemical resistance. They
are also widely used in the manufacture of reinforced plastics, in the
"potting" of electrical components, and as an adhesive for bonding many
different substances. For example, epoxies rather than rivets are used to
bond the outer skin of aluminum on high-speed aircraft.

The most common epoxy resin is made by condensing epichlorohydrin
with bisphenol A according to the equation

$$CH_2 \underset{\diagdown \;\; \diagup}{\overset{O}{\phantom{-}}} CH-CH_2Cl + HO-\bigcirc-\overset{\overset{\displaystyle CH_3}{|}}{\underset{\underset{\displaystyle CH_3}{|}}{C}}-\bigcirc-OH +$$

$$NaOH \rightarrow NaCl + H_2O +$$

$$\cdots -CH_2-\overset{\overset{\displaystyle OH}{|}}{CH}-CH_2-O-\bigcirc-\overset{\overset{\displaystyle CH_3}{|}}{\underset{\underset{\displaystyle CH_3}{|}}{C}}-\bigcirc-O-\cdots$$

A substantial excess of the epichlorohydrin is normally used to ensure
that the chains are terminated by epoxide groups. In addition to bisphenol A, other hydroxyl compounds such as resorcinol, glycols, hydroquinone and glycerol can be used. However, epichlorohydrin is the only
epoxide available commercially at a reasonable cost.

Equipment required to produce epoxy resins is similar to that used for
the manufacture of phenolics. Thus, to prepare solid epoxy polymers for
surface coatings, a mixture of epichlorohydrin and bisphenol A is charged
to an agitated heated reaction vessel. The molar ratio of epichlorohydrin
to bisphenol A varies from about 1.2-2.0 or higher, depending on the
desired molecular weight of the polymer. The solution is heated to 200-
220°F and maintained at this temperature during the addition of about
1 mole NaOH/mole epichlorohydrin as a 40 per cent NaOH solution.
Overhead vapors consisting of water and epichlorohydrin are condensed,
separated by decantation, and the epichlorohydrin layer returned to the
reactor. When the desired molecular weight is obtained, excess epichlorohydrin is removed by distillation and the salt and excess caustic removed
by washing with water at temperatures above the melting point of the
resin.

Resins produced in this way are thermoplastic and soluble. The resins
may be cured (converted to a cross-linked thermosetting plastic) by
heating under pressure with a suitable curing agent such as a polyamine,
polysulfide, polyamide, acid anhydride or another polymer such as
phenol-formaldehyde. The curing reactions involve opening the epoxide

ring to give a hydroxyamino linkage, esterification of the secondary hydroxyl groups, esterification of the epoxide groups, etc. Normally, no volatile products are evolved during curing, a substantial advantage since it minimizes shrinkage strains.

## POLYAMIDES (NYLON)

The word "nylon" is now accepted as a generic term for the synthetic polyamides. The nylons are named on the basis of the number of carbon atoms in the monomer chain. Polymers based on amino acids are designated by a single number such as nylon 6 for polycaprolactam. Polymers based on diamines and dibasic acids are designated by two numbers, the first giving the number of carbon atoms in the diamine monomer and the second the number of carbon atoms in the acid monomer. Thus, nylon 66, the most common in the United States, is made from hexamethylenediamine and adipic acid. The nylons of commercial importance are the 66, 6, 610 and 11.

The development of nylon goes back to fundamental research carried out by W. H. Carothers starting about 1928. Carothers was interested primarily in the basic principles of polymerization processes. The first synthetic polymers produced by Carothers and his co-workers were polyesters produced by the condensation of glycols with dibasic acids and polyamides produced by the condensation of amino acids. These first polymers had molecular weights ranging from about 2500-5000, but later work produced "superpolymers" having molecular weights as high as 25,000. At this point it was recognized that the superpolymers were of commercial interest, and further work was directed largely toward the development of a polymer which could be used as a textile fiber.

The polyesters were considered to be unsuited for textile fibers because of their poor mechanical properties, so that future work was concentrated on the polyamides. In 1935 the polyamide of hexamethylenediamine and adipic acid was first made. Textile fibers having excellent physical properties could be produced either by melt spinning or by dry spinning from phenol solutions. These fibers melted at about 510°F and were insoluble in all common solvents. Because of the good physical properties of the fiber and the potential availability of the raw materials, this polymer (nylon 66) was selected for future commercial development.

### Raw Materials for Nylon 66

The manufacture of adipic acid was described in Chapter 16. The first commercial process for the manufacture of hexamethylenediamine used adipic acid as a raw material according to the equation

$$HOOC—(CH_2)_4—COOH + 2NH_3 \rightarrow N\equiv C—(CH_2)_4—C\equiv N + 4H_2O$$

$$\xrightarrow{\text{H}_2} H_2N—(CH_2)_6—NH_2$$

From patents, adiponitrile is produced by a vapor-phase catalytic reaction between ammonia and adipic acid at temperatures of 600-700°F, using about a 20:1 molar ratio of ammonia to adipic acid. A fixed-bed dehydration catalyst such as boron phosphate or silica gel is used. The yield is 85-90 per cent, based on adipic acid. Adiponitrile is purified by distillation and hydrogenated to hexamethylenediamine in the liquid phase, using a catalyst of Raney Ni or Raney Co. Temperatures of 200-250°F and pressures of about 1500 psig are used, with a yield of 95 per cent or better. Product is purified by fractionation, and any unreacted adiponitrile is recycled.

A competing process for the manufacture of hexamethylenediamine is based on butadiene. This process is used by du Pont, and it is reported that because of the increased availability and lower cost of butadiene, du Pont has decided to concentrate all present and future production of nylon intermediates on the butadiene route (estimated consumption of 160 million pounds/year of butadiene by 1965). The first step involves a chlorination of butadiene according to the equation

$$CH_2\!=\!CH—CH\!=\!CH_2 + Cl_2 \begin{cases} \rightarrow Cl—CH_2—CH\!=\!CH—CH_2—Cl \\ \rightarrow Cl—CH_2—CHCl—CH\!=\!CH_2 \end{cases}$$

The chlorination is carried out at 500-650°F, using a substantial excess of butadiene; the two isomers are produced in about equal amounts.

The mixture of dichlorobutylenes is purified by distillation and reacted with a 35 per cent sodium cyanide solution containing some free HCN:

$$CH_2Cl—CH\!=\!CH—CH_2Cl + 2NaCN \rightarrow$$

$$N\equiv C—CH_2—CH\!=\!CH—CH_2—C\equiv N + 2NaCl$$

Although the patents are a little hazy, evidently the unsymmetrical dichlorobutylene isomerizes to also yield the 1,4-dicyanobutylene. The reaction is carried out at about 285°F, using a cuprous chloride catalyst. The yield is reported to be as high as 96 per cent. The 1,4-dicyanobutylene may then be converted to adiponitrile by mild hydrogenation, or may be converted all the way to hexamethylenediamine by hydrogenation as above for adiponitrile.

### Manufacture of Nylon 66

Hexamethylenediamine and adipic acid are polymerized according to the equations

$$H_2N-(CH_2)_6-NH_2 + HOOC-(CH_2)_4-COOH \rightarrow$$

$$NH_3^+-(CH_2)_6-NH_3^+-{}^-O-\overset{\overset{\displaystyle O}{\|}}{C}-(CH_2)_4-\overset{\overset{\displaystyle O}{\|}}{C}-O^- \rightarrow 2H_2O +$$

*nylon salt*

$$\cdots -NH-(CH_2)_6-NH-\overset{\overset{\displaystyle O}{\|}}{C}-(CH_2)_4-\overset{\overset{\displaystyle O}{\|}}{C}-\cdots$$

*nylon polymer*

To obtain polymers of high molecular weight, it is essential that the re-actants be mixed in stoichiometric quantities. In the case of nylon 66, this is easily achieved by first forming the 1:1 "nylon salt" which is relatively insoluble in methanol. The salt is filtered, dissolved in water and 0.5-1.0 mole per cent acetic added as a viscosity stabilizer. The solution is then heated in an agitated autoclave for 2-3 hr at about 530°F and 250 psig until all the water has been evolved as steam. The final polymerization is completed by applying a vacuum and raising the temperature to about 570°F. An inert atmosphere must be maintained above the melt at all times to prevent oxidation and discoloration. When the viscosity (molecular weight) of the nylon has reached the desired value, the molten polymer is extruded as a ribbon and cut into chips.

Nylon 66 can either be molded to form a thermoplastic resin or melt spun and cold drawn to form a highly oriented fiber having high strength and elasticity. In 1963, the total production of polyamide resins in the United States was about 62 million pounds, with an additional 692 million pounds going into the manufacture of nylon fiber. About half of all fiber goes into the production of tire cord, and about a third of the fiber goes into apparel uses. Other important uses include the manufacture of carpets, rope, thread, belting, filter cloth, etc., where high strength and good resistance to abrasion and chemical attack are required. Nylon plastic finds modest use as a substitute for metals in bearings, gears, cams, etc., particularly where light weight is desired.

### Raw Materials for Nylon 6

Nylon 6 is based on the single monomer caprolactam, which is derived from an amino acid:

$$H_2N-(CH_2)_5-COOH \rightarrow H_2O + \begin{matrix} CH_2-CH_2-CO \\ | \qquad\qquad | \\ CH_2 \qquad\qquad | \\ | \qquad\qquad | \\ CH_2-CH_2-NH \end{matrix}$$

*ε-aminocaproic acid*

*ε-caprolactam or 2H-azepin-2-one, hexahydro*

The chief advantage of the lactam is that it can be purified by distilla-

tion whereas the amino acid would have to be purified by a recrystalliza-
tion process. In a six- or seven-membered lactam, there is an equilibrium
between the lactam and the amino acid; during polymerization to form
nylon, water acts as a catalyst to open the ring and thus permit the
growth of the polymer. However, in the case of the higher lactams, this
equilibrium does not exist and there is little tendency to reform the
lactam once the ring is opened.

Manufacture of nylon 6 started in Europe, but substantial quantities
are now being produced in the United States. Reportedly, three different
processes are now being used commercially in the United States to manufacture caprolactam. Allied Chemical hydrogenates phenol according to
the equation

$$\text{C}_6\text{H}_5\text{—OH} + 2\text{H}_2 \rightarrow \begin{array}{c} \text{O} \\ \| \\ \text{C} \\ \text{H}_2\text{C} \quad \text{CH}_2 \\ \text{H}_2\text{C} \quad \text{CH}_2 \\ \text{CH}_2 \end{array}$$

From patents, the reaction is carried out at 365°F and 70 psig, using a
solution of phenol in ethanol. The hydrogenation is directed primarily
to the formation of cyclohexanone by the use of a palladium catalyst
which is promoted with sodium and supported on activated carbon.
Cyclohexanone is purified by distillation and converted to cyclohexanone
oxime by the reaction

$$\begin{array}{c} \text{O} \\ \| \\ \text{C} \\ \text{H}_2\text{C} \quad \text{CH}_2 \\ \text{H}_2\text{C} \quad \text{CH}_2 \\ \text{CH}_2 \end{array} + \text{NH}_2\text{OH} \rightarrow \text{H}_2\text{O} + \begin{array}{c} \text{N—OH} \\ \| \\ \text{C} \\ \text{H}_2\text{C} \quad \text{CH}_2 \\ \text{H}_2\text{C} \quad \text{CH}_2 \\ \text{CH}_2 \end{array} \xrightarrow{\text{H}_2\text{SO}_4} \begin{array}{c} \text{CH}_2\text{—CH}_2\text{—CO} \\ \text{CH}_2 \\ \text{CH}_2\text{—CH}_2\text{—NH} \end{array}$$

The oximation of cyclohexanone occurs at about room temperature,
using a solution of hydroxylamine sulfate, with addition of ammonia to
neutralize the acid. The oxime is then added to 98-100 per cent sulfuric
acid to obtain caprolactam by the Beckmann rearrangement. The reaction is strongly exothermic, and the maximum temperature must be
limited to about 280°F to prevent excessive decomposition. Product

caprolactam is then obtained by vacuum distillation of the organic layer.

E. I. du Pont produces caprolactam by a nitration of cyclohexane, followed by a reduction-dehydration reaction:

$$
\begin{array}{c}
CH_2 \\
\diagup \quad \diagdown \\
H_2C \qquad CH_2 \\
| \qquad\qquad | \\
H_2C \qquad CH_2 \\
\diagdown \quad \diagup \\
CH_2
\end{array}
+ HNO_3 \rightarrow H_2O +
\begin{array}{c}
HCNO_2 \\
\diagup \quad \diagdown \\
H_2C \qquad CH_2 \\
| \qquad\qquad | \\
H_2C \qquad CH_2 \\
\diagdown \quad \diagup \\
CH_2
\end{array}
\xrightarrow{H_2}
$$

$$
\begin{array}{c}
CH_2-CH_2-CO \\
| \qquad\qquad\qquad | \\
CH_2 \qquad\qquad\quad | \quad + H_2O \\
| \qquad\qquad\qquad | \\
CH_2-CH_2-NH
\end{array}
$$

The nitration of cyclohexane may be carried out in either the liquid or vapor phase. Liquid-phase nitration uses about 35 per cent $HNO_3$ at 250°F and 75 psig; vapor-phase nitration is at about 500°F, using an excess of cyclohexane. In either case, precise control of nitrating conditions is essential to minimize formation of by-product adipic acid. The nitrocyclohexane can be converted to cyclohexanone oxime by mild liquid-phase hydrogenation; however, du Pont reportedly converts the nitrocyclohexane directly to caprolactam by passing the vapors over a hydrogenation-dehydration catalyst such as borophosphoric acid. From patents, the reaction is carried out at atmospheric pressure and about 550-650°F in the presence of hydrogen or nitrogen. The yield is increased by the addition of about 1 mole of "adjuvant" per mole of nitrocyclohexane. Adjuvants which can be used include methanol, acetonitrile, acetone, cyclohexanone, etc. Evidently the adjuvant is oxidized, thereby favoring the reduction of nitrocyclohexane to caprolactam. The yield is about 40 per cent, based on nitrocyclohexane.

However, the process which now appears to be most favored for the manufacture of caprolactam is based on cyclohexane. The first step involves an air oxidation of cyclohexane to a mixture of cyclohexanone and cyclohexanol as described previously under the manufacture of adipic acid. A crude cyclohexanol fraction is separated by distillation, and this crude fraction is then dehydrogenated to cyclohexanone by passing it over ZnO pellets at about 750°F. From patents, the conversion is 99 per cent with a selectivity to cyclohexanone of 82 per cent. The cyclohexanone is purified by distillation and converted to the oxime and caprolactam as described above. This process is being used commercially by Dow-Badische at Freeport, Texas, and is also widely used in Europe.

## Manufacture of Nylon 6

The polymerization of a lactam[1] is substantially different from the polymerization of an amino acid. In the case of a lactam, a catalyst is always needed to start the reaction. In practice, water is always used as catalyst in the polymerization of caprolactam. The water opens the ring to form a small amount of the amino acid, and polymerization then proceeds in the following way:

$$CH_2—CH_2—CO$$
$$CH_2 \qquad\qquad\qquad + H_2N—(CH_2)_5—COOH \rightarrow$$
$$CH_2—CH_2—NH$$

$$\overset{O}{\overset{\|}{H_2N—(CH_2)_5—C—NH—(CH_2)_5—COOH}} \quad etc.$$

The growth of the polymer is achieved by a direct addition of caprolactam onto the $NH_2$ groups of the chain, thus lengthening the chain one unit at a time. The addition reaction is believed to be catalyzed by the carboxyl groups present in the monomer.

Another feature of the polymerization of a lactam is the fact that polymerization is never complete. At the usual polymerization temperatures, about 10 per cent of the caprolactam monomer is unreacted; in addition, small quantities of the dimer and trimer are also present. These low molecular-weight materials substantially modify the properties of the nylon 6 polymer, and they normally must be removed before further processing of the polymer.

In the commercial production of nylon 6, caprolactam is polymerized at about 430°F, using water (and possibly acid) as a catalyst. After polymerization, the unreacted monomer and the low molecular-weight polymers are removed by extraction with water, and the nylon 6 thoroughly dried by heating under vacuum. The crystalline melting point of nylon 6 is 437°F, and it is softer and less stiff than nylon 66. Nylon 6 is the leading form in Europe where it was first produced commercially. The survey by Haines (*op. cit.*) estimated a capacity of 152 million pounds/year of nylon 6 in the United States, as compared with 466 million pounds/year of nylon 66. Capacity for both grades of nylon is now undergoing rapid expansion. However, with the improved processes now available for the production of caprolactam, nylon 6 appears to have a cost advantage over nylon 66, and it is possible that strong future competition may develop between thes two polymers.

[1] R. Aelion, *Ind. Eng. Chem.*, **53**(10), 826 (1961); P. H. Hermans, *et al.*, *J. Polymer Sci.*, **30**, 81 (1958).

## Other Nylons

The two other nylons produced commercially are the nylon 11 and nylon 610. Although these are both more expensive, their properties are sufficiently different that they have found limited commercial application.

Nylon 11 is manufactured by the polymerization of 11-aminoundecanoic acid, which is produced from castor oil by the reactions

$$\text{Castor oil} \rightarrow CH_2{=}CH{-}(CH_2)_8{-}COOH + CH_3(CH_2)_5CHO$$
$$undecylinic\ acid$$

$$CH_2{=}CH(CH_2)_8COOH + HBr \rightarrow BrCH_2(CH_2)_9COOH \xrightarrow{NH_3}$$
$$H_2N(CH_2)_{10}COOH$$

Castor oil is heated to 570°F in a vacuum to form undecylinic acid by thermal decomposition of glyceryl ricinoleate, the chief ester present in castor oil. The undecylinic acid is reacted with HBr in the presence of a peroxide catalyst, and then converted to 11-aminoundecanoic acid by heating with aqueous ammonia at about 110°F. Nylon 11 is produced by polymerizing the amino acid at about 420°F either alone or as a solution in xylenol. The polymer is less water-sensitive than other nylons because of the longer hydrocarbon chain in the monomer. Nylon 11 finds some use in Europe as a textile fabric.

Nylon 610 is manufactured by the polymerization of hexamethylenediamine and sebacic acid. The polymer is not used as a textile fiber, but has found limited use in the production of monofilaments for brushes, bristles, sporting equipment, etc. Sebacic acid monomers may be produced by heating castor oil with strong caustic to obtain sodium sebacate and 2-octanol. It is also possible to produce sebacic acid from butadiene by a series of steps involving the intermediate formation of isomers of dicyanooctadiene, followed by hydrogenation to yield sebacic acid.

## LINEAR POLYESTERS

Linear polyesters can be produced either by polymerization of a hydroxyacid or by polymerization of a dibasic acid with a glycol. The aliphatic polyesters were among the first polymers studied by Carothers and his co-workers over the period 1928-32. Various polyesters were prepared such as polyethylene succinate, polyethylene sebacate, etc. However, these materials were unsuited for the manufacture of synthetic fibers because they were too easily hydrolyzed and their softening temperatures were too low to permit ironing. For these reasons, Carothers rejected them as possible fiber-forming materials.

However, research in Britain showed that the physical properties of the polyesters could be improved by the use of aromatic dicarboxylic acids, since the benzene ring gives greater stability and stiffness to the polymer. Thus, in 1942, Whinfield and Dickson produced polyethylene terephthalate, which is the only commercially important linear polyester. The chief uses of the polymer are for the manufacture of fibers ("Terylene" and "Dacron") and the manufacture of film ("Melinex" and "Mylar"). The importance of this polymer can be appreciated from the fact that about 331 million pounds of dimethyl terephthalate were produced in the United States in 1963, substantially all of which was used in the manufacture of polyethylene terephthalate.

Although polyethylene terephthalate can be prepared in principle by polymerizing ethylene glycol and terephthalic acid, this reaction is not used for two reasons. First, the polymerization equilibrium is not particularly favorable, and stoichiometry is more difficult to achieve because there is no formation of a salt. Second, the terephthalic acid is hard to purify because of its low solubility and high melting point. However, both of these difficulties can be circumvented by first esterifying the terephthalic acid with methanol, then purifying the dimethyl terephthalate by distillation or crystallization. This is then polymerized with ethylene glycol to produce a linear polymer by ester interchange according to the equation

$$H_3C-O-\overset{\overset{O}{\|}}{C}-\!\!\!\!\bigcirc\!\!\!\!-\overset{\overset{O}{\|}}{C}-O-CH_3 + 2HO-C_2H_4-OH \rightarrow$$

$$2CH_3OH + HO-C_2H_4-O-\overset{\overset{O}{\|}}{C}-\!\!\!\!\bigcirc\!\!\!\!-\overset{\overset{O}{\|}}{C}-O-C_2H_4-OH$$

$$\downarrow$$

$$\cdots\ -O-C_2H_4-O-\overset{\overset{O}{\|}}{C}-\!\!\!\!\bigcirc\!\!\!\!-\overset{\overset{O}{\|}}{C}-\ \cdots$$

In practice, a two-step process is used. First, the dimethyl terephthalate is condensed with excess ethylene glycol to form a mixture of bis-(2-hydroxyethyl) terephthalate and low molecular-weight polymers. The condensation is carried out at about 400°F, using a catalyst such as caustic, lithium hydride or zinc acetate. The reaction involves an ester interchange with the splitting off of methyl alcohol which distills as it is formed. When ester interchange is complete, a catalyst such as antimony trioxide or manganous naphthenate is added and the material heated to about 530-540°F under 1 mm Hg pressure to distill off ethylene glycol and complete the polymerization. From the patent literature, materials such as $H_3PO_4$ may also be added to prevent coloration of the polymer.

The polymer is amorphous when first formed, and retains this structure if rapidly cooled. It can be converted to a crystalline polymer by reheating or by treatment with suitable organic liquids. The thermoplastic crystalline polymer melts at 482°F and is soluble in only a few polar organics such as o-chlorophenol, trifluoroacetic acid, etc. It is converted to fibers by melt spinning under dry conditions to avoid hydrolysis. The polyethylene terephthalate also finds some application as a plastic film, although here it encounters much competition from polyethylene.

## POLYURETHANES

The polyurethanes were first developed commercially in 1937 by Farben-fabriken-Bayer A. g. The polymers[1] are named from the German word "urethane" (ethyl carbamate), which was synthesized by Wurtz in 1858. Polyurethane fibers and foams were used rather extensively in Germany during World War II. Development in the United States started in 1945 when reports of the German work first became available. In recent years the polyurethanes have shown a spectacular growth, commercial production in the U.S. increasing from essentially zero in 1954 to an

TABLE 19-2.  ESTIMATED POLYURETHANE END USES
IN MILLIONS OF POUNDS/YEAR*

|  | 1962 | 1967 |
|---|---|---|
| Foams | | |
|     Flexible | 120 | 260 |
|     Semirigid | 5 | 15 |
|     Rigid | 18 | 135 |
| Elastomers | 9 | 35 |
| Coatings | 8 | 18 |
| Other | 5 | 12 |
|     Total | 165 | 475 |

\* J. Gordon, op. cit.

estimated 475 million pounds/year by 1967. Table 19-2 gives estimated end uses of the polyurethanes.

[1] R. E. Knox, Chem. Eng. Progr., 57(10), 40 (1961); J. Gordon, Hydro. Proc. Petrol. Refiner, 41(11), 171 (1962); 42(2), 123 (1963); I. A. Eldib, Ibid., 42(12), 121 (1963).

### Polyurethane Chemistry

The chemistry of the polyurethanes is quite complex because various types of reaction may occur during polymerization. However, the fundamental reaction is a condensation of an isocyanate group with a hydroxyl group according to the general equation

$$RNCO + R'OH \rightarrow R-\overset{\overset{\displaystyle H}{|}}{N}-\overset{\overset{\displaystyle O}{\|}}{C}-O-R'$$

*urethane*

If both reactants are monofunctional, the reaction stops with the formation of urethane. If both reactants are bifunctional, linear polymers are obtained having the general formula

$$OCN-R-NCO + HO-R'-OH \rightarrow$$

$$\cdots -R-\underset{\underset{\displaystyle H}{|}}{N}-\underset{\underset{\displaystyle O}{\|}}{C}-O-R'-O-\overset{\overset{\displaystyle O}{\|}}{C}-\overset{\overset{\displaystyle }{}}{N}-\cdots$$

*polyurethane*

Synthetic fibers and thermoplastics are usually linear polymers of this type. Note that the interunit group in the polyurethanes is —NH—CO—O— as compared with —NH—CO— in the polyamides. The additional oxygen atom imparts greater flexibility to the polyurethane chains, and lowers the crystalline melting point to about 125°F less than the corresponding polyamide.

Cross-linked three-dimensional polyurethanes may be produced in several ways. One possible way would be to use a polyfunctional isocyanate such as a triisocyanate monomer. However, these are difficult and expensive to manufacture, and thus are not used commercially. The normal method of producing cross-linking is to use a polyfunctional alcohol (polyol), either a polyether or polyester, which contains more than two hydroxyl groups per molecule. Thus, triols, tetrols, etc., may be used, depending on the desired properties of the polymer.

A certain amount of cross-linking is also produced by secondary reactions. Thus, at temperatures of about 175°F or greater, a cross-linking reaction known as an allophonate linkage can occur between an isocyanate group and a hydrogen atom on the nitrogen of the urethane group. The equation is as follows:

$$\cdots -R-\overset{\overset{\displaystyle H}{|}}{\underset{\underset{\displaystyle }{}}{N}}-\overset{\overset{\displaystyle O}{\|}}{C}-O- \cdots + -NCO \rightarrow \cdots -R-\underset{\underset{\displaystyle O=C-N-}{|}}{N}-\overset{\overset{\displaystyle O}{\|}}{C}-O- \cdots$$

The formation of allophonate linkages is affected by the temperature, the nature of the polyol which is used, and the ratio of isocyanate to hydroxyl groups in the polymer. Allophonate linkages may alter substantially the physical and mechanical properties of the polymer.

### Blowing Agents

A suitable blowing agent must be used for the manufacture of a polyurethane foam. In the case of rigid foams, blowing is usually done during polymerization by means of a volatile blowing agent such as a fluorocarbon. However, in the case of flexible foams, blowing is usually accomplished by the addition of water during polymerization to generate carbon dioxide by the reaction

$$\text{RNCO} + \text{HOH} \rightarrow \text{R}-\overset{\overset{\displaystyle H}{|}}{N}-\overset{\overset{\displaystyle O}{\|}}{C}-\text{OH} \rightarrow \text{RNH}_2 + \text{CO}_2$$

The amine then reacts with an additional isocyanate group by the reaction

$$\text{RNH}_2 + \text{RNCO} \rightarrow \text{R}-\overset{\overset{\displaystyle H}{|}}{N}-\overset{\overset{\displaystyle O}{\|}}{C}-\overset{\overset{\displaystyle H}{|}}{N}-\text{R}$$

*substituted urea*

The actual reactions are undoubtedly more complex than this simple theory indicates, since experiments have shown that carbon dioxide continues to be generated even when no free isocyanate remains in the polymer.

Depending on temperature and the availability of isocyanate groups, a secondary cross-linking reaction can occur in a water-blown foam. This is the "biuret" reaction in which hydrogens on the urea react with isocyanate according to the equation

$$\text{R}-\overset{\overset{\displaystyle H}{|}}{N}-\overset{\overset{\displaystyle O}{\|}}{C}-\overset{\overset{\displaystyle H}{|}}{N}-\text{R} + -\text{NCO} \rightarrow \text{R}-\overset{\overset{\displaystyle H}{|}}{N}-\overset{\overset{\displaystyle O}{\|}}{C}-\underset{\underset{\displaystyle \underset{\underset{\displaystyle H}{|}}{N-}}{\overset{\displaystyle |}{\underset{\displaystyle O=C}{}}}}{N}-\text{R}$$

Thus, the biuret reaction also introduces cross-linking, and thereby modifies the properties of the polymer.

### Monomers

Diisocyanates which may be used for the production of polyurethanes include aliphatic derivatives such as hexamethylene diisocyanate and aromatic derivatives such as *p,p'*-diphenylmethane diisocyanate, naphthyl-1,5-diisocyanate, and toluene diisocyanate. The latter is used almost exclusively in the United States because of its low cost, low toxicity and greater reactivity.

Many different polyols may be used in the polymerization such as polyesters, polyethers, and even nitrogen-containing materials such as the alkanolamines. In addition to supplying functional groups, the polyols also must meet the following requirements: (a) The polyols must supply the major portion of the materials requirements; thus, a flexible foam consists of about 70 per cent polyol and 30 per cent diisocyanate. (b) The unit cost of the polyol is less than half the cost of 80/20 toluene diisocyanate. Thus, a moderately high molecular-weight polyol is desirable to reduce the cost of the finished polymer. (c) The nature of the polyol will determine the molecular weight, degree of elasticity, extent of cross-linking, etc. of the final polyurethane. Since many different polyols may be used in the polymerization, the physical properties of the polyurethanes can be varied over wide limits.

Typical raw materials for the manufacture of polyurethanes are listed in Table 19-3. The most important polyols are the polyethers which are cheaper than the polyesters and now account for about 90 per cent of the polyurethane flexible foam. The polyethers usually have molecular weights in the range from 400-5000 and have a functionality ranging from about 2 to 6. They are produced chiefly by condensation reactions between propylene oxide and glycols, although the properties may be modified by the use of other olefin oxides or other polyols. Polyesters are obtained from glycols by esterification with a dibasic acid such as adipic, phthalic or sebacic acid.

## Urethane Polymerization

The isocyanate group is extremely reactive, which is rather unusual for an organic compound. To explain this high reactivity, it has been suggested that the isocyanate group consists of a polarized electronic structure having an electronegative oxygen and electropositive carbon. In the reaction with an alcohol, the proton is attracted to the negative oxygen atom and the RO-radical is attracted to the positive carbon atom. Rearrangement then occurs spontaneously to yield the urethane structure.

Polymerization of a diisocyanate and a polyol occurs readily at room temperature even when uncatalyzed. On the average, primary hydroxyl groups react several times as fast as secondary; however, primary and secondary amines are even more reactive. Catalysts may be used to maintain a balance between chain extension and cross linking. The following two types of catalyst have been employed: (a) organic bases, especially tertiary amines such as triethylene diamine; (b) organic tin compounds

TABLE 19-3. TYPICAL MONOMERS FOR POLYURETHANES

*Diisocyanates*

Toluene diioscyanate

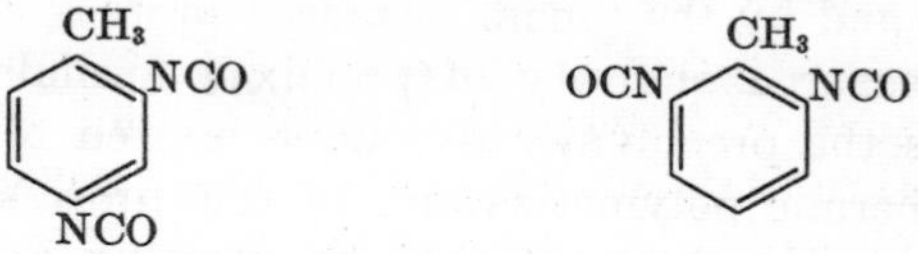

p,p'-Diphenyl methane diisocyanate

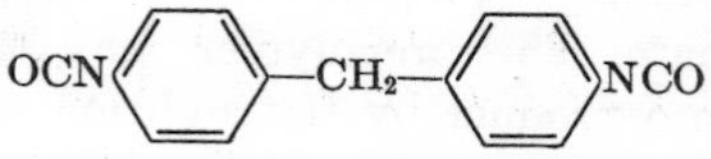

Naphthyl-1,5-diisocyanate

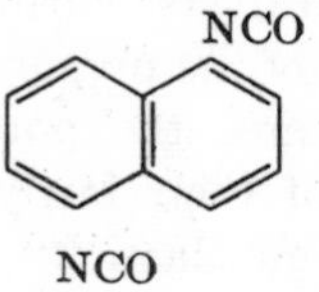

*Polyester*
Ethylene glycol + adipic acid → polyethylene adipate

*Polyethers*
Polyethylene glycol
Polypropylene glycol
Trimethylolpropane

*Higher polyols*

Sorbitol

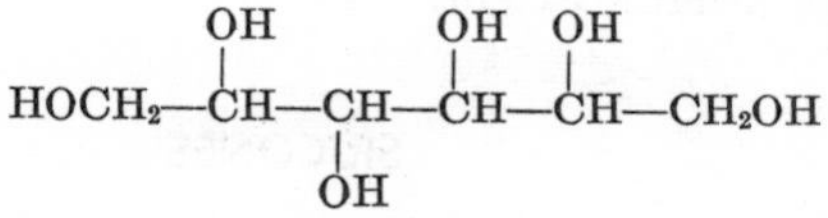

"Quadrol"

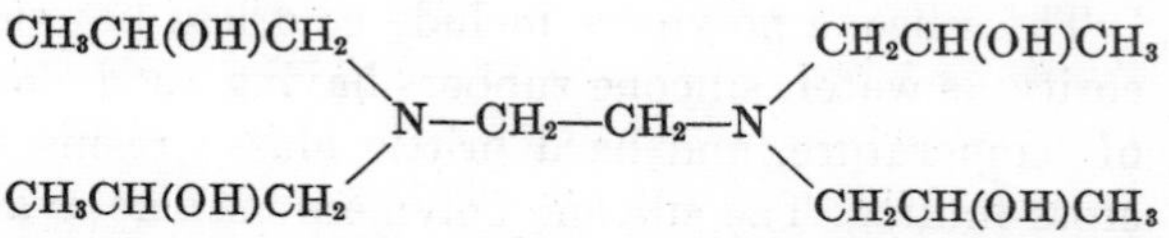

such as stannous octoate. The tin catalysts are used almost entirely in foams.

In the manufacture of a polyurethane foam, the chief goal is to achieve the lowest possible density consistent with other requirements. Flexible foams require relatively less cross-linking, and are made chiefly from triols in the 3000-4000 molecular-weight range. Rigid foams are much more cross-linked, and require polyols of low molecular weight but high functionality. The chief applications of the polyurethane foams have been in furniture cushions, bedding, padding, as a buoyant material in boats and for insulation of refrigeration equipment. Polyurethane foams also have a large potential market in building construction where they can be used for wall panels, roofs, etc.

Commercially, most flexible foam has been produced by the "free rise" technique in which the monomer streams are fed directly to a mixing head located above a moving conveyer. Flexible foam may also be produced by the "one shot" process which mixes the reactants in a mixing gun, and by the "foam in place" process which involves the addition of a measured quantity of premixed formulation into a cavity. In some cases the prepolymer technique is used to obtain better control of the exothermic polymerization. In this process, a relatively low molecular-weight adduct is prepared by reacting part of the polyol with all the diisocyanate. The prepolymer may then be stored, and converted as needed into product by the addition of the remaining polyol plus additives such as catalysts, curing agents and blowing agents. Most rigid foams are made by the prepolymer technique.

Outside of foams, the polyurethanes have found only limited use, chiefly because of their fairly high cost. Polyurethane elastomers have high strength, high elasticity and good chemical resistance; these have found limited use for special purposes as film, sheeting and castings. Polyurethane coatings have excellent physical properties, but practical uses were held back for some time by problems of cost and formulation of suitable products. The polyurethanes also have potential value for the manufacture of plastics and fibers, but these uses have not as yet developed to any appreciable extent.

## SILICONES

The silicone polymers include colorless liquids of about the same viscosity as water, silicone rubbers having good elasticity over a wide range of temperature, and hard brittle glassy resins having a high degree of cross-linking. The silicone polymers became available commercially during the war, and attracted considerable interest because of their unique physical properties. However, the growth of the silicones has been quite modest, chiefly because of their high cost. Thus, in 1963, the total U.S. production of silicone resins was about 10 million pounds and production of silicone elastomers was about 8 million pounds. Thus, the silicones remain more or less of a specialty, and it is hard to see any substantial future increase unless production costs can be lowered.

As in the case of carbon, atoms of silicon can form either Si—Si or Si—C covalent bonds. However, silicon does not form double or triple bonds, and thus silicone polymers can be produced only by condensation-type reactions. The monomers used to produce the silicone polymers are usually compounds of the type $SiR_nCl_{4-n}$, where R is an alkyl or aryl group. These compounds are easily hydrolyzed by water to form polymers having siloxane linkages. Thus, taking dimethyldichlorosilane as an example,

$$\begin{matrix} & \text{CH}_3 & & & & \text{CH}_3 & & & \text{CH}_3 & \text{CH}_3 \\ & | & & & & | & & & | & | \\ \text{Cl}-&\text{Si}-\text{Cl} + 2\text{H}_2\text{O} \rightarrow 2\text{HCl} + \text{HO}-&\text{Si}-\text{OH} \rightarrow \cdots -&\text{Si}-\text{O}-\text{Si}- \cdots \\ & | & & & & | & & & | & | \\ & \text{CH}_3 & & & & \text{CH}_3 & & & \text{CH}_3 & \text{CH}_3 \end{matrix}$$

The first step is a splitting off of HCl from the chlorosilane; however, the hydroxyl groups are unstable and react with each other to split off water and form siloxane linkages. The properties of the polymers will be determined by the monomers which are used. Thus, dichlorosilanes will produce linear polymers, trichlorosilanes will produce cross-linked polymers, etc.

The monomers may be produced in several ways. In the direct synthesis, an alkyl or aryl halide reacts directly with silicon according to the typical equation

$$2\text{RCl} + \text{Si} \rightarrow \text{SiR}_2\text{Cl}_2$$

The reaction is carried out at temperatures of 500-800°F, using a metal catalyst such as copper or silver. Numerous side reactions can occur, and maximum yields of about 70 per cent are typical. Problems are also encountered in the separation of the products, since there may be little difference in the boiling points and azeotropes may be formed. For example, the normal boiling points of methyltrichlorosilane and dimethyldichlorosilane differ by only about 7°F.

Another method of producing silicone monomers is by the classical Grignard reaction

$$\text{CH}_3\text{Cl} + \text{Mg} \rightarrow \text{CH}_3\text{MgCl}$$

$$2\text{CH}_3\text{MgCl} + \text{SiCl}_4 \rightarrow (\text{CH}_3)_2\text{SiCl}_2 + 2\text{MgCl}_2$$

The Grignard reaction is a favorite of laboratory chemists because it is direct and gives a high yield. However, it is not very well suited for plant operations because of the high cost and the problems of handling ether solutions.

### Polymerization of Silanes

Silicone polymers are produced by polymerizing a mixture of water and silane at temperatures ranging from room temperature up to about 300°F, depending on the nature of the silane that is used. Low molecular-weight polymers are obtained by the use of a dichlorosilane plus some monochlorosilane which acts as a "chain stopper." Elastomers are obtained by the use of a carefully purified dichlorosilane monomer to permit the formation of high molecular-weight linear polymers. Resins are obtained by the addition of trichlorosilane to produce cross-linking.

Some of the most important silicone products are as follows:

(1) Silicone Oils. The silicone oils are colorless liquids having viscosities as high as a million centistokes. The most common are linear polymers of dimethyldichlorosilane with a small amount of trimethylchlorosilane to limit the molecular weight of the polymer. Silicone oils are essentially nonvolatile, can be used to temperatures of about 500°F and show very little change in physical properties (such as viscosity) over wide temperature limits. The materials are widely used as special purpose lubricants, antifoaming agents, and as additives to paints and automobile polishes. Since the silicones have high water repellency, they are also commonly applied to fabrics, paper and leather to make them more water repellent.

(2) Silicone Resins. The silicone resins have a three-dimensional structure resulting from the use of a mixture of di- and trichlorosilanes. Often the polymerization is carried out in the presence of an organic solvent such as toluene which dissolves the resin and thereby prevents the formation of a gel. The resin is then brought to the desired degree of polymerization by heating the solution in the presence of a catalyst. Silicone resins are used in surface coatings, as high temperature laminating resins, in electrical insulation, as mold-release agents and in water-repellent coatings.

(3) Silicone Elastomers. The silicone elastomers are usually prepared by the hydrolysis of very pure dimethyldichlorosilane to obtain polymers having molecular weights ranging from about 100,000-500,000. These are then mixed with a filler such as powdered silica and a curing agent such as benzoyl peroxide to give a plastic mass which is molded and cured. Silicone elastomers will withstand temperatures as high as 600°F, yet they will also retain their elastic properties down to temperatures as low as − 130°F. The materials find considerable use as gaskets, seals, power cables, tubing, etc., where extremes of temperature are encountered.

(4) "Nutty putty." The unique properties which can be obtained in a silicone polymer are perhaps best exemplified by the nutty putty which was widely advertised several years ago as a children's plaything. The material flows like a very viscous liquid on storage, can be drawn out into long threads when moderate tension is applied, is brittle when sudden tension is applied, yet bounces like a rubber ball when dropped on a hard surface.

## POLYCARBONATES

The linear polycarbonates are produced by the condensation of aromatic hydroxy compounds with either phosgene or diphenyl carbonate.

These polymers were first produced commercially in 1957 as a result of research carried out in Germany and the United States. In recent years the polycarbonates have shown a modest, but not spectacular growth. The polycarbonates are crystalline thermoplastic polymers having good mechanical and electrical properties.[1] They can be cast, molded, or extruded to produce various articles such as telephone parts, machinery housings, electrical insulation, etc. Polycarbonates also can be spun and drawn to form a textile fiber, although this use has been very limited to date.

Commercially, the most important polycarbonate is produced by the condensation of phosgene and bisphenol A according to the equation

$$\text{HO}-\!\!\!\left\langle\bigcirc\right\rangle\!\!\!-\!\!\overset{\overset{\displaystyle CH_3}{|}}{\underset{\underset{\displaystyle CH_3}{|}}{C}}\!\!\!-\!\!\!\left\langle\bigcirc\right\rangle\!\!\!-\text{OH} + COCl_2 \xrightarrow{\text{NaOH}} 2NaCl +$$

$$2H_2O + \cdots -O-\!\!\!\left\langle\bigcirc\right\rangle\!\!\!-\!\!\overset{\overset{\displaystyle CH_3}{|}}{\underset{\underset{\displaystyle CH_3}{|}}{C}}\!\!\!-\!\!\!\left\langle\bigcirc\right\rangle\!\!\!-O-\overset{\overset{\displaystyle O}{\|}}{C}-\cdots$$

The condensation is carried out at about room temperature in the presence of caustic solution to react with the liberated HCl. In addition, an inert chlorinated solvent such as $CH_2Cl_2$ is used to dissolve the phosgene and the polycarbonate. The molecular weight of the polymer is about 200,000. The salt is washed out of the mixture, and the polymer recovered either by precipitation with a nonsolvent or by removal of the solvent by distillation.

A slightly different process is used by General Electric Co. in its 5 million pounds/year polycarbonate plant at Mount Vernon, Indiana. Pyridine is used in place of caustic, and the liberated HCl is tied up as pyridine hydrochloride. The condensation is carried out at about 100°F over the period of 1-3 hr, polycarbonate solution is decanted from the pyridine hydrochloride, and an antisolvent added to precipitate the polymer.

Polycarbonates may also be produced by ester interchange between diphenyl carbonate and bisphenol A according to the reaction

[1] W. F. Christopher and D. W. Fox, "Polycarbonates," New York, Reinhold Publishing Corp., 1962.

The reaction is carried out under vacuum at 300-550°F, using a catalyst such as manganese, calcium or zinc. Phenol is removed by distillation during the polymerization. The ester-interchange process produces directly a polymer in the molten state, but the molecular weight of the polymer is lower and there is a greater tendency for side reactions because of the higher polymerization temperature.

## CHAIN-REACTION (ADDITION) POLYMERIZATION

The addition polymers include polyethylene, polystyrene, polyvinyl chloride, the diene polymers, etc. As we have already seen, these polymers are produced by a typical chain reaction involving initiation, propagation and termination of the polymer chains. As illustrated in Table 19-4, various types of chain-reaction polymerization are possible, depending on the nature of the chain carriers. The classical type of addition polymerization involves free radicals which act as the chain carriers. Thus, in the case of polyvinyl chloride, we have seen that the free radical opens the double bond to permit polymerization by the reactions

$$R^• + CH_2{=}CHCl \rightarrow RCH_2CHCl^• \begin{cases} \rightarrow RCH_2CHClCH_2CHCl^• \\ \rightarrow RCH_2CHClCHClCH_2^• \end{cases} \text{etc.}$$

In the growth of the polymer chain, the successive addition of monomer units can occur in two ways. The first produces a head-to-tail polymer in which the substituents (in this case, chlorine atoms) occur on alternate carbon atoms. The second produces a head-to-head, tail-to-tail structure in which the substituents occur on adjacent carbon atoms. In practice, most polymers are made up chiefly of head-to-tail linkages, only a very small number of head-to-head and tail-to-tail linkages being present.

The growth of a polymer chain can be terminated in two ways. The first is known as combination or coupling, whereby two free radicals react with each other to form a saturated covalent bond according to the typical equation

TABLE 19-4. TYPE OF CHAIN POLYMERIZATION SUITABLE
FOR COMMON MONOMERS*

| *Free Radical Only* | | *Cationic Only* |
|---|---|---|
| Halogenated vinyls | | Isobutylene and derivatives |
| $CH_2{=}CHX$ | (where X = halo- | $CH_2{=}C(CH_3)R$ |
| $CH_2{=}CX_2$ | gen or hydrogen, | Alkyl vinyl ethers |
| $CF_2{=}CFX$ | but ethylene not | $CH_2{=}CHOR$ |
| $CF_2{=}CX_2$ | included). | $CH_2{=}C(R)OR$ |
| Vinyl esters | | $CH_3OCH{=}CHOCH_3$ |
| $CH_2{=}CHOCOR$ | | Coumarone, indene |
| | | Derivatives of $\alpha$-methylstyrene |

| *Anionic Only* | | *Cationic or Free Radical* |
|---|---|---|
| Vinylidene cyanide | | N-vinylcarbazole |
| $CH_2{=}C(CN)_2$ | | N-vinylpyrrolidone |
| $CH_2{=}C(CN)Y$ | (where Y = $SO_2R$, | |
| | $CF_3$, or COOR). | |
| Nitroethylenes | | |
| $CH_2{=}C(NO_2)R$ | | |

| *Free Radical or Anionic* | *Cationic, Free Radical, or Anionic* |
|---|---|
| Acrylic and methacrylic esters | Ethylene |
| Vinylidene esters | Butadiene |
| $CH_2{=}C(COOR)_2$ | Styrene |
| Derivatives of acrylonitrile | $\alpha$-Methylstyrene |
| $CH_2{=}CRCN$ | Methyl vinyl ketone |
| $CH_2{=}CRCONH_2$ | |

*Coordination or Supported Metal Oxide Catalyst*
$\alpha$-Olefins, including ethylene, dienes, alkyl vinyl ethers

* C. E. Schildknecht, *Ind. Eng. Chem.*, **50**, 107 (1958); F. W. Billmeyer, Jr., *op. cit.*, p. 292.

$$\text{—CH}_2\text{—}\underset{\underset{\text{Cl}}{|}}{\overset{\overset{\text{H}}{|}}{\text{C}}}{}^{\bullet} + {}^{\bullet}\underset{\underset{\text{Cl}}{|}}{\overset{\overset{\text{H}}{|}}{\text{C}}}\text{—CH}_2\text{—} \rightarrow \text{—CH}_2\text{—}\underset{\underset{\text{Cl}}{|}}{\overset{\overset{\text{H}}{|}}{\text{C}}}\text{—}\underset{\underset{\text{Cl}}{|}}{\overset{\overset{\text{H}}{|}}{\text{C}}}\text{—CH}_2\text{—}$$

The second way in which chain growth can be terminated is by disproportionation in which a hydrogen atom is transferred from one chain to the other according to the typical equation

$$\text{—CH}_2\text{—}\underset{\underset{\text{Cl}}{|}}{\overset{\overset{\text{H}}{|}}{\text{C}}}{}^{\bullet} + {}^{\bullet}\underset{\underset{\text{Cl}}{|}}{\overset{\overset{\text{H}}{|}}{\text{C}}}\text{—CH}_2\text{—} \rightarrow \text{—CH}_2\text{—}\underset{\underset{\text{Cl}}{|}}{\overset{\overset{\text{H}}{|}}{\text{C}}}\text{—H} + \underset{\underset{\text{Cl}}{|}}{\overset{\overset{\text{H}}{|}}{\text{C}}}{=}\text{CH—}$$

Both types of termination are encountered in practice: thus, polystyrene terminates chiefly by combination whereas polymethyl methacrylate terminates entirely by disproportionation at temperatures over about 140°F.

Free radicals required to initiate polymerization may be generated in several ways. The usual way is to add a material such as an organic peroxide, hydroperoxide, or azo-compound which decomposes thermally to produce free radicals. Such a material is known as an initiator. A second way to initiate polymerization is by the use of a photochemical initiator such as benzoin which is decomposed into free radicals by ultraviolet light. To be effective, a free radical must be sufficiently reactive to activate the particular reaction, and it should have a fairly long average lifetime. In general, primary radicals are more reactive than secondary, and these in turn are more reactive than tertiary. Unfortunately, however, the average lifetimes of the radicals are inversely proportional to their reactivity, so the choice of the best initiator involves several compromises.

### Inhibitors and Retarders

A free-radical polymerization will be strongly affected by any substance which can react with free radicals to form products incapable of adding monomer. Such a substance is known as an inhibitor or retarder. Theoretically, an inhibitor completely stops the polymerization whereas a retarder simply slows it down; however, in practice, the distinction between the two is one of degree only, and the two words are often used more or less interchangeably.

An inhibitor is often merely a material which produces free radicals such as triphenylmethyl which are themselves too unreactive to initiate a polymer chain, yet can react with the other free radicals which are present and thereby stop the polymerization. In principle, inhibitors can interact either with the free radicals which initiate the polymerization or with the growing polymer chains. However, it is now believed that the chief action of an inhibitor is to stop the growth of the chains, and that inhibitors have little effect on the rate of initiation of chains. Examples of inhibitors are the quinones, particularly benzoquinone, nitrobenzene, nitrosobenzene, amino derivatives, phenols, etc. In some cases, a given material may act as an inhibitor under some conditions and as an initiator under others. For example, oxygen acts as an inhibitor in the polymerization of vinyl acetate, but is an initiator in the polymerization of ethylene.

### Redox Initiators

When a peroxide initiator is used in aqueous solution, its effectiveness can be greatly increased by the addition of a reducing agent. Such a combination is known as a "redox" system. A typical example is the combination of ferrous iron with hydrogen peroxide to produce free radicals in the following way:

$$H_2O_2 + Fe^{+2} \rightarrow OH^{\bullet} + OH^- + Fe^{+3}$$

Other systems which have been used include the following: (a) persulfate initiator with a thiosulfate or bisulfite reducing agent; (b) cumene hydroperoxide with a ferrous or cuprous salt; (c) peroxide initiator plus a heavy metal salt plus a reducing agent such as sugar or thiosulfate.

The great advantage of the redox initiators is that they produce a high rate of radical formation at a fairly low temperature. Since low temperatures inhibit side reactions, normally the properties of a polymer are improved by going to lower polymerization temperatures. Probably the most successful application of redox systems has been in the manufacture of synthetic rubber by the "cold rubber" emulsion process which has essentially replaced the "hot" process used during World War II. This has permitted the continued operation of the synthetic rubber industry, since cold rubber is equal to natural rubber for most applications whereas the hot rubber was definitely inferior to the natural product.

### Ionic Polymerization

Chain-reaction polymerization can occur by several mechanisms other than those involving free radicals. For example, certain ethylene derivatives polymerize readily in the presence of very small quantities of Friedel-Crafts catalysts. In fact some monomers such as isobutylene can only be polymerized in this way. Typical catalysts which may be used include $AlCl_3$, $BF_3$, $AlBr_3$, $TiCl_4$, $SnCl_4$ and $H_2SO_4$. All of these are good electron acceptors and strong lewis acids. In most cases a cocatalyst, usually a proton-yielding substance, must also be used; the cocatalyst evidently reacts with the catalyst to form the true initiator.

The mechanism of the polymerization is usually considered to involve a carbonium ion exchange between the monomer and the catalyst-cocatalyst complex. For example, the $BF_3$-catalyzed polymerization of isobutylene involves first the formation of active complex between the catalyst and cocatalyst

$$BF_3 + RH \rightarrow BF_3R^-H^+$$

This complex then donates a proton to an isobutylene molecule to initiate polymerization according to the reaction

$$BF_3R^-H^+ + (CH_3)_2C{=}CH_2 \rightarrow BF_3R^- + (CH_3)_3C^+ \rightarrow$$

$$H_3C-\underset{\underset{CH_3}{|}}{\overset{\overset{CH_3}{|}}{C}}-CH_2-\underset{\underset{CH_3}{|}}{\overset{\overset{CH_3}{|}}{C}}{}^+ \quad \text{etc.}$$

The polymerization then proceeds by head-to-tail addition of monomer to give a growing chain which is at all times a carbonium ion.

This type of polymerization is known as cationic polymerization, and has several very remarkable features. Thus, cationic polymerization is often extremely rapid; for example, isobutylene may be polymerized in a few seconds at $-150°F$ to yield a polymer having molecular weights up to several million. Both the rate of polymerization and the molecular weight of the polymer increase with decrease of temperature; in fact, cationic polymerization often proceeds best at temperatures as low as $-180°F$. The rate of polymerization tends to increase with the dielectric constant of the solvent in which the polymerization is carried out. Free-radical inhibitors often have little effect on cationic polymerization; however, any material which reacts with the catalyst can prevent the reaction, and many compounds are known which will inhibit cationic polymerization.

In addition to those polymerizations which are catalyzed by cations, there are also some monomers such as acrylonitrile and styrene in which the polymerization is catalyzed by anions. Typical catalysts include sodium in liquid ammonia, alkali-metal alkyls, triphenylmethylsodium and various Grignard reagents. Such catalysts are all capable of providing negative ions, and it is assumed that the mechanism of the polymerization is the same as in the case of cationic polymerization. It is of interest to note that anionic polymerization was carried out commercially before the mechanism of the polymerization was known. Thus, the buna-type of synthetic rubber had been produced for many years in Germany and the Soviet Union by the polymerization of butadiene with a catalyst of either sodium or potassium, and some time later it was shown that this polymerization involves an anionic chain reaction.

### Cross-linked Addition Polymers

Since a double bond is bifunctional, addition polymers such as polyethylene and polystyrene should consist of linear chains only. In practice, a growing chain may interact with one which has previously been terminated, or else a hydrogen atom may transfer from one chain to another, thereby opening up a double bond which can cause branching. Another example is the case of polyethylene, which is found to be quite branched when polymerized at a high temperature. Here the branching is attributed to transient ring formation, with subsequent polymerization to produce branches containing only a few chain atoms.

However, a cross-linked addition polymer can be readily obtained by the use of a polyfunctional monomer such as a divinyl or diene. For example, 0.1 per cent divinylbenzene in polystyrene leads to the formation of an insoluble, thermosetting, cross-linked polymer in which divinyl bridges link linear polystyrene chains. The polymerization of a diene always leaves one double bond which does not take part in the polymerization. Thus, in the case of natural rubber, these double bonds can be cross-linked by the use of materials such as sulfur which can link chains together by adding across the double bonds. Cross-linking strongly affects the strength, hardness, elasticity and other properties of the polymer.

### Thermodynamics and Kinetics of Addition Polymerization

The heat of polymerization can be obtained either by calorimetric experiments, by measurements of the heats of combustion of monomer and polymer or by calculation of the bond energies. The polymerization reactions are quite exothermic, heats of polymerization ranging roughly from 10,000-25,000 cal/mole of monomer. Similarly, the free energies of reaction are also quite favorable, so that the thermodynamic equilibrium is virtually 100 per cent to the right.

In the case of free-radical polymerization, the rate of formation of free radicals by decomposition of the initiator is proportional to the concentration of the initiator in the monomer. Thus,

$$\frac{dC_r}{dt} = k_1 C_i \tag{19-4}$$

where $C_i$ is the concentration of the initiator and $C_r$ is the concentration of free radicals in the material. Of the free radicals which are formed, a certain fraction $f$ will initiate chains. Thus, if $C_p$ is the concentration of growing polymer chains,

$$\frac{dC_p}{dt} = f k_1 C_i \tag{19-5}$$

The termination step involves combination or disproportionation, both of which involve an interaction of one chain with another. Thus, the rate of disappearance of polymer chains is proportional to the square of the concentration, namely,

$$-\frac{dC_p}{dt} = k_2 C_p^2 \tag{19-6}$$

Under steady-state conditions, the rate of formation of polymer chains must equal the rate of disappearance. Hence,

$$k_2 C_p^2 = f k_1 C_i \quad \text{or} \quad C_p = (f k_1 C_i / k_2)^{1/2} \tag{19-7}$$

Thus, the concentration of growing polymer chains and hence the initial rate of polymerization is theoretically proportional to the square root of the initiator concentration. This has been confirmed experimentally for many different polymers; typical results are given in Fig. 19-3.

Ionic polymerizations are so fast that it is difficult to measure experimentally the kinetics of the polymerization. In some cases the rate appears to be directly proportional to the catalyst concentration, indicating that the termination reaction is also first-order. However, other rate equations have been observed, so there is still some uncertainty concerning the mechanism of these polymerizations.

Activation energies have been measured for both types of reaction. In free-radical polymerizations, activation energies are about 4000-8000 cal/mole for the propagation reaction and from 0-5000 cal/mole for the termination reaction. In ionic polymerizations, activation energies are usually quite low; in fact, some negative activation energies have been reported. The fact that these polymerizations take place rapidly at very low temperature is, of course, possible only if the activation energies are very small.

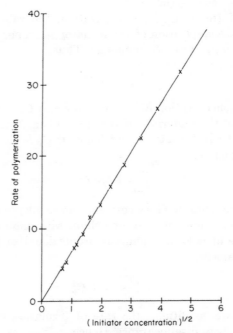

FIG. 19-3. Rate of polymerization of methyl methacrylate with $\alpha,\alpha'$-azobisisobutyronitrile initiator [L. M. Arnett, *Jour. Am. Chem. Soc.*, **74**, 2027 (1952)].

## COPOLYMERIZATION

Several of the most important addition polymers are obtained by polymerizing a mixture of two different monomers to obtain a copolymer in which the polymer chains contain repeating units derived from both monomers. The properties of a copolymer are entirely different from a physical mixture of the two individual polymers. Thus, it is often possible in a copolymer to combine the good qualities of each polymer, whereas a physical mixture often merely emphasizes the bad ones. For example, the copolymer of vinyl acetate and vinyl chloride combines the higher softening point of polyvinyl chloride with the greater thermal stability of polyvinyl acetate.

When two monomers are polymerized together, the composition of the copolymer, in general, will not be the same as that of the monomer mixture. The difference in composition results from the fact that one monomer will usually tend to polymerize more rapidly than the other (higher reactivity), and thus the copolymer formed in the early stages will be richer in the more reactive monomer. If we consider the copolymerization of two monomers A and B, the polymerization occurs by a combination of the following four reactions: (a) A adds to A. (b) A adds to B. (c) B adds to A. (d) B adds to B. The composition of the copolymer will depend on the relative rates of these four reactions.

If the system is ideal, the rate of addition depends only on the concentration and reactivity of each monomer, and is not affected by the nature of the end group on the growing chain. Under these conditions, the repeating units will occur at random along the chains, and there will be no ordered structure in the polymer. However, in some cases, a polymer radical reacts more readily with a monomer of a different type than with its own type. This produces an alternating copolymer in which the monomer units tend to alternate regularly in the chain regardless of the composition of the monomer solution. Theoretically, a third type of polymerization is also possible in which the polymer radicals tend to react only with similar monomer units; however, this type of copolymerization is not encountered in practice, and all cases which have been studied lie somewhere between ideal and alternating.

The composition of a copolymer is not significantly affected by changes in temperature, solvents, initiator or the possible presence or absence of inhibitors. However, changing from a free-radical to an ionic polymerization causes a substantial change in the reactivities of the monomers, and thus usually affects the nature of the copolymer. In commercial practice, if one monomer is appreciably more reactive than the other, copolymerization is carried out by starting with a solution having such a concentration as to produce a copolymer having the desired composition; the more reactive monomer is then fed continuously to the reactor so that the composition of the copolymer remains essentially constant during the course of the polymerization.

### Block and Graft Copolymers

A block copolymer consists of one in which blocks of repeating units of one type alternate with blocks of another type. Thus, a typical block copolymer would have a structure . . . -AAAAAAABBBBBBBBBAAAAA- . . . . Block copolymers are produced by the introduction of end groups which can be made to react under different conditions. This is simple in the case of condensation polymerization, since it is necessary only to prepare two low molecular-weight homopolymers, and then mix them to allow further polymerization to form a block structure. However, it is much harder to produce an addition copolymer in a block structure. Various techniques which have been used include the use of end groups which can be later induced to form free radicals, the use of an initiator which decomposes in two separate steps, etc.

From a commercial standpoint, the graft copolymers are more important because they are easier to manufacture. A graft copolymer consists of a linear polymer chain of one type to which has been grafted side chains of a different type of polymer. Graft copolymers may be produced by chemical grafting, radiation grafting or chain transfer. In chemical grafting, a unit such as a peroxide group is introduced into the polymer chain, and this is then used for attaching a second type of polymer. In radiation grafting, gamma radiation is used to produce active centers for attaching the second polymer. In chain transfer, polymerization of a monomer is carried out in the presence of a preformed polymer of a different type, and a suitable catalyst is used to graft the growing chains onto the preformed polymer by chain transfer. In practice, chain transfer is the usual method of producing graft copolymers.

The importance of the block and graft copolymers is that the resultant material tends to exhibit the properties of each homopolymer. For example, pure polystyrene is quite brittle, whereas polymerization in the presence of about 5 per cent rubber produces a material which is strong and tough. Polyacrylonitrile is an excellent textile fiber, but is difficult to dye; by copolymerization or by grafting on a second polymer, it is possible to maintain the desirable properties of the fiber, yet produce a textile which can be processed in the usual way.

## STEREOSPECIFIC POLYMERIZATION

From measurements of the crystal structure of hydrocarbons, it is known that unsubstituted paraffin chains have a zig-zag planar structure of the form

$$\cdots C \diagup^{C} \diagdown_{C} \diagup^{C} \diagdown_{C} \diagup^{C} \diagdown_{C} \cdots$$

In studying the structure of polymers, it is convenient to similarly depict the polymer chain in the fully extended planar state, and locate substituent groups with reference to this plane. Two different types of geometrical arrangement are observed. Some arrangements such as *cis* vs. *trans* isomers and head-to-head vs. head-to-tail polymerization can only be changed by the breaking of chemical bonds. Such arrangements are commonly called "configurations." However, other arrangements such as the location of a constituent above or below the plane of the polymer can be changed by rotation about a single bond. Such arrangements are commonly called "conformations."

Consider now the case of a polymer such as polystyrene, and assume that the polymerization is all of the head-to-tail type. In solution or in the molten state, the individual polymer chains will be in constant motion, and the phenyl radicals which are attached to the chain will assume many different conformations. When the polymer becomes solid, this free motion is restricted and the polymer chains assume a conformation such as the following:

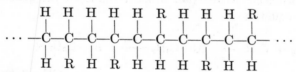

where the phenyl groups R are located at random either above or below the plane of the polymer chain. Such a random arrangement is known as an atactic polymer. Because the bulky phenyl group prevents close approach of the chains, atactic polystyrene is noncrystalline.

However, under some conditions, it is possible to obtain polystyrene in a stereoregular form in which all the phenyl groups are located on the same side of the plane:

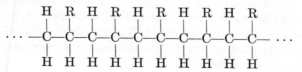

Such an arrangement is known as an isotactic polymer. Isotactic polymers are crystalline because of the ordered structure and the fact that the polymer chains can approach each other more closely.

Another ordered structure which is possible in a polymer is one in which the groups alternate regularly along the chain:

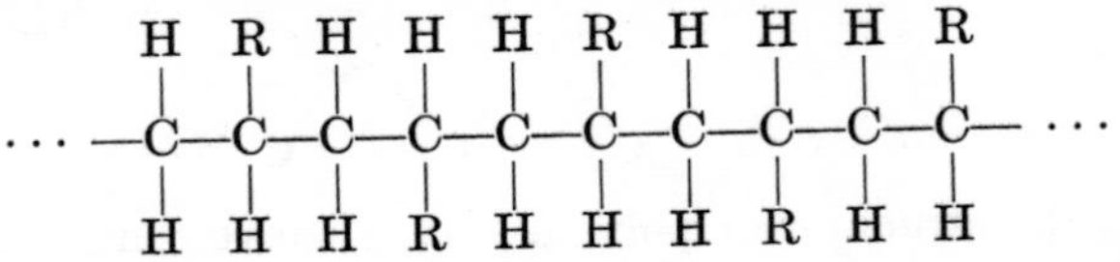

Such an arrangement is known as a syndiotactic polymer. This type of structure is commonly found in the natural polymers, but is rather rare in the synthetic polymers. However, by the proper choice of catalyst, it is possible to produce syndiotactic forms of polymethyl methacrylate, poly-1,2-butadiene and others to a lesser degree.

### Ziegler Catalysts

In 1949, K. Ziegler and his co-workers at the Max Planck Institute for Coal Research discovered that aluminum alkyls will react with ethylene to form higher alkyls, which can then be converted to alcohols or linear $\alpha$-olefins. This reaction was discussed in Chapter 18. In the course of one of Ziegler's experiments, ethylene and aluminum triethyl were reacted in an autoclave which accidentally contained traces of colloidal nickel. Instead of forming the expected higher alkyls, an almost quantitative yield of 1-butylene was obtained. Evidently the presence of the nickel caused a displacement reaction which terminated the growth of the alkyls by the equation

$$\text{Al—C}_2\text{H}_5 + \text{C}_2\text{H}_4 \rightarrow \text{Al—C}_4\text{H}_9 \xrightarrow{\text{C}_2\text{H}_4} \text{Al—C}_2\text{H}_5 + \text{CH}_2\text{=CH—CH}_2\text{—CH}_3$$

Further investigation of this unexpected "nickel effect" showed that cobalt and platinum were also active catalysts for the displacement reaction. An experiment was then carried out using zirconium acetylacetonate as cocatalyst, and instead of obtaining a lower $\alpha$-olefin, a white mass of polyethylene was formed. Further study of this second unexpected result showed that the combination of an aluminum alkyl and a transition metal of Groups IV-VIII of the periodic table served as an active catalyst for the polymerization of olefins. However, of even greater importance was the discovery by G. Natta and his co-workers that the Ziegler catalysts produce crystalline stereospecific polymers which have unique physical properties.

A Ziegler catalyst contains the following two types of metallic compounds: (a) metal hydrides or metal alkyls of Groups I-III of the periodic table; (b) transition-metal compounds from Groups IV-VIII of the periodic table. A particularly active catalyst is obtained by the use of a mixture of trialkylaluminum and titanium tetrachloride. In addition to forming a stereopolymer, the Ziegler catalysts also have the great advantage that the polymerization can be carried out at moderate temperature and pressure. For example, the free-radical polymerization of ethylene requires pressures of 1000 atm or more at temperatures as high as 500°F; however, the Ziegler polymerization of ethylene can be carried out at about atmospheric pressure and room temperature.

## Alfin Catalysts

In addition to the Ziegler catalysts, others have been found to yield stereoregular polymers. Probably the most important of these is the Alfin (*al*cohol + ole*fin*) catalyst which consists of a combination of sodium chloride, an alkylenylsodium compound such as allyl sodium, and an alkoxide of a secondary alcohol such as sodium isopropoxide, in an inert solvent such as pentane. The Alfin catalysts are particularly effective in the polymerization of dienes where they show high activity for stereospecific 1,4-polymerization.

## POLYETHYLENE

The total production of polyethylene in the United States in recent years is illustrated in Fig. 19-4. Note the rapid growth of the material. In 1963, the total production of conventional low-density polyethylene was 1754 million pounds, about 35 per cent going into the manufacture of film and sheet, 17 per cent going into export, 12 per cent for extrusion coating on paper and other materials, 11 per cent for injection molding, 10 per cent for coating wire and cable and the remainder for all other minor uses. In addition, 516 million pounds of high-density polyethylene were produced, about 43 per cent of this material going into blow molding and 16 per cent going into injection molding.

The history of polyethylene[1] is extremely interesting and is another example of the unexpected results which can come from research, and of the importance of the role of chance in such work. Up until about 1935, it was generally believed that ethylene could not be polymerized. In 1932, J. C. Swallow and M. W. Perrin of Imperial Chemical In-

[1] A. Renfrew and P. Morgan, "Polythene," London, Iliffe and Sons, Ltd., 1960; S. L. Aggarwal and O. J. Sweeting, *Chem. Rev.*, **57**, 665 (1957).

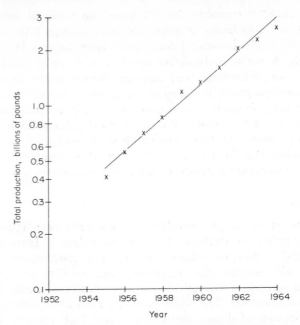

FIG. 19-4. Total United States production of polyethylene in recent years (United States Tariff Commission, Synthetic Organic Chemicals).

dustries, Ltd., suggested that research be carried out on chemical reactions at ultrahigh pressures in the hope that novel effects might be obtained. Some 50 reactions were tried during 1932 and 1933, but the results were all disappointing. However, one of the experiments carried out in March 1933 involved the reaction between ethylene and benzaldehyde at 170°C and 1400 atm pressure. The walls of the vessel were coated with a thin layer of a "white waxy solid" which was recognized as a polymer of ethylene. However, when the experiment was repeated with ethylene alone, there was an explosive decomposition into carbon, hydrogen and methane which destroyed the apparatus. Experiments were then temporarily suspended while more suitable apparatus was designed.

In December 1935 the experiment was again tried, and 8 grams of white powdery polyethylene were obtained. Later it was found that the success of the experiment was the result of a leak at one of the joints in the apparatus. This necessitated the addition of fresh ethylene to replace that which had leaked out, and by a coincidence the added ethylene contained about the right amount of oxygen necessary to catalyze the polymerization.

## High-pressure Process

The high-pressure process involves the direct reaction

$$nC_2H_4 \rightarrow \cdots -\underset{\underset{H}{|}}{\overset{\overset{H}{|}}{C}}-\underset{\underset{H}{|}}{\overset{\overset{H}{|}}{C}}-\underset{\underset{H}{|}}{\overset{\overset{H}{|}}{C}}-\underset{\underset{H}{|}}{\overset{\overset{H}{|}}{C}}- \cdots$$

$$\Delta H^{\circ}_{298} = -22,300 \qquad \Delta F^{\circ}_{298} = -12,200$$

with various possible side reactions such as

$$C_2H_4 \rightarrow 2C + 2H_2 \qquad \Delta H^{\circ}_{298} = -12,500 \qquad \Delta F^{\circ}_{298} = -16,282$$

$$C_2H_4 \rightarrow C + CH_4 \qquad \Delta H^{\circ}_{298} = -30,385 \qquad \Delta F^{\circ}_{298} = -28,422$$

Thus, the polymerization is possible only by the use of a selective polymerization catalyst. Free-radical catalysts which may be used as initiators include oxygen, peroxides such as benzoyl peroxide, hydroperoxides, azo compounds, etc.

Commercially, the polymerization is carried out at pressures of about 1500 atm, temperatures of 375-410°F, using 0.03-0.10 per cent $O_2$ as catalyst. The ethylene must be of high purity ($\sim$99.5 per cent $C_2H_4$) and free from unsaturates such as acetylene. Since the critical temperature of ethylene is about 50°F, it cannot be liquefied at the temperatures used for the polymerization.

Because of the high pressures and the necessity of maintaining close temperature control, the polymerization is commonly carried out continuously in stainless steel tubular reactors. A diluent such as benzene or water may be added to permit better control of the exothermic reaction. If an organic diluent is used, both the monomer and polymer are soluble at the temperatures and pressures which are used, so that a true solution polymerization is obtained.

The ICI (Imperial Chemical Industries) high-pressure polyethylene process is illustrated in Fig. 19-5. Ethylene feed is purified by distillation to give 99.8 per cent $C_2H_4$ or better, and is then mixed with oxygen and compressed to 1500 atm. The polymerization takes place at 375°F with special means to maintain isothermal conditions. About 25 per cent of the ethylene is converted per pass. Reactor effluent passes to a separator which recycles ethylene back to an intermediate stage of the gas compressor. Liquid from the separator consists of viscous water-white polyethylene which is extruded, cooled, and chopped for storage and shipment. The product has a molecular weight of 18,000-30,000 and the over-all yield based on ethylene is about 95 per cent.

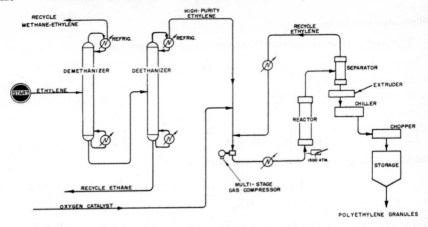

FIG. 19-5. I.C.I. high pressure polyethylene process [*Hydro. Proc. Petrol. Refiner.*, **40**(11), 286 (1961)]. Copyright 1961, Gulf Pub. Co., Houston, Texas.

This process is subject to modification, depending on the particular physical properties desired for the polyethylene. For example, in the water-solvent process the feed consists of a 1.0:1.0:1.5 mixture of ethylene, benzene and water. The water contains about 100 ppm of oxygen which serves as initiator. This mixture is fed to a stainless steel tubular reactor, water carrying additional initiator being injected at multiple points along the reactor. About 17 per cent of the ethylene is converted to polymer. The polyethylene dissolves in the benzene, and is ultimately separated by distilling off benzene from the nonvolatile polymer.

### Properties of High-pressure Polyethylene

The ICI process still accounts for most of the world's production of polyethylene. The characteristic feature of high-pressure polyethylene is its lower density (0.91-0.94) and moderate crystallinity (50-60 per cent). It melts at about 240°F and is soluble in many solvents at temperatures over about 200°F. Although no room-temperature solvents are known to exist, several materials cause swelling and/or cracking of polyethylene at room temperature.

Low-density polyethylene contains branched chains of two distinct types. The first type of branching is produced by intermolecular chain transfer of the type

$$R_1\text{—}CH_2\text{—} \cdots \text{—}CH_2^{\bullet} + R_2CH_2 \cdots CH_2R_3 \rightarrow$$

*propagating chain*      *"dead" polymer chain*

$$R_1\text{—}CH_2\text{—} \cdots CH_3 + R_2CH^{\bullet} \cdots CH_2R_3$$

*new propagating chain*

This type leads to branches which are approximately as long as the main polymer chain. However, the second type of branching is far more common, and involves the formation of short branches normally containing 4 or 2 carbon atoms in the branch. This type of branching is attributed to intramolecular chain transfer involving transient ring formation such as

## High-density Polyethylene

The development of the Ziegler catalysts permitted the polymerization of ethylene to be carried out at low temperatures and pressures. The resultant polymer is referred to variously as linear polyethylene, low-temperature polyethylene or high-density polyethylene. The characteristic features of the polymer are an essentially linear structure with very little branching, over 90 per cent crystallinity, a density of 0.95-0.97 and a melting point of about 275°F.

In spite of the advantage of operating at a lower temperature and pressure, high-density polyethylene is more expensive because of the added costs of catalyst preparation and separation of polymer from the reaction mixture. High-density polyethylene is harder, stiffer, and has a greater tensile strength than the low-density material. Because of these advantages, it is widely used for injection molding of housewares and toys, production of bottles by blow molding and the manufacture of pipe. Increasing quantities of linear polyethylene are going into the manufacture of fibers; however, the material has the substantial disadvantage that it cannot be ironed because of the low melting point.

The original Ziegler process for the polymerization of ethylene has undergone many modifications, and several versions are now being operated commercially. In general, the polymerization is carried out at pressures ranging from atmospheric to less than 100 atm and at temperatures ranging from room temperature to about 200°F. The first step in the process involves the preparation of the catalyst. This is commonly done by adding a solution of a metal salt such as titanium tetrachloride to a metal alkyl such as triethylaluminum. An exothermic reaction occurs in which a colored precipitate is formed and the titanium is reduced to a lower valence, predominantly the trichloride. On the addition of a solvent such as a hydrocarbon, part of the precipitate is dispersed as a colloidal suspension which is an active catalyst for the polymerization.

The polymerization is carried out continuously in an agitated reactor, cooling being provided to remove the heat of reaction. Because of the high reactivity of the aluminum alkyls, it is essential that all reactants be dry and free from oxygen and other unsaturates such as acetylene. Ethylene is fed under moderate pressure, dissolves in the solvent and is converted to the polymer. The solvent helps in the dispersion of the catalyst, and permits better agitation of the reaction mixture as it becomes full of solid polymer. Since titanium trichloride is insoluble, the actual polymerization is a surface reaction in which ethylene diffuses to the surface of the titanium trichloride where the reaction occurs. However, there is still considerable uncertainty as to the actual mechanism of the reaction, in spite of a large amount of work which has been reported in the literature.

One substantial disadvantage of the Ziegler process is the fact that the catalyst tends to color the polymer, and hence a fairly elaborate purification is required. Thus, after polymerization, the catalyst is destroyed or "killed" to permit removal from the product. This may be done by the addition of either alcohol or water to react with the alkyls, followed by filtration of the polymer slurry. Further purification is then carried out by washing with water or dilute acid to remove metallic impurities, heating under vacuum to remove volatile solvent, etc. The purified polymer is then dried, mixed with pigments and antioxidants, and processed to give the conventional molding powder required by the plastics industry.

An annoying problem which is encountered in the polymerization of ethylene or propylene using Ziegler catalysts is the sticking or "bagging" of the polymer to the walls of the reactor, agitator and processing vessels. These deposits reduce the transfer of heat and increase the horsepower required for agitation. Periodically the reactor must be shut down and the accumulated deposits cleaned by heating in the presence of a suitable solvent.

It must be emphasized that the above description of the Ziegler process gives only typical operating conditions, and each manufacturer operates in a different way, depending on the availability of patents and proprietary information. Thus, the catalyst may be either premixed, or the alkyl and metal chloride may be charged separately to the reactor. The nature of the catalyst and the method of preparation are both very important, since these determine the catalyst activity and the molecular weight of the product. Polymerization conditions are variable over wide limits, and may be deliberately changed to modify the nature of the polymer.

## Other Low-pressure Processes

The Phillips Petroleum Co. process involves the use of an inorganic catalyst such as $Cr_2O_3$ on a silica-alumina support. Catalyst, ethylene and a solvent such as cyclohexane or xylene are charged to a reactor at a temperature of 200-300°F and a pressure of 100-500 psig. Both ethylene and polyethylene are soluble in the solvent under these conditions. Reactor effluent passes to a flash drum which vaporizes dissolved ethylene and some solvent, and the polymer solution is then filtered to remove catalyst. The solution is cooled, and an antisolvent such as water added to facilitate precipitation of polymer from the solution. Polymer is then dried and converted to molding powder in the usual way. Over-all yield of polymer is about 98 per cent, based on ethylene feed.

The success of the Phillips process is very much dependent on the catalyst. From patents, the catalyst consists of 1-3 per cent $Cr_2O_3$, possibly stabilized with SrO, supported on a commercial cracking catalyst base of 90:10 silica-alumina. Various metal oxides can be used as promoters. The catalyst is activated by heating for several hours at temperatures over 750°F, using a mixture of steam and air. Both the molecular weight and the physical properties of the polymer are dependent on the type of catalyst which is used and the temperature of activation.

Standard Oil of Indiana has developed a similar process for the manufacture of polyethylene. The following two types of catalyst are described in patents: (a) nickel and/or cobalt supported on activated charcoal; (b) molybdenum oxide supported on alumina and other oxides. The molybdenum catalyst is more effective, and is presumably the one used commercially. Various promoters, chiefly alkali and alkaline earth compounds, have been disclosed in patents. Activation is carried out by heating in a reducing atmosphere at temperatures of about 600°F or greater to convert the hexavalent molybdenum to valences in the range of 3-5.

The polymerization is carried out at temperatures of 450-520°F and pressures of 40-80 atm in the presence of a solvent. Unconverted ethylene is flashed, the polymer solution filtered to remove catalyst and solvent stripped by distillation. Molten polymer is extruded, cooled and processed in the conventional way.

## POLYPROPYLENE

Polymers of propylene range all the way from low polymers such as the trimer and tetramer through polymer gasoline and polymer oils up to crystalline polymers similar to polyethylene. Early attempts to produce high polymers of propylene resulted only in liquid or semiliquid polymers of no value. However, the development of Ziegler catalysts permitted the production of crystalline polypropylene having molecular weights up to about 100,000. First commercial production was by Montecatini in Italy starting in 1957. Since then there has been a modest growth, with a total United States production of about 197 million pounds in 1963. About half the polypropylene goes into injection molding and about 40 per cent is extruded to form rope, fibers, seat covers, etc.

Polypropylene has a density of about 0.90, and is the lightest plastic known. It has a higher tensile strength and greater rigidity than polyethylene, excellent electrical properties and good chemical resistance. Polypropylene also shows less shrinkage during cooling, a substantial advantage in injection molding. However, in spite of these advantages, there is no denying the fact that polypropylene has been a disappointment in recent years. Thus, the 1963 polypropylene capacity in the United States was estimated to be 465 million pounds/year, more than twice the 1963 production.

Why is there this great discrepancy between capacity and production? First, polypropylene is more expensive than polyethylene, and hence has had problems in competing in markets where polyethylene is firmly entrenched. Second, much polypropylene capacity is probably based on the desire of the HPI to dispose in some way of the large quantities of propylene available from refinery operations. Third, polypropylene is made in essentially the same way as low-temperature polyethylene, and hence the same equipment may be used interchangeably for the two olefins. Most manufacturers are still optimistic about the future of polypropylene, and there appears to be a general feeling that polypropylene may be just entering a period of very rapid growth.

### Manufacture of Polypropylene

Polypropylene is produced commercially[1] by low-temperature polymerization using Ziegler catalysts. The polymerization is carried out in the presence of a diluent such as a $C_6$ or $C_7$ paraffinic hydrocarbon at tem-

---

[1] The Montecatini process is described in the *Hydro. Proc. Petrol. Refiner*, **42**(11), 219 (1963); see also M. Sittig, *Ibid.*, **40**(3), 129 (1961); H. W. Haines, Jr., *Ind. Eng. Chem.*, **55**(2), 31 (1963).

peratures ranging from room temperature to about 250°F and pressures from atmospheric to about 150 psig. The usual catalyst is a mixture of titanium tetrachloride and an aluminum alkyl. However, it is desirable that the alkyl contain the same number of carbon atoms as the monomer; thus, aluminum tripropyl should be used, not aluminum triethyl. If the latter were used for the polymerization of propylene, the ethyl groups would be replaced by propylene and ethylene would be incorporated into the polymer.

Following polymerization, unreacted propylene is flashed from solution, the catalyst is killed by the addition of alcohol or water and the polymer is purified as in the case of polyethylene. Depending on the catalyst which is used and the reaction conditions, polypropylene can be made in the isotactic, syndiotactic or atactic form. Isotactic polypropylene is a linear polymer having a melting point of about 349°F. The crystallinity of the commercial product normally varies from about 90-98 per cent.

Polypropylene may also be produced by both the Phillips process and the Standard Oil process, using the conventional fixed-bed supported catalyst. However, the polymer produced by these processes is considerably less crystalline than that produced by the Ziegler process. Copolymers of ethylene and propylene may also be produced by any of the processes used to produce propylene. The copolymers have properties intermediate between the two homopolymers. These copolymers have potentially a very large market in the rubber industry, and hence are discussed in more detail in the section on synthetic elastomers.

## OTHER POLYOLEFINS

Relatively low molecular-weight polymers may be produced by polymerization of butylenes. These have found limited use in the manufacture of adhesives, cements, sealing and insulating materials, etc. It is also possible to produce high molecular-weight isotactic polymers of olefins such as 1-butylene, but these have not achieved any commercial importance. In practice, the only important $C_4$ olefin polymer is butyl rubber, a copolymer of isobutylene and isoprene. This will be discussed in the section on elastomers.

## POLYVINYL CHLORIDE

Polyvinyl chloride is by far the most important of the vinyl polymers. Thus, total production of polyvinyl chloride and copolymer resins in the United States for 1963 was about 1386 million pounds. Polyvinyl chloride has been growing at an average annual rate of 11 per cent over the past 10 years. The chief uses of polyvinyl chloride are as follows: (a) About 36 per cent of the material is calendered to form film, sheet and floor covering. These go into the manufacture of raincoats, handbags, shower curtains, vinyl flooring, etc. (b) About 23 per cent of the material is extruded in the form of insulation for wire and cable, garden hose, plastic pipe, etc. (c) About 13 per cent of the material goes into coating and adhesive resins such as in the manufacture of coated fabrics, as a coating for paper and flooring, etc. (d) About 10 per cent of the material goes into conventional and "slush" molding of phonograph records, dolls, rainboots, etc.

### Polymerization of Vinyl Chloride

The commercial production of polyvinyl chloride[1] started in the early 1930's in Germany and the United States. Initial work was directed largely toward the production of a material having elastomeric properties. However, it was soon found that the properties of the polymer could be varied from rubbery products to rigid plastics; this opened up additional markets for the polymer, and hence the growth has been very rapid in recent years.

Pure vinyl chloride is a relatively insensitive monomer. However, traces of oxygen or water lead to the formation of peroxides which are shock sensitive and which can initiate polymerization and side reactions in the monomer. The first attempts to polymerize vinyl chloride were based on bulk and solution polymerization methods. These were commercially unsatisfactory because of problems of heat removal, solvent recovery and product handling. However, it was found that polymerization could be readily achieved with little rise in temperature by the use of a suspension or emulsion of vinyl chloride in water. This basic process is still used, and has changed little over the past 30 years.

In practice, most polyvinyl chloride is manufactured in a batch process, using suspension polymerization. A typical flow diagram is illustrated in Fig. 19-6. Water and vinyl chloride monomer are charged to a several thousand gallon jacketed glass-lined or stainless steel autoclave fitted with an anchor agitator. The ratio of water to vinyl chloride varies from 1.5 to 3.5, depending on the suspending agent which is used. The three principal suspending agents are gelatin, methyl cellulose and polyvinyl alcohol. Approximately 0.1-0.3 per cent lauroyl or caproyl peroxide is added as a free-radical initiator, agitation is started and the material

---

[1] John T. Barr, Jr., "Polyvinyl Chloride," chapter in J. J. McKetta, Jr., Vol. 7, *op. cit.*

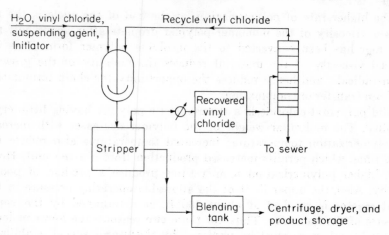

FIG. 19-6. Flowsheet for polyvinyl chloride.

heated to 120-140°F to start the polymerization. The pressure varies from about 75-125 psig, as determined by the temperature and the vapor pressure of vinyl chloride monomer.

For a successful polymerization, the monomer must be present as small droplets which do not agglomerate during polymerization. An inert atmosphere such as nitrogen or carbon dioxide is commonly maintained above the liquid to give a faster polymerization and a better product. After the reaction starts, cooling must be provided to remove the heat of polymerization. The total reaction time is usually 10-20 hr. After about 90 per cent conversion to polymer has been obtained, the pressure has dropped by some 40 psig and the cycle is terminated, since further reaction is harmful to resin color and porosity. The batch is dropped to a stripper, 8-10 per cent unreacted monomer is recovered, and the stripped batch is blended with other batches to form a more uniform product. The polymer slurry is then centrifuged, washed, dried and sent to product storage. All parts of the plant in contact with monomer or polymer are stainless steel or glass lined to prevent iron pickup, and insure the production of a quality product.

The rate of polymerization of vinyl chloride shows a rather interesting relationship with time. Thus, about 25 per cent of the polymerization occurs in the last hour and about 50 per cent in the last 3 hours, which results in a high heat load in the last portion of the cycle. This effect is partly caused by the presence of inhibitors and impurities in the original charge, and also partly by an increase in the number of initiating radicals from the decomposition of the peroxide. However, the chief reason for the higher rate of polymerization at the end of the cycle is the increased viscosity of the monomer-polymer droplets after about half the monomer has been converted to the insoluble polymer form. This increased viscosity of the material reduces the mobility of the growing chain-radicals, and hence reduces the opportunity for chain termination by chain transfer or combination.

Solid polyvinyl chloride is a thermoplastic polymer having little crystallinity. The molecular weight of the polymer decreases with increase in polymerization temperature; increased temperatures also reduce the cycle time, which permits increased production from a given unit. However, higher polymerization temperatures produce a product of poorer quality. Also, the upper limit of the allowable operating pressure in the usual reactor is reached at about 160°F, as determined by the vapor pressure of the monomer. Thus, for these two reasons, the lower molecular-weight polymers must be prepared by the use of special stabilizers or chain transfer agents during the polymerization.

### Emulsion Polymerization

Historically, the first commercial production of polyvinyl chloride was by emulsion polymerization. Although it became less popular after suspension methods were developed, emulsion polymerization is widely used for the manufacture of other polymers, and still finds some use in the manufacture of polyvinyl chloride.

Emulsion polymerization differs from suspension polymerization in two ways, namely, the initiator is located in the aqueous phase and the individual particles in the dispersed organic phase are much smaller than in the case of suspension polymerization. The emulsion is obtained by the use of soap to stabilize the small droplets of monomer. In addition, the soap has the important function of forming "micelles", which are layered aggregates of perhaps 50-100 soap molecules containing a very thin layer of monomer. Polymerization starts within the micelles by diffusion of monomer through the aqueous phase. Soon the polymer particles grow larger than the original micelles, and further polymerization takes place within the polymer particles which are already formed. The rate of polymerization is roughly constant until about 60-80 per cent of the monomer has polymerized; by this time the individual monomer droplets have disappeared, and any further polymerization occurs as a result of unconverted monomer which exists within the polymer particles.

In the emulsion polymerization of vinyl chloride, an approximately 2:1 mixture of water and vinyl chloride is agitated with about 1.0 per cent ammonium stearate soap and 0.1 per cent ammonium persulfate initiator. The mixture is polymerized at 105-130°F for 12-18 hr, and the resulting latex stripped of monomer and spray dried to produce a finely divided product. This basic process is subject to many variations such as the use of sulfated esters or other synthetic emulsifiers in place of the soap, etc. In some cases, a chain transfer agent such as dodecyl mercaptan is also used to control molecular weight and aid in the transfer of free radicals from the aqueous to the polymer phases.

## POLYVINYL ACETATE

Polyvinyl acetate was first developed commercially by Shawinigan Chemicals, Ltd., in Canada in 1925, and production in the United States and Germany started in about 1930. The polymer has had a modest growth in recent years, and is expected to continue to grow at a rate of about 9 per cent a year over the immediate future. Total production in the United States for 1963 was about 241 million pounds. About 42 per cent of the polyvinyl acetate goes into adhesives of both the emulsion and hot-melt type, 33 per cent goes into the production of water-based emulsion paint, and smaller quantities are used as a binder for textiles, in the coating of paper, in industrial finishes, for chewing gum, etc. The present growth of polyvinyl acetate is largely the result of the increased use of the latex paints, particularly the outdoor paints.

Vinyl acetate undergoes free-radical polymerization to form a thermoplastic atactic linear polymer. However, vinyl acetate has a tendency to undergo chain transfer with the abstraction of hydrogen either from the acetate group or from the tertiary hydrogen on one of the carbon atoms of the main polymer chain. Thus, polyvinyl acetate contains two types of branches, namely, those attached to the main chain and those attached to acetate groups. The extent of branching during polymerization depends on the per cent conversion and whether or not a solvent is used. Branching is nearly absent if the conversion of monomer is limited to about 20-30 per cent, but increases substantially with higher conversions.

About 90 per cent of the polyvinyl acetate produced in the United States is made by emulsion polymerization. Either batch or continuous polymerization is easily carried out in a jacketed kettle fitted with an agitator. The reaction is carried out at temperatures of 160-200°F, using the conventional soap emulsifier and a water-soluble peroxide or redox initiator. Polymerization is normally stopped at about 70-80 per cent conversion to minimize branching and cross-linking. Residual monomer is then stripped from the emulsion, and the polymer normally sold as an emulsion containing 50-55 per cent by weight of dry resin. All process equipment is usually stainless steel or glass-lined to prevent coloration of the product.

Polyvinyl acetate can also be produced by suspension polymerization and by solution polymerization, using a solvent such as benzene or methanol. In addition, bulk polymerization was carried out commercially in Germany, but the process was not very satisfactory because of problems of heat transfer and sticking of polymer to the surface of processing vessels.

## POLYVINYL ALCOHOL

Vinyl alcohol monomer does not exist because any chemical reaction capable of yielding vinyl alcohol gives instead either acetaldehyde or ethylene oxide by tautomeric interchange of a hydrogen atom:

$$CH_2{=}CHOH \rightarrow CH_3{-}CHO \quad \text{or} \quad CH_2\underset{\diagdown \diagup}{\overset{O}{\phantom{x}}}CH_2$$

However, the polymer of vinyl alcohol is quite stable, and this may be produced from vinyl acetate by an alcoholysis reaction which involves replacement of acetyl groups by hydroxyl groups. Thus, if polyvinyl acetate is reacted with methanol, the following interchange occurs:

$$\cdots -CH_2-CH- \cdots + CH_3OH \rightarrow$$
$$\cdots -CH_2-CH- \cdots + CH_3COOCH_3$$

(with pendant groups: $O$, $C{=}O$, $CH_3$ on the left structure, and $OH$ on the right structure)

The reaction is catalyzed by about 0.5 per cent of either caustic or a mineral acid. In practice, polyvinyl acetate is simply dissolved in the alcohol (methanol or ethanol), the catalyst is added, and the solution is heated. Polyvinyl alcohol precipitates, and can be removed by filtration.

Polyvinyl alcohol is soluble in water, and finds some use as a thickening agent for emulsions, as an adhesive and in the grease-proofing of paper. Since the hydroxyl groups are fairly small, polyvinyl alcohol can also be drawn into a crystalline fiber having essentially the same lattice as polyethylene. The fiber is spun using a solution containing formaldehyde, which introduces formal groups by the reaction

$$\cdots -CH_2-CH-CH_2-CH- \cdots + HCHO \rightarrow$$
$$\qquad\qquad |\qquad\qquad |$$
$$\qquad\quad OH\qquad\quad OH$$

$$\cdots -CH_2-CH-CH_2-CH- \cdots + H_2O$$
$$\qquad\qquad\qquad\quad O\qquad\qquad O$$
$$\qquad\qquad\qquad\qquad \diagdown\qquad\diagup$$
$$\qquad\qquad\qquad\qquad\quad CH_2$$

About one-third of the hydroxyl groups are reacted to render the fiber insoluble. Since polyvinyl alcohol fibers have high water absorption, they have found moderate use as a replacement for cotton where the fiber is in contact with the body.

Another important use of polyvinyl alcohol is in the manufacture of polyvinyl acetals. The most important of these is polyvinyl butyral which is used for the manufacture of safety glass. Polyvinyl alcohol is condensed with butyraldehyde in the presence of a sulfuric acid catalyst to give the reaction

$$\cdots -CH_2-CH-CH_2-CH- \cdots + C_3H_7CHO \rightarrow$$
$$\qquad\qquad |\qquad\qquad |$$
$$\qquad\quad OH\qquad\quad OH$$

$$\cdots -CH_2-CH-CH_2-CH- \cdots + H_2O$$
$$\qquad\qquad\qquad\quad O\qquad\qquad O$$
$$\qquad\qquad\qquad\qquad \diagdown\qquad\diagup$$
$$\qquad\qquad\qquad\qquad\quad CH$$
$$\qquad\qquad\qquad\qquad\quad |$$
$$\qquad\qquad\qquad\qquad\quad C_3H_7$$

The condensation is stopped when about one-fourth of the hydroxyl groups are still left in the polymer; this is essential for the material to have adequate strength and adhesion to glass. The final laminate is made by mixing the polyvinyl butyral with a plasticizer such as dibutyl sebacate, and extruding the material in the form of sheets of approximately 0.015-in. thickness.

## VINYL COPOLYMERS

Several different vinyl copolymers have been developed in order to modify the properties of the individual homopolymers. The most important of these are based on vinyl chloride. For example, a copolymer of 90 per cent vinyl chloride and 10 per cent vinyl acetate can be obtained by solution polymerization; this copolymer has the good mechanical properties of polyvinyl chloride plus the heat stability of polyvinyl acetate. Such copolymers are marketed under names such as "Acrilan," "Zefran," vinyon, "Tygon," etc. A copolymer of 60 per cent vinyl chloride and 40 per cent acrylonitrile is widely used as a textile fiber ("Dynel").

It is also possible to modify the properties of polyvinyl chloride by the use of plasticizers. The most commonly used plasticizers include dioctyl phthalate, trioctyl phosphate, dioctyl sebacate and low molecular-weight polymers such as esters of polypropylene glycol. The plasticizer lowers the glass transition temperature to below room temperature, and thus changes the material from a hard brittle solid to a flexible tough solid. Plasticizers also improve the flow characteristics and hence the processability of the polymer. The plasticizer content varies with the nature of the material, but typically ranges from about 10-30 per cent.

## POLYSTYRENE

Although it was shown as early as 1845 that styrene could be polymerized to a solid transparent polymer, it was not until 1925 that the Naugatuck Chemical Co. started commercial production of styrene monomer. This initial production was short-lived because of problems encountered in the handling of the material, but in the early 1930's Dow Chemical Co. and I. G. Farben in Germany independently started research programs which resulted in the successful production of styrene monomer and polymer. In 1942, the U.S. government decided that emergency wartime production of synthetic rubber would be based on the GR-S (government rubber-styrene) copolymers of butadiene with about 30 per cent styrene. By the end of the war, the production of styrene had increased to 432 million pounds/year, and increasing demands for polystyrene and styrene copolymers have resulted in a further growth which is expected to continue over the immediate future.

In 1963, total production of polystyrene resins in the United States was 1494 million pounds, including 515 million pounds of straight polystyrene, 564 million pounds of rubber-modified polystyrene, 188 million pounds of styrene-butadiene copolymers and 227 million pounds of other copolymers such as ABS (acrylonitrile-butadiene-styrene) and SAN (styrene-acrylonitrile). Approximately half the polystyrene goes into molding powder where it is used to fabricate various plastics such as toys, novelties, housewares, radio and television sets, trays and liners for refrigerators, small containers, etc. About 13 per cent of the polystyrene goes into extrusion materials, 8 per cent goes into the surface treatment of paper and textiles, 3 per cent goes into emulsion paints and the remainder goes into hundreds of other small uses, including export.

## Polymerization of Styrene

Polystyrene may be produced by either free-radical, cationic or anionic polymerization according to the equation

$$CH{=}CH_2 \quad \cdots \; -CH-CH_2-CH-CH_2- \; \cdots$$

$$\Delta H_{298}^{\circ} = -16,500$$

Although isotactic polystyrene can be produced by the use of Ziegler catalysts, the isotactic material is more expensive and offers no significant advantage over the atactic polymer. For this reason, commercial polystyrene is produced as a linear, thermoplastic, atactic polymer. Polystyrene is a hard, clear plastic having good chemical resistance, good dimensional stability and moderate tensile strength. Polystyrene is exceptionally easy to process, and has good stability and flow under injection-molding conditions. It is a good electrical insulator and shows low dielectric loss at moderate frequencies. However, straight polystyrene is quite brittle, undergoes heat distortion at temperatures of about 185°F, has poor resistance to outdoor weathering and is readily attacked by many solvents including the standard dry cleaning solvents.

Commercially, styrene can be polymerized [1] using any of the standard methods including bulk, solution, suspension or emulsion polymerization; however, bulk and suspension polymerization are used most commonly. In the continuous bulk process, styrene monomer is first washed with caustic to remove the inhibitor (*p-tert*-butylcatechol) and is charged to an agitated stainless steel or glass-lined kettle. A peroxide initiator is added, and polymerization allowed to continue at a temperature of 175-185°F until the material becomes as viscous as can be conveniently handled (30-35 per cent polymerization). The kettle product is then discharged to a vertical tower which maintains a temperature gradient from about 220°F at the top to 400°F at the bottom. The viscous polymer slowly passes down the tower, and is extruded at the bottom as a rod which is chopped and made into molding powder.

Suspension polymerization of styrene is carried out in the usual way using agitated kettles up to several thousand gallon capacity. An oil-

[1] N. N. T. Samaras and E. Perry, *J. Appl. Chem.*, **1**, 243 (1951).

soluble initiator is used, and the temperature is normally limited to about 200°F to maintain the pressure below atmospheric. Unreacted monomer is removed by steam distillation, and the small beads or pearls of polystyrene centrifuged and thoroughly dried.

In practice, the molecular weight and physical properties of the polymer are strongly affected by the temperature of polymerization. High temperatures result in a faster reaction, but the polymers are of low molecular weight and are quite brittle. At low temperatures the polymerization is slower, the polymer is of high molecular weight and is tough and difficult to fabricate. Thus, a compromise must be struck between the time of reaction and the properties desired in the final product.

### Modified Polystyrene

In order to overcome the disadvantages of polystyrene such as its brittleness and low softening point, several modified forms of polystyrene are produced commercially. For example, both styrene and polystyrene are compatible with various types of natural and synthetic rubber. Up to 10 or 12 per cent synthetic rubber can be incorporated into the polymer either by mastication of the polymer and the rubber under suitable conditions or by dissolving the rubber in styrene monomer before polymerization. The rubber-modified polystyrene is tougher and has better physical properties, but has a slightly lower softening point and is nontransparent.

The physical properties of polystyrene can also be improved by the use of copolymers. The most important of these is the ABS resin, a copolymer containing 20-30 per cent acrylonitrile, 20-30 per cent butadiene and 40-60 per cent styrene. About 125 million pounds were produced in 1963. The ABS resins are rigid, tough, have high tensile strength, good thermal stability and good resistance to abrasion. The resins are easily processed by extrusion or molding.

The other important copolymer is the SAN resin which contains about 73 per cent styrene and 27 per cent acrylonitrile. About 32 million pounds were produced in 1963. The major use of this copolymer is for household and industrial articles that must stand attack by polishes, detergents, and cleaning agents.

Two other forms of polystyrene have shown rapid growth in recent years. Polystyrene foam is made by incorporating about 10 per cent of a volatile hydrocarbon such as pentane or butane in polystyrene granules or beads. The material can then be expanded to a density as low as 1 lb/ft$^3$. Foamable polystyrene is sold as a rigid board which has found considerable use in refrigeration and packing.

Bi-oriented polystyrene film is made by extruding a thin sheet or

:ube of polystyrene, stretching it sideways while still in the plastic range and allowing it to cool under tension. The resultant sheet ("Polydex," "Styroflex") is not as brittle as conventional polystyrene, and is used as a packaging film, as a laminating material, and in the manufacture of electrical condensers.

## ACRYLIC POLYMERS

The acrylic polymers were first developed commercially in the early 1930's in Britain and the United States. These polymers are all based on acrylic acid, which may be prepared by condensation of ethylene oxide with HCN, followed by reaction with sulfuric acid at about 320°F:

$$CH_2\text{---}CH_2 + HCN \rightarrow HOCH_2\text{---}CH_2CN$$

$$HOCH_2\text{---}CH_2\text{---}CN + H_2SO_4 + H_2O \rightarrow$$
$$CH_2\text{=}CH\text{---}COOH + (NH_4)HSO_4$$

Acrylic acid can be polymerized directly to give a hard polymer. However, the best polymers are obtained by the use of esters of acrylic acid such as methyl acrylate, ethyl acrylate, lauryl methacrylate, cyclohexyl methacrylate and methyl methacrylate. The latter is by far the most important commercially.

In practice, methyl methacrylate monomer is produced,[1] using a continuous process developed by ICI in Britain. The first step is a condensation of acetone with HCN, using a basic catalyst at about 80-120°F, to give acetone cyanohydrin by the equation

$$CH_3\text{---}\overset{\overset{\displaystyle O}{\|}}{C}\text{---}CH_3 + HCN \rightarrow CH_3\text{---}\overset{\overset{\displaystyle OH}{|}}{\underset{\underset{\displaystyle CN}{|}}{C}}\text{---}CH_3 \xrightarrow{H_2SO_4}$$

$$CH_2\text{=}\overset{\overset{\displaystyle CH_3}{|}}{C}\text{---}\overset{\overset{\displaystyle O}{\|}}{C}\text{---}NH_2 \cdot H_2SO_4$$

$$CH_2\text{=}\overset{\overset{\displaystyle CH_3}{|}}{C}\text{---}\overset{\overset{\displaystyle O}{\|}}{C}\text{---}OCH_3 + NH_4HSO_4$$

The acetone cyanohydrin is purified by distillation, and sulfuric acid added to form a salt of methacrylamide sulfate. This salt is not isolated, but is heated with methanol at 200-220°F, using a catalyst such as cop-

[1] M. Salkind, *et al., Ind. Eng. Chem.,* **51,** 1232, 1328 (1959).

per to form methyl methacrylate and ammonium bisulfate. An inhibitor such as hydroquinone is added to prevent polymerization, and the methyl methacrylate purified by distillation.

Polymethyl methacrylate is made commercially by either suspension or bulk polymerization using a peroxide free-radical initiator:

$$CH_2{=}C\overset{\overset{\displaystyle CH_3}{|}}{\phantom{C}}{-}\overset{\overset{\displaystyle O}{\|}}{C}{-}OCH_3 \rightarrow \cdots -CH_2{-}\overset{\overset{\displaystyle CH_3}{|}}{\underset{\underset{\displaystyle O{=}C{-}OCH_3}{|}}{C}}{-} \cdots$$

$$\Delta H^{\circ}_{298} = -13,300 \qquad \Delta F^{\circ}_{298} = -11,800$$

In the bulk polymerization process, the rate of polymerization remains essentially constant from zero to about 15 per cent conversion, and then increases rapidly with further conversion of the monomer. Cast sheets, rods and tubes are commonly made by first producing a syrup of partially polymerized material, pouring the syrup in place and heating to 150-200°F to finish the polymerization. Care must be taken to exclude oxygen, since this acts as an inhibitor for the polymerization.

Although both isotactic and syndiotactic polymethyl methacrylate have been prepared, the commercial polymer is always atactic because of the random arrangement of the bulky side groups. Polymethyl methacrylate has good mechanical and thermal properties, good electrical properties, good resistance to weathering, and can be molded at temperatures only slightly above those used for polystyrene. However, its outstanding property is its clearness and excellent light transmission. The one major disadvantage of the material is its softness, which limits the use in optical lenses because it is so easily scratched.

Polymethyl methacrylate molding powder finds wide use in the manufacture of lenses for automobile taillights and medallions, plastic jewelry, small signs, brush backs, molded dentures, etc. Cast and extruded polymer is used for signs, glazing, skylights and for decorative purposes in the building industry. The commercial material is marketed under trademarks such as "Plexiglas" (Rohm & Haas), "Acrylite" (Allied Chemical), and "Lucite" (du Pont).

### Polyacrylonitrile

Acrylonitrile was practically unknown until the late 1940's when acrylonitrile-butadiene copolymers were first produced in Germany, and found considerable use as an oil-resistant synthetic rubber. Production started in the United States in 1940, and expanded rapidly because of the use of the material as a self-sealing liner for aircraft fuel tanks. Although there is still a substantial use of acrylonitrile in the manufacture of synthetic rubber, the growth since 1950 has been almost entirely due to the development of polyacrylonitrile fibers. Thus, data presented by the Textile Economics Bureau shows a total production of acrylic and modacrylic fiber in the United States of 210 million pounds for 1963 and 288 million pounds for 1964. With the increasing expansion and possibly lower cost of acrylonitrile monomer, this rapid growth of acrylic fiber will probably continue for some time.

The early development of polyacrylonitrile was held back because of the insolubility of the polymer in ordinary solvents. Thus, it could not be dissolved or plasticized, and since it is insoluble in the monomer, it could not be polymerized by casting. Furthermore, the polymer softens only slightly below its decomposition temperature, and this prevents the production of fiber by melt spinning.

However, an intensive search for suitable solvents was made in the 1940's, and this showed that polyacrylonitrile can be dissolved by highly polar solvents such as dimethylsulfone, dimethylformamide, sulfolane, etc. In addition, concentrated inorganic salt solutions such as 55 per cent sodium thiocyanate, and strong mineral acids will dissolve polyacrylonitrile. These discoveries permitted the spinning of polyacrylonitrile, and commercial production of the fiber started in 1950.

Since acrylonitrile is appreciably soluble in water, it may be polymerized by either solution or suspension polymerization in water, using a water-soluble redox initiator. From patents, a typical process involves the use of a 6 per cent solution of acrylonitrile in water, with the addition of 0.03 per cent ammonium perdisulfate, 0.06 per cent sodium metabisulfite and enough sulfuric acid to bring the pH to 3.2. Other initiators such as sodium alkoxides, $H_2O_2 + FeSO_4$, etc., may be used; also, traces of metallic ions such as $Cu^{++}$ and $Fe^{+++}$ have been found to greatly accelerate the polymerization. The polymerization is exothermic ($\Delta H°_{298} = -18,400$), and cooling must be provided to maintain a temperature of 100-120°F. The polymer is insoluble, and separates as a fine powder having an average molecular weight in the range of 32,000-110,000. The relatively small size of the nitrile group permits close approach of individual chains in the polymer, and hydrogen bonding produces strong interchain forces which result in a difficulty-soluble polymer.

A recent development in the polymerization of acrylonitrile is the use of a medium which is a solvent for both the monomer and the polymer. This avoids the necessity of separating, drying and redissolving polymer in order to produce a spinning dope. Solvents which have been used include dimethyl sulfoxide, dimethylformamide and strong nitric acid. Any solvent which is used must not, of course, interfere with the polymerization and must be satisfactory for spinning the fiber.

Polyacrylonitrile has one severe disadvantage for use as a textile fiber, namely, that the pure polymer is very difficult to dye. For this reason, copolymers are normally used in which a second material such as vinyl acetate, vinyl chloride, vinylidene chloride or an acrylic ester is added to permit dyeing of the resultant fiber. In the textile industry, the "acrylic" fibers are those containing at least 85 per cent acrylonitrile and the "modacrylic" fibers are those containing from 35-85 per cent acrylonitrile. Acrylic fibers are strong, tough and resilient, and have excellent weatherability. The chief uses are in the manufacture of knit sweaters, broad-woven goods and apparel, blankets, carpets and rugs. The acrylics compete directly with wool, and much of the growth of the acrylics is undoubtedly due to the fact that the synthetic fibers are substantially cheaper than wool. Acrylics are marketed under such familiar trade names as "Acrilan" (Chemstrand), "Creslan" (American Cyanamid), "Zefran" (Dow), "Dynel" (Union Carbide), "Orlon" (du Pont), etc.

## COUMARONE-INDENE POLYMERS

These resins are made by polymerizing a mixture of coumarone and indene to obtain a random copolymer

coumarone
(benzofuran)          indene

The coumarone-indene resins were produced commercially in Germany as early as 1900, and have been produced in the United States since World War I. Total production in the United States for 1963 was about 344 million pounds. The chief uses are in the manufacture of surface coatings such as floor tiles, as an additive to synthetic rubber, in adhesives, printing inks, waxed paper, etc. These resins are among the cheapest available, the quoted average price in 1963 being 10 cent/lb.

The original production of these resins involved the separation of a naturally-occurring coumarone-indene fraction of approximately 338-365°F boiling range from the solvent naphtha fraction of coal-tar light oil. This fraction is then polymerized at about 300°F or greater, using a catalyst such as sulfuric acid, anhydrous HF, aluminum chloride, or boron trifluoride. The catalyst is then neutralized, volatiles removed by distillation and the resulting polymer steam distilled to remove dimers, trimers, etc., until a resin with the desired softening point is obtained (normal range from about 40-420°F). The polymers are of fairly low molecular weight, normally less than 1000, and vary in color from pale amber to dark brown, depending largely on the temperature of polymerization.

In addition to the resins based on coal tar, it is also possible to produce similar polymers from certain by-products of petroleum refining. The "petroleum polymers" are based more on the polymerization of unsaturates such as the turpenes, but the properties and uses of the petroleum polymers are essentially the same as those of the coumarone-indene polymers.

## ACETAL RESINS

The acetal resins include those polymers produced by addition-polymerization of aldehydes through the carbonyl group. In practice, formaldehyde is the most important raw material because of its low cost. The acetals have been introduced commercially only in recent years under such trade names as Delrin and Celcon. The resins can be used for injection molding or extrusion, and have found wide use in the manufacture of plastic objects such as gears, bearings, plastic moldings, door knobs, etc. In 1964 over 100 million lbs of 37 per cent formaldehyde went into the acetal resins, and this consumption is expected to triple within 5 years.

The polymerization of formaldehyde occurs by the equation

$$n\text{H}-\overset{\text{O}}{\underset{}{\text{C}}}-\text{H} \rightarrow \cdots -\text{O}-\text{CH}_2-\text{O}-\text{CH}_2- \cdots$$

Since the polymers normally contain hydroxyl end groups, they were referred to in the early literature as "polyoxymethylene glycols." Formaldehyde polymerizes readily either in bulk, from a nonreactive solvent, or directly as a vapor. Many different ionic initiators may be used such as common acids and bases, amines, organic acids, etc. However a monomer of high purity must be used, since small traces of impurities have a strong influence on the stability and molecular weight of the polymer produced.

Acetals may also be produced from higher aldehydes. In this case, the repeating unit is a substituted oxymethylene ...—OCRH—....

In the commercial production of acetals, formaldehyde is first purified by such techniques as scrubbing with an inert solvent, dehydration by $P_2O_5$, partial polymerization to remove chain-transfer impurities, etc. The purified formaldehyde is then introduced as a vapor into a polymerization vessel containing an inert solvent such as dry heptane. An initiator such as triphenyl phosphine (20 ppm) is used, and a stabilizing agent may be added to control the molecular weight of the polymer. The polymer is filtered, washed with heptane and acetone, dried, and an antioxidant added. Although the mechanical properties of the polymer are not materially affected by the nature of the end groups, these do affect the chemical and thermal stabilities of the polymer. Thus the raw polymer is often reacted with a material such as acetic anhydride in order to convert the hydroxyl end groups to the more stable acyl groups.

## FLUOROCARBON POLYMERS

The fluorocarbon polymers have exceptional chemical and thermal stability because of the high stability of the carbon-fluorine bond. The most important of these polymers is polytetrafluoroethylene, which finds considerable use in the chemical industry for the manufacture of gaskets, pump packing, valve seals, nonlubricated bearings, filter cloths, etc., where high chemical and heat resistance is required. Polytetrafluoroethylene also has unique electrical properties, and thus finds some use in the electronics industry and as an insulator for motors, generators, transformers and capacitors. The one disadvantage of polytetrafluoroethylene is its high cost, which has limited the total production to about 10 million pounds/year.

Polytetrafluoroethylene was discovered accidentally in 1938 by R. J. Plunkett, who was carrying out research using a cylinder of compressed tetrafluoroethylene gas. In the middle of an experiment the cylinder suddenly ran "dry," even though the weight of the cylinder indicated that plenty of gas should be left. When the cylinder was cut open with a hacksaw, it was found to contain a waxy white powder which was shown to be the polymer. As the result of this discovery, a pilot plant to manufacture polytetrafluoroethylene was completed in 1943 and commercial production started in 1949.

Tetrafluoroethylene monomer is a nontoxic gas having a normal boiling point of $-105°F$. It is made commercially by pyrolysis of chlorodifluoromethane according to the equation

$$2CHClF_2 \rightarrow CF_2{=}CF_2 + 2HCl$$

The reaction is carried out at 1200-1500°F, followed by absorption of the HCl in water and separation of product by fractionation.

Tetrafluoroethylene polymerizes according to the reaction

$$CF_2{=}CF_2 \rightarrow \cdots \; {-}\underset{\underset{\displaystyle F}{|}}{\overset{\overset{\displaystyle F}{|}}{C}}{-}\underset{\underset{\displaystyle F}{|}}{\overset{\overset{\displaystyle F}{|}}{C}}{-}\underset{\underset{\displaystyle F}{|}}{\overset{\overset{\displaystyle F}{|}}{C}}{-}\underset{\underset{\displaystyle F}{|}}{\overset{\overset{\displaystyle F}{|}}{C}}{-} \; \cdots$$

$$\Delta H_{298}^{\circ} = -48{,}620$$

The polymerization is carried out at temperatures ranging from room temperature up to about 200°F in the presence of water to obtain a granular or a finely-powdered polymer. Water-soluble free-radical initiators are used such as hydrogen peroxide, persulfates, organic peroxides or redox initiators. Tetrafluoroethylene gas is admitted at pressures of 100-700 psig, with efficient agitation to prevent any local overheating or buildup of monomer. Explosions have occurred in the polymerization of tetrafluoroethylene because the heat of polymerization is quite high, and temporary overheating may cause explosive disproportionation of the monomer into carbon and carbon tetrafluoride.

Polytetrafluoroethylene is a linear highly crystalline polymer having a melting point of about 620°F. It is believed that branching is completely absent, and that the average molecular weight is up in the millions. The polymer is extremely difficult to fabricate because of its high melting point and almost complete insolubility. In practice, the polymer is molded using techniques similar to those employed in powder metallurgy. Thus, powdered polymer is first compressed at room temperature to give a preform, which is then sintered at a temperature above the crystalline melting point to compact the material. This is another factor which leads to the fairly high cost of the finished material.

## SYNTHETIC ELASTOMERS

The history of the synthetic rubber industry[1] goes back to World War I when the Allied blockade cut Germany off from access to the rubber plantations of the Far East. In desperation the Germans developed "methyl rubber," which was based on the polymerization of dimethylbutadiene synthesized from acetone and polymerized in the presence of air for 10-12 weeks at about room temperature. The material was so bad that military trucks could not be left standing on their tires overnight!

[1] For recent reviews, see W. W. Crouch, and R. S. Hammer, "The New Elastomers," chapter in J. J. McKetta, Jr., Vol. IX, *op. cit.*; J. D. D'Ianni, "Elastomers," ibid., Vol. IV; M. E. Samuels, "Hydrocarbons in the Stretch," paper presented at Feb. 7-11, 1965 Houston meeting of Amer. Inst. Chem. Engrs.

Having learned the hard way, Germany (and also the Soviet Union) carried out intensive research starting in the 1920's on a possible substitute for natural rubber. In 1933, a butadiene-styrene copolymer known as "buna S" was introduced in Germany; this polymer is still the most important by far of the synthetic rubbers. In 1936, the Germans introduced "buna N," an oil-resistant copolymer of butadiene and acrylonitrile. Meanwhile, the first synthetic elastomers introduced in the United States were "Thiokol," an oil-resistant organic polysulfide elastomer introduced in 1930 and neoprene, the polymer of chloroprene, which was introduced in 1931. Although both of these polymers are still produced in substantial amounts, they cannot compete with the other synthetics for most applications. In 1940, butyl rubber was introduced in the United States. This is a copolymer of isobutylene with about 3 per cent isoprene; it is still produced in substantial quantities, and finds wide use as an innertube rubber where it is far superior to natural rubber.

Suddenly in 1942 the United States in turn found itself cut off from the supplies of natural rubber. Fortunately, the possible loss of access to natural rubber had been foreseen, and four synthetic rubber plants based on butadiene-styrene were already in operation. The decision was made to base the wartime production on the GR-S (government rubber-styrene) type of synthetic, and rapid expansion followed with an eventual design capacity of about 700 thousand tons/year. With the end of the war, there was a return to the use of natural rubber at the expense of synthetic. However, better processes for the manufacture of synthetic rubber resulted in products equal to or superior to natural rubber for most applications, and with the development of stereospecific catalysts, it is now possible to produce a synthetic "natural rubber." Thus, synthetic rubber now acounts for about three-fourths of the market in the United States, and it is probable that most of the future growth in the use of rubber will be in the synthetic material.

## Natural Rubber

Before discussing the synthetic rubbers, let us first briefly discuss natural rubber. Rubber is a natural exudation from various plants when they are cut or injured. The ordinary rubber comes from the tree *Hevea braziliensis*, a native of South America which is now grown commercially chiefly in the Far East. Two other forms of natural rubber are also known, namely, gutta-percha and balata. All three of these natural rubbers are polymers of isoprene, 2-methyl-1,3-butadiene; however, it is now known that ordinary rubber is formed by *cis* 1,4-addition whereas gutta-percha and balata are formed by *trans* 1,4-addition. This is illustrated diagrammatically in Fig. 19-7 which gives the structural formula

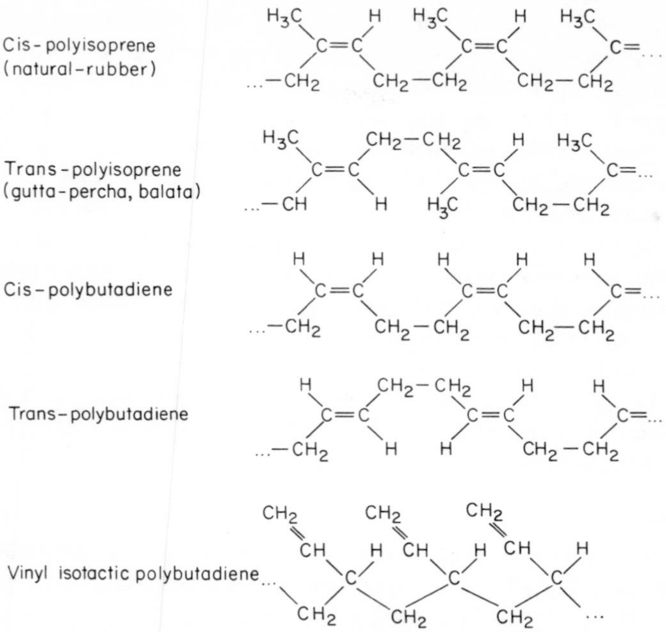

Fig. 19.7. Structural formulas for important elastomers.

for several important elastomers. Note that in the *cis* form, the H and CH₃ radicals are on the same side of the double bond, whereas in the *trans* form they are on opposite sides. This difference in stereo structure causes substantial differences in the physical properties of the polymer. Thus, rubber is by definition "rubbery," whereas balata and gutta-percha are hard, nonelastic materials. The chief use of balata is as a golfball cover where it is hard, tough and produces the "click" when the club meets the ball.

Pure rubber cannot be used because it is much too soft and plastic. In 1839, Goodyear found that rubber could be vulcanized by the use of sulfur. The effect of sulfur is to react with the double bonds to form a cross-linked structure having greater strength and hardness. Although other materials can be used, sulfur still remains the principal vulcanizing agent. However, accelerators such as derivatives of mercaptothiazole are also used to permit lower vulcanizing temperatures and a faster curing time for the vulcanized rubber.

Another factor which must be considered is the fact that the processing of any rubber involves the incorporation of reinforcing agents such as carbon black, inert fillers such as heavy oils, softening agents, antioxidants, pigments, etc. The rubber industry has developed certain standard techniques for processing natural rubber, and any deviation from the standard procedure will substantially increase the cost of the processed rubber. It has been found that certain synthetic rubbers are compatible with natural rubber, and can also be processed in the same manner as natural rubber. These synthetics have a substantial advantage over those which are incompatible with natural rubber, and thus require special methods of processing.

When it was recognized that rubber is a diene polymer, it was logical to base the manufacture of synthetic rubber on those dienes which could be produced economically. However, it was soon found that synthetic "rubbers" could be produced from materials substantially different from isoprene such as the sulfides, silicones, urethanes, etc. Thus, it is becoming increasingly common to refer to the materials as "elastomers" rather than as "synthetic rubbers," although the diene polymers are still by far the most important commercially.

### SBR Rubber

Total production of elastomers in the United States for 1963 is given in Table 19-5. Note that the butadiene-styrene copolymer (former GR-S, now usually called SBR) accounts for about two-thirds of the total synthetic production. Approximately 61 per cent of the total synthetic and natural rubber consumed in the United States goes into tires and tire products; in the past about 90 per cent of the tire market has been filled by natural and SBR rubber, although there is now increasing use of stereo rubber for tires.

The butadiene polymers were first developed in Germany, using alkali metals as initiators. The polymers were called the "buna" rubbers, the name coming from the first two letters of butadiene and the symbol Na for sodium. Straight polymers of butadiene were found to be quite unsatisfactory. The polymerization was slow and hard to control, and the resultant elastomer was hard to process and gave an inferior grade of rubber. For these reasons, a search was made for copolymers of butadiene which might have better mechanical properties, and in 1933, the butadiene-styrene copolymers (buna S) were first introduced. These copolymers were produced by emulsion polymerization, using 68-70 per cent butadiene, 30-32 per cent styrene, a soap emulsifier and a persulfate initiator.

In 1942, the U.S. government decided that wartime production of synthetic rubber would be based on a polymer similar to buna S, except that a product of lower viscosity would be produced to permit direct use in existing rubber-processing machinery (the German product required a

TABLE 19-5.  U.S. PRODUCTION AND USE OF ELASTOMERS
FOR 1963*

|  | Production (thousands of lb) |
|---|---|
| Synthetic elastomers, cyclic | |
| Polybutadiene-styrene (S-type) | 2,149,823 |
| Polybutadiene-styrene-vinylpyridine | 18,301 |
| Polyurethane | 6,059 |
| Synthetic elastomers, acyclic | |
| Polybutadiene-acrylonitrile (N-type) | 108,368 |
| Polychloroprene (Neoprene) | 288,714 |
| Polyisobutylene-isoprene (Butyl) | 242,235 |
| Silicone elastomers | 8,234 |
| Stereo elastomers | 312,807 |
| All other acyclic elastomers | 50,373 |
| Total synthetic | 3,184,914 |
| Natural rubber (consumption) | 1,022,191 |
| Reclaimed rubber (consumption) | 590,616 |
| Grand total | 4,797,721 |
| Consumption of new rubber | |
| Tire and tire products, natural rubber | 660,800 |
| Tire and tire products, synthetic | 1,760,640 |
| Non-tire products, natural | 362,880 |
| Non-tire products, synthetic | 1,167,040 |
| Total consumption | 3,951,360 |

* Data from U.S. Tariff Commission and from the Rubber Manufacturers Association, Inc.

preliminary heat-softening step). All plants and processes were to be standardized as much as possible to obtain a uniform product. Emulsion polymerization was used at a pressure of 125 psig and a temperature of 122°F with about 75 per cent conversion in 12 hours. The standard recipe consisted of 75 parts of butadiene, 25 styrene, 180 water, 5.0 soap, 0.5 lauryl mercaptan and 0.3 potassium persulfate. The polymerization was carried out batchwise, using agitated stainless steel or glass lined kettles of several thousand gallons capacity. When the conversion and polymer viscosity reached the proper value, a "shortstop" of hydroquinone and sodium sulfite was added to terminate the polymerization, and the latex was stripped of volatiles. An antioxidant was then added, the latex coagulated by the use of brine and dilute acid and the product washed and dried.

Although it had been recognized that a better rubber could probably be made by lowering the polymerization temperature, this was not possible with the "hot" recipe because the catalyst became less active at lower temperatures. After the war, it was found that German production of buna S had been carried out at increasingly lower temperatures, with a corresponding improvement in the quality of the rubber. This led to the development of the "cold" rubber process which involves the use of a more active initiator such as cumene hydroperoxide or a redox system. Thus, most SBR production is now carried out at temperatures of 0-40°F. A typical flow sheet for the production of cold rubber is illustrated in Fig. 19-8. The basic process is essentially the same except that

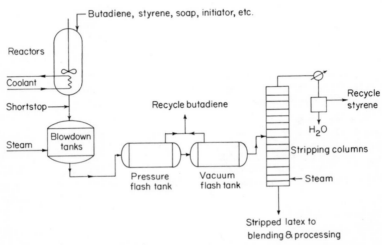

Fig. 19-8. Typical cold rubber process (J. D. Sutherland, *op. cit.*).

a lower temperature and a more complicated recipe are used, and the polymerization is normally continuous using a series of reactors. Thus, Table 19-6 gives a typical recipe for a modern emulsion cold rubber process. Judging from the number of ingredients, it is apparent that the production of cold rubber is more or less of an art.

The purpose of the various ingredients used to manufacture cold rubber is as follows: (a) The soap acts as an emulsifier to hold the monomer and subsequently the polymer in emulsion form. The soap also enters into the activation system through its ability to form micelles which solubilize a small amount of monomer, thereby making it available to the free radicals which are in the aqueous phase. (b) A secondary emulsifier such as a sodium alkyl aryl sulfonate is used to reduce the amount of solid rubber that falls out of suspension and is deposited in the vessels, pipes, pumps, etc. In practice, this is one of the severest

TABLE 19-6.  TYPICAL RECIPE FOR COLD RUBBER
BY EMULSION POLYMERIZATION*

| Component | Parts by Weight |
|---|---|
| Water | 200 |
| Butadiene | 70 |
| Styrene | 30 |
| Soap | 4.5 |
| Trisodium phosphate dodecahydrate | 0.80 |
| "Tamol" N | 0.15 |
| Sodium formaldehyde sulfoxylate | 0.15 |
| Ferrous sulfate heptahydrate | 0.05 |
| Versene | 0.07 |
| p-Methane hydroperoxide | 0.10 |
| tert-Dodecyl mercaptan | 0.20 |

(Run at 41°F to 60 per cent conversion and shortstop
with 0.15 parts sodium dimethyl dithiocarbamate.)

* J. D. Sutherland, "The Basics of SBR Production," paper presented
at New Orleans meeting of Southern Rubber Group, Oct. 8, 1960.

problems in the production of SBR. (c) Mercaptan compounds such as
lauryl mercaptan are used to control the molecular weight of the polymer by reducing cross-linking. The mercaptan acts as a chain transfer
agent. This is the mechanism by which the "Mooney viscosity" or toughness of the polymer is controlled. (d) For cold rubber polymerization,
the sulfoxylate initiation system is now considered to be the best because
of its high activity and the fact that it does not color the product. The
sulfoxylate system uses an oxidizing agent such as a hydroperoxide, a
reducing agent such as sodium formaldehyde sulfoxylate, a sequestering
agent and trace quantities of iron in the form of ferrous sulfate. (e)
Since oxygen is a strong inhibitor of the polymerization, a reducing agent
such as sodium hydrosulfite is added to the soap solution to react with
any molecular oxygen which may be present. (f) An electrolyte such as
trisodium phosphate or potassium chloride is added to buffer the emulsion system to hold the pH at the proper value and stabilize the emulsion
against changes in pH. The electrolyte also reduces the viscosity of the
reaction mixture, thereby improving agitation and heat transfer.

The SBR copolymer is produced by free-radical polymerization, and
is hence a random copolymer. Because of the higher reactivity of butadiene, the SBR polymers contain only about 24 per cent bound styrene
when a 30 per cent charge is used. Depending on the temperature of
polymerization, the butadiene units in the polymer are about 60 per cent
*trans*-1,4 and 20 per cent *cis*-1,4; in addition, about 20 per cent of the
butadiene polymerizes by 1,2-addition. The polymer is compatible with
natural rubber and the other major elastomers. Cold-process SBR is

equal to natural rubber for automobile tires, but is inferior to natural rubber for heavy-duty truck tires. Since SBR is easy to process, it is also widely used for rubber belting, hose, flooring, molded goods, rubber soles, coated fabrics, etc.

SBR has accounted for most of the production of synthetic rubber in the United States, and is still by far the most important synthetic. However, in 1955 the government sold the original wartime plants to private industry at a profit, and since then there has been increased competition in the rubber industry. These original plants are now presumably fully amortized, and can thus continue to be operated at a modest cost. However, it is probable that SBR has passed its peak, and that future growth in the synthetic rubber industry such as the EPT (ethylene-propylene terpolymer) and stereo rubbers will come partially at the expense of SBR.

### Nitrile Rubbers

The nitrile rubbers (N-type) are copolymers of butadiene and acrylonitrile. The chief use of these elastomers is in the manufacture of fuel tanks, gasoline hoses, in the food industry, etc., where good resistance to oils, fats and solvents is required. They also find some use in adhesives and for impregnating paper, leather and textiles. However, the nitrile rubbers are not suited for use in tires because of their low resilience and relatively high cost.

The nitrile rubbers are produced commercially in various grades ranging from about 18-40 per cent acrylonitrile. Those having a higher acrylonitrile content have greater oil resistance, but are also more expensive. The rubbers are produced by emulsion polymerization in the same general way as SBR. Since acrylonitrile is more reactive than butadiene, the polymer is richer in acrylonitrile than the monomer solution from which it is formed. The nitrile rubbers are compatible with natural rubber, and they can be compounded and vulcanized in the same way as natural rubber.

### Neoprene

Neoprene is one of the oldest of the synthetic elastomers, and still finds moderate use in the manufacture of wire and cable coatings, gaskets, belts for power transmission, industrial hoses, solid tires, rubber gloves, etc. Neoprene is used primarily where resistance to heat and solvents is required. In addition, neoprene has good weather resistance, good ozone resistance and a remarkably high tensile strength for an elastomer (to 4000 psig). Although neoprene does make excellent tires, it cannot compete in this market because of its cost.

Neoprene is produced commercially by the low-temperature emulsion polymerization of chloroprene, using a rosin emulsifying agent and a persulfate initiator. When the desired conversion is obtained, a shortstop of tetramethylthiuram disulfide is added, unreacted chloroprene is stripped by vacuum steam distillation, and the neoprene coagulated, washed and dried. Because of asymmetry induced by the chlorine atom on chloroprene, the polymer is produced almost 100 per cent as a head-to-tail *trans*-1,4-polychloroprene. The vulcanization of neoprene is different from that of natural rubber, and is usually done by the use of metal oxides such as zinc or magnesium oxide. Various grades of neoprene are commercially available, depending on the additives which are used, method of vulcanization, etc.

### Butyl Rubber

Butyl rubber was developed commercially by Standard Oil Co. of New Jersey just before the war. It consists of a copolymer of isobutylene with 1-3 per cent isoprene to permit vulcanization. The chief characteristic of butyl rubber is its low permeability to gases such as air and water vapor. Thus, most tire inner tubes are made of butyl rubber, although this market has suffered since the introduction of the tubeless tire. In addition, butyl rubber has good electrical properties, and has found considerable use for wire and cable insulation. There has been some use of butyl rubber in the manufacture of tires; these have good ozone resistance, give a smooth ride and there is no "squeal" when turning corners. Even in conventional tires, butyl is used as an inner liner and a trim rubber. About one-fourth of the rubber parts that go into new automobiles are now made of butyl; in fact, a Ford is quieter than a Rolls Royce because of butyl engine mounts.

Butyl rubber is made by the continuous cationic polymerization of isobutylene at temperatures as low as $-150°F$, using a Friedel-Crafts catalyst such as aluminum chloride or boron trifluoride. In practice, isobutylene containing 1-3 per cent isoprene is mixed with about 3 parts by volume of methyl chloride antifreeze, and is fed to an agitated polymerization reactor which is cooled by liquid ethylene. Aluminum chloride catalyst is added as a 0.20-0.25 per cent solution in methyl chloride. The polymer does not go through a latex stage, but separates as a fine powder or "crumb." The slurry is pumped continuously from the reactor to a tank of hot water which flashes off volatiles; the polymer is washed, an antioxidant and zinc stearate are added to prevent deterioration and agglomeration of the polymer, and the product is filtered and dried in a tunnel drier at 200-350°F.

Because of the low temperature of polymerization, butyl rubber has a relatively high molecular weight. Chain-transfer agents such as diiso-butylene are sometimes added to limit the molecular weight to the 200,000-300,000 level. Most of the isoprene units polymerize by 1,4-addition. Butyl rubber can be vulcanized, but more drastic conditions are required because of the low unsaturation. However, this low unsaturation is also an advantage, since the lack of double bonds increases the resistance of the material to oxidation and chemical attack.

### Ethylene-propylene Elastomers

At present, tremendous interest is being shown in elastomers produced by copolymerization of ethylene and propylene. These copolymers are based on work in Italy by Natta and his co-workers, using Ziegler catalysts. By proper choice of catalyst, it is possible to produce polymers having either a stereo structure, a block structure, or a random structure. The latter is the one desired for an elastomer, in order to reduce any tendency for crystallinity in the material.

The mushrooming interest in these elastomers is caused by the following factors: (a) Both ethylene and propylene are readily available at low cost; hence these elastomers are potentially cheaper than the conventional rubbers. (b) The polymers have a low density, which also favors a low cost for the finished product. (c) The polymers have good resistance to heat, ozone, weathering and chemicals. (d) The polymers are easy to process, and permit a high loading of pigments and fillers.

The first semicommercial production of these elastomers was in 1958 by Montecatini at its plant in Ferrara, Italy. However, in addition to the Italian production, there are now at least four companies in the United States producing the polymer commercially, and it is reported that the total U.S. capacity is about 100 million pounds/year. The original production was based on a straight ethylene-propylene copolymer known as EPR (ethylene-propylene rubber). However, this polymer could not be vulcanized in the usual way because it lacked double bonds, and hence all manufacturers have now shifted to a terpolymer known as EPT (ethylene-propylene terpolymer) which includes a diene to permit vulcanization by sulfur. The terpolymer appears to be of much greater interest to rubber processers than were the earlier copolymers.

In practice, the polymerization is carried out in solution, using a solvent such as $n$-hexane, cyclohexane, benzene, petroleum ether or tetrachloroethylene. The ethylene-propylene ratio can be varied over fairly wide limits; however, the typical polymer will contain 50-60 weight per cent ethylene, 0.5-2.0 per cent unsaturation (expressed as $C=C$), the balance being propylene. At first glance, it might appear that isoprene or 1,3-butadiene could be used for the third monomer. However, since these are conjugated dienes, their reactivity is much higher than that of ethylene or propylene, and hence their use would result in uncontrollable polymerization plus the danger of putting double bonds in the main polymer chain by 1,4-addition. Thus, a nonconjugated diene must be used such as dicyclopentadiene, cyclooctadiene or 1,4-hexadiene. One double bond of the nonconjugated diene polymerizes in the main polymer chain, but the other double bond is left in the side chain and thus permits vulcanization with conventional sulfur systems.

The three monomers, catalyst and solvent are metered continuously into an agitated stainless steel or glass lined reactor. Normally, the concentration of the reactants in the solvent is not over 10 per cent. From patents, the catalyst consists of an aluminum alkyl or dialkyl aluminum halide plus a vanadium compound such as $VCl_4$, $VOCl_3$ or a vanadate ester. The polymerization occurs rapidly at temperatures up to 125°F and pressures less than 100 psig; the terpolymer is present as a rubber cement dissolved in the solvent. Product solution is agitated with hot water to kill any remaining catalyst, solvent is flashed and recovered, and polymer is separated as crumbs which are filtered and dried using conventional synthetic rubber equipment.

EPT elastomers have two serious disadvantages. First, they are not compatible with any highly unsaturated polymer such as SBR or natural rubber. Second, the EPT elastomers have virtually no adhesion or "tack." (In the rubber industry, tack refers to the ability of two pieces of uncured rubber to adhere together with minimum pressure; natural rubber tack is so good that two pieces practically weld together, and attempts to pull them apart usually result in tearing outside the original plane of juncture.) Thus, although there is no question that EPT will find an increasing market over the next few years, there is still considerable uncertainty as to whether EPT can be used for tires. With no tire use, the consumption of EPT by 1970 is estimated to be about 270 million pounds/year; however, if EPT is widely used for tires, the 1970 consumption could reach as much as 1400 million pounds/year.

## STEREO ELASTOMERS

In 1963, roughly 10 per cent of the total U.S. production of synthetic elastomers consisted of stereo rubber, chiefly *cis*-1,4-polybutadiene. This represented a 50 per cent increase over the previous year, and further increases are anticipated for the next few years. The interest in stereo elastomers is partly based on the discovery that Ziegler catalysts can be used to produce a *cis*-polyisoprene which is almost identical with natural rubber. However, even greater interest has resulted from the fact that polybutadiene in the *cis*-form appears to have elastomeric properties which are equal to or superior to those of natural rubber.

### Polybutadiene

In view of the availability and relative cheapness of butadiene, it is perhaps surprising that straight polybutadiene has never been an important elastomer. Actually, polybutadiene was produced commercially in the Soviet Union starting in 1932. The process used was the "rod" polymerization technique in which a cylinder was coated with a catalyst of metallic sodium, and liquid butadiene was allowed to polymerize over the period of several weeks. In 1950, experimental batches of polybutadiene were produced in the United States, using the conventional cold rubber emulsion process. The material had fairly good properties, although there was a tendency for cold flow during storage. However, the product was never developed commercially because the availability of styrene at a reasonable cost permitted the continued production of the familiar SBR.

As illustrated in Fig. 19-7, the polymerization of butadiene can occur in several ways. Because of the double bond in the polymer, 1,4-addition can be either *cis* or *trans*, depending on whether the two hydrogen atoms are on the same side or on opposite sides of the double bond. The 1,2-addition gives a vinyl structure which in theory can be either isotactic, syndiotactic or atactic, because of the asymmetry of the carbon atoms having the vinyl side chains. In conventional emulsion polymerization, the *cis*, *trans* and vinyl forms are obtained in a random structure, depending on the temperature of polymerization. Thus, at 122°F (hot process), the composition is about 18.6 per cent *cis*, 59.3 per cent *trans* and 19.7 per cent vinyl; at 14°F (cold process), the composition is about 7.4 per cent *cis*, 74.3 per cent *trans* and 17.6 per cent vinyl.

With the discovery of the Ziegler catalysts, it became possible to produce an ordered or stereo polymer. Thus, in 1956, Phillips Petroleum Co. announced the development of polybutadienes of controlled structure. However, as illustrated in Fig. 19-9, the significant feature of this work was the remarkable change in the physical properties of the polymer as the amounts of *cis* and *trans* were varied. Over the range from about 20-80 per cent *cis*, there is little change in properties such as strength and resilience. However, 95 per cent *cis*-polybutadiene has a resilience equal to that of natural rubber, and the material has found widespread acceptance in passenger tires for both tread and carcass stocks.

Although no details of commercial processes are available, it is known that *cis*-polybutadiene is made by solution polymerization, using Ziegler catalysts. Table 19-7 lists various catalysts which have been disclosed

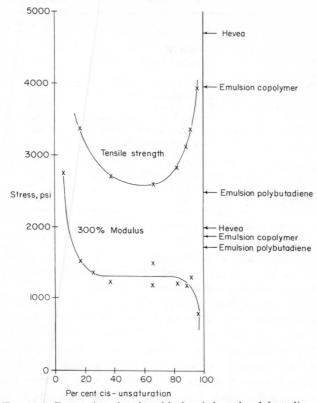

FIG. 19-9. Properties of carbon black reinforced polybutadienes as function of cis-content [W. W. Crouch and G. K. Kahle, *Hydro. Proc. Petrol. Refiner,* **37**(11), 187 (1958)]. Copyright 1958, Gulf Pub. Co., Houston, Texas.

in patents; the *cis*-form appears to be produced by the use of aluminum alkyls plus either iodide salts or soluble cobalt compounds. The polymerization is carried out at temperatures of about 40-140°F and pressures up to 50 psig, using an inert solvent such as benzene or a paraffin fraction. Normally, the conversion of monomer is virtually 100 per cent. The catalyst is then killed by the addition of water or alcohol, solvent is removed and the polymer dried in the conventional way. One serious problem in solution polymerization is the handling of the very viscous "cements" which are encountered at some stages in the process, depending on the solvent ratio that is used. These viscous solutions can be handled only in special reactors fitted with scrapers to increase the coefficient of heat transfer to the solution. This increases substantially the

TABLE 19-7.  POLYDIENE CATALYST SYSTEMS*

| Company | Catalyst | cis-Content (%) Butadiene | cis-Content (%) Isoprene |
|---------|----------|----------------------------|---------------------------|
| American Rubber and Chemical | Titanium iodide, Al alkyl | 95 | |
| Firestone Tire and Rubber | Butyl lithium | 40 | |
| | Butyl lithium | | 93 |
| General Tire and Rubber | Proprietary | 95-98 | |
| Goodrich-Gulf Chemicals | Co halides, Al alkyl halides | 98 | |
| Goodyear Tire and Rubber | Titanium iodide, Al alkyl | 95 | |
| | Titanium tetrachloride, Al alkyl | | 95 |
| Naugatuck Chemical | Proprietary | 95 | |
| Phillips Petroleum | Titanium iodide, Al alkyl | 95 | |
| Shell Chemical | Butyl lithium | | 92-93 |
| Texas-U.S. Chemical | Proprietary | 95 | |

* H. Haines, *Ind. Eng. Chem.*, **54**(11), 16 (1962).

cost of processing, and it is probable that solution polymerization will continue to be more expensive than emulsion polymerization until the technology has been more thoroughly developed.

Commercial production of *cis*-polybutadiene was started in 1960 by Phillips, and the total U.S. capacity is now about 250 million pounds/year with other plants in the design stage. The polymer is widely used in the manufacture of passenger tires, normally as a blend with SBR to improve the processability of the material. It is also possible to use *cis*-polybutadiene for truck tires if it is blended with natural rubber. Road tests have shown that *cis*-polybutadiene and its blends have better abrasion resistance than either natural rubber or SBR. There appears to be no question about the growth of *cis*-polybutadiene at the expense of SBR, depending of course on possible future competition from EPT.

## Polyisoprene

*Hevea* natural rubber is almost 100 per cent *cis*-polyisoprene. The development of Ziegler catalysts permitted for the first time the manufacture of a true "synthetic natural rubber." At present, polyisoprene is being produced commercially in the U.S. by three manufacturers having a total capacity of about 152 million pounds/year. The process involves the solution polymerization of carefully purified isoprene at about atmospheric pressure and room temperature. Two catalysts are reported to be used commercially, an alkyllithium compound and a combination of tributylaluminum and titanium tetrachloride. The polyisoprene is produced as a cement in a hydrocarbon solvent; this cement is then emulsified in water, using a suitable emulsifying agent, and the solvent steam-stripped to leave a latex of polyisoprene in water.

The kinetics of the polymerization of isoprene have been studied by Saltman[1] and his co-workers. When aluminum triisobutyl and titanium tetrachloride are mixed together, a precipitate is formed which contains most of the titanium in a reduced valence state. However, as the amount of the aluminum alkyl is increased, the solid changes from a brown $TiCl_3$ to more complex compounds in which chlorine is partially replaced by alkyl groups. The maximum rate of polymerization is obtained with a 1:1 molar ratio of aluminum to titanium. The reaction is first-order with respect to monomer, and has an activation energy of about 14,400 cal/mole.

The commercial manufacture of *cis*-polyisoprene is certainly a remarkable accomplishment by the chemical industry. The synthetic material produced to date has been inferior to natural rubber in some respects and superior in others. However, there appears to be no question that ultimately the synthetic material will be equal or superior to natural rubber for all applications. The advantages of the synthetic material are that it is lighter in color, more uniform, processes more easily and is less often contaminated by foreign materials than the natural product.

However, the future of *cis*-polyisoprene is very much in doubt because of its price. Until recently, the small amounts of isoprene required in the production of butyl rubber were produced by cracking suitable refinery fractions. With the increasing demand for isoprene monomer, considerable work has been carried out in a search for the most economic process.[2] Two processes appear to be most favored in the United States. The first is a straight thermal cracking of $C_5$ refinery fractions to produce isoprene directly; if desired, the process can be operated in conjunction with butadiene facilities, the isoprene being recovered as a byproduct. The second process was developed by Goodyear-Scientific Design, and is based on propylene. The first step involves a dimerization of propylene either in the liquid phase by the use of a trialkylaluminum catalyst or in the vapor phase by passing propylene gas over a base-treated $SiO_2$-$Al_2O_3$ catalyst at 850°F. The dimer is then isomerized to 2-methyl-2-pentene by passing it over an acid catalyst, and isoprene is produced by thermal cracking at temperatures of about 1400°F, using steam as a carrier gas. The future of polyisoprene will be strongly dependent on how well these two processes work out in practice.

[1] W. M. Saltman, *et al., J. Am. Chem. Soc.,* **80,** 5615 (1958).
[2] A. A. Di Giacomo, *et al., Chem. Eng. Progr.,* **57**(5), 35 (1961).

# Appendix

TABLE A-1. HEAT CAPACITIES OF GASES AND VAPORS IN THE IDEAL-GAS STATE $(C^{\circ}_p = a + bT + cT^{-2})$, WHERE $T$ IS IN $^{\circ}$K.*

| Material | Formula | $a$ | $b \times 10^3$ | $c \times 10^{-5}$ | Range, $^{\circ}$K |
|---|---|---|---|---|---|
| Acetylene | $C_2H_2$ | 12.13 | 3.84 | $-2.46$ | 298-2000 |
| Ammonia | $NH_3$ | 7.11 | 6.00 | $-0.37$ | 298-1800 |
| Carbon disulfide | $CS_2$ | 12.45 | 1.60 | $-1.80$ | 298-1800 |
| Carbon dioxide | $CO_2$ | 10.57 | 2.10 | $-2.06$ | 298-2500 |
| Carbon monoxide | $CO$ | 6.79 | 0.98 | $-0.11$ | 298-2500 |
| Carbon tetrachloride | $CCl_4$ | 24.17 | 1.20 | $-4.10$ | 298-1500 |
| Chlorine | $Cl_2$ | 8.85 | 0.16 | $-0.68$ | 298-3000 |
| Fluorine | $F_2$ | 8.26 | 0.60 | $-0.84$ | 298-2500 |
| Hydrogen | $H_2$ | 6.52 | 0.78 | 0.12 | 298-3000 |
| Hydrogen chloride | $HCl$ | 6.27 | 1.24 | 0.30 | 298-2000 |
| Hydrogen cyanide | $HCN$ | 9.41 | 2.70 | $-1.44$ | 298-2500 |
| Hydrogen fluoride | $HF$ | 6.55 | 0.72 | 0.17 | 298-4000 |
| Hydrogen sulfide | $H_2S$ | 7.81 | 2.96 | $-0.46$ | 298-2300 |
| Methane | $CH_4$ | 5.65 | 11.44 | 0.46 | 298-1500 |
| Nitric oxide | $NO$ | 7.03 | 0.92 | $-0.14$ | 298-2500 |
| Nitrogen | $N_2$ | 6.83 | 0.90 | $-0.12$ | 298-3000 |
| Nitrogen dioxide | $NO_2$ | 10.07 | 2.28 | $-1.67$ | 298-2000 |
| Nitrogen tetroxide | $N_2O_4$ | 20.05 | 9.50 | $-3.56$ | 298-1000 |
| Oxygen | $O_2$ | 7.16 | 1.00 | $-0.40$ | 298-3000 |
| Phosphorus | $P_2$ | 8.31 | 0.46 | $-0.72$ | 298-2000 |
| Phosphorus pentoxide | $P_4O_{10}$ | 73.60 | — | — | 298-1500 |
| Sulfur dioxide | $SO_2$ | 11.04 | 1.88 | $-1.84$ | 298-2000 |
| Sulfur trioxide | $SO_3$ | 13.90 | 6.10 | $-3.22$ | 298-1500 |
| Water | $H_2O$ | 7.30 | 2.46 | — | 298-2750 |

* Taken from K. K. Kelley, U.S. Bureau of Mines Bulletin 584 (1960).

TABLE A-2. HEAT CAPACITY OF GASES AND VAPORS IN THE IDEAL-GAS STATE $(C^{\circ}_p = p + qT + rT^2)$, WHERE $T$ IS IN $^{\circ}$K.*

| Material | Formula | $p$ | $q \times 10^3$ | $r \times 10^7$ |
|---|---|---|---|---|
| Normal paraffins | | | | |
| Methane | $CH_4$ | 3.381 | 18.044 | $-43.00$ |
| Ethane | $C_2H_6$ | 2.247 | 38.201 | $-110.49$ |

* Taken from H. M. Spencer, *Ind. Eng. Chem. 40*, 2152 (1948). See also K. A. Kobe and H. R. Crawford, *Hydro. Proc. Petrol. Refiner 37* (7) 125 (1958). All data valid 298-1500° K.

TABLE A-2. HEAT CAPACITY OF GASES AND VAPORS IN THE IDEAL-GAS STATE (*Cont'd*)
($C°_p = p + qT + rT^2$), WHERE $T$ IS IN °K.*

| Material | Formula | $p$ | $q \times 10^3$ | $r \times 10^7$ |
|---|---|---|---|---|
| Propane | $C_3H_8$ | 2.410 | 57.195 | −175.33 |
| Butane | $C_4H_{10}$ | 4.453 | 72.270 | −222.14 |
| Pentane | $C_5H_{12}$ | 5.910 | 88.449 | −273.88 |
| Hexane | $C_6H_{14}$ | 7.477 | 104.422 | −324.71 |
| Increment per C atom above 6 | | 1.572 | 15.950 | −50.69 |
| Normal monoolefins | | | | |
| Ethylene | $C_2H_4$ | 2.830 | 28.601 | −87.26 |
| Propylene | $C_3H_6$ | 3.253 | 45.116 | −137.40 |
| 1-Butylene | $C_4H_8$ | 5.132 | 61.760 | −193.22 |
| 1-Pentene | $C_5H_{10}$ | 7.175 | 76.835 | −240.03 |
| 1-Hexene | $C_6H_{12}$ | 8.609 | 93.090 | −292.19 |
| Increment per C atom above 6 | | 1.572 | 15.950 | −50.69 |
| Miscellaneous materials | | | | |
| Acetaldehyde | $CH_3CHO$ | 7.422 | 29.029 | −87.42 |
| Acetylene | $C_2H_2$ | 7.331 | 12.622 | −38.89 |
| Benzene | $C_6H_6$ | −0.409 | 77.621 | −264.29 |
| 1,3-Butadiene | $C_4H_6$ | 5.432 | 53.224 | −176.49 |
| Carbon (solid) | C | −1.265 | 14.008 | −103.31 |
| Cyclohexane | $C_6H_{12}$ | −7.701 | 125.675 | −415.84 |
| Cyclopentane | $C_5H_{10}$ | −5.763 | 97.377 | −313.28 |
| Ethanol | $C_2H_5OH$ | 6.990 | 39.741 | −119.26 |
| Ethylbenzene | $C_8H_{10}$ | 2.234 | 110.041 | −367.11 |
| Methylcyclopentane | $C_6H_{12}$ | −3.261 | 112.590 | −362.43 |
| Styrene | $C_8H_8$ | 4.074 | 99.731 | −331.08 |
| Toluene | $C_7H_8$ | 0.576 | 93.493 | −312.27 |
| *o*-Xylene | $C_8H_{10}$ | 4.573 | 104.210 | −338.40 |
| *m*-Xylene | $C_8H_{10}$ | 2.293 | 108.002 | −354.17 |
| *p*-Xylene | $C_8H_{10}$ | 2.153 | 107.559 | −350.82 |

TABLE A-3. STANDARD HEATS OF FORMATION, FREE ENERGIES OF FORMATION
AND ENTROPIES AT 298° K.*

| Material | Formula | $\Delta H°_{298}$ | $\Delta F°_{298}$ | $S°_{298}$ |
|---|---|---|---|---|
| Normal paraffins | | | | |
| Methane | $CH_4$ (g) | −17,889 | −12,140 | 44.50 |
| Ethane | $C_2H_6$ (g) | −20,236 | −7,860 | 54.85 |
| Propane | $C_3H_8$ (g) | −24,820 | −5,614 | 64.51 |
| *n*-Butane | $C_4H_{10}$ (g) | −29,812 | −3,754 | 74.10 |
| *n*-Pentane | $C_5H_{12}$ (g) | −35,000 | −1,960 | 83.27 |
| *n*-Hexane | $C_6H_{14}$ (g) | −39,960 | 50 | 92.45 |
| Increment per C atom above 6 | | −4,926 | 2,048 | 9.183 |
| Normal monoolefins | | | | |
| Ethylene | $C_2H_4$ (g) | 12,496 | 16,282 | 52.45 |
| Propylene | $C_3H_6$ (g) | 4,879 | 14,990 | 63.80 |
| 1-Butylene | $C_4H_8$ (g) | 280 | 17,217 | 73.48 |
| 1-Pentene | $C_5H_{10}$ (g) | −5,000 | 18,787 | 83.08 |
| 1-Hexene | $C_6H_{12}$ (g) | −9,960 | 20,800 | 92.25 |
| Increment per C atom above 6 | | −4,926 | 2,048 | 9.183 |

* Data from F. D. Rossini et al, National Bureau of Standards Circular C461 (1947) and Circular 500 (1952); K. A. Kobe and H. R. Crawford, Hydro. Proc. Petrol. Refiner *37* (7), 125 (1958); P. Goldfinger and G. Martens, Trans. Faraday Soc. *57*, 2220 (1961); J. H. S. Green, J. Appl. Chem. *11*, 397 (1961); J. H. S. Green, Quart. Rev. Chem. Soc. Lond. *15*, 125 (1961).

TABLE A-3. STANDARD HEATS OF FORMATION, FREE ENERGIES OF FORMATION
AND ENTROPIES AT 298° K.* *(Cont'd)*

| Material | Formula | $\Delta H°_{298}$ | $\Delta F°_{298}$ | $S°_{298}$ |
|---|---|---|---|---|
| Miscellaneous organic compounds | | | | |
| Acetaldehyde | $CH_3CHO$ (g) | −39,760 | −31,960 | 63.5 |
| Acetic acid | $CH_3COOH$ (l) | −116,400 | −93,800 | 38.2 |
| Acetone | $CH_3COCH_3$ (g) | −51,720 | −36,300 | 70.5 |
| Acetonitrile | $CH_3CN$ (g) | 21,000 | 25,200 | 58.18 |
| Acetylene | $C_2H_2$ (g) | 54,194 | 50,000 | 47.997 |
| Benzene | $C_6H_6$ (g) | 19,820 | 30,989 | 64.34 |
| 1,3-Butadiene | $C_4H_6$ (g) | 26,330 | 36,010 | 66.59 |
| *iso*-Butane | $C_4H_{10}$ (g) | −31,452 | −4,296 | 70.42 |
| *n*-Butanol | $C_4H_9OH$ (g) | −66,920 | −37,370 | 86.90 |
| Carbon tetrachloride | $CCl_4$ (g) | −25,500 | −15,300 | 73.95 |
| Chlorobenzene | $C_6H_5Cl$ (g) | 12,860 | 24,180 | 74.85 |
| Chloroform | $CHCl_3$ (g) | −24,000 | −16,000 | 70.86 |
| Cumene | $C_9H_{12}$ (g) | 940 | 32,738 | 92.87 |
| Cyclohexane | $C_6H_{12}$ (g) | −29,430 | 7,590 | 71.28 |
| Cyclopentane | $C_5H_{10}$ (g) | −18,460 | 9,230 | 70.00 |
| Dimethyl ether | $CH_3OCH_3$ (g) | −44,300 | −27,300 | 63.72 |
| Ethanol | $C_2H_5OH$ (g) | −56,240 | −40,300 | 67.4 |
| Ethyl chloride | $C_2H_5Cl$ (g) | −25,100 | −12,700 | 65.9 |
| Ethylbenzene | $C_8H_{10}$ (g) | 7,120 | 31,208 | 86.15 |
| Ethylene dichloride | $(CH_2Cl)_2$ (g) | −31,400 | −18,090 | 73.8 |
| Ethylene glycol | $HOC_2H_4OH$ (l) | −108,580 | −77,120 | 39.9 |
| Ethylene oxide | $C_2H_4O$ (g) | −12,190 | −2,790 | 58.1 |
| Formaldehyde | $HCHO$ (g) | −27,700 | −26,300 | 52.26 |
| *n*-Hexanol | $C_6H_{13}OH$ (g) | −76,750 | −33,330 | 105.52 |
| Ketene | $CH_2CO$ (g) | −14,600 | — | — |
| Methanol | $CH_3OH$ (g) | −48,080 | −38,690 | 56.8 |
| Methyl chloride | $CH_3Cl$ (g) | −19,600 | −14,000 | 55.97 |
| Methylcyclopentane | $C_6H_{12}$ (g) | −25,500 | 8,550 | 81.24 |
| Methylene dichloride | $CH_2Cl_2$ (g) | −21,000 | −14,000 | 64.68 |
| *n*-Pentanol | $C_5H_{11}OH$ (g) | −71,850 | −35,400 | 96.21 |
| Phenol | $C_6H_5OH$ (g) | −23,050 | −7,880 | 75.40 |
| *iso*-Propanol | $C_3H_7OH$ (g) | −65,400 | −34,770 | 50.64 |
| *n*-Propanol | $C_3H_7OH$ (g) | −61,820 | −39,210 | 77.59 |
| Styrene | $C_8H_8$ (g) | 35,220 | 51,100 | 82.44 |
| Thiophene | $C_4H_4S$ (g) | 27,490 | 30,120 | 66.66 |
| Toluene | $C_7H_8$ (g) | 11,950 | 29,228 | 76.42 |
| Urea | $(NH_2)_2CO$ (c) | −79,634 | −47,120 | 25.00 |
| *o*-Xylene | $C_8H_{10}$ (g) | 4,540 | 29,177 | 84.31 |
| *m*-Xylene | $C_8H_{10}$ (g) | 4,120 | 28,405 | 85.49 |
| *p*-Xylene | $C_8H_{10}$ (g) | 4,290 | 28,952 | 84.23 |
| Miscellaneous inorganic compounds: | | | | |
| Ammonia | $NH_3$ (g) | −11,040 | −3,976 | 46.01 |
| Ammonium carbamate | $NH_4COONH_2$ (c) | −154,210 | −109,470 | 39.70 |
| Ammonium chloride | $NH_4Cl$ (c) | −75,380 | −48,730 | 22.6 |
| Ammonium nitrate | $NH_4NO_3$ (c) | −87,270 | — | — |
| Calcium | $Ca$ (c) | 0 | 0 | 9.95 |
| Calcium carbide | $CaC_2$ (s) | −15,000 | −16,200 | 16.8 |
| Calcium carbonate | $CaCO_3$ (s) | −288,450 | −269,780 | 22.2 |
| Calcium chloride | $CaCl_2$ (s) | −190,000 | −179,300 | 27.2 |
| Calcium hydroxide | $Ca(OH)_2$ (s) | −235,800 | −214,330 | 18.2 |
| Calcium oxide | $CaO$ (s) | −151,900 | −144,400 | 9.5 |

TABLE A-3. STANDARD HEATS OF FORMATION, FREE ENERGIES OF FORMATION AND ENTROPIES AT 298° K.* *(Cont'd)*

| Material | Formula | $\Delta H°_{298}$ | $\Delta F°_{298}$ | $S°_{298}$ |
|---|---|---|---|---|
| Carbon | C (graphite) | 0 | 0 | 1.361 |
| Carbon dioxide | $CO_2$ (g) | −94,052 | −94,260 | 51.061 |
| Carbon disulfide | $CS_2$ (g) | 27,550 | 15,550 | 56.84 |
| Carbon monoxide | CO (g) | −26,416 | −32,808 | 47.301 |
| Chlorine | $Cl_2$ (g) | 0 | 0 | 53.286 |
| Fluorine | $F_2$ (g) | 0 | 0 | 48.6 |
| Hydrogen | $H_2$ (g) | 0 | 0 | 31.211 |
| Hydrogen bromide | HBr (g) | −8,660 | −12,720 | 47.437 |
| Hydrogen chloride | HCl (g) | −22,063 | −22,769 | 44.617 |
| Hydrogen cyanide | HCN (g) | 31,200 | 28,700 | 48.23 |
| Hydrogen fluoride | HF (g) | −64,200 | −64,700 | 41.47 |
| Hydrogen iodide | HI (g) | 6,200 | 310 | 49.314 |
| Hydrogen peroxide | $H_2O_2$ (l) | −44,750 | −28,100 | 26.17 |
| Hydrogen sulfide | $H_2S$ (g) | −4,815 | −7,892 | 49.15 |
| Nitric acid | $HNO_3$ (l) | −41,404 | −19,100 | 37.19 |
| Nitric oxide | NO (g) | 21,600 | 20,719 | 50.339 |
| Nitrogen | $N_2$ (g) | 0 | 0 | 45.767 |
| Nitrogen dioxide | $NO_2$ (g) | 8,091 | 12,390 | 57.47 |
| Nitrogen tetroxide | $N_2O_4$ (g) | 2,309 | 23,491 | 72.73 |
| Nitrosyl chloride | NOCl (g) | 12,570 | 15,860 | 63.0 |
| Oxygen | $O_2$ (g) | 0 | 0 | 49.003 |
| Phosgene | $COCl_2$ (g) | −53,300 | −50,310 | 69.13 |
| Phosphoric acid | $H_3PO_4$ (c) | −306,200 | — | — |
| Phosphorus | P (white) | 0 | 0 | 10.6 |
| Phosphorus pentoxide | $P_4O_{10}$ (c) | −720,000 | −654,400 | 65.9 |
| Sodium | Na (c) | 0 | 0 | 12.2 |
| Sodium bicarbonate | $NaHCO_3$ (c) | −226,500 | −203,600 | 24.4 |
| Sodium carbonate | $Na_2CO_3$ (c) | −270,300 | −250,400 | 32.5 |
| Sodium chlorate | $NaClO_3$ (s) | −85,730 | — | — |
| Sodium chloride | NaCl (s) | −98,232 | −91,785 | 17.30 |
| Sodium cyanide | NaCN (s) | −21,460 | — | — |
| Sodium hydroxide | NaOH (s) | −101,990 | −90,600 | 14.09 |
| Sulfur | S (rhombic) | 0 | 0 | 7.62 |
| Sulfur dioxide | $SO_2$ (g) | −70,960 | −71,790 | 59.40 |
| Sulfur trioxide | $SO_3$ (g) | −94,450 | −88,520 | 61.24 |
| Sulfuric acid | $H_2SO_4$ (l) | −193,910 | — | — |
| Water | $H_2O$ (g) | −57,798 | −54,636 | 45.106 |
| Water | $H_2O$ (l) | −68,317 | −56,690 | 16.716 |

# Index